Field Guide to the
Caterpillars
of Great Britain and Ireland

BARRY HENWOOD AND PHIL STERLING

ILLUSTRATED BY RICHARD LEWINGTON

B L O O M S B U R Y   W I L D L I F E
LONDON · OXFORD · NEW YORK · NEW DELHI · SYDNEY

To my late parents Doug and Rene, who encouraged my love of wildlife from a young age and who would have loved to have seen this book. To my wife Mandy for her tolerance and patience, which have made this book possible. BH

To my late father Col. Dougie Sterling, to my mother Audrey, and to my brother Mark for our shared interest in moths and butterflies across the world. To my wife Carol for her support and her tolerance of my obsession with bugs and maggots. PS

BLOOMSBURY WILDLIFE
Bloomsbury Publishing Plc
50 Bedford Square, London, WC1B 3DP, UK

BLOOMSBURY, BLOOMSBURY WILDLIFE and the Diana logo are trademarks of
Bloomsbury Publishing Plc

First published in the United Kingdom 2020

Copyright © Barry Henwood and Phil Sterling, 2020
Illustrations © Richard Lewington, 2020
Maps © Chris Manley, 2020

Barry Henwood and Phil Sterling have asserted their right under the Copyright, Designs and Patents Act, 1988, to be identified as Authors of this work

For legal purposes the photographic credits on p. 413
constitute an extension of this copyright page

A catalogue record for this book is available from the British Library

Library of Congress Cataloguing-in-Publication data has been applied for

ISBN: HB: 978-1-4729-3358-4; PB: 978-1-4729-3356-0;
ePDF: 978-1-4729-3355-3; ePUB: 978-1-4729-3357-7

4 6 8 10 9 7 5

Designed by D & N Publishing, Baydon, Wiltshire
Printed and bound in Great Britain by Bell and Bain Ltd, Glasgow

To find out more about our authors and books visit www.bloomsbury.com and sign up for our newsletters

CONTENTS

ACKNOWLEDGEMENTS   5

INTRODUCTION   7
Using this field guide   8
Glossary   11
Format of the species accounts   18
Rearing techniques   23
How to find larvae   26
Life cycles: early stages   30
Coping with winter   38
Number of generations in a year   39
What do larvae eat?   40
Defence mechanisms   42
Parasites   60
Diseases   61

USEFUL RESOURCES   63
Further reading   63
Societies, recording schemes and groups   65

AT-A-GLANCE GUIDE   68

SUPERFAMILY HEPIALOIDEA   72
Hepialidae Swift moths   72

SUPERFAMILY COSSOIDEA   74
Cossidae Goat and leopard moths   74
Sesiidae Clearwing moths   76

SUPERFAMILY ZYGAENOIDEA   85
Limacodidae Slug moths   85
Zygaenidae Forester and burnet moths   86

SUPERFAMILY PAPILIONOIDEA   90
Papilionidae Swallowtail butterflies   90
Hesperiidae Skippers   91
Pieridae White butterflies   95
Nymphalidae Brown, fritillary, admiral and
    tortoiseshell butterflies   98
Riodinidae Metalmark butterflies   108
Lycaenidae Copper, hairstreak and blue butterflies   109

SUPERFAMILY DREPANOIDEA — 116
Drepanidae Hook-tip and lutestring moths — 116

SUPERFAMILY LASIOCAMPOIDEA — 121
Lasiocampidae Eggar and lappet moths — 121

SUPERFAMILY BOMBYCOIDEA — 125
Endromidae — 125
Saturniidae Emperor moths — 126
Sphingidae Hawk-moths — 127

SUPERFAMILY GEOMETROIDEA — 132
Geometridae Looper moths — 132

SUPERFAMILY NOCTUOIDEA — 205
Notodontidae Prominent, kitten and processionary moths — 205

PLATE SECTION — 212

Erebidae Tussock, ermine, tiger, footman, snout, fan-foot, marbled, blackneck and underwing moths — 276
Noctuidae Noctuid moths — 293
Nolidae Black arches, silver-lines and nycteoline moths — 366

CHECKLIST OF THE MACRO-MOTHS AND BUTTERFLIES OF GREAT BRITAIN AND IRELAND — 369

SCIENTIFIC NAMES OF PLANTS AND THEIR ASSOCIATED BUTTERFLY AND MOTH SPECIES — 386

PHOTOGRAPHIC CREDITS — 413

APPENDIX 1: Separating *Xanthorhoe* carpets — 414

APPENDIX 2: Separating pug moths (genera *Gymnoscelis* and *Eupithecia*) — 416

APPENDIX 3: Separating sallows and chestnuts — 418

APPENDIX 4: Separating readily confused pale-striped green noctuids — 421

APPENDIX 5: Separating external-feeding wainscots — 424

INDEX OF ENGLISH NAMES — 428

INDEX OF SCIENTIFIC NAMES — 436

ACKNOWLEDGEMENTS

We could not have written and illustrated this field guide on our own. Many people have offered their knowledge, expertise, material and time to help us get to this finished product, and we are grateful to you all.

Much has changed in the publishing world since the British Wildlife Publishing field guides became part of Bloomsbury Publishing's list, and there were doubters who worried whether the same quality and attention to detail that Andrew and Anne Branson consistently achieved would still be possible 'under new management'. They need have no fear. Our guide has been Katy Roper, Commissioning Editor at Bloomsbury Wildlife, and we are hugely indebted to her for her support. Her experience in providing guidance to us as authors has ensured that we have maintained the high standards expected of field guides in the Bloomsbury Wildlife Guides series. We are also very grateful to David Campbell for his support during the proof stages while Katy has been away.

There are many who deserve mention here for their support. In particular, a big thank you to Darryl Rush for painstakingly putting together a spreadsheet of larval foodplants from the main reference texts on larvae. We have benefitted hugely from the IT expertise of Phil Dean; he has found digital solutions to checking proofs, and his advanced spreadsheet manipulation has enabled the creation of the index of plant names and their associated moth and butterfly species. Chris Manley spent much of the winter of 2018/19 producing the species distribution maps for us. These maps drew information from Butterfly Conservation's National Moth Recording Scheme and Butterflies for the New Millennium databases, and from Moths Ireland maps. We thank Dr Nigel Bourn, Les Evans-Hill, Richard Fox and Dr Zoë Randle at Butterfly Conservation for so willingly allowing us access to these data, as well as recorded foodplant data. We are also grateful to Julie Williams, Chief Executive Officer at Butterfly Conservation, for her support for our endeavours.

We needed living material from various parts of Great Britain and Ireland, and relied on local enthusiasts for their knowledge and their much-needed additional pairs of eyes to join us on our many forays into the countryside looking for larvae. A number of international, national and local experts on Lepidoptera natural history, diversity and fieldcraft gave their advice freely, as well as photographic images, especially of species we could not find ourselves, and we have depended on almost daily access to websites showing larvae. We are very grateful to the following for their part in helping us put together the different facets we required to create this field guide: Nicola Bacciu, Phil Barden, Nick Bowles, Paul Butter, Dr Paul Cannon (Kew Gardens), Tony Davis, Bryan Edwards, Dave Foot, Reg Fry, Dave Green, Gerry Haggett, Sharon Hearle, Bob Heckford, Prof. Daniel Janzen, Rachel Jones, Ian Kimber, Roy Leverton, Roy McCormick, Lorraine Munns, Mark Parsons, Dr Tom Prescott, Phil Sansum, Dr Malcolm Scoble, Dr Mark Shaw, Ben Smart, Alan Stubbs (Kent), Prof. Jeremy Thomas, Martin Townsend, Prof. Dick Vane-Wright, Jeroen Voogd, Wolfgang Wagner, John Walters, Dr Paul Waring, Dr Mark Young and Dr Alberto Zilli.

While the authors have written this work in their spare time, for the illustrator this has been his day (and night) job. We are hugely grateful to the Golden Bottle Trust and to Tony Hoare for their generous financial support, without which this field guide would remain languishing in the bottom drawer of good ideas lacking support. We are also indebted to the British Entomological and Natural History Society for a grant from the Maitland Emmet BENHS Research Fund towards the scanning required for converting several thousand 35mm transparencies to digital format to provide additional reference material for the illustrations.

Barry Henwood, Phil Sterling and Richard Lewington

INTRODUCTION

This field guide covers the caterpillars of most of the butterflies and macro-moths found in the British Isles. It has been written and illustrated as a stand-alone reference, though it can also be seen as a companion volume to *Field Guide to the Moths of Great Britain and Ireland* (Waring, Townsend & Lewington, 2017), *Concise Guide to the Moths of Great Britain and Ireland* (Townsend, Waring & Lewington, 2019) and *The Butterflies of Britain and Ireland* (Thomas & Lewington, 2014).

We hope we appeal to a broad audience of those interested in natural history. The guide is certainly for the amateur naturalist keen on Lepidoptera and for students and professionals in ecology, but it is also for the many casual observers who just want to know the name of a caterpillar they have encountered or a bit more about it.

The terms caterpillar and larva are commonly used to refer to this early stage of the life cycle of a butterfly or moth, and similarly chrysalis and pupa for the following stage. Throughout this field guide we have preferred to use the shortest possible terms for the four stages of the life cycle, so we refer to them as egg, larva, pupa and adult.

Interest in adult moths has grown very rapidly in recent decades with the ready availability of moth traps, field guides, the internet and social media providing almost instant access to identification. Most people study moths from the comfort of their garden or patio, looking through what the light attracted to their trap the night before. By contrast, the recording of larvae generally requires more effort, unless they are stumbled across during a walk or in the garden. They are also relatively hard to identify, with few printed or online references available to assist. The disproportionate effort in favour of adult moths is reflected in data recording. For example, in the Devon moth database, just one in 250 records is of a larva, and that is in the county where BH lives, so Devon probably has a higher proportion of larval records than most!

We hope this field guide will stimulate a growing interest in larvae, and in searching for and recording them. Studying larvae, what they feed on, where and how they live, and their defence mechanisms will, we trust, add a new dimension to your interest in natural history. Generally, moths and butterflies spend a disproportionate amount of time as a larva compared with other life stages, and it is the commonest stage in which to spend the winter. In reality, there is no day or night of the year when larvae cannot be found somewhere, and the middle of winter is a surprisingly good time to have a look. There is also much to be discovered about the habits and behaviour of larvae in the wild.

This guide for the most part does not cover micro-moths, however desirable that may be. Micro-moths are a loose, non-scientific grouping of 50 families of moths that are generally smaller than the macro-moths. Most adults and a number of larvae of micro-moths are included within the *Field Guide to the Micro-moths of Great Britain and Ireland* (Sterling, Parsons & Lewington, 2012). It has been difficult enough to find sufficient material for RL to illustrate larvae of all the macro-moth species; it would be a league harder to achieve the same for over twice as many micro-moths, and take several years extra to write the accompanying species accounts. Treat that as a challenge! We do occasionally describe and illustrate micro-moth larvae in this guide, where we feel they are sufficiently similar to a macro-moth species. We also provide a few notes in this Introduction on separation of larvae of macro-moths and micro-moths. There is no easy distinction because there is no scientific basis for separating the groups in the first place. We have also included life history information of a few micro-moth species in the Introduction where it is particularly interesting.

On the subject of finding illustrative material for this field guide, in addition to our own extensive collections of photographs we are in the fortunate position to have been able to benefit from the explosive growth in the internet from the mid- to late 1990s. Since then there has been the advent of a few, but excellent, websites that cover life histories of butterflies and moths, using mostly high-quality digital images. These websites are referenced on p. 65

These websites are referenced on p. 65

OPPOSITE: **Larvae of (A) Pebble Prominent, (B) Large White, (C) Peppered Moth, (D) Scarce Footman, (E) Painted Lady, (F) Poplar Kitten, (G) Heath Fritillary, (H) Scarlet Tiger, (I) Rosy Marsh Moth and (J) Coxcomb Prominent**

under *Further reading*. Jim Porter's book *Colour Identification Guide to Caterpillars of the British Isles* (Porter, 1997) was the magnum opus of its day, showing photographs of larvae of almost all the macro-moths recorded at the time. Jim was restricted to using mostly 35mm transparencies, and his book is all the more remarkable when you realise the very limited amount of photographic material available to him, and the absence of websites.

When we started compiling this field guide, we knew the quantity of photographic material available for larvae would be just a fraction of what is available for adult macro-moths and butterflies. For adults, not only is there a plethora of digital images, but there are also drawers full of reference specimens in museums. While it is possible to preserve larvae using a technique known as 'blowing', and some collections do have them, such dried larvae are typically distorted and discoloured, so of little use as references for illustration and description.

We have done our best to synthesise what we have found to provide you with illustrations and supporting descriptive text, together with a number of photographs of feeding patterns and larval behaviours. Above all, we hope you enjoy using this book and that it helps to expand your knowledge and interest in the early stages of butterflies and moths.

USING THIS FIELD GUIDE

How many species are covered?

In this field guide we have included 832 species of butterfly and moth. These are either the species resident in Great Britain and Ireland or those that migrate here and result in larvae during the summer. The Channel Islands are also included. The number of residents will undoubtedly become out of date quickly following publication as more species arrive from Europe and colonise, and we continue to experience a warming climate. Some resident species may also become extinct.

Not every resident species is illustrated and described. For example, there are a few species that have never been found in the wild, such as Marsh Oblique-barred, Pinion-streaked Snout and White-line Snout. Also, Large Blue is not illustrated because the last-instar larva lives underground in the nests of ants.

Identifying a larva from its last instar

With a few exceptions, this field guide covers only the final instar of each species. An instar is the stage between successive ecdyses or sheddings of the skin: the first instar is the stage after hatching from the egg and before the first ecdysis; the final instar is the last stage after the larva has been through several skin changes, before it changes into a pupa (see *Life cycles*, p. 30).

Limiting illustrations to the final instar is a deliberate choice for several reasons:

■ Last-instar larvae exhibit the greatest contrast in colour and markings in comparison with earlier instars, which are invariably plainer.
■ Last-instar larvae offer the best characters that enable diagnosis to species; even then, some species are so similar that larvae must be reared to adult to confirm which species they are.
■ Last-instar larvae are mostly large enough to handle easily, and examine with the naked eye or under a low-power hand lens.
■ Only a small number of species can be identified with certainty from earlier instars.

If a larva is suspected not to be last instar it should be either reared to final instar or returned to where it was found. There is no easy way of telling what instar a larva is in, but larvae not in final instar will always be rather smaller than the illustration in this guide (taking account of the magnification), and generally rather plainer. Also, if the larva stops feeding for a few days and you notice a small head with a larger one behind underneath the skin, then it is about to change its skin into another instar (see photo p. 23). Extensive notes on rearing larvae are given on pp. 23–5. For a few species, we have included illustrations of earlier instars because they are distinctive and substantially different from the final instar.

Where to start to identify a larva

The starting point is the colour plate illustrations (pp. 212–75). For the novice this may present a bewildering range of possibilities. There are a substantial number of green and brown larvae, and at a very basic level all can look similar to one another. The accompanying species descriptions must be read as they contain the information that will help rule in or out a long list of possibilities. With practice, the task gets much easier. Once you have narrowed down identification to a few possible species, it is worth asking yourself the following questions about your unidentified larva:

- Is it within the known geographical distribution?
- Does it fit well with the illustrations and descriptions or are there missing or additional features?
- Is it possible to locate the different structures referred to in the text – if not, see the section on *Structure of a larva* (below).
- Is it in one of the appropriate habitats?
- Is it feeding or likely to be feeding on the appropriate plants?
- Should it be a last-instar larva at this date?
- Are there any other field notes to help?

We have included illustrations of the main colour forms, patterns and structures that we are aware of, and identification of many species can be straightforward. However, some larvae can be very variable and it has not been practicable, or indeed helpful, to illustrate or describe all known variations. For example, the larva of Green-brindled Crescent is very variable in colour and pattern, yet all forms possess a pair of raised points on the dorsum of abdominal segment A8. Illustrating all known forms would distract from the diagnostic feature.

The structure of a larva may also be variable. Brimstone Moth often has a large, divided dorsal projection on abdominal segment A3. However, this may be reduced to no more than a pair of slightly enlarged pinacula (raised bumps). In this instance, the larva of Brimstone Moth should present no great difficulty in identification, but it should be remembered that the soft structures can vary markedly within a species.

For some species we have seen only limited material, and where this is so we have mentioned this in the relevant accounts. It is inevitable that we will have not seen all variants of all species, so please bear this in mind when reading the text. Also, if you are using this guide in Europe, remember that some species show much greater variation in larval characters than populations in Great Britain and Ireland.

We have also included photographs of the feeding damage caused by larvae where this is helpful in finding the species in the field. For example, in the clearwing moths, Sesiidae, the larvae are never free-living, but are contained within their foodplant and may form a gall or other feeding sign that is characteristic and identifiable.

Once the reader has reached a conclusion about identity, we recommend consulting other sources of images of larvae, and particularly websites, as further confirmation. A list of websites we use regularly is given in the *Useful resources* list (p. 65).

Structure of a larva

The larva is the feeding stage of the moth or butterfly and its structure reflects the need to eat and digest, grow, move and deal with the risk of predation. At the front end is the head with the chewing mouthparts for ingestion; behind this is a long, expandable bag, the body; and at the back end is the anus for egestion. The body is supported on a number of pairs of legs, three pairs towards the front and up to five pairs behind.

While we have reduced the number of technical terms used in the species descriptions, there are many we consider essential to learn to identify larvae and get the best out of this guide (see *Glossary* opposite). The illustrations below show the basic structures and anatomical positions that we use in the descriptions.

Typical noctuid larva

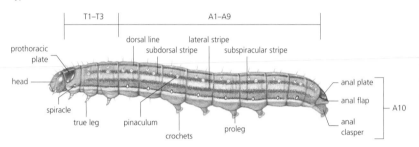

Larval head

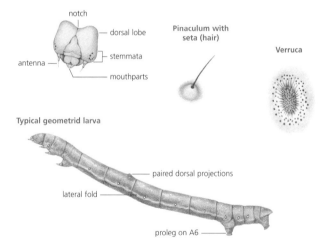

Pinaculum with seta (hair)

Verruca

Typical geometrid larva

Noctuid larva showing male gonad

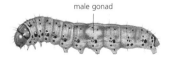

male gonad

Diagrams showing typical relative widths of a line, stripe and band

dorsal line   dorsal stripe   dorsal band

GLOSSARY

Adventive	Species that has appeared in a region, which may have been introduced accidentally or deliberately by human activity
Anal clasper	Fleshy outgrowth on A10 used in movement
Anal comb	Structure above anus, hidden beneath anal plate, used to flick away faecal pellets
Anal flap	Central structure on A10, dorsally covering the anus
Anal plate	Sclerotised area on anal flap
Anal point	Point on A10 either centrally at the end of the anal flap or paired arising from the base of the anal clasper or dorsolaterally from the anal flap
Antenna	Sensory organ on the head
Anterior	Nearer to or towards the front end of the larva or body segment, the position relative to a larval structure, or the front end of the larva
Aposematic	Animal with bright warning coloration or markings that warn or repel predators
Band	Marking wider than a stripe
Biennial	Occurring every other year
Bristle	Stiff hair
Butterfly	Member of a group of families in the superfamily Papilionoidea
Calyx (pl. calyces)	Protective outer layer of a flower bud
Chitin	Large structural polysaccharide that is a major component of an insect's exoskeleton
Cocoon	Structure constructed of silk, sometimes mixed with soil, hairs or plant material, in which the larva will pupate
Concolorous	Same colour as specified adjacent area
Cremaster	Set of hooks at the posterior end of the pupa that help secure or anchor it during this life stage
Crochet	One of a number of hooks at the end of the proleg used for gripping
Crypsis	Ability to blend in with the background

GLOSSARY

Cuticle (of larva)	Flexible outer covering of the larva, parts of which may be sclerotised or thickened and made hard
Diapause	Dormant phase adopted during unfavourable conditions, such as winter
Dioecious	Species of plant with male and female reproductive organs on separate plants
Distal	Away from the point of attachment to the main part of the body
Dorsal	Uppermost part of the body in anatomical position
Dorsal lobe	One side of the uppermost part of a notched head
Dorsal vessel	Major structure in the circulatory system situated centrally and at the uppermost of the body in anatomical position
Dorsolateral	Between dorsal and lateral areas
Dot	Tiny round mark, smaller than a spot
Ecdysis	Act of shedding a skin
Epidermis	Outer layer of cells of a leaf, also known as the cuticle
Foliose	Leaf-like growth form of a lichen, often lobed or undulating at the margin
Frass	Larval excrement or faecal pellets
Fruticose	Coral-like growth form of a lichen, producing a bushy form
Gonad	Organ that produces the reproductive (sex) cells
Haemolymph	Fluid circulating within an insect's body that is analogous to blood within vertebrates
Hair	Fine thread-like strand growing from the skin of the larva (in this field guide we include a seta arising from a pinaculum as a hair)
Herbaceous	Plant without a woody stem that usually persists for one or a few seasons; its foliage often dies back over winter
Hibernaculum	Larval habitation constructed for diapause
Instar	Stage between successive ecdyses: first instar is the stage after hatching from the egg and before the first ecdysis; final instar is the stage before pupation
Labial palp	Structure occurring in pairs, covered in scales, usually with three segments, arising from the head of an adult, below the eye

GLOSSARY	
Lateral	Side of the body in anatomical position
Lateral flange	Fold of skin near the spiracular level (more pronounced than a lateral fold)
Lateral fold	Fold of skin near the spiracular level
Leaf mine	Chamber created within a leaf by a larva feeding internally in the leaf tissue, leaving the upper and lower surfaces intact other than possibly an entry and/or exit hole, and creating a track or blotch when viewed from above or below
Line	Marking narrower than a stripe
Macro-moth	Species in the loose, non-scientific grouping of 15 families of moths that are generally larger than the micro-moths
Micro-moth	Species in the loose, non-scientific grouping of 50 families of moths that are generally smaller than the macro-moths
Monophagous	Feeds on only one foodplant
Network cocoon	Open-weave cocoon where the pupa is easily visible within
Neotropical	Biogeographic realm including the tropical regions of the Americas and the entire South American temperate zone
Newcomer's gland	Dorsal gland on A7 of various larvae in the family Lycaenidae that produces secretions attractive to ants
Nominate subspecies	When a species is split into two or more subspecies (ssp.), the population first described becomes the nominate ssp.; the subspecific name is a repeat of the species name (e.g. Dingy Skipper *Erynnis tages tages* populations became the nominate ssp. when ssp. *baynesi* was described)
Notch	On the larval head, an indentation along the centreline; on a leaf, a nick or V-shape chewed by the larva
Oligophagous	Feeds on a small number of different foodplants
Osmeterium	Forked structure that is extruded from T1 of the larvae of species of swallowtail butterfly when attacked
Oviposition	Act of egg-laying
Ovipositor	Egg-laying organ
Parasite	Organism that lives in or on another species, gaining nutrients at the other's expense; normally it is smaller than the host, and is often not lethal to it

GLOSSARY	
Parasitoid or protelean parasite (of insects)	Insect, usually a wasp or fly, that feeds as a larva in or on the body of its host, which provides all its nourishment; the host dies at the end of the association, and the wasp or fly emerges as a larva or adult to become free-living (in this field guide, we refer to parasitoids as parasites)
Patch	Marking larger than a spot, which may be regular or irregular in outline
Peristalsis (peristaltic)	Wave-like muscular contractions
Petiole	Leaf stalk that joins the leaf to the stem
Phenology	Study of the time of year when different stages are found
Pinaculum (pl. pinacula)	Outgrowth from the larval skin giving rise to a seta
Plumose	Feather-like
Polyphagous	Feeds on a wide variety of foodplants
Pore cupola	Small glands scattered over the surface of various larvae in the family Lycaenidae that produce secretions attractive to ants
Posterior	Nearer to or towards the hind end of the larva or body segment, the position relative to a larval structure, or the hind end of the larva
Proboscis	Feeding organ of an adult butterfly or moth
Proleg	Fleshy ventral outgrowth from an abdominal segment, usually on A3–A6 of larvae, and used in movement
Prothoracic plate	Sclerotised plate on T1
Pupa	Chrysalis, the life cycle stage between larva and adult
Sclerotised	Thickened area on a larva
Sclerotised strip	Thickened transverse structure on a larva
Seta (pl. setae)	Hair arising from a pinaculum
Spine	Sharp projection
Spinneret	Larval organ that produces silk
Spiracle	Structure through which gases diffuse into and out of the body
Spiracular	In the region of the spiracles

GLOSSARY	
Spot	Roughly circular mark, larger than a dot but smaller than a patch
Stemma (pl. stemmata)	A structure on the larval head functioning as an eye
Stripe	Marking wider than a line but narrower than a band
Tentacle organ	One of a pair of eversible organs on A8 of the larvae of several species of blue butterfly; when everted it can be seen to end in a rim of filaments
Thanatosis	Behaviour of an animal that is 'playing dead'
Tine	Sharp point
Tracheal tube	Air tube leading in from the spiracle
True leg	Leg on a thoracic segment
Tubercle	Prominence on Emperor Moth larvae giving rise to bristles
Ventral	Underneath of the body in anatomical position
Ventrolateral	Between ventral and lateral areas
Verruca (pl. verrucae)	Prominence on larval skin giving rise to a tuft of diverging hairs

In describing larvae we typically use the terms dorsal to describe characters on the upperside of the larva, lateral for those at the side, and ventral for the ones on the underside. Since larvae are basically cylindrical in shape, there is no physical demarcation of dorsal, lateral and ventral parts. It is a matter of interpretation where a particular feature sits on the cylinder, but we have tried to be consistent. We sometimes refer to the combination 'dorsolateral' where the feature is halfway between the top and side of the larva.

The head has mouthparts and usually six stemmata (light-sensitive organs) on each side, which function as eyes. Behind the head are the three thoracic segments, followed by 10 abdominal segments. These are described as T1–T3 and A1–A10. The thoracic segments may be referred to as prothorax (T1), mesothorax (T2) and metathorax (T3), and in some species we describe a sclerotised (see *Glossary* opposite) dorsal plate on T1, also known as the prothoracic plate. A pair of true legs arises from each thoracic segment; these legs correspond to the legs beneath the thorax in an adult moth or butterfly.

We refer to the term prolegs for the 'legs' on A3–A6, and anal claspers for those on A10, and most larvae typically have this arrangement. Each proleg and anal clasper ends in small hooks called crochets. The function of prolegs and anal claspers is to cling onto a surface and aid the larva's locomotion. Legs and their modification are discussed further in the section on *Defence mechanisms* (p. 42). There is a reduction in the number of prolegs and anal claspers in some families, and in some species. There is never an increase in proleg number. Larvae in the families Cossidae, Sesiidae, Zygaenidae, Papilionidae, Hesperiidae, Pieridae, Nymphalidae, Riodinidae, Lycaenidae, Lasiocampidae, Endromidae, Saturniidae, Sphingidae, Notodontidae, Erebidae and Noctuidae all have prolegs on A3–A6, but there are exceptions among the Erebidae and Noctuidae and these are described in the species accounts. Larvae in the subfamily Nolinae of the Nolidae lack prolegs on A3. In some of the Notodontidae the anal claspers are modified into tails. Most Geometridae have only one pair of prolegs and that is on A6. Larvae in the subfamily Drepaninae of the Drepanidae lack anal claspers. Limacodidae larvae break the rules entirely and do not have either prolegs or anal claspers.

A pair of spiracles is present on T1 and A1–A8, but is absent on T2–T3. It is through these that oxygen diffuses in and carbon dioxide diffuses out of the larva's body. The position of the prolegs and spiracles can aid in identifying which segment is which. Above the anus is the anal flap. There may be a sclerotised shield on A10 known as the anal plate, and in some families, such as Hesperiidae, larvae have an additional structure between the flap and anus known as the anal comb.

The body has numerous wart-like structures on its surface known as pinacula (singular pinaculum), sometimes prominent, sometimes all but invisible. These give rise to setae (singular seta) or hairs, either singly or in tufts. Strictly speaking, the term setae refers to what arises from pinacula. They have a sensory function and may also contribute to the colour and pattern of the larva. Some species have hairs elsewhere not arising from pinacula. In this field guide the term hairs is used to encompass setae as well. Sometimes the point from which a hair arises is within a larger sclerotised patch. In such cases, we refer to the whole patch surrounding the central point from which a hair arises as a pinaculum (e.g. see Crescent).

There are often longitudinal lines or stripes. The position of these is described as dorsal, lateral or spiracular (see *Glossary*, p. 11). The prefixes 'sub' and 'supra' are commonly added to indicate the position of a line below or above that area or part of the body. We also distinguish the width of the feature: if thin, the term 'line' is used; if relatively wider, 'stripe'; and if very wide, 'band'. All these terms are relative to one another, and there is often variation between larvae. Again, we have tried to be consistent in our descriptions and offer the term that is most frequently observed as a description of width.

There may be single or paired anal points present. A single anal point is created by a sharp end to the anal plate. Paired anal points arise in one of two ways. Usually they are pointed projections that arise posteriorly from the bases of the anal claspers. However, in the subfamily Satyrinae of the Nymphalidae, they are processes arising dorsolaterally from the anal flap.

There may be soft swellings or projections present on various segments. These are often very useful in identification but may be variable within a species. These structures can differ in prominence from the start to the end of the final instar; just after the skin change, soft structures are usually most noticeable, but as the larva grows and its body fills out, they tend to become much less obvious. Larvae in the subfamily Ennominae of the Geometridae, including the thorns in genera *Ennomos* and *Selenia*, are good examples.

Some of the Geometridae have a fold of skin near the spiracles, which we have referred to as the lateral fold. It is even more pronounced in Satin Wave, forming a lateral flange from A2 to A5.

There are a number of species where the larva has a somewhat translucent skin with organs and viscera showing through. The dorsal vessel that carries the blood or haemolymph may be visible and we describe this as a character in some species. In White-mantled Wainscot visibility through the skin of the tracheal tube joining the spiracles is the key feature separating it from Brown-veined Wainscot. In the male of many species, the paired gonads may be visible subdorsally through the skin on A5.

Large Ear larva showing male gonads on A5

Distinguishing larvae of micro-moths

There are no obvious features that allow us to distinguish larvae belonging to families of macro-moths and butterflies from those in families of micro-moths. It is only with experience of both groups that distinguishing them becomes easy. However, here are a few pointers to help:

- Macro-moth and butterfly larvae are generally much larger than micro-moth larvae in their final instar.
- Micro-moth larvae are frequently leaf miners for part or all of their larval period, whereas this is a rare behaviour in larvae of macro-moths and butterflies (e.g. forester moths).
- Micro-moth larvae are often translucent, with the viscera and dorsal vessel showing through the skin, whereas this is a feature mostly confined to macro-moth larvae living within plant stems and roots.
- Micro-moth larvae are often very active when disturbed, whereas this is generally less so with macro-moth and butterfly larvae.
- Many macro-moth and butterfly larvae are free-living on the surface of plants, hidden away in leaf litter by day and moving up the plant to feed at night, or live under the soil surface. They often rely on intrinsic crypsis to hide from predators unless they are aposematic (see *Warning colours and mimicry*, p. 49). The majority of micro-moth larvae are rather more concealed within plant materials, often drawn together with silk, although a few are free-living, and a very few aposematic.
- Similar to a few macro-moth larvae and those of lycaenid butterflies are some free-living larvae of the plume moths in the Pterophoridae micro-moth family. Careful examination should enable these to be separated easily, and especially by noting the foodplant.
- Many micro-moth larvae make spinnings among leaves, whereas this is less common behaviour among macro-moth and butterfly larvae (e.g. the lutestrings in subfamily Thyatirinae of the Drepanidae).

There are no macro-moth or butterfly larvae in Great Britain and Ireland that make a portable case of silk, plant or mineral material, whereas this is commonplace in some families of micro-moths (e.g. it defines the 100 or so species of case-bearing Coleophoridae).

Distinguishing larvae of sawflies and beetles

Larvae of sawflies and some beetles can look similar to those of butterflies and moths. Sawflies belong to the suborder Symphyta in the order Hymenoptera and are commonly considered as the primitive forms of our more familiar ants, bees and wasps. Their larvae can be remarkably similar to those of butterflies and moths at first glance, but it is important to count the legs.

Honeysuckle Sawfly *Zaraea fasciata* larva, showing prolegs A2–A8 and large dark eye (stemma) on head

Chamomile Shark larva, showing prolegs A3–A6

A chafer beetle larva, showing the absence of prolegs and relatively long true legs

Sawfly larvae have additional prolegs on A2 and sometimes A7 and even A8. No British butterfly or moth larva has these. Sawfly larvae do not have crochets at the end of the prolegs. In addition, sawfly larvae have a single dark stemma, or eye, on each side of the head. This is easily noticeable if the head is pale, whereas butterfly and moth larvae usually have six much smaller and hardly noticeable stemmata on each side of the head.

Larvae of a number of larger beetles (Coleoptera) can be of similar size to those of butterflies and moths. They tend to live within plant tissues or the soil, although those of the leaf beetles (Chrysomelidae) are free-living on leaves. Most have soft, rather pointed bodies, and when they are uncovered in soil or dead wood, they are dirty whitish with a pale brownish head, and lying on their side in a characteristic C-shape. Free-living beetle larvae tend to be squat in shape with fat abdomens and tapering to front and back ends. Beetle larvae do not have prolegs and their true legs are often long and well developed, although sometimes absent.

FORMAT OF THE SPECIES ACCOUNTS

Taxonomic order and nomenclature

The species text is organised numerically following *Checklist of the Lepidoptera of the British Isles* (Agassiz, Beavan & Heckford, 2013). The nomenclature also follows this publication and subsequent updates. We give the superfamily name (ending in 'oidea'), which may be represented by just one or a few families. We then give the family name (ending in 'idae') at the start of each family, and then the subfamily (ending in 'inae'). There is a brief introduction to the family, setting the diversity of species in Great Britain and Ireland in a global context, together with any notes about their larvae, and if there are any common features.

Each species is headed by its common name, scientific name, checklist number and reference to the illustration. The family is coded by one or two digits before the decimal point, and the species by three or four digits after. For example, for 3.001 Orange Swift the '3' indicates family Hepialidae and the '001' the taxonomic place of Orange Swift in that family. Similarly, for 70.2841 Banded Pine Carpet the '70' indicates the species is in the family Geometridae, and the '2841' its position within the family. A four-digit species code indicates that either the species is an addition to the list since its publication or it is known or thought to be an adventive or import into the country. The number in brackets is the former checklist number from *Checklist of Lepidoptera Recorded from the British Isles* (Bradley, 2000). The scientific name is given in italics as a binomial (genus and species).

The binomial should usually be followed by the author who described the species, with the date of publication. For ease of reading, the author and date have been omitted in the main body of the text, but are given in full in the checklist at the back of the guide (p. 369).

Status and distribution

The status of each moth species is that given in Waring, Townsend & Lewington (2019). There are a few exceptions where we have updated status in the light of new information. The status definitions follow those published by the Joint Nature Conservation Committee and are listed opposite. They do not apply in Ireland. It is accepted that in many cases these statuses are badly in need of revision, but review can be carried out only under a closely defined procedure. Butterfly Conservation is in the process of carrying out that review of moths for the government agencies. So, for now, there are examples throughout the text where the status is given as 'Common' yet the species has become much rarer – for instance Spinach, which has declined severely in recent decades and is rarely seen across much of lowland England.

The status categories used are as follows:

- Red Data Book species (RDB). These are species included in the *British Red Data Books 2. Insects* (Shirt, 1987) or meeting the Red Data Book criteria subsequently.
- pRDB. Species proposed in Waring, Townsend & Lewington (2017) for RDB status at the next review as they now meet the current RDB criteria.
- Nationally Scarce A (Na) – recorded from 16–30 10km squares in Britain since 1980.
- Nationally Scarce B (Nb) – recorded from 31–100 10km squares in Britain since 1980.
- Local – recorded from 101–300 10km squares in Britain since 1960.
- Common – recorded from more than 300 10km squares in Britain since 1960.
- Uncommon on introduced foodplant (alien host) – recorded from fewer than 100 10km squares in Britain since 1980, but all known larval foodplants are non-native.
- Transitory resident – breeding population present but for only a small number of years.
- Naturalised – accidentally introduced to Britain and breeding successfully here.
- Immigrant – recorded occasionally or regularly and believed to have flown to Britain from Europe, Africa or America. Where it is not clear, then 'possible' or 'suspected' has been added.
- Rare immigrant – very few records (usually fewer than 10), but there is good evidence (e.g. weather conditions, association with known immigrant species) that migration was involved.
- Suspected rare immigrant – doubt exists that records are of genuine natural immigrants. Generally refers to species recorded on fewer than 10 occasions (often only a single record), and often those not usually regarded as migratory.
- Adventive – accidentally introduced to Britain, often with imported goods, and intercepted at, or recorded at or close by, ports of entry, airports, warehouses, etc. Adventives can become naturalised.
- Extinct – resident species that has not been recorded for a very long time in spite of many searches of known sites and other suitable habitats.

For butterflies, the status categories are taken from Fox *et al.* (2010).

- Regionally Extinct (RE) – there is no reasonable doubt that the last individual has died in the region.
- Critically Endangered (CR) – considered to be facing an extremely high risk of extinction in the wild.
- Endangered (EN) – considered to be facing a very high risk of extinction in the wild.
- Vulnerable (VU) – considered to be facing a high risk of extinction in the wild.
- Near Threatened (NT) – has been evaluated against the criteria but does not qualify for Critically Endangered, Endangered or Vulnerable now, but is close to qualifying for, or is likely to qualify for, a threatened category in the near future.
- Least Concern (LC) – has been evaluated against the criteria and does not qualify for Critically Endangered, Endangered, Vulnerable or Near Threatened. Widespread and abundant taxa are included in this category.

A species can have two statuses. This is particularly so for those that have restricted distributions where they are known to be breeding but are occasionally found a long way from known areas, and especially along the coast during periods of heightened immigrant activity.

Where we feel it helpful, we then provide a note on the current distribution of the species to add context to the distribution map (see below), and comment on recent changes in range and abundance. These comments have largely been interpreted from the two reviews of the state of Britain's larger moths published by Butterfly Conservation and Rothamsted Research (Fox *et al.*, 2006 and Fox *et al.*, 2013), and in the light of our own lifetime experiences.

Where more than one subspecies (ssp.) occurs in Great Britain and Ireland then these are listed and their distributions described very briefly. Where only one subspecies occurs in Great Britain and Ireland but it is not the nominate subspecies (see *Glossary*, p. 13), then the species is headed as the binomial and the subspecific name is written at the start of the species text.

The following species are fully protected under Schedule 5 of the Wildlife and Countryside Act 1981 and subsequent amendments. In summary, it is an offence to kill, injure, possess or sell any of their life stages or to damage or destroy their habitat.

Fiery Clearwing	Marsh Fritillary	Black-veined Moth
New Forest Burnet	Heath Fritillary	Sussex Emerald
Swallowtail	Large Blue	Reddish Buff
High Brown Fritillary	Barberry Carpet	Fisher's Estuarine Moth

Distribution maps

Thumbnail distribution maps are provided for all species, often with individual descriptions in the text. The data are drawn from maps of post-1999 records from Butterfly Conservation's Butterflies for the New Millennium and National Moth Recording Scheme, and Moths Ireland.

These maps are provided for at-a-glance reference, to see if it is likely that the species being identified would fit with the known distribution. We advise that readers do not attempt to interpret the boundaries of the coloured shapes in detail. They provide indicative distributions only and shapes have been altered to some extent to allow locations to appear at such a small scale. So, for species restricted to one site, the shape on the map is bound to cover a much greater proportion of the map than the species inhabits on the ground.

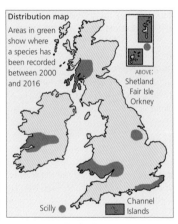

An example of a distribution map

Field characters

For each species we give a brief description of the larva, concentrating on those features that are helpful in identification. The same features are not necessarily described for all species as they are not always useful in this respect. Each description deals with one side of the larva, although the head is described whole. If present, there is one dorsal line and any dorsal structures are described as paired. Anal points are described as single or paired and the tails of some of the Notodontidae are described as paired. The ventral surface is not routinely described but on many occasions we do make a comment where we consider this useful. Ventral structures are described as paired if appropriate. Otherwise a feature is described only on one side of the body, even though it obviously occurs on the other side as well. The features we use are explained in detail in the earlier section on the structure of a larva (p. 10).

The range of larval length in last instar for each species has not been included as we do not consider it particularly helpful in diagnosis. A larva continues to grow until fully fed, and throughout last instar its length will increase noticeably before decreasing in preparation for pupation, so measurements at a point in time can be misleading. For readers who do wish to examine larval length, these are recorded next to the images on the UK Lepidoptera website (see *Further reading*, p. 65).

Similar species

Where species are likely to be confused, these are listed and the differences described, usually under the first of those species in taxonomic order. On occasions they have been dealt with slightly differently; for example, if one of these is significantly more widespread and commoner than the others, then the differences may be described under that species. If two species have similar larvae but there is no overlap of their foodplants, they are not necessarily listed as similar. The plant on which such a larva was found should prevent confusion. Conversely, species found on the same foodplant may be described under similar species when their similarities are modest.

There are many cases where we consider the larvae of two or more species as indistinguishable in the field. In such cases, we generally include a larval description only in the first of the group, and we refer to one illustration that covers the group, which is appropriately referenced under that illustration. That is not to say there aren't reliable diagnostic features, just that we haven't been able to find them.

For a few hard-to-identify groups containing several species we have produced separate tables of key features and notes. We hope the information in the tables will be helpful in guiding the reader to narrow down a wide range to a few possible species, but it is likely any larvae will need to be reared to confirm identity. There are tables for wainscots in genera *Mythimna*, *Leucania* and *Senta*, carpets in genus *Xanthorhoe*, sallows and chestnuts, and, as we have termed them, readily confused pale-striped green noctuids. Some species have larvae that are immensely variable in colour and pattern, and whose range of variation overlaps with that of other species. Various pug moths fall into this category, and they are dealt with in a table.

Habitats

We have listed terms for habitats that are mostly in general or common usage in Great Britain and Ireland. The list for each species is where we have found larvae, or where they have been recorded or published to live. The list should not be taken as comprehensive or definitive. Habitats used do not follow any defined classification system, but we have chosen those based broadly on plant composition (e.g. grassland, woodland, heathland), geological formation or soil type (e.g. acid or calcareous), and physical characteristics such as wetness or salinity (e.g. dry grasslands, saltmarsh). Some species do not fit easily into habitat categories, or they occupy a particular part of a habitat, and we add additional descriptive notes for these. We provide a few notes below on habitats that may be less familiar to some readers, and where we consider explanation about others may be helpful.

Breckland is an area of East Anglia in Norfolk and Suffolk where there is a unique combination of dry acid grassland/heathland mixed with calcareous grassland. This combination has formed where sands have been wind-blown over the underlying chalk. The area is important both for its mix of perennial plants and for its annuals that thrive on thin, impoverished soils.

Calcareous grassland refers to chalk grassland or chalk downland, and to limestone grassland. Calcareous grassland is largely restricted to southern England, with the greatest expanse in any area being on Salisbury Plain in Wiltshire.

Carr woodland is a type of wet woodland, often permanently or seasonally waterlogged, usually dominated by willows or Alder. It is often characterised by an impenetrable jungle of branches and trunks of living and dead wood, mixed with tussocky grasses and sedges, and can be surprisingly diverse in its vegetation composition. The best examples are in the Norfolk Broads.

Gardens and urban parks is used here as a catch-all for the variety of habitats that make up the more natural spaces in our urban environments where moth and butterfly larvae are found. We also add allotments, cemeteries and street trees where appropriate. London supports dozens of urban parks and retains surprisingly high biodiversity.

Hard cliff describes vegetation that clings on to sheer rock faces, in crevices or among eroded materials, including rock scree. The mineral nature of the rock, and exposure to wind and sea spray, determines what grows, but the habitat is characterised by short, sparse vegetation. Hard cliff occurs around the coastlines of Great Britain and Ireland, with spectacular examples on the Lizard (Cornwall), Gower Peninsula (Wales), Isle of Skye (Scotland) and Cliffs of Moher (Co. Clare, Ireland).

Limestone pavement refers to eroded exposures of Carboniferous limestone (c. 330 million years old), scored by deep fissures with slabs or pavement between, and where the soil has largely been washed away. The vegetation is extremely diverse, supporting calcium-loving plants, and plants characteristic of acid conditions where the soils are leached. There is a range of wetness from parched ground to bog, adding to the diversity. There is no better example in western Europe than on the Burren, Cos Clare and Galway, in the west of Ireland.

Machair is a type of dune grassland formed from calcareous seashells and seaweeds. It is often very rich in herbaceous plant species. Machair is uniquely found on the coasts of northern and western Ireland and Scotland.

Parkland is wood pasture. Trees of varying age grow in relatively open conditions among grassland or Bracken where natural woodland regeneration is suppressed by the intensity of grazing. Parkland may contain many veteran trees. The most extensive area of parkland in Britain is in the New Forest in Hampshire.

Soft cliff describes a cliff that erodes from its base through the action of the sea, and throughout via the action of rain washing the surface and seeping into porous sands. It supports a complex of habitats, often on a small scale, including open ground, dry and wet grasslands, fen, scrub and carr woodland. Perhaps the best examples are the soft cliff exposures between Lyme Regis and Bridport in Dorset.

Waste ground is also a catch-all for a wide variety of open and often sparsely vegetated habitats associated with industrial landscapes and urban development in a phase of dereliction, with varying amounts of natural succession towards revegetation. Waste ground is a subset of brownfield, or former developed land. Some mine-waste landscapes known as calaminarian grasslands are important ecologically, owing to their high concentrations of toxic heavy metals in the soil, and, in general, waste ground is an important resource for wildlife. There are good examples of this grassland type in the Peak District National Park in Derbyshire.

We list habitats in alphabetical order where we do not consider there is a particular preference across a larva's geographical range. Otherwise, the main habitats are listed first.

Foodplants

The foodplant list is derived from a number of published resources, data from the National Moth Recording Scheme and personal observations. Unless otherwise stated, they are plants that we know or presume to host the larva in the wild in Great Britain or Ireland. Where published foodplants clearly refer to captive rearing, we have not included them. It is surprisingly difficult to be certain what constitutes a foodplant and we discuss this further under *What do larvae eat?* (p. 40). Where one or a few plants are known to be the preferred hosts, these are listed first and stated as such. Where it is less clear there is a preference, or we consider there is no preference that holds true across the known geographical range of a species, we list the plant species in alphabetical order of the generic common name. In this way, for example, a species on Heath Bedstraw and Lady's Bedstraw is shown as 'on Heath and Lady's bedstraws', rather than these two plants being split as they might be if ordered by specific name. We have pluralised generic common names to prevent repetition. We have also pluralised generic common names where we do not know which species exactly is the foodplant; thus a larva known to feed on unspecified oaks is written as 'on oaks'. For species that feed on a very wide range of plants, we have listed up to 20 species of host where we are reasonably confident of that list, and have not attempted to include all known foodplants. An index of the common and scientific names of the plants, together with associated species of butterflies and moths, is given at the back of the guide (p. 386). We follow Stace (2019) where the plant names are included in that publication.

Field notes

This section includes the period when the species is a larva. If it is known that there is more than one generation a year then this is given, and also whether the larva feeds by day or night or both. Other aspects of behaviour are described that may enable the reader to decide the best way to find the larva, having read the section *How to find larvae* (p. 26). If known, the pupation site is given, and whether a cocoon is constructed. These are not always confirmed in the wild because they are hard to observe. Sometimes they are inferred from captive rearing, and there can be conflicting accounts between different literature sources, possibly because there is genuine variation within a species or inaccuracy in recording. The stage at which the species overwinters is stated unless inferred from the larval period spanning the winter. If a larva or pupa is known to overwinter more than once then this is mentioned.

REARING TECHNIQUES

We advocate rearing of difficult-to-identify larvae in many places in the text. More widely, however, it also allows observation of this fascinating and rather understudied aspect of the life cycle, and particularly larval behaviour. Although we advise caution in extrapolating observations in captivity to what happens in the wild (see *Captive rearing on plants*, p. 41), it may give important clues. In this section we set out our experiences and those of others on the best ways to care for larvae and pupae.

Care of larvae

Most larvae can be reared in plastic boxes providing their foodplant is changed every couple of days. They should be kept out of direct sunlight to prevent overheating and condensation, in which they could otherwise drown. Most larvae can be kept in the dark if necessary. If they

Grey Dagger larva ready for ecdysis – note the appearance of two heads

Sleeve on a branch and sleeve on a pot for rearing larvae

feed on plants with a relatively high water content then a piece of kitchen towel in the bottom of the box will be helpful to absorb excessive moisture from the frass (the egested material). A small paintbrush may be helpful in moving larvae when the container is cleaned out. Some larvae, such as those of Notodontidae, spin significant pads of silk on the leaves to cling onto and can be difficult to move with a paintbrush; attempting this when they are due to shed their skins may result in the process failing to be completed and death. For these larvae, cut the leaf around them with scissors.

When preparing to shed its skin, the larva stops feeding and the new, larger head becomes apparent, forming behind the old head, which is soon to be cast. When it is nearly fully grown, suitable material should be provided for pupation, so check the species account for pupation site. For those larvae that pupate on or in the ground, provision of a dry compost material is ideal. For most larvae, a depth of a few centimetres is fine, but very large species will need to burrow deeper.

Those species that pass the winter as a larva present a challenge, and it can be very difficult to get some through successfully. A number of species continue to feed slowly throughout the winter, such as Clouded Yellow and Lesser Yellow Underwing. They can continue to be fed in the usual way but should be kept in an outbuilding. Keeping them indoors may bring larvae to full growth early, resulting in the adult hatching at an inappropriate date. Keeping overwintering larvae in a plastic box may result in losses; a good alternative is to 'sleeve' them out, encaging them in a netting tube or bag either on the branch of a tree or on potted plants as appropriate to the species. If using a pot, the bottom of the pot should be lined with a permeable material to prevent ingress of predators and escape of your larvae. The sleeve can be tied around the rim of the pot and small stakes used to raise the sleeve material away from the plant. A suitable sleeve can be made from a rectangular piece of fine netting or translucent cloth, with its long edges sewn together with a fine stitch. The sleeve can then be placed over the branch or pot and tied at either end, having put the larvae inside.

Most larvae can be switched from one known foodplant to another if necessary. Check the *Further reading* list (p. 63) for sources of information. However, it is worth highlighting that there are instances when larvae refuse alternatives or die after eating them. This can happen even though they would have been fine if they had been started on the alternative from hatching. For example, Devon Carpet larvae accept Hedge Bedstraw when newly hatched, but if later switched to it from Common Marsh-bedstraw they die.

Care of pupae

Care of the pupa depends on a number of factors, such as size, whether and where the larva made a cocoon, and how soon the adult is likely to emerge. Some will emerge within a couple of weeks, whereas others will pass through the winter in this stage. Indeed, the pupa of species such Belted Beauty may survive over several winters, and can emerge in autumn in captivity as well as its normal emergence period in spring.

If the pupa is in a flimsy cocoon it can be removed from the cocoon and placed on a shallow layer of compost material in a plastic box. The advantage of opening the cocoon is that you will know whether there is a live pupa or dead larva inside and you will be able to anticipate emergence of the adult. Some species make a strong, specialised cocoon, such as those in the families Lasiocampidae, Saturniidae and some in the Notodontidae. The cocoons of these should be left intact. For those species whose larvae have buried themselves, after a couple of weeks it is worth tipping out the compost material and collecting the pupae. But check the species text to see if the species is one that remains underground in its cocoon for many weeks through the summer, or overwinters underground as a larva, before pupating. These should not be disturbed until you feel confident they will have pupated.

Very large pupae, such as those in the family Sphingidae, have low risk of dehydration and can be kept in a large plastic container such as a plant propagator. An occasional sprinkling of water is a good idea. On emergence, such a relatively heavy adult will not be able to cling to plastic easily, so some twigs should be provided for the adult to climb onto to allow its wings to expand fully and hang down.

Smaller pupae should be kept on a shallow layer of compost material in a plastic box, as described above. Desiccation is a risk, particularly for those that spend many months in this stage, but so is mould. A small amount of water can be sprinkled onto the compost occasionally, but excessive dampness should be avoided. The box must be kept out of direct light to avoid condensation and can be kept in the dark. Small geometrid moths are light enough to be able to cling to the sides of a plastic box, but this is not so for larger species. It is a good idea to line the sides of the box with some nylon netting for the adult to climb onto. A good way to achieve this is to cut one piece of netting such that when placed in a rectangular plastic box it will cover the bottom and come up the sides, and can be held in place by the lid. The compost material at the bottom will hold it in place.

Very often, the pupa will change visibly when emergence of the adult is imminent. It may darken, the wing pattern may be visible through the wing cases and it becomes soft.

Box for keeping pupae, with netting for moths to cling onto

HOW TO FIND LARVAE

A variety of methods can be employed for finding larvae. Reading the field notes in each species account should enable you to decide which technique or techniques are going to be suitable to find that particular larva and whether to look by day or night. Different species will be found at different times of the year and some can be found feeding on mild nights throughout the winter. For larvae that feed on trees and shrubs, throughout May and into early June is a time when there are particularly large numbers of larvae in the wild. Trees and shrubs do not build up full chemical defences against herbivores in their leaves until summer and this is exploited by larvae. It is also one reason why insectivorous birds nest at the same time, to feed their young on this insect bonanza.

Searching

Serendipity plays a part. While out for a walk you may be lucky enough to encounter the larva of something like a Goat Moth crossing the path in search of a pupation site, or you might happen to spot the larva of a Dark Green Fritillary crawling at high speed. More commonly, larvae are found by chance while you are weeding in the garden. Species that spend the day underground are often found in this way, such as Heart & Dart and Large Yellow Underwing.

Usually, though, to find larvae you need to spend time going out to look for them. Simply use your eyes to look at trees or plants on the ground and be prepared to get down on your hands and knees. There are clues to be found, such as leaves with holes or chunks eaten out of them, although of course many other invertebrates do that too. If a leaf has been eaten, look to see if the margin of the eaten part is brown, in which case the damage is old, or green, in which case the larva is likely to be nearby. If it is a plant on the ground that has been eaten recently, search at the base of the plant as the culprit may be resting there during the day. Finding larvae is a skill, and as time goes by you will become much better at spotting them and their signs. The eye tends to be drawn to strong, lush plants but you need to discipline yourself to look for the weak, less healthy looking plants. There are two reasons for this. First, the weak plants may look like that as a result of feeding damage. Second, stressed plants may be less able to mount a defence against insect attack and so may be favoured.

Many species feed inside the foodplants and there can be telltale signs of their presence. Those that feed internally in the stems of grasses give themselves away by a dead or dying central shoot. They do move from plant to plant, so if you do not find them in the first plant, look close by. Cock's-foot is a good grass to search for species of minors in genus *Oligia*, or young larvae of Flounced Rustic. A Foxglove wilting at the top is likely to have a larva of Frosted Orange inside the stem. Sometimes the Foxglove stems are fractured, leaving them bent over at an acute angle. Although this gives them the appearance of having been hit by a stick, in fact they have snapped at the site of the entry hole of the larva.

Typical posture for searching for larvae on the ground

Sickly shoot of Cock's-foot caused by internal feeding of Marbled Minor; INSET: Marbled Minor larva

Drooping Foxglove and hole (arrowed) in stem caused by Frosted Orange larva;
INSET: Frosted Orange larva in Foxglove stem

Another clue may be a spun leaf or several leaves spun together. Opening such a spinning will reveal the larva inside, unless it has moved on.

Spun leaves of Eared Willow, the habitation of Small Chocolate-tip larva

Small Chocolate-tip larva (Ireland)

Narrow-bordered Bee Hawk-moth frass and larva

The presence of frass suggests a larva nearby. Frass is often black, but may also be green or pale brown, and sometimes reddish, as made by larvae of Large Red-belted Clearwing. Frass may have fallen from above onto a leaf or have been left behind by a larva when it was feeding.

Searching can also be done at night and in many ways this is likely to be a more productive and rewarding method of finding larvae of moths and butterflies. That is because so many species are active only at night. Ground-dwelling species may hide at ground level or even underground during the day, coming up at night to feed. Many tree-dwellers may hide by day in a bark crevice, between spun leaves or cryptically on a branch, again coming out at night to feed. A good torch is what is needed, and a warm night helps.

Sweeping

A sweep net is made of a strong material capable of repeatedly being swiped across vegetation. It is really suitable only for habitats where plants are going to be able to withstand its use, such as grassland and heathland. The net should be swept briskly from side to side and the contents examined after about every 10 sweeps. One disadvantage of this method is that it is not possible to tell exactly which plant a larva was feeding on. Sweeping can be done by day and even more productively at night. Be careful when the vegetation is wet because larvae can drown in the moisture that collects at the bottom of the sweep net, so examine the contents regularly.

Sweep net being used on heathland

Collecting catkins

Collecting catkins of poplars and willows that fall to the ground in spring can be a productive method of finding larvae. Keep the catkins in an old pillowcase and any larvae will crawl up the material in due course. They will generally be quite small and you will have to rear them at least to final instar or maybe to adult to be certain of their identity. A variety of species may be found in this way, including Pink-barred Sallow, Sallow and Red-line Quaker. Slender Pug completes its development feeding on the catkins of willows.

Another rewarding method is to cut a few twigs of Grey Willow during February. Fill a glass jar with water and secure a lid on top. Pierce the lid sufficiently to allow the cut end of each stem to be pushed through into the water. Keep the jar in an old fish tank or similar covered with netting material to prevent larvae escaping. In due course, the twigs should start sprouting roots and the leaf buds will open. Unseen moth eggs will hatch and young larvae will start eating the new shoots.

Beating

A beating tray is essentially a white sheet, held taut by a rigid, folding framework. Either by day or at night, hold it under the branch of a tree in full leaf and give the branch a short, sharp blow with a sturdy stick. Many larvae can be dislodged this way. However, some simply grip on too tightly or hide in spinnings by day. At night additional species will have emerged from their spinnings to feed, and others that hide by day on branches or in bark crevices will be out on the leaves feeding. Beating is not suitable if the trees are wet or if conditions are windy.

It is not just trees that can be beaten. At night, try bending Common Reed over the tray and beating the leaves. This will reveal not only species that feed on the reeds but also species associated with other plants growing among them. Overhanging heathers can be beaten in a similar way, and a variation in the technique is to hold the tray or a net under a herbaceous plant and ruffle the plant with your fingers to encourage any larvae to fall.

A storm in May can provide what amounts to a natural beating on a grand scale. The strong wind may dislodge a large number of larvae from the tops of trees and they are left exposed afterwards on the understorey vegetation.

Beating tray being used on Scots Pine

Sand Dart habitat, Scilly; INSET: Sand Dart larva

Subterranean searches

Many larvae hide underground by day, coming up to feed above ground by night. Others spend their entire lives underground feeding on roots. Some of these will be encountered by chance while you weed the garden, but most are difficult to search for. However, coastal sandy habitats provide an opportunity for such searching. The larva of Shore Wainscot feeds on Marram at night, hiding in the sand by day. Running your fingers through sand at the base of the plant may uncover a larva, or more commonly its bright green frass. Once frass has been found, searching through the sand should reveal a larva. Sand Dart larvae feed on the closest flowering plants on the foredunes above the high-tide mark, such as Sea Rocket. Running your fingers through the sand underneath a foodplant in August may reveal them. Doing the same further away from the sea in a dune system may reveal other species such as Archer's Dart.

LIFE CYCLES: EARLY STAGES

The typical life cycle of a butterfly or moth is that, following mating of male and female adults, the female lays eggs that hatch into larvae. The larvae feed and grow, periodically shedding their skins to allow for further growth during each instar. When fully fed they prepare for pupation. Some spin a silken cocoon around themselves, some hang from a pad of silk and others make no such structure. They then shed their skin for the final time to become a pupa, a process known as pupation. In due course the adult moth or butterfly emerges and the cycle begins again. All butterflies and moths undergo the same process, with the exception of a few micro-moths that are parthenogenetic, where there are no males and the species breeds by asexual reproduction, the females laying viable eggs without mating. The next section describes some of the variation between species in the details of their life cycles, illustrating the wide variety of strategies adopted.

Egg

Eggs are laid singly, in batches or scattered during flight, depending on species. The oviposition site may be very precise; for example, Purple Hairstreak lays its eggs singly at the base of the terminal bud of oaks. Rivulet larvae feed on the seeds of Red Campion, a dioecious species that produces male and female flowers on separate plants. Any eggs laid on male flowers would be doomed, and somehow the female moth manages to sex the plant and lay only on the female flowers. Some species scatter their eggs as they fly, such as swift moths (Hepialidae) and Marbled White. Chimney Sweeper has been observed simply to drop its eggs. When a batch of

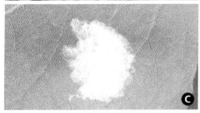

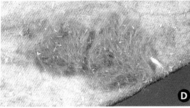

(A) Stack of Small Emerald eggs; (B) Silk-like fibres secreted by abdomen of Engrailed, covering egg mass; (C) White Satin egg mass covered with foam-like abdominal secretion; (D) Hairs from adult female covering egg mass of Yellow-tail; (E) Brown Hairstreak egg on twig of Blackthorn; (F) Lappet eggs

eggs is laid it is usually in one layer, but that of the Marsh Fritillary may have three tiers. Small Emerald lays small batches of eggs in a vertical stack, one egg wide, on Traveller's-joy.

A number of species habitually or frequently lay their eggs on plants other than their usual foodplant, such as Large Yellow Underwing, which lays large batches of eggs often high above the ground, such as on a Common Ivy leaf. The larvae feed on the ground on herbaceous plants at night, spending the day underground. Other examples are given in the section *What constitutes a larval foodplant?* (p. 40).

Engrailed lays its eggs under lichens on branches, and the egg batches are covered with curly, silk-like fibres that probably offer some protection from predators. An abdominal gland must produce these fibres. The mass consists of many separate fibres rather than one continuous fibre of silk as a larva produces from its spinnerets. White Satin Moth lays batches of eggs that it covers in a different sort of abdominal secretion, which looks like a solidified foam. Yellow-tail and Brown-tail cover their batches of eggs with abdominal hairs that will also bear some irritant larval hairs among them, derived from the hairy cocoon through which the moth pushes on emergence from the pupa. Sallow lays small batches of eggs on willow twigs near the buds, also covering them with brown hairs from its abdomen.

Eggs vary greatly in their shape and appearance. Those of many species are simply ovoid with a smooth surface, but some are intricately sculptured, such as those of the copper, hairstreak and blue butterflies. Lappet eggs are patterned.

Finally, we always think that as part of an insect's life cycle it is obligatory that a female insect lays her eggs and these eggs hatch into larvae, which then start feeding. Of course, in nature, there are always exceptions. Perhaps surprisingly there are plenty of species, especially in flies (Diptera), where the eggs hatch within the female and it is tiny larvae that are laid. This is known as larvipary. It appears to be a rare behaviour in moths. There was a species of micro-moth in Britain that did lay larvae rather than eggs, though sadly it hasn't been seen here for many decades and is now presumed extinct. This is the case-bearer *Coleophora albella* (Coleophoridae). The larvae are laid directly into the flowers, mainly of Ragged-Robin.

Larva

Function of skin changes

The traditional view of the function of skin change is that an insect has an exoskeleton that expands as it grows, but from time to time it has to be shed, revealing a new, loose skin in which further growth can take place. This is, of course, true and is undoubtedly the primary function. However, there are other benefits too. One is that it enables the larva to change its appearance as it grows to maintain its crypsis under different circumstances or to change defence strategy. Another possible benefit is that it removes any parasitoid's egg that might have been laid externally on the old skin, or indeed any build-up of pathogens such as fungi. This latter reason could be important for the many species that overwinter as larvae and are inactive over that period; for example, a Brown-tail larva is confined within its communal nest, where spread of pathogens is a significant risk. We do not know the full range of functions of skin change, but some

TOP: **Small Elephant Hawk-moth larva, fourth instar**
ABOVE: **Small Elephant Hawk-moth larva, fifth instar**

species shed their skins many more times than is necessary to allow for growth, and some species have an instar in which they do not feed at all (see below).

The larva of Elephant Hawk-moth is usually green in its first three instars, but when it sheds its skin for the third time to enter its fourth instar, it usually dramatically changes its colour to brown. This is presumably because when small it spends most of its time up among leaves of its foodplant, but when too big and heavy it is likely to have to spend most of its time on the ground. Interestingly, the Small Elephant Hawk-moth undergoes the same colour change, but being smaller this occurs when it enters the fifth instar. The colour thus matches the background at these different stages. Another example is the larva of Alder Moth, which in its early instars is black and white, closely resembling a bird's dropping, but undergoes a dramatic change in its final instar, becoming a black-and-yellow-striped larva with curious long paddle-shaped black hairs. We discuss this change further in the section *Defence mechanisms* (p. 42).

Non-feeding instars

The larva of True Lover's Knot is unique among our macro-moths in that it has a non-feeding final instar, which is actually its seventh instar. This skin change has no function as far as we can tell, and thus appears to be a futile instar. In spring when it sheds its skin for the sixth time

True Lover's Knot penultimate instar larva | True Lover's Knot final (non-feeding) instar larva, same individual

to enter this final instar, the appearance may become paler and the markings may become less well pronounced. In this seventh instar the larva can sometimes be found at night resting up on Heather, but it does not feed and in time simply descends to the ground to pupate.

The burnet moths also have a non-feeding instar. In this case it is specialised for a dormant stage known as diapause. In late summer or early autumn the young larva stops feeding and sheds its skin. It loses its yellowish-green colour and becomes dull brown. It then rests in diapause until the spring, when it sheds its skin and resumes feeding again. Most larvae will then complete their growth, producing an

Six-spot Burnet cast larval skin

adult moth later that year. However, a small proportion will feed for a short time only, before shedding their skin and entering diapause again until the following spring. Those individuals that go through a two-year life cycle thus have an extra instar. The burnet moth larva sheds its skin in a different way from those of other macro-moths. The old skin splits dorsally and the larva crawls out, as opposed to the usual mechanism of the old skin being progressively pushed back to the rear by peristaltic-type movements of the body.

The first-instar larva of Lobster Moth, although not entirely non-feeding, eats only its eggshell before its first skin change. It will not feed on leaves until the second instar.

Number of instars

The number of instars varies from species to species and there can be some variation within a species. Counting the number of instars requires very careful observation and recording, and should be repeated to check reproducibility. It is a surprisingly difficult thing to do and easy to make a mistake. For many species, the number of instars is simply not known. A common number is five but some species have only four (e.g. Purple Hairstreak), and this appears to be the minimum. Vapourer has a marked difference in size between the male and female moths. So great is this that a female larva has six instars whereas a male has five.

Dingy Footman larva in 12th and final instar, feeding on moss

Some overwintering larvae of the footman moths in the subfamily Arctiinae of the Erebidae have an unusually large number of instars. Four-dotted Footman and Dingy Footman both have a remarkable 12 instars, Small Dotted Footman has 10 and Rosy Footman has seven or eight. It is difficult to know why this should be, especially as the hairy skins require considerable energy and materials in their construction. There is still much to investigate concerning instars.

Larval hairs

There is considerable variation between and within species in the structure and function of hairs on larvae, and we have devoted a separate section to this, *Hairy larvae* (p. 55), describing the defence mechanisms for which hairs have been adapted.

The Round-winged Muslin lives in marshy habitats that are subject to inundation by water, especially between autumn and spring when the larva is around. In addition to simple hairs, it has plumose hairs that could help it survive underwater by trapping a pocket of air around its body. However, it is unlikely that this is the only benefit of plumose hairs as two other species

ABOVE: Round-winged Muslin larva showing plumose hairs and male gonads in A5
BELOW: Plumose hair of Round-winged Muslin larva (1mm long)

Round-winged Muslin larvae underwater, surrounded by air bubbles

with similar hairs, Rosy Footman and Four-dotted Footman, are not especially prone to inundation. It may be that a parasitic wasp would be unable to reach the larval skin in areas covered by such hairs.

In the subfamily Lymantriinae of the Erebidae are species that have wingless females that cannot fly (e.g. Vapourer) or that have wings that are effectively incapable of being used for flight as they are not rigid (e.g. Gypsy Moth). Their newly hatched larvae are lightweight and have long hairs. They can be blown significant distances by the wind, thus aiding dispersal.

Dealing with frass

Some relatively sedentary larvae take trouble to ensure frass does not accumulate around them; this is likely to prevent the frass acting as a signal to attract predators and parasites, and may offer an element of hygiene to prevent spread of disease.

The larva of Scalloped Hook-tip expels a frass pellet from the anus at high speed such that each pellet lands far beyond the leaf on which the larva was resting. Puss Moth does the same and for this species it is even more important, otherwise the pellet might get held up by the larval tails. In captivity, some larvae in the Pieridae, Geometridae and Noctuidae have been observed to remove frass pellets by picking them up with their mouths and dropping them clear of the leaf.

Some larvae, including those of skipper butterflies (Hesperiidae), have an anal comb. This is used to flick pellets of frass away. The comb is visible by observing the larva under a microscope and gently raising the anal flap with a thumbnail. It is otherwise completely hidden from view.

anal comb above anus

inner surface of anal flap

anal clasper

further enlargement of the anal comb showing the tines

Micro-moth *Gypsonoma dealbana* (Tortricidae) silk and frass larval tubes, pre-diapause

Large Skipper anal comb

Larvae of some species, however, make use of frass. In the section *Coping with a plant's defences* (p. 57), we describe how the White Admiral larva uses frass to construct a pier, has an aerial latrine and in the first instar uses it to adorn itself. The micro-moth *Gypsonoma dealbana* (Tortricidae) larva feeds in the autumn underneath a leaf, living within an expanding silken tube that incorporates frass and its cast head capsules.

The curious waxy secretion on skipper butterfly larvae

Larvae of the skippers in subfamily Hesperiinae of the Hesperiidae have white waxy deposits, secreted by abdominal glands positioned ventrally on the anterior part of A7 and A8. These deposits are widely described for Silver-spotted Skipper but they are present in the final instar of all five British species in this subfamily. The deposits are made up of microscopic hollow filaments and are said to have a flaky or cottony appearance. The secretions appear part way through the final instar. They must have some function, but we do not know what it is. In Lulworth Skipper the secretions have been observed to have disappeared from the larva by the time it is resting in its spinning ready for pupation. In Large Skipper they can be seen deposited as small clumps among the silk of the cocoon, mainly at the anterior end. Most species of skipper also produce wax secreted through pores in the cuticle of the pupa.

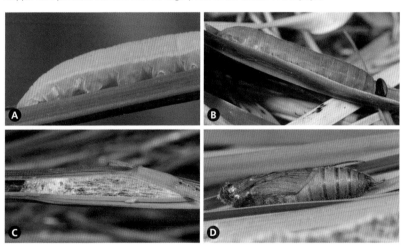

(A) Lulworth Skipper final-instar larva showing white waxy substance under A7 and A8 anteriorly;
(B) Large Skipper larva late in final instar showing white waxy substance under A7 and A8 anteriorly;
(C) Large Skipper cocoon showing the white waxy substance from the larva deposited anteriorly (left end);
(D) Large Skipper pupa showing a few patches where the white waxy substance has adhered at the head end. Note the extension of the pupa to accommodate the long proboscis

Pupation

When fully grown the larva needs to prepare for pupation. This varies a great deal from species to species. Some simply pupate where they have been feeding, whereas others wander to find a suitable pupation site. Some green larvae that have been living among leaves change colour dramatically once they have finished feeding, becoming less conspicuous on the ground or on the bark of trees. Examples include Lime Hawk-moth and Humming-bird Hawk-moth, which change from green to pinkish brown. Miller not only changes from green to a dull greenish grey, but its long white hairs also become grey. One of the most remarkable examples is Orange Underwing, which changes from green to a dark purplish grey before it pupates in dead wood.

The larvae of many butterflies in the family Nymphalidae (e.g. White Admiral) spin a silk pad from which the larva hangs upside down. Butterflies in the families Papilionidae and Pieridae and moths in genus *Cyclophora* of the Geometridae spin a silk pad, to which the larva's rear is attached, and a silk girdle around the middle of the body. Some species, such as the Marbled White, make no special provision and simply pupate low among vegetation.

Orange Underwing larva: final instar (left) and when fully fed (right). Note the colour change to be cryptic on dark-coloured wood

White Admiral pupa hanging from a silk pad

Orange-tip pupa attached to a silk pad and supported by a girdle of silk

Others make a loose spinning among the foodplant (e.g. Lilac Beauty). Eggar moths in the family Lasiocampidae make tough egg-shaped cocoons.

Members of subfamily Lymantriinae of the Erebidae, and family Lasiocampidae, include irritant larval hairs within their cocoons, adding to the protection of the pupa inside. These hairs are laid flat and woven loosely within the silken structure of the cocoon. Rosy Footman has many plumose hairs as well as some simple hairs. These are included in the cocoon but stick out perpendicularly, thus creating a most unusual structure. The Emperor Moth is the only member of the family of silk-moths (Saturniidae) in the British Isles. Its cocoon is a

Emperor Moth cocoon

Rosy Footman cocoon: under construction (left), showing how hairs have been shed from the larva for inclusion in the cocoon; completed (right), showing plumose hairs sticking out perpendicularly

remarkable structure with a ring of outward-pointing silken spurs at the exit, allowing the moth to emerge but preventing predators from entering.

In the family Notodontidae, the Puss Moth creates a cocoon on a tree trunk by chewing up pieces of bark and incorporating them within the silk it spins. Finally, it secretes a substance that causes the silk to become very hard, such that the result is a very tough and highly cryptic wood-like cocoon.

Jersey Mocha pupa attached to a silk pad and supported by a girdle of silk

Many species bury themselves in the ground for pupation. Some then make a flimsy cocoon, while others (e.g. Shark) make a tough cocoon. Poplar Hawk-moth doesn't make a cocoon at all.

During pupation the final larval skin is shed. Some species, such as Meadow Brown, retain the skin attached to the rear of the pupa. Those species pupating within a cocoon almost always retain the skin within the cocoon. However, Scalloped Hook-tip discards the larval skin completely from within the cocoon via a hole at the back.

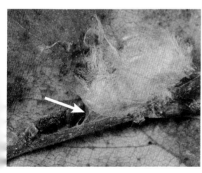

Scalloped Hook-tip cocoon, with a hole posteriorly (arrowed) through which the larval skin has been extruded

Meadow Brown pupa attached to shed larval skin, hanging from a silk pad

COPING WITH WINTER

Moths and butterflies have adopted a wide range of strategies for passing the winter and the larva is the commonest stage in which they do so. Larvae may continue to feed slowly through mild spells in the winter (e.g. Square-spot Rustic) or they may enter a dormant stage known as diapause in which they do not feed until the spring (e.g. Mottled Beauty). We have avoided using the term 'hibernation' in this guide as it is strictly a physiological state adopted by some mammals during the cold months of the year. The White Admiral larva enters diapause when partly grown, whereas some other species, such as Plain Clay, enter diapause as soon as they hatch from the egg. At the other end of the scale are species that overwinter fully fed, such as Fox Moth, which makes its cocoon in the spring without further feeding. Goat Moth overwinters for the final time as a fully fed larva inside its tough cocoon, before pupating in the spring. Sand Dart spends the winter buried in sand on a beach just above the strand-line. Winter storms may shift the sand such that it is too deep for successful emergence of the moth. The larva solves this problem in late spring by burrowing up and crawling out onto the surface of the sand, before burying itself again to an appropriate depth for pupation.

Some larvae produce specialised structures in which to spend their winter diapause. Brown-tail are gregarious as larvae from first instar in late summer and by mid-autumn they construct a dense whitish silk tent in which they diapause communally. Within the tent each larva spins its own silk cell in which it spends the winter. In areas of high population density, larvae from different females aggregate to form very large nests, up to 15cm long, and containing just under 2,000 larvae. Similarly, Yellow-tail makes a tough silken larval cocoon (hibernaculum) for diapause, but it overwinters singly, even though the larvae feed gregariously in autumn. White Admiral also constructs a hibernaculum, but it is a much weaker structure (see *Coping with a plant's defences*, p. 57).

Individual hibernaculum of Yellow-tail

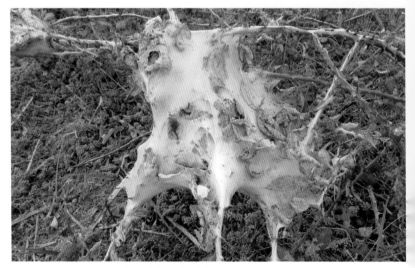

Brown-tail larval web in which larvae diapause

Many species overwinter as an egg and some of those have the larva fully formed inside throughout this period, including High Brown Fritillary and Dark Marbled Carpet. The eggs of some species will actually hatch during the winter months (e.g. Centre-barred Sallow and Grass Eggar).

Other species overwinter as a pupa, the adult usually developing when warmer weather has returned, although in some species the adult is fully formed within the pupa and the wing pattern is visible through the wing cases (e.g. Clouded Silver). The same usually applies to V-Pug, but some individuals of this species do not develop until shortly before emergence.

Sometimes a pupa will not produce an adult after the first winter has passed, but will go through another winter or sometimes more before the adult finally emerges. It is only possible to glean information on this from captive rearing, but this is undoubtedly relevant to what happens in the wild and can confer the species with a survival benefit, despite it being susceptible to predation for a greater length of time. Emperor Moth occurs on moorland as one of its habitats and flies in April and May. This habitat can be subject to harsh weather conditions at that time of year, which could result in poor breeding success. If a proportion of pupae produce moths after a second winter the weather conditions may be more favourable. Cloaked Pug larvae feed in the unripe green cones of Norway Spruce. In some years, this tree may fail to produce any cones across a wide geographical area, making it impossible for the moth to breed successfully. Larvae have weak prolegs and anal claspers, and so are simply not adapted to feed on any other part of the plant. However, a proportion of pupae overwinter twice, increasing the chances of offspring from one generation being able to survive years when the cone crop is absent.

Other species overwinter as an adult and some, such as the Winter Moth and December Moth, fly during the winter. Others are active in autumn and spring but remain in diapause during the cold months (e.g. Peacock). This species and many more mate in the spring, but for others, such as Red-green Carpet, mating occurs in the autumn and only the female moth survives the winter.

NUMBER OF GENERATIONS IN A YEAR

It is tempting to think of a species neatly fitting into a pattern of having one or two generations a year. Even in a species that appears once a year, we know that larval development can take one, two or three years to complete. Similarly, in the pupal stage, an overwintering pupa may not necessarily produce an adult the following year. For many species, we know from captive rearing that a proportion may pass two or more winters before the adult emerges, and this is likely to happen in the wild. So, in reality, describing the number of generations per year as a single number is an oversimplification of the situation in nature and it is almost impossible to follow the progress of individuals of many species through their life cycle in the wild.

Very often, it appears, second generations are partial second generations. Only some of the larvae arising from the first generation of adults produce more adults later in the same year, while the remainder produce adults in the following or subsequent years. Small Pearl-bordered Fritillary and White-spotted Pug are examples of such species. To be defined as a species producing a partial second generation, the proportion of second-generation individuals could vary from just above zero to just under 100%, and it seems likely this is what happens in nature, depending on a variety of environmental factors such as seasonal temperature.

The number of generations a year can vary with latitude, with populations of a particular species in the north almost always producing one, and in the south at least a partial second generation. In such cases, it seems likely that the proportion of the second generation would gradually reduce as latitude increases. During recent decades we have experienced exceptionally warm years and, as a result, we are increasingly seeing adults of a second generation that were previously unknown or scarce, as well as second generations appearing much further north. For example, Light Emerald previously had one generation in the British Isles, but now produces a substantial partial second generation in the autumn.

WHAT DO LARVAE EAT?

Larvae of different species feed on a huge variety of organic matter. Most use living plants, but it may be specific parts of plants. As you read through the species descriptions you will get a good idea of the range. They may feed on the leaves, internally in the stem, on flowers, or just on the internal parts of flowers, seeds and roots, either externally or internally. Some feed internally in living wood, while others among the micro-moths feed on dead wood. Some feed on fungi, algae or lichens. Some species are fussy about the condition of the plant, preferring fresh young leaves, leaves growing in sunshine or in deep shade, old green leaves, or wilting or dead leaves. There are also carnivorous species that feed on other larvae or insects. Some feed in the nests of bees. The familiar clothes moths in the wild feed in birds' nests, on owl pellets or on animal skins.

A species may be specific to one plant (known as monophagous) or to a small number of different plants (oligophagous), or may feed on a wide variety of plants (polyphagous). This is, of course, a spectrum from specialisation to generalisation.

Some larvae may be dependent upon different foods at different stages in their development. For example, Yellow-line Quaker may start feeding in the catkins of willows, but when it falls to the ground will feed on a variety of herbaceous plants.

What constitutes a larval foodplant?

There is no rigid definition of a foodplant and to create one would not be very helpful, as it couldn't be applied retrospectively to foodplants listed in existing literature. Essentially, however, a foodplant (also known as a hostplant) is a plant that the larva of a particular species has been found to be eating in the wild. Generally, larvae should be able to complete their development on such a plant, but for most foodplant records this has not been established. Also, some larvae switch foodplants between instars, or after winter, and sometimes larvae are found on surprising plants that are not necessarily suitable for successful completion of their life cycle. For example, Brindled Pug is a species usually associated with oaks, but larvae have been found on Hazel underneath an oak canopy and then found to eat Hazel in captivity. It is doubtful that they would ever use only Hazel, but presumably were able to eat it having fallen from the oak trees above. It is common to find larvae of other species blown out of the canopy in a storm that continue feeding on different plants in the understorey or on the woodland floor, particularly Bramble or Bilberry. Sometimes larvae can be observed feeding on a plant species that is not good for them. A larva of the Holly Blue found feeding on the leaves of Grey Willow produced an adult butterfly but it was diminutive and did not expand its wings properly. Similarly, larvae of Brown-tail have been observed eating Bracken in the wild in the Channel Islands, but they died the following day.

On occasion, the normal diet is not available to larvae and they seem to manage on another part of the plant. The larva of Common Emerald is regularly found feeding on Hawthorn leaves. It remains small in the autumn and overwinters, resuming feeding in the spring. On a sleeved

Common Emerald larva feeding on a Hawthorn twig

branch, larvae have come out of diapause before the spring buds have opened, and have been observed to eat the young twigs until the buds have expanded enough.

Sometimes different plants are suitable at different stages in a larva's life. For example, eggs of the Muslin Moth have been found on the leaf of an Apple tree. Although the larvae ate the leaf in their first instar, they then fell to the ground to feed on herbaceous plants. They are not equipped to continue life in a tree.

We find plenty of examples where eggs are laid somewhere other than on the foodplant. Silver-washed Fritillary lays its eggs singly in cracks in the bark of trees in summer. The larva hatches in about two weeks and remains on the tree without feeding until the following spring, when it descends to search for violets, on which it then feeds. On heathland, Silver-studded Blue often lays eggs on Bracken. Larvae hatch in spring and they are picked up by ants and taken to their nests, later emerging to feed at night on gorses and heathers. And as a final example, Fisher's Estuarine Moth lays its eggs in batches between the stem and leaf-sheath of grasses near the larval foodplant, Hog's Fennel.

The examples above are of normal egg-laying sites where larvae find the plants they require and develop successfully. However, sometimes a female adult simply makes a mistake. A Brimstone was once observed laying eggs on a dock, but this is a wholly unsuitable foodplant, and furthermore the larvae could never have found their way to the Buckthorn or Alder Buckthorn that they needed.

These examples illustrate how difficult it can be to record foodplants, and we do ask recorders to be as precise as possible, including any observations of what plant a larva was eating and the circumstances of discovery. For example, a larva beaten from a branch of a large oak tree would have almost certainly been eating that plant and it would be quite acceptable to record the finding as 'beaten from oaks', but even better if 'and not observed feeding' was added too. Simply to record a larva as on a particular plant may wrongly imply it is a foodplant, yet sadly this is commonly done, severely degrading the value of the record. Try to avoid ambiguity by stating whether or not there was evidence of feeding – for example, 'seen feeding' or 'resting on a leaf that had recent feeding damage' – or whether there was frass on the leaf. Careful observation and recording will increase what we know about larval habits in the wild. Apart from the fascination and enjoyment of discovery they provide, successful insect species conservation projects are based on detailed knowledge of life histories, so there is an important conservation incentive for precise recording.

Captive rearing on plants

Finding that a larva eats an unusual plant in captivity cannot be taken to imply that this plant would ever be used in the wild. For example, White Spot is known only to use Nottingham Catchfly in the wild, but will accept Red Campion in captivity. However, there are cases where observations in captivity are likely to hold true in the wild, but would be very difficult to demonstrate. In captivity, Square Spot and Satin Beauty will not lay eggs on leaves of their foodplants. They have long ovipositors clearly adapted for a more specialised oviposition site, and when provided with pieces of an oak branch covered in algae and lichens, they readily lay eggs under the lichen and in bark crevices.

On hatching, the larvae feed on the algae and lichens, and Square Spot has been observed to reach final instar and Satin Beauty second instar in this way. It seems highly likely that a tiny, newly hatched larva of either species travelling a considerable distance to the nearest leaf would take advantage of this readily accepted food on the way. There is no doubt that our understanding of the requirements of early-instar larvae generally lags well behind that of larger larvae and requires further study.

Satin Beauty eggs laid singly under lichen

Carnivory

Several species have larvae that are carnivorous for at least part of this life stage. For example, Dun-bar larvae feed on the leaves of a variety of trees, but also eat other larvae they may encounter. Silky Wainscot probably feeds on the leaves of Common Reed when young. Later it lives inside the reed stems, eating living and dead invertebrates. In captivity, Rosy

Silky Wainscot larva

Marbled larvae have been observed to feed at first on the petals of flowers of cinquefoils and Bramble, but by second instar they become cannibalistic, feed on micro-fungi and continue to eat petals. When presented with dead flies and moths, the larvae eat them too. It seems highly likely that in the wild they eat other small insects visiting the flowers where they live, and they are probably also scavengers. And finally, perhaps the ultimate carnivore is Large Blue. Last-instar larvae feed on ant larvae within the ants' nest (see *Living with ants*, p. 59).

DEFENCE MECHANISMS

All stages of the life cycle of butterflies and moths are vulnerable to predation from a variety of animals. We commonly think of insectivorous birds in this respect, but we should also include bats, hedgehogs, moles and shrews, as well as amphibians and reptiles. Then there are many invertebrate predators too, including dragonflies, beetles, bees and wasps. With threats to existence coming from such a wide range of predators, the evolutionary selection pressure to avoid being eaten is intense, and the responses very varied and in some cases quite remarkable.

Larvae and adults of butterflies and moths are usually mimicking, or imitating, something. This might be an inert grey or brown background colour, green leaves or an insect that is distasteful, or even a predator. Sometimes they combine a number of tactics for use at different times. Larvae are particularly vulnerable to predators because they have to feed and so most can't be completely hidden away; they also can't get out of the way as quickly as winged adults, and, in the British Isles at least, most species spend a long time in the larval stage.

Hiding

Staying out of sight is a good strategy and is adopted by many species of moth and butterfly.

HIDING		
Behavioural response	**Example**	**Comment**
Hide in a silken spinning among leaves	Bilberry Pug	Spins the shoots of Bilberry together
Burrow in wood or bark	Clearwing moths	Most insectivorous birds cannot get to the larvae. However, Great Spotted Woodpecker specialises in finding wood-boring insects and heavily preys upon Lunar Hornet Moth larvae and pupae
Feed at night	Larvae of many species of moth and butterfly	Most insectivorous birds are not active at night. However, some bats, such as Brown Long-eared Bat, specialise in locating insects, including larvae, on leaves at night

 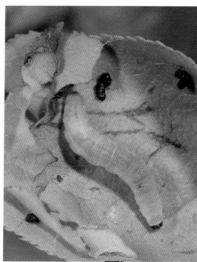

A spinning on Bilberry made by a Bilberry Pug larva   Bilberry Pug larva exposed

Movement response

Larvae of butterflies and moths exhibit a range of movement responses that appear to reduce the risk of predation.

MOVEMENT RESPONSE		
Behavioural response	**Example**	**Comment**
Drop from the plant	Dentated Pug	Larva sits on the underside of the lower leaves of Yellow Loosestrife, dropping to the ground if disturbed, and climbing up the plant again once danger has passed
Drop and secrete a silk thread	Magpie	Larva drops from a leaf or twig, hanging from a silk thread, later climbing up the thread back to the plant
Spring away from the plant to avoid danger	Star-wort	When feeding on Goldenrod in woodlands, the larva convulses if disturbed, springing away from the plant. If feeding on Sea Aster in saltmarshes, the larva stays more tightly on the plant, probably to avoid the risk of falling into tidal waters
Feigning death (thanatosis)	Small Elephant Hawk-moth	If disturbed, the larva may become limp and play dead. It is not obvious why, but the behaviour may reduce risk of predation

Crypsis

Blending into or mimicking the background is a common defence strategy and there are remarkable examples shown by larvae found in the British Isles.

CRYPSIS		
Defence mechanism	Example	Comment
Resembles leaves	Larvae of many species of moth and butterfly	By sitting on the underside of a leaf that is illuminated from above, a green larva blends in well
Countershading	Eyed Hawk-moth	Large larvae that hang upside down in vegetation sometimes exhibit 'countershading'; that is, their ventral surface (which is uppermost when upside down) is a darker shade of green than the dorsal surface. More light falls on the larva from above than is reflected from below, so the countershading helps keep a similar shade from top to bottom. The cylindrical larva appears much flatter than it would otherwise, aiding crypsis
Resembles twigs or bark	September Thorn	Various projections and markings on the larva closely resemble buds and leaf scars on oak twigs
	Early Thorn	Viewed from the side, the swelling and angles of the thoracic region resemble a thorn or a bud on a twig. Viewed from another angle, the legs on T3 appear like biting jaws
	Red Underwing	The larva feeds on the leaves of willow or poplar at night. By day, it rests low down on the trunk of the tree. It even aligns itself along the contours of the bark, enhancing its crypsis
	Lappet	At rest, the larva closely hugs a Blackthorn twig. It has hairs at the sides ventrally that enable it to blend in seamlessly with the twig without casting a shadow. It also has a brown dorsal lump on A8 resembling a bud. When disturbed, the larva flexes anteriorly, revealing black between the segments, containing blue between T2/T3 and T3/A1 but orange spots instead of the blue in an earlier instar. This reaction probably startles a would-be predator
Resembles flowers or seeds	Wormwood	The green larva with brown blotches closely resembles dead flowers and developing seeds of wormwoods
	Plain Pug	The larva rests among the fruits of oraches, sometimes curled up, leaving a gap in the middle resembling an eaten fruit

(A) Eyed Hawk-moth larva in usual resting position, showing countershading; (B) September Thorn larva resembling an oak twig with leaf scars and buds; (C) Early Thorn larva lateral view, showing metathoracic legs resembling a bud or thorn; (D) Early Thorn showing metathoracic legs, viewed such that they resemble biting jaws; (E) Red Underwing larva resting cryptically by day on trunk of Grey Willow; (F) Young Lappet larva hugging a twig and showing brown dorsal hump on A8 resembling a Blackthorn bud; (G) Plain Pug larvae, one stretched out looking cryptic among Orache and another curled up resembling a fruit that has been eaten out, like the fruit behind it

CRYPSIS		
Defence mechanism	Example	Comment
Resembles lichens	Brussels Lace	The larva closely resembles the lichens on which it feeds, the shade even varying depending upon the lichen
Larva alters its appearance in response to local environmental conditions	Scalloped Hazel	Inferred from experiments on larvae reared in captivity by Majerus (1983). The commonest form in last instar is plain brownish, which may have greenish patches resembling algae, and there is a rarer form that looks like lichens. If small pieces of white paper are introduced into the container with larvae as they grow, this induces a higher proportion of larvae to develop into the lichen form in last instar compared with not adding bits of paper

Brussels Lace larva on a bluish-grey lichen (left) and on a pale green lichen (right)

Scalloped Hazel larva, lichen-coloured form (left) and normal colour form (above)

CRYPSIS		
Defence mechanism	Example	Comment
Larva alters its appearance to maintain crypsis as the seasons change	Scarce Silver-lines	When small in late summer, the larva is green, feeding from underneath an oak leaf. In autumn and over winter it is pale brown with a darker brown saddle on T2, resembling an oak bud or leaf scar, matching an oak twig on which it sits. At bud burst in spring, it becomes green with reddish-brown subspiracular and dorsal stripes, resembling an expanding oak bud. Once the tree is in leaf, the larva becomes all green again

Scarce Silver-lines larva: (A) pre-diapause feeding under an oak leaf; (B) during diapause; (C) in spring feeding on an opening oak bud; and (D) in late spring feeding on an oak leaf

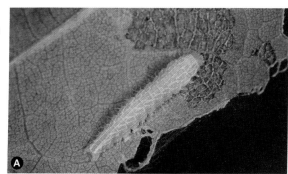

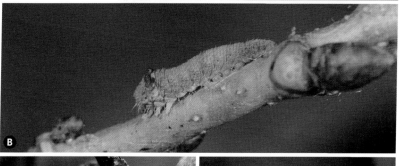

CRYPSIS		
Defence mechanism	**Example**	**Comment**
Larva adorns itself with materials from the environment	Blotched Emerald	Larva has short spiky hairs to which it attaches pieces of oak leaf or bud scales, which hide the larva while feeding
	Large Emerald and Common Emerald	During the diapause instar only, larvae have algae attached to their skins, with more at the end than at the start of winter. It is not completely clear how the algae get there, but larvae of Large Emerald have been observed attaching bark fragments to their skins. The algae may even grow on the skin. Common Emerald skin is covered with short rectangular white and black projections, raised tiny white spots, and very sparse, short spiky hairs, creating a 'sticky' surface for attachments
Resembles algae	Brimstone Moth	In contast to the previous two species, the same deception is achieved during diapause not by attaching algae to the body but by the smooth skin being grey with greenish patches, resembling algae

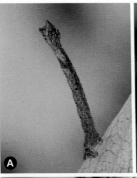

(A) Common Emerald larva in diapause, covered with living algae, aiding crypsis. Note the rough skin; (B) Large Emerald larva in diapause, covered with living algae, aiding crypsis; (C) Brimstone Moth brown larva with green patches mimicking algae. Note vestigial prolegs on A4–A5 and hair-like fleshy projections between proleg and anal clasper

Warning colours and mimicry

Warning colours are commonplace in the natural world, and the technical term used to describe their function is aposematism. In most cases warning colours and patterns are bright and contrasting against the natural background, so they advertise to a predator that the bearer should be avoided because it is distasteful or dangerous, or both. Colours such as red, yellow and black are typical.

Some butterflies, moths and their larvae have toxins in their bodies. The toxin may have been sequestered into the insect's body from the foodplants the larva ate, or it may have been synthesised within the insect's cells. These individuals are unpalatable to predators and advertise the fact with their contrasting colours. Once a bird has tasted a few it will learn to leave them alone.

As much as there is a benefit to an insect from being warningly coloured, there is also an advantage to one that can look like another animal that is unpalatable or dangerous. In this way, the mimic may be a palatable or harmless species resembling a harmful one, thus gaining protection from predators by deception. This is known as Batesian mimicry. Another type is Müllerian mimicry, where both or several species are unpleasant, and all species derive mutualistic benefit by being similar.

A frequent pattern found in moth and butterfly species is an eye-like marking. In the British Isles, well-developed examples include adult Peacock and Emperor Moth, but there are others across several families of mainly larger moths and butterflies. The functions of eyespots are probably several. They may act to startle a would-be predator to avoid the bearer, such as the flash of the eyespots surrounded by pink on the hindwings of adult Eyed Hawk-moth. Or they could be positioned on a less vulnerable part of the body, such as on the outer margin of the hindwing of a Long-tailed Blue. Here, the eyespots, together with the 'tails' looking like antennae, may lead a predator's attention away from the head and thorax in so-called 'false-head' mimicry. They may also be involved in communication between individuals of the same species, and especially courtship.

We also believe there is good circumstantial evidence for eyespots deceiving insectivorous birds into reacting as if they belong to snakes. We suggest, as a result of our observations over many years, that snake mimicry is surprisingly widespread in larvae of moths and butterflies in the British Isles and we hope our views stimulate interest in the subject. It appears that snake mimicry readily evolves, and has done so many times independently in the Lepidoptera, including in families Papilionidae, Sphingidae, Geometridae, Notodontidae, Erebidae and Noctuidae.

The theory of snake mimicry in Lepidoptera has been pioneered by Professor Daniel Janzen and colleagues, who have been working on hundreds of tropical species in Costa Rica in Central America (Janzen, Hallwachs and Burns, 2010). Snake mimicry is neither Batesian nor Müllerian, where insectivorous birds learn by experience to avoid a brightly coloured pattern. Instead, snake mimicry relies on the innate, or hard-wired, response of insectivorous birds to avoid predators such as snakes. A bird is not likely to survive its first close encounter with a snake, so cannot learn by experience. The selection pressure is for an instantaneous avoidance response. Janzen suggests that birds have a genetically determined image of a snake in their brains. This is not likely to be a sophisticated image; rather, it may be a set of visual cues created by similar patterns that elicit the escape response. The result is that larvae, even though much smaller than snakes, can get away with the mimicry providing their markings and shapes match the cues.

Nut-tree Tussock larva (above), a Batesian mimic of Vapourer; Vapourer larva (right) with irritant hairs

WARNING COLOURS AND MIMICRY

Defence mechanism	Example	Comment
Warning colours (aposematic larvae)	Cinnabar	The black-and-yellow larva sits openly on Common Ragwort and is easily seen by would-be predators. This species is also a Müllerian mimic, being distasteful itself and having a similar body pattern to a wasp
	Magpie	The larva, pupa and adult of this moth are brightly coloured, each stage warning of its distastefulness
Batesian mimicry	Nut-tree Tussock	The larva of Nut-tree Tussock has a very similar pattern of hair tufts to Vapourer, but, unlike those of Vapourer, its hairs are not irritant
Snake mimicry (*continued on p. 52*)	The tropical hawk-moth *Hemeroplanes triptolemus*	An extraordinary larva, which when disturbed adopts a posture that makes it look just like a snake. It lets go with its true legs, expands its thoracic segments that taper towards the head, and reveals impressive eyespots on its ventral surface. It also behaves like a snake, moving the false head slowly from side to side, and lunges like one
	Elephant Hawk-moth	When disturbed, A1 is expanded with the thoracic segments tapering to the head and there are eyespots on A1 and A2. It moves in a slow, rather interrupted manner, giving the impression of a snake
	Dark Spectacle	The larva has A2 more domed than other segments and a pair of yellow spots on A1
	Rosy Marbled	The larva has A1 expanded, body tapering towards the head and with eyespots subdorsally on A1
	Satin Wave	Normally the larva rests with its body curled under, revealing a conspicuous pale spot each side on the wide flange of A5 with segments tapering to the posterior

Cinnabar larva showing aposematism, and Müllerian mimicry of a wasp

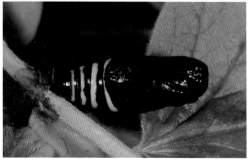

Magpie pupa showing aposematism

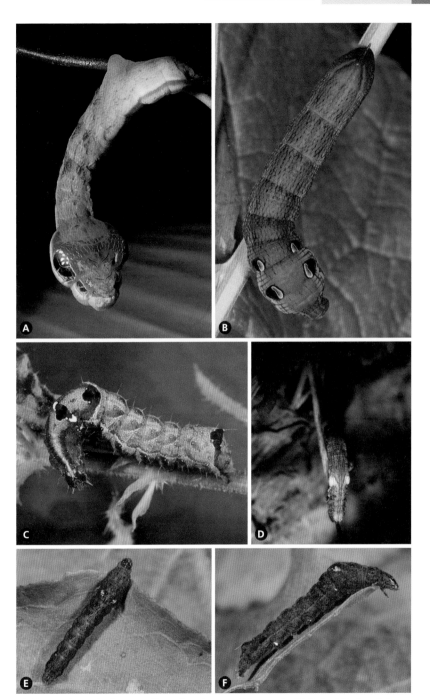

(A) *Hemeroplanes triptolemus* penultimate-instar larva mimicking a snake; (B) Elephant Hawk-moth larva showing snake mimicry; (C) Dark Spectacle larva showing snake mimicry; (D) Satin Wave larva curled in normal resting posture, showing snake mimicry; (E and F) Rosy Marbled larva, dorsal and lateral views, showing snake mimicry

WARNING COLOURS AND MIMICRY

Defence mechanism	Example	Comment
Snake mimicry (*continued*)	Blood-vein	The larva has A1 expanded in the horizontal and vertical planes, with the thoracic segments tapering towards the head
	Riband Wave	The larva is dark brown anteriorly, but from A5 posteriorly it is much lighter brown. Within this light area is a dark mark like a forked tongue, with A5 being especially wide to accommodate the fork
	Lobster Moth	The fully grown larva is brown and when disturbed spreads its legs in a threatening way. The snake mimicry becomes apparent when viewed from the rear: A7 and especially A8 are much expanded and the tails give the appearance of a forked tongue

(A) Blood-vein larva showing snake mimicry; (B) Riband Wave larva showing a mark resembling a forked tongue; (C) Lobster Moth final-instar larva showing snake mimicry.

Bird's dropping mimicry

A frequent form of deception used by invertebrates is pretending to be a bird's dropping, and this behavioural adaptation is common in moths and butterflies, in both adults and larvae. Birds ignore their faeces in the environment, so looking like a bird's dropping can prevent an insect being preyed upon. In larvae, body size is an important factor that determines the stage at which the mimicry is developed, and as the larva grows too big to mimic the typical size of a bird's dropping, the deception may be abandoned or modified in favour of another strategy.

BIRD'S DROPPING MIMICRY		
Dropping type	**Example**	**Comment**
Mimicking dark and white droppings	Alder Moth	The larva is a dropping mimic in third and fourth instars. In fifth instar it undergoes an astonishing change to black with yellow bands, with long paddle-shaped hairs. During this stage the larva has the warning coloration of stinging or distasteful insects, although is probably not distasteful itself
	Swallowtail	Early instars mimic droppings but later instars are brightly coloured as a warning of distastefulness, and the larva emits an acrid smell when alarmed

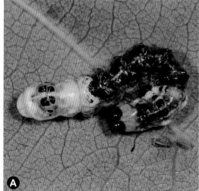 

(A) Alder Moth third-instar larva mimicking a bird's dropping; (B) Alder Moth final-instar larva showing warning coloration; (C) Swallowtail young larva mimicking a bird's dropping

BIRD'S DROPPING MIMICRY		
Dropping type	Example	Comment
Mimicking brown droppings from insectivorous birds	Scalloped Hook-tip	In early instars, the larva sits openly on the top of birch leaves, curving its body to one side like a curled dropping. The mimicry is not present in the final instar
	Peach Blossom	The larva rests on the upper leaf surface, resembling a dropping in early instars, but changes its appearance during later instars when it becomes too big to look like a dropping

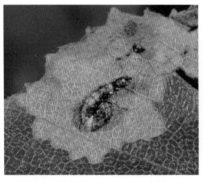

Scalloped Hook-tip young larva mimicking an insectivorous bird's dropping

Peach Blossom young larva mimicking an insectivorous bird's dropping

Defensive postures and secretions in larvae

The Puss Moth larva is impressive and especially scary to birds in its final instar. It relies on crypsis while hanging beneath a twig of its foodplant, its purplish-brown saddle helping to break up its outline. When a predator is close by and disturbs the larva, it raises its front end, revealing a bright red anterior part of T1 around the head. It also raises its tails at the posterior end, extruding red filaments from them and thrashing them around. Howse (2010) reports that salicylic acid is discharged from the tails as they are flicked forwards. If the bird attempts to get the front of the larva in its beak then the larva squirts out pungent formic acid from a gland within the red ventral part of T1.

Puss Moth larva final instar at rest

ABOVE: Rannoch Sprawler larva when alarmed
LEFT: Puss Moth larva final instar threatening posture. Note the opening of the gland on T1, from which it can eject formic acid

In a similar manner, when alarmed the larva of Rannoch Sprawler rears its head and true legs up, exposing the slit-like opening of a gland on the ventral surface of T1. This is known as a repugnatorial gland and it is likely to emit a defensive secretion.

Hairy larvae

Most larvae have hairs to a greater or lesser extent, but some are particularly hairy. For some species, defence features prominently among the various functions of the hairs, especially when the hairs are irritant. Garden Tiger is one of the hairiest larvae. Its hairs do not seem to be particularly irritant but it may be that their sheer length makes the larva difficult for birds to deal with.

Grass Eggar young larva. Note that irritant hairs are commonly found on larvae in the family Lasiocampidae

In Great Britain and Ireland, it is species in the family Lasiocampidae and subfamily Lymantriinae of the Erebidae that have particularly harmful hairs. These can cause an unpleasant itchy skin rash if the larvae are handled. In the case of the Lasiocampidae, the hairs are unbarbed and the distal points will enter the victim's skin, breaking to release the toxins within. Among the Lymantriinae, Brown-tail is the ultimate in this line of defence. It is the hairs making up the brown cushions along its back that cause the main irritation. They are c. 0.5mm long and are variously quoted as

Garden Tiger larva showing its very long hairs

Brown-tail larva with irritant hairs

numbering 500,000 to 2 million on each larva. Each hair is shaped like a needle, with a hollow centre containing a concoction of irritating and skin-dissolving compounds, and is barbed on the outside. The hairs get dislodged easily, including by a gentle breeze, so even the atmosphere around a bush heavily infested with larvae can get filled with the tiny hairs. Once a hair lands on the skin it burrows in, and any scratching only exacerbates the problem as the barbs help the hair lodge deeper within the tissue. In humans, the unpleasant reaction can last hours or sometimes days, and most birds that try to eat a larva can be seen wiping their bill, presumably experiencing something of this reaction. There is, however, one bird that specialises in eating hairy larvae, and that is the Cuckoo, which eats large numbers of Drinker larvae in the spring and early summer. It seems to prefer irritant and distasteful larvae, and will take Brown-tail and Cinnabar larvae, and adult burnet moths.

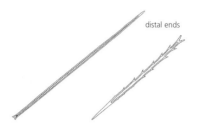

Irritant hairs of Drinker (left) larva (1.5mm long) and Brown-tail (right) larva (0.5mm long)

The larva of Pale Tussock has irritant hairs and is brightly coloured. When a predator disturbs the larva, it curls its head down, revealing black spots between the segments that may startle the predator or may possibly be an aposematic warning. The entomologist John Walters has found that the hairs fluoresce when viewed with an ultraviolet torch and the larva appears even brighter. How relevant this is in terms of defence is unclear.

Pale Tussock larva in normal light (top) and fluorescing when viewed with an ultraviolet torch (bottom)

Can a moth be deliberately defenceless?

The micro-moth family Psychidae (bagworms) has larvae that construct cases, which they carry around with them. The adult males are winged and females are wingless. One particular heathland species, *Acanthopsyche atra* (Psychidae), presents an interesting twist in the tale of defence mechanisms. The larva pupates within its case, but it may do so with its head facing the exit hole, or facing the attachment point of the case. Mating takes place soon after the female emerges from the pupa. She remains in the case if her head is facing the exit, and the male's abdomen extends down inside the case to reach around her to mate. If her head is facing the attachment, mating is easier, and her genitalia are exposed at the entrance to the case until she has mated. The females that are facing the attachment are entombed and never leave the case, but those that are facing the exit may drop from the case to lie on the ground. Extraordinarily, the female is

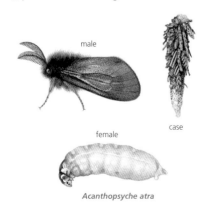

male

female

case

Acanthopsyche atra

yellowish, has no scales, no legs, no wings and no antennae, and the only movements she can perform are peristaltic contractions of her abdomen. She is defenceless yet continues her peristaltic motion, and is potentially conspicuous on dark peaty soil. In an experiment undertaken in the 1950s, females were fed to a captive Robin. Remarkably, two weeks later, out of the bird's faeces emerged tiny larvae of the moth. It appears as if this maggot-like adult moth has evolved to be eaten, by actively attracting a predator with the purpose of aiding dispersal of her progeny, using the predator and its faeces as the vector. How bizarre is that?

Coping with a plant's defences and unusual larval behaviour

Plants have evolved a wide range of physical and chemical defences in their leaves to try to thwart foraging larvae. The following are two examples of species that have overcome Honeysuckle's defence of a sticky exudation from its leaves and, in doing so, create characteristic feeding patterns that identify both species in the field.

The White Admiral female chooses stressed Honeysuckle leaves growing in shady conditions for egg-laying. In doing so, she has already selected plants with reduced defence capacity. The young larva cannot cope with the exudation from a chewed, lush Honeysuckle leaf growing in sunshine.

The eggs are usually laid on the upperside of the leaf margin. On hatching, the larva makes its way to the leaf tip. It starts feeding from the margin on either side, near the tip, leaving an arrowhead shape. It quickly produces yellow frass pellets that appear undigested, and attaches them to the leaf tip with silk, creating a pier extension to the midrib. It continues to feed by cutting a curved channel into the leaf and dropping down the flag of leaf thus created, attaching it with silk below the midrib. This pattern of feeding continues, usually on alternating sides of the leaf. Later on the first day, black frass is produced and this, as well as leaf hairs, gets added to the pier, which is complete by the end of 24 hours.

White Admiral egg on edge of Honeysuckle leaf, upper surface

As more flags are cut, they are sewn loosely together with silk, forming an aerial latrine, frass being deposited within. When not feeding, the larva rests on the pier, facing away from the leaf. It swipes hairs from the midrib or covers them with silk, and over time the junction between pier and midrib becomes harder to discern.

White Admiral larva day 1. First instar showing early feeding, and yellow frass pellets with early pier construction

During the first instar, the larva is adorned with frass pellets. The feeding signs are especially conspicuous. The midrib appears longer than it really is due to the pier extension, and the amount of leaf missing on either side of the midrib is greater than would be expected from feeding alone as flags of leaf are dropped down below the midrib.

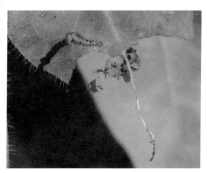

White Admiral larva day 5. First instar adorned with black frass, showing feeding method, pier, silk on midrib, and aerial latrine having been moved towards petiole

White Admiral leaf sewn to stem

White Admiral third-instar larva showing aerial latrine

The second-instar larva is not usually adorned with frass. The larva moves the aerial latrine towards the petiole as the cut edge of the leaf recedes. It does this by cutting the outer silk attachment, allowing the latrine to drop, but it remains attached to the leaf above by the inner threads. It then hitches the latrine back up to the leaf further towards the petiole. The larva continues to rest on the midrib or pier when not feeding. As it grows, it eats some of the flag once the channel has been cut, and later consumes the whole flag. It also sews the petiole of its leaf to the stem, ensuring it will not fall.

White Admiral larva constructing partial cut-and-fold hibernaculum and showing a notch cut out of both sides of base of leaf to aid folding

The third-instar larva may wander to an adjacent leaf to feed, but it returns, via a silk trail, to the original midrib to rest. It constructs a hibernaculum from the leaf it has most recently been eating or a nearby leaf. The petiole is sewn to the stem and a silk pad is spun over the midrib, on which it will rest for the winter. A notch may be cut one or both sides of the midrib at the base of the leaf to aid folding. Larvae construct four different types of hibernaculum, the commonest of which is a partial cut-and-fold where a larva eats a channel in from the leaf margin to just past the midrib, and the cut section closest to the petiole is folded up with silk. The hibernaculum is attached strongly to the stem and is unlikely to get dislodged. However, the sides may disintegrate in winter, leaving the larva exposed. In spring, the larva goes through two further instars without specialist behaviour before pupating. Further details of this complex behaviour are described in Fox (2005), Eeles (2016) and Henwood & Walters (2019).

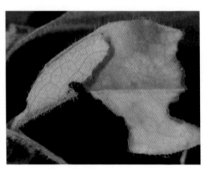

White Admiral partial cut-and-fold hibernaculum completed, showing a notch cut out of both sides of base of leaf to aid folding

Broad-bordered Bee Hawk-moth has a different strategy for dealing with the sticky substance, and the female lays her eggs on leaves of lush Honeysuckle growing in

Broad-bordered Bee Hawk-moth first-instar larval feeding signs on Honeysuckle leaf

Broad-bordered Bee
Hawk-moth final-
instar larva

sunshine. The larva at first feeds from the underside of the leaf, creating a small hole. Once the leaf exudes the sticky substance, it moves to the other side of the midrib and creates another small hole. It continues to make small holes on alternate sides until it is large enough to cope with the sticky substance, when it eats the whole leaf. The feeding pattern created is diagnostic of the species.

Living with ants

Butterflies, and especially the blue butterflies in the Lycaenidae (e.g. Holly Blue), have long been known to have largely positive associations with ants; this is known as myrmecophily. We give a few examples below, but it is a difficult area to study and there is undoubtedly much still to discover. There are also examples of moths living with ants, but these are poorly researched in comparison. For a relationship to be described as myrmecophilous, it is most likely to be one where both ant and butterfly benefit mutually, but, as with most highly evolved relationships in nature, this can vary. Relationships can also be commensal, where one party benefits but the other neither benefits nor is harmed, or parasitic, where one benefits and the other is harmed.

Among the micro-moths, larvae of the scarce *Myrmecozela ochraceella* (Tineidae) live in loose silken tubes at the edge of the nests of wood ants *Formica aquilonia* and *F. lugubris* in the central Highlands of Scotland, feeding on the nest material. The relationship is believed to be commensal, with all life stages of the moth deriving benefit from the association, and the ants apparently not doing so, but we don't really know. Oddly, in the macro-moths, larvae, pupae and freshly emerged adults of Dotted Chestnut have been found in the nests of the black ant *Lasius fuliginosus*. The larvae of Dotted Chestnut are unlike other species in the same genus, and have long hairs, but the details of the relationship with the ant are not understood at all.

Larvae of many species of blue butterfly have developed particularly close associations with ants and have special structures that are integral to their interaction. These are:

- Newcomer's gland, also known as a honey gland, dorsally on A7.
- Pore cupola over the body, these being visible under a low-power microscope.
- A pair of white eversible structures, known as tentacle organs, which end in a ring of filaments. These are situated dorsally on A8 but are not always present.

Newcomer's gland and pore cupola between them secrete sugars and amino acids, and probably other chemicals involved in communication with ants. Larvae are attended by ants, which feed on these secretions from the glands. The precise function of the tentacle organs is unclear but they are probably also involved in communication with ants. For most associations the ants derive nutrition from the larvae, and the larvae are thought to receive protection from enemies, warded off by the presence of the ants.

Among British species, the relationship is closest in Large Blue. In this example it is predatory and not mutualistic. Eggs are laid on Wild Thyme and Wild Marjoram, and young larvae feed in the flower head. They are also cannibalistic, eating other larvae occupying the same flower head. When still small, but having gone through all its three moults, each larva drops to the ground and waits. When a red ant finds the larva, the ant stimulates the larval honey gland to produce a drop of liquid, which the ant imbibes. The larva is attended by ants for up to a few hours until it rears up, adopting a new posture. The first ant then picks it up and carries it into the nest. From then on, the larva feeds on ant grubs and increases in size about 100 times until it

Holly Blue larva being attended by an ant. Note feeding signs and Newcomer's gland arrowed

is fully fed, with no further skin changes. The larva overwinters in the nest, resuming feeding in the spring, and finally pupates. It is possible that some larvae may spend two years in the nest. Although Large Blue larvae may be adopted by various species of red ant, they are most likely to survive if the ant is *Myrmica sabuleti*. In the non-British butterfly species Alcon Blue *Phengaris alcon*, the relationship has developed further. The larva is a bit like a Cuckoo chick in a bird's nest, such that the host ants actually feed the larva with regurgitations, rather than it being predatory as we see with Large Blue.

Aside from Large Blue and its complete dependence upon ants, many other species have close relationships with them. The female Silver-studded Blue lays her eggs near the nests of black ants in genus *Lasius*. On hatching, the tiny larva is picked up by an ant and taken into its nest. It is not clear exactly how the larva feeds when tiny, but it goes on to emerge from the nest at night to feed on foodplants, and returns to hide in the ants' nest by day. Pupation occurs within the nest, and when the butterfly emerges it is accompanied by ants attracted by tiny droplets of liquid on its body until just before it takes to the air for its maiden flight.

Adonis Blue and Chalk Hill Blue larvae are similar to each other and highly attractive to ants. Adonis Blue larvae may be buried in the ground by ants between bouts of feeding. Pupation is often in an ants' nest. Chalk Hill Blue larvae may pupate in a small cell created by ants under the foodplant.

Larvae of various species are known to make sounds, inaudible to the human ear, that probably function to communicate with ants. Pupae of several species also make sounds that can be heard if held close to the ear. The sounds attract ants, which in turn feed from secretions made through the pupa's cuticle. Purple Hairstreak and Green Hairstreak pupae, for example, have been found in ants' nests. We don't know for certain, but pupation may occur in the nest, or ants may transport pupae to their nest by grabbing them by the hairs on the cuticle.

PARASITES

Moths and butterflies provide hosts for parasites, as anyone who rears the early stages will know. How often have we been excited to find a larva after hours of hard search, only to find a week later a wasp grub has appeared and the larva has died? Parasites come from a range of taxa, including viruses, bacteria, protozoa, fungi and nematode worms. However, those we are most used to seeing when rearing larvae are parasitic wasps (Hymenoptera) and flies (Diptera).

Technically, parasites are defined as organisms that normally live within or on the host, so are smaller than the host, and are harmful but often not lethal to it. Wasp and fly parasites of moths and butterflies are different; they start feeding within the living tissues of a single host and end up consuming it from within. The host dies, and the parasite emerges to become free-

Cocoons of the parasitic wasp *Protapanteles hirtariae* on Belted Beauty larva

living, either in the larval or adult stage. These are formally referred to as protelean parasites or parasitoids, but we will continue here to call them insect parasites.

The life histories of insect parasites are varied and can be complex. Some are host specific while others attack a range of host species. In some cases there is one parasite per host, but in other cases there may be several. The parasite may live internally (endoparasite) or externally (ectoparasite). There are even parasites of parasites, known as hyperparasites.

Egg, larval and pupal stages are all attacked by parasites. They may emerge from the stage originally attacked, or a subsequent stage. For example, a parasite may oviposit in a host's egg and the adult parasite emerges from that egg, or the parasite may not emerge until the host is a fully fed larva. When fully fed, the endoparasitic wasp and fly larvae usually emerge through the skin of the host larva and spin their own cocoons for pupation, although some species pupate within the host larva's skin or within the pupa.

The wasps may lay their eggs on the host or inject them inside it, feeding on fluid exuding from the puncture site. Most flies lay their eggs on the host, but some have a puncturing apparatus that allows them to lay inside the body. Alternatively, they may lay eggs on foliage and will enter the body only once eaten by the host, or they may hatch into first-instar larvae, which eventually make contact with the host.

Each butterfly and moth species may provide a web of interactions with a number of different parasite species. For example, PS has reared 11 species of parasite from the early stages of Brown-tail (Wyatt & Sterling, 1988).

Much useful information can be gleaned if parasites are reared and retained, and we encourage you to send the parasites, their cocoons and any host remains, along with full data, to a parasite expert. Your County Moth Recorder should be able to give you contact details. In this way, a full picture of host–parasite associations and parasite species distributions can be built up. Useful data to include are recorder, location, grid reference, host foodplant, date of collection, stage collected, and date of emergence of parasitic larva and adult. The identity of the host should be given, but it is not always possible to be certain, in which case that doubt should also be expressed. Please put parasite specimens in a clean tube that is free of wing scales, otherwise it makes the job of identifying the wasps and flies much harder!

DISEASES

All life stages of moths and butterflies are susceptible to disease, and some of these diseases fall into the definition of parasites in that they involve carrying other organisms but do not appear to be lethal.

Viruses

In studies on Brown-tail (Sterling, 1989), two types of virus were isolated from larvae: a cytoplasmic polyhedrosis virus (CPV, or cypovirus) and a nuclear polyhedrosis virus (NPV, or baculovirus). CPVs are a group of insect-specific viruses that develop in the cytoplasm of cells in the mid-gut of the larva. NPVs are also insect-specific viruses, but these develop within the nuclei of cells. Both diseases are likely to be ingested by larvae eating leaves. In Brown-tail the NPV proved lethal and highly virulent, spreading quickly between larvae, while the CPV infection eventually led to death of the host, causing the larva to feed ever more slowly and to desiccate. CPVs in other hosts are often chronic rather than lethal, affecting pupal weight and adult fecundity, whereas NPVs are almost always lethal. Brown-tail larvae, pupae and adults have also been found to be carrying protozoa in the group Microsporidia. These are likely to have been mainly sublethal to the host, although many dead larvae collected in the field had abundant Microsporidia within them.

NPVs are often specific to the host they infect, and PS's studies on Brown-tail NPV showed no cross-infectivity in a wide range of other moths. The specificity of NPVs has value in developing biological control methods for moth outbreaks. For example, in the USA, the NPV for Gypsy Moth is known as 'Gypchek' and has been used widely for control of outbreaks by government agencies. The virus is collected from dead larvae, purified and dried as a white powder, and sprayed over foliage in a water-based suspension. Healthy larvae ingest virus particles while feeding. Shortly before larvae die their behaviour changes and they climb to the top of the tree where they have been feeding. These larvae liquefy on death, and the virus-filled droplets fall onto the vegetation below, spreading the virus naturally and causing further infection.

Fungi

Larvae and pupae of moths and butterflies frequently succumb to fungal attack, often producing white fungal hyphae that grow and cause the cuticle to burst. Perhaps the most dramatic fungal attack is from Scarlet Caterpillarclub Fungus *Cordyceps militaris*. This fungus occurs in grassland and woodland edges and produces a highly visible reproductive body in late summer or autumn arising from a dead underground larva or pupa. *Cordyceps farinosa* is another species of fungus that infects moth and butterfly larvae, and here the reproductive body may appear from the pupa.

Scarlet Caterpillarclub Fungus *Cordyceps militaris*

Scarlet Caterpillarclub Fungus *Cordyceps militaris* showing how it grows out of a larva

The fungus *Cordyceps farinosa* growing out of a Bilberry Pug pupa

USEFUL RESOURCES

FURTHER READING

Selected useful reference books are listed below, as well as websites that provide photographic images of larvae to complement the illustrations in this field guide.

Selected reference texts for British and Irish species

Asher, J., M. Warren, R. Fox, P. Harding, J. Jeffcoate, and S. Jeffcoate. 2001. *The Millennium Atlas of Butterflies in Britain and Ireland*. Oxford: Oxford University Press.

Carter, D. J., and B. Hargreaves. 1986. *A Field Guide to Caterpillars of Butterflies and Moths in Britain and Europe*. London: HarperCollins.

Emmet, A. M., and J. Heath, eds. 1989. *The Moths and Butterflies of Great Britain and Ireland. Volume 7, Part 1: Hesperiidae to Nymphalidae, The Butterflies*. Colchester: Harley Books.

Emmet, A. M., and J. Heath, eds. 1991. *The Moths and Butterflies of Great Britain and Ireland. Volume 7, Part 2: Lasiocampidae to Thyatiridae, with Life History Chart of the British Lepidoptera*. Colchester: Harley Books.

Haggett, G. M. 1981. *Larvae of the British Lepidoptera Not Figured by Buckler*. London: British Entomological and Natural History Society.

Heath, J., ed. 1976. *The Moths and Butterflies of Great Britain and Ireland. Volume 1: Micropterigidae to Heliozelidae*. Oxford: Blackwell Scientific Publications and Curwen Press.

Heath, J., and A. M. Emmet, eds. 1979. *The Moths and Butterflies of Great Britain and Ireland. Volume 9: Sphingidae to Noctuidae (Part I)*. London: Curwen Books.

Heath, J., and A. M. Emmet, eds. 1983. *The Moths and Butterflies of Great Britain and Ireland. Volume 10: Noctuidae (Part II) to Agaristidae*. Colchester: Harley Books.

Heath, J., and A. M. Emmet, eds. 1985. *The Moths and Butterflies of Great Britain and Ireland. Volume 2: Cossidae to Heliodinidae*. Colchester: Harley Books.

Howarth, T. G. 1973. *South's British Butterflies*. London: Frederick Warne & Co.

Members of the British Entomological and Natural History Society. 1981. *An Identification Guide to the British Pugs: Lepidoptera: Geometridae*. London: British Entomological and Natural History Society.

Newman, L. H., and E. Mansell. 1968. *The Complete British Butterflies in Colour*. London: George Rainbird Ltd.

Porter, J. 1997. *The Colour Identification Guide to Caterpillars of the British Isles*. London: Viking.

Randle, Z., L. Evans-Hill, M. S. Parsons, A. Tyner, N. A. D. Bourn, A. M. Davis, E. B. Dennis, M. O'Donnell, T. Prescott, G. M. Tordoff, and R. Fox. 2019. *Atlas of Britain and Ireland's Larger Moths*. NatureBureau, Newbury.

Riley, A. M., and G. Prior. 2003. *British and Irish Pug Moths*. Colchester: Harley Books.

Skinner, B. 2009. *Colour Identification Guide to Moths of the British Isles*. 3rd ed. Stenstrup: Apollo Books.

South, R. 1906. *The Butterflies of the British Isles*. London: Frederick Warne & Co.

South, R. 1961. *The Moths of the British Isles. Series 1 and 2*. 4th ed. London: Frederick Warne & Co.

Sterling, P. H., M. S. Parsons, and R. Lewington. 2012. *Field Guide to the Micro-moths of Great Britain and Ireland*. Gillingham, Dorset: British Wildlife Publishing.

Thomas, J., and R. Lewington. 2014. *The Butterflies of Britain and Ireland*. New revised edition. London: Bloomsbury Publishing.

Townsend, M., P. Waring, and R. Lewington. 2019. *Concise Guide to the Moths of Great Britain and Ireland*. 2nd ed. London: Bloomsbury Publishing.

Waring, P., M. Townsend, and R. Lewington. 2017. *Field Guide to the Moths of Great Britain and Ireland*. 3rd ed. London: Bloomsbury Publishing.

Selected references on classification, structure, status and natural history

Agassiz, D. J. L., S. D. Beavan, and R. J. Heckford. 2013. *A Checklist of the Lepidoptera of the British Isles*. Handbooks for the Identification of British Insects. Telford: Field Studies Council on behalf of the Royal Entomological Society.

Agassiz, D. J. L., S. D. Beavan, and R. J. Heckford. 2016. 'Corrigenda to *A Checklist of the Lepidoptera of the British Isles*, 2013.' *The Entomologist's Record and Journal of Variation* 128: 50–5.

Agassiz, D. J. L., S. D. Beavan, and R. J. Heckford. 2016. 'Addenda and Amendments to *A Checklist of the Lepidoptera of the British Isles* on Account of Subsequently Published Data.' *Entomologist's Record and Journal of Variation* 128: 94–8.

Agassiz, D. J. L., S. D. Beavan, and R. J. Heckford. 2019. 'Second Update to the *Checklist of the Lepidoptera of the British Isles*, 2013.' *Entomologist's Record and Journal of Variation* 131: 1–7.

Allan, P. B. M. 1979. *Larval Foodplants*. 2nd ed. Hawkhurst: Watkins & Doncaster.

Bradley, J. D. 2000. *Checklist of Lepidoptera Recorded from the British Isles*. 2nd ed. Fordingbridge and Newent: D. J. Bradley and M. J. Bradley.

Edwards, S. R. 2012. *English Names for British Bryophytes*. 4th ed. Cardiff: British Bryological Society.

Eeles, P. 2016. 'The Hibernaculum Habits of the White Admiral Butterfly *Limenitis camilla* (Linnaeus).' *Dispar: The Online Journal of Lepidoptera*. www.dispar.org/reference.php?id=120

Ford, E. B. 1957. *Butterflies*. 3rd ed. London: HarperCollins.

Ford, E. B. 1972. *Moths*. 3rd ed. London: HarperCollins.

Fox, B. W. 2005. 'The Larva of the White Admiral Butterfly, *Limenitis camilla* (Linnaeus, 1764) – A Master Builder.' *Entomologist's Gazette* 55: 225–36.

Fox, R., T. M. Bereton, J. Asher, T. A. August, M. S. Botham, N. A. D. Bourn, K. L. Cruickshanks, C. R. Bulman, S. Ellis, C. A. Harrower, I. Middlebrook, D. G. Noble, G. D. Powney, Z. Randle, M. S. Warren, and D. B. Roy. 2015. *The State of the UK's Butterflies 2015*. Wareham, Dorset: Butterfly Conservation and the Centre for Ecology and Hydrology.

Fox, R., T. M. Bereton, J. Asher, M. S. Botham, I. Middlebrook, D. B. Roy, and M. S. Warren. 2011. *The State of the UK's Butterflies 2011*. Wareham, Dorset: Butterfly Conservation and the Centre for Ecology and Hydrology.

Fox, R., K. F. Conrad, M. S. Parsons, and I. P. Woiwod. 2006. *The State of Britain's Larger Moths*. Wareham, Dorset: Butterfly Conservation and Rothamsted Research.

Fox, R., M. S. Parsons, J. W. Chapman, I. P. Woiwod, M. S. Warren, and D. R. Brooks. 2013. *The State of Britain's Larger Moths 2013*. Wareham, Dorset: Butterfly Conservation and Rothamsted Research.

Fox, R., M. S. Warren, J. Asher, T. M. Bereton, and D. B. Roy. 2007. *The State of Britain's Butterflies 2007*. Wareham, Dorset: Butterfly Conservation and the Centre for Ecology and Hydrology.

Fox, R., M. S. Warren, and T. M. Brereton. 2010. *A New Red List of British Butterflies, Species Status 12*; 1–32. Peterborough: Joint Nature Conservation Committee.

Henwood, B. P., and J. W. Walters. 2019. 'The Extraordinary Larva of the White Admiral Butterfly, *Limenitis camilla* (Linnaeus, 1764).' *Entomologist's Gazette* 70: 67–77.

Hill, M. O., T. H. Blackstock, D. G. Long, and G. P. Rothero. 2008. *A Checklist and Census Catalogue of British and Irish Bryophytes*. Cardiff: British Bryological Society.

Howse, P. 2010. *Butterflies: Messages from Psyche*. Winterbourne: Papadakis.

Howse, P. 2014. *Seeing Butterflies: New Perspectives on Colour, Pattern and Mimicry*. Winterbourne: Papadakis.

Janzen, D. H., W. Hallwachs, and J. M. Burns. 2010. 'A Tropical Horde of Counterfeit Predator Eyes.' *Proceedings of the National Academy of Sciences of the United States of America* 107, no. 26 (June): 11659–11665. www.pnas.org/cgi/doi/10.1073/pnas.0912122107

Legon, N. W., and A. Henrici. 2005. *Checklist of the British and Irish Basidiomycota*. Kew: Royal Botanic Gardens.

Leverton, R. 2001. *Enjoying Moths*. London: T. & A. D. Poyser.

Majerus, M. E. N. 1983. 'Some Observations of Lichen Marked Larvae of the Scalloped Hazel: *Gonodontis bidentata* Clerck.' *Entomologist's Record and Journal of Variation* 95: 21–3.

Majerus, M. E. N. 2002. *Moths*. London: HarperCollins.

Rothschild, M. 1985. 'British Aposematic Lepidoptera.' In *The Moths and Butterflies of Great Britain and Ireland. Volume 2: Cossidae to Heliodinidae*, edited by J. Heath and A. M. Emmet. Colchester: Harley Books.

Scoble, M. J. 1995. *The Lepidoptera: Form, Function and Diversity*. Oxford: Oxford University Press.

Shirt, D. B., ed. 1987. *British Red Data Books 2. Insects*. Peterborough: Nature Conservancy Council.

Smith, C. W., A. Aptroot, B. J. Coppins, A. Fletcher, O. L. Gilbert, P. W. James, and P. A. Wolseley. 2009. *The Lichens of Great Britain and Ireland*. London: British Lichen Society.

Stace, C. 2019. *New Flora of the British Isles*. 4th ed. Middlewood Green: C & M Floristics.

Sterling, P. H. 1989. 'Natural mortalities of *Euproctis chrysorrhoea* (L.) and use of its baculovirus in biocontrol.' Unpublished DPhil thesis, University of Oxford.

van Emden, H. F., and M. Rothschild, eds. 2004. *Insect and Bird Interactions*. Andover: Intercept Limited.

Wyatt, N. P., and P. H. Sterling. 1988. 'Parasites of the Brown-tail Moth, *Euproctis chrysorrhoea*

(L.) (Lep. Lymantriidae), Including Two Diptera (Tachinidae, Sarcophagidae) New to Britain.'
Entomologist's Monthly Magazine 124: 207–13.
Young, M. R. 1997. *The Natural History of Moths*. London: T. & A. D. Poyser.

Selected websites including photographic images of larvae

UKMoths www.ukmoths.org.uk
Images of adults and some larvae, short descriptions and key features; all moth families covered; available as an iPhone application

UK Lepidoptera www.ukleps.org
Images of early stages and adults, complementing UKMoths, often showing a range of instars and giving sizes; covers all butterfly and moth families

UK Butterflies www.ukbutterflies.co.uk
Images of all stages, including early instars

Lepiforum (Germany) www.lepiforum.de
Covers European families

Pyrgus (Germany) www.pyrgus.de
Covers European families

Lepinet (France) www.lepinet.fr
Images of adults and early stages

Moths and Butterflies of Europe and North Africa www.leps.it
Images of adults and some early stages

Fauna Europaea https://fauna-eu.org
The scientific names of all European land and freshwater animals brought together in one authoritative database

SOCIETIES, RECORDING SCHEMES AND GROUPS
Amateur Entomologists' Society

A society for all ages and experience. Publishes the *AES Bulletin*, books and leaflets; holds an annual exhibition and trade fair. Contact: AES, PO Box 8774, London SW7 5ZG. www.amentsoc.org

British Entomological & Natural History Society

The national society for field entomologists, including many active butterfly and moth recorders. Publishes the *British Journal of Entomology and Natural History* and a number of reference works; organises an annual exhibition and series of lectures and field meetings. Maintains its own library, reference collection and lecture space in Reading. Contact: The Secretary, c/o The Pelham-Clinton Building, Dinton Pastures Country Park, Davis Street, Hurst, Reading, Berkshire RG10 0TH. www.benhs.org.uk

Butterfly Conservation

The national charity for the conservation of moths and butterflies. Publishes a magazine for members, *Butterfly*, regular reports of the state of Britain's butterflies and moths, and key reference sources such as *The Millennium Atlas of Butterflies in Britain and Ireland* and *The Atlas of Britain and Ireland's Larger Moths*. Operates recording schemes for butterflies and moths (see below), and organises national recording meetings, members' days and international symposia. Has 31 branches across the UK run by volunteers, who organise over 700 events per year. Contact: Butterfly Conservation, Manor Yard, East Lulworth, Wareham, Dorset BH20 5QP. www.butterfly-conservation.org

Journals

There are three main journals, well known to most UK and Irish lepidopterists, that regularly publish articles, notes and observations on butterflies and moths: *Atropos*, the *Entomologist's Gazette*, and the *Entomologist's Record and Journal of Variation*.

Local records centres

These are the focal point within many counties for the management and dissemination of wildlife records. A few centres work as a conduit between local recording groups, County Recorders and Butterfly Conservation to coordinate records management. Find your local records centre via the Association of Local Environmental Records Centres at www.alerc.org.uk

Recording butterflies

National recording of butterflies is coordinated through Butterfly Conservation within two major schemes, Butterflies for the New Millennium (BNM) and the UK Butterfly Monitoring Scheme (UKBMS) (https://butterfly-conservation.org/butterflies/recording-and-monitoring).

BNM is the scheme for general recording of butterflies across Great Britain and Ireland, run with the Biological Records Centre (part of the Natural Environment Research Council's Centre for Ecology and Hydrology). This partnership is an example of collaboration between government, research organisations and charity and volunteer groups (such as the Dublin Naturalists' Field Club) to collect and analyse the best possible data for monitoring the state of our natural environment. From 1995 to 1999, 1.6 million butterfly sightings across Britain and Ireland were collated to produce *The Millennium Atlas of Butterflies in Britain and Ireland*. The BNM continues today, with its records contributing to the regular *State of the UK's Butterflies* reports, and the database now has over 12 million sightings. https://butterfly-conservation. org/our-work/recording-and-monitoring/butterflies-for-the-new-millennium.

UKBMS collects annual data on the population status of butterflies from three sources: butterfly transects walked on a fixed route weekly from April to September; surveys of habitat specialist butterflies, including timed counts of adults, single-species transects, and egg and larval counts; and the Wider Countryside Butterfly Survey (WCBS), involving volunteers counting butterflies in randomly selected 1km squares along two parallel 1km routes, two to four times during the year. The resulting UKBMS dataset is an important resource for understanding changes in butterfly populations, and for gaining understanding of status and long-term trends. www.ukbms.org

Recording moths

There are many local moth recording groups that are self-organised by dedicated volunteers, and some of these maintain websites offering information on latest sightings of macro- and micro-moths, recording forms and field meetings. Almost all counties in England, Wales and Scotland, and in the Isle of Man have a County Moth Recorder (CMR), often having separate individuals for micros and macros. In Northern Ireland there are separate macro- and micro-moth Recorders, and in the Republic of Ireland a Recorder covering all species. These individuals collate and verify records at the county (or vice-county) level, some also producing newsletters and organising field and indoor meetings. Often these individuals are a key coordinator of the

Wood Tiger larva

local recording group. Records should be forwarded to the relevant CMR at least at the end of each year, and some counties now operate online recording databases for you to enter your records. Many individual county moth lists have been published and these provide a good guide to species that may occur at particular localities. While some have not been updated since the Victoria History of the Counties of England (the Victoria County History) series that began publication in 1899, there are many more modern authoritative works covering counties or other geographical areas. The list and contact details for your CMR can be found via the Moths Count website (www.mothscount.org). The CMRs forward your verified records to the National Moth Recording Scheme (NMRS).

NMRS, run by Butterfly Conservation, is part of the Moths Count project. It began in 2007 and since then has amassed over 25 million records across some 900 macro-moth species from the UK, Isle of Man and Channel Islands. The enormous dataset is giving us extraordinary insight into our changing moth fauna. It is the data source for *The Atlas of Britain and Ireland's Larger Moths*. https://butterfly-conservation.org/our-work/recording-and-monitoring/nationalmoth-recording-scheme

Royal Entomological Society

The members of this society are professional entomologists and amateurs interested in research. It publishes various journals, organises international symposia and maintains a comprehensive library. Contact: RES, The Mansion House, Chiswell Green Lane, St Albans, Hertfordshire AL2 3NS. www. royensoc.co.uk

AT-A-GLANCE GUIDE

These pages provide a quick reference to the diversity of larvae across the families of macro-moths and butterflies in Great Britain and Ireland.

Hepialidae (pl. 1)

×1.25

Orange Swift/Map-winged Swift/ Ghost Moth (pp. 72–3)
Triodia sylvina/Korscheltellus fusconebulosa/Hepialus humuli

Cossidae (pl. 1)

×1.25

Goat Moth (p. 74)
Cossus cossus

Sesiidae (pl. 1)	Limacodidae (pl. 2)	Zygaenidae (pl. 2)

×1.5   ×1.5   ×1.5

Lunar Hornet Moth (p. 77)   Festoon (p. 85)   Narrow-bordered Five-spot Burnet (p. 89)
Sesia bembeciformis   *Apoda limacodes*   *Zygaena lonicerae*

Papilionidae (pl. 3)

×1.25

Swallowtail (p. 90)
Papilio machaon

Hesperiidae (pl. 3)	Pieridae (pl. 4)

×1.75   ×1.75

Grizzled Skipper (p. 92)   Orange-tip (p. 96)
Pyrgus malvae   *Anthocharis cardamines*

Nymphalidae (pl. 5–7)

×1.75

Ringlet (p. 100)
Aphantopus hyperantus

×1.75

Red Admiral (p. 104)
Vanessa atalanta

Riodinidae (pl. 7)

×1.75

Duke of Burgundy (p. 108)
Hamearis lucina

Lycaenidae (pl. 8)

×2

Green Hairstreak (p. 110)
Callophrys rubi

Drepanidae (pl. 9)

×1.25

Dusky Hook-tip/Pebble Hook-tip (p. 117)
Drepana curvatula/D. falcataria

×1.25

Yellow Horned (p. 120)
Achlya flavicornis

Lasiocampidae (pl. 10–11)

×1.25

Lackey (p. 122)
Malacosoma neustria

×1.25

Oak Eggar (p. 123)
Lasiocampa quercus

×1.25

Endromidae (pl. 11)

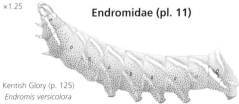

Kentish Glory (p. 125)
Endromis versicolora

Sphingidae (pl. 12–15)

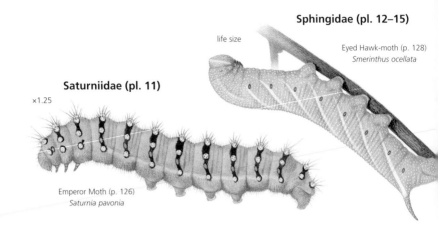

life size

Eyed Hawk-moth (p. 128)
Smerinthus ocellata

Saturniidae (pl. 11)

×1.25

Emperor Moth (p. 126)
Saturnia pavonia

Geometridae (pl. 16–34)

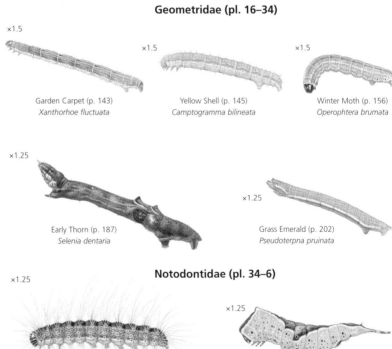

×1.5

Garden Carpet (p. 143)
Xanthorhoe fluctuata

×1.5

Yellow Shell (p. 145)
Camptogramma bilineata

×1.5

Winter Moth (p. 156)
Operophtera brumata

×1.25

Early Thorn (p. 187)
Selenia dentaria

×1.25

Grass Emerald (p. 202)
Pseudoterpna pruinata

Notodontidae (pl. 34–6)

×1.25

Oak Processionary (p. 205)
Thaumetopoea processionea

×1.25

Sallow Kitten (p. 206)
Furcula furcula

×1.25

Swallow Prominent (p. 208)
Pheosia tremula

×1.25

Chocolate-tip (p. 211)
Clostera curtula

Erebidae (pl. 37–42)

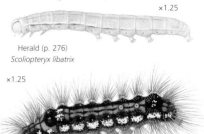

×1.25

Herald (p. 276)
Scoliopteryx libatrix

×1.25

Snout (p. 277)
Hypena proboscidalis

×1.25

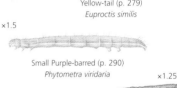

Yellow-tail (p. 279)
Euproctis similis

×1.25

Ruby Tiger (p. 282)
Phragmatobia fuliginosa

×1.5

Small Purple-barred (p. 290)
Phytometra viridaria

Red Underwing (p. 291)
Catocala nupta

×1.25

Noctuidae (pl. 43–64)

×1.25

Silver Y (p. 295)
Autographa gamma

×1.25

Knot Grass (p. 300)
Acronicta rumicis

×1.25

Mullein (p. 302)
Cucullia verbasci

×1.25

Angle Shades (p. 311)
Phlogophora meticulosa

×1.25

Brick (p. 328) *Agrochola circellaris*

×1.25

Bright-line Brown-eye (p. 343)
Lacanobia oleracea

Large Yellow Underwing (p. 358)
Noctua pronuba

Nolidae (pl. 64)

×1.5

Least Black Arches (p. 367)
Nola confusalis

×1.25

Scarce Silver-lines (p. 367)
Bena bicolorana

HEPIALOIDEA
HEPIALIDAE SWIFT MOTHS

There are five species in this family in Great Britain and Ireland out of a worldwide listing of around 500. Larvae are entirely subterranean, feeding on the roots of their foodplants, and pupation takes place in the ground. The winter is spent as a larva, and most species pass two winters in this stage. Larvae are most frequently encountered by gardeners while weeding, and those found in this way are most likely to be Orange Swift, Common Swift or Ghost Moth.

Common Swift ×1.25

Typically the larva has an orangey-brown head and a white body covered with orangey pinacula, each with a short grey hair. The prothoracic plate is orangey, the anal plate greyish brown, and spiracles black. Common Swift is more slender than others. Common Swift and a typical broader-bodied larva are illustrated. Gold Swift is shown as a photo.

ORANGE SWIFT
Triodia sylvina

PLATE 1
3.001 (15)

Common. More local in the north. Has increased significantly in abundance in recent decades. **FIELD CHARACTERS** See general description in family notes above. **HABITATS** Rough grassland in many places, including farmland, gardens, calcareous grassland, meadows and pastures, moorland and woodland. **FOODPLANTS** Roots of herbaceous plants. Has been reported on Bracken, dandelions, Broad-leaved Dock and viper's-buglosses. Probably also feeds on grass roots. **FIELD NOTES** Sep–May or Jun. Pupates in the ground. An adult has been observed emerging from a pupa in a garden lawn. In the wild considered to overwinter as a larva through two winters, but produces an adult in a one-year life cycle when reared from an egg in captivity.

COMMON SWIFT
Korscheltellus lupulina

PLATE 1
3.002 (17)

Common. Widespread and sometimes abundant in England and Wales. Much more local in Scotland and Ireland. **FIELD CHARACTERS** See general description in family notes above. **HABITATS** Grassy areas in a wide variety of habitats, including farmland, fens, gardens, calcareous grassland, meadows and pastures, moorland and woodland. **FOODPLANTS** Roots of wild and cultivated herbaceous plants including grasses. Has been reported on Red and White dead-nettles, docks, geraniums and Black Horehound. An occasional pest of agricultural crops and horticultural plants. **FIELD NOTES** Jun or Jul–May. Pupates in the ground. Overwinters as a larva once or twice.

MAP-WINGED SWIFT
Korscheltellus fusconebulosa

PLATE 1
3.003 (18)

Local. Frequent in the north and west; very local in the south and east. **FIELD CHARACTERS** See general description in family notes above. **HABITATS** Bogs, gardens, acid grassland, heathland, moorland and open woodland. Sometimes found on calcareous grassland and sand dunes. **FOODPLANTS** Roots and lower parts of stems of Bracken, and roots of Red Fescue. Probably on other herbaceous plants. **FIELD NOTES** Jul–May. Pupates in the ground. Overwinters as a larva through two winters.

GOLD SWIFT
Phymatopus hecta

SEE PHOTO BELOW
3.004 (16)

Local. **FIELD CHARACTERS** See general description in family notes (p. 72). In addition there are sclerotised patches on all thoracic segments and the pinacula are darker than in other species. **HABITATS** Most frequent in open woodland. Also found among Bracken on rough grassland, heathland and scrub. **FOODPLANTS** Roots of Bracken, and mosses. Has been found in Bracken in Apr below new growing shoots, and in spring feeding within Swan's-neck Thyme-moss. **FIELD NOTES** Jun–late May. Pupates in the ground. Overwinters as a larva through two winters.

Gold Swift larva

GHOST MOTH
Hepialus humuli

PLATE 1
3.005 (14)

Common. Has decreased significantly in abundance in recent decades. **FIELD CHARACTERS** See general description in family notes (p. 72). **HABITATS** Grassy and weedy areas. Found in farmland, gardens, heathland, meadows and pastures, moorland (but rarely at high altitude in the north) and woodland. **FOODPLANTS** Roots of many herbaceous plants, including burdocks, dandelions, dead-nettles, docks, Water Figwort, grasses, Black Horehound, Hop, nettles and Wild Strawberry. **FIELD NOTES** Jul–May. Pupates in the ground. Overwinters as a larva through two winters.

COSSOIDEA
COSSIDAE GOAT AND LEOPARD MOTHS

There are three species in the British
Isles, in a family of about 700
worldwide. Larvae feed within living
plant tissues. In two species, larvae
feed for two years before pupating in
the larval habitation. In the third, the

Leopard Moth ×1.25

larva feeds for three to four years and may pupate in the larval habitation
or elsewhere. None of the species is easy to locate in the wild.

Goat Moth larva

COSSINAE

GOAT MOTH
Cossus cossus

PLATE 1
50.001 (162)

Nb. Formerly widespread, but has declined significantly in recent
decades. Occurs very locally in widely scattered areas throughout. **FIELD
CHARACTERS** Body shiny. Head and prothoracic plate dark brown or black. Body
somewhat flattened, purplish across the dorsum and laterally, and orangey
below. **SIMILAR SPECIES** Red-tipped Clearwing. **HABITATS** Wide variety, including
bogs, soft cliffs, gardens, hedgerows, marshes, ancient parkland, scrub, river
valleys and woodland. Tends to be more frequent in areas where ground is
waterlogged. **FOODPLANTS** Feeds within living wood under bark and within
heartwood of several broadleaf trees and shrubs, including Alder, Apple, Ash, birches, Sweet Chestnut,
English Elm, Pedunculate Oak, Pear, Plum, poplars and willows. **FIELD NOTES** Eggs hatch in Jul or Aug
and larvae burrow into the wood of either the main trunk or branches. Their presence may be given
away by the exudation of frass and/or sweet-smelling sap runs, as well as old emergence holes in bark.
Some veteran oak trees may be infected with successive generations of larvae for decades, possibly much
longer, and long-infested trees support an important assemblage of other invertebrates. Larvae have been
observed occupying the same branches of Grey Willow as Red-tipped Clearwing, but the larva of the
clearwing is usually within smaller-diameter wood and forms a gall. The Goat Moth larva takes three or
four years to complete its growth. When fully fed, it may spin a cocoon in the larval habitation or leave
the tree and wander, sometimes at speed over open ground, in search of a pupation site in rotten wood
or underground. Overwinters for the final time in a strong cocoon before pupating in the spring.

ZEUZERINAE

LEOPARD MOTH
Zeuzera pyrina

PLATE 1
50.002 (161)

Common. Widely distributed in England and Wales but rarely seen in numbers. One record in Ireland. **FIELD CHARACTERS** Head and prothoracic and anal plates dark brown. Body yellow or yellowish white, covered with dark brown pinacula. **HABITATS** Gardens and urban parks, heathland, orchards and open woodland. Occasionally a pest in fruit trees. **FOODPLANTS** Wide variety of woody plants, including Apple, Ash, Beech, birches, Blackthorn, cherries, Black Currant, elms, Hawthorn, Honeysuckle, Horse-chestnut, Lilac, oaks, Pear, privets, Rowan, Sycamore, Wayfaring-tree and willows. **FIELD NOTES** Aug–May, taking two or three years to complete its growth. In living branches of the foodplant, preferring stems up to 10cm in diameter. Pupates in the larval burrow without a cocoon.

REED LEOPARD
Phragmataecia castaneae

PLATE 1
50.003 (160)

RDB. Very local in East Anglia, and occurs at one site in Dorset. **FIELD CHARACTERS** Head and prothoracic plate brown. Body whitish with a purplish subdorsal stripe. **HABITATS** Fens, marshes, margins of ponds, reedbeds and reed swamp. **FOODPLANT** Common Reed. **FIELD NOTES** Jul–May. Feeds in the roots and lower stems of the foodplant, regularly moving between stems. Takes two years to complete its growth, and overwinters in a stem, usually below water level. Pupates in the reed, and an infected stem rarely produces a flower spike.

Holes in ancient Pedunculate Oak tree indicating Goat Moth infestation

SESIIDAE CLEARWING MOTHS

There are 15 species that are resident in the British Isles, and one, Dusky Clearwing, which may be resident in the Channel Islands. Larvae feed internally in a diversity of living plant tissues, including roots, tree trunks, branches, twigs, stems and under the bark.

Lunar Hornet Moth × 1.25

All larvae in this family are very similar in shape and colour. Typically, the head is orangey brown, the prothoracic plate translucent and pale yellowish brown, and the body creamy white with short hairs. One species, Lunar Hornet Moth, is illustrated to show the general form of the larva, and to distinguish clearwing larvae

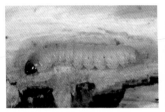

Red-belted Clearwing larva

from larvae of beetles (Coleoptera) that may be found in similar situations (see *Distinguishing larvae of sawflies and beetles*, p. 17). In addition, clearwing larvae may be distinguished from beetle larvae by carefully searching for the slight silk they produce within the feeding gallery.

Finding evidence of clearwing moth activity requires good field skills, but once these are acquired, recording of several species from larval signs can be straightforward, and achieved in winter and early spring. The text concentrates on descriptions of habits of early stages of clearwing moths and how to find them in the field. Dusky Clearwing is not included as its residency is uncertain.

TINTHIINAE

RASPBERRY CLEARWING
Pennisetia hylaeiformis

SEE PHOTO BELOW
52.001 (369a)

Recent colonist/Adventive. Resident in south-east England and East Anglia and spreading slowly. **FIELD CHARACTERS** See general description in family notes above. **HABITATS** Allotments, fruit farms and gardens. **FOODPLANTS** Cultivated Raspberry, including summer- and autumn-fruiting varieties. In Europe on Bramble and Raspberry. **FIELD NOTES** Aug–spring, overwintering twice as a larva. Brownish-red eggs are laid on the underside of green Raspberry leaves but it is not clear how the larva gets into the cane. There is no evidence it feeds on or in the leaf near the egg, and possibly it travels along the leaf petiole to the stem or falls to the ground to find a suitable cane. Feeds internally in a living cane, leaving no sign of its presence until after the first winter. It then feeds in the crown and the top of the root, sometimes causing a gall to

form at the base of the stem, from which orangey-brown frass is extruded. The gall may be pear-shaped or nearly spherical and is two or three times the diameter of the cane. Later that year, the larva may tunnel 15–25cm upwards from the gall, centrally in the pith. It then moves to the crown for the second winter. The exit hole for the pupa/adult is constructed in the cane, leaving a thin covering of stem. Mature larvae have also been found in spring in the base of canes without any sign of a gall. Pupation occurs in the cane without a cocoon. In

Raspberry Clearwing gall

autumn-fruiting varieties, the stems are pruned in winter, so pupation probably takes place within the gall or at the base of the cane. Canes of autumn-fruiting varieties may break near a gall, causing them to fall.

SESIINAE

HORNET MOTH
Sesia apiformis

SEE PHOTOS BELOW
52.002 (370)

Nb. Widespread and sometimes frequent in the Midlands, East Anglia and south-east England. **FIELD CHARACTERS** See general description in family notes (p. 76). **SIMILAR SPECIES** Lunar Hornet Moth rarely uses poplars, and Hornet Moth rarely uses willows. Lunar Hornet Moth usually bores deeper into the wood, pupates higher in its tunnel, and does not make a substantial cocoon. **HABITATS** A variety of open situations where poplars are planted, including fens, large gardens, hedgerows, plantations, shelterbelts, street trees and urban parks. **FOODPLANTS** Mature trees of Aspen, balsam-poplars, Black-poplar, Hybrid Black-poplar, Lombardy-poplar, and Grey and White poplars. Occasionally willows, including Siberian Violet-willow. **FIELD NOTES** Jul–autumn, overwintering two or three times as a larva. Makes extensive tunnels between the living bark and wood at the base of the tree and upper part of the roots, and may bore deeper if the tree is heavily infested. When fully fed, bores to the pupal exit point, leaving a thin layer of bark at the end of the tunnel, and constructs a cocoon of chewed bark, wood and silk just before the exit. Sometimes the bark covering is lost and the cocoon is visible. Occasionally makes a cocoon in the ground using soil particles, or may bore in the trunk up to 1m above ground. Overwinters in the cocoon and pupates Apr–May. Infested trees may be found by searching for old exit holes c. 10mm in diameter near the tree base and for piles of reddish-brown frass. Sometimes, empty cocoons may be found at the base of trees in the spring, the pupae having been predated. Adults emerge mid-Jun–mid-Jul, rarely Aug, from 7 to 11am.

Hornet Moth old exit holes at base of Hybrid Black-poplar trunk

Hornet Moth extruded pupal case

LUNAR HORNET MOTH
Sesia bembeciformis

PLATE 1
52.003 (371)

Common. Widespread throughout, but local in Scotland and southern and western Ireland. **FIELD CHARACTERS** See general description in family notes (p. 76). **SIMILAR SPECIES** Hornet Moth. **HABITATS** Wide variety, including bogs, soft cliffs, fens, marshes, scrub, margins of waterbodies, and open woodland. **FOODPLANTS** Mainly Goat and Grey willows, occasionally Hybrid Crack-willow and other willows. Also Black-poplar and Lombardy-poplar. **FIELD NOTES** Aug–spring, overwintering twice as a larva. Lives in small and mature trees, and sometimes

Lunar Hornet Moth old exit holes and signs of woodpecker predation in Goat Willow trunk

smaller stems *c.* 3cm in diameter. Feeds under the bark in the first year, sometimes below ground level. The following year it tunnels upwards in the wood up to 50cm. When fully fed, bores down to the pupal exit point, leaving a thin layer of bark at the end of the tunnel. Pupates head down, high in the tunnel, in a cocoon of silk and wood scrapings, sealing the tunnel below the pupa. An infested tree is most easily detected by finding old exit holes, and orangey frass extruding from cracks in the bark. Holes are round, *c.* 10mm in diameter, usually near the base of the tree, but sometimes up to 2m above ground. Rough oval-shaped holes indicate predation by woodpeckers. A single large tree can produce over 30 adults in a year. Adults emerge end Jun–Jul, usually in the first half of the period, *c.* 8.30am.

WELSH CLEARWING
Synanthedon scoliaeformis

SEE PHOTOS BELOW

52.005 (376)

RDB. Very local. Further colonies probably await discovery. **FIELD CHARACTERS** See general description in family notes (p. 76). **SIMILAR SPECIES** There are several clearwing species whose larvae feed in birches, and where distributions overlap, rearing to confirm identity is advised. Larvae of different species can occur even in the same birch stump. However, the following notes may help distinguish larval feeding habits. Bark-feeding species: Welsh Clearwing occurs in mature trees, not stumps, and makes a cocoon of roundish bark particles; Yellow-legged Clearwing, which occasionally feeds on birches, makes a cocoon of granular, woody frass. Wood-feeding species: White-barred Clearwing pupates without making a cocoon; Large Red-belted Clearwing makes a cocoon from long, thin fragments of wood. **HABITATS** Open birch woodland on wet grassland, heathland and moorland. **FOODPLANTS** Downy and Silver birches. **FIELD NOTES** Aug–May, overwintering twice as a larva. Feeds in contorted tunnels on the inner bark of mature trees with thickened bark, and when nearly fully fed may eject reddish frass from cracks in the bark. When fully fed, constructs the pupal exit hole, leaving a thin layer of bark covering the tunnel. Pupates in a reddish-brown cocoon of roundish bark particles and silk, constructed under the bark. Cocoon construction is Jul–Aug of the second year, and pupation in the spring of the third year. Old exit holes and extruded pupal cases provide evidence of an infested tree. Empty cocoons may persist for several years. Exit holes are *c.* 5mm in diameter and are usually 1–2m above ground, sometimes as high as 6m.

Welsh Clearwing extruded pupal case

Welsh Clearwing old exit holes in bark of a mature birch tree

WHITE-BARRED CLEARWING
Synanthedon spheciformis

SEE PHOTO BELOW

52.006 (375)

Nb. Found in three discrete areas only. **FIELD CHARACTERS** See general description in family notes (p. 76). **SIMILAR SPECIES** Welsh Clearwing, Large Red-belted Clearwing and Yellow-legged Clearwing. **HABITATS** In various habitats including copses, marshes, scrub on heathland, trees growing along streamsides, and open areas in dry and wet woodland. **FOODPLANTS** Alder and birches. **FIELD**

Old pupae of White-barred Clearwing. Note wood fragments ejected by the larva from its feeding gallery onto the stump

NOTES Aug–May, overwintering at least twice as a larva. Lives within suckering young growth, young trees, old trees and cut stumps, feeding at the base and in the roots. Tunnels between the bark and wood, eating the wood. It may descend into the roots, boring up above ground level in spring after the first winter. When fully fed, constructs the pupal exit hole, which is covered with a thin layer of bark or with chewed wood at the surface of a cut stem. Pupation occurs at the top of the burrow, which is lined with chewed wood and silk, but there is no cocoon. Old exit holes c. 5mm in diameter and piles of frass on the ground provide evidence of its presence. In areas where young birches are cut cyclically in winter for brushwood, chewed wood may be piled above the cut stem by the larva in spring before pupation.

LARGE RED-BELTED CLEARWING
Synanthedon culiciformis

SEE PHOTOS BELOW

52.007 (381)

Nb. Widely recorded across much of southern England away from the south-west, and in East Anglia, the Midlands and central areas in Scotland. Rare in Wales. **FIELD CHARACTERS** See general description in family notes (p. 76). **SIMILAR SPECIES** Welsh Clearwing, White-barred Clearwing and Yellow-legged Clearwing. **HABITATS** Scrub on heathland and moorland, and in open woodland and woodland rides. **FOODPLANTS** Downy and Silver birches. Less often Alder. **FIELD NOTES** Jul–May in the south, but possibly over two winters in the north as this is the behaviour noted elsewhere in northern Europe. Lives in stems and cut stumps, and can be especially common in the latter where they have not been treated with herbicide. Tunnels between the bark and wood, eating the wood, and may later enter the wood. Reddish frass may be seen extruding from the top of a stump or in crevices in the bark. When fully fed, constructs its future exit hole, leaving a thin layer of bark or covering it with silk. This may be situated in the bark, or between the bark and wood in a stump, or more centrally in a stump. Pupates in a cocoon made of silk and long strands of wood.

Large Red-belted Clearwing frass extruding from Silver Birch stump

Large Red-belted Clearwing frass extruding from Silver Birch stump, and parasitic wasp egg-laying

RED-TIPPED CLEARWING
Synanthedon formicaeformis

SEE PHOTOS ON P.80

52.008 (380)

Nb. Widespread over much of England, but very local in the north and far west, and in Wales and Ireland. No recent record from Scotland. **FIELD CHARACTERS** See general description in family notes (p. 76). **SIMILAR SPECIES** In Grey Willow, most likely to be confused with the weevil *Cryptorhynchus lapathi* (Coleoptera), which produces circular scars around the branches and, like Red-tipped Clearwing, extrudes elongated woody frass. Where beetle and moth larvae have been found in the same tree, the weevil larva has not caused the branch to swell into a gall; otherwise the signs were similar. However, the weevil larva is known to cause a gall to be formed, and while the gall is often irregular in shape, it may not be possible to confirm identity of the moth based on the presence of a gall alone. Goat Moth larvae frass has also been found extruding from a 4cm diameter branch of Grey Willow, without a gall. The gall of Sallow Clearwing on Goat and Grey willows is always smaller and on a narrower twig, and has a horseshoe-shaped scar on one side. The longhorn beetle *Saperda populnea* (Coleoptera) makes a similar-shaped gall to Sallow Clearwing on narrow twigs of Goat and Grey willows, but without the horseshoe scar. Yellow-legged Clearwing is also reported rarely on broadleaf willows. The micro-moth *Cydia servillana* (Tortricidae) makes a slender gall in a one-year-old stem of Goat and Grey willows, and there is

Red-tipped Clearwing gall on Grey Willow, with extruded pupal case

Grey Willow branch showing frass from the weevil *Cryptorhynchus lapathi*

Micro-moth *Cydia servillana* (Tortricidae) gall on Grey Willow

a silk-capped emergence hole just above a dead leaf bud at the widest part of the gall. **HABITATS** Various habitats where willows grow in open situations with poor drainage, including soft cliffs, Osier beds, scrub in fens, heathland and marshes, and margins of waterbodies. **FOODPLANTS** Various willows, including Osier, and Almond, Goat, Grey and Tea-leaved willows. Also noted on Creeping Willow. **FIELD NOTES** Aug–May, overwintering twice as a larva. Lives within branches 2–5cm in diameter or in trunks, sometimes in sufficient abundance to kill a thin stem, and in situations where the plant produces little growth and appears stressed, or is already damaged. In Goat and Grey willows, the young larva bores around the stem just under the bark, creating a circular scar. It then bores centrally in the wood. The stem thickens above the scar, forming a gall 2–3cm in diameter from which elongated woody frass extrudes. When fully fed, creates the pupal exit hole in the gall, leaving a covering of a thin layer of bark. Pupation occurs without a cocoon. In Osier there is little external evidence of larvae within, and their presence is more likely to be detected from old emergence holes nearby or woody frass at the edge of a broken stem or stump. In Scandinavia, the larva causes gall formation low down on Creeping Willow, and adult moths have been seen flying around this plant in the British Isles.

SALLOW CLEARWING
Synanthedon flaviventris

SEE PHOTOS BELOW

52.009 (377)

Nb. From Dorset to Kent and north to the south Midlands. **FIELD CHARACTERS** See general description in family notes (p. 76). **SIMILAR SPECIES** Red-tipped clearwing, micro-moth *Cydia servillana* (Tortricidae) and longhorn beetle *Saperda populnea* (Coleoptera). **HABITATS** Willows growing in open situations with poor drainage, especially in bogs, heathland, road verges, waste ground and woodland rides. **FOODPLANTS** Goat and Grey willows, in bushes from 1m high to tall trees, preferring to inhabit long, straight shoots. **FIELD NOTES** Aug– Jun, overwintering twice as a larva. Lives within narrow stems, 0.5–1.5cm in diameter. At first it tunnels around a stem, then in spring it bores into the middle and creates a vertical tunnel. It feeds centrally, causing a gall to form during the second year, and above the gall the leaves turn yellowish green and the stem may die. The full-sized gall is nearly bilaterally symmetrical, 1–2cm in diameter and 2.5cm long, with a roughly horseshoe-shaped depression on one side. When fully fed, creates the pupal exit hole, leaving a covering of a thin layer of bark. Pupates head down in a chamber above the gall without a cocoon. The galls are mainly found in odd/even winters (e.g. winter 2021/22). Galls are heavily predated by birds, so after leaf-fall in early winter is a good time to look for them.

Sallow Clearwing gall on Grey Willow (left) and opened to show larva inside (right)

ORANGE-TAILED CLEARWING
Synanthedon andrenaeformis

SEE PHOTOS BELOW
52.010 (378)

Nb. Found widely in southern England away from the far south-west, and in parts of south Wales. **FIELD CHARACTERS** See general description in family notes (p. 76). **HABITATS** Calcareous grassland, hedgerows, scrub, and edges of woodland. Also among planted areas in urban landscapes, especially on road verges. **FOODPLANTS** Mainly Wayfaring-tree and occasionally Guelder-rose. **FIELD NOTES** Jul–May, overwintering twice as a larva. Lives in stems 0.8–2.5cm in diameter, less often up to 5cm, in bushes growing in sunny situations, and also in shade. Tunnels centrally in the stem, causing a gall to form in the

narrowest but not the widest stems, and the lining of the tunnel to turn black. Frass is extruded from the tunnel. When fully fed, creates the pupal exit hole at the widest part of the gall, if present, leaving a concave cap of bark over the entrance. The cap may fall off, revealing the tunnel, which may or may not be filled with frass. The exit hole may be below the tunnel or up to 25mm above it. Pupates in the tunnel without a cocoon. Old holes are much easier to find than occupied stems and galls.

Orange-tailed Clearwing gall on Wayfaring-tree (left) and old exit hole on Wayfaring-tree (right)

RED-BELTED CLEARWING
Synanthedon myopaeformis

SEE PHOTOS BELOW
52.011 (379)

Nb. Widely distributed from the Midlands southwards, but appears to be declining in the west of its range. **FIELD CHARACTERS** See general description in family notes (p. 76). **SIMILAR SPECIES** Cherry Bark Tortrix *Enarmonia formosana* (Tortricidae) feeds under the bark of various trees in the rose family. Its larva has large grey pinacula, which Red-belted Clearwing does not. Clearwing larvae found on cherries will need to be reared to confirm identity since Yellow-legged Clearwing can also feed on the plant. **HABITATS** Allotments, gardens and urban parks, hedgerows,

Red-belted Clearwing extruded pupal case

Cherry Bark Tortrix *Enarmonia formosana* (Tortricidae) larva.
Note the large grey pinacula on the larva, which distinguish it from
Red-belted Clearwing (see photo p. 76)

Red-belted Clearwing old exit hole
and extruded pupal case, showing
how it has pushed through a thin
layer of bark covering its gallery

orchards, scrub, street trees and open woodland. **FOODPLANTS** Mainly Apple and Crab Apple, and especially Crab Apple cultivars grown as street trees. Also reported on Almond, cherries, Hawthorn, Peach, Pear and Rowan. **FIELD NOTES** Aug–May, almost certainly in an annual life cycle. In parts of Europe the life cycle is biennial. Feeds on the inner surface of the bark. When fully fed, creates the pupal exit hole, leaving a covering of a thin layer of bark. Pupates in a cocoon of bark particles and silk on the inner surface of the bark. A heavily infested tree may show many old exit holes c. 0.4cm in diameter, extruded pupal cases, and frass in bark crevices, and such infestations can be frequent in street trees in urban areas.

YELLOW-LEGGED CLEARWING
Synanthedon vespiformis

SEE PHOTO BELOW
52.012 (374)

Nb. Found throughout most of England away from the north and north-west, and very local in Wales. **FIELD CHARACTERS** See general description in family notes (p. 76). **SIMILAR SPECIES** On birches, Welsh Clearwing, White-barred Clearwing and Large Red-belted Clearwing. On cherries, Red-belted Clearwing. **HABITATS** Hedgerows, parkland and woodland. **FOODPLANTS** Mainly on Sweet Chestnut and Pedunculate Oak. Also reported on Beech, birches, cherries, Wych Elm, Holm and Sessile oaks, Walnut, and broadleaf willows. **FIELD NOTES** Aug– May, and likely to have an annual life cycle. In parts of Europe the life cycle is

biennial. Eggs are laid on cankerous swellings on the lower parts of tree trunks, at the site of wounds, and on cut stumps. Feeds on the inner bark of the tree. It is most frequently detected in cut stumps not treated with herbicide, from the summer/autumn after tree felling, and a couple of years before. Frass can be seen in heaps between the wood and bark at the cut surface and larvae of varying size can be found in the same stump. Also likely to feed in the bark of healthy, unmanaged trees since adult moths have been seen freshly emerged low down on the trunk, but larval signs are hard to detect in this situation. Pupates in a cocoon made of granular, woody frass, under the bark.

Yellow-legged Clearwing larva

CURRANT CLEARWING
Synanthedon tipuliformis

SEE PHOTOS BELOW
52.013 (373)

Nb. Widespread in England, local in Wales, and very local in Ireland and Scotland. Likely to be significantly under-recorded. **FIELD CHARACTERS** See general description in family notes (p. 76). **HABITATS** Most often recorded in allotments, fruit farms, gardens and on waste ground. Occasionally reported in semi-natural habitats such as hedgerows, scrub in fens, and streamsides in woodland. **FOODPLANTS** Wild and cultivated Black and Red currants, and occasionally Gooseberry. Prefers plants growing in sunshine. **FIELD NOTES** Aug– May. Feeds in the centre of a lateral or main stem, often leaving no evidence of

Currant Clearwing gallery in Black Currant

Currant Clearwing old exit holes in Black Currant

its presence, although sometimes brownish frass can be seen extruding from cracks in the bark or at the end of a cut stem. If a cut stem is hollow and blackened inside, this indicates a larva has fed in that stem. Overwinters in a chamber within the stem made of chewed wood and silken threads. When fully fed it constructs the pupal exit hole, leaving a covering of a thin layer of bark. There is no cocoon.

SIX-BELTED CLEARWING
Bembecia ichneumoniformis

SEE PHOTOS BELOW
52.014 (382)

Nb. Widespread in England and possibly expanding its range northwards; local in Wales. **FIELD CHARACTERS** See general description in family notes (p. 76). **HABITATS** Coastal habitats, including hard and soft cliffs, rough grassland, stabilised sand dunes and vegetated shingle. Also calcareous grassland, old quarries and brick-pits, sparsely vegetated cuttings and embankments adjacent to roads and old railways, and waste ground. It is most frequent in places without heavy grazing. **FOODPLANTS** Common Bird's-foot-trefoil and Kidney and Horseshoe vetches, preferring isolated plants. **FIELD NOTES** Jul–early Jun. Feeds internally in the roots of the foodplant and also in the lower stem of Kidney Vetch. There may be no external sign of the presence of the larva, but on Kidney Vetch the whole plant may look sickly. Frass is not extruded from the plant. When fully fed it makes a silken tube from the root to the surface of the ground, sealing the upper end and pupating within.

A sickly Kidney Vetch plant, dying because of Six-belted Clearwing larva in root

Six-belted Clearwing larva in root of Kidney Vetch

FIERY CLEARWING
Pyropteron chrysidiformis

SEE PHOTO BELOW
52.015 (384)

RDB. Protected species. On the north and south coasts of Kent and in the Channel Islands. **FIELD CHARACTERS** See general description in family notes (p. 76). **HABITATS** A variety of sparsely vegetated habitats with warm microclimates, including railway ballast, chalk spoil heaps, cliffs and undercliffs, sparse grassland, vegetated shingle and waste ground. **FOODPLANTS** Mainly Curled Dock and Common Sorrel. Also reported on Water Dock and Sheep's Sorrel. Probably on other docks. Prefers larger, more isolated plants. **FIELD NOTES** Aug–May, sometimes overwintering twice. Tunnels into the taproot, often causing the plant to look sickly. When fully fed, may ascend and bore into the stem to create the pupal exit hole, leaving a thin layer of stem over the exit. Alternatively, constructs a silken tube from the root to the surface of the ground. Pupation takes place in the stem or silk tube without a cocoon. The black eggs may be found on the stem, near the root.

Fiery Clearwing eggs on Curled Dock

THRIFT CLEARWING
Pyropteron muscaeformis

SEE PHOTO BELOW
52.016 (383)

Nb. A coastal species in south-west England, Wales, south-west and north-east Scotland, and south-west and western Ireland. Abundant in the Channel Islands. **FIELD CHARACTERS** See general description in family notes (p. 76). **SIMILAR SPECIES** The micro-moth *Lobesia littoralis* (Tortricidae) feeds in the flower heads, shoots and leaves in spring, and seedheads in autumn, whereas Thrift Clearwing is in the roots and stems. **HABITATS** Cliffs, rocky coasts, coastal grassland, and vegetated walls and banks close to the sea. **FOODPLANT** Thrift. **FIELD NOTES** Aug–May. Feeds in the root and stem in a silk-lined tunnel. Piles of reddish-brown frass may be found extruded from the infested stem in late summer and autumn. Although the plant may later become brown in the affected area, brown patches in cushions of Thrift are commonplace without larvae being the cause. Plants with larvae are often at the edge of larger patches. Pupates in a loose web with frass particles in the larval chamber.

Thrift Clearwing frass extruding from sickly foodplant

ZYGAENOIDEA
LIMACODIDAE SLUG MOTHS

The Limacodidae is a family of moths found throughout the world but concentrated in the tropics, with over 1,000 species described so far. They are known as the slug moths, after their short, fleshy, slug-like caterpillars. There are two species in the British Isles.

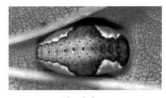

Triangle larva

The larvae are domed and oval in shape, with a tiny head and tapering posterior. The true legs are minute and prolegs absent. Larvae leave a white trail behind them when they move, in a similar way to a slug. The ventral surface of the larva secretes a thin layer of an adhesive fatty substance that enables the larva to adhere to a leaf, and creates the trail as the larva moves. The pupal cocoon has a hinged lid that opens when the moth emerges.

The adhesive forces make it unlikely that larvae will be dislodged from foliage by beating. However, at night, larvae of the two species found in the British Isles glow in ultraviolet light shone from a hand-held torch, and this may prove to be an effective way of surveying for these species.

Festoon ×1.5

FESTOON
Apoda limacodes

PLATE 2
53.001 (173)

Nb. Local in central southern and south-east England and East Anglia, and very local in the Midlands. Appears to be increasing in abundance in the west of its distribution. **FIELD CHARACTERS** Body oval, green and covered with yellow spots. Subdorsal line yellow, edged above with elongated red spots. **HABITATS** Mainly woodland. Also wooded heathland, mature oaks in hedgerows and scrub in wooded landscapes. **FOODPLANTS** Mainly Pedunculate Oak. Also reported on Beech, Silver Birch and other oaks. **FIELD NOTES** Aug–Oct. Feeds on the undersurface of a leaf. When small it leaves the upper cuticle intact, producing a brown lattice-like pattern. Later it feeds on the full thickness of the leaf at its tip. When fully fed in autumn, spins a cocoon on a leaf, pupating within in the spring.

TRIANGLE
Heterogenea asella

PLATE 2
53.002 (174)

RDB. A scarce moth of mainly ancient oak woodland in southern counties of England. Also found in Lincolnshire. **FIELD CHARACTERS** Body oval and green with a broad purplish-brown dorsal band that widens centrally to form a saddle. The band is edged yellow. **HABITATS** Woodland. **FOODPLANTS** Beech and Pedunculate Oak. Also reported on Silver Birch, Sweet Chestnut, Small-leaved Lime and poplars (although not reared successfully on poplars). **FIELD NOTES** Aug–Oct. Feeds on the undersurface of a leaf. When small it excavates almost rectangular sections, c. 1mm x 2mm, leaving the upper cuticle intact. It makes no more than four or five of these patches in one area before moving to another part of the leaf to repeat the process, and there may be 10–40 such patches on one leaf. This feeding pattern is noticeable from the upperside. As the larva grows, the excavations are up to 5mm long and go through the upper cuticle. In the final two instars, complete sections of leaf are eaten. When fully fed it spins a cocoon on a leaf or fork in a twig, pupating within in the spring.

ZYGAENIDAE FORESTER AND BURNET MOTHS

There are about 800 species worldwide and 10
recorded in Great Britain and Ireland. All are more
readily seen as day-flying adults than as larvae.
However, the stumpy yellow larvae with black spots and

Six-spot Burnet ×1.5

yellowish papery cocoons spun high on grass stems, characteristic of Six-spot Burnet,
are a very familiar sight throughout in flowery grasslands and other open habitats.

Two species, Six-spot Burnet and Narrow-bordered Five-spot Burnet, are
widespread and can be abundant. Other species are localised and tend to survive
in small, discrete colonies. Over many thousands of generations some have evolved
differences between colonies that may be recognised as subspecies or races.

All stages of the life history of burnet moths retain or produce toxins – in
particular cyanides – that deter predators, and those within larval and adult cells may
be carried forward into pupae and eggs. While most birds and other predators avoid
larvae of burnets, dipteran and hymenopterous parasitoids do not, and these insects
contain an enzyme that detoxifies the cyanide compounds.

The presence and abundance of burnet and forester moths is dependent
on land management and they require the maintenance of open, semi-natural
habitats. Many colonies of both groups have been lost to agricultural improvement
as well as to scrub encroachment. If grazing pressure is intense and over a long
period, particularly where habitat conservation is the primary motive, that pressure
is often too high for burnet and forester moths and it leads to local extinction
of colonies, which often contain small numbers of individuals. Thanks to a good
understanding of the ecology of New Forest Burnet in western Scotland, and a
reduction in grazing pressure, numbers of this species at its only site are stable
or increasing. However, many colonies of Five-spot Burnet have been lost from
calcareous grassland across south-east England.

Scotch Burnet/Mountain Burnet larva

PROCRIDINAE

SCARCE FORESTER
Jordanita globulariae

PLATE 2
54.001 (165)

Na. A moth restricted as a breeding species to just a few areas in southern and south-east England. **FIELD CHARACTERS** Body pale greyish brown, covered with numerous tiny, dark brown dots, and with large pinkish-brown verrucae from which arise tufts of pinkish-brown hairs. Dorsal line dark brown, and subdorsal stripes whitish or yellow. **HABITATS** Unimproved chalk grassland. Herb-rich grasslands must be relatively long and rough, and subject to light, extensive grazing, to support Scarce Forester colonies. **FOODPLANTS** Common and Greater knapweeds. **FIELD NOTES** Jul–May. Mines leaves of the foodplant and lives within the blistered leaf it creates, with most of the frass produced remaining in the blister. Feeds until Sep, then goes into diapause, resuming feeding in the spring. Pupates either on the ground or just below the surface, in a brownish-grey silk cocoon enclosed within an outer spinning of silk and earth.

FORESTER
Adscita statices

PLATE 2
54.002 (163)

Local. Scattered widely in England and Wales, but many colonies have been lost since the 1950s as a result of agricultural intensification. Very local in Scotland and Ireland. **FIELD CHARACTERS** Body yellow subdorsally and yellow, pale brown, pinkish brown or dirty whitish laterally, and covered with numerous tiny black dots. There are large yellow, or sometimes dirty whitish, verrucae subdorsally from which arise tufts of grey hairs, and the verrucae are ringed clear yellow at the bases. Laterally, the verrucae are yellow, brownish or whitish depending on body colour. **HABITATS** Calcareous grassland inland and on the coast, damp or wet neutral grasslands, limestone pavement (the Burren, Cos Clare and Galway, Ireland), stabilised sand dunes and woodland rides. Most frequent in areas with light, extensive grazing. **FOODPLANTS** Common and Sheep's sorrels. **FIELD NOTES** Jul–May. Mines leaves at first, usually from the underside, forming short galleries. Later it feeds externally. Pupates in a loosely spun cocoon near the ground.

CISTUS FORESTER
Adscita geryon

PLATE 2
54.003 (164)

Nb. Found very locally in England and Wales, but can be abundant where it occurs. **FIELD CHARACTERS** Body black or brown, covered with numerous tiny black dots. Subdorsal stripe yellow or white, with large verrucae similarly coloured and from which arise tufts of yellow or grey hairs. Laterally there are purple or brown verrucae giving rise to tufts of grey or brown hairs. **SIMILAR SPECIES** The butterflies Brown Argus and Northern Brown Argus, and the case-bearing micro-moth *Coleophora ochrea* (Coleophoridae). These species mine leaves but the entrance holes to the mines are smaller than those made by Cistus Forester. **HABITATS** Calcareous grassland. Prefers warm, south-facing slopes, and relatively short turf (up to 5cm tall). **FOODPLANT** Common Rock-rose. **FIELD NOTES** Jul–May. Mines the leaves at first, forming blotches, and later in the summer feeds externally on the underside, leaving the upper cuticle intact. In spring the entire leaf is eaten. Pupates in a loosely spun cocoon low down.

ZYGAENINAE

The larva hatches from the egg in summer and feeds through to the end of the third instar. Then it changes its skin for the third time and the larva takes on a dull appearance. In this fourth instar the larva enters winter diapause and does not feed. Occasionally the diapause happens in the fifth instar. In the spring it sheds its skin again before feeding resumes. Most larvae then continue to feed until ready to make their cocoons. However, a proportion feed for a short time in spring, moult again and then re-enter diapause until the following spring, and this process may be repeated the following year. There are usually seven instars if there is one winter diapause, eight instars if there are two, and nine instars if there are three. Larvae feed by day.

TRANSPARENT BURNET
Zygaena purpuralis

PLATE 2
54.004 (172)

Ssp. *segontii* RDB. North Wales, presumed extinct. Ssp. *caledonensis* Na. Scotland, mainly on the Hebridean Islands. Ssp. *sabulosa* Ireland. **FIELD CHARACTERS** Body greyish yellow or greyish green with groups of short white hairs. Dorsal line pale and often indistinct, with black subdorsal spots T2–A10, and yellow lateral spots T3–A8. **HABITATS** Inland limestone grassland, coastal heathland and acid grassland on steep south- or south-west-facing slopes, limestone pavement (the Burren, Cos Clare and Galway, Ireland) and sand dunes. Areas with extensive grazing are preferred. **FOODPLANT** Wild Thyme. **FIELD NOTES** Jul–May, sometimes overwintering twice as a larva. Feeds on the leaves. Can be found by searching low down among the foodplant. Pupates in a cocoon spun near the ground and usually concealed among the vegetation, or less often on a rock. Populations may fluctuate considerably, especially in response to changing grazing pressure.

SLENDER SCOTCH BURNET
Zygaena loti

PLATE 2
54.005 (167)

Ssp. *scotica* RDB. Endemic to Scotland and found in a few sites on the Isle of Mull and nearby Isle of Ulva. **FIELD CHARACTERS** Body dark grey or greenish grey with groups of short grey hairs. Two black subdorsal spots and one yellow lateral spot on each segment T2–A9, sometimes with a dusting of yellow between. **HABITATS** On south- or south-west-facing coastal grassland slopes on basalt (a volcanic rock formed from lava). The moth and foodplant tend to be most frequent in areas of slippage where the ground is disturbed and where there is moderate grazing pressure. **FOODPLANT** Common Bird's-foot-trefoil. **FIELD NOTES** Jul–May, sometimes overwintering twice as a larva. Prefers to feed on plants shorter than 6cm, and avoids lush growth. Can be found by searching among the foodplant. Pupates in a cocoon spun on the ground and concealed by vegetation. Heavy grazing pressure leads to local extinction of colonies.

SCOTCH BURNET/MOUNTAIN BURNET
Zygaena exulans

PLATE 2
54.006 (166)

Ssp. *subochracea* RDB. In Scotland found only in the eastern Cairngorms at altitudes of 700–850m. **FIELD CHARACTERS** Body grey to black, and dark greenish laterally, with tufts of short grey or black hairs. Yellow subdorsal spots T2–A8, with inconspicuous black shading above and between the spots. **HABITATS** Mountains, on the higher slopes and summits. Inhabits areas where the vegetation comprises prostrate Crowberry and heathers, lichens and scattered Bilberry, Mountain Everlasting and Trailing Azalea. **FOODPLANTS** Mainly Crowberry. Also reported on Bilberry, Cowberry and heathers. **FIELD NOTES** Jul or Aug–late May or Jun, overwintering once or more, perhaps several times, before completing its feeding. Feeds on the terminal shoots and unripe berries. Pupates in a yellowish-white cocoon low down among the foodplant.

NEW FOREST BURNET
Zygaena viciae

PLATE 2
54.007 (168)

Ssp. *ytenensis* Extinct. Formerly in the New Forest, Hampshire. Ssp. *argyllensis* RDB. Protected species. In Scotland, at one site in western Argyllshire (no distribution map is shown owing to the sensitivity of the location). **FIELD CHARACTERS** Body green, sparsely covered with tufts of white hairs. Dorsal stripe whitish and rather diffuse. Subdorsal stripe whitish and incorporating a yellow spot posteriorly on each segment T2–A8, with black spots above A1–A8. Spiracles black. **HABITATS** Unimproved coastal grassland on a steep, south-facing slope that includes rock ledges. The grassland is flushed by calcareous groundwater. Requires moderate grazing and periods without animals to allow the herb-rich grassland to flower. **FOODPLANTS** Common Bird's-foot-trefoil and Meadow Vetchling. **FIELD NOTES** Jul–early Jun, sometimes overwintering more than once as a larva. Feeds on the leaves. Pupates in a yellowish cocoon under leaves or on a grass stem low down. Heavy grazing in the past at the one known site reduced the population to about 15 individuals.

SIX-SPOT BURNET
Zygaena filipendulae

PLATE 2
54.008 (169)

Ssp. *stephensi* Common. Widespread in England, Wales and Ireland, and spreading in Scotland. Ssp. *pulcherrima* Channel Islands. **FIELD CHARACTERS** Body yellow, and covered with tufts of short white hairs. Two black subdorsal spots on each segment T2–A9, and one yellow lateral spot on each segment T2–A7, with a row of black lateral spots below. **SIMILAR SPECIES** Narrow-bordered Five-spot Burnet has hairs twice as long as those of Six-spot Burnet and Five-spot Burnet. Larvae of Six-spot Burnet and Five-spot Burnet (and especially ssp. *palustrella*) cannot be separated in the field with certainty; ssp. *decreta* feeds mainly on Greater Bird's-foot-trefoil, so larvae on this foodplant are likely to be Five-spot Burnet. **HABITATS** Unimproved grassland on acid and calcareous soils, on the coast and inland. Also old quarries, rail and road cuttings and embankments, sand dunes, waste ground and woodland rides. **FOODPLANTS** Mainly Common Bird's-foot-trefoil. Also reported on Greater Bird's-foot-trefoil, clovers, and Horseshoe and Kidney vetches. **FIELD NOTES** Aug–Jun, sometimes overwintering more than once as a larva. Feeds on the leaves. Pupates in a white or yellowish-white cocoon high on a grass stem, other vegetation or fencing.

NARROW-BORDERED FIVE-SPOT BURNET
Zygaena lonicerae

PLATE 2
54.009 (171)

Ssp. *lonicerae* Channel Islands. Ssp. *latomarginata* Common. Widely throughout England and Wales, but more local in the west. Talisker Burnet ssp. *jocelynae* RDB. Isle of Skye. Ssp. *insularis*. Ireland, mainly in the north, and in decline. **FIELD CHARACTERS** Body whitish green, with tufts of long white hairs. Two black subdorsal spots on each segment T1–A9, and one yellow lateral spot on each segment T2–A8, with a row of black lateral spots below. **SIMILAR SPECIES** Six-spot Burnet and Five-spot Burnet. **HABITATS** Prefers rough grassland in a range of situations on acid, chalk, limestone and neutral soils, on dry or wet ground, and coastal or inland, including fens, rail and road cuttings and embankments, road verges and woodland rides. **FOODPLANTS** Most frequently Red Clover and Meadow Vetchling, and found occasionally on Common Bird's-foot-trefoil, Bitter-vetch, White Clover and Sainfoin. In some wetlands in southern England larvae are found exclusively on Greater Bird's-foot-trefoil. **FIELD NOTES** Jul–Jun, sometimes overwintering more than once as a larva. Feeds on the leaves and sits exposed. Pupates in a relatively translucent, whitish-yellow or white cocoon spun on a grass stem or other herbage.

FIVE-SPOT BURNET
Zygaena trifolii

PLATE 2
54.010 (170)

Has declined significantly since the 1950s as a result of agricultural intensification and loss of semi-natural habitats. Ssp. *decreta* Local. Southern and south-west England, coastal parts of Wales, and the south Midlands, but distribution not well understood owing to confusion between this species and Narrow-bordered Five-spot Burnet. Ssp. *palustrella* Local. Calcareous grasslands from Dorset to Kent and in the south Midlands. Ssp. *subsyracusia* Channel Islands, widespread. **SIMILAR SPECIES** Six-spot Burnet. Also Narrow-bordered Five-spot Burnet. **HABITATS** Ssp. *decreta* Bogs, wet grassland, heathland, moorland, sand dunes and woodland. Ssp. *palustrella* and ssp. *subsyracusia* Coastal and inland calcareous grasslands. Ssp. *subsyracusia* Herb-rich grasslands. **FOODPLANTS** Ssp. *decreta* Mainly Greater Bird's-foot-trefoil; less often Common Bird's-foot-trefoil. Ssp. *palustrella* and ssp. *subsyracusia* Common Bird's-foot-trefoil. **FIELD NOTES** Sometimes overwinters more than once as a larva. Pupates in a white papery cocoon. Ssp. *decreta* Aug–early Jun, and in some colonies May. The cocoon is spun high on Soft-rush or other herbage. Ssp. *palustrella* and ssp. *subsyracusia* Jun–Apr. The cocoon is spun low down, near the ground and well concealed.

PAPILIONOIDEA (Butterflies)

There are around 18,000 butterfly species in the world, and over 550 in Europe. In Great Britain there are 59 and in Ireland 31 species, including two migrant species that breed regularly in both areas, Clouded Yellow and Painted Lady. There are several other species that arrive as irregular immigrants, and yet more that turn up through accidental importation or deliberate release. There is nothing morphologically to distinguish between larvae of butterflies and moths.

PAPILIONIDAE SWALLOWTAIL BUTTERFLIES

Worldwide this is a family of around 600 species, with just one in Great Britain. The larvae of all members of the family are characterised by the presence of a forked structure on the dorsum on T1, known as the osmeterium. This is often brightly coloured and appears to be used in defence. When disturbed, larvae of most species are able to evert this structure, and there may be a pungent odour emitted at the same time.

Swallowtail larva

Swallowtail, early instar, ×1.5

PAPILIONINAE

SWALLOWTAIL   PLATE 3
Papilio machaon   56.003 (1539)

NT. Protected species. Ssp. *britannicus* Endemic. Confined to the Norfolk Broads. Ssp. *gorganus* Immigrant and transitory resident. Mainly in coastal counties of south-east England. **FIELD CHARACTERS** Head pale green or pale yellowish green with two vertical black stripes each side and black spots low down between. Body pale green or pale yellowish green, with a series of transverse black stripes interrupted by orange spots. Black spot on each proleg and anal clasper. Forked orange osmeterium dorsally on T1, which is extruded when the larva is irritated and releases an acrid smell. In the first three instars the larva is mainly black with a white saddle A3–A4, creating the impression of a bird's dropping. **HABITATS** Ssp. *britannicus* Fens. Occasionally gardens. Ssp. *gorganus* Allotments, gardens and chalk grassland. **FOODPLANTS** Ssp. *britannicus* Milk-parsley, and occasionally cultivated Carrot. Reported on Wild Angelica, Burnet-saxifrage, Caraway, Wild Carrot, Fennel, Hog's Fennel and Cow Parsley in the second generation when Milk-parsley is going over. Ssp. *gorganus* Cultivated Carrot, Wild Carrot, Dill, Fennel, Garden Parsley and cultivated Parsnip, and rarely other plants in the Apiaceae. **FIELD NOTES** Ssp. *britannicus* Jul–Aug, and occasionally Sep in a partial second generation in warm years. Feeds at first on the upper surface of the leaves, but from the fourth instar on the flowers. Pupates head up on a reed or other plant stem, attached to a silk pad and held in place with a silken girdle. Overwinters as a pupa. Ssp. *gorganus* Rarely Jun–Aug, most often Sep. Currently not able to survive the winter as a pupa, but this situation may change.

HESPERIIDAE SKIPPERS

Butterflies in this family are known as the skippers owing to their characteristic darting flight. There are over 3,000 species worldwide, and eight species within our shores.

Dingy Skipper ×1.75

Larvae of species in Great Britain and Ireland share a number of common characters that together help separate them from larvae in other families, and between genera within the family. For example, all larvae have the head larger than the prothorax (T1), giving the appearance of a distinct neck. They also bear an anal comb, a chitinous plate structure with pointed projections. It is used to flick frass well away from the larva. The structure is not easily visible as the anal flap must be lifted in order to reveal it. In the subfamily Hesperiinae there is also a curious white substance ventrally across the anterior part of A7 and A8 in last-instar larvae. The substance, which appears as a mass of tightly packed white waxy filaments, is produced part way through the last instar, but its function is not known.

Additionally, larvae of the three *Thymelicus* species show very fine brown spotting anteriorly. This is visible under a hand lens or microscope (×10). The brown spotting is found on T1–A1 and is denser on T2–T3.

Larvae of skippers in Great Britain and Ireland all feed in a similar manner, spinning some form of a fold in a leaf or spinning leaves together to create a retreat in which they hide, and from which they emerge to feed.

Large Skipper larva, early in final instar. Note waxy substance underneath A7 and A8 has not yet been produced, in contrast to the older larva shown on p. 35

PYRGINAE

DINGY SKIPPER
Erynnis tages

PLATE 3
57.001 (1532)

VU. Ssp. *tages* Widespread but declining in England and Wales, and very local in the eastern half of Ireland. Very local and mainly coastal in south-west Scotland and along the southern border of the Moray Firth. Ssp. *baynesi* Very local on limestone in the west of Ireland. **FIELD CHARACTERS** Head notched, and mottled pale and dark brown. Body plump, green and covered with numerous tiny white dots. Dorsal line dark green and subdorsal line pale green. Spiracles black or brown. **HABITATS** Wide variety of open habitats, including hard and soft cliffs, calcareous grassland, heathland, old quarries and railway cuttings, sand dunes, waste ground, and woodland clearings and rides. Prefers sparse swards with areas of bare ground, within a mosaic of taller vegetation. **FOODPLANTS** Most commonly Common Bird's-foot-trefoil. Also reported on Greater Bird's-foot-trefoil and Horseshoe Vetch. **FIELD NOTES** May–Apr in a single generation, with a partial second generation in warm years in the south. Constructs a loose spinning low down among the foodplant, from which it ascends to feed, retreating when disturbed. When fully fed, it constructs a more substantial spinning, within which it overwinters, pupating in the spring.

GRIZZLED SKIPPER
Pyrgus malvae

PLATE 3
57.002 (1534)

VU. Fairly widespread in central, southern and south-east England, but declining. Very local in Wales. **FIELD CHARACTERS** Head black with white hairs, and prothoracic plate black, brown or greenish. Body dull greenish or brownish green, covered with numerous tiny white dots and short white hairs. Dorsal line dark green; subdorsal, lateral and spiracular lines paler. **HABITATS** Mainly in three distinct types: calcareous grassland on chalk and clay; woodland clearings and rides; and waste ground including landfills, calaminarian grasslands (including former mine-waste sites) and railway cuttings. Occasionally also heathland, wet grassland and sand dunes. **FOODPLANTS** Wide variety of plants in the rose family, most often Agrimony, Creeping Cinquefoil and Wild Strawberry. Also reported on Wood Avens, Bramble, Salad Burnet, Dog-rose, Raspberry, Silverweed, Barren Strawberry and Tormentil. Prefers sparse swards with areas of bare ground, within a mosaic of taller vegetation (often including scrub), and where there are abundant nectar sources. **FIELD NOTES** May–Sep, growing very slowly. At first it creates a spinning on the upper surface of a leaf, and on a soft leaf like Barren Strawberry it folds the edges together. Feeds within the spinning, leaving the lower cuticle intact. Later it may spin leaves together, leaving its retreat to feed, mainly in the evening and early morning. When on Bramble, found on the leaves of runners lying close to the ground, not on leaves in thickets. Palatability of leaves during the summer is critical to larval survival; in dry spells some foodplants can wither or die back, and larger larvae are known to wander some distance in search of fresh leaves. Larvae have been observed on Barren Strawberry; this plant usually wilts in dry weather in Jun and these larvae would not be able to complete their development on this species alone. Pupates in a loose cocoon spun among leaves near the ground. Overwinters as a pupa.

HETEROPTERINAE

CHEQUERED SKIPPER
Carterocephalus palaemon

PLATE 3
57.004 (1525)

EN. Resident in western Scotland, population stable, and possibly under-recorded. Became extinct in central England in the 1970s, but was reintroduced to a woodland complex in Northamptonshire in 2018. **FIELD CHARACTERS** Head green. Body green with a dark green dorsal line, edged white, and pale lateral and spiracular lines. When fully fed, the green coloration becomes entirely replaced by brown. **HABITATS** In Scotland, in wet grassland at the margins of open woodland in low-lying areas. In England, woodland clearings and rides. **FOODPLANTS** In Scotland, almost exclusively on Purple Moor-grass although eggs have been found on False Brome in woodland. In former colonies in England, on False and Upright bromes, Hairy-brome and Tor-grass. **FIELD NOTES** Jul–Mar. On hatching, the young larva creates a tube in the grass by folding the edges over with silk. Emerges to feed above and below the tube, at first eating V-shaped notches, then eating the entire blade but leaving the midrib intact. Once it has fed as much as it can, it moves to another leaf to repeat the process. Growth is very slow, the larva becoming fully fed in early Oct. The colour gradually changes to brown and it constructs a hibernaculum by spinning a few grass blades together. Emerges late Mar but does not feed again, and spins several old grass blades together, in which it pupates.

HESPERIINAE

ESSEX SKIPPER
Thymelicus lineola

PLATE 3
57.005 (1527)

LC. Widespread in much of England, gradually spreading into the south-west and north, and into Wales. Now recorded in southern Scotland. Also in south-east Ireland. **FIELD CHARACTERS** Head grey, sometimes green, with a pair of whitish or yellowish vertical stripes and a thin central line, all edged brownish laterally. Body green with a dark green dorsal stripe incorporating a pale central line and edged with yellow shading. Subdorsal line yellow and subspiracular line white. There is a white substance ventrally across the anterior part of A7 and A8. **HABITATS** Prefers rank, open grassland in a range of usually dry situations, including acid and chalk grasslands, embankments such as flood defences and sea walls, road verges, saltmarshes, waste ground and woodland rides. **SIMILAR SPECIES** Small Skipper and Lulworth Skipper lack the brownish-edged yellow or white vertical stripes on the head. They have pale lines with no brownish edging, although these may be absent in Small Skipper. These two species are very similar, but are not known to share a foodplant, and Lulworth Skipper occurs in only a small part of the range of Small Skipper. **FOODPLANTS** Mainly Cock's-foot and others grasses, including False Brome, Common Couch, Meadow Foxtail, Creeping Soft-grass, Timothy and Tor-grass. Has been reported on Yorkshire-fog, and two larvae were once beaten from Ribbed Melilot and continued to thrive on it in captivity. **FIELD NOTES** Apr–Jun. Females prefer to lay their eggs in tightly wrapped leaf sheaths, and the larva overwinters fully formed within the egg. In spring, constructs a tube by spinning the edges of a leaf blade together, and emerges from the tube to feed. Pupates in a loose spinning low down among leaf blades, attached by a silk pad and girdle.

SMALL SKIPPER
Thymelicus sylvestris

PLATE 3
57.006 (1526)

LC. Widespread throughout England and Wales and spreading northwards into southern Scotland. Has been recorded rarely in Ireland. **FIELD CHARACTERS** Head green, occasionally with a thin pale central line or a pair of faint white vertical lines. Body green with a dark green dorsal stripe incorporating a pale central line and edged with white or pale yellowish lines. Subdorsal and subspiracular lines white. There is a white substance ventrally across the anterior part of A7 and A8. **SIMILAR SPECIES** Essex Skipper and Lulworth Skipper. **HABITATS** In areas where grasses grow lush and tall, such as unimproved grassland on any soil type, road verges, margins of scrub and woodland rides. **FOODPLANTS** Most frequently Yorkshire-fog. Occasionally on other grasses, including False Brome, Cock's-foot, Meadow Foxtail, Creeping Soft-grass and Timothy. **FIELD NOTES** Sep–May. Females lay their eggs in leaf sheaths. Immediately after hatching the larva spins a hibernaculum inside the grass sheath, where it remains until Apr. It then constructs a tube by spinning the edges of a leaf together, and emerges from the tube to feed. Pupates in a loose spinning among leaf blades at the base of the foodplant.

LULWORTH SKIPPER
Thymelicus acteon

PLATE 3
57.007 (1528)

NT. Confined to Dorset, with the largest colonies in warm, south-facing coastal locations. Has declined significantly in abundance in recent decades, but has expanded its range slightly westwards and onto the Isle of Portland. **FIELD CHARACTERS** Head green or pale greenish brown with a pair of pale yellow or white vertical lines, sometimes with a thin central line. Body green with a dark green dorsal stripe incorporating a pale central pale line and edged with pale yellow lines. Subdorsal line pale yellow and subspiracular line white. There is a white substance ventrally across the anterior part of A7 and A8. **SIMILAR SPECIES** Essex Skipper and Small Skipper. **HABITATS** Tall grassland in coastal areas on calcareous soils, and on cliffs, old quarries and undercliff. Less numerous on a few inland chalk grasslands in Purbeck and coastal neutral grassland west of Portland. **FOODPLANT** Tor-grass. **FIELD NOTES** Sep–May. Females prefer to lay their eggs on tall clumps up to 50cm in height. Immediately after hatching, the larva spins a silken hibernaculum around the eggshell inside the grass sheath, within which it remains until spring. In Apr, it eats its way out and spins the edges of a leaf together, forming a tube, and emerges to feed only at night. It makes V-shaped notches in the leaf below the tube and eats the leaf blade above the tube. Later tubes incorporate more than one leaf. Pupates close to the ground in a loose spinning of leaves, attached with a silk pad and girdle.

SILVER-SPOTTED SKIPPER
Hesperia comma

PLATE 3
57.008 (1529)

NT. Confined to the calcareous grasslands of southern and south-east England. Has declined in range very significantly in the twentieth century to become confined to the south, but here it has started to spread locally in recent decades. **FIELD CHARACTERS** Head black with a pale brown vertical line either side of the middle. Prothoracic plate black. Body dull greenish brown and covered in numerous tiny black dots. Dorsal line darker, indistinct, and there is an indistinct pale spiracular line. There is a white substance ventrally on the anterior parts of A7–A8. **HABITATS** Chalk grassland, preferring short sparse

turf, except in the warmest years when a more closed turf may be selected. **FOODPLANT** Sheep's-fescue.
FIELD NOTES Late Mar–early Jul. Females usually lay their eggs on small tufts of grasses in otherwise bare
patches in or near shallow depressions. Eggs remain on the grass over winter. On hatching, the larva
constructs a habitation of leaves of the foodplant spun together. Larvae are usually solitary but up to four
may be found within one spinning. From there, feeds on surrounding leaves, constructing new habitations
as it grows. Pupates in a silken cocoon, incorporating grass blades, spun low in a small tussock.

LARGE SKIPPER
Ochlodes sylvanus

PLATE 3

57.009 (1531)

LC. Widespread in England and Wales and spreading northwards in southern
Scotland. **FIELD CHARACTERS** Head notched, and dark brown or blackish, with
pale brown or dirty whitish patches either side of the middle. Body green,
covered with numerous tiny black dots. Dorsal line dark green, subdorsal stripe
pale and indistinct, and subspiracular stripe greenish white and indistinct.
There is a row of dark dots, one on each segment, between the dorsal and
subdorsal lines, and one row above and one below the level of the spiracles
A1–A8. Spiracles pale brown, and much larger on A8 than the rest. There is a
white substance ventrally on the anterior parts of A7–A8 that begins to appear about a third of the way
through the final instar. **HABITATS** In tall grassy areas in dry or damp conditions on any soil type, favouring
unimproved areas. Frequently occurs in fens, gardens and urban areas, calcareous grassland, heathland,
marshes, road verges, margins of scrub and woodland rides. **FOODPLANTS** Mainly Cock's-foot. Also on
False Brome, Purple Moor-grass, Wood Small-reed and Tor-grass, and has been reported on Common
Couch, Red Fescue, Creeping Soft-grass, Timothy, Hairy Wood-rush and Yorkshire-fog. **FIELD NOTES** Jul–
May. On hatching, creates a tube in the grass by folding the edges over with silk, and emerges to feed
on the edge of the grass bade. When larger, several grass blades are spun together to form a tube.
Overwinters partly grown in a hibernaculum of spun leaves. Pupates in a loose cocoon within a spinning
of several grass leaves.

PIERIDAE WHITE BUTTERFLIES

Worldwide, there are some 1,200 species of 'whites' and 'sulphurs', as they are commonly known, and eight species in Great Britain and Ireland. They include the well-known long-distance travellers to our shores, Small White and Large White (the 'cabbage' whites) and Clouded Yellow.

Orange-tip ×1.75

There are no easy and distinguishing features for larvae of Pieridae, but careful examination will reveal that the cuticle of each abdominal segment is divided into a number of rings or folds, usually six. These are perhaps easiest to see in the wood whites and Brimstone.

Small White larva

DISMORPHIINAE

WOOD WHITE
Leptidea sinapis

PLATE 4
58.001 (1541)

EN. A rare species in England and Wales, and found in the Burren, Cos Clare and Galway, Ireland. Has undergone a very significant decline in recent decades, except in western Ireland. Occurs in discrete colonies and numbers fluctuate considerably within a colony. **FIELD CHARACTERS** Head green. Body green with a dark green dorsal line, edged with pale yellow shading, and a yellow spiracular line. **SIMILAR SPECIES** Cryptic Wood White is indistinguishable in the field. Although absent from the Burren, its distribution may overlap with that of Wood White in Co. Galway. The two species occupy rather different habitats, but larvae may need to be reared to confirm identity where overlap is considered a possibility. **HABITATS** Mainly in limestone pavement (western Ireland), hard and soft undercliffs (Devon and Dorset), and woodland clearings and rides. Colonies are also known in rough field margins, tall grasslands, an old clay quarry, scattered scrub and old railway cuttings. **FOODPLANTS** Mainly Meadow Vetchling. Also Common and Greater bird's-foot-trefoils, Bitter-vetch and Tufted Vetch. Notably, Bush and Common vetches are avoided. **FIELD NOTES** Jun–Sep, including a partial second generation. Feeds from the tip of a shoot downwards, resting on the stem or petiole when not feeding. Pupates head up on surrounding vegetation, attached to a silk pad and held in place with a silken girdle. Overwinters as a pupa.

CRYPTIC WOOD WHITE
Leptidea juvernica

PLATE 4
58.002 (1541b)

Widely distributed across Ireland away from the Burren, Cos Clare and Galway. **SIMILAR SPECIES** Wood White. **HABITATS** Variety of open habitats, including fens, unimproved grassland, margins of hedgerows, old quarries, railway and road verges, sand dunes, waste ground and wide woodland rides. Typically prefers areas with scattered scrub or some other shelter. **FOODPLANTS** Mainly Meadow Vetchling. Also reported on Common Bird's-foot-trefoil on sand dunes (the only foodplant at Murlough National Nature Reserve, Co. Antrim, Northern Ireland), Greater Bird's-foot-trefoil and Bitter-vetch. **FIELD NOTES** Jun–Jul. Feeds from the tip of a shoot downwards. Adults of a second generation are rare. Pupates head up, attached to a silk pad and held in place with a silken girdle. Overwinters as a pupa.

PIERINAE

ORANGE-TIP
Anthocharis cardamines

PLATE 4
58.003 (1553)

LC. Ssp. *britannica* Widespread in England and Wales. More local in Scotland, but expanded its range northwards. Ssp. *hibernica* Widespread in Ireland. **FIELD CHARACTERS** Head green with numerous black pinacula giving rise to short white hairs, and with a short white stripe in line with the subspiracular stripe on the abdomen. Body green with numerous black pinacula giving rise to hairs that are either black or white. Body is darker dorsally, paler laterally, and the subspiracular stripe is white. **HABITATS** Damp grassy places, including banks of canals and rivers, ditches, wet grassland and woodland rides. Also drier habitats, including allotments, gardens and urban parks, hedgerows and waste ground. **FOODPLANTS** Wide variety of plants in the cabbage family, especially Cuckooflower in wetter habitats and Garlic Mustard in drier areas. Reported occasionally on Large Bitter-cress, Charlock, Hedge and Tower mustards, Hairy Rock-cress, Turnip, Water-cress, Weld and Winter-cress. Larvae may also be found on Dame's-violet and Honesty, but appear not to thrive. **FIELD NOTES** May–Jul. Feeds on the flowers and developing seeds, sitting exposed and usually aligned on the fruits of the foodplant. Pupates head up on tall vegetation, attached to a silk pad and held in place with a silken girdle. Overwinters as a pupa, sometimes over four winters.

LARGE WHITE
Pieris brassicae

PLATE 4
58.006 (1549)

LC. Widespread throughout, but has declined in abundance in recent decades and does not breed in upland areas. Populations are boosted annually by immigration. **FIELD CHARACTERS** Head grey, speckled with black. Body greyish yellow or grey with a yellow dorsal line. Body covered with black spots of various sizes and shapes, and short grey hairs, but from the supraspiracular area ventrally body more yellow and black spots generally smaller. **HABITATS** Found in most habitats but breeds mainly in allotments, arable fields, gardens and waste ground. Also rough calcareous grassland, old quarries and railway lines, sand dunes and vegetated shingle. **FOODPLANTS** Mainly plants in the cabbage family; also several species in pea, mignonette and nasturtium families. Feeds especially on cultivated Cabbage, including Broccoli and Brussels-sprout; also on Horse-radish, and rapes including Oil-seed Rape. In gardens frequently on cultivars of Nasturtium, and occasionally Dame's-violet, geraniums and Spiderflower. Less often on wild plants such as Wild Cabbage, Wild Mignonette, Black, Garlic and Hedge mustards, Field Penny-cress, Sea Radish, Sea Rocket, Sea-kale, Perennial Wall-rocket and Water-cress. **FIELD NOTES** May–Jan, in two or possibly three generations. Larvae feed gregariously at first, dispersing when larger. On Cabbage they tend to feed on the outer leaves. Pupates head up on any suitable upright surface, attached to a silk pad and held in place with a silken girdle. Overwinters as a pupa, although larvae are sometimes found into early Jan.

SMALL WHITE
Pieris rapae

PLATE 4
58.007 (1550)

LC. Widespread throughout, away from upland areas, but not frequently seen in the far north of Scotland. Numbers are boosted annually by immigration. **FIELD CHARACTERS** Head green with dark green and white pinacula giving rise to short black and white hairs. Body green and covered with numerous small pinacula. Most pinacula are black, with a few white, except ventrally where they are all white. They give rise to short hairs that are mainly white, but a few black. Dorsal line yellow, with a yellow spot on T2 and T3 at the spiracular level. Small and large yellow spots adjacent to spiracles A1–A8. **SIMILAR SPECIES** Green-veined White lacks the yellow dorsal line, has yellow rings around the spiracles, and is otherwise without yellow spots. **HABITATS** Found in most habitats where wild and cultivated plants in the cabbage family grow. Mostly seen in allotments, arable fields, gardens and waste ground. Less often on cliffs, rough calcareous grassland, hedgerows, old quarries and railway lines, sand dunes, vegetated shingle and woodland rides. **FOODPLANTS** Cultivated Cabbage and Oil-seed Rape, and on wild plants in the cabbage family, including Wild Cabbage, Charlock, Flixweed, Hoary Cress, Horse-radish, Wild Mignonette, Garlic and Hedge mustards, and Water-cress. In gardens on cultivars of Nasturtium, and has been reported on Spiderflower. **FIELD NOTES** Apr–Oct or later, usually in two or possibly three generations. On Cabbage it may be in the centre of the plant or fully exposed on a leaf. Usually pupates on a suitable upright surface, head up, attached to a silk pad and held in place with a silken girdle, but larvae of the spring generation may also pupate on the foodplant. Overwinters as a pupa, although larvae have been found feeding in Dec.

GREEN-VEINED WHITE
Pieris napi

PLATE 4
58.008 (1551)

LC. A widespread species that appears to exist in fairly discrete colonies and does not readily disperse. There is noticeable regional variation, with the brightly coloured yellow forms of the adults being recognised by some authors as distinct subspecies in Scotland and Ireland. Ssp. *sabellicae* Widespread throughout. Ssp. *britannica* Ireland. Ssp. *thomsoni* Scotland. **FIELD CHARACTERS** Head green with pinacula giving rise to short white and black hairs. Body green and covered with numerous black dots and short white hairs. Dorsal line dark and ill-defined. Each spiracle is surrounded by a yellow ring. **SIMILAR SPECIES** Small White. **HABITATS** Prefers lush and damp habitats, including ditches, fens, wet grassland, hedgerows, margins of lakes and ponds, riverbanks and woodland rides. Sometimes found in gardens. **FOODPLANTS** Wide variety of wild plants in the cabbage family, including Hairy and Large bitter-cresses, Wild Cabbage, Charlock, Cuckooflower, Horse-radish, Wild Mignonette, Garlic and Hedge mustards, Wild Radish, Sea Rocket, Water-cress and Winter-cress. Occasionally on cultivated Cabbage, and Nasturtium in gardens. **FIELD NOTES** Apr–Oct, in two or possibly three generations, although just one above 250m. Feeds openly on leaves of the foodplant. Pupates low down on a suitable surface, away from the foodplant, head up, attached to a silk pad and held in place with a silken girdle. Overwinters as a pupa.

COLIADINAE

CLOUDED YELLOW
Colias croceus

PLATE 4
58.010 (1545)

LC. A regular immigrant and seen most frequently in England, Wales and southern Ireland, and only occasionally in Scotland. **FIELD CHARACTERS** Head green. Body green and covered with numerous tiny black dots. Dorsal line dark green and indistinct. Spiracular stripe white above and yellow below, with an orange dash on each segment. Below the dashes there may be a black dot on a variable number of segments from T2 to A8. **HABITATS** Most often seen in coastal habitats where Common Bird's-foot-trefoil is abundant, and in arable fields growing leguminous crops. Also inland in unimproved grassland, old quarries and railway lines, road verges and waste ground. **FOODPLANTS** Wide variety of plants in the pea family, including Common and Hairy bird's-foot-trefoils, wild and cultivated clovers, Lucerne, Black and Spotted medicks and Ribbed Melilot. **FIELD NOTES** Jun–Oct, or sometimes over the winter in favourable conditions. Feeds on the leaves. Pupates on a stem of the foodplant, head up, attached to a silk pad and held in place with a silken girdle. Many young larvae have been found in late autumn on hot, south-facing cliff slopes on the south coast of Dorset, and some have been observed closely and found to feed up successfully during the winter to produce adults in Apr. These go on to produce a further generation in summer. Adults seen in early spring along the south coast may indicate local residency over winter, and it is likely this happens inland occasionally during mild winters.

BRIMSTONE
Gonepteryx rhamni

PLATE 4
58.013 (1546)

LC. Ssp. *rhamni* Widespread in England and Wales, and occasionally recorded in southern Scotland. Its range has expanded significantly in recent decades. Ssp. *gravesi* is recognised by some authors as a separate subspecies in Ireland, where it is quite widespread but uncommon due to the rarity of the foodplants. **FIELD CHARACTERS** Head green with tiny black dots. Body green and covered with numerous tiny black dots. Dorsal line barely discernible, and spiracular stripe greenish white. **HABITATS** Associated with scrub in a wide variety of habitats, including bogs, fens, gardens and urban areas (especially where foodplants are planted), calcareous grassland, heathland, limestone pavement, moorland and woodland rides. **FOODPLANTS** Buckthorn and Alder Buckthorn. **FIELD NOTES** May–Jul, resting openly over the midrib of the upper surface of a leaf of the foodplant. Its presence may be given away by feeding damage in the form of holes in the leaf when the larva is small or sections eaten from the edge when larger. Usually pupates on the underside of a leaf or stem attached to a silk pad and held in place with a silken girdle. Overwinters as an adult.

NYMPHALIDAE BROWN, FRITILLARY, ADMIRAL AND TORTOISESHELL BUTTERFLIES

This is an extremely diverse family of butterflies with around 6,000 species worldwide. There are 26 species resident or regularly breeding in Great Britain and Ireland.

Speckled Wood ×1.75

They exhibit high diversity in terms of larvae. For example, the Satyrinae are rather similar, simple in form and near unicolorous, with short, bristly hairs and paired anal points. The Nymphalinae, in contrast, are complex, with a variety of colours and structures, including spines, bumps and horns. Larvae in the Satyrinae are solitary but in the Nymphalinae many are gregarious, at least in early instars. Our one representative in the Limenitidinae, the White Admiral, exhibits remarkable behaviour as a larva, described in the *Introduction* (see p. 57).

Silver-washed Fritillary ×1.75

Large Heath larva

White Admiral larva

SATYRINAE

WALL
Lasiommata megera

PLATE 5
59.002 (1615)

NT. Still widespread in England and Wales, commonest on or near the coast, but has declined significantly in recent decades from central lowland areas. Mainly coastal in Ireland and south-west Scotland. **FIELD CHARACTERS** Head pale bluish green. Body pale bluish green and covered with short, straight white hairs. Dorsal stripe bluish green, incorporating a pale central line and edged with a whitish-green line. Subdorsal line greenish white with indistinct lateral lines and a clear white subspiracular line. Spiracles pale orange. Paired anal points pale bluish green, often tipped with white. **HABITATS** Found in open grassy areas where there is broken ground, in a range of habitats, including cliffs and slopes, rocky coastlines, field margins, coastal grassland, heathland, hedgerows, old quarries and railway lines, undercliffs, waste ground, and occasionally in open woodland. **FOODPLANTS** A range of grasses, including bents, False Brome, Cock's-foot, Common Couch, Wavy Hair-grass, Annual Meadow-grass, Tor-grass and

Yorkshire-fog. **FIELD NOTES** Jun–Apr, in two generations per year. A partial third generation of adults is sometimes seen in the far south in mid-autumn. Feeds mainly at night. Pupates suspended from a silk pad attached to grass. Usually overwinters as a larva, but sometimes as a pupa.

SPECKLED WOOD
Pararge aegeria

PLATE 5

59.003 (1614)

LC. Widespread and often found commonly. Ssp. *aegeria* Channel Islands. Ssp. *tircis* Widespread in England, Wales, Ireland, and expanding rapidly northwards into southern Scotland. Ssp. *oblita* Fairly widespread in central and northern Scotland and expanding in range. Ssp. *insula* Scilly. **FIELD CHARACTERS** Head green. Body bright green and covered with short white and black hairs. Dorsal stripe dark green, incorporating a pale central line and edged with a yellowish or white line. Subdorsal, lateral, an indistinct spiracular and slightly wavy subspiracular lines may be yellowish or white. Spiracles orange. Paired anal points white. **HABITATS** In the north, a species of woodlands. In the south, found more widely in gardens and urban parks, overgrown hedgerows, scrub and woodland, often preferring slightly damper areas. **FOODPLANTS** Several grasses, including False Brome, Cock's-foot, Common Couch, Creeping Bent, Tufted Hair-grass, meadow-grasses and Yorkshire-fog. Also recorded on Tufted-sedge. **FIELD NOTES** The larva can be found in any month, in two generations and a partial third in autumn. Feeds by day and night. Pupates suspended head down from a silk pad attached to a grass leaf or surrounding vegetation. Regularly overwinters as a third-instar larva or pupa.

LARGE HEATH
Coenonympha tullia

PLATE 5

59.004 (1628)

VU. Occurs in isolated colonies in the north and west, and is separable into three subspecies based on geographical distribution. Overall, the species is declining in its range. Ssp. *davus* Small colonies in the West Midlands, northern England and the far south-west of Scotland. Ssp. *polydama* Found in north-east England, mid- and north Wales, southern Scotland (away from the south-west) and throughout Ireland. Ssp. *scotica* Widespread in northern half of Scotland. **FIELD CHARACTERS** Head green. Body green and covered in numerous tiny white dots. Dorsal stripe dark green, edged with white or yellowish lines. Subdorsal stripe white or yellowish, edged dark green above. A dark green supraspiracular stripe and a white or yellowish subspiracular stripe. Paired anal points pink. **SIMILAR SPECIES** Small Heath shows no obvious and consistent differences but is associated with different foodplants and is smaller when fully fed. **HABITATS** Below 500m (600m in northern Scotland) in upland blanket bogs, lowland raised bogs, and wet areas on moorland. Sites are normally characterised by having a carpet of *Sphagnum* mosses with tussocks of Hare's-tail Cottongrass, and plenty of Cross-leaved Heath that is used as the principal nectar source by the adult. **FOODPLANTS** Mainly Hare's-tail Cottongrass. Occasionally Common Cottongrass and Jointed Rush. Also reported on White Beak-sedge and Purple Moor-grass. **FIELD NOTES** Jul–May, sometimes overwintering twice as a larva in Scotland. Feeds by day and hides at the base of a tussock when not feeding. It is most easily found in the middle of the day. Pupates suspended head down from a pad of silk attached to the foodplant or nearby vegetation.

SMALL HEATH
Coenonympha pamphilus

PLATE 5

59.005 (1627)

NT. Ssp. *pamphilus* Widespread but has declined in abundance in recent decades, although its range remains stable. Ssp. *rhoumensis* is recognised by some authors from the far north and west of Scotland. **FIELD CHARACTERS** Head green. Body green and covered in numerous tiny white dots. Dorsal stripe dark green, edged with yellow or whitish. Subdorsal stripe yellowish or whitish, edged above with dark green, with a dark green spiracular stripe above a yellowish or whitish subspiracular stripe. Paired anal points pink **SIMILAR SPECIES** Large Heath. **HABITATS** A species of open, dry grasslands. Found in greatest numbers in acid and calcareous grasslands, heathland and sand dunes. Also parkland, road verges, waste ground, and rides in open woodland. **FOODPLANTS** A range of fine grasses, including bents, fescues and meadow-grasses. Also reported on Crested Dog's-tail, Mat-grass and Tor-grass. **FIELD NOTES** Jun–Apr, in one generation in Scotland, and two or possibly three in the south. Feeds at night. Pupates suspended head down from a pad of silk attached to the foodplant or nearby vegetation.

MOUNTAIN RINGLET/
SMALL MOUNTAIN RINGLET
Erebia epiphron

PLATE 5
59.007 (1617)

NT. Occurs in discrete colonies, sometimes in high numbers. There is some evidence of a decline in numbers at known sites in Scotland. Some authors recognise two subspecies in Great Britain. Ssp. *mnemom* Lake District, England. Ssp. *scotica* Scottish Highlands. **FIELD CHARACTERS** Head green. Body pale green and covered with short black hairs. Dorsal stripe dark green, edged with yellowish lines, and with a white subdorsal line and a yellowish or white subspiracular stripe. Paired anal points pale brown. **HABITATS** On mountains, usually 500–700m in the Lake District, and 350–900m in Scotland. In open grassland dominated by Heath Bedstraw and Mat-grass. **FOODPLANTS** Mainly on Mat-grass, but may also be on Sheep's-fescue. **FIELD NOTES** Aug–May, and sometimes overwinters twice. Feeds at night and may also be found basking in the sun. Pupates in a loose cocoon made of silk and grass blades at the base of a tussock.

SCOTCH ARGUS
Erebia aethiops

PLATE 5
59.008 (1618)

LC. Ssp. *aethiops* Two sites in England and widespread in north-east Scotland. Ssp. *caledonia* Widespread in western and south-west Scotland. **FIELD CHARACTERS** Head brown. Body pale brown and covered with white pinacula from which arise short, pale brown bristle-like hairs. Dorsal line dark brown, with brown subdorsal and lateral lines, often indistinct. Below the lateral line is a pale stripe and brown dashes, the latter especially on A2–A8. A pale spiracular line may be visible just above the black spiracles and there is a pale subspiracular stripe. Paired anal points short and pale brown. **SIMILAR SPECIES** Ringlet, and brown forms of Gatekeeper/Hedge Brown and Marbled White. Ringlet has dark stripes on the head, longer anal points, and lacks the lateral line and thicker brown dashes below. It also has longer hairs that are recurved and paler in the lower half of each hair, compared with the short bristle-like and unicolorous hairs of Scotch Argus. Gatekeeper/Hedge Brown is distinguished from Ringlet by its brown (not black) spiracles, unicolorous pale hairs and less stumpy appearance. Brown and green forms of Marbled White do not have dark stripes or rows of dark speckling on the head, distinguishing them from brown and green forms of both Ringlet and Gatekeeper/Hedge Brown. The distribution of Scotch Argus shows little overlap with either Marbled White or Gatekeeper/Hedge Brown. **HABITATS** Found only in tall open grasslands that are either lightly grazed or ungrazed. In Scotland, up to 500m on the fringes of bogs, in wet acid or neutral grasslands, including those on raised beaches on the west coast, moorland, and in open woodlands and clearings. In England, in mosaics of limestone grassland, scrub and woodland. **FOODPLANTS** In Scotland, mainly Purple Moor-grass, but also on Common Bent, Tufted and Wavy hair-grasses, Sheep's-fescue and Sweet Vernal-grass. In England, on Blue Moor-grass only. **FIELD NOTES** Aug–Jun. Feeds on the tips of grasses by day and night before the winter, but just at night from the spring, and drops readily if disturbed. Pupates in a thin cocoon among leaf litter or moss on the ground.

RINGLET
Aphantopus hyperantus

PLATE 5
59.009 (1629)

LC. Widespread in England, Wales and Ireland, and in Scotland away from the far north and west. Its range is expanding. **FIELD CHARACTERS** Head pale brown, brown or purplish brown with darker stripes. Body pale greyish brown and covered in recurved brownish hairs, each of which is pale in the lower half and darker in the upper half. Dorsal stripe dark brown with a pale lateral and white subspiracular stripe. Spiracles black. Paired anal points white. **SIMILAR SPECIES** Scotch Argus, and brown forms of Gatekeeper/Hedge Brown and Marbled White. **HABITATS** Inhabits tall grassland, usually on damp, clayey soils. In the north in more open, wet grasslands. In the south prefers shaded, rather sheltered wet grasslands and damp woodland rides, and is found in parkland, riverbanks, road verges, and open areas among scrub. **FOODPLANTS** Several grasses, including Creeping Bent, False Brome, Cock's-foot, Common Couch, Tufted Hair-grass, meadow-grasses and Wood Millet. Also reported on Wood-sedge. **FIELD NOTES** Aug–Jun. Overwinters when small. It can be found feeding at night in the spring. Pupates at the base of a grass clump or on the ground, in a slight cocoon.

MEADOW BROWN
Maniola jurtina

PLATE 5
59.010 (1626)

LC. Ssp. *insularis* Widespread over much of Great Britain and Ireland. Ssp. *splendida* Hebrides, Orkney, and mainland Scotland north of the Great Glen. Ssp. *cassiteridum* Scilly. Ssp. *iernes* South-west Ireland and the Atlantic Isles. **FIELD CHARACTERS** Head green and unmarked. Body green and covered with longish, curved white hairs. Dorsal stripe dark green and subspiracular line greenish white. Spiracles orangey brown. Paired anal points white or pink. **SIMILAR SPECIES** Green forms of Gatekeeper/Hedge Brown and Marbled White both have a brown head and shorter, straighter hairs. Gatekeeper/Hedge Brown has dark speckling on the head, unlike Meadow Brown and Marbled White. **HABITATS** Wide variety, including soft cliffs, unimproved grassland on a range of soil types, heathland, road verges, sand dunes, urban habitats such as allotments, cemeteries, gardens and urban parks, waste ground, and in open areas and rides in woodland. A coastal species in northern Scotland. **FOODPLANTS** Wide variety of grasses, showing preference for fine species, including bents, fescues and meadow-grasses, especially Smooth Meadow-grass, with larger larvae also feeding on False Brome, Cock's-foot, Common Couch, Downy Oat-grass and rye-grasses. **FIELD NOTES** Jul–Jun. Feeds slowly by day through the winter, but from about Mar feeds at night. Pupates suspended head down, attached to the shed larval skin, which is attached to a grass blade or stem.

GATEKEEPER/HEDGE BROWN
Pyronia tithonus

PLATE 5
59.011 (1625)

LC. Ssp. *britanniae* Widespread in England and Wales and expanding northwards to the border with Scotland. Mainly in southern coastal counties in Ireland. **FIELD CHARACTERS** Head brown with rows of dark speckling. Body usually brown, sometimes green, with short pale hairs. The brown form is patterned with numerous short, darker wavy dashes, with a dark brown dorsal, yellowish lateral and white subspiracular stripe. Spiracles brown. Paired anal points whitish with a pink tinge. The green form differs in having a dark green dorsal stripe, an indistinct green lateral stripe and a greenish-white subspiracular stripe. **SIMILAR SPECIES** Green form: Meadow Brown and green form of Marbled White. Brown form: Scotch Argus, Ringlet and brown form of Marbled White. **HABITATS** A species of tall grassland in close proximity to scrub. Found in a variety of habitats, including rough coastal areas and especially undercliff, acid and calcareous grasslands, heathland, hedgerows, old quarries and railway lines, and woodland rides. Also in gardens. **FOODPLANTS** A range of grasses, showing preference for fine species such as bents, fescues and meadow-grasses. Also feeds on Cock's-foot and Common Couch. **FIELD NOTES** Aug–Jun. Feeds by day until Oct, and by night in the spring. Pupates suspended head down, joined to the shed larval skin, which is attached to a grass blade.

MARBLED WHITE
Melanargia galathea

PLATE 5
59.012 (1620)

LC. Ssp. *serena* Widespread in much of England, but rarely common except in parts of the south. Scarce in East Anglia, and local in Wales. Expanding its range northwards in the Midlands and into Yorkshire. **FIELD CHARACTERS** Head pale brown and unmarked. Body usually brown, sometimes green, and covered with short white hairs. The brown form has a pale brown body with a blackish-brown dorsal stripe, a dark and often faint subdorsal line, and a pale band beyond. Adjacent to the pale band is a darker lateral stripe, often darkly marked only at its upper margin. Subspiracular line pale. Spiracles black. The pale band, lateral stripe and subspiracular line converge towards a pair of pinkish anal points. The green form is similar, with the brown replaced by green, and pinkish anal points. The colour of the penultimate instar is usually green. **SIMILAR SPECIES** Green form: Meadow Brown and green form of Gatekeeper/Hedge Brown. Brown form: Scotch Argus, Ringlet and brown form of Gatekeeper/Hedge Brown. **HABITATS** A species of unmanaged or infrequently managed grasslands where Red Fescue is common. Found most frequently on cliffs, calcareous grassland and undercliffs. Also occurs in acid grassland, old quarries and railway lines, road verges, waste ground and woodland rides. **FOODPLANTS** Red Fescue or Sheep's-fescue appear to be an important component of the diet, but larvae are frequently found on Tor-grass. Also reported on Cock's-foot, Timothy, Tufted-sedge and Yorkshire-fog. **FIELD NOTES** Aug–Jun. Enters diapause immediately after eating most of its eggshell. Leaf-feeding begins as early as Jan. Ascends a grass blade after dark and feeds at night. Pupates on the ground with no attachment.

GRAYLING
Hipparchia semele

PLATE 5
59.013 (1621)

VU. Occurs in discrete colonies, and several subspecies are recognised. Its range is declining in some areas. Ssp. *semele* Widespread along the coasts of England and Wales, and inland on heathlands in southern England, in breckland grassland, and in derelict industrial sites in the Midlands. Ssp. *scota* Coastal areas in the northern half of Scotland. Ssp. *thyone* Great Ormes Head peninsula, north Wales. Ssp. *atlantica* The Hebridean Islands, Scotland. Ssp. *clarensis* The Burren, Cos Clare and Galway, Ireland. Ssp. *hibernica* Coastal areas in Ireland. **FIELD CHARACTERS** Head brown with three dark vertical stripes each side. Body pale brown with a dark brown dorsal stripe incorporating a pale central line. Subdorsal and lateral stripes dark brown, the latter edged above and below with whitish lines. Paired anal points pale brown or white. **SIMILAR SPECIES** Clay group of wainscots (see *Separating external-feeding wainscots* table, pp. 424–7) and Square-spot and Six-striped rustics are superficially similar, but all lack the anal points, and none of these larvae taper posteriorly like Grayling. **HABITATS** In all cases in dry habitats with sparse vegetation and much bare ground. In coastal locations, on cliffs, rocky coastlines, short-turf grassland, old quarries, saltmarshes, sand dunes and undercliffs. Inland, on acid and calcareous grasslands, heathland, former industrial sites with waste heaps, and open woodland on stony ground. **FOODPLANTS** Mainly fine grasses, and particularly Bristle Bent, Red Fescue, Early and Tufted hair-grasses and Sheep's-fescue. Marram is favoured on sand dunes. Also reported on False Brome, Common Couch and Annual Meadow-grass. **FIELD NOTES** Sep–May. Feeds mainly at night, but also by day during mild winter weather. Pupates just below the surface of the ground.

HELICONIINAE

PEARL-BORDERED FRITILLARY
Boloria euphrosyne

PLATE 6
59.014 (1601)

EN. Has declined significantly in range in England and Wales in recent decades and is now very local. Remains widespread in much of Scotland and frequent in the Burren, Cos Clare and Galway, Ireland. **FIELD CHARACTERS** Head black. Body black with a spiracular row of white spots, the white sometimes more extensive, forming a spiracular band. Elsewhere there may be a scattering of small white spots. Body covered with cone-shaped pinacula from which arise black spines. Pinacula yellow subdorsally with black tips, and all black elsewhere. **HABITATS** Areas on free-draining soils supporting a mosaic of Bracken, grass and scattered scrub, recently cleared or regularly coppiced woodland, and, in Scotland, in broadleaf parkland. In all cases, the ground layer must have abundant leaf litter and violets. **FOODPLANTS** Most commonly on Common Dog-violet, but reported on Heath Dog-violet, Wild Pansy and Sweet Violet, and on Marsh Violet in northern populations. **FIELD NOTES** Jun–Apr. Feeds in summer and autumn on the leaves until fourth instar, and then goes into diapause in leaf litter. In spring it spends much of its time basking in sunshine, as well as feeding, and hides among leaf litter at other times. Pupates in leaf litter, suspended from a silk pad within a light silken structure.

SMALL PEARL-BORDERED FRITILLARY
Boloria selene

PLATE 6
59.015 (1600)

NT. Has declined significantly in England in recent decades but remains widespread in the south-west and the Lake District. Widespread in Scotland. **FIELD CHARACTERS** Head black. Body grey, more or less mixed with orangey brown, usually with a pale grey dorsal stripe and black subdorsal and lateral patches. Body covered with orangey, sometimes black, cone-shaped pinacula that give rise to short black spines, and the subdorsal pinacula on T1 are especially long and forward-pointing. **HABITATS** Various habitats, including grassland with Bracken and scattered scrub, wet grassland and moorland (in the west and north), clearings and open areas in woodland (in the south), and broadleaf parkland and woodland edges (in Scotland). Also on cliffs and dune-slacks. In all habitats there is a strong preference for damp grassy areas with abundant violets. **FOODPLANTS** Common Dog-violet and Marsh Violet, especially in northern populations. **FIELD NOTES** Jul–May. Feeds by day when warm, hiding among leaf litter at other times. Diapause is in the fourth instar, but a proportion of larvae complete their growth in summer and produce a second generation of adults in Aug. Pupates low down among vegetation, suspended from a silk pad within a light silken structure.

SILVER-WASHED FRITILLARY
Argynnis paphia

PLATE 6
59.017 (1608)

LC. Most frequent in southern England and the southern half of Wales, and undergoing a significant expansion in range, especially in the east Midlands and East Anglia. Widespread in Ireland. **FIELD CHARACTERS** Head black. Body pale yellowish brown with a pale yellowish dorsal stripe incorporating a central black line and edged with black, forming rounded patches A2–A8. Laterally, there are irregular short black marks outlined in yellow. Body covered in long orangey pinacula from which arise dark brown spines, and the subdorsal pinacula on T1 are darker, longer and forward-pointing. **HABITATS** Mainly broadleaf woodland; less often in wooded hedgerows and mixed woodland. Females choose sites for egg-laying where there is total or partial shade and scattered violets growing on the woodland floor. **FOODPLANTS** Common Dog-violet and Sweet Violet. **FIELD NOTES** Sep–Jun. Eggs are laid in a crevice on the bark of a tree or on moss, and when the larva hatches it spins a pad of silk and immediately enters diapause. In late Mar or early Apr it descends to the ground to begin feeding by day on nearby violets. Between bouts of feeding it may bask in the sun on dead leaves. Pupates suspended head down from a silk pad attached to vegetation.

DARK GREEN FRITILLARY
Argynnis aglaja

PLATE 6
59.019 (1607)

LC. Widely distributed throughout but very local in central England and East Anglia, and mainly coastal in Ireland. **FIELD CHARACTERS** Head black. Body black with an interrupted white or pale orange dorsal stripe incorporating a central black line. Orange spots adjacent to spiracles A1–A8, usually with orange dashes below. Body covered in long cone-shaped black pinacula from which arise black spines. **HABITATS** Various unimproved habitats, including acid grassland with Bracken, calcareous grassland, coastal grassland, moorland and sand dunes. Occasionally in woodland rides. **FOODPLANTS** Widely on Common Dog-violet; also Hairy Violet on calcareous grassland, and Marsh Violet on wet grassland and moorland. **FIELD NOTES** Aug–May. On hatching, eats its eggshell and enters diapause immediately. It begins to feed as soon as the temperature is warm enough in early spring, and is between half and fully grown Apr–May. It is most often encountered wandering at high speed across the ground. Pupates suspended from a silk pad within a light cover of spun leaves.

HIGH BROWN FRITILLARY
Argynnis adippe

PLATE 6
59.020 (1606)

CR. Protected species. A rare species that has declined very severely from being widespread in the 1950s to a point where it requires sustained conservation management across the landscape to maintain the few remaining populations in Dartmoor, Exmoor, Wales and Morecambe Bay. **FIELD CHARACTERS** Head orangey brown. Body pale brown with white dorsal and interrupted subdorsal lines, between which there is a black patch anteriorly on each segment. There is a whitish-grey transverse band between segments. Body covered with long pinkish-brown pinacula from which arise brown spines. **SIMILAR SPECIES** Heath Fritillary is similar to non-final-instar larvae but has long dorsal pinacula with spines A1–A9, which are absent in High Brown Fritillary. **HABITATS** Now only in two habitat types: areas of dense Bracken and mixed Bracken and grass on moorland slopes, and among limestone rock outcrops where scrub and woodland have recently been cleared or coppiced. **FOODPLANTS** Widely on Common Dog-violet, and Hairy Violet in limestone areas. It may occasionally feed on Heath and Pale dog-violets, and is reported on Sweet Violet. **FIELD NOTES** Apr–May. Overwinters as a fully developed larva within the egg. Hatches in spring, feeds on the leaves, and may be found basking in sunshine on dead fronds of Bracken on the ground, where it is especially cryptic. Pupates suspended from a pad of silk within a loose structure of spun leaves.

LIMENITIDINAE

WHITE ADMIRAL
Limenitis camilla

PLATE 6
59.021 (1584)

VU. Fairly widespread in England away from the far south-west and far north, and in the east of Wales, but its range is expanding, especially northwards. **FIELD CHARACTERS** Head pale brown with dark markings, and spiny. Body green with cone-shaped brown pinacula giving rise to brown spines. The pinacula are subdorsal on T2–T3 and A2–A8, and those on A3–A6 are shorter than the others. There is a white subspiracular stripe from A2 posteriorly, containing a yellow spot on each segment, edged below with brown A2–A6. **HABITATS** Broadleaf and mixed woodland, especially where there is Bramble in rides for nectar. **FOODPLANT** Honeysuckle, where this grows in partial or deep shade within the woodland. **FIELD NOTES** Aug–May. An account of the remarkable habits of this larva are described in the *Introduction* (p. 57). Pupates suspended from a silk pad on the underside of a leaf or stem, usually of the foodplant.

APATURINAE

PURPLE EMPEROR
Apatura iris

PLATE 6
59.022 (1585)

NT. Mainly in central southern England and the south Midlands, but expanding its range northwards and into East Anglia. **FIELD CHARACTERS** Head green with a pair of long green or bluish-green horns tipped with brown, with vertical white stripes down the face at the base of the horns. Body green and covered with numerous yellow spots. Subdorsal line yellow or white T1–T3 and extending onto the horns of the head. There are yellow diagonal lines laterally, that spanning A2–A4 being the widest and longest and extending onto the dorsum, where there are small yellow projections. A yellow line extends from A9 into a single anal point. **HABITATS** Mainly extensive broadleaf and mixed woodlands and in wooded landscapes. Also in young conifer plantations, and more recently in abandoned fields and farmland where Goat Willow becomes abundant. **FOODPLANTS** Mainly Goat Willow; also Grey Willow, and occasionally Hybrid Crack-willow and White Poplar. Reported on Aspen. **FIELD NOTES** Aug–Jun. After hatching, sits at the tip of a leaf facing the petiole and feeds by day from the edge of that leaf. In following instars, it tends to travel to feed on a different leaf from the one it rests on. In autumn, usually in early Nov, the colour changes from green to brown and the larva attaches itself to a pad of silk in the fork of a branch for the winter. In spring it resumes feeding, and rests between feeding bouts on a leaf, facing the petiole. Pupates suspended from a pad of silk beneath a leaf of the foodplant.

NYMPHALINAE

RED ADMIRAL
Vanessa atalanta

PLATE 7
59.023 (1590)

LC. A regular two-way migrant in Great Britain and Ireland and widespread throughout. **FIELD CHARACTERS** Head black and not notched. Body black and covered with whitish or yellowish dots, tiny on some individuals and larger on others. On larvae with largest dots, the dots coalesce to give an overall pale grey or yellowish appearance to the body. A series of broad yellow marks in the subspiracular region from A1–A8 may coalesce to form a stripe in some individuals. Body also covered with cone-shaped yellow, brownish, grey or blackish pinacula from which arise blackish spines. **SIMILAR SPECIES** Painted Lady, which occasionally feeds on Common Nettle, has a much hairier and notched head, a slenderer body, and a narrower subspiracular stripe. **HABITATS** Wide variety, from seashore to the tops of mountains and in man-made and semi-natural habitats. Regularly in gardens. **FOODPLANTS** Widely on Common Nettle, but also reported on Hop, Small Nettle and Pellitory-of-the-wall. **FIELD NOTES** Apr–Oct. When feeding on the leaves of Common Nettle, constructs a tent made by spinning the edges of a single leaf together and upwards, and sometimes partially eats through the petiole at the base of the leaf, causing wilting. It constructs new habitations as it grows. Alternatively, and especially in the final instar, it constructs a retreat by spinning the upper leaves of a shoot together, chewing part of the way through the stem so the top of the plant or leaf droops down. Pupates suspended from a silken pad among spun leaves. In recent decades it has overwintered in numbers as an adult, at least in the southern part of its range, and can be seen flying on cold sunny days in the winter.

PAINTED LADY
Vanessa cardui

PLATE 7
59.024 (1591)

LC. A regular two-way migrant in Great Britain and Ireland and widespread throughout. **FIELD CHARACTERS** Head black or brown, deeply notched and hairy. Body very variable in colour, usually blackish, or pale yellowish with black marks, and covered with numerous tiny white or yellow dots. Dorsal line black, often edged with yellow, and there may be yellow subdorsal and lateral stripes, and brown lateral spots. Yellow subspiracular stripe A1–A8. The body has cone-shaped black, pinkish-brown or grey pinacula from which arise black, yellow or grey spines. **SIMILAR SPECIES** Red Admiral. **HABITATS** Wide variety, from seashore to the tops of mountains, and in man-made and semi-natural habitats. Regularly breeds in intensively farmed grasslands with thistles. **FOODPLANTS** Mainly on thistles (*Carduus* and *Cirsium* spp.), particularly Creeping, Marsh, Musk and Spear thistles. Reported on a wide variety of herbaceous plants in years of great immigration (such as 2009), including Globe Artichoke, Greater and Lesser burdocks, Common Cudweed, Common and Greater knapweeds, mallows, Common Nettle, Carline Thistle and Viper's-bugloss. **FIELD NOTES** Apr–Oct. Feeds at first under a silk pad on the underside of a leaf. Later it feeds within one or several silken tents incorporating folded leaves. These are conspicuous and contain frass. Pupates suspended from a silk pad under a tent of spun leaves. Does not overwinter but migrates south.

PEACOCK
Aglais io

PLATE 7
59.026 (1597)

LC. Widespread throughout England, Wales and Ireland, but rather more local and expanding northwards in Scotland. It is a short-distance wanderer rather than a long-distance, two-way migrant, and adults seldom cross the sea. **FIELD CHARACTERS** Head black, notched and hairy. Body black and covered with numerous white dots, and long cone-shaped black panicula from which arise black spines. Prolegs brown and anal clasper black, all with pale brown crochets. **SIMILAR SPECIES** Small Tortoiseshell has yellow markings and yellowish pinacula. **HABITATS** Found in many open, sunny habitats. Most frequent where Common Nettle abounds in allotments, gardens and urban parks, hedgerows on farmland, and in clearings among scrub and woodland. **FOODPLANTS** Widely on Common Nettle, but reported on Hop, and occasionally Small Nettle. **FIELD NOTES** May–Jul, and rarely as a second generation in Sep. Feeds by day and night, at first gregariously under a communal web. Later, the larvae disperse and become solitary, sitting fully exposed on leaves. Pupates suspended from a silk pad under vegetation. Overwinters as an adult.

SMALL TORTOISESHELL
Aglais urticae

PLATE 7
59.027 (1593)

LC. Widespread throughout and often common, but currently undergoing substantial decline in abundance that may be related to parasitism of larvae by a fly that has recently colonised the British Isles. There is also evidence that adults are increasingly entering diapause by midsummer rather than in autumn, and are not producing a further generation in late summer, perhaps in response to a warming climate. Low numbers from July onwards may reflect this behavioural change in comparison with counts from previous decades. **FIELD CHARACTERS** Head black with yellowish speckles and hairy. Body black with variable intensity of yellow markings. Body covered with numerous yellow dots. Dorsal line black, edged with yellow dots, lines or stripes, with or without a yellow lateral stripe or line. Subspiracular line yellow. The body has long cone-shaped yellow or black pinacula from which arise yellowish or black pines. Prolegs and anal clasper yellowish green. **SIMILAR SPECIES** Peacock. **HABITATS** Found in many open, sunny habitats. Most frequent where Common Nettle abounds in allotments, farmland, gardens and urban parks, hedgerows, scrub, waste ground and open woodland. **FOODPLANTS** Common and small nettles. **FIELD NOTES** May–Aug, in two generations in the south, and one in the north. Feeds by day and night, at first gregariously under a communal web. Later it disperses, becomes solitary and sits fully exposed on leaves. Pupates suspended from a silk pad under vegetation or on a hard surface. Overwinters as an adult.

COMMA
Polygonia c-album

PLATE 7
59.031 (1598)

LC. Widespread in England and Wales, and expanding rapidly through Scotland and along the eastern seaboard of Ireland. **FIELD CHARACTERS** Head black and deeply notched, with near-vertical orange stripes laterally and on the face either side of the mouthparts. There is a black wart-like protuberance on each dorsal lobe, giving rise to a tuft of pale hairs. Body bluish black with transverse orange bands T1–A2, and a broad white dorsal band A3–A8. Subspiracular line orange and wavy. Body covered with long cone-shaped pinacula that are pale yellowish T1–A2, giving rise to pale yellowish spines, and white A3–A8, giving rise to white spines. **HABITATS** Wide variety, but most frequently in banks of canals and rivers, hedgerows, scrub and open woodland. Also in allotments, gardens and urban parks. **FOODPLANTS** Most commonly on Common Nettle, and frequently elms and Hop, but also reported on Black and Red currants, Gooseberry and willows. Has once been found on Hazel, but the larva produced a small adult. Sunny, sheltered spots are seen commonly feeding on cultivated Hop, and was known as the 'Hop cat'. **FIELD NOTES** Apr–Jun and Jul–Aug, in two generations. Some of the earliest larvae of the first generation feed up quickly, resulting in a partial second generation of adults with a brighter golden colour to the upper surface of the wings than typical examples in spring and autumn. This seasonal summer form is known as *hutchinsoni*, and these adults become sexually mature quickly without having to overwinter, leading to larvae that are seen in late summer. The larva sits on the underside of a leaf and, when large, occasionally the upperside. Pupates suspended from a silk pad under vegetation. Overwinters as an adult.

MARSH FRITILLARY
Euphydryas aurinia

PLATE 7
59.033 (1610)

VU. Protected species. A species in decline in range and abundance, not only in Great Britain and Ireland but also across Europe. Now it is a species mainly of western areas, and is fairly widespread in Ireland. Numbers fluctuate considerably over decades and the species needs sites managed across wide landscapes to enable it to thrive. **FIELD CHARACTERS** Head black. Body black with a broad band of white spots dorsally and at the spiracular level, and a scattering of tiny spots between. Body covered with long cone-shaped black pinacula from which arise black spines. **HABITATS** A range of open grassy habitats where foodplants are common, including bogs, fens, calcareous grassland, lowland and upland wet grasslands on peaty or clayey soils, and heathland. Occasionally found in large clearings in woodland. **FOODPLANTS** Widely on Devil's-bit Scabious. Occasionally on Field and Small scabiouses in calcareous grassland. Also reported on Honeysuckle, Greater Knapweed, plantains, Wild Teasel and Marsh Valerian. **FIELD NOTES** Jul–Apr. At first, larvae feed inside a communal web, and by the third instar they bask in sunshine outside the web. On entering fourth instar in late summer, they construct a communal web for diapause that may be at ground level, or raised in, for example, a Purple Moor-grass tussock. Larvae begin to emerge on sunny days in Feb, retreating when cooler, and start feeding from Mar in discrete groups, forming webs and basking together in the sun. In the final, sixth instar they disperse to feed alone. Pupates hanging from vegetation, to which it is attached by a silk pad.

GLANVILLE FRITILLARY
Melitaea cinxia

PLATE 7
59.034 (1612)

EN. Restricted as a native resident to coastal habitats in the south of the Isle of Wight, and in the Channel Islands. **FIELD CHARACTERS** Head reddish brown with a black spot laterally and black central triangle. Body black with transverse bands of white spots, and covered with long cone-shaped black pinacula from which arise black spines. Prolegs and anal clasper reddish brown. **HABITATS** Mainly on hard and soft undercliffs. Also on chalk grassland, cliff tops and in steep coastal river valleys (chines). **FOODPLANTS** Mainly Ribwort Plantain and in last instar also on Buck's-horn Plantain. Reported on Sea Beet, hawkweeds and Sea Plantain. **FIELD NOTES** Jun–May. Larvae form a dense communal web over the foodplant, spending much time basking on top of the web, and feeding in the sunshine. In late summer, in the fifth instar, they spin a denser web for diapause. Feeding resumes in Mar when they construct a fresh web. In the final, seventh instar they abandon the web and feed alone, resting conspicuously on vegetation. Pupates suspended from a silk pad, in a loosely spun shelter.

HEATH FRITILLARY
Melitaea athalia

PLATE 7
59.036 (1613)

EN. Protected species. A rare species, confined to Cornwall (one site), Devon (one site on the edge of Dartmoor), Somerset (several sites on Exmoor), and several sites in Essex and Kent. Its range has declined very significantly in recent decades. **FIELD CHARACTERS** Head black. Body black with numerous white geometric shapes that vary in size among individuals such that white is sometimes the dominant colour. Body covered in long cone-shaped, pale orangey-brown pinacula with paler or whitish tips. These pinacula give rise to black spines. **SIMILAR SPECIES** High Brown Fritillary in non-final instar. **HABITATS** Unimproved grassland with Ribwort Plantain or Germander Speedwell growing where the vegetation is short or sparse; sheltered heathland valleys on Exmoor where Common Cow-wheat grows among Bilberry; recently cleared or coppiced woodland where Common Cow-wheat is abundant. **FOODPLANTS** Mainly on Common Cow-wheat, Ribwort Plantain and Germander Speedwell. Also reported on a variety of herbaceous plants, especially in years when larvae are locally abundant, including Lesser Celandine, Foxglove, Wood Sage, Ivy-leaved Speedwell, vetches and Yarrow. **FIELD NOTES** Jun–May. Larvae feed at first in an inconspicuous communal web, dispersing in smaller groups in the second instar. They are solitary by the third instar, feeding by day and hiding under dead leaves at night or in poor weather. In Sep, each larva constructs a hibernaculum in a tightly rolled dead leaf near the ground. In spring, it feeds in warm weather by day, spending much time basking in sunshine. Pupates suspended beneath a leaf, attached by a pad of silk.

RIODINIDAE METALMARK BUTTERFLIES

There is just one species in the British Isles, but many species occur in Asia, Africa and North America, and especially in the Neotropical region. The larvae are of similar shape to the Lycaenidae but the Newcomer's gland is absent.

Duke of Burgundy larva

RIODININAE

DUKE OF BURGUNDY
Hamearis lucina

PLATE 7
60.001 (1582)

EN. Mainly in the south Midlands and central southern England, with small populations in Kent and in northern England. This species has declined significantly in range in recent decades. **FIELD CHARACTERS** Head orangey brown with longish grey hairs. Body brown and covered with grey hairs. Dorsal line dark grey and expanded to form a black spot on each segment A1–A8. There is a round yellowish subdorsal patch on each segment T2–A8. **HABITATS** Calcareous grassland containing scrub or other shelter, wide rides in recent plantations, and recently cleared or coppiced woodland. There is a preference for north- and west-facing slopes of grasslands, or tussocky grasslands, where the foodplants on which the larvae depend to complete their feeding successfully are able to maintain lush growth over the summer. **FOODPLANTS** Cowslip and Primrose, and occasionally on hybrids of these two species. **FIELD NOTES** Jun–Aug. Rests at the base of the foodplant by day and ascends to feed on the leaves at night. It creates multiple holes in the lamina, leaving most of the veins intact. Pupates on the ground or low down in a grass tussock.

LYCAENIDAE COPPER, HAIRSTREAK AND BLUE BUTTERFLIES

There are about 6,000 species in this family, and 15 resident in Great Britain and Ireland, containing the coppers, hairstreaks and blues. In addition, Long-tailed Blue is an occasional immigrant to southern coastal counties and is sometimes accidentally imported with edible green beans, and the Geranium Bronze sometimes establishes itself in gardens and urban parks following accidental importation on geraniums.

Common Blue ×2

Larvae are similar-shaped between species, all rather grub-like and tapering to front and back ends. The head is particularly small and usually tucked underneath the first thoracic segment. Larvae of a number of species have associations with ants, and on the dorsum they may bear associated structures such as microscopic pore cupola over the body, a Newcomer's gland on A7, and eversible tentacle organs on A8, as described in the *Introduction* (p. 59). Much field work still needs to be carried out to elucidate the complexity of interactions of the Lycaenidae with ants; the field notes below provide short descriptions for each species where these are at least partly known.

Black Hairstreak ×2

Brown Hairstreak larva

LYCAENINAE

SMALL COPPER
Lycaena phlaeas

PLATE 8
61.001 (1582)

LC. Ssp. *eleus* Widespread and common throughout, but rather coastal in Scotland, and rare in the far north and west. Ssp. *hibernica* Widespread in Ireland. **FIELD CHARACTERS** Head pale brown with black markings. Body green and covered in numerous tiny white dots and short bristle-like hairs. One form has a dark green dorsal line and no other significant markings. Another form has pink dorsal and subspiracular stripes, and the pink coloration is continuous across T1 dorsally and on the anal flap. **HABITATS** Wide variety, including cliffs and undercliffs, unimproved grassland on all soil types, heathland, moorland, sand dunes, and clearings in woodland. Also in allotments, cemeteries, rough parts of improved grassland, old quarries and railway embankments, road verges and waste ground. **FOODPLANTS** Common and Sheep's sorrels. Occasionally on Broad-leaved Dock. Reported on Fiddle Dock and Common Ragwort. **FIELD NOTES** May–Jul and Aug–Apr, in two or three generations, the last of which may be partial. At first feeds from the underside of the leaf, excavating many short, curved grooves and leaving the upper epidermis as an opaque window. These windows are quite easy to spot from above in the field. Later, it eats the full thickness of the leaf. First-brood adults lay their eggs on the foodplant well above the ground, whereas subsequent broods lay close to the ground. Pupates attached to a silk pad by its cremaster and a silk girdle. A natural pupation site has not been found.

THECLINAE

BROWN HAIRSTREAK
Thecla betulae

PLATE 8
61.003 (1556)

VU. A species mainly of the south Midlands, Lancashire, southern and south-west England and south-west Wales. Also in Cos Clare and Galway in Ireland. Has declined in range overall in recent decades, but is now showing signs of rapid expansion in parts of south-east England. Also, systematic search for eggs in the winter regularly reveals hitherto unknown colonies. **FIELD CHARACTERS** Head black or brown. Body green and wedge-shaped, rising from T1 to its highest point on A1 then sloping gradually down to A10. Dorsal stripe green, edged each side with white or yellow lines on ridges that diverge from A1 anteriorly. Diagonal white or yellow subdorsal streaks T2–A8, and a similar, lateral row A1–A7. Subspiracular line white or yellow. When fully fed the body colour changes to purple. **HABITATS** On clayey and calcareous soils in hedgerows, scrub, urban parks, and woodland edges and rides, in coastal and inland situations. Egg-laying sites are frequently less than 1.5m above ground, and often on suckering growth from Blackthorn. **FOODPLANTS** Mainly Blackthorn and occasionally Bullace and Wild Plum. **FIELD NOTES** Apr–Jun. Feeds at first in an opening leaf bud. It then moves to the underside of a leaf, resting by day on a silk pad, and feeds at night on nearby leaves before usually returning to the same pad to rest. Pupates on the ground, the pupa being tended by ants. Overwinters as an egg.

PURPLE HAIRSTREAK
Favonius quercus

PLATE 8
61.004 (1557)

LC. Widespread in much of England and Wales. More local in northern England and Scotland but its range is expanding quickly northwards. Local in Ireland. **FIELD CHARACTERS** Head black. Body orangey brown, dark brown or pale greyish brown, with a dark dorsal line. There may be a grey dorsal patch on T1. Whitish subdorsal markings on T2 and T3 variable in shape and size, and can be short curves, diagonal streaks, smudges or V-shapes. Pale diagonal subdorsal streaks A1–A6, inwardly shaded paler towards the dorsal line, and outwardly edged or shaded darker brown. Body colour from A7 posteriorly is paler brown. **HABITATS** Oak woodland. **FOODPLANTS** Mainly Pedunculate and Sessile oaks. Also Holm and Turkey oaks. **FIELD NOTES** Apr–Jun. Feeds at first inside an opening flower bud, leaving a hole in the side. Later it feeds at night on young leaves, resting when not feeding under a nearby silken web that incorporates discarded scales that covered the bud. Pupae have been found in the nests of ants, several metres from the trunk of the tree. Overwinters as a fully developed larva in the egg.

GREEN HAIRSTREAK
Callophrys rubi

PLATE 8
61.005 (1555)

LC. Widespread throughout, but rather locally distributed in north-east England, Scotland and Ireland. **FIELD CHARACTERS** Head black or brown. Body green and covered with short hairs that are white, grey and reddish brown or purplish brown. Dorsal stripe green, incorporating a pale green or yellowish central line. Whitish or yellowish subdorsal markings T3–A6 are variable in size, shape and intensity, and can be dashes, smudges or diagonal streaks, with or without darker green shading along the outer edges. Subspiracular line white or yellow. The contrast between body colour and markings may be slight or marked. There is a small dorsal gland on A7. **SIMILAR SPECIES** Holly Blue shares some foodplants, but Green Hairstreak has more obvious reddish-brown or purplish-brown hairs. **HABITATS** Usually in association with scrub in a wide variety of habitats, including bogs, fens, unimproved grassland on all soil types, heathland, moorland, old quarries and railway embankments, undercliffs and woodland rides. **FOODPLANTS** Wide variety, usually dependent on habitat type. Common Bird's-foot-trefoil and Common Rock-rose (preferring flowers to leaves) on calcareous grassland, Bilberry on Scottish moorland, and Broom, Gorse, Dwarf Gorse, Dyer's Greenweed and Petty Whin on neutral grassland and heathland. Also reported on the buds of Bramble and Dogwood, the berries of Buckthorn and Alder Buckthorn, and Cross-leaved Heath. Has been observed egg-laying on Cranberry. **FIELD NOTES** May–Aug. Feeds on the soft parts of the foodplant, including flowers, developing fruits, buds and young leaves. Pupates on the ground, the pupa being tended by ants, which cover it with soil particles, and it has been found deep within an ants' nest. Overwinters as a pupa.

WHITE-LETTER HAIRSTREAK
Satyrium w-album

PLATE 8
61.006 (1558)

EN. Widespread in much of England and Wales, expanding its range north and west, and was recorded in 2018 in southern Scotland. **FIELD CHARACTERS** Head black or brown. Body usually pale green or yellowish green and dome-shaped, with subdorsal projections T2–A6, the tallest on A3. Dorsal line pale green or yellowish green and edged dark green, especially on the inner margin of each projection. A white or yellow line runs along the ridge formed by the projections. A series of white or yellow diagonal lateral streaks T2–A7. Subspiracular line white or yellow. Rarely the larva may be tinged more or less reddish or brownish, and a greenish-white form has been recorded. When fully fed the body colour changes to greyish brown. **HABITATS** Hedgerows, scrub and woodland clearings, glades and rides. Also on individual planted trees and copses, in both rural and urban settings. **FOODPLANTS** Wych Elm is the preferred foodplant, but other native elms, and some introduced species of elm resistant to Dutch elm disease, are also eaten. **FIELD NOTES** Mar–Jun. Feeds at first in an opening bud. Later it feeds on the leaves, resting on a silk pad on the underside of a leaf. At this stage it forms a dark silhouette against the light when viewed from below, and is fairly easy to spot, especially on Wych Elm. Pupates attached by a silk pad and girdle under a leaf of the foodplant or sometimes in the fork of a twig. Overwinters as a fully developed larva in the egg.

BLACK HAIRSTREAK
Satyrium pruni

PLATE 8
61.007 (1559)

EN. Very local and restricted to the east and south Midlands, and a recently discovered large colony in Sussex. A species hard to locate in all stages of its life cycle. **FIELD CHARACTERS** Head brown. Body green and dome-shaped, with subdorsal projections A2–A6, the tops and inner margins of which are usually pink or red, and the outer edges white. The extent of reddish coloration is variable, from a slight tinge on the projections to more extensive subdorsal shading on other abdominal segments, dorsal marks on T2 and A9, and shading across the anal flap. A series of faint diagonal yellowish lateral streaks A2–A6. Subspiracular line yellow and interrupted. **HABITATS** Found in dense mature stands of Blackthorn at the margins of woodland, and in woodland glades and rides. Also in patches of Blackthorn scrub in more open landscapes associated with unmanaged copses and hedgerows on farmland, railway lines and road verges. **FOODPLANTS** Mainly Blackthorn, and occasionally larvae of some populations on Bullace and Wild Plum. **FIELD NOTES** Mar–Jun. Feeds at first via a hole bored into a developing flower bud. Later rests exposed on a leaf, feeding by day. Pupates on a twig or sometimes on a leaf. The pupa resembles a bird's dropping. Overwinters as a fully developed larva in the egg.

POLYOMMATINAE

LONG-TAILED BLUE
Lampides boeticus

PLATE 8
61.008 (1567)

LC. Rare immigrant; adventive. Increasingly recorded, including the early stages along the south coast. **FIELD CHARACTERS** Head brown. Body dull green, covered in numerous tiny dark dots. Dorsal line purplish, indistinct slight purplish shading dorsally and subdorsally. Subspiracular line pale. Newcomer's gland is present on A7 and a pair of tentacle organs on A8. When fully fed the whole body becomes a purplish colour. **HABITATS** Mainly coastal, also gardens. **FOODPLANTS** Bladder-senna, Broom, Broad-leaved and Narrow-leaved everlasting-peas. Also as an adventive on Mange-tout peas. **FIELD NOTES** Aug–Sep. At first feeds on the flower and later the seedpods. Pupates among withered leaves, attached by a silk girdle. Does not survive the winter in Great Britain.

SMALL BLUE
Cupido minimus

PLATE 8
61.010 (1569)

NT. A local species mainly found in the south Midlands and southern England. Very local and usually coastal in south Wales, northern England, Scotland and Ireland. Its range has declined in recent decades. **FIELD CHARACTERS** Head black or brown with black markings. Body whitish brown with a grey or pinkish dorsal line. Subdorsal, lateral and supraspiracular lines faint, wavy and pink or brown, and white subspiracular line edged above with pink or brown. Newcomer's gland is present on the dorsum of A7. **HABITATS** The foodplant is a species of bare or disturbed and broken ground and the butterfly occurs in similar places, including cliffs and undercliffs, calcareous grassland, old quarries and railway lines, gravel deposits from rivers, road verges supporting sparse vegetation, sand dunes and vegetated shingle. **FOODPLANT** Kidney Vetch. **FIELD NOTES** Jun–Apr, in one and a partial second generation in the south, and a single generation in the north. On hatching, bores into a flower and feeds on the developing fruit within. When larger, it rests on the outside of a flower with its head and anterior burrowed into the flower from the side. Larvae are rarely attended by ants in Great Britain and Ireland, while this is a common sight in Europe. When fully fed in Jul, the larva finds a place on or just under the soil surface to rest for many months of diapause. Pupates in the spring, head up and attached by a silk pad and girdle of silk on moss or a leaf.

HOLLY BLUE
Celastrina argiolus

PLATE 8
61.012 (1580)

LC. Ssp. *britanna* Widespread in most of England, Wales and Ireland, and rapidly increasing its range into southern Scotland. Its abundance seems to fluctuate on a cycle of about six to seven years. **FIELD CHARACTERS** Head black. Body green with paired dorsal humps T2–A6. It is usually devoid of markings apart from a dark green dorsal line and a pale subspiracular line, and there may be rows of short whitish hairs along the ridges of the dorsal humps, and low down laterally. More strongly marked examples have the dorsal line broadly edged whitish green T2–T3, a transverse dark green band on A1, narrowing across the dorsum, and dark green diagonal subdorsal streaks A2–A6, inwardly shaded whitish green towards the dorsal line. Sometimes the green may be tinged pinkish dorsally, or there are pinkish spots along the dorsum and a pink subspiracular line. In Europe, larvae occur that have a pink or purplish ground colour when feeding on Heather or Purple-loosestrife. Newcomer's gland is present on A7 and a pair of tentacle organs on A8. When fully fed the larva changes colour to purple. **SIMILAR SPECIES** Green Hairstreak shares some foodplants. **HABITATS** Wide variety, including allotments, cemeteries, churchyards, field margins, gardens and urban parks, hedgerows, marshes, scrub, undercliffs and woodland. In Ireland it appears to be more restricted to woodland. **FOODPLANTS and FIELD NOTES** The following extended notes and observations are provided to encourage field work beyond reconfirming the traditional view that this butterfly has two generations per year, where it feeds on Holly in the first generation in May–Jun, and Common Ivy in the second in Jul–Sep. The butterfly is widely associated with Holly and Common Ivy. On female Holly trees, the larva feeds on the flowers and young fruits via a hole in the side, while on male Holly trees it feeds on the young tender leaves. On Common Ivy, it usually feeds on the flower buds via holes in the side. The presence of a larva may be given away by these holes or by an attendant ant.

First-generation larvae
First-generation larvae have been found feeding on young Common Ivy leaves. In the west of England both generations have been found feeding on the flowers and developing seedpods of gorses, and those of the second are confirmed to be on Western Gorse. On Scilly, where the butterfly is common and Holly is rare, egg-laying has been observed on the tender shoots of Gorse and flower buds of Bramble, and first-instar larvae have been observed to make a hole in the side of Bramble flower buds. Feeding on the pollen of Bramble flowers has been noted elsewhere. First-generation larvae have also been found on Alder Buckthorn flowers, Wall Cotoneaster, Dogwood and *Escallonia* flowers, and one has been found with its front end within the flesh of a raspberry that subsequently produced a perfect butterfly.

Second-generation larvae
A second-generation larva has been found in late Aug feeding on the leaves of Grey Willow, although it produced a small adult that failed to expand its wings properly. A final-instar larva has been found in a flower of Western Gorse. Egg-laying has been observed on Heather and Lucerne and the resulting larvae reared on those plants in captivity. They bit holes in the base of the Heather flowers, putting their heads through and apparently eating the inside of the flowers. They were pinkish green in the final instar. Egg-laying has also been observed on a range of non-native garden shrubs, including brooms, dogwoods,

Firethorn, Lewis's Hebe, Cherry Laurel, Snowberry and Evergreen Spindle. It is not known whether larvae can successfully complete their life cycle on these plants.

Foodplant preference requires more observations, but the larva appears to be truly polyphagous. Pupates attached by a silk pad and girdle deep among vegetation. The colour change before pupation suggests that the larva may also pupate on the ground, and a freshly emerged adult has been observed low down among grasses. Overwinters as a pupa. There remains much to be discovered about the life history of this widespread and increasingly common species.

LARGE BLUE
Phengaris arion

NOT ILLUSTRATED
61.013 (1581)

CR. Protected species. Ssp. *eutyphron* Became extinct in 1979. Ssp. *arion* Introduced from 1983 and is now well established in a number of areas and is spreading to new sites under favourable management. **FIELD CHARACTERS** Body unmarked and whitish in the final instar, but will not be found openly in the field as it lives within the nest of the red ant *Myrmica sabuleti*. **HABITATS** Unimproved acid grassland on the coast, and limestone grassland inland. Critical to survival is a warm, sparsely vegetated microhabitat with abundance of the host ant and foodplants. **FOODPLANTS** Mainly flowers of Wild Thyme. A few populations are solely on flowers of Wild Marjoram, and some are on a mix of the two. Feeds on flowers until end of third instar. Then on the brood of *M. sabuleti*. Larvae are often carried into the nests of other species of *Myrmica* red ants, but these rarely survive as larvae release the scent of *M. sabuleti*, and are usually killed. **FIELD NOTES** Jul–May. The life history is described in the *Introduction* (p. 60).

SILVER-STUDDED BLUE
Plebejus argus

PLATE 8
61.014 (1571)

VU. Ssp. *argus* Very local and found in three distinct habitats in England and Wales. Ssp. *caernensis* Great Ormes Head peninsula and Dulas Valley, north Wales. Overall, the range of this species has declined very significantly in the past 50+ years, and two subspecies (*masseyi* and *cretaceus*) have become extinct. **FIELD CHARACTERS** Head black. Body green or purplish brown with a dark purplish-brown dorsal stripe, edged with a white line T2–A6, and sometimes broadened into a dark purplish-brown patch on T1 and A7. In the green form there may be slightly oblique, dark green dashes laterally, more or less forming one or two lateral stripes, and these may be edged paler, or sometimes there may be only slightly oblique pale streaks laterally. Subspiracular line white. In the brown form, there is one dark purplish-brown lateral stripe formed of slightly oblique dashes, edged paler. Newcomer's gland is present on A7 and a pair of tentacle organs on A8. **HABITATS** Ssp. *argus* Limestone grassland and old quarries, dry and damp heathland, and sand dunes. Ssp. *caernensis* Limestone grassland. The species is most frequent where habitats are short and sparsely vegetated, except on humid heaths in the south where vegetation is taller. **FOODPLANTS** Gorses, Cross-leaved Heath, Heather and Bell Heather on heathland, Common Bird's-foot-trefoil, Common Rock-rose and Horseshoe Vetch on limestone grassland, and Common Bird's-foot-trefoil on sand dunes. Also reported on Broom and restharrows. **FIELD NOTES** Mar–Jun. As soon as the egg hatches, the larva is attractive to the black ants *Lasius alienus* and *L. niger*, and is likely to be taken into the ants' nest almost immediately. Spends the day in the nest, emerging at dusk to feed, and is possibly carried by the ants to do so. Pupates within the ants' nest. Overwinters as a fully developed larva in the egg.

BROWN ARGUS
Aricia agestis

PLATE 8
61.015 (1572)

LC. Formerly a very local species but now widespread in much of England. Expanding its range northwards, but remains local and coastal in the south-west and in Wales. **FIELD CHARACTERS** Head black. Body green with a dark green dorsal line and indistinct pale green lateral streaks. Subspiracular line white, edged above and below with red to a variable extent such that either colour may dominate. Newcomer's gland is present on A7 and a pair of tentacle organs on A8. **HABITATS** Arable field margins and rough, disturbed grassland, calcareous grassland, old quarries and railway lines, road verges, sand dunes, and open areas in woodland. **SIMILAR SPECIES** Northern Brown Argus is indistinguishable, but their ranges do not currently overlap. On calcareous grassland sites, the leaf mine on Common Rock-rose made by Cistus Forester has a larger entry hole than that of either brown argus species. In addition, the leaf mines of the micro-moth *Coleophora ochrea* (Coleophoridae) are usually much larger. The mines are also usually associated with the tubular case made with the leaves of the plant, which are up to 1–1.5cm long, and in which the larva lives. **FOODPLANTS** Common Rock-rose on calcareous grassland. In other habitats on Dove's-foot Crane's-bill and Common Stork's-bill. Egg-laying has been observed on Cut-leaved, Hedgerow and Meadow crane's-bills, so these may be foodplants. **FIELD NOTES** Jun–Jul and Sep–Apr, in two generations, except in the north of its range where one is the norm. Eggs are normally laid on the underside of the leaves, though some are on the upperside on Dove's-foot Crane's-bill and Common Stork's-bill. On hatching, feeds on the underside of the leaf, making a small hole from which it mines a small area within the leaf that is visible from the upper surface. Only the anterior part of the larva enters the leaf. Later it feeds on the whole leaf, resting on the underside. Has been observed feeding on the seeds of Dove's-foot Crane's-bill. Its presence may be given away by attendant ants, which, unlike the larva, are conspicuous. Pupates on the ground, most pupae being taken away by ants and buried in earthen cells.

NORTHERN BROWN ARGUS
Aricia artaxerxes

PLATE 8
61.016 (1573)

VU. Ssp. *artaxerxes* Very local in northern England and Scotland, and declining in range, especially in the south. Ssp. *salmacis* Described from Durham populations. **SIMILAR SPECIES** Brown Argus. The feeding damage caused by Cistus Forester is also similar. The ranges of the micro-moth *Coleophora ochrea* (Coleophoridae) and Northern Brown Argus do not overlap. **HABITATS** Associated with free-draining, unimproved grasslands where Common Rock-rose grows, and in ungrazed or lightly grazed situations. Favoured areas include the foodplant in association with some bare ground, and scattered scrub or boulders for shelter. Typical habitat includes exposed coastal locations, steep grassland slopes, limestone pavement, old quarries and sand dunes. **FOODPLANT** Common Rock-rose. **FIELD NOTES** Jul–May. Eggs are laid on the upperside of the leaves. At first the larva feeds on the underside of the leaf, making a small hole from which it mines a small area within the leaf that is visible from the upper surface. It diapauses over winter when small, and in spring basks in sunshine before resuming feeding. It continues to mine leaves at first, but when larger it feeds on the whole leaf, resting on the underside. Occasionally attended by ants in spring. Pupates on a silk pad on the ground, or among vegetation attached by silk.

COMMON BLUE
Polyommatus icarus

PLATE 8
61.018 (1574)

LC. Ssp. *icarus* Widespread and sometimes abundant. Ssp. *mariscolore* Widespread in Ireland and north-west Scotland. **FIELD CHARACTERS** Head black. Body green with T2–A6 raised along the dorsum. Dorsal line dark green, edged pale green. There are indistinct dark green diagonal streaks laterally and a white subspiracular line. Newcomer's gland is present on A7 and a pair of tentacle organs on A8. **SIMILAR SPECIES** The leaf mines on Common Bird's-foot-trefoil made when the larva is small are similar to those of the micro-moth *Coleophora discordella* (Coleophoridae). The feedings of *Coleophora* are usually found along with the somewhat pistol-shaped tubular case, made of leaves, in which the larva lives. Recording of either species should not be made from finding the whitish blotches alone. **HABITATS** Grassy places in a wide variety of habitats, including unimproved grassland on all soil types, old quarries and railway embankments, sand dunes, vegetated shingle, waste ground, and open areas in woodland. Also in urban areas such as cemeteries, and occasionally gardens, especially where wildflowers are introduced. **FOODPLANTS** Widely on Common Bird's-foot-trefoil. Also reported on Bird's-foot, Greater Bird's-foot-trefoil, Burnet-saxifrage, Red and White clovers, Black Medick, Common and other restharrows, Lesser Trefoil and Yarrow. May switch foodplants between generations. **FIELD NOTES** There are two or three generations in the south and one in the north. The phenology is complex. The larva may be seen in any month of the year, with some becoming fully fed in summer months and producing a second generation, while others remain small and overwinter at this size. At first feeds on the underside of the leaf, making a small hole from which it mines a small area within the leaf that is visible from the upper surface. Only the anterior part of the larva enters the leaf. Later, it feeds on the whole leaf, flowers and fruits. Final-instar larvae are attractive to ants, but ants are not always found with them. Pupates on the ground or on the lower stem of the foodplant.

ADONIS BLUE
Polyommatus bellargus

PLATE 8
61.019 (1576)

NT. Very local in the south Midlands, and southern and south-east England. Currently undergoing a slight expansion in range. **FIELD CHARACTERS** Head black. Body green with a dark central line, either side of which is a yellow dash on a raised ridge T2–A6. Subspiracular line yellow, with yellow dashes below ventrally. Newcomer's gland is present on A7 and a pair of tentacle organs on A8. The colour changes to dull brown for diapause. **HABITATS** Requires hot microhabitats on calcareous grassland, on the coast and inland, preferring short turf (1–4cm in height). Also in old quarries where vegetation height is variable. **SIMILAR SPECIES** Chalk Hill Blue shows no obvious constant differences. However, Adonis Blue larvae will be near fully fed in spring when Chalk Hill Blue is hatching from the egg, and larvae of Chalk Hill Blue will be fully fed by the time the first-generation larvae of Adonis Blue are starting to feed. Also, Adonis Blue larvae feed during the day, and Chalk Hill Blue mainly at night. **FOODPLANT** Horseshoe Vetch. **FIELD NOTES** Jun–Jul and Sep–Apr, in two generations. It is likely that the second generation is partial, as a first-brood larva reared in captivity from an egg developed slowly over the summer and was still small in its fourth out of five instars in early Sep. At first feeds on the upperside of the leaf, making a small hole from which it mines a small area within the leaf. Only the anterior part of the larva enters the leaf. It may also graze the leaf surface. Later, it eats the whole leaf, by day. Between feeding bouts and at night the larva may be buried in the ground by attendant ants. The most frequent ant species in attendance are the red ant *Myrmica sabuleti* and the black ant *Lasius niger*. Pupates in the ground, having been buried by ants, or within the brood chambers of an ants' nest.

CHALK HILL BLUE
Polyommatus coridon

PLATE 8
61.020 (1575)

NT. Very local in the Midlands, and southern and south-east England. It appears to be declining in some areas, especially in the west of its range. **SIMILAR SPECIES** Adonis Blue. **HABITATS** Calcareous grassland, on the coast and inland, and old quarries; inhabits any aspect although prefers south- and west-facing. Egg-laying is on vegetation in turf 2–10cm in height. **FOODPLANTS** Almost exclusively Horseshoe Vetch, but Common Bird's-foot-trefoil and Kidney Vetch also reported historically as principal foodplants. Larvae have been found feeding on Red and White clovers, and are reported on Bird's-foot, Wild Liquorice and Crown Vetch. **FIELD NOTES** Apr–Jun. At first grazes the leaf surface, usually from the underside and leaving the opposite epidermis intact. Later, the larva eats the whole leaf, feeding mostly at dusk and at night. Ants attend it and may bury it during the day. Red *Myrmica* and black *Lasius* ants attend the larva, as well as the subterranean yellow ant *Lasius flavus*, which pursues larvae above ground at night. Pupates in the ground under the foodplant in a cell of soil created by ants, or within an ants' nest. Overwinters as a fully developed larva in the egg.

DREPANOIDEA
DREPANIDAE HOOK-TIP AND LUTESTRING MOTHS

This family has about 1,000 species worldwide, with 16 resident in the British Isles. The larvae have notched heads. In the subfamily Drepaninae they rest with their rear ends raised. The anal claspers are absent and the abdomen ends in a single point. The larva sits exposed on the upper surface of a leaf. In the subfamily Thyatirinae the larvae have weak anal claspers and rest exposed or in spun leaves.

Scarce Hook-tip ×1.25

Scalloped Hook-tip larva, contrast with earlier instar (p. 54)

Common Lutestring larva

DREPANINAE

SCALLOPED HOOK-TIP
Falcaria lacertinaria

PLATE 9
65.001 (1645)

Common. Increasingly recorded in Scotland and Ireland. **FIELD CHARACTERS** In early instars, the body is alternating pale brown or whitish and dark brown. Rests in a curled position, resembling an insectivorous bird's dropping. The final instar is pale brownish or orangey brown, heavily mottled black. Pinacula pale brownish or whitish, broadly surrounded with orangey-brown shading, and forming a variably raised subdorsal row, especially on T2–T3 where strongly raised pinacula are paired, and on A8. Dorsal line pale brown T1–T3 and comprising black dashes on most abdominal segments. Anal clasper absent. Abdomen ends in a short red projection. **HABITATS** Bogs, heathland, scrub and woodland. **FOODPLANTS** Downy and Silver birches, preferring smaller bushes. **FIELD NOTES** Jun–Jul and Aug–Sep where there is a partial second generation (most of its range), and Jul–Aug where there is one generation (Scotland). Sits exposed on the upper leaf surface. In early instars it feeds from the upper surface, leaving the lower surface brown and intact, and it sits in the brown patch. In final instar it eats the full leaf thickness. Pupates in a silken cocoon within a folded leaf of the foodplant. Overwinters as a pupa.

OAK HOOK-TIP
Watsonalla binaria

PLATE 9
65.002 (1646)

Common. Has declined significantly in abundance in recent decades. **FIELD CHARACTERS** Body various shades of brown. Dorsal line brown, and sometimes faint or broken. Three broad, rounded dorsal patches, with the middle one at least paler than the body colour: T1–A2, tapering posteriorly to a point on the dorsum, where usually edged white; A3–A7, tapering at either end and usually edged with a dark line; A7–A9, usually edged paler. A dorsal projection with two points on T3. Anal clasper absent. Abdomen ends in a narrow point.

SIMILAR SPECIES Barred Hook-tip is indistinguishable but feeds on Beech. **HABITATS** Mainly oak woodland. Also hedgerows in wooded landscapes, parkland and occasionally gardens. **FOODPLANTS** Pedunculate and Sessile oaks, and possibly Turkey Oak. Also occasionally recorded on Silver Birch. **FIELD NOTES** Jun–Jul and Aug–Sep, in two generations. Sits exposed on the upper surface of a leaf. Pupates in a cocoon spun into a folded leaf of the foodplant. Overwinters as a pupa.

BARRED HOOK-TIP
Watsonalla cultraria

PLATE 9
65.003 (1647)

Local. Appears to be spreading in the north of its range, and in Ireland. **SIMILAR SPECIES** Oak Hook-tip. **HABITATS** Mainly Beech woodland. Also among mature Beech trees in well-wooded landscapes. **FOODPLANT** Beech. **FIELD NOTES** Jun–Jul and Aug–Sep, in two generations. Sits exposed on the upper surface of a leaf. Pupates in a cocoon spun into a folded leaf of the foodplant. Overwinters as a pupa.

DUSKY HOOK-TIP
Drepana curvatula

PLATE 9
65.004 (1649)

Immigrant; recent colonist. Appears to have established at least temporarily in Kent. **SIMILAR SPECIES** Pebble Hook-tip. **HABITATS** Woodland in Kent. **FOODPLANTS** Alder, birches and oaks on the Continent. **FIELD NOTES** Larva has yet to be found in Great Britain. Jun–Jul and Sep on the Continent. Overwinters as a pupa.

PEBBLE HOOK-TIP
Drepana falcataria

PLATE 9
65.005 (1648)

Common. Widespread, but rare or absent at high altitude. **FIELD CHARACTERS** Body green with sparse dark hairs and whitish pinacula. Pinacula on T2–A2 are raised on reddish-brown projections. A broad brownish or purplish-brown band across the dorsal area, sometimes less extensive T1–A1. Anal clasper absent. Abdomen ends in a blunt point. **SIMILAR SPECIES** Dusky Hook-tip is indistinguishable in the field. Where distributions overlap, larvae should be reared to confirm identity. **HABITATS** Gardens, heathland and wooded heathland, riverbanks and streamsides, scrub, and carr and other woodlands. **FOODPLANTS** Mainly Alder, and Downy and Silver birches. Also reported on Aspen, oaks and White Willow. **FIELD NOTES** Late Jun–late Jul and Sep in two generations in the south, the second being partial. Jul–Aug in one generation in the north. Sits exposed on the upper surface of a leaf. Pupates in a cocoon spun into a folded leaf or between leaves of the foodplant. Overwinters as a pupa.

SCARCE HOOK-TIP
Sabra harpagula

PLATE 9
65.006 (1650)

RDB; suspected immigrant. Resident in the lower Wye Valley. **FIELD CHARACTERS** Body brown. Dorsal line brown with an irregular yellow or pale brown band across the dorsal area, wide on T3, narrow on A2, wide between A4 and A5, narrow between A5 and A6, and expanded on A7. There is a subdorsal brown spot within the yellow band on A8. A dorsal projection with paired points on T3. Anal clasper absent. Abdomen ends in a narrow point. **HABITATS** Woodland where the foodplant is common. **FOODPLANTS** Small-leaved Lime in Great Britain. Known to feed also on Alder, birches and oaks in Europe. **FIELD NOTES** Late Jul–late Sep, or occasionally mid-Oct. Rarely seen on lower branches or epicormic growth (young stems growing directly from the trunk) at the base of trees, so the larva is presumed to prefer the tree canopy. Pupates in a cocoon spun between leaves of the foodplant. Overwinters as a pupa.

CHINESE CHARACTER
Cilix glaucata

PLATE 9
65.007 (1651)

Common. **FIELD CHARACTERS** Body varies from greyish to brownish. Dorsal line dark brown, sometimes whitish and thicker on T3, with paired projections on either side T2–T3, A3 and A8–A9, with the largest being on T3. A pale, oval-shaped dorsal patch T3–A2. Spiracular line dark, edged paler above T1–T3, and lying diagonally across A1, and subspiracular line whitish, from A6 posteriorly. Anal clasper absent. Abdomen ends in a narrow point. **HABITATS** Gardens, hedgerows, scrub and woodland. **FOODPLANTS** Mainly Blackthorn and Hawthorn. Also reported on Crab Apple, Bramble, Pear, Rowan and occasionally birches. **FIELD NOTES** Mid-Jun–mid-Jul and late Aug–Oct, in two generations. Pupates in a cocoon spun in a bark crevice or between leaves. Overwinters as a pupa.

THYATIRINAE

PEACH BLOSSOM
Thyatira batis

PLATE 9
65.008 (1652)

Common. **FIELD CHARACTERS** When small the body is brownish grey with a large pale dorsal patch T2–T3 and smaller pale patches A2–A6. In final instar the head is notched. Body brown with a dorsal hump and a paired projection on T2, and dorsal humps A2–A6, the smallest on A6. The sides of these abdominal humps are darker, with similar shading on A1. When viewed from above, there are pale forward-pointing triangles A1–A6. A dark dorsal patch on A8 with a slight hump posteriorly. **HABITATS** Mainly scrub and woodland. Also gardens, derelict ground and other urban habitats. **FOODPLANTS** Bramble and Raspberry. Also reported on Meadowsweet. **FIELD NOTES** Early Jul–mid-Sep. Sits exposed on the foodplant when young, resembling a bird's dropping, later hiding on the ground by day and feeding at night. Pupates in or on the ground. Overwinters as a pupa.

BUFF ARCHES
Habrosyne pyritoides

PLATE 9
65.009 (1653)

Common. Scarce in southern Scotland. Has declined significantly in abundance in recent decades. **FIELD CHARACTERS** Head notched. Body brown. Dorsal line black with a white spot laterally on A1, sometimes with further, smaller spots A2–A3. **HABITATS** Gardens, scrub and woodland, apparently preferring shaded areas. **FOODPLANTS** Mainly Bramble and Dewberry. Also recorded on Hawthorn, Hazel and Raspberry. **FIELD NOTES** Late Jul–Nov. Feeds at night. Pupates in the ground. Overwinters as a pupa.

FIGURE OF EIGHTY
Tethea ocularis

PLATE 9
65.010 (1654)

Ssp. *octogesimea* Common. Appears to be spreading in Scotland. **FIELD CHARACTERS** Head notched and orange, with shiny prothoracic and anal plates body-coloured. Body bluish green, whitish green or pale green. Dorsal line darker green. Two small black spots laterally on T1, and often another subdorsally on T2. Black spots on other segments have been reported. Spiracular line whitish. **SIMILAR SPECIES** Poplar Lutestring has a range of variation that overlaps Figure of Eighty, making reliable separation difficult. Figure of Eighty does not occur in the far north. **HABITATS** Gardens, hedgerows, riverbanks, scrub, shelterbelts, and carr and other woodlands. **FOODPLANTS** Aspen, black-poplars and White Poplar. **FIELD NOTES** Mid-Jul–Sep. Hides between spun leaves by day and emerges to feed at night. Pupates between leaves that fall to the ground in autumn. Overwinters as a pupa.

POPLAR LUTESTRING
Tethea or

PLATE 9
65.011 (1655)

Ssp. *or* Local. Extends to the Scottish border. Ssp. *scotica* Local. Scottish Highlands and the Hebrides. Ssp. *hibernica* Ireland. **FIELD CHARACTERS** Head notched and orange, with shiny prothoracic and anal plates body-coloured. Body bluish green or pale green. Small black spots laterally T1–A9, or limited to one on T1, or entirely absent. Spiracular line whitish. **SIMILAR SPECIES** Figure of Eighty. **HABITATS** Established scrub on heathland and moorland, and woodland, including recent plantations. **FOODPLANTS** Mainly Aspen. Also reported on poplars. **FIELD NOTES** Mid-Jul–Oct. Hides between spun leaves by day and emerges to feed at night. Pupates between leaves that fall to the ground in autumn. Overwinters as a pupa.

SATIN LUTESTRING
Tetheella fluctuosa

PLATE 9
65.012 (1656)

Local. **FIELD CHARACTERS** Head notched with two rounded lobes, orangey brown, and sometimes black above. Prothoracic plate white or whitish brown. Body dark greenish grey with paler speckling, especially over the dorsal area, and pale greenish white ventrally. **HABITATS** Woodland on former heathland in south-east England, and mature woodland. **FOODPLANTS** Alder and birches. **FIELD NOTES** Late Jul–Oct. Feeds at night, hiding between spun leaves by day. Pupates between leaves that fall to the ground in autumn. Overwinters as a pupa.

COMMON LUTESTRING
Ochropacha duplaris

PLATE 9
65.013 (1657)

Common. Has increased significantly in abundance in recent decades. **FIELD CHARACTERS** Head notched and orange. Prothoracic plate black. Body greyish green over the dorsal area and greyish white below. Pinacula small and pale with black centres, giving them the appearance of being pale dorsally and black below. **SIMILAR SPECIES** Yellow Horned has large white pinacula and feeds in late spring and early summer. **HABITATS** Scrub on heathland and in river valleys, and woodland, including coppice. **FOODPLANTS** Mainly birches. Also reported on Alder, Hazel and oaks. **FIELD NOTES** Late Jul–early Oct. Feeds at night, hiding between spun leaves by day. Pupates between leaves that fall to the ground in autumn. Overwinters as a pupa.

OAK LUTESTRING
Cymatophorina diluta

PLATE 9
65.014 (1658)

Ssp. *hartwiegi* Local. Has declined significantly in abundance in recent decades. **FIELD CHARACTERS** Head black. Body pale yellowish grey or greenish grey, with a dark grey dorsal line and an indistinct dark greyish lateral band. **HABITATS** Woodland, especially ancient woodland, with mature oak trees. **FOODPLANTS** Pedunculate and Sessile oaks. **FIELD NOTES** Apr–Jun. Hides between spun leaves by day and emerges to feed at night. Pupates in a cocoon among leaves in the tree. Overwinters as an egg on a twig.

FROSTED GREEN
Polyploca ridens

PLATE 9
65.015 (1660)

Local. Rare in northern England. **FIELD CHARACTERS** Head notched and orange. Body greenish grey, grey or greenish white, with large whitish pinacula. Well-marked examples have a thin grey dorsal line, broadly edged with yellow, and interrupted yellow subdorsal, lateral and spiracular stripes, and there may be black spots subdorsally and laterally. Greenish-white forms may be unmarked or have subdorsal and supraspiracular rows of black spots. **HABITATS** Mature hedgerow trees in wooded landscapes, and woodland, especially ancient woodland. **FOODPLANTS** Pedunculate and Sessile oaks. **FIELD NOTES** Late May–mid-Jul. Rests by day within a spun leaf and emerges to feed at night. Pupates in or on the ground. Overwinters as a pupa, sometimes for two years.

YELLOW HORNED
Achlya flavicornis

PLATE 9
65.016 (1659)

Ssp. *galbanus* Common. England, Wales and Ireland. Ssp. *scotica* Common. Mainland Scotland and Inner Hebrides. **FIELD CHARACTERS** When very small the larva is black with white pinacula. The final instar has a notched orange head. Prothoracic plate black. Body greenish grey, and sometimes blackish or greyish over the dorsal area, with large white pinacula. Dorsal line pale, and there may be subdorsal and lateral rows of black spots. **SIMILAR SPECIES** Common Lutestring. **HABITATS** Scrub on heathland and moorland, and woodland, including coppice. **FOODPLANTS** Downy and Silver birches, often on low-growing vegetation. **FIELD NOTES** Mid-May–mid-Jul. Hides between tightly spun leaves by day and emerges to feed at night. Pupates on or in the ground. Overwinters as a pupa, sometimes for two years.

LASIOCAMPOIDEA
LASIOCAMPIDAE EGGAR AND
LAPPET MOTHS

This is a family of about
2,200 species worldwide,
with 11 residents in the
British Isles. The larvae
are cylindrical and hairy. Some

Lackey ×1.25

species spin communal webs and live
gregariously until the final instar. They
are hairy to a greater or lesser extent.
The hairs are irritant and can cause an
unpleasant itchy rash.

Fox Moth larva early instar ×1.25

Fox Moth larva

POECILOCAMPINAE

DECEMBER MOTH
Poecilocampa populi

PLATE 10
66.001 (1631)

Common. **FIELD CHARACTERS** Body greyish, mottled black and yellowish or
whitish. There is a sparse covering of short dark hairs above the spiracular level
and longer pale hairs below. Dorsal line grey, mottled black, and sometimes
ill-defined, with a subdorsal row of orange or whitish spots, and sometimes a
yellowish lateral line with yellowish or whitish spots. There is a transverse reddish-
brown band across the dorsum on T1. **HABITATS** Hedgerows, scrub and woodland.
Sometimes in gardens. **FOODPLANTS** Wide variety of woody plants, including Alder,
Ash, Aspen, birches, Blackthorn, elms, Hawthorn, limes, oaks, poplars and willows.
FIELD NOTES Apr–Jun. Feeds at night, resting by day on a twig or tree bark. Pupates in a cocoon among loose
bark, or on or just in the ground. Flies in the early winter, spending the rest of the winter as an egg.

PALE EGGAR
Trichiura crataegi

PLATE 10
66.002 (1632)

Common. Widely distributed over much of England and Scotland, but has
declined significantly in abundance in recent decades. Local in Wales and very local
in Ireland. **FIELD CHARACTERS** Body bluish grey with a sparse covering of long and
short pale hairs. Markings very variable. Often there is a subdorsal orange line or
row of orange spots and dashes, above which are orange verrucae and markings.
There may be bright yellow transverse bands or dull orange lines across the
dorsum. The larva may be extensively shaded whitish laterally or have white lateral
spots T1–A8. There may be a yellow lateral line. If present, subspiracular line or
spots orange or yellow. **FOODPLANTS** Frequently on birches, Blackthorn and Hawthorn. Also reported on Crab Apple, Bilberry,
Bramble, Hazel, Heather, Bell Heather, oaks, poplars and willows. **FIELD NOTES** Apr–Jun, and in northern areas
until spring of the second year. Pupates in an oval cocoon on the ground. Overwinters as an egg, but in the
Scottish Highlands and possibly northern England a second winter is passed as a near fully grown larva.

MALACOSOMATINAE

LACKEY
Malacosoma neustria

PLATE 10
66.003 (1634)

Common. Has declined severely in abundance in recent decades. Widely distributed in southern and eastern England, local and coastal in Wales, and local in Ireland. **FIELD CHARACTERS** Head bluish grey with two black spots. Body dull bluish with a sparse covering of dark hairs above the spiracular level and denser, orangey-brown hairs below. Dorsal stripe white, edged with a black line and an orange stripe beyond. Subdorsal stripe orange, blackish above and edged below with a black line. Subspiracular stripe orange, edged with black lines. Two black dorsal spots on T1 and a black hump on A8. **HABITATS** Open habitats, including gardens, hedgerows, scrub and open woodland. **FOODPLANTS** Mainly on woody plants in the rose family such as Apple, Blackthorn, Bramble, cherries, ornamental Shrubby Cinquefoil, Wall Cotoneaster, Dog-rose, Gooseberry, Hawthorn and Raspberry. Also reported on Silver Birch, elms, Hazel, oaks including Holm Oak, Grey Poplar and willows. **FIELD NOTES** Apr–Jun. Lives gregariously in a conspicuous white silken tent. Late in final instar the larva disperses to complete feeding singly. Pupates among the foodplant in a silken cocoon, the outside of which is loosely woven and contains a yellow powder. Overwinters as an egg in a batch encircling a twig.

GROUND LACKEY
Malacosoma castrensis

PLATE 10
66.004 (1635)

Na. Restricted to coastal parts of north Kent, Essex and Suffolk, and Axmouth in Devon. **FIELD CHARACTERS** Head grey. Body bluish black with orangey-brown hairs. Extent of markings very variable. Dorsal line or stripe white, edged black, with a variable amount of orange subdorsally, a variable amount of bluish or bluish grey laterally, and an orange lateral stripe. **HABITATS** Coastal and estuarine saltmarshes, and vegetated shingle. **FOODPLANTS** A variety of low-growing herbaceous plants, including Sea Arrowgrass, Sea Campion, Wild Carrot, Curled Dock, Golden-samphire, grasses, Grass-leaved Orache, Sea Plantain, Common Sea-lavender, Sea-purslane, Thrift and Sea Wormwood. Also recorded on willows. **FIELD NOTES** Apr–Jul. Lives gregariously when young in a web spread across the vegetation, and larvae disperse to feed singly when larger. Pupates low down among vegetation in a transparent silken cocoon, the outside of which is loosely woven and contains a yellow powder. Overwinters as an egg in a batch encircling a stem.

LASIOCAMPINAE

SMALL EGGAR
Eriogaster lanestris

PLATE 10
66.005 (1633)

Nb. Has decreased in abundance and distribution very significantly over the past 50 years. Now found in a few broad geographical areas in England, Wales and Ireland. Populations fluctuate annually in any one area. **FIELD CHARACTERS** Body bluish grey, or blackish tinged bluish, with long brown hairs and cushions of short orangey-brown hairs subdorsally T2–A9. A whitish-yellow lateral line and transverse dashes between each cushion. Young larvae are velvety black with a whitish-yellow lateral line and transverse dashes. **HABITATS** Mainly in hedgerows and scattered banks of scrub on grasslands. Sometimes in gardens, planted bushes on roadside verges, and woodland rides. **FOODPLANTS** Most frequently on Blackthorn, and regularly also on Dog-rose and Hawthorn. Also reported on Almond, Apple, birches, elms, Juneberry, Plum, Spindle and Grey Willow. **FIELD NOTES** Apr–Jul. Lives gregariously in a conspicuous and densely woven white tent until part way through last instar, when the larva disperses to complete feeding singly. Pupates in a hard oval brown cocoon among the foodplant near the ground. Overwinters as a pupa, sometimes over two or three winters, or even up to seven.

GRASS EGGAR
Lasiocampa trifolii

PLATE 10
66.006 (1636)

Ssp. *trifolii* Na. Scattered along the south and west coasts of England and Wales. Also on heathland in Dorset. Pale Grass Eggar ssp. *flava* RDB. Dungeness, Kent, and a similar form occurs among populations in the Channel Islands. **FIELD CHARACTERS** Body densely covered with short orangey-brown hairs and longer whitish hairs. An orange transverse band, speckled with brown, on T1, and an orange anal plate, speckled with brown. **HABITATS** Cliffs, heathland, sand dunes and vegetated shingle. **FOODPLANTS** Wide variety, but varies between colonies. Main foodplants at specific sites are: Bramble (Prawle Point, Devon), Tree Lupin (Hayling Island, Hampshire), Marram (Studland, Dorset) False Oat-grass (Dungeness) and Creeping Willow (Formby, Lancashire). Also reported on Common Bird's-foot-trefoil, Blackthorn, Broom, clovers, Gorse, Heather, Lucerne, Sickle Medick, Ribbed Melilot, Wild Plum, Spiny Restharrow, Sheep's Sorrel, Thrift, Kidney Vetch and other willows. **FIELD NOTES** Late Mar–Jul. Feeds at night, resting by day fully exposed. Pupates in an oval brown cocoon on the ground. Overwinters as an egg, but hatches from late Jan.

OAK EGGAR
Lasiocampa quercus

PLATE 10
66.007 (1637)

Ssp. *quercus* Common. One-year life cycle. Northern Eggar ssp. *callunae* Common. Two-year life cycle. Northern Eggar is typically a moorland moth of northern England, Wales and Scotland, and Oak Eggar is typically found widely elsewhere, away from intensively farmed land. However, the situation is complex, with either one- or two-year life cycles in the Midlands and Welsh borders, and examples resembling Northern Eggar occurring in south-west England and Ireland. **FIELD CHARACTERS** Markedly different in appearance before and after winter diapause. Pre-diapause, the body is bluish, covered with orangey-brown hairs. Forward-pointing dorsal triangles or diamonds on each segment, and these are orange, sometimes mixed whitish anteriorly, and surrounded by black. Post-diapause and in the final instar, the body is densely covered in pale brown hairs, but in some examples these are chocolate brown or dark brown, with black bands between segments that become more apparent when the larva curls up. Lateral stripe comprises white dashes. Spiracles white. **HABITATS** Wide variety, including cliffs, fens, breckland and other grasslands, heathland, hedgerows, moorland, sand dunes, scrub and vegetated shingle. **FOODPLANTS** Wide variety, including Alder, Bilberry, birches, Common Bird's-foot-trefoil, Blackthorn, Bramble, Broom, cherries, Dogwood, Gorse, Hawthorn, Hazel, Heather, Honeysuckle, Common Ivy, montbretias (seeds), oaks, roses, Rowan, Sea-buckthorn, Common Sorrel and willows. **FIELD NOTES** Ssp. *quercus* Aug–Jun. Ssp. *callunae* Jul–Sep of the second year then overwintering as a pupa. Pupates in a tough oval brown cocoon among vegetation or on the ground.

FOX MOTH
Macrothylacia rubi

PLATE 11
66.008 (1638)

Common. **FIELD CHARACTERS** Early instars have a black body, covered in brown hairs, with conspicuous orange bands between segments. The final instar is densely covered in short orangey-brown and longer grey or brown hairs. The orange bands are reduced to small orangey transverse dashes, with narrow black bands between segments that become more apparent when the larva curls up. **HABITATS** Wide variety, including fens, heathland, moorland, sand dunes, vegetated shingle, open woodland, and coastal, chalk, limestone and wet grasslands. **FOODPLANTS** Bilberry, birches, Greater Bird's-foot-trefoil, Blackthorn, Bog-myrtle, Bramble, Salad Burnet, Creeping Cinquefoil, Bloody Crane's-bill, Cross-leaved Heath, Heather, Bell Heather, Knotgrass, Meadowsweet, Pedunculate Oak, Burnet Rose, Wood Sage, Wild Strawberry, Creeping Thistle and willows. **FIELD NOTES** Jun–Apr, and fully fed in Sep. Often seen openly in summer and autumn, and basking in sunshine in early spring. Young larvae have been nicknamed Devil's Gold-rings because of the skin irritation caused by their hairs. Pupates in the spring without feeding again, in a long greyish cocoon.

PINARINAE

PINE-TREE LAPPET
Dendrolimus pini

PLATE 11
66.009 (1639)

Immigrant, and probably long-overlooked resident in one area of Scotland near Inverness – it is not known whether this is as a result of immigration and subsequent colonisation, or accidental importation. The species is a serious forest pest in Europe. **FIELD CHARACTERS** Body various shades of brown, with whitish flecks or more extensive whitish patches across the dorsal area. Short tufts of dark bluish hairs and longer grey hairs dorsally, long brown or grey hairs anteriorly on T1, posteriorly on A10 and below the spiracular level on all segments, and black and white hair tufts dorsally on T2–A1. When the larva flexes anteriorly, black areas mixed with blue are revealed dorsally between segments T2 and T3 and between T3 and A1. **HABITATS** Remnant Caledonian pine forest and mature mixed woodland in Scotland. **FOODPLANT** Recorded on Scots Pine in Scotland. **FIELD NOTES** Jul–May. Feeds on poor-quality needles, ignoring young growth. Captive rearing from the egg in Scotland resulted in larvae overwintering either two or three times. Overwintering for the last time is as a large larva, either in the penultimate or final instar. Pupates in a tough brown cocoon on a branch or the bark of the tree, or in debris on the ground. Overwinters as a larva in moss at the base of a conifer tree.

DRINKER
Euthrix potatoria

PLATE 11
66.010 (1640)

Common. Widespread in much of England, Wales and Ireland; much more local in Scotland. **FIELD CHARACTERS** In early instars, body bluish grey with tufts of short grey hairs and longer hairs arising from T2 and A9. Black across the dorsal area T2–T3 with a central white or yellow patch, and white or yellowish subdorsal dots T2–T3. Subdorsal stripe comprises alternating yellow spots and white or yellow dashes, with yellow spots laterally T1–T3, and short diagonal white or yellow lateral stripes A1–A7. Prolegs yellow. In the final instar, body bluish grey with dorsal and subdorsal stripes of yellow speckles and short subdorsal tufts of blackish hairs A1–A8, two dorsal tufts of long brown or black hairs on T2, a dorsal tuft of long black hairs on A8, and tufts of short white hairs at the spiracular level T2–A8. Prolegs grey. **HABITATS** Wide variety of grassy habitats, with a preference for damp or wet areas, including bogs, ditches, fens, gardens, dry grassland, lowland and upland wet grasslands, heathland, moorland (not at high altitude), scrub, reedbeds, river valleys, and plantation and woodland rides. **FOODPLANTS** Wide variety of mainly coarse grasses, rushes and sedges, including False Brome, Reed Canary-grass, cultivated Ribbon-grass, Cock's-foot, couches, Tufted Hair-grass, Marram, meadow-grasses, Purple Moor-grass, Greater and Lesser pond-sedges, Common Reed, Pendulous Sedge, Wood Small-reed and Greater Tussock-sedge. **FIELD NOTES** Aug–Jun. Often encountered by day at rest, but ascends to feed at night. Pupates in a tough buff-coloured cocoon attached to a stem. Overwinters as a small larva.

LAPPET
Gastropacha quercifolia

PLATE 11
66.012 (1642)

Common. Has declined significantly in recent decades, and is now locally distributed in England from the south-west to East Anglia. **FIELD CHARACTERS** Final instar has a grey body, covered with short grey hairs, with longer brown or grey hairs anteriorly on T1 and below the spiracular level on all segments. A reddish-brown hump on A8 and much smaller paired, slightly projecting reddish-brown spots A1–A7. There are paired white dorsal marks anteriorly on T3. When the larva flexes anteriorly, black areas mixed with blue are revealed dorsally between segments T2 and T3 and between T3 and A1. Occasionally the larva is orangey brown with extensive white patches laterally. In the previous instar each black area between these segments contains a pair of bright orange subdorsal spots. **HABITATS** Hedgerows, and scrub in various situations such as coastal and calcareous grasslands, old quarries, vegetated shingle and in open woodland. **FOODPLANTS** Mainly Blackthorn and Hawthorn, and less often apples. Also reported on Buckthorn, Alder Buckthorn, cherries, Pear and willows. Shows a preference for small, isolated bushes. **FIELD NOTES** Jul–late May. Rests by day low down and closely appressed to the main stem of the foodplant, climbing to feed at night. Pupates in a tough cocoon attached to the stem or twig of the foodplant, usually low down. Overwinters as a small larva.

BOMBYCOIDEA
ENDROMIDAE

This family is known only from the Palearctic region and includes just one species. This species is distributed from the British Isles eastwards across Europe to southern Siberia and the Far East. The larva is characteristically broad-bodied and tapers strongly towards the head.

Kentish Glory egg batch on birch twig

Kentish Glory larva

KENTISH GLORY
Endromis versicolora

PLATE 11
67.001 (1644)

Na. Resident in the eastern and central Scottish Highlands. **FIELD CHARACTERS** Head green with whitish stripes. Body green, paler green without speckles across the dorsum, and green with dark green speckles laterally. Whitish subdorsal stripe on T1. Dorsal line green, with diagonal whitish stripes on abdominal segments, and one at a shallower angle, rising from T3 to T1. There is a hump on A8, with a black line over the tip, and from which descends a whitish stripe to the spiracular level. Spiracles white. When the larva is fully fed the green colour changes to reddish. The newly hatched larva is black with a pair of orange spots on T1. **HABITATS** Moorland and open woodland. Requires plenty of young, regenerating scrub. **FOODPLANTS** Mainly Silver Birch. Also Alder and Downy Birch. **FIELD NOTES** Mid-May–mid-Aug. Feeds gregariously at first, but is solitary in the final instar. Twigs stripped of leaves can indicate the presence of a larva. Eggs are laid in a batch encircling a twig from the outer part of a bush, and selected bushes are less than 2m in height and in sunny situations. Pupates in a rough dark cocoon among leaf litter on the ground. Overwinters as a pupa, sometimes for up to five winters.

SATURNIIDAE EMPEROR MOTHS

There are about 1,300 species in the world, mainly found in the tropics. This family contains some of the largest moths in the world, including the giant silk-moths and moon moths. Larvae have rows of tubercles that give rise to spines and they often spin elaborate cocoons. There is just one species resident in the British Isles.

Emperor Moth larva

SATURNIINAE

EMPEROR MOTH
Saturnia pavonia

PLATE 11
68.001 (1643)

Common. Widespread throughout, but scarce away from semi-natural habitats and in areas of agricultural intensification in lowland England. **FIELD CHARACTERS** Body green with transverse rows of white, yellow or pink tubercles, each tubercle surrounded by a black ring or with black markings more extensive, and sometimes in transverse bands across the dorsum. Black bristles arise from the tubercles. The first-instar larva is black. **HABITATS** Mostly habitats on acidic soils, including bogs, fens, field margins, heathland, hedgerows, moorland, sand dunes, scrub, waste ground and woodland rides. Sometimes also calcareous grassland. **FOODPLANTS** Wide variety, including Mountain Avens, Bilberry, birches, Blackthorn, Bog-myrtle, Bramble, Alder Buckthorn, Salad Burnet, Marsh Cinquefoil, elms, Hawthorn, Hazel, Cross-leaved Heath, Heather, Bell Heather, Hemp-agrimony, Meadowsweet, Purple-loosestrife, Raspberry, Rowan, Tormentil and willows. **FIELD NOTES** Late May–Aug. Feeds gregariously at first, sitting exposed on the foodplant. Pupates among the foodplant, in a brown cocoon with a circle of spiny, forward-pointing fibres at the top that allow exit of the moth but prevent entry of invertebrate predators. Overwinters as a pupa, sometimes over two winters.

SPHINGIDAE HAWK-MOTHS

There are over 1,000 species
so far described worldwide in
this mainly tropical family,
with just nine species
resident in the British Isles.
Several others are frequent or
occasional residents during summer
months following immigration, and a generation of
larvae may be found on appropriate foodplants, often
along the south coasts but sometimes inland. Death's-head
Hawk-moth is more frequently encountered as a larva on Potato
plants in allotments and arable fields than it is as an adult at moth
traps, and is often found well away from the coast. Of those immigrant
species, Humming-bird Hawk-moth is a familiar sight as an adult and a larva, and
appears regularly to be able to survive the winter here as an adult, while other
immigrant species that overwinter on the Continent as a pupa cannot survive.

Eyed Hawk-moth life size

   Larvae of hawk-moths in the British Isles characteristically have a horn at their
tail end, although it is very small in Small Elephant Hawk-moth. Larvae may be
frequently encountered while searching foodplants, and it is often their black frass
resting on leaves or on the ground below that gives away their location rather
than the larvae themselves, which tend to be remarkably cryptic against their
background. Larvae usually pupate near the foodplant and pupae can be found by
sorting through debris or the soil below.

Convolvulus Hawk-moth larva

SMERINTHINAE

LIME HAWK-MOTH
Mimas tiliae

PLATE 12
69.001 (1979)

Common. Widespread in much of England, more local in Wales, and in Ireland only in Dublin. **FIELD CHARACTERS** Body green, with yellow diagonal stripes on abdominal segments, above which are paler green or red marks. Horn on A8 blue above and red below, and a raised yellow or red area on the anal flap. In fully fed larvae, the green colour changes completely to pinkish brown. **SIMILAR SPECIES** Eyed Hawk-moth and Poplar Hawk-moth both lack the raised area on the anal flap. Poplar Hawk-moth has a yellow horn and usually yellow diagonal stripes, whereas Eyed Hawk-moth has a blue horn and usually white diagonal stripes. **HABITATS** Gardens, urban streets and parks, trees in open countryside, and woodland. **FOODPLANTS** Mainly on elms and limes. Also reported on Alder, Downy and Silver birches, cherries, Hazel and oaks, and in the London area on planes. **FIELD NOTES** Late Jun–mid-Sep. Usually pupates in the ground near the tree, but has been found high up in trapped leaf litter. Overwinters as a pupa.

EYED HAWK-MOTH
Smerinthus ocellata

PLATE 12
69.002 (1980)

Common. Widespread in Wales and Ireland, and over much of England except in the far north, and very local in south-west Scotland. **FIELD CHARACTERS** Body green with white, occasionally pale yellow, diagonal stripes on the abdominal segments. Rarely there may be red spots on the body. Horn on A8 blue. When fully fed, the larva develops a somewhat reddish-brown hue dorsally, but does not change colour as dramatically as the Lime Hawk-moth. **SIMILAR SPECIES** Lime Hawk-moth and Poplar Hawk-moth. **HABITATS** Dune-slacks, gardens and urban parks, heathland, orchards, scrub in fens and marshes, river valleys and woodland. **FOODPLANTS** Mainly Apple, Crab Apple and willows. Also reported on Aspen and other poplars, Blackthorn and Wild Privet. **FIELD NOTES** Late Jun–Sep or Oct. Pupates in the ground near the foodplant. Overwinters as a pupa.

POPLAR HAWK-MOTH
Laothoe populi

PLATE 12
69.003 (1981)

Common. **FIELD CHARACTERS** Body green with diagonal yellow, occasionally whitish, stripes on the abdominal segments. There is a form with large red spots around the spiracles and a variable number of red subdorsal spots. Horn on A8 yellow. **SIMILAR SPECIES** Lime Hawk-moth and Eyed Hawk-moth. **HABITATS** Dune-slacks, gardens and urban parks, heathland, moorland, orchards, scrub in fens and marshes, river valleys and woodland. **FOODPLANTS** Aspen and other poplars, and willows, especially Goat and Grey willows. **FIELD NOTES** Late Jun–Sep or Oct. Pupates in the ground near the foodplant. Some adults emerge in the same year as a partial second generation. Overwinters as a pupa.

SPHINGINAE

CONVOLVULUS HAWK-MOTH
Agrius convolvuli

PLATE 12
69.004 (1972)

Immigrant. Regularly recorded as a larva in autumn along the south coast of England. **FIELD CHARACTERS** Early instars are mostly green. The final instar is variable. Body of the usual form is brown, speckled paler, sometimes with a row of black subdorsal spots, and pale diagonal stripes on abdominal segments. Spiracles usually black, occasionally orange, and horn black. There is a green form with a black-tipped orange horn, with or without blackish diagonal stripes. There is also a black form with an orange head and spiracles. **HABITATS** Larvae have been found in open coastal habitats such as cliffs, gardens, grasslands, cultivated ground including allotments, old quarries and vegetated shingle. **FOODPLANTS** Mainly found on Field and Hedge bindweeds. Also reported on Sea Bindweed and Morning-glory. **FIELD NOTES** Jul–early Nov. Eggs and young larvae are readily findable on the underside of Field

Bindweed leaves on the coast following a large influx of adult moths. Pupates in the ground. Does not survive the winter in the British Isles.

DEATH'S-HEAD HAWK-MOTH
Acherontia atropos

PLATE 13
69.005 (1973)

Immigrant. Larvae are regularly found in small numbers in summer and autumn throughout its known range. **FIELD CHARACTERS** Early instars are mostly green. The final instar has two main colour forms, yellow and brown. The yellow form has blue diagonal stripes, sometimes edged white below, on the abdominal segments. The horn on A8 is yellow with a rough surface. The brown form has grey diagonal stripes on the abdominal segments. The thoracic segments are white with brown patches either side of a white dorsal line. The horn on A8 is brown with a rough surface. **HABITATS** Larvae may be found in a variety of open habitats, including allotments, gardens, Potato fields (particularly those not treated with insecticides) and waste ground. **FOODPLANTS** Mainly Potato. Also reported on Ash, Bittersweet, dogwoods, Forsythia, Summer Jasmine, Lilac, Deadly Nightshade, Chilli Pepper, Snowberry, Spindle and Duke of Argyll's Teaplant. **FIELD NOTES** Jul–Oct. Pupates in the ground. Does not survive the winter in the British Isles.

PRIVET HAWK-MOTH
Sphinx ligustri

PLATE 13
69.006 (1976)

Common. Well distributed in southern England and south Wales. **FIELD CHARACTERS** Body green, with purplish diagonal stripes, edged white below, on the abdominal segments. The horn on A8 is black above, yellow below and black at the tip, sometimes more extensively black. When fully fed it develops a reddish-brown hue dorsally. **HABITATS** Cliffs, fens, gardens and urban parks, hedgerows, old quarries, scrub on the coast and inland grasslands, especially on calcareous soils, and open woodland. **FOODPLANTS** Frequently on Ash (especially saplings and regrowth following cutting), Forsythia, Guelder-rose, Lilac, and Garden and Wild privets. Also reported on brideworts, Butterfly-bush, Dogwood, Holly, Honeysuckle, Hop, jasmines, Laurustinus, mock-privets, Holm Oak, Rowan, Snowberry, teasels, Wayfaring-tree and willows. **FIELD NOTES** Jul–Sep. Pupates in the ground. Overwinters as a pupa, sometimes over two winters.

PINE HAWK-MOTH
Sphinx pinastri

PLATE 14
69.007 (1978)

Local. Mainly in southern counties and the eastern half of England. Spreading slowly. **FIELD CHARACTERS** In early instars, body green with white subdorsal, lateral and subspiracular stripes. In the final instar, body usually green, occasionally brown, with a broad brown dorsal band, edged with white dashes. Lateral and subspiracular stripes white. Spiracles orange. Horn on A8 black, forked at the tip. **HABITATS** Mainly self-sown pine scrub on heathland, wooded heathland and coniferous woodland. Sometimes in cemeteries and other urban situations where pines are planted. **FOODPLANTS** Mainly Scots Pine. Also reported on Atlas Cedar, Cedar-of-Lebanon, firs, Maritime and Monterey pines, and Norway Spruce. **FIELD NOTES** Late Jun–mid-Sep. Pupates in the ground. Overwinters as a pupa.

MACROGLOSSINAE

NARROW-BORDERED BEE HAWK-MOTH
Hemaris tityus

PLATE 14
69.008 (1982)

Nb. Has declined considerably in the south and east, but still found locally elsewhere, sometimes in numbers where unimproved habitats are widespread, such as Salisbury Plain, the Scottish Highlands and western Ireland. **FIELD CHARACTERS** Body green, with or without purple markings. Dorsal line dark green, subdorsal stripe white. Where purple is present, it may be in a stripe above the subdorsal stripe, or as patches around the abdominal spiracles and below, including on the prolegs. Spiracles orange with a white dot above and below. Horn on A8 purple. When fully fed the larva develops a reddish-brown hue dorsally. **HABITATS** Bogs, chalk grassland, upland wet grassland, wet heathland, limestone pavement (the Burren, Cos Clare and Galway, Ireland) and woodland rides. **FOODPLANTS** Mainly Devil's-bit Scabious, and frequently Small Scabious on chalk grassland. Less often Field Scabious. **FIELD NOTES** Late May–mid-Aug. Rests on the ground, a stem or the underside of a leaf of the foodplant. Pupates in leaf litter or in the ground. Overwinters as a pupa.

BROAD-BORDERED BEE HAWK-MOTH
Hemaris fuciformis

PLATE 14
69.009 (1983)

Nb. Has declined in recent decades as woodland management has declined, but is still found in numbers in East Anglia, Lincolnshire, the New Forest in Hampshire, and Dorset. **FIELD CHARACTERS** Body green, covered in yellow dots, with or without purple patches around the abdominal spiracles. Dorsal line dark green, subdorsal line white or yellow, and ventral area brown. Spiracles orange with a white dot above and below. Horn on A8 purple. In fully fed larvae the green colour changes completely to purplish brown. **HABITATS** Scrub edges on acid grassland and heathland, and woodland edges and rides.

FOODPLANTS Mainly Honeysuckle. Occasionally reported on cultivars of honeysuckles and Snowberry, and on bedstraws, Red and White campions, Ragged-Robin and Field Scabious. **FIELD NOTES** Late Jun–Aug. The female prefers to lay eggs on the underside of leaves on outer stems of Honeysuckle bushes growing in full sunshine. The young larva feeds from the underside, creating a series of conspicuous holes either side of the midrib. Pupates in the ground. Overwinters as a pupa.

HUMMING-BIRD HAWK-MOTH
Macroglossum stellatarum

PLATE 14
69.010 (1984)

Immigrant and temporary resident. Larvae are regularly found in summer and autumn, and the adult overwinters, but there is no evidence for continuous breeding in the British Isles. **FIELD CHARACTERS** Body green or brown, covered in white dots. Dorsal line dark, subdorsal stripe white, and subspiracular stripe yellow. Horn on A8 dark blue, tipped with orange. In fully fed larvae the green colour changes completely to pinkish brown. **HABITATS** Open habitats almost anywhere. **FOODPLANTS** Frequently Hedge and Lady's bedstraws; less often Cleavers and Wild Madder. **FIELD NOTES** Jun–Oct. Pupates on the ground. Overwinters as an adult.

SPURGE HAWK-MOTH
Hyles euphorbiae

PLATE 14
69.013 (1986)

Immigrant. Larvae are found very occasionally in the British Isles in coastal parts of the south-east and East Anglia. **FIELD CHARACTERS** There are black and green forms, with considerable variation within these. The black form usually has a black body densely covered with white dots. Dorsal stripe one of various shades from yellow to red. There is a reddish, yellow or white subdorsal spot T1–A9, and a smaller red, yellow or white spot below, except on A9, and the colour of the subdorsal and lateral spots may be the same or different. The spots are within transverse black bands lacking the dense white dots. The green form has a red or yellow dorsal stripe, and white subdorsal and lateral spots, usually with some black shading and dense white dots dorsally. Horn on A8 orange, tipped with black. True legs and prolegs usually red. **SIMILAR SPECIES** Bedstraw Hawk-moth and Striped Hawk-moth. Only Spurge Hawk-moth has the double row of lateral spots. In the final instar, Striped Hawk-moth has an orange horn with a black tip, whereas Bedstraw Hawk-moth has a red horn. **HABITATS** Open habitats in Europe. In the British Isles, the larva is most likely to be found in hot, sunny situations. **FOODPLANTS** Perennial herbaceous spurges. **FIELD NOTES** Aug–Sep. Pupates in the ground. Does not survive the winter in the British Isles.

BEDSTRAW HAWK-MOTH
Hyles gallii

PLATE 14
69.014 (1987)

Immigrant; transitory resident. Occasionally establishes temporarily, and currently believed to be resident in coastal parts of East Anglia and Lincolnshire. **FIELD CHARACTERS** Body brown, black, grey or green, speckled with white or yellow dots. Dorsal stripe pale with a black-edged yellow subdorsal spot, T2–A8. Subspiracular stripe white or yellow, sometimes only on T1–T3. Horn on A8 red. True legs black; prolegs vary with the body colour. **SIMILAR SPECIES** Spurge Hawk-moth and Striped Hawk-moth. **HABITATS** Can occur as an immigrant anywhere, but temporary establishment is usually on the coast, or inland on waste ground. **FOODPLANTS** Bedstraws, fuchsias, Godetia, Wild Madder, and Rosebay and other willowherbs. **FIELD NOTES** Jul–Sep. Basks in sunshine. Pupates in the ground. Overwinters as a pupa.

STRIPED HAWK-MOTH
Hyles livornica

PLATE 15
69.015 (1990)

Immigrant. The larva is very occasionally seen in the British Isles. **FIELD CHARACTERS** Extremely variable in colour and markings. Body black or greenish, with dense yellow spotting laterally. Dorsal line variable in colour and width, from a pale line to a black band. Subdorsal stripe yellow or white and may be expanded on each segment to form a spot of varying colour. Subspiracular stripe yellow, with an orange spot on each segment. Horn on A8 orange, with a black tip. True legs and prolegs usually black. **SIMILAR SPECIES** Spurge Hawk-moth and Bedstraw Hawk-moth. **HABITATS** Larvae have been found in warm habitats, including on the coast, in gardens and in open woodland rides. **FOODPLANTS** Most often on Hedge Bedstraw, and Rosebay and other willowherbs. Also reported on a wide variety of other herbaceous plants, including other bedstraws, Buckwheat, docks, fuchsias, Grape-vine, Knotgrass, Devil's-bit Scabious, Snapdragon, sorrels, Perennial Sowthistle, strawberries and Common Toadflax. **FIELD NOTES** Jun–Oct. Pupates in the ground. Does not survive the winter in the British Isles.

ELEPHANT HAWK-MOTH
Deilephila elpenor

PLATE 15
69.016 (1991)

Common, and has spread throughout most of Scotland in recent decades. **FIELD CHARACTERS** Young larva has a green body until the fourth instar, when it usually becomes brown. In the final instar the body is usually brown with darker patterning, or less often green. There are darker subdorsal patches A3–A8, and subdorsal eyespots A1–A2. Segment A1 is expanded, allowing the head and thoracic segments to retract into it. Horn on A8 brown with a white tip. **SIMILAR SPECIES** Small Elephant Hawk-moth has a much smaller horn on A8. **HABITATS** Wide variety of open habitats, including recently burnt ground, various coastal habitats, fens, gardens, grasslands, heathland, marshes, edges of scrub, waste ground and woodland rides. **FOODPLANTS** Most frequently encountered on fuchsias, and Great, Rosebay and other willowherbs. Also reported on a wide variety of other herbaceous plants, including Himalayan and Orange balsams, bedstraws, Hedge Bindweed, Bogbean, Cabbage, Enchanter's-nightshade, Common Evening-primrose, Godetia, Grape-vine, Purple-loosestrife, roses, tobaccos, Virginia-creepers and water-lilies. **FIELD NOTES** Late Jun–Sep. When small, rests on the underside of leaves of the foodplant, but when large, rests on the ground, climbing to feed at night. May also climb during late afternoon on warm days to rest conspicuously on the foodplant. Pupates in or on the ground. Overwinters as a pupa.

SMALL ELEPHANT HAWK-MOTH
Deilephila porcellus

PLATE 15
69.017 (1992)

Local. Widespread but local in England and Wales. In Scotland, mainly away from the west, and in Ireland, mainly coastal. **FIELD CHARACTERS** Young larva has a green body until the fifth instar, when it usually becomes brown with darker patterning, but some larvae remain green. Subdorsal eyespots A1–A2. Segment A1 is expanded, allowing the head and thoracic segments to retract into it. Horn on A8 is very small and hardly visible. **SIMILAR SPECIES** Elephant Hawk-moth. **HABITATS** Wide variety of open habitats, especially cliffs, coastal and calcareous grassland, upland wet grassland, heathland, moorland, old quarries, sand dunes and vegetated shingle. **FOODPLANTS** Mainly Heath and Lady's bedstraws. Also reported on Hedge Bedstraw, Cleavers, marsh-bedstraws, Purple-loosestrife and willowherbs, and has been observed feeding on the flowers of Red Campion. **FIELD NOTES** Late Jun–early Sep. Feeds at night, hiding by day among debris. Occasionally seen openly by day on vegetation, lying limp and apparently feigning death, although the reason for this behaviour is not understood. Pupates in or on the ground. Overwinters as a pupa.

GEOMETROIDEA
GEOMETRIDAE LOOPER MOTHS

There are at least 20,000 described species in this family worldwide, with over 300 species recorded in the British Isles. The vast majority of larvae in this family have their prolegs reduced to a pair on A6 and the anal claspers. They are often referred to as loopers because they move by bringing the prolegs on A6 up close to the true legs while the body arches up in a loop. There are a few exceptions that have additional prolegs. Orange Underwing and Light Orange Underwing have additional prolegs on A3–A5, these becoming progressively better developed from A3 to A6. Scalloped Hazel has vestigial pairs on A4 and A5, those on A5 being larger. March Moth has a vestigial pair on A5, Light Emerald an extra functional pair on A5, and Barred Red and Banded Pine Carpet a small extra pair on A5.

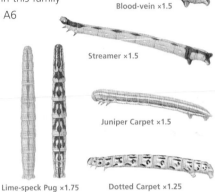

Blood-vein ×1.5

Streamer ×1.5

Juniper Carpet ×1.5

Lime-speck Pug ×1.75

Dotted Carpet ×1.25

Early Thorn ×1.25

Lilac Beauty larva

Brindled Beauty larva

STERRHINAE

NOTE ON WAVES (GENERA *IDAEA* AND *SCOPULA*)

Larvae of most species in these genera are rarely encountered in the wild, and some have not yet been found. For those that have, larvae tend to live near the ground and several eat withered and dead leaves. Their small size, general pale grey, grey or brown coloration and retiring habits make all of them hard to find. Those in genus *Scopula* are generally longer and thinner than those in *Idaea*, but species in both genera usually have noticeable transverse ridges across the body. There are no such ridges in Blood-vein.

Most species are easy to rear to adult from eggs obtained from females, perhaps discouraging field studies of the early stages. It is likely that there is more variation within species in field characters than has been observed currently, which in turn reduces confidence in determining species in the field. If there is doubt, larvae in these genera should be reared to confirm identity.

PURPLE-BORDERED GOLD
Idaea muricata

PLATE 16
70.002 (1698)

Nb. **FIELD CHARACTERS** Head brown, speckled darker and notched. Body pale greyish brown with small black marks, and with numerous transverse ridges that are raised into warty projections dorsally T1–T3. Dorsal line white edged with black lines, and there are wavy whitish subdorsal and lateral lines. Lateral fold whitish, and ventral area brownish with whitish lines. **HABITATS** Bogs, fens, damp grassland, damp heathland, marshes and mosses. **FOODPLANT** Has been found on Marsh Cinquefoil. **FIELD NOTES** Jul–late May. Pupates in a cocoon among plant debris.

BRIGHT WAVE
Idaea ochrata

PLATE 16
70.003 (1696)

RDB; immigrant. Resident on the Kent coast and Channel Islands only. **FIELD CHARACTERS** Head notched with rounded dorsal lobes. Body pale greyish brown with a pale lateral fold and numerous transverse ridges. Dorsal line whitish, edged with dark lines, and there is one wavy pale lateral line. There is also a green form. **HABITATS** Sand dunes, open golf-course 'roughs', ungrazed vegetated shingle and sandy undercliff. **FOODPLANT** Has been found on Smooth Tare. **FIELD NOTES** Aug–May. Pupates in a cocoon among plant debris.

LEAST CARPET
Idaea rusticata

PLATE 16
70.004 (1699)

Local. Has increased very significantly in range and abundance in recent decades. **FIELD CHARACTERS** Body noticeably wrinkled with many transverse ridges, and covered with yellowish warty pinacula. The pinacula give rise to hairs modified into short, pale yellowish fleshy projections, especially anteriorly, and there are similar projections from the black head. Body dark brown or blackish, mixed with pale yellow-brown patches, especially posteriorly. Transverse blackish bands between segments A1 and A5. **SIMILAR SPECIES** Based on the limited material examined, Silky Wave is very similar and no obvious difference has been found, and Dwarf Cream Wave has whitish and dark, rather than yellowish, fleshy projections. **HABITATS** Wide variety, including gardens, hedges, old coastal quarries, and scrub on calcareous grassland. **FOODPLANTS** Has been found on Sweet Alison, Groundsel, Common Ivy and Traveller's-joy. **FIELD NOTES** Aug–late May or Jun, or sometimes Jul–Aug and Oct–May. Overwinters half-grown. Pupates in a cocoon among plant debris.

SILKY WAVE
Idaea dilutaria

PLATE 16
70.005 (1704)

RDB. In three isolated areas in the west of England and Wales. **FIELD CHARACTERS** Body dark greyish brown, yellowish brown posteriorly, covered in yellowish or paler warty pinacula, and noticeably wrinkled with many transverse ridges. Pinacula are brighter posteriorly and give rise to hairs modified into short, pale yellow fleshy projections, and there are similar projections from the black head. **SIMILAR SPECIES** Least Carpet and Dwarf Cream Wave. **HABITATS** Limestone cliffs and grassland, where the foodplant is not tightly grazed, and generally facing south. **FOODPLANT** Common Rock-rose. **FIELD NOTES** Aug–end May. Overwinters as a part-grown larva. Pupates in a cocoon on the ground.

DWARF CREAM WAVE
Idaea fuscovenosa

PLATE 16
70.006 (1705)

Local. Has increased significantly in abundance in recent decades. **FIELD CHARACTERS** Body noticeably wrinkled with many transverse ridges. Lines of small, pale greyish or whitish warty pinacula give rise to hairs modified into short whitish or dark fleshy projections. Body mixed pale and dark grey, or yellowish brown and dark brown, sometimes arranged in paler diamonds dorsally, with darker shading forming X-shaped marks between segments. The dorsal patch on A5 is especially pale and may be whitish. **SIMILAR SPECIES** Least Carpet and Silky Wave. **HABITATS** Tall herbaceous areas in gardens, grasslands with scrub, hedgerows, marshes and woodland rides. **FOODPLANTS** Not known in the wild. On herbaceous plants and Bramble in captivity. **FIELD NOTES** Aug–May. Pupation site not recorded.

SMALL DUSTY WAVE
Idaea seriata

PLATE 16
70.008 (1707)

Common. Has increased significantly in abundance in recent decades. **FIELD CHARACTERS** Body with numerous transverse ridges and pale greyish brown, speckled darker, with a pale dorsal line that is indistinct in the middle segments and edged with black lines on posterior segments. There is faint wavy patterning subdorsally. Usually a large black mark laterally on A2, and paired black dorsal pinacula, and sometimes there are other black marks dorsally and laterally on abdominal segments. **HABITATS** Most frequent in urban areas, including gardens, hedges and waste ground. **FOODPLANTS** Several larvae have been beaten from Common Ivy, and one found on Elder. On withered leaves and plant debris in captivity. **FIELD NOTES** Sep–May and Jul, in two generations. Pupates in a cocoon on the ground.

SATIN WAVE
Idaea subsericeata

PLATE 16
70.009 (1709)

Common. **FIELD CHARACTERS** Body pale greyish brown, often tinged orangey brown, with numerous transverse ridges. Dorsal line pale, edged with dark lines, usually with a wavy dark subdorsal line. Lateral flanges, A2–A5, increasing in width posteriorly, with a yellow or white spot on the flange on A5, and a prominent black pinaculum on A6. **HABITATS** Heathland, hedgerows, rough calcareous grassland, scrub and open woodland. **FOODPLANTS** On herbaceous plants in captivity. **FIELD NOTES** Aug–May. Pupates in a network cocoon.

DOTTED BORDER WAVE
Idaea sylvestraria

PLATE 16
70.010 (1701)

Nb. **FIELD CHARACTERS** Body pale greyish brown, dark greyish brown ventrally, with numerous transverse ridges. Dorsal line pale, edged with dark lines, interrupted A2–A4 with small pale marks, and on A5 by a large pale patch. A row of small, dark brown subdorsal marks A1–A4. **HABITATS** Heathland. **FOODPLANTS** Not known in the wild. On Bramble and herbaceous plants in captivity. **FIELD NOTES** Aug–end May. Pupates on the ground.

SINGLE-DOTTED WAVE
Idaea dimidiata

PLATE 16
70.011 (1708)

Common. **FIELD CHARACTERS** Body pale greyish or pale orangey brown, mottled darker, with numerous transverse ridges. Dorsal line pale, edged with darker lines except on T1–T3, with a row of dark subdorsal marks, and the mottling concentrated into V-shapes across the dorsum on abdominal segments. A whitish lateral fold. Short hairs arise from pale pinacula. **SIMILAR SPECIES** Small Fan-footed Wave shows no obvious difference. **HABITATS** Fens, marshes, and damper areas in gardens, scrub and woodland. **FOODPLANTS** Recorded on flowers of Hedge Bedstraw, Burnet-saxifrage and Cow Parsley. Has also been found on comfreys, and beaten from Common Ivy. **FIELD NOTES** Aug–May. Pupates in a cocoon in plant debris.

TREBLE BROWN SPOT
Idaea trigeminata

PLATE 16
70.012 (1711)

Local. Has increased very significantly in abundance in recent decades. **FIELD CHARACTERS** Body with numerous transverse ridges, and mainly dark brown, with pale yellow-brown markings posteriorly, and with a sparse covering of moderately long curved hairs. Blackish V-shaped markings across the dorsum on abdominal segments A1–A4. **HABITATS** Mainly woodland edges and rides; also gardens, calcareous grassland and hedgerows. **FOODPLANT** Recorded on withered and dead leaves of Common Ivy. **FIELD NOTES** Aug–May. Pupates in the ground.

SMALL FAN-FOOTED WAVE
Idaea biselata

PLATE 16
70.013 (1702)

Common, but not found at higher altitudes. **FIELD CHARACTERS** Body pale brown, mottled reddish brown or orangey brown, with numerous transverse ridges. Dorsal line pale, edged with dark lines, and blackish V-shaped markings across the dorsum A1–A6, sometimes obscured anteriorly on each segment by dark grey shading forming bands between segments. A whitish lateral fold. Short hairs arise from whitish pinacula. **SIMILAR SPECIES** Single-dotted Wave. **HABITATS** Mainly scrub on heathland, and woodland; also gardens and hedgerows in well-wooded countryside. **FOODPLANTS** Unknown in the wild. Prefers withered leaves of herbaceous plants in captivity. **FIELD NOTES** Aug–May. Pupates in leaf litter.

WEAVER'S WAVE
Idaea contiguaria

PLATE 16
70.014 (1710)

Ssp. *britanniae* Na. **FIELD CHARACTERS** Body pale greyish brown, with numerous transverse ridges. Dorsal line pale, edged with dark grey shading A1–A5 and dark lines A6–A9. Dark grey dorsal pinacula A1–A5. A curved black subdorsal line T1–T2. Ventral area dark grey. **HABITATS** Moorland. Seems to prefer foodplants growing among exposed lichen-covered rocks. **FOODPLANTS** Mainly Heather. Also on Crowberry and Navelwort. **FIELD NOTES** Aug–May. Pupates in a cocoon. Overwinters part-grown.

SMALL SCALLOP
Idaea emarginata

PLATE 16
70.015 (1712)

Local. Usually occurs sparingly. **FIELD CHARACTERS** Body pale brown, brown or purplish brown, with a whitish dorsal line edged with dark stripes, and numerous transverse ridges. Subdorsal line whitish edged above with a black line. Lateral fold whitish. **HABITATS** Prefers damp areas, including hedgerow ditches, fens, scrub on heathland, and damp woodland rides. **FOODPLANTS** Bedstraws and Field Bindweed. **FIELD NOTES** Aug–May. Pupates in a cocoon in plant debris.

RIBAND WAVE
Idaea aversata

PLATE 16
70.016 (1713)

Common. **FIELD CHARACTERS** Body with numerous transverse ridges, and brown or dark brown T1–A4, paler A5–A10, sometimes more so on A5, where it may form a whitish V-shape centrally. A dark dorsal band from posterior A5 to A9. Dorsal line whitish, usually with dark brown scissor-shaped markings across the dorsum A1–A4. A5 is somewhat expanded laterally, with a diagonal dark line extending forwards from the dorsal line. **SIMILAR SPECIES** Portland Ribbon Wave (brown form) and Plain Wave are indistinguishable in the field. **HABITATS** Wide variety of lowland habitats, including gardens. **FOODPLANTS** Various low-growing herbaceous plants, including Wood Avens, bedstraws, Common Chickweed, dandelions, docks, Knotgrass, Ribwort Plantain and Primrose. Also recorded on Common Ivy. **FIELD NOTES** Jul–May. Pupates in a slight cocoon in plant debris.

PORTLAND RIBBON WAVE
Idaea degeneraria

PLATE 16
70.017 (1714)

RDB; immigrant. Has been resident in two locations in Dorset for many years and now appears to be established elsewhere along the south coast. **FIELD CHARACTERS** Body with numerous transverse ridges, and pale brown or brown T1–A4, with a broad pale area centrally on A5. A brown dorsal band or marks from posterior A5 to A9, paler laterally. Dorsal line pale with scissor-shaped, dark brown markings across the dorsum A1–A4. A5 is somewhat expanded laterally with a pair of dark dorsal pinacula. A whitish form occurs, with strongly contrasting brown patches across the dorsum A1–A4. **SIMILAR SPECIES** Riband Wave and Plain Wave are indistinguishable from the brown form. **HABITATS** Open coastal habitats, including grasslands, old quarries and scattered scrub. **FOODPLANTS** In the Channel Islands, larvae have been found in autumn on yellowing leaves of Hybrid Crack-willow. On a variety of plants in captivity. **FIELD NOTES** Late Jul–late May. In one or two generations per year, depending on location. Pupates in the ground.

PLAIN WAVE
Idaea straminata

PLATE 16
70.018 (1715)

Local. Has increased significantly in abundance in recent decades. **SIMILAR SPECIES** Riband Wave and Portland Ribbon Wave. **HABITATS** Mainly scrubby heathland and woodland; less often rough grassland and hedgerows. **FOODPLANTS** One larva has been swept from Mugwort. On a variety of plants in captivity. **FIELD NOTES** Aug–May. Pupates in plant debris.

SUB-ANGLED WAVE
Scopula nigropunctata

PLATE 16
70.020 (1684)

RDB; immigrant. **FIELD CHARACTERS** Body pale grey or pale brown, with numerous transverse ridges. Dorsal line pale, edged with dark lines, and a number of other indistinct lines elsewhere. Sometimes a variable number and position of small black marks. **SIMILAR SPECIES** Sub-angled Wave, Small Bloodvein, Lesser Cream Wave, Smoky Wave and Rosy Wave are so similar to each other that it is not possible to give easy, reliable differences. The habitat and distribution may provide some identification clues. Chevron is distinguished from all of these by having transverse ridges confined to the areas between segments. **HABITATS** Scrub in coastal grassland, and flower-rich woodland rides. **FOODPLANTS** Unknown in the wild. The adult moth has been beaten from Traveller's-joy and, in captivity, larvae feed on this and a variety of herbaceous plants. **FIELD NOTES** Aug–May. Pupates between leaves and in soil.

LACE BORDER
Scopula ornata

PLATE 16
70.021 (1687)

Na. Has declined with loss of suitable habitat. **FIELD CHARACTERS** Body dark brown or dark greyish brown, with numerous transverse lines. Dorsal line pale, edged with black lines and indistinct in the middle segments. A pale orangey-brown subdorsal stripe on head and T1, and orangey-brown patches beside the dorsal stripe A6–A9. Lateral fold pale. **HABITATS** Calcareous grassland; also on a disused railway bank. **FOODPLANTS** Wild Marjoram, Wild Thyme and probably other herbaceous plants. **FIELD NOTES** Jun–Jul and Aug–Apr. Pupates in a slight cocoon on the ground.

TAWNY WAVE
Scopula rubiginata

PLATE 16
70.022 (1688)

RDB; immigrant. Breeding appears confined to breckland grassland and the Suffolk coast. **FIELD CHARACTERS** Body pale brown, with numerous transverse ridges. Dorsal line thin and pale, edged with dark brown lines that are darker between segments. Subdorsal line whitish on the head and T1–T3, shaded dark brown below. Dark brown subdorsal mark A2–A5. Lateral fold with a clearly defined whitish stripe. **HABITATS** Breckland grassland, open forest rides and sand dunes. **FOODPLANTS** Unknown in the wild. A variety of herbaceous plants in captivity. **FIELD NOTES** Jul–Aug and Sep–May. Pupates in a slight cocoon on the ground.

MULLEIN WAVE
Scopula marginepunctata

PLATE 16
70.023 (1689)

Local. Mainly coastal but spreading inland in south-east England. Has declined in abundance significantly in recent decades. **FIELD CHARACTERS** Body whitish grey or pale greyish brown, speckled darker, especially laterally, and with numerous transverse ridges. Dorsal line pale, edged with black lines or shading that obscures the line on some abdominal segments. Blackish and brownish marks subdorsally. **HABITATS** Various coastal habitats, including grasslands, old quarries, rocky places and saltmarshes. Also allotments, sheltered walls and waste ground in urban areas. **FOODPLANTS** Various herbaceous plants, including Wild Marjoram, Mugwort, Wood Sage, stonecrops, Ivy-leaved Toadflax, Horseshoe Vetch and Yarrow. **FIELD NOTES** Jul and Sep–May. On Ivy-leaved Toadflax small larvae seem to eat from the leaf edge, whereas larger larvae nip the petiole and eat from the wilted leaf. Pupates in the ground.

SMALL BLOOD-VEIN
Scopula imitaria

PLATE 16
70.024 (1690)

Common. **FIELD CHARACTERS** Body with numerous transverse ridges, and in two colour forms. The orangey-brown form has a pale dorsal line edged with dark lines and shading, obscuring the dorsal line in places, and is darker between segments with a pale subdorsal line and lateral fold. The pale grey form is similar but has a dark subdorsal line. Either form may have large blackish smudges around the spiracles A2–A5. **SIMILAR SPECIES** Sub-angled Wave, Lesser Cream Wave, Smoky Wave, Rosy Wave and Chevron. **HABITATS** Wide variety of lowland habitats, including gardens. **FOODPLANTS** Has been found on cherries, Hawthorn, Honeysuckle and Garden Privet. On various herbaceous plants in captivity. **FIELD NOTES** Aug–May. May spring away from the foodplant if disturbed. Pupates on the ground.

LESSER CREAM WAVE
Scopula immutata

PLATE 16
70.025 (1692)

Local. **FIELD CHARACTERS** Body pale orangey brown with a pale dorsal line edged with dark shading, and with numerous transverse ridges. The shading often obscures most of the line, creating a dark band, except in the regions between segments from A1 to A5, where there are short black dashes. Subdorsal lines pale greyish and rather wavy, and lateral fold yellowish or cream. **SIMILAR SPECIES** Sub-angled Wave, Small Blood-vein, Smoky Wave, Rosy Wave and Chevron. **HABITATS** Mainly ditches in wet meadows, tall-herb fens, marshes and damp pastures. Also breckland and calcareous grasslands. **FOODPLANTS** Recorded in the field on Meadowsweet and Common Valerian. On various plants in captivity. **FIELD NOTES** Late Aug–May. Feeds at night. Pupates in plant debris on the ground.

SMOKY WAVE
Scopula ternata

PLATE 16
70.026 (1694)

Local. **FIELD CHARACTERS** Body usually pale brown, sometimes dark brown, and with numerous transverse ridges. Dorsal line pale, edged with dark lines that may have blurred edges, but with dark dashes between the segments. There may be a pale subdorsal line only, or one with blackish marks above. There is a form with a broad, dark greyish band across the dorsal area. Lateral fold with a clearly defined whitish stripe. **SIMILAR SPECIES** Sub-angled Wave, Small Blood-vein, Lesser Cream Wave, Rosy Wave and Chevron. **HABITATS** Mainly heathland and moorland; also very locally on rocky limestone grassland with short turf. **FOODPLANTS** Recorded on Bilberry, Cross-leaved Heath and Heather. **FIELD NOTES** Aug–May. Feeds at night. Pupates on the ground.

CREAM WAVE
Scopula floslactata

PLATE 16
70.027 (1693)

Ssp. *floslactata* Local. Widespread in England, Wales and southern Ireland. Ssp. *scotica* Local. Widespread in central and western Scotland. **FIELD CHARACTERS** Very variable. Body pale grey, pale brownish grey, reddish brown or blackish, with variable intensity of markings, and with numerous transverse ridges. Dorsal line thin, pale and edged with black lines that may fuse in places, obscuring the dorsal line but leaving a pair of black dashes between segments. Subdorsal markings vary from a pale stripe to a line of blackish marks, with or without black patches laterally. In reddish-brown and blackish forms there may be cream or yellowish-white marks subdorsally, forming triangles or oblique stripes A5–A6, or larvae may be uniformly dark except for paler coloration A8–A9. A transverse ridge with raised pinacula dorsally on A8. **HABITATS** Scrub within damp grassland, hedgerows and woodland. **FOODPLANTS** Has been found on bedstraws including Woodruff, and Bush Vetch. On various herbaceous plants in captivity. **FIELD NOTES** Jul–Apr. Pupates in the ground. Overwinters as a fully fed larva.

ROSY WAVE
Scopula emutaria

PLATE 16
70.028 (1691)

Nb. **FIELD CHARACTERS** Body pale greyish brown, with numerous transverse ridges. Dorsal line pale, edged with darker lines, and with short black dashes between segments. Ill-defined wavy, alternating paler and darker subdorsal and lateral lines; the darker lines may include blackish dots or dashes. **SIMILAR SPECIES** Sub-angled Wave, Small Blood-vein, Lesser Cream Wave, Smoky Wave and Chevron. **HABITATS** Mainly coastal and estuarine saltmarshes and sand dunes; also boggy heathland inland. **FOODPLANTS** Unknown in the wild. On various herbaceous plants in captivity. **FIELD NOTES** Aug–May. Pupates in plant debris on the ground. Larvae have been found overwintering on stems of Sea Beet.

BLOOD-VEIN
Timandra comae

PLATE 17
70.029 (1682)

Common; suspected immigrant. Has declined significantly in abundance in recent decades but is expanding northwards in England. **FIELD CHARACTERS** Body pale brown, reddish brown or dark greyish brown. Dorsal line brown or grey, edged broadly with whitish shading. Whitish V-shapes across the dorsum and laterally A2–A5, broadly shaded posteriorly with blackish on dorsum, and whitish laterally. A1 appears bloated, with the body tapering anteriorly to the head. **HABITATS** Wide variety, preferring damper situations, including ditches, tall-herb fens, gardens, hedgerows, marshes and woodland rides. **FOODPLANTS** Recorded from Common Chickweed, docks, Common Orache, Redshank and Common Sorrel. **FIELD NOTES** Jul and Sep–Apr. Pupates in a cocoon on the ground.

NOTE ON MOCHAS AND ALLIES (GENUS *CYCLOPHORA*)

Larvae of this genus are characterised by a notch along the centreline of the head, with the dorsal lobes domed or rounded. The face is at a right angle to the outstretched body, and the head is brownish, often with two pale vertical lines. In the material we have examined, green forms, except those of Mocha and Jersey Mocha, have reddish-brown or pinkish prolegs and anal claspers, with paler markings. These characters can help separate green *Cyclophora* larvae from other green geometrids.

Within the group, however, the colour, extent and intensity of body markings are particularly variable. It is difficult to separate with certainty the oak-feeding group: Blair's Mocha, Jersey Mocha, False Mocha, Maiden's Blush and Clay Triple-lines. Larvae may also change foodplant in captivity; for example, Maiden's Blush is known to switch from oaks to birches. If there is any doubt, *Cyclophora* larvae should be reared to confirm identity.

Larvae in this group rest openly on the upper surface of leaves without obvious silk pads fixing them in place. They are often found, and preferentially so in Dingy Mocha, on small bushes, saplings or low branches. Their resting habits suggest they are not adapted for feeding in the canopy.

Pupae of *Cyclophora* are remarkably similar to those of most butterflies, being angular in appearance. The larvae pupate exposed, attached to a pad of silk by the pupal cremaster and by a girdle of silk around the middle (see p. 37).

DINGY MOCHA
Cyclophora pendularia

PLATE 17
70.030 (1675)

RDB; suspected immigrant. **FIELD CHARACTERS** Head pale brown mottled darker, or orangey brown. Body greenish or brownish. Dorsal and wavy subdorsal and lateral lines pale or whitish. Brownish, blackish or dark green subdorsal/lateral patches anteriorly A1–A6, sometimes joined across the dorsum with dark shading. Spiracular stripe whitish, often with pinkish patches, and with whitish colour sometimes extended above. **HABITATS** Mainly humid and wet heathlands road verges, and open woodland rides in heathland areas. Rarely on damp grasslands. **FOODPLANTS** Mainly Eared and Grey willows. Also recorded on Alder, and Creeping and Goat willows. Prefers bushes 0.3–2m high in open, sunny situations, but rarely where there is spring and summer grazing. **FIELD NOTES** Jun–Jul and Aug–Sep or Oct in two generations. Overwinters as a pupa.

MOCHA
Cyclophora annularia

PLATE 17
70.031 (1676)

Nb. **FIELD CHARACTERS** Head pale brown, mottled darker. Body green, or occasionally pale brownish, with small black pinacula. Dorsal, subdorsal and spiracular lines whitish or yellowish, sometimes faint. Proleg and anal clasper green. **HABITATS** Long-established hedgerows, scrub and woodland. **FOODPLANT** Field Maple. **FIELD NOTES** Jun–Jul and late Aug–Sep in two generations. Overwinters as a pupa.

BIRCH MOCHA
Cyclophora albipunctata

PLATE 17
70.032 (1677)

Local. Apparently in decline in the Midlands and Wales. **FIELD CHARACTERS** Head brownish with paler markings. Body green, orangey brown, reddish brown or grey. Green and orangey-brown forms have dorsal and wavy subdorsal, lateral and spiracular lines that comprise pale dots and dashes. Reddish-brown and grey forms have pale dorsal and subdorsal lines formed similarly, and usually have white lateral marks A1–A6, sometimes extended to form an irregular lateral band, and often with black and/or brown marks above, sometimes extended across the dorsum. **HABITATS** Scrub on heathland, and woodland; occasionally gardens. **FOODPLANTS** Downy and Silver birches. **FIELD NOTES** Late Jun–Jul, and late Aug–mid-Oct as a partial second generation in the south. Overwinters as a pupa.

BLAIR'S MOCHA
Cyclophora puppillaria

PLATE 17
70.033 (1678)

Immigrant; recent colonist along the south coast. Likely to become more widespread. **FIELD CHARACTERS** Head brownish with paler markings. Body greenish or greyish, sometimes brownish, and covered with whitish or yellowish dots. Dorsal and wavy subdorsal, lateral and spiracular lines comprise pale dots and dashes, more or less discernible among the pale dots. Dark forms may have whitish or pale oblique extensions to the spiracular line A1–A5, sometimes with brownish shading posteriorly. Plain green forms may have some contrasting brownish markings on the dorsum. Proleg pinkish. **SIMILAR SPECIES** Jersey Mocha, False Mocha, Maiden's Blush and Clay Triple-lines. Maiden's Blush and Blair's Mocha differ from others in this oak-feeding group in their abundant pale speckling. Maiden's Blush differs from all the others by its orangey-brown lateral spots present in the green form and usually present in the brown form. Jersey Mocha, False Mocha and Clay Triple-lines may be indistinguishable from one another in the field, although based on the material available Jersey Mocha differs from the others by having little or no pink coloration on the proleg. **HABITATS** Open coastal situations, coastal gardens and woodland. **FOODPLANTS** Has been found on Chilean Myrtle and Holm Oak in Great Britain, and reared in captivity on Pedunculate Oak and privets. Also on rock-roses and Strawberry-tree in mainland Europe. **FIELD NOTES** Life history not fully understood. Has been found overwintering as a larva on Chilean Myrtle. It is also likely to be a larva during summer months.

JERSEY MOCHA
Cyclophora ruficiliaria

PLATE 17
70.034 (1678a)

Immigrant; recent colonist along the south coast. Likely to become more widespread. **FIELD CHARACTERS** Head greyish or brown, with paler markings. Body greyish or greenish, with dark pinacula. Pale yellowish oblique lateral marks A1–A6, which are sometimes joined to form a spiracular stripe, and may be shaded dark greyish, brown or dark greenish posteriorly, sometimes joined across the dorsum to form dark transverse bands. The grey form has an often faint whitish dorsal line. The green form has dorsal and wavy subdorsal and lateral lines comprising whitish dots and dashes. Both forms have yellowish or whitish prolegs with no hint of pink coloration. **SIMILAR SPECIES** Blair's Mocha, False Mocha, Maiden's Blush and Clay Triple-lines. **HABITATS** Woodland, and well-wooded gardens and parks. **FOODPLANTS** In Europe on oaks. **FIELD NOTES** Probably May–Oct in two generations. Overwinters as a pupa.

FALSE MOCHA
Cyclophora porata

PLATE 17
70.035 (1679)

Nb. Appears to be in decline. **FIELD CHARACTERS** Head brown with paler markings. Body green or brown with small black or dark brown pinacula. Dorsal and wavy subdorsal and lateral lines comprise whitish dots and dashes. Spiracular stripe paler than ground colour, incomplete and indistinct, sometimes with small oblique extensions above, shaded darker posteriorly and joined across the dorsum. Proleg has a reddish coloration. **SIMILAR SPECIES** Blair's Mocha, Jersey Mocha, Maiden's Blush and Clay Triple-lines. **HABITATS** Mainly wooded heathland and oak woodland. Also carr woodland. Appears to prefer coppice regrowth and scrubby oaks within large areas of mature habitat. **FOODPLANTS** Pedunculate Oak and probably Sessile Oak. **FIELD NOTES** Mid-Jun–late Jul, and late Aug–early Oct as a partial second generation. Overwinters as a pupa.

MAIDEN'S BLUSH
Cyclophora punctaria

PLATE 17
70.036 (1680)

Local. Has increased significantly in abundance in recent decades. **FIELD CHARACTERS** Head brownish with paler markings. Body green, greyish green, brownish or greyish brown. Dorsal and, if present, wavy subdorsal and lateral lines comprise whitish or paler dots and dashes. Spiracular stripe whitish or sometimes yellowish, incomplete, with oblique extensions above, sometimes shaded darker posteriorly and across the dorsum, and showing strong contrast in brownish forms. In the green form and usually the brown forms, the oblique whitish marks usually adjoin orangey-brown lateral spots, noticeably larger on A1. Proleg has a pinkish coloration. **SIMILAR SPECIES** Blair's Mocha, Jersey Mocha, False Mocha and Clay Triple-lines. **HABITATS** Wooded hedgerows and oak woodland. **FOODPLANTS** Pedunculate and probably Sessile oaks, and possibly Turkey Oak. **FIELD NOTES** Late Jun–Jul, and mid-Aug–Sep, in two generations. Overwinters as a pupa.

CLAY TRIPLE-LINES
Cyclophora linearia

PLATE 17
70.037 (1681)

Local. Has expanded its range in Ireland recently. **FIELD CHARACTERS** Head orangey brown or brown. Body green, brown or occasionally grey, with dorsal and wavy subdorsal and lateral lines comprising whitish or yellowish dots and dashes, and a reddish coloration to the proleg. Spiracular stripe whitish or pale, incomplete, with oblique extensions above A1 or A2–A5, and sometimes with distinct brownish marks or weaker shading posteriorly. **SIMILAR SPECIES** Blair's Mocha, Jersey Mocha, False Mocha and Maiden's Blush. **HABITATS** Mainly woodland; also gardens and urban parks, and hedgerows. **FOODPLANTS** Beech. Also recorded on Sweet Chestnut and oaks. **FIELD NOTES** Late Jun–late Aug, and Sep–Oct as a partial second generation. Overwinters as a pupa.

VESTAL
Rhodometra sacraria

PLATE 17
70.038 (1716)

Immigrant; temporary colonist. Establishes in the south in some years following large-scale immigration. Has increased significantly in abundance in recent decades. **FIELD CHARACTERS** Head brown with pale stripes, dark brown laterally and paler below. Body green or brown. The green form has a white or pale dorsal line that is interrupted but increasingly complete posteriorly, and edged dark brown A6–A8 and pale brown elsewhere, with white spots between the segments A1–A7. There are darker subdorsal and lateral lines, usually hardly discernible. Spiracular stripe indistinct. Proleg and anal clasper pinkish brown. The brown form is similar, with darker or paler subdorsal and lateral lines, a pale brown or whitish spiracular stripe, and pinkish-brown or whitish-grey proleg and anal clasper. **HABITATS** Open, sunny places such as arable fields and coastal grassland. **FOODPLANT** Has been found on Knotgrass. **FIELD NOTES** Rarely observed in the wild but likely to be present through summer and autumn. Pupates among leaf litter in captivity. Unable to survive the winter in Great Britain and Ireland.

LARENTIINAE

OBLIQUE STRIPED
Phibalapteryx virgata

PLATE 17
70.039 (1718)

Nb. Has disappeared from some areas in central southern England. **FIELD CHARACTERS** Body brown or purplish brown, yellow or whitish below, with a dark or blackish dorsal line and a dark brown or blackish lateral band or stripe. Proleg and end of anal clasper pinkish. **HABITATS** Calcareous grassland including breckland, and sand dunes. **FOODPLANT** Lady's Bedstraw. **FIELD NOTES** Jun–Jul and Sep. Pupates in or on the ground. Overwinters as a pupa.

LEAD BELLE
Scotopteryx mucronata

PLATE 17
70.040 (1733)

The combined records for Lead Belle and July Belle show a significant decline in abundance in recent decades. Ssp. *umbrifera* Local in the south-west and on the south Wales coast. Ssp. *scotica* Local. **FIELD CHARACTERS** Body dirty whitish or pale brown, with variable intensity of dark or reddish-brown speckling. Dorsal stripe comprises ill-defined dark dashes, broadly edged pale grey with dark marks. Subdorsal stripe pale brown, within which is a reddish-brown line. Spiracular stripe greyish and faint, with an irregular margin above and ill-defined below.

Spiracles black, with pale grey or blackish spots posteriorly on abdominal segments, varying in intensity from obvious to faint. **SIMILAR SPECIES** July Belle is indistinguishable on field characters, but is not fully fed until later in spring. **HABITATS** Mainly heathland and moorland; less often rough pastures and scrub. **FOODPLANTS** Broom, Gorse, Dyer's Greenweed and Petty Whin. **FIELD NOTES** Aug–Mar. Feeds at night, and throughout winter in mild conditions. Pupates in a network cocoon among the foodplant or on the ground.

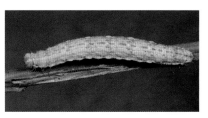

Lead Belle larva

JULY BELLE
Scotopteryx luridata

PLATE 17
70.041 (1734)

Ssp. *plumbaria*. The combined records for Lead Belle and July Belle show a significant decline in abundance in recent decades. Common. Widespread from the west Midlands and Wales southwards, in East Anglia, and in much of Scotland. Rare elsewhere, including in south-east England. **SIMILAR SPECIES** Lead Belle. **HABITATS** Calcareous grassland, heathland, moorland, scrub, vegetated shingle and open woodland. **FOODPLANTS** Gorse, Dyer's Greenweed and Petty Whin. **FIELD NOTES** Sep–May. Feeds at night. Pupates in a network cocoon among plant debris.

SPANISH CARPET
Scotopteryx peribolata

PLATE 17
70.042 (1730)

Immigrant; resident in the Channel Islands. May have established once, albeit temporarily, on the south coast of England. **FIELD CHARACTERS** Body pale brown. Dorsal line dark greyish brown, broadly shaded pale brown, with white dots posteriorly A2–A7. The line comprises dashes on abdominal segments, the dashes significantly broader A4–A5. Pale brown subdorsal stripe, lateral line and subspiracular stripe with brownish speckling between. Spiracles black, and there may be darker spots posterior to the spiracles on anterior abdominal segments. **HABITATS** Exposed parts of cliffs. **FOODPLANTS** Broom (prostrate form) and Gorse. **FIELD NOTES** Sep–May. Eggs have been found on the spines of Gorse. Probably pupates in the ground.

CHALK CARPET
Scotopteryx bipunctaria

PLATE 17
70.043 (1731)

Ssp. *cretata* Nb. **FIELD CHARACTERS** Body greyish brown, with black pinacula and short, pale, bristle-like hairs that point forwards and backwards. Dorsal line dark brown or dark grey. Subdorsal stripe pale brown, within which there may sometimes be a faint reddish-brown line. Lateral line pale and from below spiracles ventrally pale brown. Spiracles black with dark spots posterior to the spiracles A1–A6, the spots varying in intensity from obvious to faint, or sometimes absent. **SIMILAR SPECIES** Shaded Broad-bar is indistinguishable in the field. **HABITATS** Cliffs, embankments, calcareous and coastal grasslands with bare ground or exposed rocks and stones, and old quarries. **FOODPLANTS** Various clovers, trefoils and vetches, including Common Bird's-foot-trefoil, Black Medick and Horseshoe Vetch. **FIELD NOTES** Aug–Jun. Feeds at night. Pupates in a cocoon on the ground.

Chalk Carpet larva

SHADED BROAD-BAR
Scotopteryx chenopodiata

PLATE 17
70.045 (1732)

Common. Very local in the north-west. **SIMILAR SPECIES** Chalk Carpet. **HABITATS** Open, dry grassy areas on acid, calcareous and neutral grasslands, heathland, road verges, sand dunes and waste ground. **FOODPLANTS** Clovers and vetches. **FIELD NOTES** Aug–Jun. Pupates in a spinning.

OBLIQUE CARPET
Orthonama vittata

PLATE 17
70.046 (1719)

Local. More widespread in western areas. Has declined significantly in abundance in recent decades. **FIELD CHARACTERS** In two colour forms, both with variable intensity of markings. The green form has a green body, often shaded pinkish purple between segments and sometimes more extensively, a dark green dorsal line, and a pale subdorsal line and subspiracular stripe, with blackish or darker dashes above the stripe. Proleg reddish or brownish. Body of the brown form entirely brown or replaced with green A6–A10. Dorsal line brown, subdorsal line pale, and subspiracular stripe whitish or pale green, with smudged black dashes above. Proleg dark brown. **SIMILAR SPECIES** Red Carpet is shorter and broader. The green form has pinkish bands between segments, but with proleg green. **HABITATS** Bogs, ditch banks, fens, marshes, water meadows and damp woodland; less often dry grassland. **FOODPLANTS** Heath Bedstraw, Common Marsh-bedstraw, and possibly other bedstraws. **FIELD NOTES** Jul and Sep–Apr in the south, Aug–early Jun in northern Scotland.

NOTE ON CARPETS IN GENUS *XANTHORHOE*

Larvae of the eight species in genus *Xanthorhoe* have very similar markings and could readily be misidentified in the field. Red Carpet and Balsam Carpet are described in detail and illustrated as their habitat and foodplant requirements should make them easier to identify. Garden Carpet is also included as an example of a common species. The other species are not illustrated nor described but they all bear a resemblance to Garden Carpet. The table on pp. 414–15 summarises key characters, habitats, foodplants and phenology. Garden Carpet, Red Twin-spot Carpet, Dark-barred Twin-spot Carpet and Flame Carpet are especially variable and little reliance can be placed on identification based on larval features alone. Separating larvae of carpets in *Xanthorhoe* from *Epirrhoe* is rather easier: species in *Xanthorhoe* usually have a darker dorsal line from A6 posteriorly, and anterior to this there are variations along its length; species in genus *Epirrhoe*, except Small Argent & Sable, have a dark dorsal stripe from A6 posteriorly. Small Argent & Sable has a dark dorsal stripe running the full length of the dorsum.

RED CARPET
Xanthorhoe decoloraria

PLATE 18
70.048 (1723)

Ssp. *decoloraria* Common. Has declined significantly in abundance in recent decades. Ssp. *hethlandica* Shetland. **FIELD CHARACTERS** In two colour forms with variable intensity of markings. The green form has a green body, often shaded orangey or pinkish brown between segments. Dorsal line dark green, edged paler, sometimes incorporating darker or blackish dashes. Subdorsal line pale green, sometimes with black dashes above, subspiracular stripe greenish white, and proleg on A6 green, sometimes tinged pinkish around crochets. The brown form is similar, with green replaced by brown and the dorsal line edged whitish. **SIMILAR SPECIES** See *Separating* Xanthorhoe *carpets* table (pp. 414–15). **HABITATS** Usually at higher altitudes on grasslands in rocky situations and moorland. In the Northern Isles also on road verges and sand dunes. **FOODPLANTS** Lady's-mantles. **FIELD NOTES** Aug–late May. Pupates in a cocoon among plant debris.

GARDEN CARPET
Xanthorhoe fluctuata

PLATE 18
70.049 (1728)

Common. Has declined significantly in abundance in recent decades. **FIELD CHARACTERS** In two colour forms with variable intensity of markings. The green form has a green body with a dark green dorsal line, edged paler, and sometimes incorporating darker or blackish dashes. There may be faint, paler subdorsal and lateral lines. Paler or whitish below spiracles. The greyish-brown form may be more or less shaded blackish brown across the dorsum, with a dark dorsal line incorporating short black or brown dashes or spots. In darker examples, dashes may be broadly edged pale, and pale across the dorsum from A6 posteriorly. There may be faint, paler subdorsal and lateral lines. Whitish below spiracles. **SIMILAR SPECIES** See *Separating* Xanthorhoe *carpets* table (pp. 414–15). **HABITATS** Wide variety, especially allotments, gardens and rough ground, and including woodland. **FOODPLANTS** Cabbage family, including Sweet Alison, cultivated Cabbage and Honesty, and wild species such as Hairy Bitter-cress, Flixweed, wild Horse-radish, Garlic Mustard and Shepherd's-purse. Also on cultivars of Nasturtium. **FIELD NOTES** Apr–early Nov, in one to three generations depending on latitude. Feeds at night. Pupates in the ground. Overwinters as a pupa.

BALSAM CARPET
Xanthorhoe biriviata

PLATE 18
70.050 (1721)

Uncommon; suspected immigrant. Range appears to be spreading slowly. **FIELD CHARACTERS** In three colour forms with variable intensity of markings. The green form has a green body with a dark green dorsal line, edged paler, and sometimes incorporating darker or blackish dashes, and with paler subdorsal and lateral lines and pale yellowish below spiracles. Brown and grey forms may be more or less shaded blackish across the dorsum, with a dark dorsal line incorporating short black or brown dashes or spots, pale subdorsal and lateral lines and pale yellowish below spiracles. In darker examples, dashes may be broadly edged pale, and pale across the dorsum from A6 posteriorly. **SIMILAR SPECIES** See *Separating* Xanthorhoe *carpets* table (pp. 414–15). **HABITATS** Ditches, damp pastures, scrub, margins of waterbodies and woodland. **FOODPLANTS** Orange Balsam; less often Small Balsam. **FIELD NOTES** Jun, and Aug–Oct in a partial second generation. Feeds at night. Rests by day on the foodplant, especially along the midrib of the upperside of the leaf when larger. Pupation site unknown. Overwinters as a pupa.

RED TWIN-SPOT CARPET
Xanthorhoe spadicearia

NOT ILLUSTRATED
70.051 (1724)

Common. **SIMILAR SPECIES** See *Separating* Xanthorhoe *carpets* table (pp. 414–15). **HABITATS** Wide variety, including calcareous grassland, fens, hedgerows, moorland, sand dunes and woodland. **FOODPLANTS** Variety of herbaceous plants, especially Lady's and Heath bedstraws. Also reported on Wild Carrot, Cleavers, Ground-ivy, Knotgrass and Woodruff. **FIELD NOTES** Jun–Jul and Sep in two generations as far north as south-west Scotland, and Jun–late Aug elsewhere. Feeds at night. Pupates in a cocoon in plant debris. Overwinters as a pupa.

DARK-BARRED TWIN-SPOT CARPET
Xanthorhoe ferrugata

NOT ILLUSTRATED
70.052 (1725)

Common. Has declined severely in abundance in recent decades in southern England. **SIMILAR SPECIES** See *Separating* Xanthorhoe *carpets* table (pp. 414–15). **HABITATS** Wide variety, including calcareous grassland, fens, hedgerows, moorland, sand dunes and woodland. **FOODPLANTS** Variety of herbaceous plants, including bedstraws, dandelions, docks, Ground-ivy and Knotgrass. **FIELD NOTES** Jun–Jul and Sep–Oct in two generations. Feeds at night. Pupates in a cocoon in plant debris. Overwinters as a pupa.

FLAME CARPET
Xanthorhoe designata

NOT ILLUSTRATED
70.053 (1722)

Common. More numerous in the north and west. **SIMILAR SPECIES** See *Separating* Xanthorhoe *carpets* table (pp. 414–15). **HABITATS** Wide variety, including calcareous grassland, upland grassland, hedgerows, moorland and lowland woodlands. **FOODPLANT** Larvae have been found feeding on Mugwort, hiding in the twisted and withered leaves on the lower part of the stem. **FIELD NOTES** Early Jun–mid-Jul and Aug–Sep in two generations, except in Scotland where Jul–Aug. Feeds at night. Pupates in or on the ground. Overwinters as a pupa.

SILVER-GROUND CARPET
Xanthorhoe montanata

NOT ILLUSTRATED
70.054 (1727)

Ssp. *montanata* Common. Ssp. *shetlandica* Shetland. **SIMILAR SPECIES** See *Separating* Xanthorhoe *carpets* table (pp. 414–15). **HABITATS** Prefers sheltered areas among tall herbaceous vegetation within fens, gardens, grasslands, heathland, hedgerows, scrub and woodland rides. **FOODPLANTS** Herbaceous plants, including Hedge Bedstraw, Cleavers, Cowslip, Primrose, Tansy and Yarrow. **FIELD NOTES** Jul–May. Feeds at night. Pupates in a cocoon in the ground.

LARGE TWIN-SPOT CARPET
Xanthorhoe quadrifasiata

NOT ILLUSTRATED
70.055 (1726)

Local. More frequent in the east. **SIMILAR SPECIES** See *Separating* Xanthorhoe *carpets* table (pp. 414–15). **HABITATS** Scrub on heathland, ancient woodland, and carr and other wet woodlands. **FOODPLANTS** Herbaceous plants, including bedstraws, Primrose and violets. **FIELD NOTES** Aug–May. Pupates in the ground.

ROYAL MANTLE
Catarhoe cuculata

PLATE 18
70.056 (1736)

Local. Very local in eastern Scotland and western Ireland. **FIELD CHARACTERS** Body black with yellow dorsal and spiracular stripes, and green ventrally. **HABITATS** Dry calcareous areas including breckland calcareous grassland, and lower slopes of upland valleys. Also cliffs, old chalk and limestone quarries, and wide woodland rides. **FOODPLANTS** Mainly on the flowers of Hedge and Lady's bedstraws. **FIELD NOTES** Jul–early Sep. Pupates in the ground. Overwinters as a pupa.

Yellow Shell larva (see opposite)

RUDDY CARPET
Catarhoe rubidata

PLATE 18
70.057 (1735)

Nb. Has declined in abundance and distribution since mid-twentieth century. **FIELD CHARACTERS** Body pale brown or pale grey, usually heavily speckled darker T1–A6 and pale beyond, or sometimes pale or dark throughout. Dorsal line dark, continuous T1–T3 and A7–A9, with dark spots between. Whitish V-shapes across the dorsum A2–A6, edged blackish anteriorly and increasingly well defined towards A6, sometimes with a black mark laterally on A6. Subdorsal line pale and continuous T1–T3 and A6–A9 but interrupted and indistinct between. Pinacula white. Spiracles black. **SIMILAR SPECIES** Common Carpet and Wood Carpet have incomplete whitish ovals on the dorsum and a noticeably paler subspiracular stripe. However, given variation in intensity of markings, larvae should be reared to confirm identity. **HABITATS** Mainly dry calcareous places, including cliffs, breckland and calcareous grasslands, hedge banks, hedgerows, scrub and woodland rides. **FOODPLANTS** Hedge and Lady's bedstraws. **FIELD NOTES** Jul–Aug. Pupates in an earthen cocoon in the ground. Overwinters as a pupa.

YELLOW SHELL
Camptogramma bilineata

PLATE 18
70.059 (1742)

Has increased significantly in abundance in recent decades. Ssp. *bilineata* Common. Ssp. *atlantica* Shetland, Outer Hebrides. Ssp. *hibernica* Sea cliffs in Cos Cork and Kerry. Ssp. *isolata* Blasket Islands, Ireland. **FIELD CHARACTERS** Usually green, or occasionally grey or brown. The green form has a pale or dark green body, covered sparsely with conspicuous short grey hairs. Dorsal stripe dark green, edged whitish green, and subdorsal stripe whitish green. Subspiracular stripe whitish, sometimes edged above with a black line. Grey and brown forms are similarly patterned. **HABITATS** Wide variety, including cliffs, gardens, coastal and inland grasslands, heathland, hedgerows, marshes, moorland and woodland. **FOODPLANTS** Various herbaceous plants, including Garden Arabis, Aubretia, bedstraws, Wild Cabbage, Lesser Celandine, Cowslip, dandelions, docks, Pot Marjoram, Annual Meadow-grass, sorrels, Wild Strawberry, restharrows, wormwoods and Yarrow. **FIELD NOTES** Jul–late May. Feeds at night. Pupates in the ground.

NOTE ON CARPETS IN GENUS *EPIRRHOE*

Larvae of species in genus *Epirrhoe* are similar to those in *Xanthorhoe* – see *Note on carpets in genus Xanthorhoe* (p. 142) for differences. Of the following four species, it is only Common Carpet and Wood Carpet larvae that cannot be distinguished in the field.

SMALL ARGENT & SABLE
Epirrhoe tristata

PLATE 18
70.060 (1737)

Common. **FIELD CHARACTERS** Body brown or greyish brown with white pinacula. Dorsal line dark brown, and subdorsal stripe, lateral line and subspiracular stripe pale brown. Spiracles black. **SIMILAR SPECIES** Galium Carpet has a dorsal line that widens to a stripe A6–A9, the subspiracular stripe edged above with black dashes, and brown spiracles. **HABITATS** Mainly upland habitats, including high limestone grassland, moorland, and upland woodland and hedgerows. Also limestone pavement (the Burren, Cos Clare and Galway, Ireland), and rarely on heaths and mosses. **FOODPLANT** Heath Bedstraw. **FIELD NOTES** Late Jun–Aug, with a partial second generation in autumn in south-west England and Ireland. Pupates in a cocoon on the ground. Overwinters as a pupa.

COMMON CARPET
Epirrhoe alternata

PLATE 18
70.061 (1738)

Ssp. *alternata* Common. Ssp. *obscurata* Outer Hebrides. **FIELD CHARACTERS** Body brown, sometimes paler A6–A9. Dorsal stripe dark brown, continuous T1–T3 and A7–A9, with dark marks and near-complete white ovals between. Subdorsal stripe whitish, continuous T1–T3 and A6–A9, and indistinct between. Lateral line whitish, indistinct. Subspiracular stripe whitish mixed with brownish, with ill-defined margins. Pinacula white, spiracles black. **SIMILAR SPECIES** Ruddy Carpet and Wood Carpet. **HABITATS** Wide variety, including fens, gardens, calcareous and acidic grasslands, heathland, marshes, moorland, sand dunes, scrub and woodland. **FOODPLANTS** Hedge and Lady's bedstraws, Cleavers and Flixweed. **FIELD NOTES** Jun–Jul and Sep–Oct in two generations in the south, Jul–Aug in one generation in the north. Pupates in a cocoon on the ground. Overwinters as a pupa.

WOOD CARPET
Epirrhoe rivata

PLATE 18
70.062 (1739)

Local. **SIMILAR SPECIES** Ruddy Carpet and Common Carpet. **HABITATS** Mainly in calcareous areas, including cliffs and grasslands, hedgerows and boundary banks, old quarries, road verges, sand dunes, scrub and woodland rides. **FOODPLANTS** Hedge and Lady's bedstraws. **FIELD NOTES** Late Jul–late Sep. Pupates in a cocoon on or in the ground. Overwinters as a pupa.

GALIUM CARPET
Epirrhoe galiata

PLATE 18
70.063 (1740)

Local. Most frequent in coastal areas. Has declined significantly in abundance in recent decades. **FIELD CHARACTERS** Body brown with small white pinacula. Dorsal line dark brown or black, widening to a clear stripe A6–A9. Subdorsal stripe whitish. Lateral line comprising whitish dashes, and spiracular stripe whitish, edged above with blackish dashes. Spiracles brown, with darker surrounds. **SIMILAR SPECIES** Small Argent & Sable. **HABITATS** Mainly cliffs and grasslands in coastal areas, sand dunes and vegetated shingle. Less often in calcareous grassland and moorland. **FOODPLANTS** Heath, Hedge and Lady's bedstraws. **FIELD NOTES** Late Jun–Jul and Sep in two generations in the south and Ireland, Aug in the north. Pupates in the ground. Overwinters as a pupa.

CLOAKED CARPET
Euphyia biangulata

PLATE 18
70.064 (1793)

Nb. Seldom seen in numbers. **FIELD CHARACTERS** Body brown. From T3 posteriorly, dorsal line dark brown edged with a pale brown line, usually incorporating broad blackish dashes on A4 or A5–A6. Subdorsal stripe pale brown and lateral line similar, sometimes edged with a black line or shading below. Subspiracular stripe pale brown, with lower margin ill-defined. Spiracles black. **SIMILAR SPECIES** Sharp-angled Carpet is pale greyish brown with blackish spots rather than dashes along the dorsum and these are greater in number. **HABITATS** Hedge banks, hedgerows, wooded rocky ravines, and damp woodland edges and rides. **FOODPLANTS** Mainly stitchworts. Also Hedge Bedstraw and Common Chickweed. **FIELD NOTES** Late Jul–mid-Sep. Feeds at night. Pupates in a cocoon on the ground. Overwinters as a pupa.

Cloaked Carpet larva

SHARP-ANGLED CARPET
Euphyia unangulata

PLATE 18
70.065 (1794)

Local. Usually occurs in small numbers. **FIELD CHARACTERS** Body pale greyish brown or greyish. From T3 posteriorly, dorsal line grey or dark grey edged with a pale grey line, incorporating black spots A2–A5, or sometimes A1–A6. Subdorsal stripe, lateral line and subspiracular stripe pale grey or whitish. Spiracles black. **SIMILAR SPECIES** Cloaked Carpet. **HABITATS** Wooded hedgerows and woodland. **FOODPLANTS** Unknown in the wild. Feeds on Common Chickweed and stitchworts in captivity. **FIELD NOTES** Jul–Sep. Pupates in a cocoon on or in the ground. Overwinters as a pupa.

SHOULDER STRIPE
Earophila badiata

PLATE 18
70.066 (1746)

Common. **FIELD CHARACTERS** Head orangey brown, usually with a dark spot laterally. Body whitish green, green, blackish green or dark grey, with white pinacula. Paler examples may be shaded darker laterally. Pale or whitish below the spiracles, with obvious black spots A1–A7 below and in front of the whitish spiracles. **HABITATS** Wide variety, including gardens, hedgerows, scrub and woodland. **FOODPLANTS** Wild roses, including Dog-rose, Burnet Rose and Sweet-briar. **FIELD NOTES** Apr–Jul. Feeds at night. Pupates in a cocoon in the ground. Overwinters as a pupa.

STREAMER
Anticlea derivata

PLATE 18
70.067 (1747)

Common. **FIELD CHARACTERS** Body greenish with reddish or purplish markings that are variable in extent. Often a dark dorsal band T1–T3, broken into ovals on abdominal segments, and with a T-shape across the dorsum A6–A8. Proleg wholly or partly reddish or purplish. Anal flap and anal clasper dorsally reddish or purplish. **HABITATS** Wide variety, including gardens, hedgerows, scrub, and open areas or rides in woodland. **FOODPLANTS** Mainly Dog-rose. Also recorded on Blackthorn, Sherard's Downy-rose, Hawthorn and Honeysuckle. **FIELD NOTES** May–Jul. Feeds at night. Pupates in a cocoon in the ground. Overwinters as a pupa.

BEAUTIFUL CARPET
Mesoleuca albicillata

PLATE 18
70.068 (1748)

Common. Seen in small numbers only. **FIELD CHARACTERS** Body green with moderately long hairs. Usually there are orangey-brown dorsal triangles, edged brownish laterally, on T3–A7, but these may be faint in some examples. Subspiracular line reddish T1–T3 and from A6 posteriorly, and white or white mixed reddish A1–A5. Proleg and anal clasper variably reddish. Anal flap reddish. **HABITATS** Mainly in conifer plantations on ancient woodland sites, and open broadleaf woodland. Also old hedgerows and long-established scrub. **FOODPLANTS** Bramble, Dewberry, Hazel, Raspberry and Wild Strawberry. **FIELD NOTES** Jul–Sep. Feeds at night. Pupates in the ground. Overwinters as a pupa.

DARK SPINACH
Pelurga comitata

PLATE 18
70.069 (1749)

Common. Has declined severely in abundance in recent decades, especially in southern England, but remains widespread. **FIELD CHARACTERS** Body brown or grey, occasionally greenish, and mottled darker, with abdominal segments A1–A5 somewhat swollen laterally. Dorsal line dark, sometimes formed of dashes, with raised white or pale oval spots A2–A4. Often there are V-shaped blackish stripes across the dorsal area and, subdorsally, orangey spots A1–A4 and whitish pinacula. Subspiracular stripe whitish and wavy, linking above to each spiracle on A1–A4 or A5. **HABITATS** Mainly associated with cultivated ground such as allotments, arable fields and farmland, gardens, and waste ground in coastal and inland places. **FOODPLANTS** On flowers and seeds of goosefoots and oraches. **FIELD NOTES** Late Aug–Oct. Feeds at night. Pupates in or on the ground. Overwinters as a pupa.

MALLOW
Larentia clavaria

PLATE 19
70.070 (1745)

Common. Local or very local away from its core distribution. **FIELD CHARACTERS** Body pale green, with numerous transverse whitish dashes. May be tinged with yellow, and occasionally extensively with reddish-brown shading. Dorsal line dark green. Pinacula raised and white. Spiracles black, surrounded by white rings. **HABITATS** Rough coastal grassland, marshes, riverbanks, roadside verges, vegetated shingle and waste ground. **FOODPLANTS** Hollyhock, Common Mallow, Marsh-mallow and Tree-mallow. **FIELD NOTES** Mar–Jun. Feeds at night, hiding by day at the base of the plant. Pupates in the ground. Overwinters as an egg.

YELLOW-RINGED CARPET
Entephria flavicinctata

PLATE 19
70.071 (1743)

Ssp. *flavicinctata* Nb. West coast of mainland Scotland and Inner Hebrides, northern England, north Wales and the Black Mountains (Breconshire and Herefordshire), and Northern Ireland. Ssp. *ruficinctata* Local. Central and north-west Scotland, and an isolated population with two generations per year in West Dunbartonshire. **SIMILAR SPECIES** Grey Mountain Carpet, Northern Spinach and Phoenix. **HABITATS** Associated with sparsely vegetated limestone rock strata. Cliffs, gorges, rocky ravines, scree; also waste ground. **FOODPLANTS** Ssp. *flavicinctata* Mossy Saxifrage (Yorkshire) and English Stonecrop (mainland Scotland, Inner Hebrides). Ssp. *ruficinctata* Mossy, Purple and Yellow saxifrages. **FIELD NOTES** Jun–Jul and Sep–Apr where there are two generations, Sep–early Jun where there is one. Pupates in a spinning among the foodplant, in a rock crevice or in the ground. Overwinters as a larva.

GREY MOUNTAIN CARPET
Entephria caesiata

PLATE 19
70.072 (1744)

Ssp. *caesiata* Common. An upland species. Has declined severely in abundance in recent decades. Ssp. *hethlandicaria* Northern Scotland, including Shetland. **FIELD CHARACTERS** Body green or brown. Forward-facing triangles along the dorsum T3–A8, smaller and less well defined on T3 and A8. In the green form, triangles are yellowish anteriorly and reddish brown, pinkish and whitish posteriorly, and in the brown form they are orangey or yellow anteriorly and whitish and greyish or pinkish posteriorly. Triangles are usually shaded brownish laterally. Spiracular stripe white. In the green form, anterior part of T1 and anal flap are red or brown. **SIMILAR SPECIES** Yellow-ringed Carpet has similar markings but uses different foodplants. Northern Spinach has a more slender larva with fainter dorsal markings and spiracular line, and usually has a brown transverse stripe on T2. Phoenix is indistinguishable from Northern Spinach but is in different habitats on different foodplants. **HABITATS** Mountains and moorland, usually among rocky terrain. **FOODPLANTS** Bilberry, Crowberry, Cross-leaved Heath, Heather and Bell Heather. Also recorded on Lodgepole Pine. **FIELD NOTES** Jul–Jun, in one generation. Pupates in a spinning among the foodplant. Overwinters as a small larva.

WHITE-BANDED CARPET
Spargania luctuata

PLATE 19
70.073 (1786)

Na. Resident in south-east England and breckland area of East Anglia. **FIELD CHARACTERS** Body green or brown. The brown form can be pale yellowish or orangey brown, and has a brown head, a dark brown dorsal line that is indistinct A1–A7, X-shaped marks dorsally and a broken yellowish-brown subdorsal line. The green form has a pale brown head, faint X-shaped marked and complete, dark green dorsal and subdorsal lines. **HABITATS** Coniferous plantations and broadleaf woodlands, preferring clearings and wide rides. **FOODPLANTS** Rosebay Willowherb. **FIELD NOTES** Mid-Jun–late Jul, and late Aug–Sep as a partial second generation. Pupates on the ground among debris. Overwinters as a pupa.

JULY HIGHFLYER
Hydriomena furcata

PLATE 19
70.074 (1777)

Common. **FIELD CHARACTERS** Body purplish brown or black, often with whitish bands between segments. Subdorsal stripe, lateral line and subspiracular stripe white. Spiracles black. Prothoracic plate brown or black, anal plate brown and true legs black. **SIMILAR SPECIES** May Highflyer and Ruddy Highflyer (which do not share the same foodplant) both have brown true legs and feed at a different time of year than July Highflyer. Dark forms of Argent & Sable have a subdorsal line rather than a stripe, and pale spiracles with dark outlines that are surrounded by white or yellow blotches, and they feed later in the year. **HABITATS** In the south, mainly in broadleaf woodland, especially mature Hazel coppice. Also fens, heathland, conifer plantations, scrub and carr woodland. In the north, mainly on moorland. On the Isle of Man, prefers hedges around meadows and pastures. **FOODPLANTS** Bilberry, Downy Birch, Hazel, Heather, poplars and willows. Also recorded on Lodgepole Pine and Sitka Spruce. **FIELD NOTES** Apr–Jun, or slightly later in the north. Hides in a spinning by day and feeds at night. Pupates in the ground. Overwinters as an egg.

MAY HIGHFLYER
Hydriomena impluviata

PLATE 19
70.075 (1778)

Common. **FIELD CHARACTERS** Body pinkish grey with broad greenish-grey bands between segments. Dorsal line dark; subdorsal stripe, if present, whitish, faint and interrupted, and subspiracular stripe whitish and faint. Prothoracic and anal plates brown and true legs brown. **SIMILAR SPECIES** July Highflyer, Ruddy Highflyer and Argent & Sable. **HABITATS** Fens, wooded margins of waterbodies, and carr and other wet woodlands. **FOODPLANT** Alder. **FIELD NOTES** Jul–Oct or Nov, feeding slowly. Hides in a spinning by day and feeds at night. Pupates in the ground or under loose bark. Overwinters as a pupa.

RUDDY HIGHFLYER
Hydriomena ruberata

PLATE 19
70.076 (1779)

Local. Most frequent in the north and west. **FIELD CHARACTERS** Body greyish or pale brown. Dorsal line black, either within a broad, dark dorsal band, or with a black subdorsal line outwardly edged with a whitish or pale line or stripe. Dark forms have a pale subspiracular stripe. Prothoracic and anal plates brown and true legs brown. **SIMILAR SPECIES** July Highflyer, May Highflyer and Argent & Sable. **HABITATS** Bogs, acid grassland with scrub, heathland, marshes, moorland, and carr and open woodlands. **FOODPLANTS** Mainly Eared and Grey willows; also Tea-leaved Willow. Recorded on Heather in Orkney. Often prefers bushes less than 0.3m high. **FIELD NOTES** Jul–Sep, feeding slowly. Hides in a spinning by day and feeds at night. Pupates on the ground. Overwinters as a pupa.

NOTE ON CONIFER-FEEDING CARPETS AND OTHER SIMILAR-LOOKING GEOMETRIDS

Larvae of conifer-feeding species are remarkably cryptic against the foliage on which they feed, and larvae of different species can look similar to one another. Fortunately, in Great Britain and Ireland species feeding on Common Juniper do not feed on other conifers, and vice versa, so listings under similar species reflect foodplants and the likelihood of different species being found together.

PINE CARPET
Pennithera firmata

PLATE 19
70.077 (1767)

Common. Has increased significantly in abundance in recent decades. **FIELD CHARACTERS** Head brown. Body green with a dark green dorsal line, edged paler, and with a yellow or white subdorsal line and subspiracular stripe. The subspiracular stripe is broader, with orangey-brown shading above T1–T3, reaching the subdorsal line T1–T2. True legs orangey, blackish or green. Abdomen with a pair of long anal points. **SIMILAR SPECIES** Spruce Carpet and Grey Pine Carpet have a greenish head, and both lack the white and orangey-brown lateral patch T1–T3. Spruce Carpet has green true legs, Grey Pine Carpet has reddish true legs. Tawny-barred Angle, Bordered White and Banded Pine Carpet lack anal points. Dusky Peacock and Tawny-barred Angle have a rather bulbous head that is greenish centrally and brownish laterally, but are indistinguishable from each other in the field and where distributions overlap in south-east England they should be reared to confirm identity. Banded Pine Carpet has rudimentary prolegs on A5. Bordered White has a somewhat flattened head that is green with white stripes. **HABITATS** Pine plantations and woodland, and scrub on heathland and moorland. Also gardens and urban parks. **FOODPLANTS** Corsican, Lodgepole and Scots pines. **FIELD NOTES** Usually autumn–Jul, or sometimes Aug. Feeds at night. Pupates in a spinning among needles in the tree or on the ground. Overwinters as an egg or a small larva.

CHESTNUT-COLOURED CARPET
Thera cognata

PLATE 19
70.078 (1770)

Nb. Widely distributed in Scotland; local elsewhere. **FIELD CHARACTERS** Head pale brownish green. Body green, with a green dorsal line, broadly edged whitish. Subdorsal and subspiracular stripes white or yellow. True legs reddish or green. Abdomen with a pair of very short anal points. **SIMILAR SPECIES** Juniper Carpet has at least some red coloration above the subspiracular stripe, and a red lateral spot on the head. It is fully fed much later in the year. The green form of Juniper Pug has reddish coloration centrally on the anal flap, and lacks white edging to the dorsal line. **HABITATS** Cliffs, limestone pavement, moorland, and scrub on hillsides. **FOODPLANT** Common Juniper. **FIELD NOTES** Sep–early Jun but eggs have been recorded as hatching late Nov. Pupates in a spinning in the bush or on the ground. Overwinters as a small larva.

SPRUCE CARPET
Thera britannica

PLATE 19
70.079 (1769)

Common. Has increased very significantly in abundance in recent decades. **FIELD CHARACTERS** Head green or brownish green. Body green with a dark green dorsal line, narrowly edged with white lines. Subdorsal stripe white and there may be a darker green line within. Subspiracular stripe yellow. True legs green. Abdomen with a pair of short anal points. **SIMILAR SPECIES** Pine Carpet, Grey Pine Carpet, Tawny-barred Angle, Bordered White and Banded Pine Carpet. **HABITATS** Mainly conifer plantations and woodland. Also gardens and urban parks. **FOODPLANTS** Mainly Western Hemlock-spruce and Norway and Sitka spruces. Also recorded on Lawson's Cypress, Douglas Fir, Giant Fir, Noble Fir, Scots Pine, Western Red-cedar and European Silver-fir. Also reported that captive rearing from eggs on Lawson's Cypress and Western Red-cedar was unsuccessful. **FIELD NOTES** Autumn–May and Jun–Jul, in two generations. Feeds at night. Pupates in a spinning on or below the ground. Overwinters as a small larva.

GREY PINE CARPET
Thera obeliscata

PLATE 19
70.081 (1768)

Common. **FIELD CHARACTERS** Head green. Body green with a dark green dorsal line, narrowly edged with white lines. Subdorsal stripe white, sometimes mixed yellowish, and there may be a dark green line within. Subspiracular stripe white or yellowish. True legs red. Abdomen with a pair of short anal points. **SIMILAR SPECIES** Pine Carpet, Spruce Carpet, Tawny-barred Angle, Bordered White and Banded Pine Carpet. **HABITATS** Gardens and urban parks, and conifer plantations and woodland. **FOODPLANTS** A variety of conifer species, including Lawson's and Monterey cypresses, Douglas Fir, Western Hemlock-spruce, Scots Pine, Western Red-cedar, European Silver-fir and Norway Spruce. Also reported that captive rearing from eggs on Lawson's Cypress and Western Red-cedar was unsuccessful. **FIELD NOTES** Sep–Jun and Jul–Aug, in two generations. Pupates in a spinning in the ground.

JUNIPER CARPET
Thera juniperata

PLATE 19
70.082 (1771)

Ssp. *juniperata* Common. Has increased significantly in abundance in recent decades, particularly in England in urban areas. Ssp. *scotica* Local in mainland Scotland. Ssp. *orcadensis* Possibly extinct, Orkney. **FIELD CHARACTERS** Head green with a lateral red spot close to the mouthparts. Body green with a green dorsal line, broadly edged with whitish shading, and a yellow subdorsal stripe. Subspiracular stripe white with patchy yellow shading, and often edged above with a red stripe, or with red spots T1–T3. Legs red. Abdomen with a pair of short anal points. **SIMILAR SPECIES** Chestnut-coloured Carpet. **HABITATS** Cliffs, gardens and urban parks, limestone and upland grassland, moorland, sand dunes, and scrub on chalk. Populations can thrive on isolated bushes in gardens. **FOODPLANTS** Junipers, including cultivars. **FIELD NOTES** Mid-Jul–early Sep. Pupates in a spinning among the foodplant. Overwinters as an egg.

CYPRESS CARPET
Thera cupressata

PLATE 19
70.083 (1771a)

Recent colonist, spreading northwards. **FIELD CHARACTERS** Head green. Body green with a green dorsal line, edged with curved paler green lines or shading. A white subdorsal crescent on each segment, with irregular pale green blotches laterally. Abdomen with a pair of short, broad triangular anal points. True legs pink. **SIMILAR SPECIES** Cypress Pug is smaller when fully fed, has green true legs, and lacks white subdorsal crescents and anal points. **HABITATS** Mainly cemeteries, gardens and urban parks. Sometimes in rural places such as arboreta and in shelterbelts. **FOODPLANT** Monterey Cypress. **FIELD NOTES** Nov–May and late Jul–Sep, in two generations. Feeds at night. Pupates in a slight spinning.

BLUE-BORDERED CARPET
Plemyria rubiginata

PLATE 19
70.084 (1766)

Has increased significantly in abundance in recent decades. Ssp. *rubiginata* Common. Lowland England, Wales and Ireland. Ssp. *plumbata* Local. Northern England and Scotland. **FIELD CHARACTERS** Head green with a central notch and rounded dorsal lobes, and T1 has a pair of forward-facing subdorsal points. Body green, dorsal line darker. Subdorsal stripe pale yellow, spiracular line pale yellow. Abdomen with a pair of long anal points. **SIMILAR SPECIES** Barred Yellow has pale edging to the dorsal line, somewhat shorter anal points and different foodplants. **HABITATS** Banks of rivers and streams, gardens, hedgerows, lakesides, marshes, orchards, scrub and woodland. **FOODPLANTS** Mainly Alder and Blackthorn. Also recorded on Apple, birches, cherries and hawthorns. **FIELD NOTES** Late Apr–early Jun. Pupates in a spinning among twigs of the foodplant. Overwinters as an egg.

BARRED YELLOW
Cidaria fulvata

PLATE 19
70.085 (1765)

Common. Local in Ireland. **FIELD CHARACTERS** Head brownish green with a central notch and rounded dorsal lobes, and T1 has a pair of small subdorsal points. Body green and dorsal line darker, edged whitish green or yellowish green. Subdorsal line yellowish, sometimes interrupted, and subspiracular line yellowish. Abdomen with a pair of short anal points. **SIMILAR SPECIES** Blue-bordered Carpet. **HABITATS** Gardens and urban parks, scrub on calcareous grassland, and woodland. **FOODPLANTS** Dog-rose, Burnet Rose and probably other wild and cultivated roses. **FIELD NOTES** May–Jun. Feeds at night. Pupates in a slight silken cocoon among leaves of the foodplant. Overwinters as an egg.

BROKEN-BARRED CARPET
Electrophaes corylata

PLATE 19
70.086 (1773)

Common. **FIELD CHARACTERS** Head green, sometimes brown, with a central notch and forward-pointing dorsal lobes. Body yellowish green. Dorsal line dark green and often faint, with purplish or dark brown shading T1–T3 and A6–A9 and spots A1–A5. Subdorsal stripe pale yellowish green, and often there are black or purplish spots A1–A5 below the level of the spiracles. The extent of darker markings is variable. True legs red or green, and proleg green or occasionally purple. Anal flap pointed. **SIMILAR SPECIES** Small Phoenix, White-pinion Spotted and Clouded Silver. Small Phoenix has black markings on the head and a darker or black leg on T3. Broken-barred Carpet has a notched head, black or purple spots A1–A5 below the level of the spiracles, and a pointed anal plate. White-pinion Spotted has a speckled green head and a rounded anal flap. Clouded Silver has dark pear-shaped markings on the head and a rounded anal flap. **HABITATS** Hedgerows, scrub and woodland. **FOODPLANTS** Various broadleaf trees and shrubs, including Downy Birch, Blackthorn, Sweet Chestnut, Hawthorn, Midland Hawthorn, limes, Pedunculate Oak and willows. **FIELD NOTES** Jul–Sep or early Oct, feeding slowly. Pupates in the ground. Overwinters as a pupa.

PURPLE BAR
Cosmorhoe ocellata

PLATE 19
70.087 (1752)

Common. **FIELD CHARACTERS** Head mottled brown with two pale lines. Body brown, with a dark brown dorsal line edged with whitish shading, and with backward-facing V-shaped white stripes A1–A5. Subspiracular stripe white, extending onto the proleg and anal clasper. Spiracles black. **HABITATS** Wide variety, including gardens, breckland and other grasslands, heathland, hedgerows, sand dunes, scrub and woodland rides. **FOODPLANTS** Recorded on Heath, Hedge and Lady's-bedstraws, and marsh-bedstraws. **FIELD NOTES** Jun–Jul and Sep–Apr in two generations in the south, and Jul–Aug in one generation in the north. Pupates in a cocoon in the ground in Apr. Overwinters fully fed within the cocoon.

NETTED CARPET
Eustroma reticulata

PLATE 19
70.088 (1772)

RDB. Confined to the Lake District. Now extinct in Wales. **FIELD CHARACTERS** Head pale brownish green. Body green. Dorsal line dark green with red or reddish-brown marks T1–T3 or down to A3 and on A7–A8, and sometimes with red spots between. Subdorsal stripe white and spiracular line thin and pale green. Anal clasper edged anteriorly yellowish. **HABITATS** Shaded areas where the foodplant grows, in flushes, lake shores, seepages, streamsides and wet woodland. **FOODPLANT** Touch-me-not Balsam. **FIELD NOTES** Late Jul–early Sep, sometimes later. Feeds at night, at first making holes in leaves, and later on in developing seedpods. Overwinters as a pupa in an earthen cocoon on the damp soil surface.

PHOENIX
Eulithis prunata

PLATE 19
70.089 (1754)

Common. Local in Ireland. Occurs at low density. **FIELD CHARACTERS** Head with a central notch and rounded dorsal lobes, mottled brownish, and often with a pair of pale stripes. Body brownish, greyish or yellowish green. In the brown form the anterior portion of each segment is greyish, and in the greyish form uniformly grey, with a grey dorsal line, edged paler or whitish. There is a black transverse band on T2, enclosing six whitish pinacula, and short, forward-pointing V-shaped blackish or brown dorsal stripes T3–A6. Pinacula white. The yellowish-green form has a dark green dorsal line, with dark brown dorsal V-shapes sometimes reduced to spots on anterior segments, and a strongly contrasting dark band on T2. **SIMILAR SPECIES** Yellow-ringed Carpet, Grey Mountain Carpet and Northern Spinach are found in different habitats and on different plants. **HABITATS** Allotments, gardens and in woodland, where it prefers streamsides. **FOODPLANTS** Black and Red currants, and Gooseberry, preferring shaded plants. **FIELD NOTES** Apr–Jun. Feeds at night. Pupates in spun leaves of the foodplant.

CHEVRON
Eulithis testata

PLATE 20
70.090 (1755)

Common. **FIELD CHARACTERS** Head with a shallow central notch and rounded dorsal lobes, mottled brownish or pale greyish, and often with a pair of dark stripes. Body brownish or pale greyish with a darker or blackish dorsal line, whitish or pale brown subdorsal stripe, and interrupted white lateral line. Spiracles black. **SIMILAR SPECIES** Sub-angled Wave, Small Blood-vein, Lesser Cream Wave, Smoky Wave and Rosy Wave. **HABITATS** Scrubby upland grassland and moorland. Also found on heathland, and less often in dune-slacks, fens, marshes and open woodland. **FOODPLANTS** Aspen, and Creeping, Eared, Goat and other willows. Also reported on Bilberry, birches, Hazel, Heather, roses and Rowan (in the Hebrides). **FIELD NOTES** May–Jun. Pupates in spun leaves of the foodplant. Overwinters as an egg.

NORTHERN SPINACH
Eulithis populata

PLATE 19
70.091 (1756)

Common. A northern and western species. **FIELD CHARACTERS** Head greenish or brownish, with a central notch and rounded dorsal lobes. Body brownish or greenish. In the brown form the dorsal line is dark brown with a dark brown or blackish transverse band on T2, enclosing six whitish pinacula, and short, forward-pointing V-shaped whitish stripes or lines T3–A6, often shaded darker anteriorly. Pinacula white. In the green form the dorsal line is dark green or reddish brown, and the V-shaped stripes or lines are whitish and/or reddish brown, and sometimes form dorsal triangles. The band on T2 may be absent. **SIMILAR SPECIES** Yellow-ringed Carpet, Grey Mountain Carpet and Phoenix. **HABITATS** Moorland. **FOODPLANTS** Mainly Bilberry. Also recorded on Cowberry, and Goat and Grey willows. **FIELD NOTES** Apr–Jun. Pupates in a slight cocoon in spun leaves or debris. Overwinters as an egg.

SPINACH
Eulithis mellinata

PLATE 20
70.092 (1757)

Common. Has declined severely in abundance in recent decades, especially in northern England and Scotland, but remains widespread in East Anglia, and in London, Birmingham and Liverpool/Manchester conurbations. **FIELD CHARACTERS** Head green. Body green with a darker dorsal line, a faint yellow subdorsal stripe or line, and sometimes a yellow lateral line. **SIMILAR SPECIES** Currant Pug is covered with tiny white dots and has a pair of short, blunt anal points. **HABITATS** Allotments, gardens, acid grassland and woodland. **FOODPLANTS** Black and Red currants, and Gooseberry. **FIELD NOTES** Apr–May. Pupates in a loose spinning among the foodplant or on the ground. Overwinters as an egg.

BARRED STRAW
Gandaritis pyraliata

PLATE 20
70.093 (1758)

Common. Local in north-west Scotland. **FIELD CHARACTERS** Head green. Body green with a dark green, brown or black dorsal line, and a white or yellow subdorsal stripe. There are transverse yellow rings between abdominal segments. **HABITATS** Ditches, gardens, rough grassland, hedgerows, roadside verges, scrub and woodland rides. **FOODPLANTS** Hedge and Lady's bedstraws, Cleavers, Crosswort and Woodruff. **FIELD NOTES** Mid-Apr–mid-Jun. Pupates in a spinning among debris. Overwinters as an egg.

SMALL PHOENIX
Ecliptopera silaceata

PLATE 20
70.094 (1759)

Common. Has declined significantly in abundance in recent decades. **FIELD CHARACTERS** Head greenish, usually with bold black markings. Body green, occasionally reddish brown, with a dark green dorsal line, usually with small blackish spots between abdominal segments; may form a continuous blackish line from A6 posteriorly. Subdorsal line white. Pinacula white, and one behind the spiracle on A1–A5 is edged with black, forming a small spot. A black or reddish-brown transverse band on A8 with white pinacula. True legs on T1–T2 brown and on T3 darker or black. Proleg on A6 purplish, and anal clasper with a white stripe anteriorly, edged posteriorly with brown or black. Anal flap triangular and pointed. **SIMILAR SPECIES** Broken-barred Carpet, White-pinion Spotted and Clouded Silver. **HABITATS** Mainly open woodland and rides. Also allotments, banks of canals and rivers, ditches, fens, gardens, heathland, hedgerows and roadside verges. **FOODPLANTS** Broad-leaved, Great and Rosebay willowherbs. Also reported on Himalayan and Touch-me-not balsams and Enchanter's-nightshade. **FIELD NOTES** Apr–Oct, in one to three generations depending on latitude and summer temperatures. Pupates among debris. Overwinters as a pupa.

RED-GREEN CARPET
Chloroclysta siterata

PLATE 20
70.095 (1760)

Common. Has increased significantly in abundance in recent decades and is more frequent and widespread in southern and central England than formerly. **FIELD CHARACTERS** Head green with a central notch and rounded dorsal lobes. Body yellowish green, with or without a line of red dorsal spots. Subdorsal line yellowish green, on T1–T2 only, with darker green above and below. Ventral surface green or reddish brown. Abdomen with a pair of long green or pink anal points. True legs and proleg green or red. **SIMILAR SPECIES** Based on material examined, Autumn Green Carpet does not have red dorsal spots, but is otherwise indistinguishable from the plain form of Red-green Carpet. Common Marbled Carpet and Dark Marbled Carpet are distinguished from Red-green Carpet and Autumn Green Carpet by the presence of white pinacula, which are particularly conspicuous laterally. Common Marbled Carpet and Dark Marbled Carpet are very similar but, based on material examined, if there is a red subspiracular stripe the larva is Common Marbled Carpet. Without the stripe it could be either species, but differences between phenologies may be helpful to separate them. **HABITATS** Wooded gardens and hedgerows, well-wooded landscapes (especially in upland areas) and broadleaf woodland. **FOODPLANTS** Wide variety of broadleaf trees and shrubs, including Apple, Ash, birches, Blackthorn, cherries, Dog-rose, Hornbeam, limes, oaks, Rowan and Sycamore. **FIELD NOTES** Jun–Aug. Pupates in debris. Overwinters as a female adult only.

AUTUMN GREEN CARPET
Chloroclysta miata

PLATE 20
70.096 (1761)

Local. A northern and western species. Formerly widespread in the south and east; now rare or absent. **FIELD CHARACTERS** Very like the form of Red-green Carpet that lacks red dorsal spots. Based on material examined, legs and proleg red. **SIMILAR SPECIES** Red-green Carpet, Common Marbled Carpet and Dark Marbled Carpet. **HABITATS** Woodland, scrub and moorland. **FOODPLANTS** Frequently recorded on Rowan. Also on other broadleaf trees and shrubs, including Alder, birches, limes, oaks, roses and willows. **FIELD NOTES** Jun–Aug. Pupates in debris. Overwinters as a female adult only.

COMMON MARBLED CARPET
Dysstroma truncata

PLATE 20
70.097 (1764)

Ssp. *truncata* Common. Arran Carpet ssp. *concinnata* Na. Endemic in the far west of Scotland, including Inner and Outer Hebrides. **FIELD CHARACTERS** Head green with a central notch and rounded dorsal lobes. Body green with white pinacula, especially conspicuous laterally. Dorsal line dark green, and subdorsal line white or yellowish green. A red subspiracular stripe may be present, the red colour occasionally extending up as far as the subdorsal line. Abdomen with a pair of long white or red anal points. **SIMILAR SPECIES** Red-green Carpet, Autumn Green Carpet and Dark Marbled Carpet. **HABITATS** Wide variety, including fens, gardens, heathland, hedgerows, moorland, scrub on the coast and in grasslands, and woodland. Arran Carpet occurs on moorland. **FOODPLANTS** Woody and, less often, herbaceous plants, including Alder, Bilberry, birches, Bramble, Red and Black currants, docks, geraniums, Hawthorn, heathers, Meadowsweet, Round-leaved Mint, oaks, privets, Raspberry, roses, Wild Strawberry, and Goat and Grey willows. Arran Carpet feeds on Bilberry and Heather. **FIELD NOTES** Sep–May and Jun–Aug, in two generations, or Aug–Jun in one generation at high altitude in Scotland and parts of Ireland, low altitude in northern Scotland, and where Arran Carpet occurs. Pupates among leaves or on the ground.

DARK MARBLED CARPET
Dysstroma citrata

PLATE 20
70.098 (1762)

Ssp. *citrata* Common. Local in the south. Ssp. *pythonissata* Orkney and Shetland. **FIELD CHARACTERS** Very similar to Common Marbled Carpet. Based on material examined, there were no examples with a red subspiracular stripe, and the anal points were white tinged with pink. **SIMILAR SPECIES** Red-green Carpet, Autumn Green Carpet and Common Marbled Carpet. **HABITATS** Mainly heathland, moorland and woodland. Also found in hedgerows, scrub and gardens. **FOODPLANTS** Mainly woody plants, including Bilberry, birches, Heather, Alpine Lady's-mantle (flowers), Wild Strawberry and willows. **FIELD NOTES** Apr–Jun. Pupates in debris on the ground. Overwinters as a fully formed larva within the egg.

BEECH-GREEN CARPET
Colostygia olivata

PLATE 20
70.099 (1774)

Local. Very local in the south; more widespread in mainland Scotland. **FIELD CHARACTERS** Head brown and speckled. Body stumpy and rough in appearance, and pale brown with dark purplish-brown markings. Dorsal line dark purplish brown and interrupted. Pinacula comprise brownish-white bumps with black centres, and short brown hairs that point forwards and backwards on each segment. True legs black. Anal flap with a pair of large, dark brown spots. **SIMILAR SPECIES** Green Carpet has small, pale, forward-pointing triangles on the dorsum A1–A5. **HABITATS** Calcareous grassland and undercliff, moorland, old quarries, road verges and broadleaf woodland. **FOODPLANTS** Heath, Hedge and Lady's bedstraws. **FIELD NOTES** Sep–Jun. Feeds at night. Pupates in the ground. Overwinters as a small larva.

GREEN CARPET
Colostygia pectinataria

PLATE 20
70.100 (1776)

Common. Has increased significantly in abundance in recent decades.
FIELD CHARACTERS Head brown and speckled. Body stumpy and rough in
appearance, and pale brown with darker brown or purplish-brown markings.
Dorsal line dark brown and interrupted. Small, pale, forward-pointing triangles
on the dorsum A1–A5, edged dark brown anteriorly. The dorsum is paler
A6–A9. Pinacula comprise brownish-white bumps with black centres, with
short brown hairs that point forwards and backwards on each segment. True
legs black or brown. Anal flap with a pair of large brown spots. **SIMILAR
SPECIES** Beech-green Carpet. **HABITATS** Wide variety, and frequent in gardens. **FOODPLANTS** Heath,
Hedge and Lady's bedstraws, White Dead-nettle, Wild Marjoram, plantains and Woodruff. Probably also
on Cleavers, and on Sheep's Sorrel in Orkney. **FIELD NOTES** Jun–Jul and Sep–May in two generations in
the south, and Aug–May in mainly one generation in the north, with an occasional second generation.
Pupates in a cocoon in the ground.

MOTTLED GREY
Colostygia multistrigaria

PLATE 20
70.101 (1775)

Common. Very local in southern and south-east England. **FIELD
CHARACTERS** Head brown, speckled darker. Body brown. Dorsal line dark
brown, edged whitish brown. Subdorsal stripe and lateral line whitish brown,
and subspiracular stripe white or whitish brown, sometimes edged blackish
above. Spiracles black. **SIMILAR SPECIES** Striped Twin-spot Carpet usually has
a distinct dark supraspiracular stripe, and the larva feeds later in the year.
Slender-striped Rufous is distinguished from Mottled Grey and Striped Twin-
spot Carpet by its numerous conspicuous black pinacula. **HABITATS** Calcareous
grassland and undercliff, heathland, moorland and woodland. **FOODPLANTS** Heath and Lady's bedstraws,
and Cleavers. **FIELD NOTES** May–Jun. Overwinters as a pupa, although moths may emerge as early as
Dec.

STRIPED TWIN-SPOT CARPET
Coenotephria salicata

PLATE 20
70.102 (1753)

Ssp. *latentaria*. Common; possible rare immigrant. **FIELD CHARACTERS** Head
brown, speckled darker. Body brown. Dorsal line dark brown, edged with
mottled white. Subdorsal stripe whitish, sometimes with conspicuous
blackish pinacula adjacent, A1–A6. Lateral line white and often ill-defined.
Supraspiracular stripe dark brown, usually well defined, and subspiracular
stripe white. Spiracles black. **SIMILAR SPECIES** Mottled Grey and Slender-
striped Rufous. **HABITATS** Upland grassland, limestone pavement (the Burren,
Cos Clare and Galway, Ireland), moorland, sand dunes and open woodland.
FOODPLANTS Heath, Hedge and Lady's bedstraws. **FIELD NOTES** Jul–early Aug, and in Aug–early Sep
where there is a second generation at low altitude. Feeds at night. Constructs a silken cocoon on the
ground in autumn, overwinters as a larva in the cocoon, and pupates in spring.

WATER CARPET
Lampropteryx suffumata

PLATE 20
70.103 (1750)

Common. Rarely seen in numbers. **FIELD CHARACTERS** Head dark brown,
or pale brown with dark brown stripes. Body rough in appearance, mostly
greyish brown or dark brown, but paler or whitish brown A6–A9. Dorsal line
whitish T1–T3, and blackish A6–A9. In darker examples there are whitish and
reddish-brown dorsal diamonds with black centres A2–A5. In paler examples
the diamonds may be all dark brownish. Pinacula black. Spiracles black.
SIMILAR SPECIES Devon Carpet is very similar but has larger black pinacula,
and these are especially prominent in transverse lines of four on A4 and A5.
HABITATS Ditches, fens, wet grassland, heathland, hedgerows, limestone pavement (the Burren, Cos Clare
and Galway, Ireland), moorland and damp woodland. **FOODPLANTS** Heath, Hedge and Lady's bedstraws,
and Cleavers. **FIELD NOTES** May–Jun. Pupates in a substantial silken cocoon spun among the foodplant.
Overwinters as a pupa.

DEVON CARPET
Lampropteryx otregiata

PLATE 20
70.104 (1751)

Nb. Has increased very significantly in abundance in recent decades and is increasing its range eastwards and northwards. **FIELD CHARACTERS** Head brown with dark mottling. Body brown with whitish mottling, but pale brown to whitish A6–A8. Dorsal line whitish T1–T3, and dark brown beyond. There are whitish dorsal triangles with brown centres between segments A1 and A5. Pinacula black, and especially prominent in transverse rows of four on A4 and A5. Spiracles black. **SIMILAR SPECIES** Water Carpet. **HABITATS** Damp habitats, including grassland, heathland and woodland. **FOODPLANTS** Common Marsh-bedstraw, and very likely Fen Bedstraw. **FIELD NOTES** Jun–Jul and Sep–Oct in two generations. Pupates on the ground. Overwinters as a pupa.

NORTHERN WINTER MOTH
Operophtera fagata

PLATE 20
70.105 (1800)

Common. Much more local than Winter Moth, and appears to be getting rarer. **FIELD CHARACTERS** Head greenish grey with black markings. Body tapers towards anterior and posterior ends, and is pale or dark green. Dorsal line dark, and subdorsal stripe and lateral and subspiracular lines whitish or yellow. Spiracles black. In the penultimate instar the head is black. **SIMILAR SPECIES** Final-instar Winter Moth has whitish spiracles, and the penultimate instar does not have a black head. March Moth is distinguished from Northern Winter Moth and Winter Moth by its pair of rudimentary prolegs on A5, and its more rectangular body shape. **HABITATS** Heathland, moorland, orchards, scrub and broadleaf woodland. Also recorded in gardens. **FOODPLANTS** Mainly Alder, and Downy and Silver birches. Also reported on Apple, Beech, cherries and Rowan. **FIELD NOTES** Apr–Jun. Feeds by day between spun leaves. Pupates in the ground. An adult in early winter, spending the remainder as an egg.

WINTER MOTH
Operophtera brumata

PLATE 20
70.106 (1799)

Common. Some years occurs as a larva in huge numbers in oak woodland. Can be a pest in Apple orchards, and Lodgepole Pine and Sitka Spruce plantations in the north. **FIELD CHARACTERS** Head green and unmarked, or greenish grey with dark markings. Body tapers towards anterior and posterior ends, and is pale or dark green. Dorsal line dark, and subdorsal stripe and lateral and subspiracular lines whitish or yellow. Spiracles whitish, encircled with brown. **SIMILAR SPECIES** Northern Winter Moth and March Moth. **HABITATS** Wide variety, but not at high altitude. **FOODPLANTS** Wide variety of broadleaf woody plants, including Alder, Apple, Beech, Bilberry, birches, Blackthorn, Bog-myrtle, Sweet Chestnut, Hawthorn, Hazel, Heather, Hornbeam, larches, Field Maple, oaks, Lodgepole Pine, Rowan, Sitka Spruce, Sycamore and willows. **FIELD NOTES** Apr–Jun. Feeds by day between spun leaves. Pupates in the ground. An adult in early to midwinter, and an egg for the remainder.

NOTE ON NOVEMBER MOTH *EPIRRITA* GROUP, AND SIMILARITIES WITH WINTER MOTH *OPEROPHTERA* SPECIES

The November Moth group comprises four species: November Moth, Pale November Moth, Autumnal Moth and Small Autumnal Moth. Larvae of November Moth, Pale November Moth and Autumnal Moth are indistinguishable in the field, and are described under November Moth. Of the three, Autumnal Moth is less likely to have any reddish-brown coloration within the green, but this does not provide a reliable difference. The larva of Small Autumnal Moth can be separated with reasonable certainty from the other three. It feeds on Heather and Bilberry on moorland and tends to be darker green, with subdorsal and lateral lines bright yellow and more contrasting, while they are white or yellowish white and often fainter in the other species.

Larvae in the November Moth group may be confused with the two Winter Moth species. November Moth group larvae are all bigger in last instar and have greenish-white ventral surfaces, while in the Winter Moths these are the same shade as or slightly darker than the dorsal body colour.

NOVEMBER MOTH
Epirrita dilutata

PLATE 20
70.107 (1795)

Common. **FIELD CHARACTERS** Head green. Body green, ventral surface greenish white or greyish white. Dorsal line green, subdorsal and lateral lines whitish, usually faint and interrupted, and subspiracular stripe white. Pinacula white, with short white hairs. Spiracles orangey or brownish. Some examples also have scattered reddish-brown spots, and very occasionally this colour is dominant. **SIMILAR SPECIES** Pale November Moth, Autumnal Moth and Small Autumnal Moth – see notes on p. 156. Tissue has white lines bordering the dorsal line and black or green pinacula. **HABITATS** Most frequent in broadleaf woodland, but also found in gardens and urban parks, hedgerows, parkland and scrub. **FOODPLANTS** Wide variety, including Apple, Crab Apple, Ash, Aspen, birches, Blackthorn, cherries, Dog-rose, Hawthorn, Hazel, Hornbeam, elms, oaks and willows. Also reported on Rhododendron. **FIELD NOTES** Late Apr–Jun. Pupates in the ground. Overwinters as an egg.

PALE NOVEMBER MOTH
Epirrita christyi

PLATE 20
70.108 (1796)

Common. Can be abundant, but more locally distributed than November Moth. **SIMILAR SPECIES** November Moth, Autumnal Moth, Small Autumnal Moth and Tissue. **HABITATS** Mostly recorded in broadleaf woodland. **FOODPLANTS** Seems to prefer areas where Beech and Wych Elm are common. Also known to feed on Alder, birches, Blackthorn, elms, hawthorns, Hazel, Hornbeam, Field Maple, oaks and willows. **FIELD NOTES** Late Apr–Jun. Pupates in the ground. Overwinters as an egg.

AUTUMNAL MOTH
Epirrita autumnata

PLATE 20
70.109 (1797)

Common. Can be locally abundant. **SIMILAR SPECIES** November Moth, Pale November Moth, Small Autumnal Moth and Tissue. **HABITATS** Heathland, moorland, scrub and broadleaf woodland, apparently preferring relatively open situations. **FOODPLANTS** Preference for Alder, Downy and Silver birches (especially young regrowth and Scottish birch woods) and Heather. Also recorded on Hawthorn, European Larch and Scots Pine. **FIELD NOTES** Late Apr–Jun. Pupates in the ground. Overwinters as an egg.

SMALL AUTUMNAL MOTH
Epirrita filigrammaria

PLATE 20
70.110 (1798)

Common. Endemic to the British Isles. Has declined significantly in abundance in recent decades. **FIELD CHARACTERS** Head brown. Body dark green, with ventral surface greenish white, and with a darker green dorsal line, yellow subdorsal and lateral lines, and white or yellowish-white subspiracular stripe. Pinacula white, with short white hairs. Spiracles orangey. Occasionally with reddish-brown dorsal line or spots and lateral spots. **SIMILAR SPECIES** November Moth, Pale November Moth, Autumnal Moth and Tissue. **HABITATS** Moorland, preferring tall vegetation. **FOODPLANTS** Bilberry, Heather, Bell Heather and willows. Also recorded on larches. **FIELD NOTES** Mid-Apr–late May. Pupates in the ground. Overwinters as an egg.

SMALL WHITE WAVE
Asthena albulata

PLATE 21
70.111 (1875)

Common. Appears to have declined in abundance in southern England. Very local from the Midlands northwards. **FIELD CHARACTERS** Head brown with black markings. Body pale green or whitish green, sparsely covered with conspicuous black hairs. Often there is a reddish dorsal band T1–T3 and A6–A10 and reddish blotches throughout, but markings are variable in extent and may be reduced to a small lateral spot on A1. Proleg and anal clasper green or red. **SIMILAR SPECIES** Waved Carpet has a black head and prothoracic plate, and a broad purplish area with white markings A1–A5. Welsh Wave has an unmarked brownish-green head, and reddish dorsal and lateral patches T1–T3 and A2–A4. Blomer's Rivulet has a dark brown, speckled head, with dark dorsal shading T1–T3, dark lateral shading A2–A4, and a small, dark dorsal patch on A8. **HABITATS** Mainly broadleaf woodland, and especially frequent in abandoned Hazel coppice in ancient woodland. Also hedgerows. **FOODPLANTS** Birches, Hazel, Hornbeam and wild roses. **FIELD NOTES** Late Jun–Aug, and sometimes in Sep as a partial second generation in the south. Pupates on the ground among debris. Overwinters as a pupa.

DINGY SHELL
Euchoeca nebulata

PLATE 21
70.112 (1874)

Local. Very local in Scotland and Ireland. Has increased significantly in abundance in recent decades. **FIELD CHARACTERS** Head green with a black spot either side. Body green with yellowish subdorsal stripe, and usually a broad black dorsal band. The extent of black is variable and may be reduced to a row of black subdorsal spots. Pinacula white. **HABITATS** Fens, wooded margins of waterbodies, and carr and other wet woodlands. **FOODPLANT** Alder. **FIELD NOTES** Late Jun–Sep. Pupates in debris on the ground or in moss at the base of trees. Overwinters as a pupa.

WAVED CARPET
Hydrelia sylvata

PLATE 21
70.113 (1877)

Nb. Has declined in the north of its range. **FIELD CHARACTERS** Head and prothoracic plate black. Body green or yellowish green with white dorsal line. A dark purplish-brown dorsal band T1–T3, broadening laterally and ventrally A1–A5, and narrowing abruptly to border the dorsal line A6–A8. The dark shading on A1–A5 incorporates white markings dorsally, and some green or yellowish-green patches laterally. **SIMILAR SPECIES** Small White Wave, Welsh Wave and Blomer's Rivulet. **HABITATS** Mainly in coniferous plantations, scrub and broadleaf woodland, often by water or in damp situations. Also in wooded coastal habitats including undercliff. **FOODPLANTS** Alder, birches, Sweet Chestnut, Hazel, Sycamore and willows. Also reported on Blackthorn. **FIELD NOTES** Jul–Sep. Pupates on the ground. Overwinters as a pupa.

SMALL YELLOW WAVE
Hydrelia flammeolaria

PLATE 21
70.114 (1876)

Common. Very local in Scotland and Ireland. **FIELD CHARACTERS** Head pale brown or green. Body green with dark green pinacula and sparse whitish hairs, and yellow bands between segments. Dorsal line dark green. Spiracles white. **HABITATS** Gardens and urban parks, hedgerows, scrub, wooded margins of waterbodies, and broadleaf woodland including plantations. Occurs in Alder carr woodland in the north. **FOODPLANTS** Alder, Field Maple and Sycamore. Also reported on Rowan. **FIELD NOTES** Late Jul–Sep. Feeds at night. Pupates in debris on the ground. Overwinters as a pupa.

WELSH WAVE
Venusia cambrica

PLATE 21
70.115 (1873)

Local. **FIELD CHARACTERS** Head brownish green. Body green, sparsely covered with short black hairs. Dorsal line dark green and subdorsal stripe yellow. Reddish dorsal and lateral patches T1–T3 or A1, separate from those on A2–A4, and sometimes with further patches laterally A7–A8. Proleg and anal clasper may be green or red. **SIMILAR SPECIES** Small White Wave, Waved Carpet and Blomer's Rivulet. **HABITATS** Moorland and open woodland. **FOODPLANTS** Birches and Rowan. Also recorded on Alder. **FIELD NOTES** Jul–Sep. Pupates in a spinning. Overwinters as a pupa.

BLOMER'S RIVULET
Venusia blomeri

PLATE 21
70.116 (1872)

Nb. Mainly associated with Wych Elm on calcareous soils with high rainfall. **FIELD CHARACTERS** Head dark brown, speckled with black. Body green, sparsely covered with short white hairs. A dark purplish dorsal patch T1–T3, extending laterally on T2. A mixed purple, brown and black lateral patch A2–A4, sometimes joining across the dorsum. A dark purplish-brown dorsal patch on A8, edged with brown. Proleg and anal clasper green. **SIMILAR SPECIES** Small White Wave, Waved Carpet and Welsh Wave. **HABITATS** Hedgerows in wooded landscapes, and broadleaf woodland. **FOODPLANTS** Wych Elm. Also reported on other elms.
FIELD NOTES Late Jul–mid-Sep. Pupates in a cocoon in the ground. Overwinters as a pupa.

DRAB LOOPER
Minoa murinata

PLATE 21
70.117 (1878)

Nb. Has declined in distribution. **FIELD CHARACTERS** Body dark grey with large, pale grey pinacula and tufts of short whitish hairs. Dorsal line pale grey, and subspiracular stripe T3–A8 or up to T1 yellow or orange, with the pale grey pinacula prominent along its length. **HABITATS** Open woodland and along rides, especially in sunny, sheltered areas where there is frequent management, such as coppicing that encourages the foodplant. **FOODPLANT** The flowers and floral leaves of Wood Spurge. **FIELD NOTES** Late Jun–early Sep. Pupates in a silken and earth cocoon on the ground. Overwinters as a pupa.

BROWN SCALLOP
Philereme vetulata

PLATE 21
70.118 (1791)

Local. **FIELD CHARACTERS** Body black with black pinacula and sparse, short grey hairs. Dorsal stripe black, edged with white stripes, and a faint and often interrupted white subdorsal line. A broad, irregularly margined spiracular stripe, whitish mixed orangey, incorporating black spots arranged in a row just below the spiracles. A transverse orange band on T1. **SIMILAR SPECIES** Black form of Dark Umber lacks white stripes on the dorsum. **HABITATS** Hedgerows, road verges, scrub and open woodland on calcareous soils. Occasionally in gardens on planted Buckthorn. **FOODPLANT** Buckthorn. **FIELD NOTES** May–Jun. Feeds at night and hides by day in a spinning. Pupates in a cocoon in the ground. Overwinters as an egg.

DARK UMBER
Philereme transversata

PLATE 21
70.119 (1792)

Ssp. *britannica* Local. Very local in Wales and Ireland. **FIELD CHARACTERS** Body usually green, or occasionally black. The green form may have a purplish-brown hue. It has sparse, short black hairs and white pinacula. Dorsal stripe dark green, edged with faint paler lines. Spiracular stripe or line white or yellowish white, below which is dark purplish shading A6–A9 and on the anal clasper. A white stripe ventrally. The black form has a broad black dorsal band and is greyish white mixed yellowish laterally, with black spots. **SIMILAR SPECIES** Black form of Brown Scallop. **HABITATS** Fens, hedgerows, road verges, scrub and open woodland, mainly on calcareous soils, but also on acidic and neutral types. **FOODPLANTS** Mainly Buckthorn. Recorded on Alder Buckthorn. **FIELD NOTES** May–Jun. Feeds at night and hides by day in a spinning. Pupates in a cocoon in the ground. Overwinters as an egg.

ARGENT & SABLE
Rheumaptera hastata

PLATE 21
70.120 (1787)

Ssp. *hastata* Nb. Now scarce in southern England. Has declined sharply in birch woodland in recent decades alongside decline in regular woodland management. Ssp. *nigrescens* Nb. Widespread in the western half of Scotland. **FIELD CHARACTERS** Body black or brown. The black form has a black or brown head. Dorsal stripe black, edged with white dashes, and subdorsal line whitish comprising dashes. Spiracular band brownish, mixed with white and black markings, and edged above and below with white stripes that may be more or less complete. The brown form has a dark brown dorsal stripe and lateral band, and similar pale lines and markings that are pale brown or yellowish instead of white. **SIMILAR SPECIES** July Highflyer, May Highflyer and Ruddy Highflyer. **HABITATS** Bogs, acid grassland, heathland, moorland, open broadleaf woodland including coppice, and recently replanted coniferous woodland. **FOODPLANTS** Ssp. *hastata* prefers seedlings and very young regrowth of Downy and Silver birches. Also Bog-myrtle in Somerset, and Grey Willow in Shropshire. Ssp. *nigrescens* Birches and Bog-myrtle. Has once been found on Himalayan Knotweed in Ireland. **FIELD NOTES** Late Jun–mid-Aug in southern England, early Jul–early Sep further north. Feeds between spun leaves. Pupates in the spinning or on the ground. Overwinters as a pupa.

SCALLOP SHELL
Rheumaptera undulata

PLATE 21
70.121 (1789)

Local. Very local in north-east England and Scotland. **FIELD CHARACTERS** Head brown. Body varies from pale brown or grey to dark brown. In paler forms, the dorsal stripe is often darker than the body colour, edged with interrupted white lines, and there is a dark lateral band, edged above with an interrupted white subdorsal line. In darker forms the dorsum is less contrasting. Spiracular band pale greyish or pale reddish brown, mixed whitish, and spiracles whitish with black surrounds. **HABITATS** Fens, heathland, carr woodland, and rides in open, damp woodland. **FOODPLANTS** Aspen, Bilberry, and Goat and Grey willows. **FIELD NOTES** Aug–Oct. Pupates in the ground. Overwinters as a pupa.

SCARCE TISSUE
Rheumaptera cervinalis

PLATE 21
70.122 (1788)

Local. Searches for larvae may show the moth to be more widespread. **FIELD CHARACTERS** Head brown. Body grey. Dorsal stripe grey, edged with interrupted white lines, and lateral band dark grey, edged above with an interrupted white subdorsal line. Spiracular band pale greyish, mixed yellowish. Spiracles black. **HABITATS** Gardens and urban parks, hedgerows and scrub. **FOODPLANTS** Mainly ornamental barberries, including Hedge, Thunberg's and Mrs Wilson's barberries. Also wild Barberry and Oregon-grape. Prefers bushes in sunny positions. **FIELD NOTES** Jun–Jul, or occasionally to mid-Sep. Pupates in the ground. Overwinters as a pupa.

TISSUE
Triphosa dubitata

PLATE 21
70.123 (1790)

Local. **FIELD CHARACTERS** Head brownish green. Body green or yellowish green, with pinacula varying from black to green, and with short grey hairs. Dorsal line green, edged with white lines. Subdorsal line white, and supraspiracular stripe white mixed with yellow. Spiracles orange or white. **SIMILAR SPECIES** November Moth, Pale November Moth, Autumnal Moth and Small Autumnal Moth. **HABITATS** Road verges, scrub on acidic, calcareous and neutral soils, and open woodland. **FOODPLANTS** Buckthorn and Alder Buckthorn. **FIELD NOTES** May–early Jul. Hides by day in a spinning. Pupates in the ground. Overwinters as an adult.

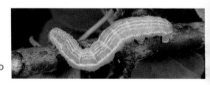

Tissue larva

BARBERRY CARPET
Pareulype berberata

PLATE 21
70.124 (1785)

RDB. Protected species. Suspected immigrant. A rare species with few extant colonies, and subject to conservation efforts to sustain and re-establish local populations. **FIELD CHARACTERS** Head pale brown, mottled black. Body varies from pale grey or pale brown to pinkish brown, with noticeable transverse skin ridges between segments A1 and A5. Dorsal line darker than the body colour, edged with paler shading, especially on A6–A8, and with black speckling and shading laterally. In contrasting examples there are paler dorsal triangles A1–A4. Plainer examples may be almost uniform in colour and markings. Pinacula prominent. **HABITATS** Mainly hedgerows. Also scrub on calcareous grassland, and woodland edges. **FOODPLANTS** Mainly Barberry. Known to feed additionally at one site on *Berberis turcomanica*. **FIELD NOTES** Early Jun–mid-Jul or later, and late Aug–late Sep, in two generations. Larvae bask in sunshine. Pupates in the ground or in debris. Overwinters as a pupa.

SLENDER-STRIPED RUFOUS
Coenocalpe lapidata

PLATE 21
70.125 (1780)

Na. Likely to be under-recorded. **FIELD CHARACTERS** Head pale brown, speckled darker. Body pale greyish brown with conspicuous black pinacula. Dorsal line dark greyish brown, edged yellowish, subdorsal line yellow, lateral stripe white or yellow and spiracular stripe yellow. Spiracles black. **SIMILAR SPECIES** Mottled Grey and Striped Twin-spot Carpet. **HABITATS** Rush pastures in upland areas, and moorland. **FOODPLANTS** Has been found once feeding on the flowers of Lesser Spearwort. On buttercups, dandelions and Traveller's-joy in captivity. **FIELD NOTES** Apr–early Aug. Pupates in an earthen cocoon in or on the ground. Overwinters as an egg.

SMALL WAVED UMBER
Horisme vitalbata

PLATE 21
70.126 (1781)

Common. Has increased significantly in abundance in recent decades. **FIELD CHARACTERS** Head pale grey and there may be a central darker band. Body pale brown or grey, sometimes paler A6–A8, with conspicuous black pinacula. Dorsal line dark grey, sometimes edged with dark shading that may extend subdorsally on central abdominal segments. Subdorsal stripe pale, sometimes obscured by the dark shading, and an inconspicuous lateral line may be present. **SIMILAR SPECIES** Fern shows no consistent differences in markings, but in the material examined the larva tends to be browner whereas Small Waved Umber tends to be greyer. Rearing is advised to be certain of identity. Pretty Chalk Carpet has diverging darker stripes on the head. **HABITATS** Hedgerows, road verges, scrub on calcareous soils, and open woodland. **FOODPLANT** Traveller's-joy. **FIELD NOTES** Jun–Jul and Sep–Oct, in two generations. Pupates in or on the ground. Overwinters as a pupa.

FERN
Horisme tersata

PLATE 21
70.127 (1782)

Common. **FIELD CHARACTERS** Head pale greyish brown with a central darker band. Body pale brown or grey, sometimes paler A6–A8, with conspicuous black pinacula. Dorsal line dark grey throughout, or sometimes on T1–T3 and A6–A8, and broken into or expanded as thick dashes on abdominal segments. The dorsal line and dashes may be edged paler or whitish. Subdorsal stripe pale, and an inconspicuous lateral line may be present. **SIMILAR SPECIES** Small Waved Umber and Pretty Chalk Carpet. **HABITATS** Gardens, hedgerows, road verges, scrub on calcareous soils, and open woodland. Increasingly found in urban areas. **FOODPLANTS** Traveller's-joy. Also reported on Wood Anemone, Baneberry and Meadow Buttercup. Possibly on cultivated *Clematis*. **FIELD NOTES** Late Jul–Sep, probably later where there is an occasional second generation. Pupates in the ground. Overwinters as a pupa.

PRETTY CHALK CARPET
Melanthia procellata

PLATE 22
70.128 (1784)

Common. Has declined significantly in abundance in recent decades. **FIELD CHARACTERS** Head pale brown or pale grey with diverging dark stripes either side of the mouthparts. Body brown or grey with black pinacula. Dorsal line black, widening to short dashes A1–A5, narrowly edged pale brownish. Variable amounts of blackish-grey or brown shading subdorsally and laterally, sometimes obscuring a pale brown subdorsal stripe. Anal flap with a dark spot anteriorly. **SIMILAR SPECIES** Small Waved Umber and Fern. **HABITATS** Hedgerows, road verges, scrub on calcareous soils, and open woodland. Sometimes found in gardens. **FOODPLANT** Traveller's-joy. **FIELD NOTES** Aug–Sep. Pupates in or the ground. Overwinters as a pupa.

DENTATED PUG
Anticollix sparsata

PLATE 22
70.129 (1863)

Na. Widespread but very local in England, and at one site in Wales. **FIELD CHARACTERS** Head green. Body green or yellowish green, with a dark green dorsal line, broadly edged whitish green. Subdorsal and lateral lines whitish green and subspiracular stripe white. **HABITATS** Fens, wet grassland, marshes, reedbeds, riverbanks and wet woodland. **FOODPLANT** Yellow Loosestrife. **FIELD NOTES** Jul–Sep. Feeds mainly on leaves, less often flowers. Prefers plants growing in deep shade. Larvae usually drop to the ground if disturbed. Overwinters as a pupa.

CHIMNEY SWEEPER
Odezia atrata

PLATE 22
70.130 (1870)

Common. Still widespread but has declined severely in southern England through loss of unimproved grassland. Very local in Ireland. **FIELD CHARACTERS** Body usually green, sometimes brown. The green form has a dark green dorsal line, greenish-white subdorsal and lateral lines, white subspiracular stripe and reddish anal flap. Spiracles orange. The brown form has a dark brown dorsal line, brownish-white subdorsal line, lateral line and subspiracular stripe, the lateral line being edged below by a dark brown line, and a reddish-brown anal flap. **HABITATS** In southern England in herb-rich, unimproved, permanent grassland on calcareous and neutral soils, and hedgerows, moorland, and woodland edges and rides. More widely found in damp grassland areas in northern England and Scotland. **FOODPLANTS** Mainly Pignut, but does occur where this plant is absent. Also Bur and Rough chervils, and has been recorded on Cow Parsley. **FIELD NOTES** Apr–early Jun. Feeds on the flowers and seeds. Pupates in the ground. Overwinters as an egg. A female has been observed simply dropping the eggs to the ground while at rest.

TWIN-SPOT CARPET
Mesotype didymata

PLATE 22
70.131 (1809)

Ssp. *didymata* Common. Widespread in the north and west; rather scarcer and local in the south and east, where it has declined. Ssp. *hethlandica* Shetland. **FIELD CHARACTERS** Head green. Body green, sparsely covered with short but conspicuous black hairs. Dorsal line dark green; subdorsal and lateral lines pale and indistinct. Subspiracular line white, indistinct anteriorly, and extending onto anal flap. Spiracles orange. **HABITATS** Wide variety, including hedgerows, rough grassland, limestone pavement (the Burren, Cos Clare and Galway, Ireland), moorland, sand dunes, sea cliffs and woodland. **FOODPLANTS** Wide variety, including Wood Anemone, Bilberry, Bog-myrtle, Red and Sea campions, Lesser Celandine, Rough Chervil, docks, Heather, Common Nettle, Cow Parsley, Primrose (flowers), Wood Sage, Alpine Saxifrage (flowers), Greater Stitchwort, willows and Wood-sorrel. Also reported on flowers of coarse grasses and wood-rushes, and on Lodgepole Pine and Sitka Spruce. **FIELD NOTES** Apr–Jun. Pupates in debris on the ground. Overwinters as an egg.

RIVULET
Perizoma affinitata

PLATE 2
70.132 (1802)

Common. Rarely seen in numbers. **FIELD CHARACTERS** Head and prothoracic and anal plates dark brown. Body whitish, shaded dull pinkish dorsally. Dorsal line grey, subspiracular line pink. Spiracles dark brown. **SIMILAR SPECIES** Sandy Carpet is more strongly coloured, with obvious purplish subdorsal and lateral stripes. **HABITATS** Hedgerows, road verges, vegetated sea cliffs (in Scotland), scattered scrub and open woodland. **FOODPLANTS** Red Campion. Also reported on White Campion and Ragged-Robin. **FIELD NOTES** Jul–early Sep. At first feeds on the flowers and later is concealed within a capsule, feeding on the developing seeds. Pupates in the ground. Overwinters as a pupa.

SMALL RIVULET
Perizoma alchemillata

PLATE 22
70.133 (1803)

Common. Fairly frequent throughout. **FIELD CHARACTERS** Head and prothoracic and anal plates black or brown. Body green or greenish white. Dorsal line green and subdorsal stripe purple, sometimes with purple lateral and supraspiracular lines or stripes. **HABITATS** Gardens, hedgerows (especially along rural lanes), marshes, scrub and open woodland. **FOODPLANTS** Common Hemp-nettle, and reported on Field Woundwort. Probably also on Hedge Woundwort. **FIELD NOTES** Jul–early Sep. Feeds among the flowers and fruits. Pupates in the ground. Overwinters as a pupa.

BARRED RIVULET
Perizoma bifaciata

PLATE 22
70.134 (1804)

Local. Widespread in England and Wales, more coastal elsewhere. **FIELD CHARACTERS** Head pale brown or pale grey, speckled darker. Body usually pale brownish grey, sometimes brown, with black pinacula surrounded by paler or whitish circles. Dorsal line dark brown, edged paler. Subdorsal and lateral lines dark brown, with dark brown patches above the subdorsal line A1–A5, and sometimes with more general dark brown shading across the dorsum A5–A9. Subspiracular stripe whitish, and dark brown ventrally. There is a form that is green below the brown dorsal area. **SIMILAR SPECIES** Heath Rivulet is smaller when fully fed, and lacks the dark brown patches above the subdorsal line. The two species are usually on different foodplants and there is little overlap of their geographical ranges. **HABITATS** Abandoned arable land on thin soils, hard and soft cliffs, sparsely vegetated dry grassland, especially on calcareous soils, limestone pavement (the Burren, Cos Clare and Galway, Ireland), stabilised sand dunes and waste ground. **FOODPLANTS** Mainly Red Bartsia. Also recorded on eyebrights. **FIELD NOTES** Aug–Oct. Initially within the fruits, and later when larger lives externally with the anterior end burrowed into the capsule, feeding on developing seeds. Holes in the capsules may indicate presence of larvae. Pupates in the ground. Overwinters as a pupa, sometimes for up to five winters.

HEATH RIVULET
Perizoma minorata

PLATE 22
70.135 (1805)

Ssp. *ericetata* Nb. Very local and possibly declining in Scotland. **FIELD CHARACTERS** Head brown with black markings. Body pale brown with black pinacula surrounded by white circles. Dorsal line pale brown, broadly edged with white, and subdorsal and lateral lines white. Subspiracular stripe white, edged darker brown below, and paler brown ventrally. **SIMILAR SPECIES** Barred Rivulet. **HABITATS** Limestone pavement (the Burren, Cos Clare and Galway, Ireland), moorland and upland pastures. **FOODPLANTS** Eyebrights. **FIELD NOTES** Mid-Aug–Sep. Feeds on the flowers and within the fruits at first, but later when larger feeds externally on the developing seeds. Pupates in the ground. Overwinters as a pupa.

PRETTY PINION
Perizoma blandiata

PLATE 22
70.136 (1806)

Ssp. *blandiata* Local. Widespread in the northern half of Scotland, but very local elsewhere. Ssp. *perfasciata* Hebrides. **FIELD CHARACTERS** Head pale brown. Body green or yellowish green with minute, darker pinacula surrounded by small pale circles. Dorsal band purplish, reddish or brown, tapering anteriorly, with a darker central line. Lateral line dark green. Anal clasper brown. **HABITATS** Limestone pavement (the Burren, Cos Clare and Galway, Ireland), machair, moorland and upland pastures. Seems to avoid habitats where turf is short and foodplant dominates. **FOODPLANTS** Eyebrights. **FIELD NOTES** Early Aug–mid-Sep. Feeds on the flowers and fruits, initially internally, but later externally when too large to fit within the fruits. Pupates in the ground. Overwinters as a pupa.

GRASS RIVULET
Perizoma albulata

PLATE 22
70.137 (1807)

Ssp. *albulata* Local. Has declined severely in abundance in recent decades, especially in northern England and Scotland. Ssp. *subfasciaria* Shetland. **FIELD CHARACTERS** Head and prothoracic and anal plates brown. Body pale yellow with some grey shading across the dorsum between segments. Dorsal line grey, subspiracular line darker yellow. **HABITATS** Hard and soft cliffs, fens, grasslands (especially calcareous), sand dunes and vegetated shingle. **FOODPLANT** Yellow-rattle. **FIELD NOTES** Mid-Jun–Aug. Feeds within the ripening fruits, causing discoloration. Pupates in the ground. Overwinters as a pupa.

SANDY CARPET
Perizoma flavofasciata

PLATE 22
70.138 (1808)

Common. Local and mainly coastal in Ireland. **FIELD CHARACTERS** Head and prothoracic and anal plates brown. Body whitish with a purplish or grey dorsal line, and purplish subdorsal, lateral and subspiracular stripes. Spiracles brown. **SIMILAR SPECIES** Rivulet. **HABITATS** Calcareous grassland, hedgerows (especially along rural lanes), sand dunes, and open areas and rides in woodland. Occasionally in gardens and urban areas. **FOODPLANTS** Mainly Red Campion. Also Bladder and White campions. **FIELD NOTES** Mid-Jul–early Sep. Feeds on ripening seeds within the capsules. Pupates in the ground. Overwinters as a pupa.

BARRED CARPET
Martania taeniata

PLATE 22
70.139 (1801)

Na. Occurs in widely scattered locations. **FIELD CHARACTERS** Based on very limited material examined, larva pale brownish, tinged pinkish, with short bristly hairs and dark brown pinacula. Dorsal line whitish, interrupted on abdominal segments by darker brownish diamonds across the dorsum. **HABITATS** Damp and sheltered habitats, especially woodlands, on base-rich geological formations such as limestone, serpentine and calcareous schists. **FOODPLANTS** Has once been found on the seed capsules of mosses. In captivity feeds on moss capsules and various herbaceous plants. **FIELD NOTES** Aug–May. Overwinters as a small larva.

MARSH CARPET
Gagitodes sagittata

PLATE 22
70.140 (1810)

Na. Very local in the east and north-east. Populations fluctuate in abundance. Extensive vegetation management during the larval period can cause local extinctions. **FIELD CHARACTERS** Head green. Body pale green with darker green transverse bands posteriorly A1–A6, and pink suffusion laterally T1–T2. At the spiracular level there are pinkish spots and shading, more or less forming a zigzag spiracular line bordered below with darker green. A pink, brown or green diagonal line on the anal clasper. **HABITATS** Banks of dykes and rivers, ditches, fens, marshes and wet meadows. **FOODPLANTS** Common and Lesser meadow-rues. Prefers the larger plants growing without competition from other vegetation and in open situations. **FIELD NOTES** Aug–Sep. Feeds externally on the ripening seeds. The larva is remarkably cryptic when resting in the seedhead. Pupates in the ground. Overwinters as a pupa.

NOTE ON PUG MOTHS (GENERA *GYMNOSCELIS*, *CHLOROCLYSTIS*, *PASIPHILA* AND *EUPITHECIA*)

The pugs comprise a large number of species (c. 50). The larvae of most should be reasonably straightforward to identify, based on the combination of field characters, habitats, foodplants and time of year of appearance. Nevertheless, several species feed on a wide variety of plants, and are variable in appearance. These are grouped on pp. 416–17 in the *Separating pug moths* table. Comments in the table aid identification where this is possible, and otherwise give clues as to larval identity even though the larva will need to be reared to be certain of the species. Rearing of all species in captivity is straightforward. Foodplants are listed in greater detail under the species accounts.

Shaded Pug is included in the table although it varies only in colour and not markings; it will be found on the same plants as other polyphagous species, some of which will have forms similar to Shaded Pug.

Bleached Pug is included even though it is not polyphagous, because it may be found in association with other variable, polyphagous species.

DOUBLE-STRIPED PUG
Gymnoscelis rufifasciata

PLATE 22
70.141 (1862)

Common. **FIELD CHARACTERS** Very variable in colour and markings. Rather short and stumpy in appearance, being noticeably fatter centrally and posteriorly. Body pink, yellow, white or green, depending on foodplant. Dorsal line dark, often with forward-pointing arrow-shaped markings across the dorsum. Where the ground colour is pale there may be dark subdorsal and lateral lines, and where the ground is colour dark, white subdorsal and lateral lines may be present. Subspiracular stripe white. A plain green form occurs on oraches and a plain white form on Maize. **SIMILAR SPECIES** See *Separating pug moths* table (pp. 416–17). **HABITATS** Wide variety, including grasslands, heathland, hedgerows, moorland, saltmarshes, urban habitats and woodland. **FOODPLANTS** Flowers of a wide variety of plants, including Ash (and among the galls of Ash Key Gall-mite *Aceria fraxinivora*), Sea Aster, Field Bindweed, Broom, Butterfly-bush, Gorse, Hawthorn, Heather, Holly, Common Ivy, Maize (within the cobs), Wild Marjoram, oraches, Lodgepole Pine, ragworts, roses, Rowan, Sitka Spruce, Tansy and Traveller's-joy. **FIELD NOTES** Early May–late Oct, mainly in two generations and a partial third generation in the south, and May–Jul in one generation in the far north. Feeds on the flowers and ripening fruits, sometimes concealed within. Pupates in the ground. Overwinters as a pupa.

V-PUG
Chloroclystis v-ata

PLATE 22
70.142 (1858)

Common. Has increased significantly in abundance in recent decades. **FIELD CHARACTERS** Head brownish. Body extremely variable in colour and markings, even within the three general forms described here. The first form has a greenish-white body, with or without an interrupted dark dorsal line, which is expanded in places. The second form has a brown body with a dark dorsal line, yellowish transverse dorsal bands between segments A1 and A6, and variable dark brown, pale brown and yellowish markings. The third form has a greyish-white or green body with dark dorsal line, whitish transverse dorsal bands, brown subdorsal lines, sometimes interrupted, and forward-facing brown dorsal triangles. **SIMILAR SPECIES** A white larva of V-Pug with dorsal line comprising dark expanded dashes anteriorly has been found on Common Valerian; this form could be confused with Valerian Pug, which has a complete dorsal line of constant width. **HABITATS** Wide variety, including fens, gardens, unmanaged grassland, hedgerows, marshes, scrub and woodland rides. **FOODPLANTS** Flowers of a wide variety of plants, including Wild Angelica, Bramble, Sweet Chestnut, Dog-rose, Elder, Goldenrod, Hawthorn, Hemp-agrimony, Yellow Loosestrife, Mugwort, Purple-loosestrife, Perforate St John's-wort, Wild Thyme, Traveller's-joy and Common Valerian. **FIELD NOTES** Mid-Jun–mid-Jul and late Aug–early Oct in two generations in the south, and late Jun–Oct in one generation further north. Feeds among the flowers. Pupates in the ground. Overwinters as a pupa, usually fully developed with the wing markings visible, but some do not develop until shortly before emergence.

SLOE PUG
Pasiphila chloerata

PLATE 22
70.143 (1859)

Common. Widespread in central parts of England; local or rare elsewhere. **FIELD CHARACTERS** Head brown. Body whitish green or whitish with a darker green, reddish or blackish-purple dorsal line. The reddish or blackish purple line may be continuous, broken or confined anteriorly, and sometimes broadens anteriorly into a stripe. Occasionally the red may be more extensive, extending subdorsally T1–A5, with a broken red subspiracular stripe. **SIMILAR SPECIES** Green Pug, when found on Blackthorn, tends to be green rather than whitish green, but larvae should be reared to confirm identity. **HABITATS** Mature hedgerows, scrub and woodland margins. **FOODPLANT** Flowers of Blackthorn. **FIELD NOTES** Mid-Mar–Apr. Feeds among the flowers. Pupates in or on the ground. Overwinters as an egg.

GREEN PUG
Pasiphila rectangulata

PLATE 22
70.144 (1860)

Common. **FIELD CHARACTERS** Head brown. Body green with a darker green, red or purple dorsal line. The red or purple line may be continuous, or broken into short lengths. **SIMILAR SPECIES** Sloe Pug. **HABITATS** Gardens and urban habitats, hedgerows, orchards, scrub and woodland. **FOODPLANTS** Flowers of Apple, Crab Apple, Blackthorn, cherries, Hawthorn and Pear. **FIELD NOTES** Late Mar–May. In the flowers. Pupates in the ground. Overwinters as an egg.

BILBERRY PUG
Pasiphila debiliata

PLATE 23
70.145 (1861)

Nb. Very local. **FIELD CHARACTERS** Head black or dark brown, and prothoracic and anal plates blackish, brown or concolorous with a broad central division in the prothoracic plate. Body pale green, with the dorsal vessel visible as a darker line, and spiracular line whitish green. Pinacula grey. **HABITATS** Heathland, moorland and woodland. Mainly found where Bilberry grows in abundance under trees. **FOODPLANT** Bilberry. **FIELD NOTES** Apr–May. Lives within spun leaves of the foodplant and has been found in a flower. Pupates in the ground or among the foodplant. Overwinters as an egg.

HAWORTH'S PUG
Eupithecia haworthiata

PLATE 23
70.146 (1813)

Local. **FIELD CHARACTERS** Body white or whitish green with dark brown, dark green or pink dorsal, subdorsal and spiracular stripes. The spiracular stripe may be absent. The larva turns pinkish when fully fed prior to pupation. **HABITATS** On calcareous soils, including rough grassland, hedgerows, old quarries, scrub and woodland. **FOODPLANTS** Traveller's-joys. **FIELD NOTES** Jul–Aug. Feeds within the flower bud when small, and frass extruding from a bud indicates its presence within. When larger, feeds externally on the bud contents via an entry hole. Pupates in the ground. Overwinters as a pupa, sometimes over two winters.

SLENDER PUG
Eupithecia tenuiata

PLATE 23
70.147 (1811)

Common. **FIELD CHARACTERS** Head black or brown. Body whitish with a band of dense, dark grey or brown speckling across the dorsum, within which is a dark dorsal line. Subdorsal stripe dark grey or brown, and a supraspiracular stripe comprising dense, dark grey or brown speckling, these markings interrupted between segments. There is a pale green form with slight grey speckling on the dorsum and a green subdorsal line. **HABITATS** Fens, heathland, marshes, margins of waterbodies, and carr and other woodlands. Occasionally in gardens. **FOODPLANTS** Catkins of Eared, Goat and Grey willows. Also Osier. **FIELD NOTES** Mar–Apr. Feeds in the catkins, including when fallen on the ground. Pupates in or on the ground. Overwinters as an egg.

MAPLE PUG
Eupithecia inturbata

PLATE 23
70.148 (1812)

Local. **FIELD CHARACTERS** Head green. Body green with a dark green dorsal line, and sometimes with pinkish-brown dorsal patches. Subdorsal line and subspiracular stripe whitish green or yellowish green. Spiracles yellow. **HABITATS** On chalk, clay and limestone soils, including in hedgerows, scrub and woodland. On trees producing an abundance of flowers. **FOODPLANT** Flowers of Field Maple. **FIELD NOTES** May–Jun. Feeds among the flowers. Pupates in a cocoon among the flowers. Overwinters as an egg.

CLOAKED PUG
Eupithecia abietaria

PLATE 23
70.149 (1815)

Uncommon; suspected immigrant. Rarely recorded as a larva, but likely to be found wherever Norway Spruce is common. **FIELD CHARACTERS** Head and prothoracic plate black or brown. Body greenish grey or purplish brown with brown pinacula. Dorsal line faint and dark. Proleg and anal clasper reduced in size and weak. **SIMILAR SPECIES** The larva of micro-moth *Dioryctria abietella* (Pyralidae) looks superficially similar but has additional prolegs to the pair Cloaked Pug has on A6. **HABITATS** Plantations and mixed woodland. **FOODPLANTS** Mainly Norway Spruce. Also Noble Fir, larches, European Silver-fir and Sitka Spruce. **FIELD NOTES** Late Jul–early Sep. Feeds on developing seeds within a green cone, usually towards the top of a tree. There may be several larvae in one cone, and, viewed through binoculars, infested green cones have brown patches with greyish-brown frass adhering. Pupates in a slight cocoon in debris on the ground. Overwinters as a pupa, sometimes over two winters. Delayed emergence to another year enables some individuals to survive over seasons when the Norway Spruce cone crop fails entirely across a forest area.

TOADFLAX PUG
Eupithecia linariata

PLATE 23
70.150 (1816)

Common. Very local in Scotland. **FIELD CHARACTERS** Head brown or black. Body various shades of yellow, white or pale green, with a black, brown or purplish patch across the dorsum on each segment, varying in size and shape and extending down to the spiracular level. In some larvae, patches are reduced in extent to dorsal V-shapes and subdorsal dashes. Spiracles black. **HABITATS** Cliffs, calcareous grassland, old quarries and railway lines, road verges, stabilised sand dunes and waste ground. Occasionally in gardens. **FOODPLANTS** Mainly Common Toadflax. Reported on Pale Toadflax, and Snapdragon (in gardens). **FIELD NOTES** Aug–Sep. Feeds at first within the flowers, and later on the seeds, with the whole or anterior part of the larva within the fruit. Makes neat round holes in the fruit. Pupates in the ground. Overwinters as a pupa.

FOXGLOVE PUG
Eupithecia pulchellata

PLATE 23
70.151 (1817)

Common. **FIELD CHARACTERS** Head brown with dark markings. Body pale purplish brown, sometimes whitish or tinged greenish, with a dark purplish-brown dorsal band, often broken into shield-shaped or oval markings. Subdorsal line dark purplish brown and there is sometimes a similar supraspiracular line. A plain green form is known in Europe. **HABITATS** Wide variety, including cliffs, rough grassland, heathland, moorland, mosses, sand dunes, waste ground, and open and recently cleared woodland. **FOODPLANT** Foxglove. **FIELD NOTES** Late Jun–mid-Aug. Feeds within the flower, especially on the stamens. When larger, the larva may feed on the seeds with its anterior part buried within the fruit, and it makes neat round holes in the fruit. An occupied flower often has a hole visible in the side of the flower tube, and its open front is usually slightly closed. Pupates in the ground. Overwinters as a pupa.

CHANNEL ISLANDS PUG
Eupithecia ultimaria

PLATE 23
70.152 (1855a)

Immigrant; recent colonist. **FIELD CHARACTERS** Head green or brown. Body slender, green or orangey brown, and subtly shaded whitish, yellowish or reddish brown dorsally, sometimes forming greenish or brownish shield-shaped marks along the dorsum that match the scale-like leaves of the foodplant. Sometimes there are whitish dorsal and subdorsal lines. Usually there are subdorsal reddish spots T3–A6, sometimes extended into diagonal dashes towards the dorsum. Some examples have diagonal whitish dashes laterally that join a whitish subspiracular stripe interrupted with larger reddish-brown spots A1–A5. Anal flap reddish centrally, edged yellowish. **SIMILAR SPECIES** Angle-barred Pug is less slender and rather larger when fully grown, and it may be much plainer or with bolder, less intricate markings. Subdorsal reddish spots are absent, whereas they are usually present in Channel Islands Pug. **HABITATS** Variety of coastal locations where the foodplant is naturalised or has been planted. **FOODPLANT** Tamarisk. **FIELD NOTES** Jul–Sep. Feeds on the leaves. Pupates on the ground. Overwinters as a pupa.

LEAD-COLOURED PUG
Eupithecia plumbeolata

PLATE 23
70.153 (1814)

Nb. Sparsely scattered throughout. **FIELD CHARACTERS** Head pale brown with a lateral black spot. Body whitish or greyish white, with a purple dorsal stripe varying in width up to a broad band. Subdorsal stripe purple. **HABITATS** Mainly open woodland. Also dune-slacks, meadows and sand dunes. **FOODPLANTS** Common Cow-wheat. Reported on Field Cow-wheat (now a rare plant) and Yellow-rattle. **FIELD NOTES** Late Jun–mid-Aug. Feeds completely enclosed within a flower. Occupied flowers of Common Cow-wheat partly fill with dark frass, but there is otherwise no external evidence. Pupates in or on the ground. Overwinters as a pupa.

MARSH PUG
Eupithecia pygmaeata

PLATE 23
70.154 (1822)

Nb. Very local although probably overlooked. Apparently not found in the far south of England. **FIELD CHARACTERS** Head pale brown and speckled. Body dull green or greyish green, sometimes brownish, with darker dorsal and subdorsal lines, and a pale subspiracular stripe. **HABITATS** Dune-slacks, fens, breckland and limestone grasslands, limestone pavement (the Burren, Cos Clare and Galway, Ireland), marshes, sand dunes, waste ground and woodland rides. **FOODPLANTS** Field Mouse-ear and probably other mouse-ears. Also reported on Greater Stitchwort. Has been observed laying eggs on flowers of eyebrights, but it is not known whether it can feed successfully on this plant. **FIELD NOTES** Jun–Jul. At first within the flowers and fruits without any external sign. Later, feeds externally on the seeds by inserting its anterior end into the open end of an old flower or by eating a hole in the side of a fruit. Pupates in or on the ground. Overwinters as a pupa, sometimes over two winters.

NETTED PUG
Eupithecia venosata

PLATE 23
70.155 (1823)

Ssp. *venosata* Local in England and Wales, and scattered in Scotland. Ssp. *hebridensis* Hebrides. Ssp. *fumosae* Orkney/Shetland. Ssp. *ochracae* Orkney. Ssp. *plumbea* Ireland. **FIELD CHARACTERS** Head brown with dark markings. Body greyish white, usually with a broad, dark grey dorsal band. Sometimes the band is reduced to dark subdorsal stripes with shading between, or occasionally it is absent. Spiracles white with dark surrounds. **HABITATS** Cliffs and rocky coasts, calcareous grassland, hedgerows, old quarries and railway cuttings, vegetated shingle and woodland rides. **FOODPLANTS** Bladder and Sea campions. Also reported on Moss, Red and White campions, and Nottingham and Small-flowered catchflies. **FIELD NOTES** Jun–Jul. Feeds within the flowers and fruits, eating the developing seeds. Pupates in the ground. Overwinters as a pupa, sometimes over two winters.

BRINDLED PUG
Eupithecia abbreviata

PLATE 23
70.156 (1852)

Common. **FIELD CHARACTERS** Head mottled brown. Body various shades of brown, covered with tiny white dots and often with dark brown dorsal and subdorsal lines. There are forward-pointing, dark brown dorsal triangles, sometimes edged white posteriorly, and sometimes diagonal whitish lateral streaks. A plain form occurs, almost devoid of markings, except for faint, dark dorsal and subdorsal lines. **SIMILAR SPECIES** Oak-tree Pug shows no consistent differences but appears not to have a plain form. A larva on oaks is more likely to be Brindled Pug, and on hawthorns Oak-tree Pug, and their distributions currently do not overlap over much of Scotland. Common Pug differs from these two species by its diamond-shaped markings with dark brown anterior margins. **HABITATS** Mainly woodland; also gardens and hedgerows. **FOODPLANTS** Pedunculate and Sessile oaks; less often hawthorns. Has been recorded on Holm Oak. Has also been found beneath oak canopy on Hazel that it ate in captivity. **FIELD NOTES** May–Jul. Pupates behind loose bark or in the ground. Overwinters as a pupa.

OAK-TREE PUG
Eupithecia dodoneata

PLATE 23
70.157 (1853)

Common. Spreading northwards. **SIMILAR SPECIES** Brindled Pug and Common Pug. **HABITATS** Gardens, hedgerows, scrub and woodland. **FOODPLANTS** Hawthorn and Pedunculate Oak. **FIELD NOTES** Late Jun–early Aug. Feeds mainly on flowers and on calyces of the fruit of Hawthorn. Also on leaves. Pupates in the ground, or in bark or wood. Overwinters as a pupa.

JUNIPER PUG
Eupithecia pusillata

PLATE 23
70.158 (1854)

Common. Spreading north. Local in Ireland. **FIELD CHARACTERS** Very variable, with three forms described here. The first form has a green head and body, with a dark green dorsal line and yellowish-white subdorsal stripe. Subspiracular stripe white; absent T1–T3. Anal flap reddish centrally. The second form has a green or dark green head. Body green with a dark or black dorsal line, and brown dorsal blotches edged yellowish. The third form has a brown head. Body pinkish brown or orangey brown, with a dark brown or black dorsal line, usually expanded to form dark blotches A1–A6. Subdorsal line whitish, often with dark brown patches laterally, and subspiracular stripe white. Sometimes the whitish is more extensive. **SIMILAR SPECIES** Chestnut-coloured Carpet and Juniper Carpet. Edinburgh Pug is shinier in appearance and lacks reddish coloration on the anal flap; it is fully fed in autumn, whereas Juniper Pug feeds in spring. **HABITATS** Cliffs, gardens, calcareous grassland, moorland and open woodland (in Scotland). **FOODPLANTS** Common Juniper. Also other junipers, including cultivars, and cypresses and red-cedars. **FIELD NOTES** Feb–Jun. Overwinters at first as an egg, hatching from early Feb. The young larva eats out the contents of buds by inserting its head from the top. Pupates in a cocoon among the foodplant.

CYPRESS PUG
Eupithecia phoeniceata

PLATE 23
70.159 (1855)

Recent colonist. Slowly spreading northwards. **FIELD CHARACTERS** Head green, speckled brown. Body green with subtly shaded darker and lighter patterning. Dorsal line dark green, edged whitish in patches, with whitish spots at the spiracular level A1–A6. Proleg reddish. Anal flap may be reddish centrally. **SIMILAR SPECIES** Cypress Carpet. **HABITATS** Mainly cemeteries, gardens and urban parks. Sometimes in rural places such as arboreta and in shelterbelts. **FOODPLANTS** Monterey Cypress. May use other cypresses, and junipers, in the wild. **FIELD NOTES** Oct–Jun. Feeds on the leaves. Pupates in a slight spinning among the needles. Overwinters as a part-grown larva, continuing to feed in mild weather.

WHITE-SPOTTED PUG
Eupithecia tripunctaria

PLATE 23
70.160 (1835)

Local. **FIELD CHARACTERS** Head greenish white, or brownish with darker mottling. Body whitish green or greyish green, brown or whitish. The whitish-green/greyish-green form has green dorsal and subdorsal lines, with forward-pointing green or dark brown dorsal triangles, and there may be brown patches laterally. The brown and whitish forms have similar markings that are dark brown. **SIMILAR SPECIES** See *Separating pug moths* table (pp. 416–17). **HABITATS** Fens, breckland grassland, marshes, riverbanks, scrub and woodland rides. **FOODPLANTS** Elder in first generation. In second generation on Wild Angelica, Wild Carrot, Goldenrod, Hogweed, Wild Parsnip and Common Ragwort. **FIELD NOTES** Jun–Aug, and Sep–Oct as a partial second generation. Feeds on the flowers and developing seeds. Pupates in the ground. Overwinters as a pupa.

GOLDEN-ROD PUG
Eupithecia virgaureata

PLATE 23
70.161 (1851)

Local. Rare or absent, except Devon and Cornwall, in much of the south, south-east and East Anglia. **FIELD CHARACTERS** Head brown and mottled. Body varying shades of brown and grey and covered with numerous tiny white or pale dots. Dorsal line and forward-pointing dorsal triangles grey or brown. Contrasting white or whitish diagonal lateral stripes that join the interrupted subspiracular stripe. These diagonal stripes strongly suggest, but are not diagnostic of, this species. Body dark ventrally. **SIMILAR SPECIES** See *Separating pug moths* table (pp. 416–17). **HABITATS** Rough, acidic grasslands, waste ground, and recently cleared areas and rides in woodland. **FOODPLANTS** A wider range of foodplants than commonly believed. Reported on Wild Angelica, Red Campion, Dahlia, Goldenrod, Hawthorn, Heather, Yellow Loosestrife, oaks, Cow Parsley, Pignut, Common Ragwort, toadflaxes, Grey Willow and Yarrow. First-generation larvae have been found on Hawthorn, oaks, Cow Parsley, Pignut and Grey Willow, and second-generation larvae may be found readily on Goldenrod and Common Ragwort. **FIELD NOTES** Jun–Jul and Aug–Oct, as a partial second generation. Feeds on flowers and fruits of herbaceous plants and on leaves of shrubs and trees in the first generation, and among flowers in the second generation. Pupates in the ground. Overwinters as a pupa, sometimes twice.

DWARF PUG
Eupithecia tantillaria

PLATE 24
70.162 (1857)

Common. Increasing in distribution. Local in Ireland. **FIELD CHARACTERS** Head orangey brown. Body orangey brown with a blackish dorsal line, varying in width along its length, and including a central white line anteriorly. Subdorsal line brownish white, often shaded below with dark brown, and subspiracular stripe brownish white. Anal flap pale brown edged whitish or paler laterally. Body chocolate brown ventrally. **SIMILAR SPECIES** Brown form of Larch Pug, and Ochreous Pug. The brown form of Larch Pug is distinguished from Ochreous Pug and Dwarf Pug by the central dark area on the anal flap and the black ventral colour. Ochreous Pug has a narrower, less black dorsal line than Dwarf Pug, and is purplish brown ventrally. Caution is advised in using these features to separate species as the descriptions are based on limited material. **HABITATS** Mainly coniferous woodland. Also gardens and urban parks, and shelterbelts. **FOODPLANTS** Most commonly associated with Douglas Fir, Norway Spruce and Sitka Spruce. Also reported on Lawson's Cypress, Giant Fir, Western Hemlock-spruce, Common Juniper, larches, Scots Pine and Western Red-cedar. **FIELD NOTES** Late Jun–late Aug. Feeds among the needles. Pupates in the ground. Overwinters as a pupa.

LARCH PUG
Eupithecia lariciata

PLATE 24
70.163 (1856)

Common. **FIELD CHARACTERS** There are green and brown forms. The green form has a pale brown head and green body, with a dark green dorsal line, including a central white line anteriorly. Subdorsal line pale green or yellowish, and subspiracular stripe white. Anal flap reddish centrally, edged white laterally. Body dark green ventrally. The brown form has a brown head and body, with a dark brown dorsal line, including a central white line anteriorly. Subdorsal line brownish white, shaded below with dark brown, and spiracular stripe white. Anal flap blackish red or dark brown centrally, edged white laterally. Body black ventrally. **SIMILAR SPECIES** Dwarf Pug and Ochreous Pug. **HABITATS** Most numerous in coniferous and mixed woodlands. Also in arboreta, gardens and urban parks, and shelterbelts. **FOODPLANTS** European Larch, and probably other larches. Also reported on Norway Spruce. **FIELD NOTES** Mid-Jun–Sep, or possibly later where there is a partial second generation. Feeds on the leaves. Pupates in or on the ground. Overwinters as a pupa.

FLETCHER'S PUG/PAUPER PUG
Eupithecia egenaria

PLATE 24
70.164 (1824)

RDB. Very local, overlooked, but also spreading. **FIELD CHARACTERS** Head green. Body green, dorsal line dark green and spiracles white. **HABITATS** Variety of situations, including arboreta, planted avenues in open countryside, parkland, street trees and ancient woodland. **FOODPLANTS** Lime, and Large-leaved and Small-leaved limes. **FIELD NOTES** Late Jun–Jul. Feeds within the flowers, eating mainly the stamens and styles. Pupates in or on the ground. Overwinters as a pupa.

PIMPINEL PUG
Eupithecia pimpinellata

PLATE 24
70.165 (1845)

Local. Scattered throughout, but overlooked and likely to be more widespread. **FIELD CHARACTERS** Head green or brown. Body green or purplish, and covered in numerous tiny white dots. Dorsal and subdorsal lines dark, and subspiracular stripe white, whitish green or yellowish, and extending onto the anal flap, which is purplish centrally. The green form has a purplish tinge dorsally on T1. **HABITATS** Calcareous grassland, cliff-top and rough grasslands, limestone pavement (the Burren, Cos Clare and Galway, Ireland), old quarries and railway lines, and dry woodland rides, mainly on calcareous soils. **FOODPLANTS** Burnet-saxifrage. Reported on Greater Burnet-saxifrage. **FIELD NOTES** Late Jul–mid-Oct. Feeds on the flowers and developing fruits. Prefers plants growing in taller swards, often in association with light scrub. Pupates in the ground. Overwinters as a pupa.

PLAIN PUG
Eupithecia simpliciata

PLATE 24
70.166 (1842)

Local. More frequent in coastal areas than inland. **FIELD CHARACTERS** There are green and brown forms. The green form has a green or yellowish-green head and body, with numerous fine white speckles. Dorsal line dark green, sometimes with forward-pointing V-shaped, dark green marks across the dorsum. Pinacula black. Spiracles black. Anal flap with a central dark mark, edged white laterally. The brown form is similar, with brown replacing green markings, and more frequently has marks across the dorsum. **HABITATS** Open, disturbed ground in coastal and inland situations (e.g. allotments, recently abandoned arable areas), tidal riverbanks, upper parts of saltmarshes, vegetated shingle and waste ground. **FOODPLANTS** Goosefoots and oraches, preferring prostrate species. Also recorded on glassworts. **FIELD NOTES** Aug–Sep. Feeds on the seeds. Neat round holes in the sides of the fruits may indicate the presence of larvae, although similar holes are produced by micro-moths in genus *Coleophora* (Coleophoridae). Pupates in the ground. Overwinters as a pupa.

NARROW-WINGED PUG
Eupithecia nanata

PLATE 24
70.168 (1846)

Common. **FIELD CHARACTERS** Head brownish. Body colour and pattern variable within two main forms, one whitish or pale greenish, heavily patterned with dark reddish, and the other green with more subtle yellowish and white markings. The heavily patterned form has jagged-edged, dark reddish transverse bands on each segment, and these may coalesce so that red becomes the dominant colour in some examples. Lateral streaks white. Anal flap red, darker centrally. The plainer form has white and yellowish markings dorsally, and white lateral streaks. Anal flap red centrally, edged yellow or white laterally. **HABITATS** Heathland and moorland. Not known to be resident in gardens. **FOODPLANTS** Heather, and has been recorded on Lodgepole Pine. **FIELD NOTES** Jul–Oct, including a partial second generation. Feeds on the flowers. Pupates in the ground. Overwinters as a pupa.

ANGLE-BARRED PUG
Eupithecia innotata

PLATE 24
70.169 (1848)

Common. Can be frequent in coastal areas from Kent to Yorkshire, otherwise rather local and infrequent, especially inland. **FIELD CHARACTERS** Head green. Body green and variably marked. Plainer examples are green with a white or yellow subspiracular stripe, and a red anal flap, edged white or yellow laterally. More contrasting examples may have one or both of the following features: yellow subdorsal dashes, edged above with dark green A2–A8; red or brown lateral spots A1–A8, each edged posteriorly with white. **SIMILAR SPECIES** If on Tamarisk, Channel Islands Pug. **HABITATS** Open habitats in a variety of situations, including coastal areas, gardens and urban parks, hedgerows, sand dunes, isolated trees in open countryside, and woodland. **FOODPLANTS** In different areas Ash, Sea-buckthorn and Tamarisk, but Cornwall have been found feeding on Sea-buckthorn and Tamarisk in the same place at the same time. Occasionally Blackthorn, Elder and hawthorns. **FIELD NOTES** Mid-Jun–late Jul and late Aug–Sep, in two generations. Feeds on the leaves. Pupates in the ground. Overwinters as a pupa.

MARBLED PUG
Eupithecia irriguata

PLATE 24
70.170 (1818)

Nb. Most frequent in central southern and south-west England; scarce elsewhere. **FIELD CHARACTERS** Head brown. Body green with reddish-brown dorsal patches between segments, each usually edged yellowish. Markings on dorsum T1–T3 variable. A purplish-black or reddish-brown band from posterior A6 to A10, edged white laterally on the anal flap. **SIMILAR SPECIES** Mottled Pug, Pinion-spotted Pug, Little Emerald, Small Grass Emerald and Southern Grass Emerald. The emeralds have a notched head that the pugs do not. Mottled Pug is distinguished from the other two pugs by having a reddish-brown subspiracular stripe. Marbled Pug does not share a foodplant with Pinion-spotted Pug and has brown dorsal markings, usually edged paler, whereas Pinion-spotted Pug has a continuous red or purple dorsal stripe. **HABITATS** Mainly woodland where there are concentrations of mature oaks. Also hedgerow oak trees in wooded landscapes. **FOODPLANTS** Pedunculate and Sessile oaks. Reported on Beech. **FIELD NOTES** Late May–early Jul. Pupates in the ground. Overwinters as a pupa.

OCHREOUS PUG
Eupithecia indigata

PLATE 24
70.171 (1844)

Common. Widespread in mainland Great Britain; very local in Ireland. **FIELD CHARACTERS** Head brown. Body brown with a darker dorsal line, a brownish-yellow subdorsal line, edged below with a dark brown line, and a white or brownish-yellow subspiracular stripe. Body purplish brown ventrally. **SIMILAR SPECIES** Dwarf Pug and Larch Pug. **HABITATS** Gardens and urban parks, pine scrub on heathland and moorland, and native Scots Pine woodland. **FOODPLANTS** Scots Pine and other pines. Also reported on Common Juniper, European Larch and spruces. **FIELD NOTES** Mid-Jun–mid-Sep. Based on observations on Scots Pine, larvae feed on the buds and emerging tender needles, but do not eat mature needles. Pupates in a slight cocoon among needles on or below the foodplant, or in a bark crevice. Overwinters as a pupa.

THYME PUG
Eupithecia distinctaria

PLATE 24
70.172 (1843)

Nb. Very local and mainly coastal and western in distribution. **FIELD CHARACTERS** Head pale brown. Body green with a red dorsal stripe. **SIMILAR SPECIES** Satyr Pug has a green form with a reddish dorsal line, but this is much narrower than the dorsal stripe of Thyme Pug, and is not such a bright red colour. **HABITATS** In sparsely vegetated calcareous areas, including cliffs, grasslands and old quarries. Also sand dunes and vegetated shingle. **FOODPLANT** Wild Thyme. **FIELD NOTES** Mainly Jul–Sep, but young larvae have been recorded as early as mid-Jun. Feeds on the flowers. Pupates in the ground. Overwinters as a pupa.

LIME-SPECK PUG
Eupithecia centaureata

PLATE 24
70.173 (1825)

Common. More coastal in the north, west and Ireland. **FIELD CHARACTERS** Body colour and pattern variable within two main forms, one whitish, whitish green or yellowish, heavily patterned with dark reddish, and the other plain greenish. The plain form has a greenish head and green body, with a faint, darker dorsal stripe, and sometimes an interrupted dark subdorsal line. There are usually yellowish skin folds between abdominal segments. The patterned forms have a variable extent of reddish, purplish or brown angular markings across the dorsum, often arranged in a distinctive geometric pattern. **SIMILAR SPECIES** See *Separating pug moths* table (pp. 416–17). **HABITATS** Wide variety of open habitats, including gardens, grasslands, hedgerows, old quarries, sand dunes, scattered scrub, vegetated shingle and open woodland. **FOODPLANTS** Wide variety of herbaceous plants, including Wild Angelica, Clustered Bellflower burnet-saxifrages, Wild Carrot, Common Fleabane, Goldenrod, Canadian Goldenrod, Groundsel, hawkbits, hawkweeds, Hemp-agrimony, knapweeds, Mugwort, Greater Plantain, Common Ragwort, Field Scabious, Rock Sea-lavender, Traveller's-joy, Sea Wormwood and Yarrow. **FIELD NOTES** May–Oct with two generations in the south. Feeds among flowers. Pupates in or on the ground. Overwinters as a pupa.

PINION-SPOTTED PUG
Eupithecia insigniata

PLATE 24
70.174 (1820)

Nb. Very local, and rarely observed in numbers. **FIELD CHARACTERS** Head and body green. Dorsal line red or purple, expanded into a band T1–T3 and A6–A10, and into a blotch on each of A1–A5. Subspiracular line yellow. Proleg red. **SIMILAR SPECIES** Marbled Pug, Mottled Pug, Little Emerald, Small Grass Emerald and Southern Grass Emerald. **HABITATS** Prefers open habitats such as isolated Hawthorn trees in grassland, old hedgerows, orchards, and edges of scrub and woodland. **FOODPLANTS** Mainly Hawthorn. Occasionally Apple, Crab Apple and pears. **FIELD NOTES** Mid-Jun–early Aug. Pupates on the ground, among moss or bark. Overwinters as a pupa.

TRIPLE-SPOTTED PUG
Eupithecia trisignaria

PLATE 24
70.175 (1826)

Local. Widely distributed. Not observed frequently but probably overlooked. **FIELD CHARACTERS** Head pale brown. Body green with dark green dorsal and subdorsal lines, and a white subspiracular stripe, extending onto the anal flap. **HABITATS** Fens, wet grassland, marshes and woodland rides. **FOODPLANTS** Mainly Wild Angelica; less often Hogweed. Also reported on Burnet-saxifrage and Wild Parsnip. **FIELD NOTES** Aug–early Oct. Feeds on the flowers and developing fruits, resting immediately below along the umbel stalks. Pupates in or on the ground. Overwinters as a pupa.

EDINBURGH PUG
Eupithecia intricata

PLATE 25
70.176 (1827)

Ssp. *intricata* Common. Mere's Pug ssp. *hibernica* The Burren, Cos Clare and Galway, Ireland. **FIELD CHARACTERS** Head green or brown. Body shiny green with a dark green dorsal line, dark green, white or yellow subdorsal line or stripe, and white subspiracular stripe. **SIMILAR SPECIES** Green forms of Juniper Pug. **HABITATS** Gardens and urban parks, moorland and coniferous woodland. Mere's Pug: limestone pavement. **FOODPLANTS** Mainly junipers and cypresses. Also Douglas Fir, Western Red-cedar and Chinese Thuja. Mere's Pug: prostrate form of Common Juniper. **FIELD NOTES** Aug–Sep. Feeds on the needles. Pupates in a cocoon among the foodplant. Overwinters as a pupa.

SATYR PUG
Eupithecia satyrata

PLATE 25
70.177 (1828)

Ssp. *satyrata* Local. Widespread and frequent from Northumberland northwards. More local further south, and scarce in lowland England. Ssp. *curzoni* Shetland. **FIELD CHARACTERS** There are two main forms, one plain pale green, the other patterned. Both are covered in numerous tiny pale dots. The plain form has a dark dorsal line, sometimes tinged pinkish. The patterned forms all have a whitish-green, yellowish-green or whitish-pink to dark pink body, with a dark pink or brown dorsal stripe and forward-pointing dorsal triangles. Whitish or yellowish diagonal lateral stripes join the interrupted pale subspiracular stripe. In some examples the stripes may be indistinct. **SIMILAR SPECIES** See *Separating pug moths* table (pp. 416–17). **HABITATS** Most frequent in upland grassland and moorland, and also found in other upland habitats. In lowland areas, in fens, calcareous grassland, heathland, marshes, waste ground and woodland rides. **FOODPLANTS** Wide variety of flowers of herbaceous plants, including Bearberry, bedstraws, gentians, hawkweeds, Cross-leaved Heath, Heather, hemp-nettles, knapweeds, Meadowsweet, mulleins, Common Ragwort, Common Rock-rose, scabiouses, St John's-worts, Wild Thyme and Yellow-rattle. Also on the soft young shoots of Lodgepole Pine and Sitka Spruce, and leaves of Bog-myrtle and willows. **FIELD NOTES** Jul–Oct. Overwinters as a pupa.

SCARCE PUG
Eupithecia extensaria

PLATE 25
70.178 (1847)

Ssp. *occidua* RDB. Restricted to the coast around the Wash. **FIELD CHARACTERS** Head green and mottled. Body green and covered in numerous tiny white dots, with dark green dorsal and subdorsal stripes and a white subspiracular stripe. **HABITATS** Higher ground on saltmarsh and saline flood banks. **FOODPLANT** Sea Wormwood. **FIELD NOTES** Jul–Sep. Feeds on the flowers and leaves. Pupates in a cocoon in debris or in the ground. Overwinters as a pupa.

WORMWOOD PUG
Eupithecia absinthiata

PLATE 25
70.179 (1830)

Common. **FIELD CHARACTERS** Head brown and mottled. Body various shades of green, brown or pink, and covered in numerous tiny pale dots, with dark dorsal and subdorsal lines and a more or less continuous pale subspiracular line. There are brown dorsal markings that may be oval with lateral extensions or triangular. In some pale greenish examples the dorsal markings are absent other than faint, darker dorsal and subdorsal lines. **SIMILAR SPECIES** See *Separating pug moths* table (pp. 416–17). **HABITATS** Wide variety of open habitats, including gardens, grasslands, heathland, moorland, old quarries, saltmarshes, sand dunes, waste ground and open woodland. **FOODPLANTS** Wide variety, including Bilberry, Common Fleabane, goldenrods, goosefoots, Gypsywort, Heather, Hemp-agrimony, Black Horehound, Wild Marjoram, mayweeds, Mugwort, Common Ragwort, Devil's-bit Scabious, Tansy, wormwoods and Yarrow. **FIELD NOTES** Late Jul–Oct. Feeds on the flowers. Pupates in the ground. Overwinters as a pupa.

BLEACHED PUG
Eupithecia expallidata

PLATE 25
70.180 (1833)

Nb. Most frequent in a band between south Wales and Kent; very local or scarce elsewhere. **FIELD CHARACTERS** Head brown and mottled. Body green, yellowish green or whitish and covered in numerous tiny pale dots. The green and yellowish-green forms have dark dorsal and subdorsal lines and a pale subspiracular line. The whitish form has a pale brown dorsal line, oval or diamond-shaped, dark brown dorsal marks, a dark brown subdorsal line and a whitish subspiracular line. **SIMILAR SPECIES** See *Separating pug moths* table (pp. 416–17). **HABITATS** Open woodland, especially in recently cleared areas and rides. Also reported in coastal scrub. **FOODPLANT** Goldenrod. **FIELD NOTES** Late Aug–mid-Oct. Feeds on the flowers. Pupates in the ground. Overwinters as a pupa.

VALERIAN PUG
Eupithecia valerianata

PLATE 25
70.181 (1821)

Nb. Scattered distribution. Rarely observed frequently, and may have declined, though also likely to be overlooked. **FIELD CHARACTERS** Head pale brown and speckled. Body dull pale greenish, or dull whitish. The pale green form has dark green, sometimes faint dorsal and subdorsal lines. The whitish form has brown dorsal and subdorsal lines. **SIMILAR SPECIES** V-Pug when on Common Valerian. **HABITATS** Most frequent in open wetland habitats such as broads, fens and marshes; also damp woodland rides. Occurs in old limestone quarries on the coast at Torquay. **FOODPLANTS** Common and Marsh valerians. Almost certainly on Red Valerian in the coastal quarries. **FIELD NOTES** Jul–mid-Aug. Feeds on the flowers and developing seeds. Pupates on the ground. Overwinters as a pupa.

Mottled Pug larva (see opposite)

CURRANT PUG
Eupithecia assimilata

PLATE 25
70.182 (1832)

Common. **FIELD CHARACTERS** Head pale brownish green, sometimes speckled. Body usually green with numerous tiny white dots, dorsal line dark green and subdorsal line white. There may be darker markings across the dorsum, including forward-pointing V-shapes, diamond shapes and dark brown subdorsal spots. Rarely the green coloration may be partly or completely replaced with brown. A pair of short, blunt anal points. **SIMILAR SPECIES** Spinach. **HABITATS** Allotments, fens, gardens, hedgerows, waste ground and open woodland. **FOODPLANTS** Black and Red currants, Gooseberry, and Hop and its garden cultivars. **FIELD NOTES** Early Jun–late Jul and late Aug–Oct, in two generations. Feeds on the underside of a leaf, eating multiple small holes in the leaf. Pupates in the ground. Overwinters as a pupa.

COMMON PUG
Eupithecia vulgata

PLATE 25
70.183 (1834)

Common. **FIELD CHARACTERS** Head brown and mottled. Body usually pale brown, sometimes pale green, or occasionally dark brown, covered in numerous tiny white dots. Dorsal line brown or green, expanded into diamond shapes A1–A5, with anterior edges usually shaded darker, especially A3–A5. Short diagonal white marks laterally A1–A5. In the dark brown form the markings are hard to discern, but there is a dark brown subdorsal line and the white dots stand out clearly. **SIMILAR SPECIES** Brindled Pug and Oak-tree Pug. **HABITATS** Wide variety, including gardens, fens, heathland, hedgerows, marshes, moorland, and open areas in scrub and woodland. **FOODPLANTS** Wide variety of woody and herbaceous plants, including Bilberry, Bramble, Bladder Campion, Goldenrod, Hawthorn, Hogweed, Orpine, ragworts, Raspberry, willows and Yarrow. Has also been found indoors eating a cactus stem. **FIELD NOTES** Jun–Jul and late Aug–early Oct, in two generations. On the flowers and leaves. Pupates in or on the ground. Overwinters as a pupa.

MOTTLED PUG
Eupithecia exiguata

PLATE 25
70.184 (1819)

Common. Very local in central and northern Scotland. **FIELD CHARACTERS** Head brown. Body green with a faint green dorsal line edged with darker shading. The dorsal line and shading are expanded between segments T3 and A5, and sometimes beyond, forming oval reddish-brown shapes with yellowish centres. A reddish-brown or purplish-black dorsal band A8–A10. Subspiracular stripe reddish brown, thinly edged above with yellow, and extending onto the anal clasper. A pair of short, blunt anal points. **SIMILAR SPECIES** Marbled Pug, Pinion-spotted Pug, Little Emerald, Small Grass Emerald and Southern Grass Emerald. **HABITATS** Gardens and urban parks, hedgerows, scrub and woodland. **FOODPLANTS** Wide variety of woody plants, including Alder, Apple, Ash, Barberry, birches, Blackthorn, currants, Dogwood, Guelder-rose, hawthorns, Field Maple, Pedunculate Oak, Pear, Rowan, Snowberry, Stranvaesia, Sycamore, Weigelia and willows. Has also been recorded feeding on the berries of Elder. **FIELD NOTES** Jul–Oct. Pupates in the ground. Overwinters as a pupa.

CAMPANULA PUG
Eupithecia denotata

PLATE 25
70.185 (1836)

Na. Central and southern England, western coasts, Channel Islands, Scilly and Isle of Man. **FIELD CHARACTERS** Head dark brown. Body pale brown and sparsely covered with short, spiky hairs. Dorsal line dark brown, edged with brown shading or widening to a dark brown band T1–T3 and A8–A10. O-shaped dark brown dorsal markings A1–A6 that may be filled dark brown in darker, well-marked examples. Spiracles dark brown. **HABITATS** On calcareous soils in hedgerows, scrub, woodland rides and occasionally gardens. Also on the coast on rocky cliffs, hedge banks and vegetated stone walls. **FOODPLANTS** Giant Bellflower, Nettle-leaved Bellflower and Sheep's-bit. Also found on introduced bellflowers in gardens. **FIELD NOTES** Jul–Sep. On bellflowers, in the developing seed capsules within the flower, with little evidence of occupation. On Sheep's-bit, in the ripening seedheads when small and externally when large. Pupates in the ground. Overwinters as a pupa.

YARROW PUG
Eupithecia millefoliata

PLATE 25
70.186 (1841)

Nb. Resident and suspected immigrant, and appears to be spreading slowly. **FIELD CHARACTERS** Head brown. Body stumpy and brown, with prominent white pinacula and numerous tiny white dots. Broad, forward-facing triangular, dark brown marks on dorsum A1–A6, with a dark brown dorsal stripe on remaining segments. Subspiracular stripe white and interrupted. **HABITATS** Rough grassland, open areas along coasts, upper parts of saltmarsh, vegetated shingle and waste ground. **FOODPLANT** Yarrow. **FIELD NOTES** Aug–late Oct. When young, feeds on the flower heads. Later, sits under and feeds on the brown seedheads, preferring those where the florets are tightly bunched. Pupates on the ground. Overwinters as a pupa.

TAWNY SPECKLED PUG
Eupithecia icterata

PLATE 25
70.187 (1838)

Common. Rarely seen in numbers. Very local in Ireland. **FIELD CHARACTERS** Head brown, mottled darker. Body brown, covered with numerous tiny white dots. Dark brown dorsal stripe and diamond- or oval-shaped markings, these sometimes absent. Subdorsal line dark brown and usually with a white subspiracular stripe, or sometimes a line. **SIMILAR SPECIES** Bordered Pug is indistinguishable. Grey Pug is very similar but has a pale subspiracular line rather than a white stripe. **HABITATS** Fens, gardens, grasslands, open areas along coasts, upper parts of saltmarsh, vegetated shingle, waste ground and open woodland. **FOODPLANTS** Mainly Yarrow. Also reported on Mugwort, Common Ragwort, Sneezewort, Southernwood and Wormwood. **FIELD NOTES** Aug–Oct. Feeds on the flowers and leaves. Pupates in the ground. Overwinters as a pupa.

BORDERED PUG
Eupithecia succenturiata

PLATE 25
70.188 (1839)

Common. Rarely seen in numbers. Widely distributed in England; local or very local elsewhere. **SIMILAR SPECIES** Tawny Speckled Pug and Grey Pug. **HABITATS** Gardens, rough grassland, open areas along coasts, upper parts of saltmarsh, vegetated shingle and waste ground. **FOODPLANTS** Mugwort, Common Ragwort, Sneezewort, Southernwood, Tansy, wormwoods and Yarrow. **FIELD NOTES** Mid-Aug–mid-Oct. Feeds at night on the upper surface of the leaves. When large, hides by day at the base of the plant. Pupates in the ground. Overwinters as a pupa.

SHADED PUG
Eupithecia subumbrata

PLATE 26
70.189 (1840)

Local. Distributed widely on calcareous soils, and in coastal areas. **FIELD CHARACTERS** Head pale brown, mottled darker. Body very slender, and brown or pale greyish green. The brown form has a pale brown body with a dark brown dorsal stripe incorporating a pale, often ill-defined central line anteriorly. Subdorsal line thin and brown, and subspiracular line whitish. Anal flap reddish brown posteriorly. The green form is similar, with brown replaced by greyish green, and the anal flap reddish posteriorly. **SIMILAR SPECIES** See *Separating pug moths* table (pp. 416–17). **HABITATS** Hard and soft cliffs, fens, breckland and chalk grasslands, recently disturbed ground including field margins, old quarries and railways, saltmarshes and woodland rides. **FOODPLANTS** Wide variety of herbaceous plants, including Spanish Catchfly, Flixweed, hawkbits, hawk's-beards, Wild Marjoram, Dark Mullein, ragworts, Field Scabious and St John's-worts. **FIELD NOTES** Jul–Sep. Feeds in the flowers. Pupates in the ground. Overwinters as a pupa.

GREY PUG
Eupithecia subfuscata

PLATE 26
70.190 (1837)

Common. **FIELD CHARACTERS** Head brown, mottled darker. Body brown, covered with numerous tiny white dots, and with dark brown dorsal and subdorsal lines. There are diamond-shaped, dark brown dorsal markings and the subspiracular line is pale brown. **SIMILAR SPECIES** Tawny Speckled Pug and Bordered Pug. **HABITATS** Wide variety, including coastal habitats, gardens, grasslands, heathland, hedgerows, moorland, scrub, wetlands and woodland. **FOODPLANTS** Wide variety of herbaceous and woody plants, including Wild Angelica, Aspen, Barberry, Nettle-leaved Bellflower, Betony, Blackthorn, Burnet-saxifrage, Common Fleabane, Goldenrod, goosefoots, hawk's-beards, Hawthorn, Hemp-agrimony, knapweeds, Wall Lettuce, Mugwort, Wild Parsnip, Common Ragwort, willows and Yarrow. **FIELD NOTES** Late Jun–Oct, including a partial second generation. Feeds on the flowers and leaves. Pupates in debris or in the ground. Overwinters as a pupa.

MANCHESTER TREBLE-BAR
Carsia sororiata

PLATE 26
70.191 (1866)

Ssp. *anglica* Nb. Widespread in central and northern Scotland, more local elsewhere, and rare in Ireland. **FIELD CHARACTERS** Head brown, sometimes with heavy black speckling. Body brown with a black dorsal line, broadly edged grey A2–A9, or in paler examples edged with white shading in patches A1–A8. Subdorsal line dark brown, sometimes faint. Spiracular band white or pale yellow, extending onto the anal flap, and shaded black above T1–T3. **HABITATS** In the wetter parts of raised bogs, dune-slacks, heathland, moorland and mosses. **FOODPLANTS** Bilberry, Cowberry and Cranberry. **FIELD NOTES** Late Apr–Jun. Feeds at night on the flowers and leaves. Pupates in a cocoon among the foodplant. Overwinters as an egg.

TREBLE-BAR
Aplocera plagiata

PLATE 26
70.192 (1867)

Ssp. *plagiata* Common. Ssp. *scotica* Common. **FIELD CHARACTERS** Body yellowish brown, greyish brown or pinkish brown. Dorsal line dark brown, sometimes continuous and edged with dark shading, especially posteriorly. In other examples the dorsal line is interrupted, faint and reduced to dark spots, and edged with greyish-white shading, especially between segments. Subdorsal stripe pale brown, and one or two dark lateral lines. Subspiracular stripe white or yellowish, the upper margin ill-defined and lower margin sharply edged with blackish. Body purplish brown ventrally. **SIMILAR SPECIES** Lesser Treble-bar is indistinguishable, but location may help separate species. **HABITATS** Prefers open, dry areas in a wide variety of habitats, including soft cliffs, acid and calcareous grasslands, recently disturbed ground, heathland, moorland, old quarries and railway lines, sand dunes, waste ground, and open areas and rides in woodland. **FOODPLANTS** St John's-worts. **FIELD NOTES** Late Jun–early Aug and Sep–Apr in two generations in the south, and Aug–Jun in one generation in the north. Pupates in the ground. Overwinters as a part-grown larva.

LESSER TREBLE-BAR
Aplocera efformata

PLATE 26
70.193 (1868)

Common. Widespread in the southern half of England away from western parts, local or rare elsewhere, and not recorded in Ireland. **SIMILAR SPECIES** Treble-bar. **HABITATS** As Treble-bar. **FOODPLANTS** St John's-worts. **FIELD NOTES** Late Jun–early Aug and Sep–Apr, in two generations. Pupates in the ground. Overwinters as a part-grown larva.

STREAK
Chesias legatella

PLATE 26
70.195 (1864)

Common. Has decreased significantly in abundance in recent decades. Remains widespread, but local or very local in parts of the west, Wales and Ireland. **FIELD CHARACTERS** There are two forms, green and yellowish. The green form has a green head, mottled with brown above. Body green with a dark green dorsal line, and a whitish-green subdorsal line with a darker green lateral stripe below. Subspiracular stripe white, extending onto the anal flap. Spiracles orange. The yellowish form has a yellowish head, somewhat speckled, with a yellowish body faintly marked with darker lines. **SIMILAR SPECIES** Broom-tip is indistinguishable from green forms of Streak. However, material examined indicates that Broom-tip may lack or have much-reduced mottling on the head, and it appears not to have a plain yellowish form. Larval periods of the two species are different, but there is considerable overlap, and well-developed larvae of both species have been found on the same plant at the same time. **HABITATS** Mainly habitats on acidic soils, including acid and breckland grassland, heathland, moorland, sand dunes, scrub and open woodland. Occasionally in calcareous habitats and gardens. **FOODPLANTS** Broom. Also recorded on Tree Lupin. **FIELD NOTES** May–Aug. Feeds on the leaves. Pupates in the ground. Overwinters as an egg.

Streak larva

BROOM-TIP
Chesias rufata

PLATE 26
70.196 (1865)

Ssp. *rufata* Nb. Very local in England and Wales and rare in Ireland. Has declined significantly in abundance in recent decades. Ssp. *scotica* Nb. Local, and probably under-recorded. **SIMILAR SPECIES** Streak. **HABITATS** Similar to Streak, but appears not to have colonised gardens. **FOODPLANT** Broom. **FIELD NOTES** Jul–Sep. Feeds on the leaves. Pupates in the ground. Overwinters as a pupa.

GREY CARPET
Lithostege griseata

PLATE 26
70.197 (1871)

RDB; suspected immigrant. Resident in breckland areas of East Anglia. **FIELD CHARACTERS** Head pale brown, mottled darker. Body green with a dark green dorsal line, and a white or whitish-green subdorsal line, sometimes ill-defined. Subspiracular stripe white or yellow, sometimes broadened towards the dorsum on abdominal segments. **HABITATS** Recently disturbed and sparsely vegetated areas, especially arable field margins and fields left fallow. Also on road verges and in open areas of woodland specifically managed by rotovation to encourage proliferation of annual plants, and following ground disturbance caused by roadworks and timber extraction. **FOODPLANT** Flixweed. Records on Treacle-mustard are considered to arise from misidentification of the foodplant. **FIELD NOTES** Late Jun–Aug. Feeds in the seedpods. Pupates in the ground. Overwinters as a pupa.

SERAPHIM
Lobophora halterata

PLATE 26
70.198 (1879)

Local. **FIELD CHARACTERS** Head pale brown or green and notched, with dorsal lobes rounded. Body dull whitish green without a dorsal line. Subdorsal stripe yellowish white, extending onto the anal flap. Subspiracular line absent. Anal flap edged laterally with a yellow line. A pair of long anal points. **HABITATS** Woodland, including plantations. **FOODPLANTS** Aspen and Black-poplar. Also reported on other poplars and willows. **FIELD NOTES** Late Jun–Jul. Feeds at night. Pupates in a cocoon on the ground. Overwinters as a pupa.

SMALL SERAPHIM
Pterapherapteryx sexalata

PLATE 26
70.199 (1882)

Local. Widespread in southern parts of England and Wales; local or scarce elsewhere. **FIELD CHARACTERS** Head whitish green and distinctly notched. Body whitish green with a whitish-green dorsal line, edged with dark green. Subdorsal stripe pale yellow, and subspiracular line white. A pair of long anal points. **HABITATS** Fens, wet heathland, marshes, scrub and wet woodland. **FOODPLANTS** Goat, White and other willows. **FIELD NOTES** Mid-Jun–mid-Sep in two generations in the south, and early Jul–mid-Aug in one generation in the north. Feeds at night. Pupates in debris on the ground. Overwinters as a pupa.

YELLOW-BARRED BRINDLE
Acasis viretata

PLATE 26
70.200 (1883)

Local. Has increased significantly in abundance in recent decades, and is spreading northwards. **FIELD CHARACTERS** Head brown. Body stumpy and usually yellowish or pale green, rarely white, with red or brown markings that are very variable in extent, usually in the form of transverse dorsal bands, edged whitish posteriorly, between T2 and A5. The dorsal markings may extend laterally or may be reduced to backward-pointing triangles, or spots. Usually there are red patches dorsally A8–A9, and sometimes on T1. **HABITATS** Gardens, parks and other urban areas, hedgerows, old quarries, scrub and woodland. **FOODPLANTS** Variety of woody plants, including Buckthorn, Alder Buckthorn, Dogwood, Guelder-rose, Hawthorn, Holly, Common Ivy, Wild Privet, Rowan and Sycamore. Has been found in the flowers of Olive. **FIELD NOTES** Jun–Jul and Sep–Oct in two generations in the south, and Jun–Jul in the north. Feeds in the buds, flowers and leaves. Pupates in a spinning in the foodplant. Overwinters as a pupa.

BARRED TOOTH-STRIPED
Trichopteryx polycommata

PLATE 26
70.201 (1880)

Na. Very localised, often occurring in small, isolated colonies. **FIELD CHARACTERS** Head green. Body green with a dark green dorsal line, and a very pale and indistinct, or absent, subdorsal line. Subspiracular stripe white or yellow and extending onto the anal flap. A pair of short anal points. **SIMILAR SPECIES** Early Tooth-striped is identical in appearance but has different foodplants. However, larvae on Honeysuckle may need to be reared to confirm identity, since larvae of Barred Tooth-striped feed on this plant in captivity and it is possible they do so in the wild. **HABITATS** Coastal chalk cliffs, breckland and chalk grasslands, hedgerows, scrub, and in open woodland and woodland rides. **FOODPLANTS** Ash and Wild Privet. Seems to prefer low privet scrub on chalk sites in the south, and Ash trees in the north. **FIELD NOTES** Mid-Apr–early Jun. Feeds at night. Pupates in a cocoon in the ground. Overwinters as a pupa.

EARLY TOOTH-STRIPED
Trichopteryx carpinata

PLATE 26
70.202 (1881)

Common. Has increased significantly in abundance in recent decades. **SIMILAR SPECIES** Barred Tooth-striped. **HABITATS** Fens, gardens, heathland, scrub and woodland. **FOODPLANTS** Alder, birches, Honeysuckle and willows. **FIELD NOTES** May–Jul. Feeds at night. Pupates in or on the ground. Overwinters as a pupa.

ARCHIEARINAE

ORANGE UNDERWING
Archiearis parthenias

PLATE 26
70.203 (1661)

Local. Widespread in England and Wales; more local in Scotland. **FIELD CHARACTERS** Head and prothoracic plate green. Body green. Dorsal stripe green edged with yellowish lines, which are sometimes rather faint. Subdorsal and lateral lines yellowish or yellowish white, and subspiracular stripe white or yellow. Spiracles black. There are additional prolegs on A3–A5, these becoming progressively better developed A3–A6. In fully fed larvae the body colour changes to a dark greyish green, with purplish between segments. **HABITATS** Scrub on heathland and waste ground, and in open and regenerating woodland. **FOODPLANTS** Downy and Silver birches. Also reported on Beech, oaks and Rowan. **FIELD NOTES** Apr–Jun. Feeds at first in the catkins and later on the young foliage, hiding by day between spun leaves. Pupates in a cocoon on the surface of soft bark, or in dead or rotten wood. Overwinters as a pupa.

LIGHT ORANGE UNDERWING
Boudinotiana notha

PLATE 26
70.204 (1662)

Nb. Very local in England. **FIELD CHARACTERS** Head pale brown or brown with vertical black bands laterally and a black spot above the mouthparts. Prothoracic plate black, or pale brown with a subdorsal black spot. Body various shades of green, grey or reddish brown. Dorsal stripe darker than ground colour, edged with white lines. Subdorsal and lateral lines white, and subspiracular stripe white. Black markings variable in number and extent above the subspiracular stripe. Spiracles white, surrounded with black. There are additional prolegs on A3–A5, these becoming progressively better developed A3–A6. **HABITATS** Scrub on heathland, and woodland. **FOODPLANTS** Aspen. Also reported on willows. **FIELD NOTES** Apr–Jun. Feeds on the foliage, hiding by day between spun leaves. While adults are usually observed around mature trees, larvae can be found on saplings, including sucker growth close to the ground. Pupates in a cocoon on the surface of soft bark, or in dead wood. Overwinters as a pupa, sometimes for up to three winters.

ENNOMINAE

MAGPIE
Abraxas grossulariata

PLATE 26
70.205 (1884)

Common. Has declined in recent decades in lowland England. **FIELD CHARACTERS** Head black. Body white with an interrupted black dorsal band, broken into oblong blocks and spots. There are black dashes laterally and an orange subspiracular stripe edged above and below with black spots. **HABITATS** Wide variety, including allotments, gardens and other urban areas, heathland, hedgerows, moorland, scrub and woodland. **FOODPLANTS** Wide variety of mainly woody shrubs and trees, including Crab Apple, Blackthorn, Bramble, Black and Red currants, elms, Gooseberry, Hawthorn, Midland Hawthorn, Hazel, Heather (in northern Scotland), Common Ivy, Navelwort, Plum, Garden Privet, Spindle, Evergreen Spindle, Orpine and ornamental stonecrops, and willows. **FIELD NOTES** Late Aug–mid-Jun. May sit openly on a leaf or hang by a silk thread. Pupates in a slight cocoon among foliage, with the yellow-and-black-striped pupa easily visible. Overwinters as a small larva on the foodplant.

CLOUDED MAGPIE
Abraxas sylvata

PLATE 26
70.206 (1885)

Local; suspected immigrant. Quite widespread, but scarce in some parts of southern England. Local in Ireland. **FIELD CHARACTERS** Head black. Body white with a black dorsal stripe edged yellowish and white, and with three black stripes laterally. Subspiracular stripe yellowish. A transverse yellowish band on T1 with black pinacula. **HABITATS** Mainly woodland. Also recorded in parkland and scrub. **FOODPLANTS** Mainly Wych Elm, but also English Elm, and the introduced Japanese Golden Elm. Also reported on Beech. **FIELD NOTES** Mid-Jul–early Oct. Pupates in or on the ground. Overwinters as a pupa.

CLOUDED BORDER
Lomaspilis marginata

PLATE 26
70.207 (1887)

Common. **FIELD CHARACTERS** Head greenish with a large triangular reddish-brown mark on each side. Body pale greyish green, covered with small black pinacula. Dorsal line pale greyish green, edged with dark green wavy lines, and with wavy dark green subdorsal and lateral lines. Subspiracular line white. Anal flap red or reddish brown, edged yellowish. **HABITATS** Wide variety. **FOODPLANTS** Aspen, poplars and willows. Also reported on Hazel. **FIELD NOTES** Jul–Sep. Pupates in the ground, and possibly also in spun leaves. Overwinters as a pupa.

SCORCHED CARPET
Ligdia adustata

PLATE 26
70.208 (1888)

Local. **FIELD CHARACTERS** Head mixed dark brown and pale brown or whitish. Body green with a faint and dark green dorsal stripe, sometimes mixed with pale brown. There are paired white subdorsal spots A2–A4, sometimes with a brown spot between, and a large brown spot laterally between segments A2 and A3, sometimes more extensively shaded pale brown or mixed whitish. A brown ventral mark adjacent to the true leg on T3. True legs pinkish brown, and proleg brown and sometimes more extensively shaded brownish above. **HABITATS** Mainly on chalk, clay and limestone soils, in hedgerows, scrub, woodland and occasionally gardens. **FOODPLANT** Spindle. **FIELD NOTES** Jun–Sep in two generations in the south, and Jul–Aug in one generation in the northern part of its range. Feeds at night and often hangs from a short silk thread among the foliage. Pupates in a spinning, in or on the ground. Overwinters as a pupa.

RINGED BORDER
Stegania cararia

NOT ILLUSTRATED
70.209 (1888b)

Immigrant; recent colonist. Very local in Europe but extending its distribution northwards and now resident in one area of Kent. **FIELD CHARACTERS** No material examined. **HABITATS** Wet woodland. **FOODPLANTS** Alder, Aspen and poplars in Europe. **FIELD NOTES** In Europe, Jul–Oct. Pupation site unknown. Overwinters as a pupa.

PEACOCK MOTH
Macaria notata

PLATE 27
70.211 (1889)

Local; possible immigrant. Has increased very significantly in abundance in recent decades. **FIELD CHARACTERS** Very variable in colour and markings. Head brown or, in the green form, green anteriorly and edged brown. Body various shades of brown, grey or green and noticeably shiny. The brown and grey forms have black spots at the spiracular level on a variable number of segments and each may be edged anteriorly with a green, yellowish or white spot. The green forms may be plain or have brownish subdorsal streaks, and brownish spots at the spiracular level. All forms have black prolegs. **SIMILAR SPECIES** Sharp-angled Peacock shows a similar range of variation, such that there do not appear to be consistent differences. **HABITATS** Scrub and open woodland with birches on acidic and chalk soils. **FOODPLANTS** Mainly birches. Also reported on Goat and Grey willows. **FIELD NOTES** Late Jun–early Aug, and again in Sep as a partial second generation in southern England and Wales. Pupates on the ground. Overwinters as a pupa.

SHARP-ANGLED PEACOCK
Macaria alternata

PLATE 27
70.212 (1890)

Local. Frequent in much of southern England and East Anglia; very local elsewhere. **SIMILAR SPECIES** Peacock Moth. **HABITATS** Scrub among soft cliffs, fens, heathland, marshes, reedbeds, sand dunes and in open woodland. **FOODPLANTS** Alder, Blackthorn, Bog-myrtle, Alder Buckthorn, sea-buckthorn and willows. Also reported on larches. **FIELD NOTES** Jul, and Sep as a partial second generation. Pupates in a cocoon in the ground. Overwinters as a pupa.

DUSKY PEACOCK
Macaria signaria

PLATE 27
70.213 (1891)

Immigrant; recent colonist in Kent. **FIELD CHARACTERS** Head bulbous, and greenish with brown streaks laterally, or brownish green and dark brown laterally. Body green with a dark green dorsal stripe, edged white, and incorporating a pale central line. There is a faint white line below, a white subdorsal stripe, and two thin black lateral lines. The subdorsal stripe extends onto the anal flap. Subspiracular stripe white, yellowish or greenish white. True legs brown. Some examples have transverse bands of pinkish or purplish suffusion. **SIMILAR SPECIES** Pine Carpet, Spruce Carpet, Grey Pine Carpet, Tawny-barred Angle, Bordered White and Banded Pine Carpet. **HABITATS** Coniferous woodland in Kent. **FOODPLANTS** Various conifers, including Scots Pine and Norway Spruce. **FIELD NOTES** Aug–Sep. Pupates in a silken cocoon. Overwinters as a pupa.

TAWNY-BARRED ANGLE
Macaria liturata

PLATE 27
70.214 (1893)

Common. **FIELD CHARACTERS** The green form is indistinguishable from Dusky Peacock. There is a dark greyish form with whitish stripes and lines. **SIMILAR SPECIES** Pine Carpet, Spruce Carpet, Grey Pine Carpet, Dusky Peacock, Bordered White and Banded Pine Carpet. **HABITATS** Coniferous woodland. Also places where conifers are planted, including urban parks. **FOODPLANTS** Mainly Scots Pine and Norway Spruce. Also reported on Douglas Fir, Western Hemlock-spruce, larches, Corsican Pine, Japanese Red-cedar and Sitka Spruce. **FIELD NOTES** Late Jun–early Aug and Sep–early Oct in two generations in the south, and Jul–Aug in one generation in the north. Pupates in or on the ground.

V-MOTH
Macaria wauaria

PLATE 27
70.215 (1897)

Local. Formerly widely distributed but has declined severely in abundance in recent decades. Remains fairly widespread but continues to decline in the north Midlands and northern England. **FIELD CHARACTERS** Head greenish grey with black markings. Body whitish green or brown, covered with large black pinacula. Dorsal and subdorsal line white, and lateral line, if present, white and faint. Spiracular stripe broad and yellow. Pale green ventrally. True legs black. When fully fed, the green colour turns purplish brown. **HABITATS** Mainly allotments and gardens. Occasionally in soft-fruit farms. **FOODPLANTS** Black and Red currants, and Gooseberry. **FIELD NOTES** Mid-Apr–mid-Jun. Feeds on the young shoots. Pupates in a silken cocoon among leaves of the foodplant. Overwinters as an egg.

NETTED MOUNTAIN MOTH
Macaria carbonaria

PLATE 27
70.216 (1895)

RDB. Probably under-recorded in the Scottish Highlands. **FIELD CHARACTERS** Head pale brown. Body green or dark grey with a series of interrupted white lines. Spiracular stripe white, darker between creases, giving a reticulated appearance, and with an ill-defined margin below. Anal flap reddish brown. **HABITATS** Moorland and mountains. **FOODPLANT** Bearberry. **FIELD NOTES** Late May–Jul. Feeds at night, and, when young, only on the young shoots. Pupates in moss, lichen and debris on the ground. Overwinters as a pupa.

RANNOCH LOOPER
Macaria brunneata

PLATE 27
70.217 (1896)

Na; immigrant. Resident in central Scotland. **FIELD CHARACTERS** Head brown, mottled darker. Body various shades of brown or grey. Dorsal line pale, edged with black lines, with further pale and wavy subdorsal and lateral lines that are increasingly edged darker laterally. Subspiracular stripe whitish, mixed yellowish, and sometimes interrupted. **SIMILAR SPECIES** Common Heath is fully fed in late summer, when Rannoch Looper is an egg. **HABITATS** Where there is abundant growth of Bilberry, in native birch and Scots Pine woodland, and less often in areas of birch regeneration and open moorland. **FOODPLANTS** Bilberry and possibly Cowberry. Also reported on Scots Pine. **FIELD NOTES** Late Apr–late May. Pupates in the ground. Normally overwinters as an egg and, based on observations in captivity, may also remain as a pupa over several winters.

LATTICED HEATH
Chiasmia clathrata

PLATE 27
70.218 (1894)

Ssp. *clathrata* Common. Has declined significantly in abundance in recent decades throughout much of its range, but is increasing and spreading in north-east Scotland. Ssp. *hugginsi* Widespread in Ireland. **FIELD CHARACTERS** There are green and brown forms. The green form has a green head, with the white subspiracular stripe extended onto the head and with black lines or a band above. Body green with a dark green dorsal stripe incorporating a central pale line, and edged with white lines. A series of subdorsal and lateral white lines, less well defined laterally, and a broad white subspiracular stripe. Spiracles orange. The brown form is similar but has a brown head, mottled black, and the green is replaced with brown. **SIMILAR SPECIES** Green form: Speckled Yellow feeds on different plants. It is very similar but has a white subspiracular line or narrow stripe. Ringed Carpet lacks the white stripe and black lines or band on the head, and has a pale and inconspicuous spiracular line, and also feeds on different plants. **HABITATS** Arable fields planted with Lucerne (where the moth may be common), cliffs, fens, acid calcareous grassland, heathland, moorland, old quarries, sand dunes, waste ground and open woodland. **FOODPLANTS** Clovers, including White Clover, Lucerne, Sainfoin, trefoils, vetches including Tufted Vetch, and Meadow Vetchling. **FIELD NOTES** Jun–Jul and mid-Aug–Sep in two generations in the south, and late May–early Aug in the north and Ireland, in one generation. Pupates in the ground. Overwinters as a pupa.

LITTLE THORN
Cepphis advenaria

PLATE 27
70.221 (1901)

Nb. Resident in southern England, south Wales and around the Bristol Channel, and very locally in Ireland. **FIELD CHARACTERS** Head brown, sometimes mixed whitish, and mottled darker. Body various shades of brown, with dark brown pinacula. Dorsal line rather indistinct, with small white subdorsal spots A1–A8, and additional white marks anteriorly on A2. Irregular white patches at the spiracular level, sometimes shaded dark brown between on A1–A4, and extended as stripes onto the proleg and anal clasper. A divided hump dorsally on A8. **HABITATS** In open woodland and woodland rides; less often in scrub. **FOODPLANTS** Bilberry, Bramble, Dog-rose and Dogwood. Also reported on Ash and willows. **FIELD NOTES** Late Jun–Aug. Pupates in the ground. Overwinters as a pupa.

BROWN SILVER-LINE
Petrophora chlorosata

PLATE 27
70.222 (1902)

Common. **FIELD CHARACTERS** There are green and brown forms. The green form has a brown head, mottled darker. Body yellowish green, with a pale green dorsal line, several pale subdorsal and lateral lines and a greenish-yellow subspiracular stripe. There is a variable amount of blackish shading between the lateral lines and subspiracular stripe. Spiracles black. The brown form has a brown body with whitish lines and a white stripe, and dark brown lateral shading. **HABITATS** Heathland, moorland, woodland, and most places where the foodplant occurs. **FOODPLANT** Bracken. **FIELD NOTES** Mid-Jun–early Sep. Pupates in the ground. Overwinters as a pupa.

BARRED UMBER
Plagodis pulveraria

PLATE 27
70.223 (1903)

Local. Has increased significantly in abundance in recent decades. **FIELD CHARACTERS** Head brown and distinctly notched. Body brown with a pair of large dorsal projections on A5 and a much smaller pair on A6. A more or less distinct white subdorsal stripe T3–A1, and a wavy white or yellow subdorsal stripe A6–A9. Sometimes there are diagonal black streaks or marks A1–A2, running laterally and across the ventral area. **SIMILAR SPECIES** Orange Moth and Swallow-tailed Moth do not have a notched head, and are fully fed in the spring. Swallow-tailed Moth has lateral swellings on A3. Orange Moth has dorsal projections on A1 and A8, and the projections on A5 are more pointed than in Barred Umber. **HABITATS** Scrub on limestone pavement, and woodland, especially ancient woodland. **FOODPLANTS** Mainly Hazel. Also reported on Ash, Downy and Silver birches, Wild Cherry, Hawthorn, oaks and willows. **FIELD NOTES** Mid-Jun–mid-Aug. Pupates in or on the ground. Overwinters as a pupa.

SCORCHED WING
Plagodis dolabraria

PLATE 27
70.224 (1904)

Local. Increasing in range in Scotland. **FIELD CHARACTERS** Body brown mixed with pale grey, with lateral and dorsal swellings on T2, and a large oval dorsal swelling and smaller lateral swellings on A5. The swellings may be similarly coloured to the body, or much darker. **HABITATS** Scrub and woodland. Also in gardens and urban parks where there is substantial woodland cover. **FOODPLANTS** Mainly Downy and Silver birches, and oaks. Also reported on Beech, Sweet Chestnut, Rowan and willows. **FIELD NOTES** Late Jun–mid-Sep. Pupates on the ground. Overwinters as a pupa.

HORSE CHESTNUT
Pachycnemia hippocastanaria

PLATE 27
70.225 (1905)

Nb. Sometimes very common in heathland areas of southern England. May disperse into other habitats, including gardens. **FIELD CHARACTERS** Body pale brown or chocolate brown, with an irregularly margined darker dorsal stripe, sometimes incorporating a paler central line, and edged with white subdorsal lines or stripes. An interrupted white lateral line may be present. Subspiracular stripe white, may be interrupted and usually extends onto the anal clasper. **SIMILAR SPECIES** Scalloped Hazel, Scalloped Oak and Dusky Scalloped Oak have a dorsal projection on A8. **HABITATS** Heathland. **FOODPLANTS** Cross-leaved Heath and Heather. **FIELD NOTES** Late May–early Jul and Sep, in two generations, the second one partial. Feeds at night. Pupates in the ground. Overwinters as a larva or a pupa and has been recorded as an adult in Jan.

BRIMSTONE MOTH
Opisthograptis luteolata

PLATE 27
70.226 (1906)

Common. **FIELD CHARACTERS** Head brown and slightly notched, with a forward-facing point on each dorsal lobe. Body green, grey or mixed green and grey, resembling a twig with algae. There are lateral swellings on T2 and paired brown dorsal projections on A3. The size of the projections on A3 varies considerably, from being no more than a pair of slightly enlarged pinacula to being large and prominent, resembling a plant bud, and on green larvae they are usually orangey brown. There may be small, paired brown dorsal projections on A4, A5 and A8. Vestigial prolegs A4–A5. A fringe of hair-like fleshy projections extends downward between the proleg and anal clasper. **HABITATS** Wide variety, including gardens, hedgerows, scrub and woodland. **FOODPLANTS** Mainly Blackthorn, Hawthorn and Rowan. Also reported on apples, birches, Bramble, cherries, Sweet Chestnut, cotoneasters, elms, Midland Hawthorn, Hazel, limes, oaks, Wild Service-tree and Wayfaring-tree. **FIELD NOTES** Any month in two or three generations in the south, and summer–autumn in one generation in the north. Pupates in a cocoon among the foodplant, or on the ground among moss. Overwinters as a larva or a pupa in the south, and as a pupa in the north.

BORDERED BEAUTY
Epione repandaria

PLATE 28
70.227 (1907)

Common. Local in northern England and southern Scotland. **FIELD CHARACTERS** Body pale brown or dark brown. Dorsal line pale, edged with black on A1 and darker brown shading elsewhere. Pale brown dorsal diamond shapes A1–A5, better defined anteriorly. Subdorsal line white, well defined on A1 and faint elsewhere, with a small white spot on each segment A1–A7. A2 is somewhat swollen, with a transverse ridge of four dark brown or blackish bumps. Proleg whitish anteriorly and dark brown or black posteriorly. **SIMILAR SPECIES** Dark Bordered Beauty is indistinguishable in appearance, but has a very restricted distribution and is associated with Creeping Willow and Aspen. **HABITATS** Scrub in fens, marshes, reedbeds and along rides in open, damp woodland, and in carr woodland. **FOODPLANTS** Mainly willows. Also Alder, Black-poplar and Hazel. **FIELD NOTES** Early May–mid-Jul. Pupates among leaves or on the ground. Overwinters as an egg.

DARK BORDERED BEAUTY
Epione vespertaria

PLATE 28
70.228 (1908)

RDB. Confined to small areas in northern England and Scotland. Requires targeted conservation efforts to maintain a population at its known site in Yorkshire. **SIMILAR SPECIES** Bordered Beauty. **HABITATS** Open, damp areas on wet acid grassland, heathland and moorland. **FOODPLANTS** Aspen in Scotland, where larvae live on Aspen suckers less than 50cm in height. Creeping Willow and possibly other willows in England. **FIELD NOTES** May–early Jul. Pupates in debris on or in the ground. Overwinters as an egg.

SPECKLED YELLOW
Pseudopanthera macularia

PLATE 28
70.229 (1909)

Common. Locally frequent in southern England and in Wales, widespread in central and western Scotland, and local in northern England and Ireland. **FIELD CHARACTERS** Head green, with the white subspiracular line or stripe extended onto the head and sometimes edged above with black. Body green with a dark green dorsal stripe incorporating a pale central line, and edged with white lines. A series of white subdorsal and lateral lines, less well defined laterally, and a white subspiracular line or narrow stripe. Spiracles white or orange. **SIMILAR SPECIES** Latticed Heath and Ringed Carpet. **HABITATS** Prefers Bracken-dominated areas and the margins of scrub. Found in coastal areas, acid grassland, heathland, moorland, and in open woodland and woodland rides. **FOODPLANTS** Mainly Wood Sage. Also reported on Yellow Archangel, White Dead-nettle and woundworts. **FIELD NOTES** Mid-Jun–early Aug. Pupates in debris or in the ground. Overwinters as a pupa.

ORANGE MOTH
Angerona prunaria

PLATE 28
70.230 (1924)

Local. Most frequent in southern England, the Wye Valley and parts of East Anglia. **FIELD CHARACTERS** Body brown or greyish brown and slender, with variable darker and paler markings. Paired dorsal projections on A1 and a larger pair on A5, with much smaller projections on A4 and A7–A8. **SIMILAR SPECIES** Barred Umber and Swallow-tailed Moth. **HABITATS** Mainly mature woodland. Also wooded heathland, ancient hedgerows, scrub and occasionally gardens. **FOODPLANTS** Mainly woody plants, including Beech, birches, Blackthorn, Broom, Hawthorn, Heather, Honeysuckle, Lilac, Wild Plum, Garden Privet and Traveller's-joy. Also reported on mints. **FIELD NOTES** Aug–late May. Feeds at night. Pupates in a spinning among leaves on the plant. Overwinters as a small larva.

LILAC BEAUTY
Apeira syringaria

PLATE 28
70.231 (1910)

Local. Increasing in Scotland. **FIELD CHARACTERS** Body various shades of grey or brown, often pale or orangey brown, with a brown dorsal band that is most obvious anteriorly. Large paired dorsal projections on A2, a smaller pair on A3, and the largest pair on A4, curved backwards. There are small subdorsal projections A2–A4. **HABITATS** Scrub and woodland, and occasionally in gardens. **FOODPLANTS** Ash, Elder, Honeysuckle (including garden varieties), Lilac, Wild and Garden privet, and Snowberry. **FIELD NOTES** Aug–end May, though larvae producing a partial second generation in the south probably start feeding Jul. Feeds at night. Pupates in a network cocoon among the foodplant. Overwinters as a small larva.

LARGE THORN
Ennomos autumnaria

PLATE 28
70.232 (1911)

Nb; suspected immigrant. Rather erratic in appearance and may temporarily establish and then decline. Increasing its range in the Midlands. **FIELD CHARACTERS** Head greyish brown, speckled darker. Body greyish brown and rather uniform in colour, or with darker pinacula, and sometimes with darker shading. Dorsal swellings on A2 and A5, sometimes edged white laterally, a pair of prominent dorsal pinacula on A8, and slight paired ventral swellings on A3. **SIMILAR SPECIES** August Thorn usually has a dorsal swelling on A3, though this may be absent, and lacks paired ventral swellings on A3. Brown forms of Large Thorn and Canary-shouldered Thorn are indistinguishable, but as a green form is not known in Large Thorn, the green form of Canary-shouldered Thorn can be separated from August Thorn in the field by the presence of paired ventral swellings on A3. **HABITATS** Gardens, scrub and woodland. **FOODPLANTS** Wide variety of trees and shrubs, including Alder, Apple, birches, Blackthorn, cherries, elms, hawthorns, Hazel, oaks, poplars, Sycamore and willows. **FIELD NOTES** Late Apr–early Aug. Feeds at night. Pupates in a network cocoon among the foodplant or on the ground. Overwinters as an egg.

AUGUST THORN
Ennomos quercinaria

PLATE 28
70.233 (1912)

Local. Widespread in England, Wales and Ireland; very local in Scotland. Has declined significantly in abundance in recent decades. **FIELD CHARACTERS** There are brown and green forms. The brown form has a brown head, mottled darker. Body brown with dorsal swellings on A2, A3 and A5 and a prominent pair of dorsal pinacula on A8. Lateral swellings on A2 and A3. The dorsal swelling on A3 may be absent and all swellings may be greatly reduced. Spiracles orange. The green form has a green head and body and the swellings may be greatly reduced. **SIMILAR SPECIES** Large Thorn and Canary-shouldered Thorn. **HABITATS** Hedgerows, scrub on calcareous grassland, and woodland. Sometimes in gardens. **FOODPLANTS** Beech, birches, Blackthorn, elms, Hawthorn, Lilac, limes and Pedunculate Oak. **FIELD NOTES** Early May–mid-Jul. Feeds at night. Pupates in a network cocoon among the foodplant. Overwinters as an egg.

CANARY-SHOULDERED THORN
Ennomos alniaria

PLATE 28
70.234 (1913)

Common. **FIELD CHARACTERS** There are brown and green forms. The brown form has a brown head. Body dark brown with dorsal swellings on A2 and A5 and paired ventral swellings on A3. Spiracles orange. The green form has a green head and body and the swellings are brown. **SIMILAR SPECIES** Large Thorn and August Thorn. **HABITATS** Hedgerows, scrub and woodland. Also gardens and urban parks. **FOODPLANTS** Alder, Downy and Silver birches, elms, Hornbeam, limes, Sessile Oak and Goat Willow. **FIELD NOTES** Early May–Jul. Feeds at night. Pupates among debris or plants on the ground. Overwinters as an egg.

DUSKY THORN
Ennomos fuscantaria

PLATE 28
70.235 (1914)

Common. A widespread species that has declined severely in abundance in recent decades. **FIELD CHARACTERS** There are green and brown forms. The green form has a green head and body, with brown dorsal swellings on A2 and A5, sometimes edged white laterally, and an obliquely angled brown lateral swelling on T2. Often there is a small brown swelling laterally on A2, and also ventrolaterally on A3. True legs brown or black, and proleg brown. The swellings and brown marks may be reduced or absent. The brown form is very similar, with head and body brown and the swellings brown or black. **HABITATS** Gardens and urban parks, hedgerows, scrub and woodland. **FOODPLANT** Ash. **FIELD NOTES** Early May–Aug with eggs hatching up to mid-Jun. Feeds at night. Pupates in a network cocoon among the foodplant. Overwinters as an egg.

SEPTEMBER THORN
Ennomos erosaria

PLATE 28
70.236 (1915)

Common. Has declined significantly in abundance in recent decades, especially in southern England, but remains widespread. Very local in Scotland. **FIELD CHARACTERS** Head brownish or greyish. Body grey or brownish grey, often more brownish from A7 posteriorly, and with brown pinacula. Brownish dorsal swellings on A2 and A5, a subdorsal swelling on T2, and paired ventral swellings on A3. A pair of brown dorsal projections on A8. **SIMILAR SPECIES** Great Oak Beauty has a notched head and lacks the dorsal projection on A5. **HABITATS** Gardens and urban parks, and woodland. **FOODPLANTS** Beech, birches, limes and oaks. **FIELD NOTES** Late Apr–early Jul. Feeds at night. Pupates in a spinning between leaves. Overwinters as an egg.

EARLY THORN
Selenia dentaria

PLATE 29
70.237 (1917)

Common. **FIELD CHARACTERS** Colours and markings are very variable. Head brown or grey above, and yellowish or greyish white below. Body generally brownish or grey, with T1–T2 yellowish or greyish white below, and with a white patch or paired white marks dorsally on A2 anteriorly, but no swelling. T3 has a substantial swelling ventrally, from which the true leg arises. There are dorsal and lateral swellings A4–A5, with whitish semicircles at the base of the paired dorsal projections. Projections and swellings become less prominent towards full growth. **SIMILAR SPECIES** Lunar Thorn and Purple Thorn can usually be distinguished from Early Thorn by their dorsal swellings on A2. Lunar Thorn has dorsal projections or swellings on A2 and sometimes A1, the latter very small, and Purple Thorn has dorsal projections or swellings on A1 and A2 that are similar sized, large or small. Lunar Thorn also has the dorsal projections on A2 edged anteriorly with white, whereas Purple Thorn does not. However, since the presence and size of projections and swellings change as the larva grows, and colour and markings are variable, it will not always be possible to identify these species in the field and they may need to be reared. **HABITATS** Gardens and urban parks, hedgerows, scrub and woodland. **FOODPLANTS** Wide variety of woody trees and shrubs, including Alder, Downy and Silver birches, Blackthorn, Bog-myrtle, Bramble, Sweet Chestnut, Hawthorn, Hazel, Honeysuckle, Raspberry and willows. **FIELD NOTES** May–Jun and Aug–early Oct in two generations in the south, and Jun–Aug in one generation in northern England and Scotland. Feeds at night. Pupates in a spinning between leaves, or among debris on the ground. Overwinters as a pupa.

LUNAR THORN
Selenia lunularia

PLATE 29
70.238 (1918)

Local; suspected immigrant. Widespread in south-west and south-east England, in Wales, and in northern parts of Great Britain and Ireland; very local elsewhere. **FIELD CHARACTERS** Head brown. Body colour various shades of grey and brown with very variable markings. T3 has a substantial swelling ventrally, from which the true leg arises. There is a ventrolateral projection or swelling on A1 and dorsal projections or swellings on A2, edged white anteriorly, and there may be very small dorsal projections on A1. Dorsal projections or swellings small on A4 and large on A5. Projections and swellings become less prominent towards full growth. **SIMILAR SPECIES** Early Thorn and Purple Thorn. **HABITATS** Moorland, scrub and woodland. **FOODPLANTS** Ash, birches, Blackthorn, Dog-rose, elms, Small-leaved Lime, oaks and Wild Plum. **FIELD NOTES** Late Jun–late Aug. Feeds at night. Pupates in or on the ground. Overwinters as a pupa.

PURPLE THORN
Selenia tetralunaria

PLATE 29
70.239 (1919)

Common. Widespread in England but rarely frequent; more local in Scotland. **FIELD CHARACTERS** Colours and markings are very variable. T3 has a substantial swelling ventrally, from which the true leg arises. There is sometimes a ventrolateral projection or swelling on A1, and there are dorsal projections or swellings on A1 and A2 of similar size, large or small, and dorsal projections or swellings on A4 and A5. Projections and swellings become less prominent towards full growth. **SIMILAR SPECIES** Early Thorn and Lunar Thorn. **HABITATS** Gardens and urban parks, scrub on heathland and calcareous grassland, and woodland. **FOODPLANTS** Wide variety, including Alder, Ash, birches, Alder Buckthorn, Wild Cherry, Sweet Chestnut, cotoneasters, Hawthorn, Hazel, larches, oaks, Raspberry and willows. **FIELD NOTES** Late May–early Jul and Aug–Sep in two generations over much of its range, and Jun–Jul in one generation in northern Scotland. Feeds at night. Pupates in the ground. A pupa has also been found on the ground in Mar in a spun birch leaf. Overwinters as a pupa.

SCALLOPED HAZEL
Odontopera bidentata

PLATE 29
70.240 (1920)

Common. **FIELD CHARACTERS** Colours and markings are exceptionally variable. There is a range of variation between pale brownish or greyish and relatively plainly marked, through brownish forms with greenish patches resembling algae, to extreme forms of mixed greenish grey, white and black, resembling foliose lichens on twigs. All forms have a somewhat notched head, and vestigial prolegs on A4 and A5, with those on A5 being slightly larger. The plainer forms have a brown or grey head with a dark patch centrally, and paired dorsal projections on A8, bordered laterally by a dark line. The lichen form has a pale grey head with a black patch centrally. **SIMILAR SPECIES** Horse Chestnut, Scalloped Oak, Dusky Scalloped Oak, Engrailed, Small Engrailed and Brussels Lace may resemble forms of Scalloped Hazel, but none of

these similar species has extra prolegs on A4 and A5. Additionally, Scalloped Oak and probably Dusky Scalloped Oak will be fully fed earlier in the year, Engrailed and Small Engrailed have T2 swollen, and Brussels Lace lacks the notch in the head and has paired dorsal projections A1–A5. **HABITATS** Gardens and urban parks, hedgerows, scrub, and broadleaf and coniferous woodlands. **FOODPLANTS** Wide variety of woody plants, including Apple, Barberry, Bilberry, birches, Blackthorn, Broom, Lawson's Cypress, Douglas Fir, hawthorns, Hazel, Common Juniper, larches, limes, oaks, pines, Wild Plum, Western Red-cedar, spruces and willows. Also on lichens on trees. **FIELD NOTES** Jun–Sep. Feeds at night. Pupates among moss or debris on the ground. Overwinters as a pupa.

Scalloped Hazel larva, posterior segments showing vestigial prolegs on A4–A5 (arrowed)

SCALLOPED OAK
Crocallis elinguaria

PLATE 29
70.241 (1921)

Common. **FIELD CHARACTERS** Head brown and slightly notched. Body brown or grey with a pair of small dorsal projections on A1, and slightly larger projections on A8, bordered laterally by a dark line. Usually there are diamond-shaped dorsal markings on abdominal segments, a pair of dark brown subdorsal lines on A4 and sometimes including A5, forming an hourglass shape, and a paler area lateral to these lines. **SIMILAR SPECIES** Horse Chestnut, Scalloped Hazel, Dusky Scalloped Oak, Engrailed and Small Engrailed. Dusky Scalloped Oak may be almost indistinguishable in the field based on the limited material examined. **HABITATS** Gardens and urban parks, hedgerows, scrub and woodland. **FOODPLANTS** Wide variety of woody plants, including Crab Apple, Beech, Bilberry, Downy and Silver birches, Blackthorn, Bog-myrtle, brideworts, cherries, cotoneasters, Hawthorn, Heather, Honeysuckle, lavenders, oaks, roses, Rowan and willows. **FIELD NOTES** Late Mar–Jul. Feeds at night. Pupates on the ground. Overwinters as an egg.

DUSKY SCALLOPED OAK
Crocallis dardoinaria

PLATE 29
70.242 (1921a)

Immigrant; resident in the Channel Islands. **FIELD CHARACTERS** On the limited material examined, very similar to Scalloped Oak but lacking the distinctive hourglass shape and the paler area laterally on A4. **SIMILAR SPECIES** Horse Chestnut, Scalloped Hazel, Scalloped Oak, Engrailed and Small Engrailed. **HABITATS AND FOODPLANTS** Not known in the Channel Islands. In Europe prefers waste ground, on Broom, *Cistus*, Gorse and Common Juniper. **FIELD NOTES** Oct–early summer. Pupation site unknown. Overwinters as a small larva.

SWALLOW-TAILED MOTH
Ourapteryx sambucaria

PLATE 29
70.243 (1922)

Common. Extending its range in Scotland in the north-east. **FIELD CHARACTERS** Body brown or grey, long and slender, with slight ventral swelling on T3 from which the true leg arises. There is a lateral swelling on A3, a dorsal projection on A5 and a wavy subspiracular fold. Abdomen with a pair of long anal points. **SIMILAR SPECIES** Barred Umber and Orange Moth. **HABITATS** Gardens and urban parks, hedgerows, scrub and woodland. **FOODPLANTS** Wide variety, including Beech, Blackthorn, Bramble, Black Currant, Elder, Wych Elm, Firethorn, forget-me-nots, Canadian Goldenrod, Hawthorn, Holly, Honeysuckle, Horse-chestnut, Common Ivy, Lilac, oaks, Pear, Garden Privet, Sycamore and Goat Willow. **FIELD NOTES** Late Aug–early Jun. Feeds at night. Pupates in a spinning among the foodplant.

FEATHERED THORN
Colotois pennaria

PLATE 29
70.244 (1923)

Common. **FIELD CHARACTERS** Body varies from pale grey to pale brown, often speckled with dark grey marks, these more or less arranged in lines. There may also be pale yellowish lines, white marks, and dark grey patches or shading. The most striking feature is a pair of red or reddish-brown dorsal projections on A8. **HABITATS** Mainly woodland. Also hedgerows, scrub on heathland and grasslands, and more rarely gardens and urban parks. **FOODPLANTS** Wide variety, including Alder, Crab Apple, Bilberry, birches, Blackthorn, Bog-myrtle, Dog-rose, elms, hawthorns, Hazel, larches, Field Maple, oaks, poplars, Wild Privet, Wild Service-tree, Sitka Spruce, Sycamore and willows. **FIELD NOTES** Apr–Jun. Feeds at night. Pupates in the ground. Overwinters as an egg.

MARCH MOTH
Alsophila aescularia

PLATE 29
70.245 (1663)

Common. **FIELD CHARACTERS** Head green and unmarked. Body green with white dorsal, subdorsal, lateral and subspiracular lines. In the final instar there is a pair of vestigial prolegs on A5. **SIMILAR SPECIES** Northern Winter Moth and Winter Moth. **HABITATS** Mainly woodland. Also hedgerows, scrub on heathland, grasslands and wetlands, and in gardens and urban parks. **FOODPLANTS** Wide variety, including apples, Bilberry, Blackthorn, birches, cherries, currants, elms, Hawthorn, Hazel, Hornbeam, limes, Lilac, Field Maple, oaks, Wild Privet, roses, Rowan, Sycamore and willows. **FIELD NOTES** Late Apr–Jun. Pupates in the ground. Overwinters as a pupa.

SMALL BRINDLED BEAUTY
Apocheima hispidaria

PLATE 30
70.246 (1925)

Local. Quite widespread and occurs in large numbers in some woodlands in southern England. Much scarcer further north. **FIELD CHARACTERS** Head grey or brown, speckled paler. Body grey, or pale brown mixed pale yellowish, with dark subdorsal pinacula that are especially prominent on A2 and A8 and slightly raised on other abdominal segments. There is a dark lateral swelling on A2 with a dark pinaculum. Markings are variable in extent. Plainer forms have an ill-defined grey dorsal line, variably edged with orangey-brown marks. Contrasting forms may be covered with short dark lines arranged in a reticulated pattern. **SIMILAR SPECIES** Pale Brindled Beauty has more pronounced subdorsal pinacula, especially A1–A3, has lateral swellings A2–A3, and may have pale V-shapes across the dorsum A2–A3. **HABITATS** Hedgerow trees in wooded landscapes and woodland. **FOODPLANTS** Pedunculate and Sessile oaks. Also reported on birches, Sweet Chestnut, English and Wych elms, Hawthorn, Hazel and Hornbeam. **FIELD NOTES** Apr–mid-Jun. Feeds at night. Pupates in the ground. Overwinters as a pupa, with the moths beginning to emerge in late winter.

PALE BRINDLED BEAUTY
Phigalia pilosaria

PLATE 30
70.247 (1926)

Common. **FIELD CHARACTERS** Head grey or brown, speckled paler. Body grey, sometimes mixed orangey brown or yellowish, with black subdorsal pinacula that are especially prominent on A1–A3 and A8 and slightly raised on other abdominal segments. There are lateral swellings with black pinacula A2–A3, and a smaller one on A1. Markings are variable in extent. Dorsal line or stripe grey, often edged with orangey-brown or yellowish marks, and some forms have short grey lines arranged in a reticulated pattern. There may be V-shaped pale or whitish markings across the dorsum A2–A3. Spiracles whitish orange with black circles, and often shaded orangey brown beyond. **SIMILAR SPECIES** Small Brindled Beauty. **HABITATS** Gardens and urban parks, hedgerows, scrub and woodland. **FOODPLANTS** Wide variety, including Alder, Apple, Ash, Downy and Silver birches, Blackthorn, Buckthorn, Alder Buckthorn, Dogwood, Wych Elm, Hawthorn, Midland Hawthorn, Hazel, larches, limes, oaks, poplars, Plum, roses and Goat Willow. **FIELD NOTES** Mid-Apr–mid-Jun. Feeds at night. Pupates in a cocoon in the ground. The first part of the winter is spent as a pupa, with the moth emerging in the later part.

BRINDLED BEAUTY
Lycia hirtaria

PLATE 30
70.248 (1927)

Common. Has declined significantly in abundance in recent decades across much of England and Wales. Remains scarce in northern England and fairly widespread in central and northern Scotland. **FIELD CHARACTERS** Head purplish brown, speckled black. Body purplish grey with four purplish-brown stripes, sometimes mixed with yellow and enclosed by wavy black lines. There are yellow subdorsal and subspiracular marks anteriorly on T1 and A9, and posteriorly on A1–A5. **SIMILAR SPECIES** Rannoch Brindled Beauty has the stripes edged by black dots and dashes, not lines. Belted Beauty has a broad, continuous yellow subspiracular stripe. The habitats and foodplants of these species will help separate them from Brindled Beauty. **HABITATS** Gardens and urban parks, hedgerows, scrub and woodland. **FOODPLANTS** Wide variety, including Alder, Aspen, Beech, Downy and Silver birches, Alder Buckthorn, elms, Hawthorn, Midland Hawthorn, Hazel, Small-leaved Lime, Pedunculate and Holm oaks, Pear, Plum and willows. **FIELD NOTES** Early May–early Jul. Feeds at night. Pupates in the ground. Overwinters as a pupa.

RANNOCH BRINDLED BEAUTY
Lycia lapponaria

PLATE 30
70.249 (1929)

Ssp. *scotica* Na. Resident in the Highlands of Scotland. **FIELD CHARACTERS** Head grey, speckled black. Body grey or reddish purple, usually with three yellow or yellowish-purple stripes edged with black dots and dashes, though these stripes may be coloured more or less as the body. Subspiracular stripe interrupted, yellow and expanded to form a yellow spot adjacent to each spiracle. There are yellow subdorsal and subspiracular marks anteriorly on T1 and A9, and posteriorly A1–A7. **SIMILAR SPECIES** Brindled Beauty and Belted Beauty. **HABITATS** Bogs and moorland. **FOODPLANTS** Mainly Bilberry and Bog-myrtle. Also on Cross-leaved Heath, Heather, Bell Heather and Eared Willow. **FIELD NOTES** Mid-May–early Aug. Feeds mainly at night. Pupates in the ground. Overwinters as a pupa, sometimes for up to four winters.

BELTED BEAUTY
Lycia zonaria

PLATE 30
70.250 (1928)

Ssp. *britannica* RDB. Restricted to coastal habitats and has disappeared from a number of sites in England and Wales. Ssp. *atlantica* Na. Subspecific status questionable. Isle of Baleshare, Outer Hebrides. **FIELD CHARACTERS** Head grey, speckled black. Body grey, speckled with black across dorsal and lateral areas. Broad subspiracular stripe yellow, sometimes mixed whitish. Spiracles black. Ventral area black. **SIMILAR SPECIES** Brindled Beauty and Rannoch Brindled Beauty. **HABITATS** Machair (vegetated shell sands), among short herb-rich vegetation of sand dunes, and a single colony in Lancashire among Sea Rush patches in saltmarsh. Also on golf links. **FOODPLANTS** Mainly Common Bird's-foot-trefoil and Kidney Vetch. Also reported on Broom, cat's-ears, clovers, Colt's-foot, dandelions, docks, Autumn Hawkbit, Yellow Iris, knapweeds, Knotgrass, Sea Plantain, Burnet Rose, thistles, Wild Thyme, Meadow Vetchling, Creeping

Willow and Yarrow. **FIELD NOTES** May–Jul. Feeds by day and especially at night. Larvae can be abundant. Pupates in the ground. Overwinters as a pupa, sometimes for up to five winters.

OAK BEAUTY
Biston strataria

PLATE 30
70.251 (1930)

Common. Local in Scotland and Ireland. **FIELD CHARACTERS** Markings are variable in intensity and extent. Head brown with crescent-shaped markings on the face and a shallow notch with rounded dorsal lobes. Body grey, grey mixed with brown, or occasionally greyish green. There are paired dorsal projections anteriorly on T1, paired ventral projections A2–A5, brown lateral projections on A1 and A4–A5, the largest on A5, and small dorsal projections on A8. All projections become less obvious as the larva expands during last instar. Spiracles whitish. A pair of very short anal points. **SIMILAR SPECIES** Peppered Moth has a more deeply notched head with more pointed dorsal lobes, and lacks the crescent-shaped markings. It has orange, not white, spiracles. It is fully fed later in the year. **HABITATS** Most frequent in woodland. Also found in gardens and urban parks, hedgerows and scrub. **FOODPLANTS** Various trees and shrubs, including Alder, Aspen, birches, Alder Buckthorn, elms, Hazel, Lime, oaks and willows. **FIELD NOTES** May–Jul. Feeds at night. Pupates in the ground. Overwinters as a pupa.

PEPPERED MOTH
Biston betularia

PLATE 30
70.252 (1931)

Common. **FIELD CHARACTERS** Colour and markings are very variable. Head brown and deeply notched with pointed dorsal lobes. Body grey, brown or green. There is often a brown ventral projection on A3 and sometimes on A4, a brown lateral projection on A5, and small dorsal projections on A8. All projections become less obvious as the larva expands during last instar. Spiracles orange. A pair of short anal points. **SIMILAR SPECIES** Oak Beauty. **HABITATS** Most frequent in oak woodland. Also found in gardens and urban parks, hedgerows, scrub and other woodlands. **FOODPLANTS** Wide variety of woody and sometimes herbaceous plants, including Beech, birches, Blackthorn, Bramble, Broom, Sweet Chestnut, currants, elms, Goldenrod, Hawthorn, Hop, larches, Michaelmas-daisies, Mugwort, oaks, poplars, roses, spruces, Tamarisk and willows. **FIELD NOTES** Early Jul–late Sep. Feeds at night. Pupates in the ground. Overwinters as a pupa.

SPRING USHER
Agriopis leucophaearia

PLATE 30
70.253 (1932)

Common. **FIELD CHARACTERS** Head black, or green mottled black, and prothoracic plate black with a broad grey or green central division. Body green with prominent subdorsal black pinacula on abdominal segments. Dorsal stripe black, and formed of widely spaced dashes with lateral extensions that may join with large black lateral spots. Sometimes the black coloration is extensive and there is little green. **HABITATS** Mainly oak woodland. Also mature oaks among hedgerows in wooded landscapes, plantations and sometimes urban areas. **FOODPLANTS** Mainly Pedunculate and Sessile oaks. Also reported on Sycamore. **FIELD NOTES** Early Apr–mid-Jun. At first feeds within a spinning. Pupates in or on the ground. Overwinters initially as a pupa, with adults usually emerging from Jan and eggs laid from then on.

SCARCE UMBER
Agriopis aurantiaria

PLATE 30
70.254 (1933)

Common. Widespread in rural areas. Local in Ireland. **FIELD CHARACTERS** Head brown. Body varies from pale brown to dark grey and occasionally green, with a pair of prominent black dorsal pinacula on A8. Several pale subdorsal and lateral lines and a white supraspiracular line. Spiracles black, sometimes surrounded by pale patches, and there may be black patches adjacent. **SIMILAR SPECIES** Dotted Border and Scarce Umber are indistinguishable in the field. Mottled Umber lacks the pair of prominent black dorsal pinacula on A8, has white spiracles, and has a broad yellow spiracular stripe edged above with a black line. **HABITATS** Most frequent in woodland. Also mature trees among gardens and scrub in wooded landscapes. **FOODPLANTS** Alder, Ash, Aspen, Beech, birches, Blackthorn, Bog-myrtle, Dog-rose, English

Elm, hawthorns, Hazel, Hornbeam, larches, limes, oaks, poplars, Raspberry, Rowan, Sycamore and willows. **FIELD NOTES** Apr–Jul. Feeds at night. Pupates in or on the ground. Overwinters as an adult in early winter, then as an egg.

DOTTED BORDER
Agriopis marginaria

PLATE 30
70.255 (1934)

Common. **SIMILAR SPECIES** Scarce Umber and Mottled Umber. **HABITATS** Gardens, scrub and woodland. **FOODPLANTS** Wide variety, including Alder, Crab Apple, Aspen, Beech, Bilberry, birches, Blackthorn, Bog-myrtle, Sweet Chestnut, Dog-rose, English and Wych elms, Hawthorn, Midland Hawthorn, Hazel, Hornbeam, limes, Field Maple, Pedunculate Oak and willows. **FIELD NOTES** Apr–mid-Jun. Feeds at night. Pupates in the ground. Overwinters at first as a pupa, and adults appear from late winter.

MOTTLED UMBER
Erannis defoliaria

PLATE 31
70.256 (1935)

Common. **FIELD CHARACTERS** Head brown. Body varies from pale brown to dark grey. Several pale subdorsal and lateral lines and a broad yellow supraspiracular stripe, edged above with a black line. The spiracular stripe usually extends from T3 to A6, with patches of the body colour surrounding white spiracles. There is a form with a spiracular stripe along the full length of the body, without any body colour enclosed. **SIMILAR SPECIES** Scarce Umber and Dotted Border. **HABITATS** Most frequent in woodland. Also in gardens, heathland, hedgerows, moorland and scrub. **FOODPLANTS** Wide variety, including Apple, Aspen, Beech, Bilberry, birches, Blackthorn, Bird Cherry, Sweet Chestnut, Dog-rose, elms, hawthorns, Hazel, Honeysuckle, Hornbeam, Field Maple, oaks, Rowan, Sitka Spruce, Sycamore and willows. **FIELD NOTES** Early Apr–late Jun. Feeds at night. Pupates on the ground. The early winter is spent as an adult, the rest of the winter as an egg.

WAVED UMBER
Menophra abruptaria

PLATE 31
70.257 (1936)

Common. Frequent in England away from the far south-west and the north, and scarce in west Wales. **FIELD CHARACTERS** Head brown with a transverse yellow band. Body brown with a brown dorsal line and whitish-brown subdorsal line, edged above with dark brown shading, especially on T3–A2 and the posterior of A4–A6. Subspiracular line whitish yellow, expanded above and around each spiracle. There is a slight dorsal hump on A8 with a transverse black bar. Black lines on the proleg, and below the spiracles A7–A8. **HABITATS** Gardens and urban parks, hedgerows, scrub and woodland. **FOODPLANTS** Winter Jasmine, Lilac and Garden Privet in urban areas. In rural locations reported on Wild Privet. **FIELD NOTES** Early Jun–Oct. Pupates in a strong cocoon among the foodplant. Overwinters as a pupa.

WILLOW BEAUTY
Peribatodes rhomboidaria

PLATE 31
70.258 (1937)

Common. **FIELD CHARACTERS** Head notched and brown, with darker mottling concentrated around the margins of the dorsal lobes. Body various shades of brown, with paired ventral swellings on A2. Dorsal line pale, edged with dark brown shading, and often ill-defined where there are pale dorsal patches or on larvae with pale body colour. Two prominent black subdorsal pinacula A1–A7, sometimes very small on pale examples. **SIMILAR SPECIES** Satin Beauty has white lateral pinacula raised on small bumps and lacks ventral swellings. Mottled Beauty lacks ventral swellings and raised white lateral pinacula. **HABITATS** Gardens and urban parks, hedgerows, scrub and woodland. **FOODPLANTS** Wide variety, including birches, Bramble, Broom, Alder Buckthorn, Leyland and Monterey cypresses, Gorse, Hawthorn, Honeysuckle, Common Ivy, laurels, Lilac, pines, Plum, Garden Privet, roses, Rowan, Norway Spruce, Traveller's-joy and Yew. **FIELD NOTES** Jul–Jun. Some larvae feed up quickly in the south and are fully grown in late summer, producing a second generation of adults in the autumn. Pupates among the foodplant or in debris on the ground. Overwinters as a small larva.

FEATHERED BEAUTY
Peribatodes secundaria

PLATE 31
70.260 (1937a)

Suspected immigrant; recent colonist. Resident in south-east England. **FIELD CHARACTERS** Head notched, and brown with darker mottling. Body pale brown or orangey brown, or sometimes grey. Dorsal line whitish, edged with dark lines. Subdorsal line or stripe whitish or pale brown, formed of widely spaced dashes. There are two fine black interrupted lateral lines below, which may be obscured by a dark brown patch on each segment A1–A7 in well-marked examples. Some forms have brown diamonds with dark edges across the dorsum. **HABITATS** Coniferous woodland. **FOODPLANTS** Norway Spruce in England and a wider range of conifers in Europe. **FIELD NOTES** Late Aug–early Jun. Pupates in a cocoon among the foodplant. Overwinters as a small larva.

BORDERED GREY
Selidosema brunnearia

PLATE 31
70.262 (1938)

Ssp. *scandinaviaria* Na. A scattered and highly localised distribution in Great Britain and Ireland. Ssp. *tyronensis* Co. Tyrone, Ireland; probably extinct. **FIELD CHARACTERS** Head notched, and pale brown or pale grey with darker mottling. Body pale brown or pale greyish brown, with black pinacula above the subdorsal line. Dorsal line pale brown, edged with dark brown lines or shading. Subdorsal line whitish or yellowish brown. Lateral line whitish, and subspiracular stripe indistinct, paler than ground colour, and sometimes edged with black dashes below. **HABITATS** Bogs, chalk, coastal and limestone grasslands, heathland, limestone pavement, moorland, mosses and sand dunes. **FOODPLANTS** Common Bird's-foot-trefoil, Broom, Cross-leaved Heath, Heather, Bell Heather, Common Restharrow, and flowers of sorrels. **FIELD NOTES** Sep–Jun. Feeds at night. Pupates in a cocoon in or on the ground. Overwinters as a small larva.

RINGED CARPET
Cleora cinctaria

PLATE 31
70.263 (1939)

Ssp. *cinctaria* Na. Very local in England and Ireland. Ssp. *bowesi* Na. Very local in Scotland, with a similar form occurring in Wales. **FIELD CHARACTERS** Head green. Body green with a dark green dorsal stripe incorporating a faint, pale line, and edged with white lines. Subdorsal line white, with a faint white line above, and two or three faint white lateral lines below. A faint whitish spiracular line. Spiracles orangey white. **SIMILAR SPECIES** Latticed Heath and Speckled Yellow. **HABITATS** Bogs, heathland and moorland, usually where there is scattered young scrub. **FOODPLANTS** Bilberry, birches, Bog-myrtle (the main foodplant in Scotland), Cross-leaved Heath, Heather and Bell Heather. Also reported on Common Bird's-foot-trefoil and Goat Willow. **FIELD NOTES** Late May–early Aug. Pupates in debris or in the ground. Overwinters as a pupa.

SATIN BEAUTY
Deileptenia ribeata

PLATE 31
70.264 (1940)

Common. Has increased very significantly in range and abundance in recent decades. **FIELD CHARACTERS** Head notched, and grey or brown with a black transverse band and mottling. Body pale grey or varying shades of brown. Dorsal line pale brown, pale grey or whitish, with variable black lines along the body. Two pinacula above the pale brown subdorsal line per segment A1–A8, the anterior one black, the posterior one black or white and raised. Lateral pinacula white and raised on small bumps. There may be diagonal black streaks and shading laterally. Anal flap ends in four points, each giving rise to a hair. **SIMILAR SPECIES** Willow Beauty and Mottled Beauty. **HABITATS** Broadleaf and coniferous woodland. Also areas where there are old Yew trees, including chalk grassland and scrub. **FOODPLANTS** Conifers, especially Scots Pine and Yew, and reported on Douglas Fir, Western Hemlock-spruce, larches, European silver-fir and spruces. Broadleaf trees include Beech, birches, oaks and willows. The ovipositor is long and curved, adapted for laying eggs under lichen, not on leaves, and in captivity young larvae will feed from algae- and lichen-covered twigs devoid of leaves. This is likely to be relevant in the wild. **FIELD NOTES** Aug–late May. Pupates in the ground. Overwinters as a small larva.

MOTTLED BEAUTY
Alcis repandata

PLATE 31
70.265 (1941)

Ssp. *repandata* Common. Widespread in Great Britain and Ireland. Ssp. *muraria* Common. Mainly in north-west England and Scotland. Ssp. *sodorensium* Outer Hebrides. **FIELD CHARACTERS** Head notched, and brown with darker mottling. Body pale grey or brown. Two pinacula per segment above the subdorsal line A1–A8, both black, with the posterior one slightly raised except on A7–A8. Dorsal line pale, more or less edged with dark brown, and with a faint, pale subdorsal line. Markings very variable, from plain with faint lines to heavily patterned with pale and dark patches. **SIMILAR SPECIES** Willow Beauty and Satin Beauty. **HABITATS** Most frequent on moorland and in woodland. Also heathland, hedgerows and scrub. Occasionally in urban areas. **FOODPLANTS** Wide variety, including Wild Angelica, Ash, Barberry, Bilberry, birches, Blackthorn, Bramble, Broom, cypresses, docks, hawthorns, Hazel, Heather, Honeysuckle, Common Juniper, oaks, pines, spruces, Traveller's-joy and Yarrow. **FIELD NOTES** Late Aug–May. Pupates in the ground. Overwinters as a small larva.

DOTTED CARPET
Alcis jubata

PLATE 31
70.266 (1942)

Local. Has increased very significantly in abundance in the north and west in recent decades, but has all but disappeared from central southern England. **FIELD CHARACTERS** Body bluish green, mixed with yellowish patches. A row of black dots and dashes along the dorsum, and a subdorsal row of black dashes. There are further black marks above and below the spiracular level. **HABITATS** Mature woodland with abundant lichens. **FOODPLANTS** Beard lichens (*Usnea* spp.). **FIELD NOTES** Late Aug–Jun. Prefers feeding on the newest growth. Pupates under moss and lichens.

GREAT OAK BEAUTY
Hypomecis roboraria

PLATE 31
70.267 (1943)

Nb. Widely distributed in south-east England; very local elsewhere. **FIELD CHARACTERS** Head notched, and pale brown with darker markings. Body mixed grey and brown with a subdorsal projection on T3, a dorsal and lateral projection on A2, paired ventral projections on A3, and a pair of raised dorsal pinacula on A8. **SIMILAR SPECIES** September Thorn. **HABITATS** Long-established oak woodland. **FOODPLANTS** Pedunculate Oak. Also reported on birches and willows. **FIELD NOTES** Aug–end May. Feeds at night. Pupates in the ground. Overwinters as a larva in the tree canopy.

PALE OAK BEAUTY
Hypomecis punctinalis

PLATE 31
70.268 (1944)

Common. Widespread and frequent in south-east England and East Anglia, and local in the Midlands. **FIELD CHARACTERS** Head notched, and brown with paler and darker markings. Body grey, greenish grey or brown, often rather plain, but sometimes more patterned. A brown subdorsal projection on A2, a pair of raised dorsal pinacula on A8, and often a ventrolateral swelling on A3. **HABITATS** Mainly woodland. Also long-established scrub, and within well-wooded landscapes. **FOODPLANTS** Wide variety, including Crab Apple, Downy and Silver birches, Sweet Chestnut, Hawthorn, Midland Hawthorn, Hazel, Honeysuckle, larches, Pedunculate Oak, Raspberry, Sycamore and willows. **FIELD NOTES** Early Jul–late Aug. Feeds at night. Pupates in the ground. Overwinters as a pupa.

NOTE ON ENGRAILED/SMALL ENGRAILED (GENUS *ECTROPIS*)
The presence of one species, Engrailed, is widely accepted in Europe. In the south in Great Britain and Ireland, however, there are populations that fly between first- and second-generation Engrailed, and for the most part have just one generation per year. They appear to exist as a separate species, known as Small Engrailed, based on phenology. The map is based on combined records for both species.

ENGRAILED
Ectropis crepuscularia

PLATE 32
70.270 (1947)

Common. **FIELD CHARACTERS** Head slightly notched, and pale brown or pale grey with darker mottling. Body brown or grey, often varying in shade along the length of the body. Markings variable but there is a yellow spot at the spiracular level on A6 with the yellow extending diagonally to the proleg. T2 is swollen, forming a hump dorsally and laterally that may be obvious only at rest. T3 swollen ventrally, from which the true leg arises. A pair of pinacula on A8, slightly raised on a hump, and usually a short, forward-pointing, curved black line below. **SIMILAR SPECIES** Small Engrailed is indistinguishable on field characters, but separation on date of finding the larva may be possible. Also Scalloped Hazel, Scalloped Oak and Dusky Scalloped Oak. **HABITATS** Mainly woodland. Also hedgerows and scrub. Uncommon in urban areas. **FOODPLANTS** Wide variety, including Alder, Ash, Aspen, Downy and Silver birches, Broom, Buckthorn, Wych Elm, hawthorns, Hazel, Honeysuckle, Hornbeam, larches, oaks including Holm Oak, Scots Pine, Wild Privet, Spindle, Sitka Spruce and Yew. **FIELD NOTES** Late Apr–Jun and Aug–Sep, in two or more generations in the south. In the north, usually May–Aug in one generation, but occasionally there is a partial second. Feeds at night. Pupates in the ground. Overwinters as a pupa.

SMALL ENGRAILED
Ectropis sp. Taxon of uncertain status and currently unnamed

PLATE 32
70.271 (1948)

Local. Widely reported in England, Wales and Ireland; much more local in Scotland (see distribution map for Engrailed). **SIMILAR SPECIES** Scalloped Hazel, Scalloped Oak, Dusky Scalloped Oak and Engrailed. **HABITATS** Mainly woodland. Also hedgerows and scrub. Uncommon in urban areas. **FOODPLANTS** Beech, Downy and Silver birches, Hawthorn and willows. **FIELD NOTES** Mid-Jun–early Aug. Feeds at night. Pupates in the ground. Overwinters as a pupa.

SQUARE SPOT
Paradarisa consonaria

PLATE 32
70.272 (1949)

Local. Widespread throughout southern England and most of Wales; local or very local elsewhere. **FIELD CHARACTERS** Head pale brown, mottled darker. Body brown or grey with several wavy and incomplete pale lines, and there may be a whitish dorsal stripe. On A1 or A2–A8 there is a pinaculum anteriorly on each segment either side of the dorsal line, and another, larger pinaculum posteriorly on each subdorsally. The posterior pinaculum is black, and brown or black and slightly raised on A8. There may be blackish shading posterior to the posterior pinacula A2–A4, creating the impression of an oblique mark, and black shading around the pinaculum on A8. **HABITATS** Mainly scrub and woodland. Also within well-wooded landscapes. **FOODPLANTS** Birches, Beech, Hornbeam, larches, Small-leaved Lime, oaks, pines and Yew. The ovipositor is long, adapted for laying eggs under lichen, not on leaves, and in captivity larvae will feed from algae- and lichen-covered twigs devoid of leaves. This is likely to be relevant in the wild for young larvae. **FIELD NOTES** Mid-Jun–mid-Aug. Feeds at night. Pupates in the ground. Overwinters as a pupa.

BRINDLED WHITE-SPOT
Parectropis similaria

PLATE 32
70.273 (1950)

Local. Rather scattered in distribution from the Midlands southwards. **FIELD CHARACTERS** There are green and greyish-brown forms. The green form has a green head and body, with a reddish or black paired dorsal projection on A5, and a smaller one on A1. White subdorsal spots on most segments, with variable extent of reddish or black markings dorsally and laterally. Proleg reddish or black. The greyish-brown form is similar, with a greyish-brown body and black projections and markings, and there may be green patches around the abdominal spiracles. **HABITATS** Long-established woodland. **FOODPLANTS** Alder, Downy and Silver birches, Sweet Chestnut, Hawthorn, Midland Hawthorn, Hazel, limes, Pedunculate Oak and willows. **FIELD NOTES** Late Jul–early Sep. Pupates in the ground. Overwinters as a pupa.

GREY BIRCH
Aethalura punctulata

PLATE 32
70.274 (1951)

Common. Widely distributed in England and Wales. Local in Scotland and very local in Ireland. **FIELD CHARACTERS** There are green and greyish-brown forms. The green form has a green head, mottled yellowish. Body green with a pale green dorsal line and a white or yellow subdorsal stripe, with two white lines between. There are two lateral lines and a subspiracular line, all white or yellow. The greyish-brown form has a greenish head, mottled with black. Body greyish brown with similar white lines and a stripe, but there are transverse bands of greyish-brown shading altering the white to smoky white. Black pinacula above the subdorsal line. **HABITATS** Scrub on heathland and moorland, and woodland. Occasionally among Alder in wet woodland. **FOODPLANTS** Mainly Downy and Silver birches. Also Alder. Has been found on Hazel among birches. **FIELD NOTES** Jun–late Aug. Pupates in the ground. Overwinters as a pupa.

COMMON HEATH
Ematurga atomaria

PLATE 32
70.275 (1952)

Common. **FIELD CHARACTERS** There are greenish, brown and grey forms and the larva is very variable. The greenish form has a greenish body with a black subdorsal pinaculum on each segment A1–A8. Dorsal line green edged with yellow lines and subdorsal stripe yellow, with a yellow line between. Subspiracular stripe yellow or white, edged above by grey or purplish shading. One brown form is similar, with brown replacing the greenish. Another brown form has a brown body with a dark brown dorsal line, blackish or dark brown subdorsal stripe, and a whitish subspiracular stripe with brown patches, edged above by a black or dark brown stripe. There may be a whitish transverse band between the subdorsal stripes A1–A7. One grey form is similar, with grey replacing the brown. There is a highly patterned grey form with a dorsal band and subspiracular stripe comprising alternating black and white dashes. **SIMILAR SPECIES** Rannoch Looper. **HABITATS** Mainly heathland and moorland. Also occurs more rarely in grasslands and woodland rides on chalk, limestone and neutral soils. **FOODPLANTS** Bog-myrtle, Broom, clovers, Cross-leaved Heath, Heather, Bell Heather, Purple-loosestrife, trefoils, vetches and Eared Willow. **FIELD NOTES** Mid-Jun–mid-Sep, in one generation or a partial second, especially in the south. Pupates in a slight cocoon in or on the ground. Overwinters as a pupa.

BORDERED WHITE
Bupalus piniaria

PLATE 32
70.276 (1954)

Common. Local in Ireland. Has had occasional population outbreaks since the 1950s and is a serious pest of pines in Europe. **FIELD CHARACTERS** Head green with white dorsal and subdorsal stripes. Body green with a white or yellow dorsal stripe, a white or yellow subdorsal line with another line just below, and a white or yellow subspiracular stripe. Spiracles orange. True legs green. **SIMILAR SPECIES** Pine Carpet, Spruce Carpet, Grey Pine Carpet, Dusky Peacock, Tawny-barred Angle and Banded Pine Carpet. **HABITATS** Native Scots Pine and other coniferous woodlands. Also pine plantations and self-sown pines on heathland, favouring mature trees. **FOODPLANTS** Mainly Scots Pine, but regularly on larches and Corsican Pine. Also reported on Douglas Fir, other pines, European Silver-fir and Norway Spruce. **FIELD NOTES** Late Jun–Oct, sometimes later. Pupates in the ground. Overwinters as a pupa.

COMMON WHITE WAVE
Cabera pusaria

PLATE 32
70.277 (1955)

Common. **FIELD CHARACTERS** There are green, brownish and pale brown/pale grey forms. The green form has a green head, speckled darker and with a brown streak laterally. Body green with a series of short dark dorsal dashes edged with brown shading on a variable number of segments, and with white subdorsal spots beyond, which are joined in a faint subdorsal stripe. Spiracles white within a brown circle. True legs on T1 green, on T2 green sometimes with a hint of red and on T3 red. Proleg red and anal clasper red anteriorly. The brownish form has a brownish head that is green centrally. Body brown, reddish brown or purplish brown, with a faintly darker dorsal stripe. Subdorsal spots white, sometimes joined in a stripe. True legs greenish. Proleg and anal clasper brownish. Pale brown and pale grey forms have markings similar to the green form, except on the head, which is like that of the brown form. **SIMILAR SPECIES** Common Wave ha black dorsal dashes bordered with white, not brown. **HABITATS** Heathland and moorland (but not at high altitude), and in scrub and woodland on many soil types. **FOODPLANTS** Alder, Downy and Silver birches, Sweet Chestnut, Hazel, oaks and willows. **FIELD NOTES** Late Jun–Oct, in one extended generation, or two in the south. Pupates among debris, or in the ground. Overwinters as a pupa.

COMMON WAVE
Cabera exanthemata

PLATE 32
70.278 (1956)

Common. **FIELD CHARACTERS** There are green and brown forms. The green form has a green head, without speckling, and a brown streak laterally. Body green with a series of short black or dark green dorsal dashes, edged white and sometimes with purplish marks beyond. Subdorsal stripe yellowish white, and sometimes there is a faint purplish subspiracular stripe. Spiracles white within a brown circle. True legs green, proleg purple or green, and anal clasper purplish anteriorly or entirely green. The brown form has a brown head and body with similar markings to the green form. **SIMILAR SPECIES** Common White Wave. **HABITATS** Scrub and woodland, especially in wet areas. **FOODPLANTS** Poplars including Aspen, and Goat, Grey and other willows. Also on Alder and birches. **FIELD NOTES** Late Jun–Oct, in one generation, or a partial second in the south. Pupates in debris on the ground. Overwinters as a pupa.

WHITE-PINION SPOTTED
Lomographa bimaculata

PLATE 32
70.279 (1957)

Common. Expanding its range in northern England and Scotland. Very local in Ireland. **FIELD CHARACTERS** Head green, speckled dark grey. Body green and rather translucent, with dorsal vessel showing dark green. Purple dorsal marks on T2, T3 and A8, and there may be further purple marks or patches varying in extent along the dorsum. Subdorsal line white, but this may be absent. Spiracular line yellow and often ill-defined. Spiracles black. True legs green, and proleg and anal clasper green. **SIMILAR SPECIES** Broken-barred Carpet, Small Phoenix and Clouded Silver. **HABITATS** Hedgerows, scrub and woodland, and sometimes in more rural gardens. **FOODPLANTS** Blackthorn, Dwarf Cherry, Hawthorn, Midland Hawthorn and Wild Plum. **FIELD NOTES** Late Jun–late Aug. Pupates in or on the ground. Overwinters as a pupa, the wings of the fully developed moth visible within.

CLOUDED SILVER
Lomographa temerata

PLATE 32
70.280 (1958)

Common. Has recently expanded its range in the north. **FIELD CHARACTERS** Head green with a brown mark, edged black, on each dorsal lobe, resembling an inverted teardrop. Body green or whitish green. Dorsal stripe yellow, continuous or comprising a series of yellow spots, and edged with red. Subdorsal line absent. Spiracles yellow within a brown circle. True legs green, and proleg and anal clasper green. **SIMILAR SPECIES** Broken-barred Carpet, Small Phoenix and White-pinion Spotted. **HABITATS** Gardens and urban parks, hedgerows, scrub and woodland. **FOODPLANTS** Apple, Crab Apple, Blackthorn, Bird and Wild cherries, Hawthorn, Midland Hawthorn and Plum. Also reported on Aspen, birches and Wych Elm. **FIELD NOTES** Late Jun–late Aug. Pupates in debris on the ground. Overwinters as a pupa with the wing pattern visible.

SLOE CARPET
Aleucis distinctata

PLATE 32
70.281 (1959)

Nb. Frequent only in the eastern parts of Essex and Suffolk. In other areas it is now found only at low density. **FIELD CHARACTERS** There are pale green, pale greyish and brownish forms. The green form has a green head, mottled yellowish. Body green. Dorsal line white, indistinct and incomplete, and subdorsal stripe white, with two white lines between. There are two white lateral lines and a white subspiracular line. The brownish form has a purplish-brown head, mottled white. Body purplish brown with broad white transverse bands A4–A5, speckled darker. The white lines are similar to those of the green form, except the subdorsal stripe, which is indistinct pale brownish with a white spot on each segment. A black transverse line on A8 posteriorly. The pale greyish form has a pale grey head, mottled darker. Body pale grey with black transverse lines or dashes T2–T3, A2–A4 and posteriorly on A8, and incomplete dark brown shading across the dorsum A4–A5. The white lines are similar to those of the green form. **SIMILAR SPECIES** Early Moth (green form) is indistinguishable in the field. Early Moth (brown form) has white transverse bands on more abdominal segments, and the subdorsal stripes are more continuous white. **HABITATS** Short scrub on wet heathlands and lawns in the New Forest, Hampshire; isolated bushes on clay soils in Surrey; rough hedgerows in farmland in Essex and Suffolk. **FOODPLANT** Blackthorn. **FIELD NOTES** Mid-May–early Jul. Feeds mainly at night. Pupates in or on the ground. Overwinters as a pupa.

EARLY MOTH
Theria primaria

PLATE 32
70.282 (1960)

Common. Very local in the northern half of Scotland and local in Ireland. **FIELD CHARACTERS** There are greenish, dark greenish and brownish forms. The greenish form has a green head, with a whitish-green or yellowish-green body and a white subdorsal line or stripe, with other white lines similar to Sloe Carpet (green form). The brownish form has a pale brown head, mottled darker. Body brown or purplish brown, with broad white transverse bands A1–A7, speckled darker. The arrangement of white lines and stripes is similar to Sloe Carpet but they are more obviously white. Black subdorsal pinacula. There is a dark greenish form with the brownish replaced by dark greenish. **SIMILAR SPECIES** Sloe Carpet. **HABITATS** Hedgerows, established scrub, and woodland margins or within open woodland. **FOODPLANTS** Mainly Blackthorn and Hawthorn. Also reported on Bilberry, Midland Hawthorn, oaks and Wild Plum. **FIELD NOTES** Early Apr–late May. Pupates on or below the ground. The early part of the winter is passed as a pupa and the latter part as an adult.

LIGHT EMERALD
Campaea margaritaria

PLATE 32
70.283 (1961)

Common. **FIELD CHARACTERS** Body various shades of brownish grey with white pinacula. A fringe of hair-like fleshy projections extends down from the sides. There is a pair of white pinacula on a slight hump on A8, and a pair of functional prolegs on A5. **SIMILAR SPECIES** Beautiful Hook-tip has reduced prolegs on A3–A4. **HABITATS** Most frequent in woodland. Also found in gardens and urban parks, hedgerows and scrub. **FOODPLANTS** Alder, Ash, Beech, Downy and Silver birches, Blackthorn, Broom, Sweet Chestnut, elms, Hawthorn, Hazel, Hornbeam, Horse-chestnut, Juneberry, Pedunculate Oak, Plum, roses, Rowan and willows. **FIELD NOTES** Mid-Aug–Jun. Feeds at night. A partial second generation of smaller moths is now found regularly in the south, and fully fed larvae may be expected in late summer. Pupates on the ground. Overwinters as a small larva.

BARRED RED
Hylaea fasciaria

PLATE 33
70.284 (1962)

Common. **FIELD CHARACTERS** Body mixed brownish and grey, or grey. Colour and markings very variable between forms, from rather plain grey to contrasting orangey brown with white subdorsal stripes. There are paired brown dorsal projections on A1–A6 and A8, noticeably larger on A3–A5 and A8. There is a pair of rudimentary prolegs on A5. **HABITATS** Native Scots Pine and other coniferous woodlands. Also many places where conifers are planted in rural and urban situations. **FOODPLANTS** Mainly Scots Pine and Norway Spruce. Reported on cedars, Douglas Fir, Western Hemlock-spruce, European Larch, and Corsican and Lodgepole pines. **FIELD NOTES** Early Sep–late May. Feeds at night. Pupates among needles and debris on the ground.

BANDED PINE CARPET
Pungeleria capreolaria

PLATE 3
70.2841 (–

Immigrant; possible colonist in Dorset. **FIELD CHARACTERS** Head green with two short black lines dorsally, a white subdorsal stripe, and black marks or a wide black streak laterally. Body green with a sparse covering of moderately long dark hairs. Dorsal stripe dark green, subdorsal band white, sometimes formed of a white line thickly edged greenish white laterally, and subspiracular stripe white, sometimes tinged yellowish. Proleg green. The subspiracular strip extends onto the green anal clasper. There is a pair of rudimentary prolegs on

A5. **SIMILAR SPECIES** Pine Carpet, Spruce Carpet, Grey Pine Carpet, Dusky Peacock, Tawny-barred Angle and Bordered White. **HABITATS** In Dorset adults have been found near copses. **FOODPLANTS** In Europe on European Silver-fir and Norway Spruce. **FIELD NOTES** Autumn–spring in Europe, feeding slowly over the winter. Feeds at night on the upper surface of the needles when young, and on whole needles in last instar. Rests on the underside of a needle by day. Pupation site in the wild not known.

SCOTCH ANNULET
Gnophos obfuscata

PLATE 33
70.285 (1963)

Nb. Widespread in central and northern Scotland, and local along the west coast of Ireland. **FIELD CHARACTERS** Body pale brownish grey with darker mottling. Dorsal line pale, indistinct and edged darker, with dark brown subdorsal marks and sometimes a row of white subdorsal dots. There are two white, sometimes black, dorsal pinacula on A8, and one on A9. Subspiracular line white. Spiracles black. **SIMILAR SPECIES** Annulet has a pair of pointed dorsal projections on A8, significantly larger than the pinacula on Scotch Annulet. **HABITATS** Moorland and mountains, preferring rocky situations such as in gullies and old quarries. **FOODPLANTS** A range of low-growing plants, including Cross-leaved Heath, Heather, Bell Heather, saxifrages including Yellow Saxifrage, stonecrops, vetches and Petty Whin. **FIELD NOTES** Sep–Jun. Pupates in a cocoon among debris or in the ground.

IRISH ANNULET
Gnophos dumetata

PLATE 33
70.286 (1962a)

Ssp. *hibernica* Ireland, in Cos Clare and Galway only. **FIELD CHARACTERS** Body grey. Dorsal stripe black anteriorly and posteriorly, and grey edged with black lines between. There are paired yellow dorsal spots that may be joined on T3–A4 and shaded black anteriorly. There may also be yellow and white spots at the spiracular level on a variable number of segments. **HABITATS** Limestone pavement. **FOODPLANT** Buckthorn. Mainly on prostrate or low-growing bushes growing in open conditions. **FIELD NOTES** Apr–early Jul. Pupates in a silken cocoon. Overwinters as an egg.

ANNULET
Charissa obscurata

PLATE 33
70.287 (1964)

Local. A scattered, mainly coastal distribution, but inland in southern England and the Midlands. **FIELD CHARACTERS** Body brown or grey, with slightly raised white pinacula, especially on abdominal segments. Diagonal, dark brown lateral stripes or shading A2–A5. Paired, pointed dorsal projections on A8 and a much smaller pair on A9. Spiracles black. **SIMILAR SPECIES** Scotch Annulet. **HABITATS** Calcareous cliffs and rocky coastlines, inland calcareous grassland, coastal sandy grassland, dry heathland, moorland and old quarries. **FOODPLANTS** Common Bird's-foot-trefoil, Salad Burnet, Sea Campion, Creeping Cinquefoil, Shining Crane's-bill, Heather, Common Rock-rose, Wild Strawberry, Thrift, Wild Thyme and Kidney Vetch. **FIELD NOTES** Sep–late May. Feeds at night. Pupates among debris or in the ground. Overwinters as a small larva.

BRUSSELS LACE
Cleorodes lichenaria

PLATE 33
70.288 (1945)

Local; suspected immigrant. Widely distributed in south-west England, Wales and Ireland, and scattered throughout Scotland. Has increased in central southern England in recent decades, but declined as a resident in south-east England. **FIELD CHARACTERS** Head rounded, and greenish grey with black markings. Body various shades of green with a variable pattern of black marks, closely resembling lichen-covered twigs. Paired dorsal projections on A1–A5 and A8, largest on A5. **SIMILAR SPECIES** Scalloped Hazel. **HABITATS** Gardens and urban parks, scrub and woodland. Also hard cliffs and rocky coastal areas. **FOODPLANTS** Variety of mainly fruticose and foliose lichens growing on twigs, stems, rocks and walls. Emerged pupal cases have been found among *Ramalina* sp. lichens growing on rocks on the Cornish coast. **FIELD NOTES** Late Aug–end May. Pupates in a cocoon of silk mixed with lichens, or under moss.

BLACK MOUNTAIN MOTH
Glacies coracina

PLATE 33
70.289 (1965)

Na. Widespread in the central and north-west Highlands of Scotland. **FIELD CHARACTERS** Head brown. Body brown, and sometimes whitish brown or orangey brown across the dorsum on abdominal segments. Dorsal line dark or as body colour, and subdorsal line white, interrupted by oblique, dark brown dorsal streaks from T3 to A5. Subspiracular stripe white and wavy, edged above with black crescents. **HABITATS** Moorland and mountains, usually above 600m. **FOODPLANT** Crowberry. **FIELD NOTES** Larva probably over two seasons, Aug–May of the second year. Larvae, pupating larvae and pupae have been found under Reindeer-moss Lichen (*Cladonia* sp.) in May. Overwinters the first time as a larva, and as a larva or possibly a pupa the second time.

COMMON FOREST LOOPER
Pseudocoremia suavis

PLATE 33
70.290 (1965a)

Adventive. New Zealand endemic, introduced to Cornwall; now established and may spread. **FIELD CHARACTERS** There are two greenish forms and one brown form, all with the ventral area green. The bright green form is relatively unmarked with a white dorsal stripe that narrows between segments, whitish interrupted subdorsal and subspiracular lines, and paired brownish dorsal projections on A8. The brownish-green form has a dirty whitish dorsal stripe, sometimes edged with short black dashes, several wavy, paler and darker lines beyond, and whitish subspiracular marks. There are paired brownish dorsal projections on A4 and A8. The brown form has a mixed whitish and pale brownish dorsal stripe, edged blackish brown, forming a diamond pattern, and is mottled pale and dark brown laterally, sometimes forming indistinct stripes. There are paired dorsal projections, dark brown and whitish on A4, and whitish on A8. **HABITATS** Woodland and a rural garden in England. **FOODPLANTS** Wide variety in New Zealand; not known in England, but likely to include conifers. **FIELD NOTES** Could be found as a larva at any time of year. Pupates on the ground.

BLACK-VEINED MOTH
Siona lineata

PLATE 33
70.291 (1966)

RDB. Protected species. Confined to a few sites in Kent, but formerly more widespread in southern England. **FIELD CHARACTERS** Head whitish brown with a dark central line and dark speckling either side, a whitish-brown subdorsal stripe and darker brown lateral stripes. Body whitish brown and often speckled to a variable extent with dark brown or black, sometimes mixed purplish, and with conspicuous black pinacula. The dorsal area tends to be paler than the lateral area. Dorsal line pale and indistinct, broadly edged with dark brown shading and a white line beyond. Indistinct white subdorsal and lateral lines, and a white subspiracular stripe. Anal flap pointed. **SIMILAR SPECIES** Straw Belle and Yellow Belle both have paired anal points. The two belles cannot be reliably distinguished from one another in the field, but their distributions only overlap in a restricted area. **HABITATS** Known sites are rough, herb-rich chalk grassland. Used to occur on cliffs and in open woodland. **FOODPLANTS** Has been found on Common Bird's-foot-trefoil, Common Knapweed and Wild Marjoram. **FIELD NOTES** Late Jul–May. Pupates in a silken cocoon spun on blades or stems of grass. The adult female may be seen laying eggs on grasses, especially Tor-grass, but larvae do not eat grasses.

GREY SCALLOPED BAR
Dyscia fagaria

PLATE 33
70.292 (1969)

Local. Fairly widespread in Scotland and Ireland, local in northern England, and very local in Wales and central southern England. **FIELD CHARACTERS** Body brown, grey or mixed reddish brown and grey, and varying from rather plain to patterned with paler transverse bands. Dorsal stripe yellowish brown or speckled grey. There are very small paired dorsal projections A4–A7 and a much larger single dorsal projection on A8. Whitish stripe on the proleg and anal clasper. The body ends in a pair of long anal points. **SIMILAR SPECIES** Grass Wave is distinguished by the absence of a single prominent dorsal projection on A8. **HABITATS** Bogs, heathland, moorland and raised mosses. Often more frequent among regrowth following burns, or among short vegetation. **FOODPLANTS** Cross-leaved Heath, Heather and Bell Heather.

Also reported on White Willow. **FIELD NOTES** Jul–May. Feeds at night. Pupates among vegetation or on the ground. Overwinters as a small larva.

STRAW BELLE
Aspitates gilvaria

PLATE 33
70.293 (1967)

Ssp. *gilvaria* RDB; possible immigrant. As a resident found only on the North Downs of Surrey and Kent. Ssp. *burrenensis* Ireland. Mainly Cos Clare and Galway. **FIELD CHARACTERS** Body pale greyish brown or pale yellowish brown, usually with tiny black pinacula. Dorsal line grey, edged yellowish, subdorsal stripe pale yellowish and extending onto the head, and subspiracular stripe whitish. The body ends in a pair of long anal points. **SIMILAR SPECIES** Black-veined Moth and Yellow Belle. **HABITATS** Rough chalk grassland and old quarries in England. Limestone pavement and sand dunes in Ireland. **FOODPLANTS** Common Bird's-foot-trefoil and Fairy Flax. Also reported on Creeping Cinquefoil, Black Medick, Wild Parsnip, Wild Thyme and Yarrow. **FIELD NOTES** Sep–Jun. Feeds at night, resting on dead grass stems when not feeding. Pupates in a slight spinning. Overwinters as a small larva.

YELLOW BELLE
Aspitates ochrearia

PLATE 33
70.294 (1968)

Local. Mainly coastal and estuarine areas in England and Wales, and inland it is widespread in East Anglia, and very local in Dorset and Hampshire. **SIMILAR SPECIES** Black-veined Moth and Straw Belle. **HABITATS** Coastal areas, including dry grassland, old quarries, higher saltmarsh, sand dunes, vegetated shingle and waste ground. Inland on acid, breckland and chalk grasslands, and heathland. **FOODPLANTS** Wide variety of herbaceous plants, including Common Bird's-foot-trefoil, Wild Carrot, Nottingham and Spanish catchflies, Hare's-foot Clover, Beaked Hawk's-beard, Buck's-horn Plantain, Common Restharrow, Smooth Tare, toadflaxes and Sea Wormwood. **FIELD NOTES** Sep–May and late Jun–Aug, in two generations. Feeds at night and rests on grasses by day. Pupates in a slight spinning.

GRASS WAVE
Perconia strigillaria

PLATE 33
70.295 (1970)

Local. A scattered distribution throughout. **FIELD CHARACTERS** Body pale brown, reddish brown or greyish, with paired dorsal projections A1–A7, the largest on A5. Examples with a dark ground colour usually have noticeable pale projections. Those with a pale ground colour tend to have very small projections, except on A5 where they are slightly larger and black. Body ends in a pair of short, blunt anal points. **SIMILAR SPECIES** Grey Scalloped Bar. **HABITATS** Mainly acid grassland, and coastal and inland heathland. Less often in bogs, heathy vegetation in woodland rides, limestone pavement (the Burren, Cos Clare and Galway, Ireland) and moorland. **FOODPLANTS** Broom, Gorse (flowers), Heather, Bell Heather and Petty Whin. Also reported on Blackthorn and Creeping Willow. **FIELD NOTES** Aug–late May. Feeds at night. Pupates in a spinning attached to the foodplant. Overwinters as a small larva.

GEOMETRINAE

REST HARROW
Aplasta ononaria

PLATE 33
70.296 (1664)

RDB; suspected immigrant. Resident at two sites in Kent. **FIELD CHARACTERS** Head green with black speckling. Body stumpy, green, and covered with conspicuous white hairs. Subspiracular stripe yellow, if present. **HABITATS** Land-slipped soft cliffs and sand dunes, preferring short vegetation in hot, sheltered conditions. **FOODPLANT** Common Restharrow. **FIELD NOTES** Jul–early Jun. Pupates in a spinning at the base of the foodplant. Overwinters as a small larva.

GRASS EMERALD
Pseudoterpna pruinata

PLATE 33
70.297 (1665)

Ssp. *atropunctaria* Common. Widespread in England, Wales and Ireland, and local in Scotland, where it has also declined severely in recent decades. **FIELD CHARACTERS** Head deeply notched and green, with the pointed tips reddish and a yellow line joining the subspiracular stripe. Behind the head on T1 are paired projections with tips tinged reddish. Body green with numerous fine white dots. Dorsal line dark green, and subdorsal, lateral and ventral lines yellowish or whitish. Subspiracular stripe white, sometimes mixed with pink, or entirely yellow. The subspiracular stripe is in two parts, from T1 to anterior T3, and from base of true leg on T3 to A8. The body ends in paired anal points. **SIMILAR SPECIES** Jersey Emerald has no obvious distinguishing features but at present is confined to the Channel Islands. **HABITATS** Coastal and wet upland grasslands, heathland, moorland, scrub (including planted scrub on restored mineral and waste sites), vegetated shingle and open woodland. **FOODPLANTS** Broom, Gorse and Petty Whin. **FIELD NOTES** Jul–early Jun. Pupates in a network cocoon on the ground. Overwinters as a very small larva.

JERSEY EMERALD
Pseudoterpna coronillaria

PLATE 33
70.298 (1665a)

Channel Islands. Resident on Alderney and Jersey. **SIMILAR SPECIES** Grass Emerald. **HABITATS** Open, coastal slopes with grassland and scrub on Alderney, and a golf course containing Broom and Gorse on Jersey. **FOODPLANTS** Has been found on Prostrate Broom on Alderney. On Broom and Gorse in Europe. **FIELD NOTES** Not fully understood in the Channel Islands; likely to be similar to Grass Emerald.

LARGE EMERALD
Geometra papilionaria

PLATE 33
70.299 (1666)

Common. **FIELD CHARACTERS** Head notched and brownish. Body green or brown with numerous fine white dots. The green form has a purplish-brown dorsal stripe or band, entire or restricted to A6–A8. Paired purplish-brown or green dorsal projections as follows: two on T1, and one on each of T2 and A2–A5, the largest being on T2 and A3. There is considerable variation in the size of projections between larvae. Subspiracular stripe yellow, sometimes obscured by brown or purplish-brown lateral shading A6–A7. Anal clasper purplish brown. The brown form is brown with the white dots arranged in wavy stripes. Just before overwintering, the larva is mainly brown, with green on A2–A4. During the winter it is brown and covered with a good sprinkling of algae, and tiny flakes of bark. **HABITATS** Well-grown hedgerows, scrub on grassland, heathland and limestone pavement, woodland, and woody vegetation along lakes and streamsides. **FOODPLANTS** Alder, Beech, Downy and Silver birches (especially seed catkins of birches in late summer), and Hazel. **FIELD NOTES** Jul–Jun. The overwintering larva sits on a silk pad on a twig, chewing bark fragments from the twig and placing them on its body. Pupates in a network cocoon in debris on the ground.

BLOTCHED EMERALD
Comibaena bajularia

PLATE 34
70.300 (1667)

Local. Most frequent in central southern and south-east England; local elsewhere. **FIELD CHARACTERS** Body stumpy, brown or dark grey with white dots, and sparsely covered with short, spiky hairs. Small pieces of the foodplant are cut and attached to these hairs, obscuring most of the body. There is a small brown projection laterally on A1–A4. **HABITATS** Hedgerow trees in wooded landscapes, and woodland. **FOODPLANTS** Pedunculate and Sessile oaks. **FIELD NOTES** Late Jul–early Jun. Pupates in a network cocoon in debris on the ground. Overwinters as a small larva.

SMALL EMERALD
Hemistola chrysoprasaria

PLATE 34
70.302 (1673)

Local. Mainly in the southern half of England. Has decreased significantly in abundance in recent decades. **FIELD CHARACTERS** Head notched and brown. Body green with a pair of forward-facing, pointed dorsal projections anteriorly on T1. Dorsal line dark green. Subdorsal and lateral lines, and subspiracular and ventral stripes, comprise numerous tiny white dots. Anal flap pointed. The larva is brown during the winter. **HABITATS** Mainly on calcareous soils, in gardens, hedgerows, scrub, old quarries and open woodland. **FOODPLANTS** Traveller's-joys. **FIELD NOTES** Jul or Aug–Jun. Pupates in a network cocoon among the foodplant.

LITTLE EMERALD
Jodis lactearia

PLATE 34
70.303 (1674)

Common. Fairly widespread in the southern half of England and in Ireland. Local in northern England and very local in Scotland. **FIELD CHARACTERS** Head deeply notched, and brown with a whitish streak on the front of each lobe. Body green with a pair of forward-facing, pointed dorsal projections anteriorly on T1. The dorsal line may be red and continuous, and expanded laterally between segments, or it may comprise a series of red spots that are edged yellow laterally. The spiracular line is green and there is sometimes a red subspiracular stripe. The body ends in a pointed anal flap. **SIMILAR SPECIES** Small Grass Emerald and Southern Grass Emerald are covered in numerous fine white dots, and they are unlikely to be found on the same foodplant as Little Emerald. Southern Grass Emerald is yellowish green whereas Small Grass Emerald is green, and each occurs in different habitats. Marbled Pug, Pinion-spotted Pug and Mottled Pug do not have notched heads. **HABITATS** Well-grown hedgerows, scrub on grassland, heathland and moorland, and in open woodland and woodland rides. **FOODPLANTS** Bilberry, Downy and Silver birches, Blackthorn, Bramble, Broom, Sweet Chestnut, Dogwood, Hawthorn, Hazel, Hornbeam, oaks, Sycamore and willows. **FIELD NOTES** Late Jun–early Oct. Pupates in a network cocoon. Overwinters as a pupa.

SUSSEX EMERALD
Thalera fimbrialis

PLATE 34
70.304 (1672)

RDB. Protected species. Suspected immigrant. One known colony in Kent. **FIELD CHARACTERS** Head deeply notched and pale brown. Body green with numerous fine white dots. Body green with a pair of forward-facing, pointed dorsal projections anteriorly on T1. Dorsal line may be dark green, but often red, edged with pinkish shading, and sometimes reduced to a series of reddish patches with slight shading. Subdorsal line and spiracular stripe faint, and pale green or yellowish. The body ends in a pointed anal flap. **HABITATS** Vegetated shingle, but where the shingle has had finer chalky materials added as a result of development. **FOODPLANTS** Mainly Wild Carrot growing among sheltered, taller vegetation. Larvae are occasionally found on Common and Hoary ragworts growing near Wild Carrot. **FIELD NOTES** Aug–early Jun. Pupates in a network cocoon. Pupation site not known in the wild.

COMMON EMERALD
Hemithea aestivaria

PLATE 34
70.305 (1669)

Common. Widespread in England, Wales and Ireland, except on higher ground. Very local in Scotland. **FIELD CHARACTERS** There are green, greyish-brown and pale brown forms. Head deeply notched and brownish. The green form has a green body with a pair of pointed dorsal projections anteriorly on T1. Dorsal line green A2–A6, and greyish brown T1–A1 and posteriorly from A6. Paired whitish subdorsal marks A2–A8, and an angled greyish-brown lateral stripe on A1. There is considerable variation in the extent of greyish-brown markings, from entirely absent to dominant. The body ends in a pointed anal flap. The pale brown form has forward-pointing, V-shaped whitish or pale markings across the dorsum on abdominal segments. During the winter, the larva is brown and covered with a sprinkling of algae, and sometimes small pieces of lichen. **HABITATS** Gardens and urban parks, hedgerows, scrub and woodland. **FOODPLANTS** Wide variety, including Aspen, wild and cultivated barberries, birches, Blackthorn, cinquefoils, clovers, currants, Dog-rose, hawthorns, Hazel, Honeysuckle, jasmines, Knotgrass, limes, Mugwort, oaks, plantains, Sea-buckthorn and willows. **FIELD NOTES** Jul–early Jun. Feeds at night. Pupates in a network cocoon among the foodplant.

SMALL GRASS EMERALD
Chlorissa viridata

PLATE 34
70.306 (1670)

Na. Fairly frequent in the New Forest, Hampshire, and on the Dorset heaths; otherwise very localised. No confirmed records from the Channel Islands. **FIELD CHARACTERS** Head notched and greenish, with the pointed tips reddish. Behind the head on T1 are paired projections with tips tinged reddish. Body green with numerous fine white dots. Dorsal stripe usually reddish or purplish, sometimes comprising dashes, and edged with yellow or white between abdominal segments. It may also be reduced to a green dorsal line. Subspiracular stripe yellowish, with purplish marks below, A6–A7. The body ends in a pointed anal flap. **SIMILAR SPECIES** Little Emerald, Southern Grass Emerald, Marbled Pug, Pinion-spotted Pug and Mottled Pug. **HABITATS** Humid and wet heathland and raised mosses, preferring areas of shorter vegetation not dominated by grasses. **FOODPLANTS** Birches, Gorse, Cross-leaved Heath, Heather and Creeping Willow. Also reported on Bramble, Hawthorn, Tormentil and Petty Whin. **FIELD NOTES** Late Jul–Sep. Pupates in a delicate network cocoon among vegetation or on the ground. Overwinters as a pupa.

Small Grass Emerald lava

SOUTHERN GRASS EMERALD
Chlorissa cloraria

PLATE 34
70.307 (1670a)

Channel Islands; suspected immigrant. Resident on Guernsey and Jersey, and recorded once on Portland, Dorset. **FIELD CHARACTERS** Head notched, yellowish green and tinged pale brownish, with the pointed tips reddish. Behind the head on T1 are paired projections with tips tinged reddish. Body yellowish green with numerous fine white dots. Dorsal stripe red, and subspiracular stripe greenish yellow with reddish marks below, A6–A7. Abdomen terminates in a pointed anal flap. **SIMILAR SPECIES** Little Emerald, Small Grass Emerald, Marbled Pug, Pinion-spotted Pug and Mottled Pug. **HABITATS** On Guernsey, on open coastal cliff tops and slopes with sparse or short grassy vegetation and scattered scrub. **FOODPLANTS** Not known in the wild, but probably Common Bird's-foot-trefoil. **FIELD NOTES** Early stages have not been found in the wild. Probably late Jun–Sep. Overwinters as a pupa.

NOCTUOIDEA
NOTODONTIDAE PROMINENT, KITTEN AND PROCESSIONARY MOTHS

This is a family of 2,500–3,000 species worldwide, with 22 species resident in the British Isles and another transitory resident that may no longer be here. The larva of one species, Oak Processionary, constructs a nest when half-grown and has irritant hairs that can cause an unpleasant itchy rash. Some species have fleshy dorsal projections. In the subfamilies Cerurinae and Dicranurinae the anal claspers have been modified into tails, and in the Notodontinae and Phalerinae the anal claspers are smaller than the prolegs.

Puss Moth ×1.25

Scarce Prominent ×1.25

Lobster Moth final-instar larva, lateral view

Lobster Moth penultimate-instar larva in threatening posture. Note the opening of the gland on T1 from which it can eject formic acid

THAUMETOPOEINAE

OAK PROCESSIONARY
Thaumetopoea processionea

PLATE 34
71.001 (2022)

Immigrant; naturalised adventive in south-east England; resident in Channel Islands. The moth is considered to be a pest in Great Britain and is subject to a government-led programme of survey and management to minimise populations, spread and impacts. Larvae carry irritating hairs that cause skin rashes of concern to public health, and, when populations are high, larvae can cause defoliation of host trees. **FIELD CHARACTERS** Body dark grey in a broad dorsal band, mottled pale grey laterally, and whitish grey below the spiracular level. Pinacula yellow with tufts of long whitish hairs. **HABITATS** Urban parks and open spaces, and woodland. Occasionally in gardens. **FOODPLANTS** In England, mainly on pedunculate and Turkey oaks, and reported on Holm Oak and ornamental oak species. During outbreaks in Europe, larvae may feed on other broadleaf tree species, including Beech. **FIELD NOTES** Late Apr–late Jun. Larvae construct a communal silken nest when half-grown, usually on a trunk or branch, often high up. Usually feed at night after leaving their nest in procession, following a silk trail left by the leading larva. They pupate in the larval nest. Overwinters on a twig as an egg in a solid, single-layer egg mass known as a plaque.

CERURINAE

PUSS MOTH
Cerura vinula

PLATE 34
71.003 (1995)

Common. Widespread, but infrequent in upland areas and rare in the Channel Islands. **FIELD CHARACTERS** First-instar larva black, with subdorsal projections anteriorly on T1, and black whip-like tails formed from modified anal claspers. When the larva is disturbed, the tails extend red filaments that have a white section near the base. The final-instar larva has a green body laterally, with a saddle-shaped, white-edged purplish-brown dorsal patch. The patch extends posteriorly to A10, and laterally to a point on A4, narrowing to a red hump on T3 and broadening to T1. T1 has red encircling the head with a black subdorsal spot on either side, and below, within the red, is a slit from which formic acid can be squirted. When the larva is fully fed the whole body develops a purplish colour. **HABITATS** Wide variety, including fens, gardens and urban parks, heathland, hedgerows, marshes, moorland, sand dunes, scrub and woodland. **FOODPLANTS** Poplars including Aspen, and willows. **FIELD NOTES** Jun–Sep. Most frequently found on saplings and regrowth following cutting, and in sunny situations. Pupates in a very tough cocoon made of chewed bark and silk on a tree trunk. Overwinters as a pupa, sometimes over two winters.

SALLOW KITTEN
Furcula furcula

PLATE 34
71.005 (1997)

Common. Frequent in England and Wales, less so in Scotland and Ireland. **FIELD CHARACTERS** First instar black with two green dorsal blotches, subdorsal projections anteriorly on T1, and black whip-like tails, each with two whitish sections, formed from modified anal claspers. When the larva is disturbed, the tails extend red filaments. The final-instar larva has a green body laterally, with a saddle-shaped, yellow-edged purplish-grey or purplish-brown dorsal patch. The patch extends posteriorly to A10, and laterally, where it is mixed yellowish, to its lowest point on A4, narrowing to a hump on T2, and broadening onto T1. There is a small dark subdorsal projection on T1 anteriorly. **SIMILAR SPECIES** Alder Kitten does not share a foodplant with Sallow Kitten and Poplar Kitten. Poplar Kitten has a gap in the dorsal patch on T3, distinguishing it from Sallow Kitten, which has a continuous patch. **HABITATS** Wide variety, including fens, heathland, hedgerows, marshes, moorland, sand dunes, scrub and open woodland. Occasionally in urban areas. **FOODPLANTS** Mainly Goat, Grey and White willows, but reported on a wide variety of other willows, and poplars including Aspen. Also reported on Beech. **FIELD NOTES** May–Jul and Aug–Sep, in two generations, or Jul–Sep where there is one in Scotland and Ireland. Pupates in a very tough cocoon made of chewed bark and silk on a branch or tree trunk. Overwinters as a pupa.

ALDER KITTEN
Furcula bicuspis

PLATE 34
71.006 (1996)

Local. Regularly recorded in several discrete areas. A single record from Ireland. **FIELD CHARACTERS** First instar black with two green dorsal blotches, subdorsal projections anteriorly on T1, and black whip-like tails, each with two whitish sections, formed from modified anal claspers. When the larva is disturbed, the tails extend filaments. The final-instar larva has a green body laterally, with a saddle-shaped, yellow- or white-edged brown dorsal patch. The patch extends posteriorly to A10, laterally, where it is mixed with orangey brown, to its lowest point on A4, and to the posterior part of T3. There is a gap of green with a further brown patch from the hump on T2 and expanding onto T1. There is a small dark subdorsal projection on T1 anteriorly. **SIMILAR SPECIES** Sallow Kitten and Poplar Kitten. **HABITATS** Mainly woodland, including open birch woodland on hillsides, and streamside alders. Occasionally in gardens. **FOODPLANTS** Alder and birches. **FIELD NOTES** Late Jun–early Sep. Pupates in a very tough cocoon made of chewed bark and silk on the stem of the foodplant. Overwinters as a pupa.

POPLAR KITTEN
Furcula bifida

PLATE 34
71.007 (1998)

Local. Quite widespread in England and eastern Wales; very local elsewhere. **FIELD CHARACTERS** First instar dark brown with two green dorsal blotches, subdorsal projections anteriorly on T1, and black whip-like tails, each with two whitish sections, formed from modified anal claspers. When the larva is disturbed, the tails extend dark red filaments. The final-instar larva has a green body laterally, with a saddle-shaped, yellow- or white-edged purplish-brown dorsal patch, extending posteriorly to A10, laterally, where it is mixed with pale brown, to its lowest point on A4, and anteriorly to A1. There is a gap of green with a further purplish-brown patch from the hump on T2 and expanding onto T1. There is a small dark subdorsal projection on T1 anteriorly. **SIMILAR SPECIES** Sallow Kitten and Alder Kitten. **HABITATS** Poplar plantations and individual trees in a variety of locations, often in woodland, and sometimes in gardens and urban parks. **FOODPLANTS** Mainly poplars, including Aspen. Also reported on willows. **FIELD NOTES** Late Jun–mid-Sep. Pupates in a very tough cocoon made of chewed bark and silk on the trunk of a tree. Overwinters as a pupa.

DICRANURINAE

LOBSTER MOTH
Stauropus fagi

PLATE 35
71.009 (1999)

Common. Widespread and sometimes frequent in the south, and in south-west Ireland. **FIELD CHARACTERS** First-instar larva is ant-like in appearance, with tails formed from modified anal claspers, and long true legs. The final instar has a brown body, with very long true legs, and anal tails. Dorsal humps paired on each segment A1–A5, either a black spot below the spiracle on A1–A2 or just a black dash, and a brown spiracular line. There is a slit ventrally on T1 from which formic acid can be produced. The posterior segments from A7 are held raised over the back of the larva, and A7 and especially A8 are expanded laterally. **HABITATS** Mature and long-established woodland. **FOODPLANTS** Mainly Beech, birches, Hazel and oaks. Also reported on Alder, Apple, Crab Apple, Blackthorn, Dog-rose, Hawthorn, limes, Holm Oak, Pear, Walnut and willows. **FIELD NOTES** Late Jun–Sep. Pupates among fallen leaves. Overwinters as a pupa.

NOTODONTINAE

MARBLED BROWN
Drymonia dodonaea

PLATE 35
71.010 (2014)

Local. Widespread in much of England and Wales, very local in northern England and Scotland, and rare in Ireland. **FIELD CHARACTERS** Body green with a green dorsal stripe edged with yellow lines, and a yellow subdorsal line, most noticeable anteriorly and posteriorly. Body colour is bluish green above and yellowish green below the subdorsal line. Spiracular stripe yellow with red spots, edged above with a red line. **HABITATS** Mature and long-established woodland. **FOODPLANTS** Pedunculate and Sessile oaks. **FIELD NOTES** Late Jun–early Sep. Pupates in a cocoon in the ground. Overwinters as a pupa.

LUNAR MARBLED BROWN
Drymonia ruficornis

PLATE 35
71.011 (2015)

Common. Has increased significantly in abundance in recent decades. Widespread in much of England, Wales and Ireland. More local in northern England and Scotland. **FIELD CHARACTERS** Body bluish green with a yellow subdorsal stripe and yellow spiracular stripe, sometimes mixed with white and expanded to form a ring around each abdominal spiracle. **HABITATS** Hedgerows and woodland. Sometimes gardens and urban parks. **FOODPLANTS** Pedunculate and Sessile oaks. **FIELD NOTES** Late May–Aug. Pupates just below the surface of the ground. Overwinters as a pupa.

IRON PROMINENT
Notodonta dromedarius

PLATE 35
71.012 (2000)

Common. **FIELD CHARACTERS** Body various shades of grey, brown or green. Dorsal humps on A1–A4 and A8. Dorsal stripe variable in width and extent, always a broad brown band T1–T3, sometimes narrowing around humps to A4, and often a stripe from the hump on A8 posteriorly. Subspiracular stripe pale A2–A6, where it is angled to end at the base of the proleg. The segments from A7 posteriorly, or at least their ventral area, may be darker than the rest of the body, and are held raised when the larva is at rest. When the larva is fully fed and looking for a pupation site, the humps reduce in size and the colour darkens. **HABITATS** Wide variety, including fens, heathland, marshes, moorland, scrub and woodland. Sometimes in gardens and urban parks. **FOODPLANTS** Mainly Alder, and Downy and Silver birches. Also reported on Grey Alder, Hazel, oaks, and Eared and Grey willows. **FIELD NOTES** Mid-Jun–late Jul and Sep–early Oct, in two generations, and mainly Aug in the north where there is one. Pupates in the ground. Overwinters as a pupa.

PEBBLE PROMINENT
Notodonta ziczac

PLATE 35
71.013 (2003)

Common. **FIELD CHARACTERS** Body whitish grey or whitish brown, sometimes tinged pinkish, with dorsal humps on A2, A3 and A8. Two white lines enclose a dorsal stripe that is concolorous with the main part of the body, except broader and darker on T1–T3 and anteriorly on A2, and sometimes A3. Subspiracular line white, usually ending on A6, where it is angled to end at the base of the proleg, sometimes also extended to A9 and absent T3–A1. The segments from A7 posteriorly may contrast in colour from the rest of the body, being dark reddish brown or pale orangey brown, and are held raised when the larva is at rest. When the larva is fully fed and searching for a pupation site, the humps reduce in size. **HABITATS** Wide variety, including fens, gardens and urban parks, heathland, hedgerows, marshes, moorland, sand dunes, scrub, river valleys and woodland. **FOODPLANTS** Poplars including Aspen, and willows. **FIELD NOTES** Jun–Jul and Aug–late Sep in two generations in the south, and May–Sep in one generation in the north. Pupates in the ground. Overwinters as a pupa.

GREAT PROMINENT
Peridea anceps

PLATE 35
71.016 (2005)

Local. A widespread species in the southern half of England and in Wales; very local further north and in Scotland. **FIELD CHARACTERS** Body green with a green dorsal stripe edged with yellow lines, and subdorsal line comprising widely spaced yellow dots. Diagonal lateral stripes on abdominal segments, orange above and yellow below. There is an orange and yellow stripe running from the lower lateral part of the head across T1 and T2. Spiracles white. When the larva is fully fed the colour darkens. **HABITATS** Hedgerows, trees in well-wooded landscapes, and woodland. **FOODPLANTS** Pedunculate and Sessile oaks. **FIELD NOTES** Late May–early Aug. Pupates in the ground. Overwinters as a pupa.

SWALLOW PROMINENT
Pheosia tremula

PLATE 35
71.017 (2007)

Common. Widespread in England and Wales; local in Scotland and Ireland. **FIELD CHARACTERS** There are green and brownish forms, and both have a hump on A8 raised to a point. The green form has a shiny body and is whitish green dorsally and green laterally. Subspiracular stripe yellow with a white spot below each spiracle, a transverse black line across the hump on A8, and reddish-brown shading edging the anal flap. Spiracles mostly black, but white on T1 and A8 and sometimes A7. The dark form is very variable but generally is shiny greenish brown or greyish, sometimes mixed whitish, with brownish dorsal patches edged dark grey posteriorly. The dark grey extends laterally as transverse stripes to the spiracles. There is a transverse black line across the hump on A8, but no subspiracular stripe. **HABITATS** Wide variety, including fens, gardens and urban parks, heathland, hedgerows, marshes, moorland, sand dunes, scrub, river valleys and woodland. **FOODPLANTS** Poplars including Aspen, and willows. **FIELD NOTES** Jun–Jul and late Aug–Oct in two generations in the south, and Jul–Sep where there is one in the north. The first-generation larvae pupate in a cocoon spun among leaves and the second generation in the ground. Overwinters as a pupa.

LESSER SWALLOW PROMINENT
Pheosia gnoma

PLATE 35
71.018 (2006)

Common. **FIELD CHARACTERS** Body shiny purplish brown with a yellow subspiracular stripe. There is a hump on A8 raised to a black point, with a transverse stripe or band extending laterally to the spiracular level. Spiracles black and there is reddish-brown shading edging the anal flap. **HABITATS** Wide variety, including heathland, moorland, sand dunes, scrub, waste ground and woodland. **FOODPLANTS** Downy and Silver birches. **FIELD NOTES** Jun–Jul and late Aug–Oct, in two generations over most of the area, and Jul–Sep where there is one in northern Scotland. Pupates in a cocoon in the ground. Overwinters as a pupa.

WHITE PROMINENT
Leucodonta bicoloria

PLATE 35
71.019 (2012)

Resident. Occurs in a localised area of Co. Kerry in Ireland. **FIELD CHARACTERS** Body shiny whitish green, with darker green dorsal line and subdorsal and lateral stripes. Supraspiracular line and subspiracular stripe yellowish; the stripe may be reduced to spots A2–A5. Spiracles black. **HABITATS** Woodland with mature birch trees. **FOODPLANTS** Birches. **FIELD NOTES** Jun–Aug. Pupates among leaf litter or just below ground. Overwinters as a pupa.

PALE PROMINENT
Pterostoma palpina

PLATE 36
71.020 (2011)

Common. Widespread throughout except in northern Scotland, where it is localised. **FIELD CHARACTERS** Body bluish green with dorsal stripe as body colour, edged with white lines, and a white subdorsal line. Supraspiracular stripe yellow or white, tinged yellow, sometimes mixed pink, and edged above with a black line. **HABITATS** Wide variety, including fens, gardens and urban parks, heathland, hedgerows, marshes, moorland, sand dunes, scrub, river valleys and woodland. **FOODPLANTS** Poplars including Aspen, and willows, preferring saplings and regrowth following cutting. **FIELD NOTES** Jun–Jul and late Aug–Sep in two generations in the south, and Jul–Aug where there is one in the north. Pupates in or on the ground. Overwinters as a pupa.

COXCOMB PROMINENT
Ptilodon capucina

PLATE 36
71.021 (2008)

Common. **FIELD CHARACTERS** Body green, or occasionally pink. Dorsal line dark green, spiracular stripe yellow with red spots posterior to the spiracles A1–A8, and a white patch on T1 and T2. There is a pair of red dorsal projections on A8. True legs and crochets red. The larva has a characteristic resting posture with the posterior segments from A7 raised, and the thorax bent backwards over the abdomen, prominently exposing the red legs. **HABITATS** Gardens and urban parks, scrub and woodland. **FOODPLANTS** Wide variety of woody trees and shrubs, including Alder, Aspen, Beech, birches, Sweet Chestnut, Hawthorn, Hazel, Hornbeam, limes, Field Maple, oaks, poplars, roses, Rowan, Sycamore and willows. **FIELD NOTES** Jun–Jul and mid-Aug–Oct where there are two generations in the south, and Jun–Aug where there is one in the north and Ireland. Pupates in a cocoon in the ground. Overwinters as a pupa.

MAPLE PROMINENT
Ptilodon cucullina

PLATE 36
71.022 (2009)

Local. Appears to be increasing in parts of south-east England and the Midlands. Very local in the west. **FIELD CHARACTERS** There are green and brown forms. The green form is whitish green with yellow markings laterally on abdominal segments. Dorsal line dark green, expanded into a band T1–A2, and subdorsal line dark green A2–A9, with a yellowish-tinged whitish stripe below that extends forwards onto T1. There are dorsal humps A2–A7, and on A8 a larger hump raised to a pair of red or orangey points. The larva characteristically rests with the posterior segments from A7 raised. The brown form is whitish brown, tinged greyish, or pale orangey brown, and is otherwise similar in markings. **HABITATS** Mainly hedgerows, scrub and woodland, usually on chalk soils. Also found in gardens and urban areas on planted trees. **FOODPLANTS** Mainly Field Maple and Sycamore. Also reported on introduced maples. In north Devon, there are populations dependent on Sycamore in woodland where Field Maple is absent. **FIELD NOTES** Late Jun–Sep. Pupates in a tough cocoon in moss on a trunk, in leaf litter or in the ground. Overwinters as a pupa, sometimes over two winters.

SCARCE PROMINENT
Odontosia carmelita

PLATE 36
71.023 (2010)

Local. Quite widespread in south-east England, the Scottish Highlands and Ireland, but very local elsewhere. **FIELD CHARACTERS** Body bright green, heavily marked with yellow. Dorsal stripe green, edged with yellow patches, forming indistinct interrupted stripes. Subspiracular stripe yellow with a pinkish spot on each segment T1–A8. Body colour ventrally is mixed bluish green and dark green. Spiracles black surrounded by white rings. **HABITATS** Long-established woodland. **FOODPLANTS** Downy and Silver birches, preferring mature trees. **FIELD NOTES** May–Jul. Pupates in a cocoon in or on the ground. Overwinters as a pupa.

PLUMED PROMINENT
Ptilophora plumigera

PLATE 36
71.024 (2013)

Na. Occurs in several widely scattered locations in the south, south-east and East Anglia. **FIELD CHARACTERS** Head rather bulbous and green. Body whitish green, at least laterally. In one form there is a broad green dorsal band, edged with white subdorsal stripes, and in another form this band is whitish green. Lateral and spiracular lines white, sometimes tinged yellowish, and rather wavy. **HABITATS** Mature Field Maple trees in hedgerows and woodland, on calcareous soils. Continuous presence of mature Field Maple over several centuries may be important for this species' survival. **FOODPLANTS** Mainly Field Maple. Also reported on Sycamore. **FIELD NOTES** Apr–Jun. Rests on the underside of a leaf, in a P-shape with the anterior end curled round. Pupates in a cocoon on the ground. Overwinters as an egg.

PHALERINAE

BUFF-TIP
Phalera bucephala

PLATE 36
71.025 (1994)

Common. Widespread in England, Wales and Ireland; more local in Scotland. **FIELD CHARACTERS** Body black and covered with pale grey hairs. Subdorsal, two lateral, spiracular and subspiracular lines yellowish, although the lateral and spiracular lines are sometimes mixed whitish. Each segment has a yellowish-orange transverse band. **HABITATS** Gardens and urban parks, hedgerows, scrub and open woodland. **FOODPLANTS** Most frequently birches, Hazel, oaks and willows. Reported on a wide variety of other woody plants, including Alder, Beech, Blackthorn, cherries, Sweet Chestnut, elms, False-acacia, Hawthorn, Hornbeam, Persian Ironwood, Laburnum, limes, Wild Plum, Roble, Rowan and Sycamore. **FIELD NOTES** Jul–early Oct. Larvae are gregarious when young, and skeletonise leaves as they feed communally. Older larvae feed singly, but stripped leaves on a branch often indicate their presence. Pupates in a chamber in the ground, without a cocoon. Overwinters as a pupa.

PYGAERINAE

CHOCOLATE-TIP
Clostera curtula

PLATE 36
71.027 (2019)

Local. Widespread in the southern half of England, and into eastern Wales. Also occurs very locally in Scotland. **FIELD CHARACTERS** Covered with tufts of whitish hair. Body colour is variable and may include shades of grey, white, yellow or orange, mottled with black, with yellowish or orangey subdorsal and lateral verrucae. Dorsal line black. A pair of closely spaced black dorsal verrucae surrounded by a round black patch on A1 and A8. **SIMILAR SPECIES** In Small Chocolate-tip the black patch on A1 and A8 is oval, not round, although in Ireland this patch around the dorsal verrucae may be absent. Scarce Chocolate-tip is distinguished from the other two species by having a white spot either side of the hump on A1. **HABITATS** Wide variety, including fens, gardens and urban parks, heathland, hedgerows, marshes, plantations, sand dunes, scrub and woodland. **FOODPLANTS** Poplars including Aspen, and willows, often preferring regrowth following cutting. **FIELD NOTES** May–Jun and Aug–Sep in two generations in the south, and Jul–Aug in Scotland where there is one. Feeds at night, hiding between spun leaves by day. Pupates between spun leaves of the foodplant. Overwinters as a pupa on the ground, having fallen with the leaves in autumn.

SMALL CHOCOLATE-TIP
Clostera pigra

PLATE 36
71.028 (2017)

Nb. Occurs in widely scattered areas. Very local in England and Wales, but rather more frequent in Scotland and Ireland. It appears to have become rarer in recent decades. **FIELD CHARACTERS** Covered with tufts of whitish hair. Body colour is variable and may include shades of grey, yellow or orange, mottled with black, with yellowish or orangey subdorsal and lateral verrucae. Dorsal line grey or black. A pair of black dorsal verrucae surrounded by an oval black patch on A1 and A8. In Ireland it appears that there is no oval black patch between these verrucae. **SIMILAR SPECIES** Chocolate-tip and Scarce Chocolate-tip. **HABITATS** Open habitats, including bogs, broads, dune-slacks, fens, wet heathland, limestone pavement (the Burren, Cos Clare and Galway, Ireland), marshes, moorland, raised mosses and open woodland. **FOODPLANTS** Mainly Creeping Willow, Eared Willow and Aspen. Also reported on suckers and regrowth of poplars and other willows. Prefers plants close to the ground. **FIELD NOTES** Late May–mid-Jul and Sep–early Oct in two generations in the south, and Aug–mid-Sep in the north where there is one. Feeds at night and hides between spun leaves by day. Pupates among spun leaves. Overwinters as a pupa.

SCARCE CHOCOLATE-TIP
Clostera anachoreta

PLATE 36
71.029 (2018)

RDB; immigrant. Transitory resident for several decades in periods between 1858 and 2000, most recently at Dungeness, Kent, but may no longer be so. **FIELD CHARACTERS** Covered with tufts of grey or pale brown hairs. Body grey speckled with black, with yellowish or orangey subdorsal and lateral verrucae. Dorsal stripe black, edged with yellow or white stripes. Subdorsal stripes yellow or white, often suffused with transverse bands of yellowish or orangey shading. A black dorsal hump with a pair of brown or reddish verrucae on A1 and A8, with a white subdorsal spot below the hump on A1. Black lateral patches A2–A8. **SIMILAR SPECIES** Chocolate-tip and Small Chocolate-tip. **HABITATS** Scrub among vegetated shingle at Dungeness. **FOODPLANTS** Mainly Grey Willow in Kent. Also reported on poplars including Aspen, and other willows. **FIELD NOTES** May–Jul and Aug–Sep, in two generations. Feeds at night, hiding between spun leaves by day. Pupates between spun leaves. Overwinters as a pupa on the ground, having fallen with the leaves in autumn.

PLATE 1

HEPIALIDAE SWIFT MOTHS

All species ×1.25

Common Swift (p. 72)
Korscheltellus lupulina

Orange Swift/Map-winged Swift/Ghost Moth (pp. 72–3)
Triodia sylvina/Korscheltellus fusconebulosa/Hepialus humuli

COSSIDAE GOAT AND LEOPARD MOTHS

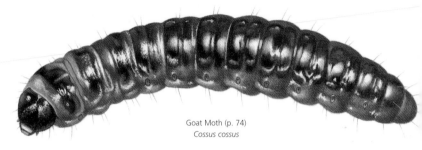

Goat Moth (p. 74)
Cossus cossus

Leopard Moth (p. 75)
Zeuzera pyrina

Reed Leopard (p. 75)
Phragmataecia castaneae

SESIIDAE CLEARWING MOTHS

Lunar Hornet Moth (p. 77)
Sesia bembeciformis

PLATE 2

LIMACODIDAE SLUG MOTHS

All species ×1.5

Festoon (p. 85)
Apoda limacodes

Triangle (p. 85)
Heterogenea asella

ZYGAENIDAE FORESTER AND BURNET MOTHS

Scarce Forester (p. 87)
Jordanita globulariae

Forester (p. 87)
Adscita statices

Cistus Forester (p. 87)
Adscita geryon

Transparent Burnet (p. 88)
Zygaena purpuralis

Slender Scotch Burnet (p. 88)
Zygaena loti

Scotch Burnet/Mountain Burnet (p. 88)
Zygaena exulans

New Forest Burnet (p. 88)
Zygaena viciae

Six-spot Burnet/Five-spot Burnet (p. 89)
Zygaena filipendulae/Zyyaena trifolii

Narrow-bordered Five-spot Burnet (p. 89)
Zygaena lonicerae

PLATE 3

PAPILIONIDAE SWALLOWTAIL BUTTERFLIES

×1.5

young larva

Swallowtail (p. 90)
Papilio machaon

HESPERIIDAE SKIPPERS all species ×1.75

Dingy Skipper (p. 91)
Erynnis tages

Grizzled Skipper (p. 92)
Pyrgus malvae

Chequered Skipper (p. 92)
Carterocephalus palaemon

diapausing

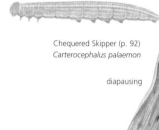

Essex Skipper (p. 92)
Thymelicus lineola

Small Skipper (p. 93)
Thymelicus sylvestris

Lulworth Skipper (p. 93)
Thymelicus acteon

Silver-spotted Skipper (p. 93)
Hesperia comma

Large Skipper (p. 94)
Ochlodes sylvanus

PLATE 4

PIERIDAE WHITE BUTTERFLIES

All species ×1.75

Wood White/Cryptic Wood White (p. 95)
Leptidea sinapis/L. juvernica

Orange-tip (p. 96)
Anthocharis cardamines

Large White (p. 96)
Pieris brassicae

Small White (p. 96)
Pieris rapae

Green-veined White (p. 97)
Pieris napi

Clouded Yellow (p. 97)
Colias croceus

Brimstone (p. 97)
Gonepteryx rhamni

PLATE 5

NYMPHALIDAE BROWN, FRITILLARY, ADMIRAL AND TORTOISESHELL BUTTERFLIES

All species ×1.75

Wall (p. 98)
Lasiommata megera

Speckled Wood (p. 99)
Pararge aegeria

Large Heath (p. 99)
Coenonympha tullia

Small Heath (p. 99)
Coenonympha pamphilus

Mountain Ringlet/Small Mountain Ringlet (p. 100)
Erebia epiphron

Scotch Argus (p. 100)
Erebia aethiops

Ringlet (p. 100)
Aphantopus hyperantus

Meadow Brown (p. 101)
Maniola jurtina

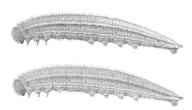

Gatekeeper/Hedge Brown (p. 101)
Pyronia tithonus

Marbled White (p. 101)
Melanargia galathea

Grayling (p. 102)
Hipparchia semele

PLATE 6

NYMPHALIDAE BROWN, FRITILLARY, ADMIRAL AND TORTOISESHELL BUTTERFLIES

All species ×1.75

Pearl-bordered Fritillary (p. 102)
Boloria euphrosyne

Small Pearl-bordered Fritillary (p. 102)
Boloria selene

Silver-washed Fritillary (p. 103)
Argynnis paphia

Dark Green Fritillary (p. 103)
Argynnis aglaja

High Brown Fritillary (p. 103)
Argynnis adippe

White Admiral (p. 104)
Limenitis camilla

Purple Emperor (p. 104)
Apatura iris

PLATE 7

NYMPHALIDAE BROWN, FRITILLARY, ADMIRAL AND TORTOISESHELL BUTTERFLIES

All species ×1.75

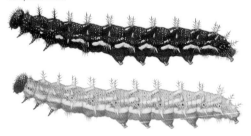

Red Admiral (p. 104)
Vanessa atalanta

Painted Lady (p. 105)
Vanessa cardui

Peacock (p. 105)
Aglais io

Small Tortoiseshell (p. 105)
Aglais urticae

young larva

Comma (p. 106)
Polygonia c-album

Marsh Fritillary (p. 106)
Euphydryas aurinia

Glanville Fritillary (p. 106)
Melitaea cinxia

RIODINIDAE METALMARK BUTTERFLIES

Heath Fritillary (p. 107)
Melitaea athalia

Duke of Burgundy (p. 108)
Hamearis lucina

PLATE 8

LYCAENIDAE COPPER, HAIRSTREAK AND BLUE BUTTERFLIES

All species ×2

Small Copper (p. 109)
Lycaena phlaeas

Brown Hairstreak (p. 110)
Thecla betulae

Purple Hairstreak (p. 110)
Favonius quercus

Green Hairstreak (p. 110)
Callophrys rubi

White-letter Hairstreak (p. 111)
Satyrium w-album

Black Hairstreak (p. 111)
Satyrium pruni

Long-tailed Blue (p. 111)
Lampides boeticus

Small Blue (p. 112)
Cupido minimus

Holly Blue (p. 112)
Celastrina argiolus

Silver-studded Blue (p. 113)
Plebejus argus

Brown Argus/Northern Brown Argus (pp. 113–14)
Aricia agestis/A. artaxerxes

Common Blue (p. 114)
Polyommatus icarus

Adonis Blue/Chalk Hill Blue (p. 115)
Polyommatus bellargus/P. coridon

PLATE 9

DREPANIDAE HOOK-TIP AND LUTESTRING MOTHS

All species ×1.25

young larva

Scalloped Hook-tip (p. 116)
Falcaria lacertinaria

Oak Hook-tip/Barred Hook-tip (pp. 116–17)
Watsonalla binaria/W. cultraria

Dusky Hook-tip/Pebble Hook-tip (p. 117)
Drepana curvatula/D. falcataria

Scarce Hook-tip (p. 117)
Sabra harpagula

Chinese Character (p. 118)
Cilix glaucata

young larva

Peach Blossom (p. 118)
Thyatira batis

Buff Arches (p. 118)
Habrosyne pyritoides

Figure of Eighty (p. 118)
Tethea ocularis

Poplar Lutestring (p. 119)
Tethea or

Satin Lutestring (p. 119)
Tetheella fluctuosa

Common Lutestring (p. 119)
Ochropacha duplaris

Oak Lutestring (p. 119)
Cymatophorina diluta

Frosted Green (p. 119)
Polyploca ridens

Yellow Horned (p. 120)
Achlya flavicornis

PLATE 10

LASIOCAMPIDAE EGGAR AND LAPPET MOTHS

All species ×1.25

December Moth (p. 121)
Poecilocampa populi

Pale Eggar (p. 121)
Trichiura crataegi

Lackey (p. 122)
Malacosoma neustria

Ground Lackey (p. 122)
Malacosoma castrensis

Small Eggar (p. 122)
Eriogaster lanestris

Grass Eggar (p. 123)
Lasiocampa trifolii

Oak Eggar (p. 123)
Lasiocampa quercus

pre-diapause

PLATE 11

LASIOCAMPIDAE EGGAR AND LAPPET MOTHS

All species ×1.25

Fox Moth (p. 123)
Macrothylacia rubi

young larva

Pine-tree Lappet (p. 124)
Dendrolimus pini

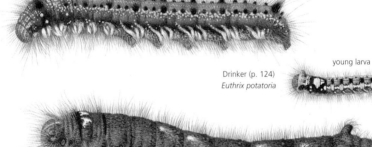

young larva

Drinker (p. 124)
Euthrix potatoria

Lappet (p. 124)
Gastropacha quercifolia

ENDROMIDAE

Kentish Glory (p. 125)
Endromis versicolora

SATURNIIDAE EMPEROR MOTHS

Emperor Moth (p. 126)
Saturnia pavonia

young larva

PLATE 12

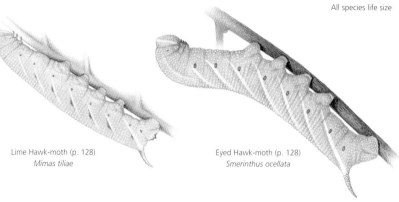

Lime Hawk-moth (p. 128)
Mimas tiliae

Eyed Hawk-moth (p. 128)
Smerinthus ocellata

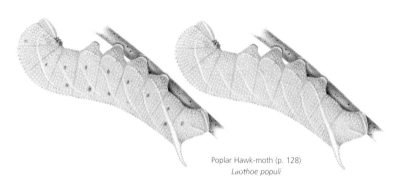

Poplar Hawk-moth (p. 128)
Laothoe populi

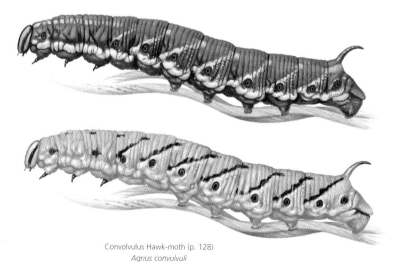

Convolvulus Hawk-moth (p. 128)
Agrius convolvuli

PLATE 13

SPHINGIDAE HAWK-MOTHS

All species life size

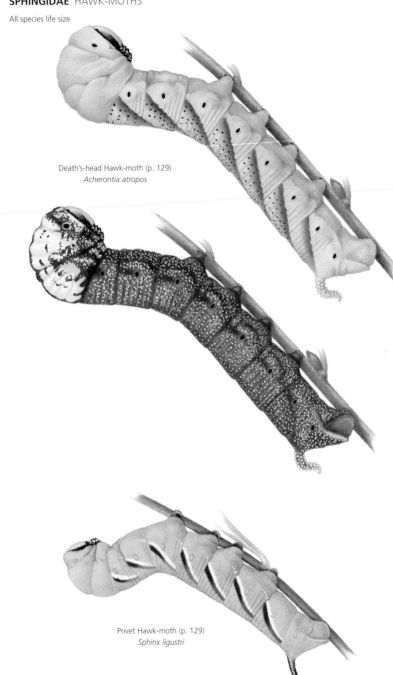

Death's-head Hawk-moth (p. 129)
Acherontia atropos

Privet Hawk-moth (p. 129)
Sphinx ligustri

PLATE 14

SPHINGIDAE HAWK-MOTHS

All species life size

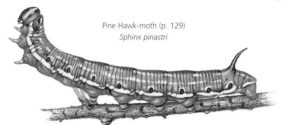

Pine Hawk-moth (p. 129)
Sphinx pinastri

Narrow-bordered Bee Hawk-moth (p. 129)
Hemaris tityus

Broad-bordered Bee Hawk-moth (p. 130)
Hemaris fuciformis

Humming-bird Hawk-moth (p. 130)
Macroglossum stellatarum

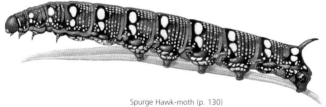

Spurge Hawk-moth (p. 130)
Hyles euphorbiae

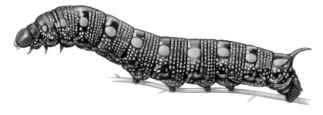

Bedstraw Hawk-moth (p. 130)
Hyles gallii

PLATE 15

SPHINGIDAE HAWK-MOTHS

All species life size

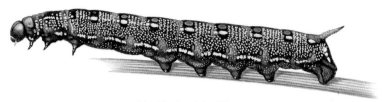

Striped Hawk-moth (p. 131)
Hyles livornica

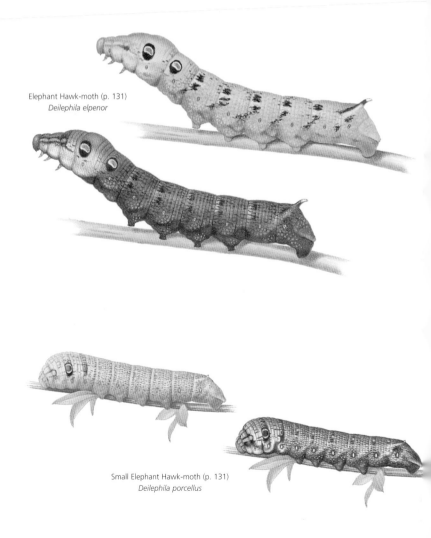

Elephant Hawk-moth (p. 131)
Deilephila elpenor

Small Elephant Hawk-moth (p. 131)
Deilephila porcellus

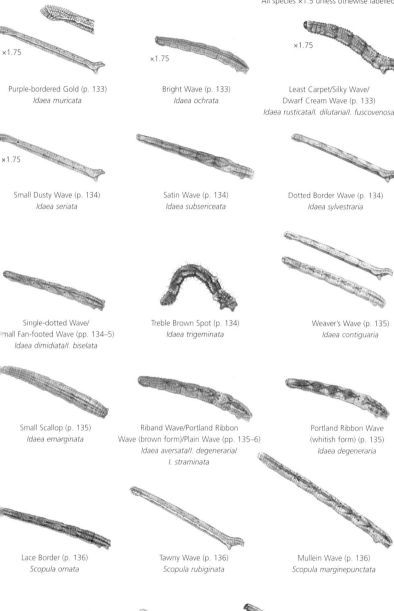

PLATE 16

GEOMETRIDAE LOOPER MOTHS

All species ×1.5 unless othewise labelled

×1.75

Purple-bordered Gold (p. 133)
Idaea muricata

×1.75

Bright Wave (p. 133)
Idaea ochrata

×1.75

Least Carpet/Silky Wave/
Dwarf Cream Wave (p. 133)
Idaea rusticata/I. dilutaria/I. fuscovenosa

×1.75

Small Dusty Wave (p. 134)
Idaea seriata

Satin Wave (p. 134)
Idaea subsericeata

Dotted Border Wave (p. 134)
Idaea sylvestraria

Single-dotted Wave/
mall Fan-footed Wave (pp. 134–5)
Idaea dimidiata/I. biselata

Treble Brown Spot (p. 134)
Idaea trigeminata

Weaver's Wave (p. 135)
Idaea contiguaria

Small Scallop (p. 135)
Idaea emarginata

Riband Wave/Portland Ribbon
Wave (brown form)/Plain Wave (pp. 135–6)
*Idaea aversata/I. degeneraria/
I. straminata*

Portland Ribbon Wave
(whitish form) (p. 135)
Idaea degeneraria

Lace Border (p. 136)
Scopula ornata

Tawny Wave (p. 136)
Scopula rubiginata

Mullein Wave (p. 136)
Scopula marginepunctata

b-angled Wave/Small Blood-vein/Lesser Cream
Wave/Smoky Wave/Rosy Wave (pp. 136–8)
*copula nigropunctata/S. imitaria/S. immutata/
S. ternata/S. emutaria*

Cream Wave (p. 137)
Scopula floslactata

PLATE 17

GEOMETRIDAE LOOPER MOTHS

All species ×1.5

Blood-vein (p. 138)
Timandra comae

Dingy Mocha (p. 138)
Cyclophora pendularia

Mocha (p. 139)
Cyclophora annularia

Birch Mocha (p. 139)
Cyclophora albipunctata

Blair's Mocha (p. 139)
Cyclophora puppillaria

Jersey Mocha (p. 139)
Cyclophora ruficiliaria

False Mocha/Clay Triple-lines (p. 140)
Cyclophora porata/C. linearia

Maiden's Blush (p. 140)
Cyclophora punctaria

Vestal (p. 140)
Rhodometra sacraria

Oblique Striped (p. 141)
Phibalapteryx virgata

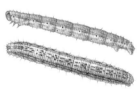

Lead Belle/July Belle (p. 141)
Scotopteryx mucronata/S. luridata

Spanish Carpet (p. 141)
Scotopteryx peribolata

Chalk Carpet/Shaded Broad-bar (p. 142)
Scotopteryx bipunctaria/S. chenopodiata

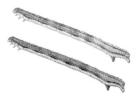

Oblique Carpet (p. 142)
Orthonama vittata

PLATE 18

GEOMETRIDAE LOOPER MOTHS

All species ×1.5

Red Carpet (p. 143)
Xanthorhoe decoloraria

Garden Carpet (p. 143)
Xanthorhoe fluctuata

Balsam Carpet (p. 143)
Xanthorhoe biriviata

Royal Mantle (p. 144)
Catarhoe cuculata

Ruddy Carpet (p. 145)
Catarhoe rubidata

Yellow Shell (p. 145)
Camptogramma bilineata

Small Argent & Sable (p. 145)
Epirrhoe tristata

Common Carpet/Wood Carpet (pp. 145–6)
Epirrhoe alternata/E. rivata

Galium Carpet (p. 146)
Epirrhoe galiata

Cloaked Carpet (p. 146)
Euphyia biangulata

Sharp-angled Carpet (p. 146)
Euphyia unangulata

Shoulder Stripe (p. 147)
Earophila badiata

Streamer (p. 147)
Anticlea derivata

Beautiful Carpet (p. 147)
Mesoleuca albicillata

Dark Spinach (p. 147)
Pelurga comitata

PLATE 19

GEOMETRIDAE LOOPER MOTHS

All species ×1.5

Mallow (p. 147)
Larentia clavaria

Yellow-ringed Carpet/
Grey Mountain Carpet (p. 148)
Entephria flavicinctata/E. caesiata

White-banded Carpet (p. 148)
Spargania luctuata

July Highflyer (p. 148)
Hydriomena furcata

May Highflyer (p. 149)
Hydriomena impluviata

Ruddy Highflyer (p. 149)
Hydriomena ruberata

Pine Carpet (p. 149)
Pennithera firmata

Chestnut-coloured Carpet (p. 149)
Thera cognata

Spruce Carpet (p. 150)
Thera britannica

Grey Pine Carpet (p. 150)
Thera obeliscata

Juniper Carpet (p. 150)
Thera juniperata

Cypress Carpet (p. 150)
Thera cupressata

Blue-bordered Carpet (p. 151)
Plemyria rubiginata

Barred Yellow (p. 151)
Cidaria fulvata

Broken-barred Carpet (p. 151)
Electrophaes corylata

Purple Bar (p. 151)
Cosmorhoe ocellata

Netted Carpet (p. 152)
Eustroma reticulata

Phoenix/Northern Spinach (p. 152)
Eulithis prunata/E. populata

PLATE 20

GEOMETRIDAE LOOPER MOTHS

All species ×1.5

Chevron (p. 152)
Eulithis testata

Spinach (p. 153)
Eulithis mellinata

Barred Straw (p. 153)
Gandaritis pyraliata

Small Phoenix (p. 153)
Ecliptopera silaceata

Red-green Carpet (p. 153)
Chloroclysta siterata

Autumn Green Carpet (p. 154)
Chloroclysta miata

Common Marbled Carpet (p. 154)
Dysstroma truncata

Common Marbled Carpet/
Dark Marbled Carpet (p. 154)
Dysstroma truncata/D. citrata

Beech-green Carpet (p. 154)
Colostygia olivata

Green Carpet (p. 155)
Colostygia pectinataria

Mottled Grey (p. 155)
Colostygia multistrigaria

Striped Twin-spot Carpet (p. 155)
Coenotephria salicata

Water Carpet (p. 155)
Lampropteryx suffumata

Devon Carpet (p. 156)
Lampropteryx otregiata

Northern Winter Moth (p. 156)
Operophtera fagata

Winter Moth (p. 156)
Operophtera brumata

November Moth/Pale November Moth/Autumnal Moth (p. 157)
Epirrita dilutata/E. christyi/E. autumnata

Small Autumnal Moth (p. 157)
Epirrita filigrammaria

PLATE 21

GEOMETRIDAE LOOPER MOTHS

All species ×1.5 unless otherwise labelled

×1.75

Small White Wave (p. 157)
Asthena albulata

×1.75

Dingy Shell (p. 158)
Euchoeca nebulata

×1.75

Waved Carpet (p. 158)
Hydrelia sylvata

×1.75

Small Yellow Wave (p. 158)
Hydrelia flammeolaria

×1.75

Welsh Wave (p. 158)
Venusia cambrica

×1.75

Blomer's Rivulet (p. 159)
Venusia blomeri

×1.75

Drab Looper (p. 159)
Minoa murinata

Brown Scallop (p. 159)
Philereme vetulata

Dark Umber (p. 159)
Philereme transversata

Argent & Sable (p. 159)
Rheumaptera hastata

Scallop Shell (p. 160)
Rheumaptera undulata

Scarce Tissue (p. 160)
Rheumaptera cervinalis

Tissue (p. 160)
Triphosa dubitata

Barberry Carpet (p. 160)
Pareulype berberata

Slender-striped Rufous (p. 161)
Coenocalpe lapidata

Small Waved Umber (p. 161)
Horisme vitalbata

Fern (p. 161)
Horisme tersata

PLATE 22

GEOMETRIDAE LOOPER MOTHS

All species ×1.5 unless othewise labelled

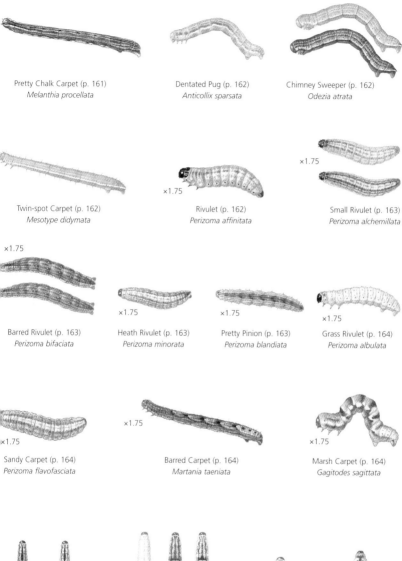

Pretty Chalk Carpet (p. 161)
Melanthia procellata

Dentated Pug (p. 162)
Anticollix sparsata

Chimney Sweeper (p. 162)
Odezia atrata

Twin-spot Carpet (p. 162)
Mesotype didymata

×1.75
Rivulet (p. 162)
Perizoma affinitata

×1.75
Small Rivulet (p. 163)
Perizoma alchemillata

×1.75
Barred Rivulet (p. 163)
Perizoma bifaciata

×1.75
Heath Rivulet (p. 163)
Perizoma minorata

×1.75
Pretty Pinion (p. 163)
Perizoma blandiata

×1.75
Grass Rivulet (p. 164)
Perizoma albulata

×1.75
Sandy Carpet (p. 164)
Perizoma flavofasciata

×1.75
Barred Carpet (p. 164)
Martania taeniata

×1.75
Marsh Carpet (p. 164)
Gagitodes sagittata

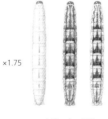

.75
ouble-striped Pug (p. 165)
Gymnoscelis rufifasciata

×1.75
V-Pug (p. 165)
Chloroclystis v-ata

×1.75
Sloe Pug (p. 165)
Pasiphila chloerata

×1.75
Green Pug (p. 166)
Pasiphila rectangulata

PLATE 23

GEOMETRIDAE LOOPER MOTHS

All species ×1.75

Bilberry Pug (p. 166)
Pasiphila debiliata

Haworth's Pug (p. 166)
Eupithecia haworthiata

Slender Pug (p. 166)
Eupithecia tenuiata

Maple Pug (p. 166)
Eupithecia inturbata

Cloaked Pug (p. 167)
Eupithecia abietaria

Toadflax Pug (p. 167)
Eupithecia linariata

Foxglove Pug (p. 167)
Eupithecia pulchellata

Channel Islands Pug (p. 167)
Eupithecia ultimaria

Lead-coloured Pug (p. 168)
Eupithecia plumbeolata

Marsh Pug (p. 168)
Eupithecia pygmaeata

Netted Pug (p. 168)
Eupithecia venosata

Brindled Pug
(plain form) (p. 168)
Eupithecia abbreviata

Brindled Pug/Oak-tree Pug (pp. 168–
Eupithecia abbreviata/E. dodoneata

Juniper Pug (p. 169)
Eupithecia pusillata

Cypress Pug (p. 169)
Eupithecia phoeniceata

White-spotted Pug (p. 169)
Eupithecia tripunctaria

Golden-rod Pug (p. 170
Eupithecia virgaureata

PLATE 24

GEOMETRIDAE LOOPER MOTHS

All species ×1.75

Dwarf Pug (p. 170)
Eupithecia tantillaria

Larch Pug (p. 170)
Eupithecia lariciata

Fletcher's Pug/
Pauper Pug (p. 170)
Eupithecia egenaria

Pimpinel Pug (p. 171)
Eupithecia pimpinellata

Plain Pug (p. 171)
Eupithecia simpliciata

arrow-winged Pug (p. 171)
Eupithecia nanata

Angle-barred Pug (p. 171)
Eupithecia innotata

Marbled Pug (p. 172)
Eupithecia irriguata

Ochreous Pug (p. 172)
Eupithecia indigata

hyme Pug (p. 172)
pithecia distinctaria

Lime-speck Pug (p. 172)
Eupithecia centaureata

Pinion-spotted Pug (p. 173)
Eupithecia insigniata

Triple-spotted Pug (p. 173)
Eupithecia trisignaria

PLATE 25

GEOMETRIDAE LOOPER MOTHS

All species ×1.75

Edinburgh Pug (p. 173)
Eupithecia intricata

Satyr Pug (p. 173)
Eupithecia satyrata

Scarce Pug (p. 174)
Eupithecia extensaria

Wormwood Pug (p. 174)
Eupithecia absinthiata

Bleached Pug (p. 174)
Eupithecia expallidata

Valerian Pug (p. 174)
Eupithecia valerianata

Currant Pug (p. 175)
Eupithecia assimilata

Common Pug (p. 175
Eupithecia vulgata

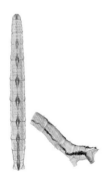

Mottled Pug (p. 175)
Eupithecia exiguata

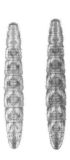

Campanula Pug (p. 175)
Eupithecia denotata

Yarrow Pug (p. 176)
Eupithecia millefoliata

Tawny Speckled Pug/
Bordered Pug (p. 176)
*Eupithecia icterata/
E. succenturiata*

PLATE 26

GEOMETRIDAE LOOPER MOTHS

All species ×1.5 unless othewise labelled

×1.75 ×1.75

Shaded Pug (p. 176)
Eupithecia subumbrata

Grey Pug (p. 177)
Eupithecia subfuscata

Manchester Treble-bar (p. 177)
Carsia sororiata

Treble-bar/Lesser Treble-bar (p. 177)
Aplocera plagiata/A. efformata

Streak/Broom-tip (p. 178)
Chesias legatella/C. rufata

Grey Carpet (p. 178)
Lithostege griseata

Seraphim (p. 178)
Lobophora halterata

Small Seraphim (p. 179)
Pterapherapteryx sexalata

Yellow-barred Brindle (p. 179)
Acasis viretata

Barred Tooth-striped/
Early Tooth-striped (p. 179)
Trichopteryx polycommata/T. carpinata

Orange Underwing (p. 180)
Archiearis parthenias

Light Orange Underwing (p. 180)
Boudinotiana notha

Magpie (p. 180)
Abraxas grossulariata

Clouded Magpie (p. 180)
Abraxas sylvata

Clouded Border (p. 181)
Lomaspilis marginata

Scorched Carpet (p. 181)
Ligdia adustata

PLATE 27

GEOMETRIDAE LOOPER MOTHS

All species ×1.5

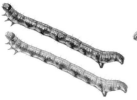

Peacock Moth/
Sharp-angled Peacock (p. 181)
Macaria notata/M. alternata

Dusky Peacock/
Tawny-barred Angle (p. 182)
Macaria signaria/M. liturata

V-Moth (p. 182)
Macaria wauaria

Netted Mountain Moth (p. 182)
Macaria carbonaria

Rannoch Looper (p. 182)
Macaria brunneata

Latticed Heath (p. 183)
Chiasmia clathrata

Little Thorn (p. 183)
Cepphis advenaria

Brown Silver-line (p. 183)
Petrophora chlorosata

Barred Umber (p. 183)
Plagodis pulveraria

Scorched Wing (p. 184)
Plagodis dolabraria

Horse Chestnut (p. 184)
Pachycnemia hippocastanaria

Brimstone Moth (p. 184)
Opisthograptis luteolata

PLATE 28

GEOMETRIDAE LOOPER MOTHS

All species ×1.25 unless otherwise labelled

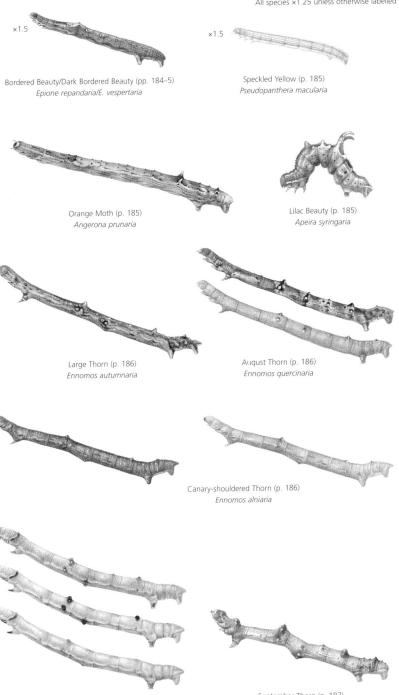

×1.5

Bordered Beauty/Dark Bordered Beauty (pp. 184–5)
Epione repandaria/E. vespertaria

×1.5

Speckled Yellow (p. 185)
Pseudopanthera macularia

Orange Moth (p. 185)
Angerona prunaria

Lilac Beauty (p. 185)
Apeira syringaria

Large Thorn (p. 186)
Ennomos autumnaria

August Thorn (p. 186)
Ennomos quercinaria

Canary-shouldered Thorn (p. 186)
Ennomos alniaria

Dusky Thorn (p. 186)
Ennomos fuscantaria

September Thorn (p. 187)
Ennomos erosaria

PLATE 29

GEOMETRIDAE LOOPER MOTHS

All species ×1.25

Early Thorn (p. 187)
Selenia dentaria

Lunar Thorn (p. 187)
Selenia lunularia

Purple Thorn (p. 187)
Selenia tetralunaria

Scalloped Hazel (p. 188)
Odontopera bidentata

Scalloped Oak/Dusky Scalloped Oak (p. 188)
Crocallis elinguaria/C. dardoinaria

Scalloped Oak (p. 188)
Crocallis elinguaria

dorsal view

Swallow-tailed Moth (p. 189)
Ourapteryx sambucaria

Feathered Thorn (p. 189)
Colotois pennaria

March Moth (p. 189)
Alsophila aescularia

PLATE 30

All species ×1.25

Small Brindled Beauty (p. 189)
Apocheima hispidaria

Pale Brindled Beauty (p. 190)
Phigalia pilosaria

Brindled Beauty (p. 190)
Lycia hirtaria

Rannoch Brindled Beauty (p. 190)
Lycia lapponaria

Belted Beauty (p. 190)
Lycia zonaria

Oak Beauty (p. 191)
Biston strataria

Peppered Moth (p. 191)
Biston betularia

Spring Usher (p. 191)
Agriopis leucophaearia

Scarce Umber/Dotted Border (pp. 191–2)
Agriopis aurantiaria/A. marginaria

PLATE 31

GEOMETRIDAE LOOPER MOTHS

All species ×1.25

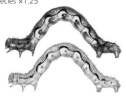

Mottled Umber (p. 192)
Erannis defoliaria

Waved Umber (p. 192)
Menophra abruptaria

A1–A3

Willow Beauty (p. 192)
Peribatodes rhomboidaria

Feathered Beauty (p. 193)
Peribatodes secundaria

Bordered Grey (p. 193)
Selidosema brunnearia

Ringed Carpet (p. 193)
Cleora cinctaria

Satin Beauty (p. 193)
Deileptenia ribeata

Mottled Beauty (p. 194)
Alcis repandata

Dotted Carpet (p. 194)
Alcis jubata

Great Oak Beauty (p. 194)
Hypomecis roboraria

Pale Oak Beauty (p. 194)
Hypomecis punctinalis

PLATE 32

GEOMETRIDAE LOOPER MOTHS

All species ×1.25

dorsal view

Engrailed/Small Engrailed (p. 195)
Ectropis crepuscularia/Ectropis sp.

Square Spot (p. 195)
Paradarisa consonaria

Brindled White-spot (p. 195)
Parectropis similaria

Grey Birch (p. 196)
Aethalura punctulata

Common Heath (p. 196)
Ematurga atomaria

Bordered White (p. 196)
Bupalus piniaria

Common White Wave (p. 196)
Cabera pusaria

Common Wave (p. 197)
Cabera exanthemata

White-pinion Spotted (p. 197)
Lomographa bimaculata

Clouded Silver (p. 197)
Lomographa temerata

Sloe Carpet (p. 197)
Aleucis distinctata

Early Moth (p. 198)
Theria primaria

Light Emerald (p. 198)
Campaea margaritaria

PLATE 33

GEOMETRIDAE LOOPER MOTHS

All species ×1.25

Barred Red (p. 198)
Hylaea fasciaria

Banded Pine Carpet (p. 198)
Pungeleria capreolaria

Scotch Annulet (p. 199)
Gnophos obfuscata

Irish Annulet (p. 199)
Gnophos dumetata

Annulet (p. 199)
Charissa obscurata

Brussels Lace (p. 199)
Cleorodes lichenaria

Black Mountain Moth (p. 200)
Glacies coracina

Common Forest Looper (p. 200)
Pseudocoremia suavis

Black-veined Moth (p. 200)
Siona lineata

Grey Scalloped Bar (p. 200)
Dyscia fagaria

Straw Belle/Yellow Belle (p. 201)
Aspitates gilvaria/A. ochrearia

Grass Wave (p. 201)
Perconia strigillaria

Rest Harrow (p. 201)
Aplasta ononaria

Grass Emerald/Jersey Emerald (p. 202)
Pseudoterpna pruinata/P. coronillaria

Large Emerald (p. 202)
Geometra papilionaria

PLATE 34

GEOMETRIDAE LOOPER MOTHS

All species ×1.25

Blotched Emerald (p. 202)
Comibaena bajularia

Small Emerald (p. 203)
Hemistola chrysoprasaria

Little Emerald (p. 203)
Jodis lactearia

Sussex Emerald (p. 203)
Thalera fimbrialis

Common Emerald (p. 203)
Hemithea aestivaria

Small Grass Emerald/
Southern Grass Emerald (p. 204)
Chlorissa viridata/C. cloraria

NOTODONTIDAE PROMINENT, KITTEN AND PROCESSIONARY MOTHS

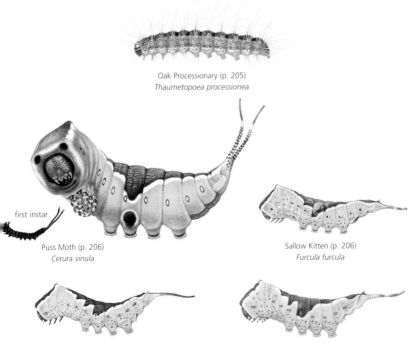

Oak Processionary (p. 205)
Thaumetopoea processionea

first instar

Puss Moth (p. 206)
Cerura vinula

Sallow Kitten (p. 206)
Furcula furcula

Alder Kitten (p. 206)
Furcula bicuspis

Poplar Kitten (p. 207)
Furcula bifida

PLATE 35

NOTODONTIDAE PROMINENT, KITTEN AND PROCESSIONARY MOTHS

All species ×1.25

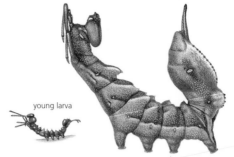

young larva

Lobster Moth (p. 207)
Stauropus fagi

Marbled Brown (p. 207)
Drymonia dodonaea

Lunar Marbled Brown (p. 207)
Drymonia ruficornis

Iron Prominent (p. 208)
Notodonta dromedarius

Pebble Prominent (p. 208)
Notodonta ziczac

Great Prominent (p. 208)
Peridea anceps

Swallow Prominent (p. 208)
Pheosia tremula

Lesser Swallow Prominent (p. 209)
Pheosia gnoma

White Prominent (p. 209)
Leucodonta bicoloria

PLATE 36

NOTODONTIDAE PROMINENT, KITTEN AND PROCESSIONARY MOTHS

All species ×1.25

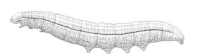

Pale Prominent (p. 209)
Pterostoma palpina

Coxcomb Prominent (p. 209)
Ptilodon capucina

Maple Prominent (p. 209)
Ptilodon cucullina

Scarce Prominent (p. 210)
Odontosia carmelita

Plumed Prominent (p. 210)
Ptilophora plumigera

Buff-tip (p. 210)
Phalera bucephala

Chocolate-tip (p. 211)
Clostera curtula

Small Chocolate-tip (p. 211)
Clostera pigra

Scarce Chocolate-tip (p. 211)
Clostera anachoreta

PLATE 37

EREBIDAE TUSSOCKS, ERMINES, TIGERS AND RELATIVES

All species ×1.25

Herald (p. 276)
Scoliopteryx libatrix

Straw Dot (p. 277)
Rivula sericealis

Snout (p. 277)
Hypena proboscidalis

Buttoned Snout (p. 277)
Hypena rostralis

Bloxworth Snout (p. 277)
Hypena obsitalis

Beautiful Snout (p. 278)
Hypena crassalis

White Satin Moth (p. 278)
Leucoma salicis

Black Arches (p. 278)
Lymantria monacha

Gypsy Moth (p. 278)
Lymantria dispar

Brown-tail (p. 279)
Euproctis chrysorrhoea

Yellow-tail (p. 279)
Euproctis similis

PLATE 38

EREBIDAE TUSSOCKS, ERMINES, TIGERS AND RELATIVES

All species ×1.25

Pale Tussock (p. 279)
Calliteara pudibunda

Dark Tussock (p. 279)
Dicallomera fascelina

Vapourer (p. 280)
Orgyia antiqua

Scarce Vapourer (p. 280)
Orgyia recens

Buff Ermine (p. 280)
Spilosoma lutea

White Ermine (p. 281)
Spilosoma lubricipeda

Water Ermine (p. 281)
Spilosoma urticae

PLATE 39

EREBIDAE TUSSOCKS, ERMINES, TIGERS AND RELATIVES

All species ×1.25

Muslin Moth (p. 281)
Diaphora mendica

Clouded Buff (p. 281)
Diacrisia sannio

Ruby Tiger (p. 282)
Phragmatobia fuliginosa

Wood Tiger (p. 282)
Parasemia plantaginis

Garden Tiger (p. 282)
Arctia caja

Cream-spot Tiger (p. 282)
Arctia villica

PLATE 40

EREBIDAE TUSSOCKS, ERMINES, TIGERS AND RELATIVES

All species ×1.25 unless otherwise labelled

Scarlet Tiger (p. 283)
Callimorpha dominula

Jersey Tiger (p. 283)
Euplagia quadripunctaria

Cinnabar (p. 283)
Tyria jacobaeae

Speckled Footman (p. 283)
Coscinia cribraria

×1.5

Rosy Footman (p. 284)
Miltochrista miniata

×1.5

Muslin Footman (p. 284)
Nudaria mundana

×1.5

similar species

White Plume (p. 284)
Pterophorus pentadactyla

×1.5

Round-winged Muslin (p. 284)
Thumatha senex

×1.5

Four-dotted Footman (p. 284)
Cybosia mesomella

×1.5

Dotted Footman (p. 285)
Pelosia muscerda

×1.5

Small Dotted Footman (p. 285)
Pelosia obtusa

Four-spotted Footman (p. 285)
Lithosia quadra

PLATE 41

EREBIDAE TUSSOCKS, ERMINES, TIGERS AND RELATIVES

All species ×1.25 unless otherwise labelled

Red-necked Footman (p. 285)
Atolmis rubricollis

Buff Footman (p. 286)
Eilema depressa

Dingy Footman (p. 286)
Eilema griseola

Common Footman (p. 286)
Eilema lurideola

Scarce Footman (p. 286)
Eilema complana

Hoary Footman (p. 287)
Eilema caniola

Pigmy Footman (p. 287)
Eilema pygmaeola

Orange Footman (p. 287)
Eilema sororcula

Dew Moth (p. 287)
Setina irrorella

×1.5

Clay Fan-foot (p. 288)
Paracolax tristalis

×1.5

Dotted Fan-foot (p. 288)
Macrochilo cribrumalis

×1.5

Fan-foot (p. 288)
Herminia tarsipennalis

×1.5

Shaded Fan-foot (p. 288)
Herminia tarsicrinalis

×1.5

Small Fan-foot (p. 288)
Herminia grisealis

×1.5

Common Fan-foot (p. 289)
Pechipogo strigilata

×1.5

Plumed Fan-foot (p. 289)
Pechipogo plumigeralis

Blackneck (p. 289)
Lygephila pastinum

Scarce Blackneck (p. 290)
Lygephila craccae

PLATE 42

EREBIDAE TUSSOCKS, ERMINES, TIGERS AND RELATIVES

All species ×1.25 unless otherwise labelled

Waved Black (p. 290)
Parascotia fuliginaria

×1.5

Small Purple-barred (p. 290)
Phytometra viridaria

×1.5

Beautiful Hook-tip (p. 290)
Laspeyria flexula

Olive Crescent (p. 291)
Trisateles emortualis

similar species

×1.5

Purple Marbled (p. 291)
Eublemma ostrina

Phycitodes saxicola (p. 291)

×1.5

Small Marbled (p. 291)
Eublemma parva

Clifden Nonpareil/Blue Underwing (p. 291)
Catocala fraxini

Red Underwing (p. 291)
Catocala nupta

Dark Crimson Underwing/
Light Crimson Underwing (p. 292)
Catocala sponsa/C. promissa

Light Crimson Underwing (p. 292)
Catocala promissa

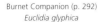

Burnet Companion (p. 292)
Euclidia glyphica

Mother Shipton (p. 292)
Euclidia mi

PLATE 43

NOCTUIDAE NOCTUID MOTHS

All species ×1.25

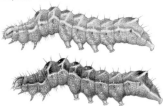

Spectacle (p. 294)
Abrostola tripartita

Dark Spectacle (p. 294)
Abrostola triplasia

Scarce Burnished Brass/Burnished Brass (p. 294)
Diachrysia chryson/D. chrysitis

Golden Plusia (p. 295)
Polychrysia moneta

Silver Y (p. 295)
Autographa gamma

Beautiful Golden Y/Plain Golden Y/
Gold Spangle (pp. 295–6)
Autographa pulchrina/A. jota/A. bractea

Scarce Silver Y (p. 296)
Syngrapha interrogationis

Gold Spot/Lempke's Gold Spot (p. 296)
Plusia festucae/P. putnami

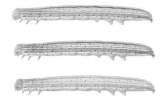

Marbled White Spot (p. 296)
Deltote pygarga

Silver Hook (p. 297)
Deltote uncula

Silver Barred (p. 297)
Deltote bankiana

Four-spotted (p. 297)
Tyta luctuosa

PLATE 44

NOCTUIDAE NOCTUID MOTHS

All species ×1.25

Nut-tree Tussock (p. 297)
Colocasia coryli

Figure of Eight (p. 298)
Diloba caeruleocephala

Scarce Merveille du Jour (p. 298)
Moma alpium

Reed Dagger/Powdered Wainscot (p. 298)
Simyra albovenosa

young larva

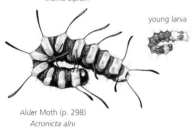

Alder Moth (p. 298)
Acronicta alni

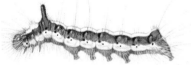

Dark Dagger (p. 299)
Acronicta tridens

Grey Dagger (p. 299)
Acronicta psi

Sycamore (p. 299)
Acronicta aceris

Miller (p. 299)
Acronicta leporina

Light Knot Grass (p. 300)
Acronicta menyanthidis

Sweet Gale Moth (p. 300)
Acronicta cinerea

Knot Grass (p. 300)
Acronicta rumicis

PLATE 45

NOCTUIDAE NOCTUID MOTHS

All species ×1.25

Poplar Grey (p. 300)
Subacronicta megacephala

Coronet (p. 300)
Craniophora ligustri

Small Yellow Underwing (p. 301)
Panemeria tenebrata

Wormwood (p. 301)
Cucullia absinthii

Shark (p. 301)
Cucullia umbratica

Chamomile Shark (p. 301)
Cucullia chamomillae

Star-wort (p. 302)
Cucullia asteris

Mullein (p. 302)
Cucullia verbasci

Water Betony (p. 302)
Cucullia scrophulariae

Striped Lychnis (p. 302)
Cucullia lychnitis

Mullein (p. 302)
Cucullia verbasci

Toadflax Brocade (p. 303)
Calophasia lunula

Anomalous (p. 303)
Stilbia anomala

PLATE 46

NOCTUIDAE NOCTUID MOTHS

All species ×1.25

Copper Underwing (p. 303)
Amphipyra pyramidea

Svensson's Copper Underwing (p. 303)
Amphipyra berbera

Mouse Moth (p. 304)
Amphipyra tragopoginis

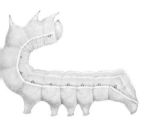

Sprawler (p. 304)
Asteroscopus sphinx

Rannoch Sprawler (p. 304)
Brachionycha nubeculosa

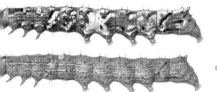

Green-brindled Crescent (p. 304)
Allophyes oxyacanthae

Early Grey (p. 305)
Xylocampa areola

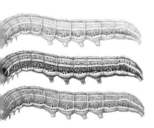

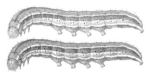

Marbled Clover/Shoulder-striped Clover (pp. 305–6)
Heliothis viriplaca/H. maritima

Bordered Sallow (p. 305)
Pyrrhia umbra

Bordered Straw (p. 306)
Heliothis peltigera

PLATE 47

NOCTUIDAE NOCTUID MOTHS

All species ×1.25

Scarce Bordered Straw/Old World Bollworm (p. 306)
Helicoverpa armigera

Reddish Buff (p. 306)
Acosmetia caliginosa

Tree-lichen Beauty (p. 307)
Cryphia algae

Marbled Beauty (p. 307)
Bryophila domestica

Marbled Green (p. 307)
Nyctobrya muralis

Rosy Marbled (p. 307)
Elaphria venustula

Mottled Rustic (p. 308)
Caradrina morpheus

Clancy's Rustic (p. 308)
Caradrina kadenii

Pale Mottled Willow (p. 308)
Caradrina clavipalpis

Uncertain (p. 308)
Hoplodrina octogenaria

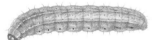

Rustic (p. 308)
Hoplodrina blanda

Vine's Rustic (p. 309)
Hoplodrina ambigua

Silky Wainscot (p. 309)
Chilodes maritima

Treble Lines (p. 309)
Charanyca trigrammica

Brown Rustic (p. 309)
Rusina ferruginea

Marsh Moth (p. 310)
Athetis pallustris

PLATE 48

NOCTUIDAE NOCTUID MOTHS

All species ×1.25

Bird's Wing (p. 310)
Dypterygia scabriuscula

Orache Moth (p. 310)
Trachea atriplicis

Old Lady (p. 310)
Mormo maura

Guernsey Underwing (p. 310)
Polyphaenis sericata

Straw Underwing (p. 311)
Thalpophila matura

Saxon (p. 311)
Hyppa rectilinea

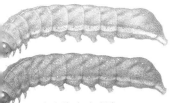

Angle Shades (p. 311)
Phlogophora meticulosa

Small Angle Shades (p. 311)
Euplexia lucipara

Burren Green (p. 312)
Calamia tridens

PLATE 49

NOCTUIDAE NOCTUID MOTHS

All species ×1.25

Haworth's Minor (p. 312)
Celaena haworthii

Crescent (p. 312)
Helotropha leucostigma

Dusky Sallow (p. 312)
Eremobia ochroleuca

Frosted Orange (p. 313)
Gortyna flavago

Fisher's Estuarine Moth (p. 313)
Gortyna borelii

Rosy Rustic/Butterbur (p. 313)
Hydraecia micacea/H. petasitis

Marsh Mallow Moth/Giant Ear (p. 314)
Hydraecia osseola

Saltern Ear/Large Ear/Ear Moth/Crinan Ear (pp. 314–15)
Amphipoea fucosa/A. lucens/A. oculea/A. crinanensis

Flounced Rustic (p. 315)
Luperina testacea

Sandhill Rustic (p. 315)
Luperina nickerlii

Large Wainscot (p. 315)
Rhizedra lutosa

Blair's Wainscot (p. 315)
Sedina buettneri

Bulrush Wainscot (p. 316)
Nonagria typhae

PLATE 50

NOCTUIDAE NOCTUID MOTHS

All species ×1.25

Fen Wainscot (p. 316)
Arenostola phragmitidis

Lyme Grass (p. 316)
Longalatedes elymi

Twin-spotted Wainscot (p. 316)
Lenisa geminipuncta

White-mantled Wainscot (p. 316)
Archanara neurica

Brown-veined Wainscot (p. 317)
Archanara dissoluta

Small Rufous (p. 317)
Coenobia rufa

Small Wainscot (p. 317)
Denticucullus pygmina

Mere Wainscot (p. 317)
Photedes fluxa

Least Minor (p. 318)
Photedes captiuncula

Small Dotted Buff (p. 318)
Photedes minima

Morris's Wainscot (p. 318)
Photedes morrisii

Concolorous (p. 318)
Photedes extrema

Fenn's Wainscot (p. 318)
Protarchanara brevilinea

Webb's Wainscot (p. 319)
Globia sparganii

Rush Wainscot (p. 319)
Globia algae

PLATE 51

NOCTUIDAE NOCTUID MOTHS

All species ×1.25

×1.25

Dusky Brocade (p. 319)
Apamea remissa

Clouded Brindle (p. 320)
Apamea epomidion

Clouded-bordered Brindle (p. 320)
Apamea crenata

Large Nutmeg (p. 320)
Apamea anceps

Rustic Shoulder-knot (p. 320)
Apamea sordens

Small Clouded Brindle (p. 320)
Apamea unanimis

Slender Brindle (p. 321)
Apamea scolopacina

Crescent Striped/Northern Arches/Exile (pp. 321–2)
Apamea oblonga/A. exulis

Dark Arches/Light Arches/Reddish Light Arches (pp. 321–2)
Apamea monoglypha/A. lithoxylaea/A. sublustris

Confused (p. 322)
Apamea furva

Double Lobed (p. 322)
Lateroligia ophiogramma

PLATE 52

NOCTUIDAE NOCTUID MOTHS

All species ×1.25

Common Rustic/Lesser
Common Rustic (pp. 322–3)
Mesapamea secalis/M. didyma

Rosy Minor (p. 323)
Litoligia literosa

Cloaked Minor (p. 323)
Mesoligia furuncula

Marbled Minor/
Tawny Marbled Minor/Rufous Minor/
Middle-barred Minor (pp. 323–4)
*Oligia strigilis/O. latruncula/
O. versicolor/O. fasciuncula*

Middle-barred Minor
(form with greenish markings) (p. 324)
Oligia fasciuncula

Beautiful Gothic (p. 324)
Leucochlaena oditis

Orange Sallow (p. 325)
Tiliacea citrago

Barred Sallow (p. 325)
Tiliacea aurago

Pink-barred Sallow (p. 325)
Xanthia togata

Sallow (p. 325)
Cirrhia icteritia

Dusky-lemon Sallow (p. 326)
Cirrhia gilvago

Pale-lemon Sallow (p. 326)
Cirrhia ocellaris

Beaded Chestnut (p. 326)
Agrochola lychnidis

Brown-spot Pinion (p. 326)
Agrochola litura

Flounced Chestnut (p. 327)
Agrochola helvola

Red-line Quaker (p. 327)
Agrochola lota

Yellow-line Quaker (p. 327)
Agrochola macilenta

Southern Chestnut (p. 327)
Agrochola haematidea

Brick (p. 328)
Agrochola circellaris

PLATE 53

NOCTUIDAE NOCTUID MOTHS

All species ×1.25

Lunar Underwing (p. 328)
Omphaloscelis lunosa

Chestnut/Dark Chestnut (p. 328)
Conistra vaccinii/C. ligula

Black-spotted Chestnut (p. 329)
Conistra rubiginosa

Dotted Chestnut (p. 329)
Conistra rubiginea

Tawny Pinion (p. 329)
Lithophane semibrunnea

Pale Pinion (p. 329)
Lithophane socia

Grey Shoulder-knot (p. 330)
Lithophane ornitopus

Blair's Shoulder-knot/Stone Pinion (p. 330)
Lithophane leautieri

Golden-rod Brindle (p. 330)
Xylena solidaginis

Sword-grass (p. 330)
Xylena exsoleta

Red Sword-grass (p. 330)
Xylena vetusta

PLATE 54

NOCTUIDAE NOCTUID MOTHS

All species ×1.25

Satellite (p. 331)
Eupsilia transversa

Angle-striped Sallow (p. 331)
Enargia paleacea

Double Kidney (p. 331)
Ipimorpha retusa

Olive (p. 331)
Ipimorpha subtusa

White-spotted Pinion (p. 331)
Cosmia diffinis

Lesser-spotted Pinion (p. 332)
Cosmia affinis

Dun-bar (p. 332)
Cosmia trapezina

Lunar-spotted Pinion (p. 332)
Cosmia pyralina

Heart Moth (p. 332)
Dicycla oo

Centre-barred Sallow (p. 333)
Atethmia centrago

Minor Shoulder-knot (p. 333)
Brachylomia viminalis

Suspected (p. 333)
Parastichtis suspecta

Dingy Shears (p. 333)
Apterogenum ypsillon

Oak Rustic (p. 333)
Dryobota labecula

Merveille du Jour (p. 334)
Griposia aprilina

PLATE 55

NOCTUIDAE NOCTUID MOTHS

All species ×1.25

Brindled Green (p. 334)
Dryobotodes eremita

Sombre Brocade (p. 334)
Dryobotodes tenebrosa

Grey Chi (p. 334)
Antitype chi

Flame Brocade (p. 335)
Trigonophora flammea

Feathered Brindle (p. 335)
Aporophyla australis

Deep-brown Dart/Northern Deep-brown Dart/Black Rustic (pp. 335–6)
Aporophyla lutulenta/A. lueneburgensis/A. nigra

Black Rustic (p. 336)
Aporophyla nigra

Brindled Ochre (p. 336)
Dasypolia templi

Feathered Ranunculus (p. 336)
Polymixis lichenea

Black-banded (p. 336)
Polymixis xanthomista

Large Ranunculus (p. 337)
Polymixis flavicincta

Dark Brocade (p. 337)
Mniotype adusta

PLATE 56

NOCTUIDAE NOCTUID MOTHS

All species ×1.25

Pine Beauty (p. 337)
Panolis flammea

Clouded Drab (p. 337)
Orthosia incerta

Blossom Underwing (p. 338)
Orthosia miniosa

Common Quaker (p. 338)
Orthosia cerasi

Small Quaker (p. 338)
Orthosia cruda

Lead-coloured Drab (p. 338)
Orthosia populeti

Powdered Quaker/Hebrew Character (p. 339)
Orthosia gracilis/O. gothica

Powdered Quaker/Northern Drab (p. 339)
Orthosia gracilis/O. opima

Hebrew Character (p. 339)
Orthosia gothica

Twin-spotted Quaker (p. 339)
Anorthoa munda

PLATE 57

NOCTUIDAE NOCTUID MOTHS

All species ×1.25

Silver Cloud (p. 340)
Egira conspicillaris

Hedge Rustic/Feathered Gothic (p. 340)
Tholera cespitis/T. decimalis

Antler Moth (p. 340)
Cerapteryx graminis

Nutmeg (p. 341)
Anarta trifolii

Broad-bordered White Underwing (p. 341)
Anarta melanopa

Beautiful Yellow Underwing (p. 341)
Anarta myrtilli

Small Dark Yellow Underwing (p. 341)
Coranarta cordigera

Pale Shining Brown (p. 341)
Polia bombycina

Silvery Arches (p. 342)
Polia hepatica

Grey Arches (p. 342)
Polia nebulosa

Light Brocade (p. 342)
Lacanobia w-latinum

Pale-shouldered Brocade (p. 342)
Lacanobia thalassina

PLATE 58

NOCTUIDAE NOCTUID MOTHS

All species ×1.25

Beautiful Brocade (p. 343)
Lacanobia contigua

Dog's Tooth (p. 343)
Lacanobia suasa

Bright-line Brown-eye (p. 343)
Lacanobia oleracea

Splendid Brocade (p. 343)
Lacanobia splendens

Dot Moth (p. 344)
Melanchra persicariae

Broom Moth (p. 344)
Ceramica pisi

Glaucous Shears (p. 344)
Papestra biren

Shears (p. 344)
Hada plebeja

PLATE 59

NOCTUIDAE NOCTUID MOTHS

All species ×1.25

Cabbage Moth (p. 345)
Mamestra brassicae

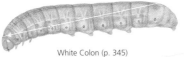

White Colon (p. 345)
Sideridis turbida

Campion (p. 345)
Sideridis rivularis

Bordered Gothic (p. 346)
Sideridis reticulata

Barrett's Marbled Coronet (p. 346)
Conisania andalusica

Broad-barred White (p. 346)
Hecatera bicolorata

Small Ranunculus (p. 346)
Hecatera dysodea

Lychnis/Marbled Coronet (p. 347)
Hadena bicruris/H. confusa

Varied Coronet (p. 347)
Hadena compta

White Spot (p. 347)
Hadena albimacula

Grey (p. 347)
Hadena caesia

Tawny Shears (p. 348)
Hadena perplexa

PLATE 60

NOCTUIDAE NOCTUID MOTHS

All species ×1.25

Double Line (p. 348)
Mythimna turca

Smoky Wainscot group (pp. 349–50)
Mythimna spp.

Southern Wainscot (p. 349)
Mythimna straminea

Clay group (pp. 348–51)
Mythimna/Leucania spp.

Shore Wainscot (p. 350)
Mythimna litoralis

Obscure Wainscot (p. 351)
Leucania obsoleta

Flame Wainscot (p. 352)
Senta flammea

Silurian (p. 352)
Eriopygodes imbecilla

Pearly Underwing (p. 352)
Peridroma saucia

Portland Moth (p. 352)
Actebia praecox

Heart & Dart (p. 354)
Agrotis exclamationis

Sand Dart (p. 355)
Agrotis ripae

Shuttle-shaped Dart (p. 355)
Agrotis puta

Flame (p. 355)
Axylia putris

PLATE 61

NOCTUIDAE NOCTUID MOTHS

All species ×1.25

Flame Shoulder (p. 356)
Ochropleura plecta

Barred Chestnut (p. 356)
Diarsia dahlii

Purple Clay (p. 356)
Diarsia brunnea

Ingrailed Clay (p. 356)
Diarsia mendica

Small Square-spot/Fen Square-spot (p. 357)
Diarsia rubi/D. florida

Red Chestnut (p. 357)
Cerastis rubricosa

White-marked (p. 357)
Cerastis leucographa

True Lover's Knot, penultimate instar (p. 358)
Lycophotia porphyrea

True Lover's Knot, final (non-feeding) instar (p. 358)
Lycophotia porphyrea

Dotted Rustic (p. 358)
Rhyacia simulans

Northern Rustic (p. 358)
Standfussiana lucernea

PLATE 62

Large Yellow Underwing (p. 358)
Noctua pronuba

Broad-bordered Yellow Underwing (p. 359)
Noctua fimbriata

Lunar Yellow Underwing (p. 359)
Noctua orbona

Lesser Yellow Underwing (p. 359)
Noctua comes

Least Yellow Underwing (p. 359)
Noctua interjecta

Langmaid's Yellow Underwing/
Lesser Broad-bordered Yellow Underwing (p. 360)
Noctua janthina/N. janthe

Stout Dart (p. 360)
Spaelotis ravida

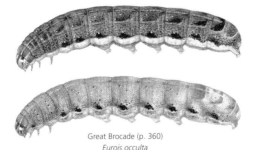

Great Brocade (p. 360)
Eurois occulta

Double Dart (p. 361)
Graphiphora augur

Green Arches (p. 361)
Anaplectoides prasina

PLATE 63

NOCTUIDAE NOCTUID MOTHS

All species ×1.25

Dotted Clay (p. 361)
Xestia baja

Square-spotted Clay (p. 361)
Xestia stigmatica

Neglected Rustic (p. 362)
Xestia castanea

Heath Rustic (p. 362)
Xestia agathina

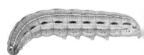

Square-spot Rustic/Six-striped Rustic (pp. 362–
Xestia xanthographa/X. sexstrigata

Setaceous Hebrew Character (p. 363)
Xestia c-nigrum

Triple-spotted Clay (p. 363)
Xestia ditrapezium

Double Square-spot (p. 363)
Xestia triangulum

Ashworth's Rustic (p. 364)
Xestia ashworthii

Northern Dart (p. 364)
Xestia alpicola

Rosy Marsh Moth (p. 364)
Coenophila subrosea

PLATE 64

NOCTUIDAE NOCTUID MOTHS

All species ×1.25 unless otherwise labelled

Autumnal Rustic (p. 364)
Eugnorisma glareosa

Plain Clay (p. 365)
Eugnorisma depuncta

Cousin German (p. 365)
Protolampra sobrina

Gothic (p. 365)
Naenia typica

NOLIDAE BLACK ARCHES, SILVER-LINES AND NYCTEOLINE MOTHS

×1.5

Small Black Arches (p. 366)
Meganola strigula

×1.5

Kent Black Arches (p. 367)
Meganola albula

×1.5

Short-cloaked Moth (p. 367)
Nola cucullatella

×1.5

Least Black Arches (p. 367)
Nola confusalis

Scarce Silver-lines (p. 367)
Bena bicolorana

Green Silver-lines (p. 368)
Pseudoips prasinana

Oak Nycteoline (p. 368)
Nycteola revayana

Cream-bordered Green Pea (p. 368)
Earias clorana

EREBIDAE TUSSOCK, ERMINE, TIGER, FOOTMAN, SNOUT, FAN-FOOT, MARBLED, BLACKNECK AND UNDERWING MOTHS

Red Underwing ×1.25

This is a large and diverse family worldwide, with 66 species resident in the British Isles and two immigrants that may establish temporarily in some years. It comprises the former families Lymantriidae (now subfamily Lymantriinae), Arctiidae (now subfamily Arctiinae) and 30 species that were formerly included in the Noctuidae. There are no common features identifying larvae as belonging to Erebidae. Larvae of the Lymantriinae and Arctiinae are hairy and some of the hairs of the former are irritant and can cause an unpleasant itchy rash.

Herald ×1.25

White Satin Moth larva

Four-spotted Footman larva

Small Fan-foot larva

SCOLIOPTERYGINAE

HERALD
Scoliopteryx libatrix

PLATE 3?
72.001 (2469

Common; more local in Scotland. **FIELD CHARACTERS** Head rather bulbous. Body elongated and green or yellowish green. Dorsal stripe dark green, and subdorsal line white or yellow and usually edged below with long black dashes. Spiracles orange, with a hint of a paler green spiracular line. **HABITATS** Wide variety. **FOODPLANTS** Poplars including Aspen, and willows; also Rowan. **FIELD NOTES** May–Sep. Pupates between leaves in a slight silken cocoon. Overwinters as an adult.

RIVULINAE

STRAW DOT
Rivula sericealis

PLATE 37
72.002 (2474)

Common; suspected immigrant. **FIELD CHARACTERS** Body green and rather stumpy with sparse, dark bristle-like hairs. Dorsal line darker, subdorsal stripe clear white and spiracular line pale green. **SIMILAR SPECIES** Several plume moths (Pterophoridae), including Yarrow Plume *Gillmeria pallidactyla* on Yarrow and Sneezewort, and Crescent Plume *Marasmarcha lunaedactyla* on restharrows. These plume larvae have a much smaller head, and are on different foodplants. **HABITATS** Wide variety of open habitats. **FOODPLANTS** Grasses, including False Brome, Purple Moor-grass and Tor-grass. **FIELD NOTES** Jul–May, in one generation in the north and at least two in the south. Feeds at night. Pupates within a folded grass blade in a slight silken cocoon. Overwinters as a small larva.

HYPENINAE

SNOUT
Hypena proboscidalis

PLATE 37
72.003 (2477)

Common. **FIELD CHARACTERS** Head green, densely speckled with brown. Body slender and green with small black pinacula and dark, bristle-like hairs. Dorsal line dark green with interrupted, or sometimes faint or obsolete, white subdorsal and spiracular lines. Intersegmental bands yellowish. Prolegs absent on A3. **SIMILAR SPECIES** Buttoned Snout has rather longer, pale hairs, and a continuous subdorsal line. Bloxworth Snout is very similar but is sometimes distinguished by slightly larger pinacula, especially anteriorly. Beautiful Snout lacks whitish on any lines. Foodplant differences should suffice to separate these species. **HABITATS** Wide variety. **FOODPLANT** Common Nettle. **FIELD NOTES** Jul–May, in one generation in the north and two in the south. Feeds at night, hiding by day between spun leaves. Pupates among leaves in a silken cocoon.

BUTTONED SNOUT
Hypena rostralis

PLATE 37
72.004 (2480)

Nb; suspected immigrant. **FIELD CHARACTERS** Head green with sparse black dots. Body slender and pale or bluish green with small black pinacula and pale hairs. Dorsal line dark green with continuous white subdorsal line, and interrupted white spiracular line. Intersegmental bands yellowish. Prolegs absent on A3. **SIMILAR SPECIES** Snout, Bloxworth Snout and Beautiful Snout. **HABITATS** Gardens, dry grassland, hedgerows, scrub, river valleys and waste ground. **FOODPLANT** Hop, including cultivars. **FIELD NOTES** Jun–Jul, resting on the underside of leaves. Pupates under a leaf in a silken cocoon. Overwinters as an adult.

BLOXWORTH SNOUT
Hypena obsitalis

PLATE 37
72.006 (2478)

RDB; recent colonist; immigrant. Established along the south coast. **FIELD CHARACTERS** Head green, densely speckled with brown. Body slender and green with black pinacula and short dark hairs. Dorsal line dark green with subdorsal line pale and rather indistinct, although more apparent on anterior segments. Spiracular line whitish and interrupted. Intersegmental bands yellowish. Prolegs absent on A3. **SIMILAR SPECIES** Snout, Buttoned Snout and Beautiful Snout. **HABITATS** Coastal slopes and cliffs, rough ground, old quarries, scrub and urban areas. **FOODPLANT** Pellitory-of-the-wall, preferring plants rowing in sheltered or shaded spots. **FIELD NOTES** Usually Jun–Sep, but has been recorded in late Nov; in wo generations. Pupates among leaves. Overwinters as an adult, often in caves and wartime bunkers.

BEAUTIFUL SNOUT
Hypena crassalis

PLATE 37
72.007 (2476)

Local. **FIELD CHARACTERS** Head green, speckled with brown. Body slender and green with small black pinacula and short dark hairs. Dorsal and subdorsal lines dark green and spiracular line appearing as faint, pale green dashes. Intersegmental bands yellowish. Prolegs absent on A3. **SIMILAR SPECIES** Snout, Buttoned Snout and Bloxworth Snout. **HABITATS** Woodland, and sometimes heathland and moorland. **FOODPLANTS** Bilberry, and confirmed on Heather in Ireland; regularly found where Bilberry is absent. **FIELD NOTES** Mid-Jul–late Sep. Feeds mainly at night. Pupates in or on the ground. Overwinters as a pupa.

LYMANTRIINAE

WHITE SATIN MOTH
Leucoma salicis

PLATE 37
72.009 (2031)

Local; suspected immigrant. Resident in the south and east. **FIELD CHARACTERS** Body black dorsally, bluish grey laterally, with orange verrucae and pale grey hair tufts. Most obvious are the large white dorsal patches. Subdorsal stripe yellow or white, interrupted and edged black below. **HABITATS** Wide variety, but found particularly in plantation woodlands, river valleys and wetlands. **FOODPLANTS** Poplars and willows. Recorded on Black-poplar, Hybrid Black-poplar, Grey and White poplars, and Bay, Creeping, Goat, Grey and White willows. **FIELD NOTES** Aug–Jun. In spring rests openly on leaves and often feeds gregariously. Eggs are laid communally within a foamy secretion that hardens to form a protective covering. Pupates in a hairy silken cocoon in a bark crevice or among leaves. Overwinters as a small larva in a communal silken web or in an individual hibernaculum.

BLACK ARCHES
Lymantria monacha

PLATE 37
72.010 (2033)

Local. Widespread in the south and has increased significantly in abundance in recent decades. **FIELD CHARACTERS** Variable. Body yellowish brown or greyish. Verrucae usually dark in subdorsal region and grey laterally. Hair tufts dark or grey. The broad greenish-brown or dark greyish dorsal band has wavy margins, and is paler on and near A5. There is a broad black dorsal mark on T2 and small red dorsal projections A6–A7. **HABITATS** Parkland and woodland. **FOODPLANTS** Mainly oaks, but also recorded on Apple, Aspen, Beech, birches, elms, hawthorns, Hornbeam, limes, Scots Pine, Norway Spruce and White Willow. **FIELD NOTES** Apr–Jun. Pupates in a silken cocoon spun in a bark crevice Overwinters as an egg.

GYPSY MOTH
Lymantria dispar

PLATE 37
72.011 (2034)

Immigrant; adventive, locally naturalised; former resident. Populations are scattered across southern and south-east England. **FIELD CHARACTERS** Very variable in colour and pattern. Body mottled grey, or sometimes black. Subdorsal verrucae are blue T1–A2, red or blackish A3–A8. Lateral verrucae may be similarly coloured, or all red, or all yellowish brown. Tufts comprise long and short, pale and dark hairs. Dorsal line yellow, subdorsal line or spots yellow, and small red dorsal projections A6–A7. **HABITATS** Parkland, scrub, urban trees and woodland. **FOODPLANTS** Mainly oaks, but also many other trees and shrubs, including Apple, birches, Bird Cherry, cotoneasters and willows. **FIELD NOTES** Apr–Jun. Rests openly on leaves. Young larva disperses in the wind and feeds solitarily. Pupates in a slight silken cocoon in a bark crevice or between leaves. Overwinters as an egg within an egg mass covered with the adult female's abdominal scales.

BROWN-TAIL
Euproctis chrysorrhoea

PLATE 37
72.012 (2029)

Local. Sometimes abundant along the south and east coasts of England, and in London, and increasingly establishing inland. **FIELD CHARACTERS** Body dark grey or blackish, sometimes paler anteriorly. Covered in cushions of short brown hairs dorsally and long pale hairs arising from verrucae elsewhere. Paired orange dorsal lines or dashes frequently from A3 posteriorly, with subdorsal tufts of short white hairs. Orange dorsal projections A6–A7. **HABITATS** Gardens, street trees and urban parks, hedgerows, and scrub in many situations. **FOODPLANTS** Wide variety of broadleaf trees and shrubs, most commonly Blackthorn, Bramble and Hawthorn; also Alder, Apple, cherries, Dog-rose, Hazel, Pear, Sea-buckthorn and willows. Has been recorded on European Larch. Following defoliation in spring, larvae disperse and may feed on herbaceous plants, including Agrimony, docks, Common Fleabane, grasses, Meadowsweet, Common Nettle, Common Ragwort and Silverweed. **FIELD NOTES** Sep–May, living gregariously in a conspicuous web. In autumn, small larvae form a tough whitish silken tent in which to overwinter communally, the only species to do so. Pupates in a hairy silken cocoon among foliage. The microscopic brown hairs are acutely irritating to most animals, including humans, where they commonly cause an intensely itchy skin rash.

YELLOW-TAIL
Euproctis similis

PLATE 37
72.013 (2030)

Common. More local or rare in the north and west. **FIELD CHARACTERS** Body black, and raised to a hump on A1, with black verrucae and tufts of long black and shorter white hairs. Paired red or orange dorsal lines or dashes T3 and A3–A7, with short, broad white hairs A1–A2 and sometimes A8, and in a band of tufts subdorsally. Orange or red dorsal projections A6–A7 and paired dorsal spots on A9. There are also variable red marks on A1, A2 and A7. **HABITATS** Wide variety, including gardens and urban parks. **FOODPLANTS** Wide variety of broadleaf trees and shrubs, including Apple, Beech, birches, Blackthorn, Bog-myrtle, Bramble, Alder Buckthorn, Sweet Chestnut, elms, Gooseberry, hawthorns, Hazel, Heather, oaks, Pear, roses and willows, and occasionally herbaceous plants such as grasses, Japanese Knotweed and nettles. **FIELD NOTES** Sep–Jun. Rests openly on leaves. Lives gregariously only in autumn. Pupates in a hairy silken cocoon among foliage. Overwinters as a larva, singly, in a tough silken hibernaculum until April.

PALE TUSSOCK
Calliteara pudibunda

PLATE 38
72.015 (2028)

Common. Frequent except in Scotland and the far north of Ireland. **FIELD CHARACTERS** Body bright or dark yellow, or green, and densely covered with long yellow, pink or grey hairs. Thick tufts of long yellow, white or pinkish-brown hairs on dorsum A1–A4. A very long, narrow tuft of red or brown hairs on A8. When disturbed the larva flexes anteriorly, revealing contrasting black patches between the dorsal tufts. **HABITATS** Wide variety, including gardens and urban parks. **FOODPLANTS** Wide variety of broadleaf trees and shrubs, including Crab Apple, Barberry, Beech, Blackthorn, elms, hawthorns, Hazel, limes, oaks, Sycamore and willows. The larva used to be seen commonly feeding on cultivated Hop, and was known as the 'Hop dog'. **FIELD NOTES** Jul–Sep. Often seen wandering on the ground in autumn prior to pupation. Pupates in a hairy silken cocoon among leaves or leaf litter. Overwinters as a pupa.

DARK TUSSOCK
Dicallomera fascelina

PLATE 38
72.016 (2027)

Local. Very local in the south, Channel Islands and in Ireland; more widespread in Scotland. **FIELD CHARACTERS** Body black, dark grey or brownish and densely covered with long grey, yellow or yellowish-brown hairs. Thick tufts of long black hairs on dorsum A1–A5, edged laterally with shorter white hairs. Sometimes the tufts on A3–A5 are entirely white. A thick tuft of very long black hairs on A8. Small pinkish-grey dorsal projections A6–A7. **HABITATS** Coastal cliffs, sand dunes and vegetated shingle, and heathland and moorland. **FOODPLANTS** Mainly Heather; also Cross-leaved Heath on heaths and moors, and a wide variety of woody plants in other habitats, including birches, Bramble, Broom, Gorse (flowers), hawthorns, Hazel, Wild Plum, and Creeping, Goat and Grey willows. **FIELD NOTES** Aug–Jun. Rests openly in spring. Pupates in a hairy silken cocoon among vegetation. Overwinters as a small larva in a silken hibernaculum, and in Scotland has been noted to overwinter twice as a larva, beginning the second diapause in early Jul.

VAPOURER
Orgyia antiqua

PLATE 38
72.017 (2026)

Common. **FIELD CHARACTERS** Body bluish grey with reddish verrucae and tufts of grey hairs. Dorsal stripe black, or sometimes brown A6–A8. Thick tufts of long white, yellow or brown hairs on dorsum A1–A4; the anterior two tufts may differ in colour from the posterior two. Tufts of very long black hairs, some with broad rounded ends, arise subdorsally on T1 and point forwards at an angle, point laterally on A2 and point backwards on the dorsum on A8. Also a compact tuft of white hairs arising laterally on A1. Small reddish projections on dorsum A6–A7. **SIMILAR SPECIES** Scarce Vapourer has a black body with orange stripes and lacks the compact white lateral tuft on A1 and the black lateral tuft on A2. **HABITATS** Wide variety, including gardens and urban parks. **FOODPLANTS** Mainly woody plants, including Bilberry, birches (the main foodplant in Scotland), Blackthorn, Bog-myrtle, young conifers, cotoneasters, Black Currant, elms, Firethorn, hawthorns, Hazel, Heather, limes, oaks, roses, Sitka Spruce, Sycamore and willows. Also reported on Bracken and herbaceous plants such as elephant-ears, lilies and Garden Strawberry. **FIELD NOTES** May–Sep. Rests openly on leaves. Pupates in a hairy silken cocoon among the foodplant or hard structures. Overwinters as an egg in an egg mass on the maternal cocoon.

SCARCE VAPOURER
Orgyia recens

PLATE 38
72.018 (2025)

RDB. Restricted to a few sites in East Anglia and the Midlands. **FIELD CHARACTERS** Body black with dark brownish or orangey verrucae and tufts of whitish-grey hairs. Thick tufts of brown or orangey hairs on dorsum A1–A4. Subdorsal and spiracular stripes orange, with subdorsal tufts of stout white or yellowish hairs T1–T3 and A5–A8. Tufts of very long black hairs, some with broad rounded ends, arise subdorsally on T1 and point forwards at an angle, and backwards on the dorsum on A8. Small pinkish or greyish projections on dorsum A6–A7. **SIMILAR SPECIES** Vapourer. **HABITATS** Bogs, fens, heathland, hedgerows and wet woodland. **FOODPLANTS** Mainly hawthorns, oaks and willows. Also recorded on a variety of other trees, shrubs and herbaceous plants, including Alder, Beech, birches, Blackthorn, Bramble, Alder Buckthorn, Water Dock, elms, Hazel, heathers, Meadowsweet, roses, Common Sorrel and Rosebay Willowherb. **FIELD NOTES** Aug–Jun, with a partial second generation. Pupates in a hairy silken cocoon spun among leaves. Overwinters as a small larva.

ARCTIINAE

BUFF ERMINE
Spilosoma lutea

PLATE 38
72.019 (2061)

Common; local in Scotland. Has decreased significantly in abundance in recent decades. **FIELD CHARACTERS** Body grey, and covered with tufts of long, pale brown hairs. A white dorsal line is sometimes present and the white lateral stripe is sometimes dashed. **HABITATS** Wide variety including gardens and urban parks. **FOODPLANTS** Wide variety of herbaceous and woody plants and shrubs, especially Balm, Barberry, birches, Elder, Honeysuckle, Hop, Common Ivy (flowers and leaves), jasmines, Common Nettle, Nipplewort, Wild Plum, Common Ragwort and Virginia-creepers. Recorded as eggs and first instar larvae on broadleaf trees including Blackthorn, Hawthorn, Pedunculate Oak, Rowan, whitebeams and Grey Willow. First instar larvae have been observed feeding on the underside of a leaf in an Apple tree; they had all fallen to the ground by second instar. Has been found on ferns. **FIELD NOTES** Jul–Oct. Feeds near the ground at night or higher in hedges. Pupates in a hairy silken cocoon on the ground. Overwinters as a pupa.

WHITE ERMINE
Spilosoma lubricipeda

PLATE 38
72.020 (2060)

Common. Has decreased significantly in abundance in recent decades. **FIELD CHARACTERS** Body blackish or dark brown, and covered with tufts of long black hairs. Dorsal stripe orangey or reddish and spiracles pale orange or white. **SIMILAR SPECIES** Water Ermine is more consistently blackish with a paler, usually whitish dorsal stripe, but these characters cannot be relied on for field identification. **HABITATS** Wide variety, including gardens and urban parks. **FOODPLANTS** Wide variety of herbaceous plants, especially docks, Common Nettle and Common Ragwort (flowers and seeds). Has been recorded on hawthorns. **FIELD NOTES** Jul–Sep. Pupates on the ground in a hairy silken cocoon. Overwinters as a pupa.

WATER ERMINE
Spilosoma urticae

PLATE 38
72.021 (2062)

Nb; suspected immigrant. Very local along coasts and occasionally found inland. **FIELD CHARACTERS** Body black or bluish black, sometimes dark brown, with tufts of long black or occasionally dark brown hairs. Dorsal stripe whitish, sometimes darker, and spiracles white. **SIMILAR SPECIES** White Ermine. **HABITATS** Dune-slacks, saltmarshes, vegetated shingle and wetlands, where often associated with ditches. **FOODPLANTS** Variety of herbaceous plants, including bedstraws, Water Dock, Yellow Iris, Yellow Loosestrife, louseworts, Water Mint, and Common and Marsh ragworts. **FIELD NOTES** Late Jun–early Sep. Pupates on the ground or among leaves of the foodplant, in a hairy silken cocoon. Overwinters as a pupa.

MUSLIN MOTH
Diaphora mendica

PLATE 39
72.022 (2063)

Common. Local in Scotland. **FIELD CHARACTERS** Head pale or orangey brown. Body greyish brown with tufts of long, pale brown hairs. Dorsal line whitish and indistinct. **SIMILAR SPECIES** Ruby Tiger has a dark brown or black head, usually a more obvious dorsal stripe, and posteriorly the hairs are longer and more swept back. Fully fed larvae found in late autumn or spring are Ruby Tiger, as Muslin Moth is a pupa over this period. **HABITATS** Wide variety of open habitats, including gardens and urban parks, grasslands, hedgerows, limestone pavement, sand dunes and open woodland. **FOODPLANTS** Wide variety of herbaceous plants, including dandelions, Red and White dead-nettles, docks, Great Mullein, Common Nettle, plantains and stitchworts. Eggs have been found in the wild on Cock's-foot and the larvae fed on it in captivity. Recorded as eggs and first-instar larvae on Apple and young larvae ate the leaves before dropping to the ground. Has also been observed on Aspen, birches, Bramble, Pedunculate Oak and roses. **FIELD NOTES** Mid-Jun–early Sep. Pupates on the ground in a hairy silken cocoon.

CLOUDED BUFF
Diacrisia sannio

PLATE 39
72.023 (2059)

Local. **FIELD CHARACTERS** Body black with tufts of black or brown hairs. Dorsal stripe is alternating white and red or white and orange, sometimes all white, or occasionally comprises white dashes or spots. Spiracles white. **HABITATS** Marshy grassland, heathland and moorland; less often on calcareous grassland and in open woodland. **FOODPLANTS** Various herbaceous and woody plants, including Bog-myrtle, dandelions, docks, Common Dog-violet, Heather, Bell Heather, Mouse-ear-hawkweed, plantains, Devil's-bit Scabious, Sheep's Sorrel and stitchworts. **FIELD NOTES** Aug–May. Pupates in a flimsy cocoon on or near the ground. Overwinters as a small larva.

RUBY TIGER
Phragmatobia fuliginosa

PLATE 39
72.024 (2064)

Has increased significantly in abundance in recent decades. Ssp. *fuliginosa* Common. Northern Ruby Tiger ssp. *borealis* Common. Scotland. **FIELD CHARACTERS** Head dark brown or black. Body greyish brown, sometimes blackish, with tufts of hairs that posteriorly are slightly longer and swept back. The hair colour may be pale brown, dark brown or black. In the south the pale brown form predominates, although dark forms do occur. In Scotland the dark forms are common. Dorsal stripe or spots yellowish. In Scotland the body and hairs are usually dark brown or black. **SIMILAR SPECIES** Muslin Moth. **HABITATS** Wide variety of open habitats, including gardens and urban parks. **FOODPLANTS** Wide variety of mainly herbaceous and some woody plants, and especially fond of ragworts. Has also been recorded on Bramble, Broom, dandelions, docks, Escallonia, Common Fleabane, Goldenrod, heathers, Purple Moor-grass, plantains, Spindle, stitchworts, Creeping Thistle, twayblades, Eared Willow and Yarrow. **FIELD NOTES** May–Jul and Aug–Apr in the south; Jul–May in the north. Basks in spring sunshine. Pupates on the ground or among heathers in a hairy silken cocoon. Usually overwinters fully fed but may feed a little in spring.

WOOD TIGER
Parasemia plantaginis

PLATE 39
72.025 (2056)

Ssp. *plantaginis* Local. Ssp. *insularum* Northern Scotland, Orkney and Shetland. **FIELD CHARACTERS** Body black. Tufts of hairs on the dorsum are usually black on one or more thoracic segments, and orangey brown from T3– or A1–A4, and sometimes –A8. Lateral hairs orangey brown or yellowish white. Exceptionally, dorsal hairs on T1 black, the remainder orangey brown. **HABITATS** Unimproved calcareous grassland, scrubby grassland, heathland, moorland, and open woodland including coppice. **FOODPLANTS** Wide variety of mainly herbaceous plants, including burdocks, Salad Burnet, dandelions, docks, Groundsel, Hound's-tongue, Dog's Mercury, Common Nettle, plantains, ragworts, Common Rock-rose and violets. Also Bell Heather. **FIELD NOTES** Jul–early Jun. Basks in spring sunshine. Pupates among vegetation in a hairy silken cocoon. Overwinters half-grown.

GARDEN TIGER
Arctia caja

PLATE 39
72.026 (2057)

Common. This species has declined severely in abundance in recent decades in inland areas of southern England, but remains frequent along coasts, and in northern England and Scotland. **FIELD CHARACTERS** Known as the 'woolly bear' owing to its exceptional hairiness. Head black. Body black, with contrasting whitish verrucae. Tufts of hairs are long and orange on T1–T2, sometimes –T3, and below spiracles on all segments, and elsewhere are very long and whitish grey. Also shorter black hairs interspersed on dorsum. Spiracles white. **HABITATS** Wide variety of open habitats. **FOODPLANTS** Recorded as eggs and first-instar larvae on broadleaf trees, including Apple, Blackthorn, Rowan, and Eared and Grey willows. Also recorded on Bracken and Water Horsetail as young larvae, and on Scots Pine and Norway Spruce. Wide variety of herbaceous plants, including burdocks, dandelions, dead-nettles, docks, Hound's-tongue, Common Nettle, plantains, Common and Marsh ragworts, Smooth Sowthistle and thistles. **FIELD NOTES** Aug–late Jun, overwintering when small. In autumn it may feed in tall vegetation, while in spring it stays close to the ground. When fully fed the larva disperses and may be seen crossing bare ground at great speed. Pupates on the ground in a hairy silken cocoon.

CREAM-SPOT TIGER
Arctia villica

PLATE 39
72.027 (2058)

Ssp. *britannica* Local. **FIELD CHARACTERS** Head, true legs and prolegs red. Body black, with grey or blackish verrucae. Tufts of hairs may be black or pale brown, although sometimes the longer hairs are black and the shorter hairs pale brown. Spiracles cream. **HABITATS** Open cliff habitats, saltmarsh grassland, heathland and sand dunes. Less often on calcareous grassland and in open woodland. **FOODPLANTS** Wide variety of herbaceous and, less often, woody plants, including cherries, Cock's-foot, dandelions, White

Dead-nettle, docks, Dogwood, young shoots of Gorse, Groundsel, hawkweeds, Black Horehound, Common Nettle, ragworts, roses and stitchworts. Recorded as eggs and first-instar larvae on Grey Willow. **FIELD NOTES** Aug–Apr. Feeds throughout winter and basks in sunshine in early spring. Pupates on the ground in a flimsy cocoon.

SCARLET TIGER
Callimorpha dominula

PLATE 40
72.029 (2068)

Local. **FIELD CHARACTERS** Body black with black verrucae and bluish spots. Tufts of bristly hairs mixed black and white. Dorsal and lateral stripes comprise yellow blotches and white spots. **HABITATS** Coastal habitats including undercliff, unmanaged dry grassland including road verges, wet grassland, riverbanks and other wetlands. Also gardens and urban parks. **FOODPLANTS** Green Alkanet, Borage, comfreys, Water Forget-me-not, Foxglove, geraniums, Hemp-agrimony, Hound's-tongue and Common Nettle. The larva disperses in last instar and feeds on various herbaceous and woody plants, including birches, Blackthorn, Bramble, cherries, docks, Wych Elm, Common Evening-primrose, Groundsel, Honeysuckle, horsetails, Meadowsweet, Creeping Thistle and willows. **FIELD NOTES** Aug–May. Feeds openly on the foodplant from early spring, often with others. Pupates on the ground in a silken cocoon. Overwinters as a part-grown larva.

JERSEY TIGER
Euplagia quadripunctaria

PLATE 40
72.030 (2067)

Local. Expanding its range east and north. **FIELD CHARACTERS** Body black with large orange verrucae. Tufts of bristly hairs whitish or creamy orange. Dorsal stripe orange, sometimes cream or yellowish, and spiracular stripe comprises white spots. **HABITATS** Wide variety, including gardens and urban parks, unimproved grassland, old quarries and waste ground. **FOODPLANTS** Wide variety of herbaceous and woody plants, including Green Alkanet, Borage, Bramble, dandelions, White Dead-nettle, elms, forget-me-nots, Ground-ivy, Groundsel, Hemp-agrimony, Honeysuckle, lettuces, Common Nettle, plantains and roses. **FIELD NOTES** Sep–May. Feeds at night, and is often found in gardens by day in spring. Pupates on the ground in a silken cocoon. Overwinters when small.

CINNABAR
Tyria jacobaeae

PLATE 40
72.031 (2069)

Common. Has decreased significantly in abundance in recent decades. Mainly coastal in northern England and Scotland. **FIELD CHARACTERS** Body yellow, with a transverse black band on each segment. Sparsely covered with short black hairs, and with long pale hairs T1–A1 and A7–A8. **HABITATS** Open habitats, including grasslands, old quarries, sand dunes and waste ground. Also gardens and urban parks. **FOODPLANTS** Mainly Common Ragwort; also recorded on Colt's-foot, Oxeye Daisy, Flixweed, Groundsel, Heath Groundsel, Hop, Great Mullein, Hoary, Marsh, Oxford and Silver ragworts, Wood Sage and Yarrow. **FIELD NOTES** Jul–Sep. Feeds openly on the foodplant, usually with others. Pupates in or on the ground in a flimsy silken cocoon. Overwinters as a pupa.

SPECKLED FOOTMAN
Coscinia cribraria

PLATE 40
72.032 (2053)

Ssp. *bivittata* RDB. Probably resident in Dorset, and resident in Jersey. Ssp. *arenaria* Immigrant. **FIELD CHARACTERS** Head black. Body black with black verrucae. Tufts of bristly hairs black and grey. Dorsal and subdorsal lines white, often with white intersegmental bands and transverse dorsal bars. **HABITATS** Heathland, and mainly sand dunes in Jersey. **FOODPLANTS** Bristle Bent in Dorset, probably other fine-leaved grasses, and reported from heathers and Bilberry. **FIELD NOTES** Sep–Jun. Basks on grass stems in sunshine in early spring. Pupates among vegetation in a flimsy silken cocoon. Overwinters as a small larva.

ROSY FOOTMAN
Miltochrista miniata

PLATE 40
72.035 (2037)

Local. Has increased significantly in abundance in recent decades. **FIELD CHARACTERS** Body greyish, and densely covered with tufts of long grey or brownish-grey hairs. The hairs are mostly plumose and just a few are straight. The tufts on A4–A8 are paler than the others. **SIMILAR SPECIES** Four-dotted Footman and Round-winged Muslin both have shorter, less dense tufts of hairs, and the tufts are uniform in colour. The body of Four-dotted Footman is much darker. **HABITATS** Wooded heathland, dense hedgerows, dense scrub and woodland. **FOODPLANTS** Algae, lichens, including the foliose species *Peltigera membranacea*, and mosses that grow on trunks and twigs of trees. **FIELD NOTES** Aug–May. Pupates in a hairy silken cocoon. The hairs project outwards, making the cocoon look particularly hairy.

MUSLIN FOOTMAN
Nudaria mundana

PLATE 40
72.036 (2038)

Local. Has increased significantly in abundance over much of its range in recent decades but remains very local in south-east England and East Anglia. **FIELD CHARACTERS** Body grey with grey verrucae and tufts of long grey hairs. There is a black dorsal patch on A4, and yellow subdorsal spots A1–A9. **SIMILAR SPECIES** White Plume *Pterophorus pentadactyla* (Pterophoridae) lacks the black dorsal patch on A4. **HABITATS** Cliffs including scree on undercliffs, old quarries, stony habitats including drystone walls, and occasionally in gardens and woodland. **FOODPLANTS** Small lichens growing on stones, and on branches of isolated trees and bushes. **FIELD NOTES** Aug–early Jun. Rests under stones, especially the top layer of a drystone wall or scree. May be found feeding openly in the early morning when the surface is damp. Pupates in a crevice in a flimsy, hairy silken cocoon.

ROUND-WINGED MUSLIN
Thumatha senex

PLATE 40
72.037 (2035)

Local. Very local away from southern, central and eastern England. **FIELD CHARACTERS** Body brown or grey, and covered with tufts of hairs, comprising a mixture of plumose grey and straight brown hairs. **SIMILAR SPECIES** Rosy Footman and Four-dotted Footman. **HABITATS** Bogs, fens, wet grassland, marshes, reedbeds, wet flushes on moorland, and slacks in sand dunes. **FOODPLANTS** Algae, lichens including foliose *Peltigera* spp., and mosses including Silky Wall Feather-moss and Common Pincushion. Larvae have been found in reedbeds, among dead leaves in tussocks of grasses and sedges, and in leaf litter. **FIELD NOTES** Late Aug–May. Pupates in a brownish, hairy silken cocoon. Overwinters as a small larva.

FOUR-DOTTED FOOTMAN
Cybosia mesomella

PLATE 40
72.038 (2040)

Local. Very local further north and in Scotland but increasing its range. **FIELD CHARACTERS** Body blackish grey or black. Tufts are black or dark brown, comprising a mixture of plumose and straight hairs. **SIMILAR SPECIES** Rosy Footman and Round-winged Muslin. **HABITATS** Fens, heathland, wet grassland, moorland and damp open woodland. **FOODPLANTS** Algae and lichens growing on plants such as heathers, willows and other woody vegetation. Has been found resting on a Bramble leaf ready to moult, following which it fed on Bramble in captivity. **FIELD NOTES** Mid-Aug–late May. Pupates among vegetation or in a bark crevice, in a loose silken cocoon.

DOTTED FOOTMAN

Pelosia muscerda

PLATE 40

72.039 (2041)

RDB; immigrant. Resident in the Norfolk Broads. **FIELD CHARACTERS** Head black. Body dark greyish with black or dark brown verrucae. Tufts comprise short, straight grey or brown hairs. The velvety-black dorsal stripe may be broken into dashes, with paired orangey or reddish spots on T1 and A9. These spots may become dull and less distinct in the final instar. Sometimes there are paired whitish spots on other segments. **SIMILAR SPECIES** Small Dotted Footman lacks orangey or reddish spots on T1 and A9 and is usually overall more brownish. **HABITATS** Fens, preferring wetter areas with scattered Alder and willow scrub. **FOODPLANTS** Unknown in the wild; probably decaying vegetation, algae and lichens. **FIELD NOTES** Aug–May. Pupates in a grey cocoon within an outer white cocoon.

SMALL DOTTED FOOTMAN

Pelosia obtusa

PLATE 40

72.040 (2042)

RDB; possible immigrant. Resident in the Norfolk Broads and adjacent fens. **FIELD CHARACTERS** Head brown. Body dark greyish brown with grey or blackish-brown verrucae. Tufts comprise short, straight brown hairs. Dorsal stripe blackish brown and lateral stripe blackish brown, sometimes edged paler. **SIMILAR SPECIES** Dotted Footman. **HABITATS** Unmanaged and cyclically cut reedbeds that are free from scrub. **FOODPLANTS** Probably decaying Common Reed and other marshland vegetation. **FIELD NOTES** Aug–May, feeding mainly at night. Pupates in a double cocoon.

FOUR-SPOTTED FOOTMAN

Lithosia quadra

PLATE 40

72.041 (2051)

Na; immigrant. Resident and sometimes locally abundant in southern coastal areas and increasingly establishing inland. **FIELD CHARACTERS** Body black with verrucae that are orange subdorsally and grey, sometimes mixed with orange, elsewhere. Hairs long and grey. Wavy yellow lines and marks all over, more pronounced along the dorsum, except on T2, T3, A4 and A8, where the body may be much blacker and often raised to slight humps. **SIMILAR SPECIES** Red-necked Footman is a smaller larva, appearing more greenish yellow, with orange verrucae laterally, and it is fully grown in autumn when Four-spotted Footman will be very small. **HABITATS** Mainly broadleaf woodland, and also scrub. Sometimes in gardens along the coast. **FOODPLANTS** Lichens, including *Flavoparmelia caperata* and *Peltigera membranacea*, and green algae, including *Pleurococcus naegelii*, that grow on trunks and branches of trees and on rocks. Sometimes feeds on foliage of oaks. **FIELD NOTES** Sep–late Jun. Pupates in a bark crevice, in a flimsy, hairy silken cocoon. Overwinters as a small larva.

RED-NECKED FOOTMAN

Atolmis rubricollis

PLATE 41

72.042 (2039)

Local; immigrant. Expanding its range. **FIELD CHARACTERS** Body black, heavily overlaid with wavy greenish-yellow lines and marks. These are more pronounced along the dorsum, except on A4 and A8, where the body is often darker or with blackish marks and may be raised to slight humps. Verrucae orangey throughout and hairs grey. **SIMILAR SPECIES** Four-spotted Footman. **HABITATS** Coniferous plantations and broadleaf woodlands. Also wooded heathland. **FOODPLANTS** Algae, including *Pleurococcus naegelii*, and lichens growing on trunks and branches of trees and on fence palings. **FIELD NOTES** Aug–Oct. Rests openly on tree trunks. Pupates in a bark crevice or on the ground in a silken cocoon. Overwinters as a pupa.

BUFF FOOTMAN
Eilema depressa

PLATE 41
72.043 (2049)

Local. Has increased very significantly in abundance in recent decades and is expanding its range northwards. **FIELD CHARACTERS** Body greenish grey, sometimes dark grey, speckled black and with grey verrucae. Tufts of hairs greyish and blackish. Dorsal band yellow, whitish or greenish white, sometimes interrupted, and edged black. The band includes black marks or wavy lines, except on T3, A4 and A8, where the body may be raised to slight humps and is often more blackish. **HABITATS** Fens, scrub on calcareous grassland and heathland, and woodland. **FOODPLANTS** Algae, including *Pleurococcus naegelii*, and lichens, including *Flavoparmelia* spp., growing on branches of deciduous and evergreen trees and scrub and on rocks. **FIELD NOTES** Sept–late Jun. Pupates among lichens or in a bark crevice, in a silken cocoon. Overwinters as a small larva.

DINGY FOOTMAN
Eilema griseola

PLATE 41
72.044 (2044)

Common. Has increased very significantly in abundance in recent decades and is expanding its range northwards. **FIELD CHARACTERS** Body greyish black or black with black verrucae. Tufts of hairs black. Dorsal line black, usually interrupted with broad orange marks on T2, or T1–T3, and on A9. Subdorsal stripe orange, often comprising broad or narrow orange spots or dashes. **HABITATS** Wide variety, especially wetlands and damp woodland. **FOODPLANTS** Lichens, including *Peltigera membranacea*, and algae growing on trees and scrub. Has also been found feeding on a *Barbula* sp. moss growing on a stone. In captivity ate bark of Apple twigs once all the algae and lichens had been consumed. **FIELD NOTES** Aug–Jun. Pupates in a silk cocoon mixed with moss and lichens. Overwinters part grown.

COMMON FOOTMAN
Eilema lurideola

PLATE 41
72.045 (2050)

Common. Local in Scotland. **FIELD CHARACTERS** Body dark grey mixed black, with dark grey verrucae. Tufts of hairs grey. Spiracular stripe orange A1–A8 or A9, with orange verrucae and hairs. **HABITATS** Wide variety of lowland habitats, including gardens and urban parks. **FOODPLANTS** Lichens and algae growing on trees and scrub, fence posts, drystone walls and rocks. Also feeds on leaves of apples, Bramble, Dogwood, hawthorns and oaks, and the flowers of Gorse. **FIELD NOTES** Aug–Jun. Basks in sunshine in the spring. Pupates in a silken cocoon. Overwinters as a small larva.

SCARCE FOOTMAN
Eilema complana

PLATE 41
72.046 (2047)

Local. Has increased very significantly in abundance in recent decades and is expanding its range in northern England. **FIELD CHARACTERS** Body dark grey with grey verrucae. Tufts of hairs grey. Dorsal stripe black. Subdorsal stripe comprising large orange spots A1–A10, with smaller white spots to a variable extent in between. A faint, interrupted orange subspiracular line and a variable number of small white spots throughout. **SIMILAR SPECIES** Hoary Footman and Pigmy Footman have a subdorsal orange stripe or dashes T1–A9. Pigmy Footman is very similar to Hoary Footman; the former usually has broader black dorsal and orange subdorsal markings, but these two species are probably indistinguishable in the field. **HABITATS** Wide variety. **FOODPLANTS** Lichens and algae growing on rocks, walls, fence posts, branches, stems and on the ground. Also recorded feeding on the flowers of Gorse, and leaves of Ploughman's-spikenard. **FIELD NOTES** Aug–Jun. Pupates on a tree or on the ground in a slight silken cocoon. Overwinters as a small larva.

HOARY FOOTMAN
Eilema caniola

PLATE 41
72.047 (2045)

Nb; immigrant. Resident in coastal areas in south-west England and Wales, and inland in central, south-east and eastern England. **FIELD CHARACTERS** Body dark grey with grey verrucae. Tufts of hairs grey. Dorsal stripe or dashes black, edged with a thin, wavy, pale line. Subdorsal stripe orange, or orange and white comprising large orange marks usually linked with small white spots. Lateral lines wavy and pale. **SIMILAR SPECIES** Scarce Footman and Pigmy Footman. **HABITATS** Cliffs, old quarries and vegetated shingle. In addition, a variety of open habitats inland, including gardens. **FOODPLANTS** Lichens, especially black lichens, and algae growing on rocks, concrete and roof tiles; also the foliage of Common Bird's-foot-trefoil, clovers and Kidney Vetch. **FIELD NOTES** Sep–late Jun. Pupates on the ground in a loose silken cocoon.

PIGMY FOOTMAN
Eilema pygmaeola

PLATE 41
72.048 (2046)

Ssp. *pygmaeola* RDB; immigrant. A coastal species resident in Kent and Norfolk. Dungeness Pigmy Footman ssp. *pallifrons* RDB. Dungeness, Kent. **FIELD CHARACTERS** Probably indistinguishable in the field from Hoary Footman. **SIMILAR SPECIES** Scarce Footman and Hoary Footman. **HABITATS** Sand dunes and vegetated shingle. **FOODPLANTS** Lichens, likely to include *Cladonia rangiformis*, and algae growing on pebbles, plant stems and fence posts. **FIELD NOTES** Aug–Jun. Rests on grass blades at night, hiding under debris by day. A silken 'nest' of small larvae has been found at the base of a dead grass stem on shingle in mid-Apr. Pupates among lichens and moss in a flimsy silken cocoon. Overwinters as a small larva.

ORANGE FOOTMAN
Eilema sororcula

PLATE 41
72.049 (2043)

Local; suspected immigrant. Expanding its range. **FIELD CHARACTERS** Body dark grey. Verrucae are orange subdorsally, except on T3, A4 and A8, where they are black. Tufts of short grey and sandy hairs throughout, interspersed with long grey hairs T1–T3 and A8–A9. Dorsal stripe black, edged with a thin, wavy whitish line and merging with whitish dorsal patches between segments T2 and T3, and on A5 and A9. Dorsum black on T3, A4 and A8 and raised to slight humps. **HABITATS** Mature scrub, broadleaf and mixed woodland, and probably gardens and urban parks. **FOODPLANTS** Lichens and algae. **FIELD NOTES** Late Jun–Sep. Larvae may be local to a particular tree and absent from surrounding ones. Pupates among moss in a slight silken cocoon. Overwinters as a pupa.

DEW MOTH
Setina irrorella

PLATE 41
72.050 (2036)

Na. Exists in scattered colonies along southern and western coasts; rarely found inland. **FIELD CHARACTERS** Body dark grey with dark grey or black verrucae. Tufts of hairs long and dark grey. Dorsal stripe bright yellow, comprising diamond-shaped marks. Subdorsal stripe comprises pale yellow spots and spiracular stripe a mix of pale and bright yellow spots. **HABITATS** Cliffs, chalk grassland, limestone pavement (the Burren, Cos Clare and Galway, Ireland) and vegetated shingle. **FOODPLANTS** Black and orange lichens on pebbles and rocks. **FIELD NOTES** Aug–Jun. Feeds and basks openly in sunshine and rests under stones. Pupates among stones or in a rock crevice in a loose cocoon.

HERMINIINAE

CLAY FAN-FOOT
Paracolax tristalis

PLATE 41
72.051 (2494)

Na; immigrant. Resident in south-east England. **FIELD CHARACTERS** Head speckled brown. Body somewhat bulbous posteriorly, and velvety brown, with indistinct darker dorsal and subdorsal lines. **HABITATS** Broadleaf woodland, preferring open areas with young regrowth. **FOODPLANTS** Oaks, and possibly other trees. **FIELD NOTES** Aug–early Jun. Has been beaten from branches in autumn and is stated to feed on damp fallen leaves. Pupates on the ground. Overwinters as a small larva in spun leaves on the ground.

DOTTED FAN-FOOT
Macrochilo cribrumalis

PLATE 41
72.052 (2493)

Nb. Most frequently found in East Anglia. **FIELD CHARACTERS** Head mottled brown. Body speckled pale brown, with a dark dorsal line edged paler and extending over anal plate. Subdorsal line pale. Pinacula small and black. **HABITATS** Variety of wetlands, including bogs, ditches, fens and marshes. **FOODPLANTS** Reported to feed on Wood-sedge and wood-rushes, eating leaves and living within stems. **FIELD NOTES** Jul–May. Pupates among vegetation on the ground. Overwinters part-grown.

FAN-FOOT
Herminia tarsipennalis

PLATE 41
72.053 (2489)

Common. **FIELD CHARACTERS** Body reddish brown speckled yellow, with a slightly darker dorsal line. Pinacula black, edged with a pale yellow halo. There is a large and conspicuous yellowish spot laterally on A7 within which is a pinaculum. **SIMILAR SPECIES** Small Fan-foot has a contrasting darker dorsal stripe. **HABITATS** Gardens and urban parks with dense undergrowth, hedgerows, scrub and broadleaf woodland. **FOODPLANTS** Withered leaves of a variety of trees and shrubs, including Beech, Bramble, Common Ivy, oaks, Raspberry and Goat Willow. **FIELD NOTES** Jul–Apr. Feeds on leaves attached to fallen or broken branches, on the ground, and in Common Ivy thickets. Overwinters fully fed, spinning a cocoon on the ground in autumn, and pupating in spring.

SHADED FAN-FOOT
Herminia tarsicrinalis

PLATE 41
72.054 (2491)

RDB; suspected immigrant. Resident in East Anglia. **FIELD CHARACTERS** Head mottled brown. Body brown or greyish brown, and pinacula black. Backward-pointing triangular, dark brown marks on dorsum at least on A1–A7, edged paler laterally. Whitish or yellowish warts subdorsally A1–A9 and conspicuous A8–A9. **SIMILAR SPECIES** Common Fan-foot and Plumed Fan-foot both lack white or yellow subdorsal warts. Plumed Fan-foot has yellowish spots in the dorsal line and a somewhat expanded body shape T3–A1. Shaded Fan-foot alone has the backward-pointing triangular marks on the dorsum. **HABITATS** Bramble thickets in open scrub, and woodland with dense Bramble understorey. **FOODPLANTS** Unknown in the wild; probably on wilted Bramble leaves. **FIELD NOTES** Late Jul–May. Pupates among leaf litter in a cocoon. Overwinters nearly fully fed.

SMALL FAN-FOOT
Herminia grisealis

PLATE 4
72.055 (2492

Common. Local in northern Scotland. **FIELD CHARACTERS** Body reddish brown speckled yellow, with a dark brown dorsal stripe. Pinacula black, edged with a pale yellow halo. There is a large and conspicuous yellow spot laterally on A7, within which is a pinaculum. **SIMILAR SPECIES** Fan-foot. **HABITATS** Mainly scrub and woodland. Also in hedgerows, and gardens and urban parks. **FOODPLANTS** Wide variety of trees and scrub, including Alder, birches including Downy Birch, Bramble, Bird Cherry, elms, hawthorns, Hazel, Hornbeam,

Small-leaved Lime, oaks including Pedunculate Oak, Raspberry, Rhododendron, Sycamore and Traveller's-joy. **FIELD NOTES** Jul–Oct. Feeds among living leaves, and withered ones attached to broken branches and on the ground. Pupates in a bark crevice or on the ground in a cocoon. Overwinters as a pupa.

COMMON FAN-FOOT
Pechipogo strigilata

PLATE 41
72.056 (2488)

Na. A much-declined species. Now recorded from scattered locations in central and southern England only. **FIELD CHARACTERS** Head brown with slight mottling. Body brown or orangey brown, pinacula black and dorsal line dark grey. Dark subdorsal and lateral markings sometimes forming diagonal shading laterally. **SIMILAR SPECIES** Shaded Fan-foot and Plumed Fan-foot. **HABITATS** Ancient woodland with bushy understorey, appearing to benefit from long-rotation coppice management. **FOODPLANTS** Withered leaves of Pedunculate Oak, and probably other species such as Hazel. **FIELD NOTES** Jul–Apr. Prefers leaves on damaged branches. Pupates in leaf litter or a bark crevice in a flimsy cocoon. Overwinters almost fully fed.

PLUMED FAN-FOOT
Pechipogo plumigeralis

PLATE 41
72.057 (2488a)

Immigrant; colonist. Probably resident in London and on the south-east coast. **FIELD CHARACTERS** Head mottled brown. Body various shades of brown, with oblique reddish streaks laterally, and somewhat expanded in shape T3–A1. Dorsal line dark with up to six yellow intersegmental spots between A1 and A7, sometimes with similar subdorsal marks adjacent. **SIMILAR SPECIES** Shaded Fan-foot and Common Fan-foot. **HABITATS** Gardens and urban parks in London. **FOODPLANTS** Unknown in the wild in England. In Europe on a variety of unrelated plants. **FIELD NOTES** Aug–Jun. Probably pupates on the ground.

HYPENODINAE

There are three species in this subfamily: Marsh Oblique-barred *Hypenodes humidalis* 72.060 (2485); Pinion-streaked Snout *Schrankia costaestrigalis* 72.061 (2484); and White-line Snout *Schrankia taenialis* 72.062 (2482). None of these species has been found as a larva in the wild in Great Britain or Ireland and they are not illustrated in this field guide. Characteristically, the larva has a reduced number of prolegs, A5–A6 only, and exhibits looping movement similar to most Geometridae. In captivity, larvae feed on flowers and leaves of healthy vegetation, and less often wilting leaves, of various herbaceous plants and shrubs. Young larvae of Marsh Oblique-barred have also fed on *Sphagnum* moss in captivity for several weeks. It is likely all species overwinter as a larva in the wild. All three species are known in captivity to pupate in suspended cocoons made of pieces of vegetation spun together.

Pinion-streaked Snout suspended cocoon

TOXOCAMPINAE

BLACKNECK
Lygephila pastinum

PLATE 41
72.063 (2466)

Local. **FIELD CHARACTERS** Body pale grey, heavily speckled with black above subspiracular stripe, dark grey or blackish below, and the dorsum may be broadly shaded darker or blackish. Dorsal line may be paler with yellow spots, subdorsal line white with yellow spots, and subspiracular stripe white with interrupted yellow above. Prolegs on A3–A4 less well developed than others. **HABITATS** Fens, calcareous grassland, damp or wet unimproved grassland, marshes, meadows and pastures, and woodland rides. **FOODPLANTS** Tufted and Wood vetches; also Marsh Pea, and milk-vetches including Wild Liquorice. **FIELD**

NOTES Aug–late May. Feeds at night. Pupates on or just beneath the ground in a cocoon. Overwinters as a small larva.

SCARCE BLACKNECK
Lygephila craccae

PLATE 41
72.064 (2467)

RDB; suspected immigrant. Resident at a few sites on the north coast of south-west England. **FIELD CHARACTERS** Body grey dorsally, pale brownish laterally and dark grey below the orangey-brown subspiracular stripe. Pinacula black, edged with a pale halo. Dorsal line black or brownish, edged whitish, subdorsal stripe brown and white, and wavy brownish stripes and black lines laterally. The pair of prolegs on A3 is less well developed than the others. **HABITATS** Rocky and steep cliff habitats, preferring recent landslips where Wood Vetch colonises, and grassy areas on the cliff top with Tufted Vetch. **FOODPLANTS** Tufted and Wood vetches. **FIELD NOTES** May–early Jul. Feeds at night. Pupates on the ground in a cocoon. Overwinters as an egg.

BOLETOBIINAE

WAVED BLACK
Parascotia fuliginaria

PLATE 42
72.066 (2475)

Nb; suspected immigrant. Increasing in range. **FIELD CHARACTERS** Body black with large orange subdorsal and lateral pinacula and sparsely covered with long, curved hairs. Paired wavy grey lines along the dorsum. Prolegs absent A3–A4. **HABITATS** Sheltered and damp places in well-wooded gardens, wooded heathland, and damp or wet woodlands. **FOODPLANTS** Mainly fungi growing on rotting timber, especially bracket fungi on birches and pines. Most frequently recorded on *Piptoporus betulinus*, *Trametes versicolor* and *Trichaptum abietinum*. Also on *Botryobasidium* spp., *Cylindrobasidium laeve*, *Daldinia concentrica*, *Phaeolus schweinitzii*, *Stereum hirsutum* and *Tapinella panuoides*. Also feeds on slime moulds and the lichen *Cladonia fimbriata*. **FIELD NOTES** Aug–mid-Jun. Rests among the foodplant and can be difficult to see unless it moves. Pupates in a cocoon made of silk, frass, wood chips and other materials, suspended by silk threads at either end, like a hammock. Overwinters as a small larva.

SMALL PURPLE-BARRED
Phytometra viridaria

PLATE 42
72.067 (2470

Local. Has declined in England except in the south. **FIELD CHARACTERS** Body elongated and green. Dorsal line dark green, edged pale green, with three wavy, pale green subdorsal/lateral lines. Spiracular stripe pale green or whitish, variably defined. Prolegs on A3 absent, and on A4 much reduced. **HABITATS** Unimproved calcareous grassland, heathland, moorland, sand dunes and woodland rides. **FOODPLANTS** Common and Heath milkworts; also Lousewort. **FIELD NOTES** Late Jun–early Sep. Feeds at night. Pupates on the ground in a strong cocoon spun among leaves. Overwinters as a pupa.

BEAUTIFUL HOOK-TIP
Laspeyria flexula

PLATE 4
72.069 (2473

Local. Increasing in range. **FIELD CHARACTERS** Body varying shades of green mixed with black markings, resembling algae and lichens. Dorsal line greyish or greenish, with raised pinacula adjacent A1–A9, prominent on A8. A fringe of hair-like whitish fleshy projections extends downwards below the spiracles. Prolegs on A3–A4 much reduced. **SIMILAR SPECIES** Light Emerald. **HABITATS** Wooded gardens, hedgerows, parkland, scrub and woodland. **FOODPLANTS** Lichens, including *Physcia stellaris* and *Xanthoria parietina*, growing on twigs and branch of various broadleaf and coniferous trees and scrub. **FIELD NOTES** Aug–late May. Pupates in a tough cocoon on a trunk or branch. Overwinters as a small larva.

OLIVE CRESCENT
Trisateles emortualis

PLATE 42
72.070 (2495)

RDB; immigrant. Resident in East Anglia and may establish elsewhere. **FIELD CHARACTERS** Body brownish or orangey brown with faint, paler wavy markings and suffused dark grey patches subdorsally. Pinacula black. Prolegs on A3–A4 much reduced. **HABITATS** Mature broadleaf woodland. **FOODPLANTS** Beech, Sweet Chestnut and oaks. On withered leaves of oaks hanging in bunches on branches above or on the ground, and dead leaves of Beech attached to twigs. **FIELD NOTES** Jul–Oct. Pupates in leaf litter on the ground in a cocoon. Overwinters as a pupa.

PURPLE MARBLED
Eublemma ostrina

PLATE 42
72.072 (2407)

Immigrant. **FIELD CHARACTERS** Head dark brown or black, and prothoracic plate brownish. Body green or yellowish grey with paler dorsal, subdorsal and lateral stripes. **HABITATS** Calcareous grassland, limestone pavement and vegetated shingle. **FOODPLANTS** The unripe seeds of Carline Thistle. **FIELD NOTES** Jul–Aug. In the flowers, causing florets to be raised and differential browning of leaves around the flower head. Larva may form a whitish chamber between a leaf and the flower head, made from silk and the cottony pubescence of the leaf. Pupates in or on the flower. Does not overwinter in Great Britain or Ireland.

SMALL MARBLED
Eublemma parva

PLATE 42
72.073 (2408)

Immigrant. Early stages sometimes recorded in summer months. **FIELD CHARACTERS** Head blackish, and prothoracic plate brown with a black posterior band. Body greyish white with purplish-red subdorsal, lateral and spiracular stripes. **SIMILAR SPECIES** The micro-moth *Phycitodes saxicola* (Pyralidae) has a brown head and a purplish-red dorsal stripe. **HABITATS** Mainly soft cliffs, coastal grassland and old quarries. Occasionally on rough ground and damp meadows inland. **FOODPLANTS** Common Fleabane and Ploughman's-spikenard. **FIELD NOTES** Aug–Sep. Feeds within the flower, causing florets to be raised. Larvae of the micro-moths *P. saxicola* (Pyralidae), *Apodia bifractella* and *Ptocheuusa paupella* (both Gelechiidae) create similar feeding signs. Pupates under a flower head in a cocoon. Not known to overwinter in Great Britain or Ireland.

EREBINAE

CLIFDEN NONPAREIL/BLUE UNDERWING
Catocala fraxini

PLATE 42
72.076 (2451)

Recent colonist; immigrant; former resident. **FIELD CHARACTERS** Head pale grey or pinkish grey, with black mottling and posterior band. Body pale grey or brownish grey, heavily speckled with blackish dots. There is usually a hump on A5, a broad blackish intersegmental band A5–A6, and a narrow W-shaped blackish band on A8. A fringe of hair-like, pale grey fleshy projections extends downwards below the spiracles. A form occurs that is heavily suffused with black. **HABITATS** Plantation and semi-natural woodland. **FOODPLANTS** Aspen and other poplars. **FIELD NOTES** Late Apr–Jul. Feeds at night and rests by day on bark. Pupates between leaves or among leaf litter in a silken cocoon. Overwinters as an egg.

RED UNDERWING
Catocala nupta

PLATE 42
72.078 (2452)

Common. Increasing in range north and west. **FIELD CHARACTERS** Head brownish or grey with a black surround. Body brownish grey or pale grey with black or grey speckles, often arranged in short wavy lines. Orange or dark wart-like subdorsal pinacula T1–A9, enlarged on A8. There is a grey or orange hump on A5, and a black bar on A8. A fringe of hair-like whitish fleshy projections extends downwards below the spiracles. **HABITATS** Large gardens and urban parks, parkland, riverside trees, scrub, and natural and plantation woodland. **FOODPLANTS** Aspen, poplars including Black-poplar and White Poplar, and willows including Hybrid Crack-willow and White Willow; also recorded from Wild Plum. **FIELD NOTES** May–Jul. Feeds at night and rests by day on the trunk. Pupates between leaves or in a bark crevice in a silken cocoon. Overwinters as an egg.

DARK CRIMSON UNDERWING
Catocala sponsa

PLATE 42
72.081 (2455)

RDB; immigrant. Resident in several woods in central England. **FIELD CHARACTERS** Head grey, or brown with a black surround. Body orangey brown, brown, grey or blackish grey, often with pale patches on A1, A5 and A6 and dark shading A5–A6 in paler examples. Pale or dark orange wart-like subdorsal pinacula A1–A9, enlarged on A8. There is a hump on A5, and often another on A8. A fringe of hair-like whitish fleshy projections extends downwards below the spiracles. **SIMILAR SPECIES** Brown forms of Light Crimson Underwing are indistinguishable. **HABITATS** Mature oak woodland. **FOODPLANTS** Pedunculate Oak and possibly Sessile Oak. **FIELD NOTES** Apr–early Jun. Feeds at night and rests on a twig or bark by day. Pupates between leaves or on bark in a silken cocoon. Overwinters as an egg.

LIGHT CRIMSON UNDERWING
Catocala promissa

PLATE 42
72.082 (2454)

RDB; immigrant. Resident in several woods in central southern England. **FIELD CHARACTERS** Body has two colour forms. The brown form with pale patches is indistinguishable in the field from Dark Crimson Underwing. The bluish-green and black form is sometimes mixed with brownish patches, and resembles lichen-covered twigs or bark. Both forms have orange, blackish or whitish wart-like subdorsal pinacula A1–A9, enlarged on A8. There is a hump on A5, and often another on A8. A fringe of hair-like whitish fleshy projections extends downwards below the spiracles. **SIMILAR SPECIES** Dark Crimson Underwing. **HABITATS** Mature oak woodland. **FOODPLANTS** Pedunculate Oak and possibly Sessile Oak. **FIELD NOTES** Apr–early Jun. Feeds at night and rests in a bark crevice or among lichen by day. Lives high up in the tree. Pupates between leaves or on a tree trunk in a silken cocoon. Overwinters as an egg.

BURNET COMPANION
Euclidia glyphica

PLATE 42
72.083 (2463)

Common. More local away from central and southern England. **FIELD CHARACTERS** Head brown, with whitish dorsal stripe on body expanding to form a white triangle on the face. Body elongated, brownish with numerous longitudinal wavy lines, dark brown or blackish subdorsally, and pale brown laterally. Subspiracular stripe pale brown. Prolegs on A3 absent and on A4 reduced. **SIMILAR SPECIES** Mother Shipton lacks pair of prolegs on A4 and white triangle on the face. Four-spotted has functional prolegs on A3–A6. **HABITATS** Grasslands, especially on calcareous soils, and open grassland in scrub and woodland. **FOODPLANTS** Pea family, including Common Bird's-foot-trefoil, clovers, Lucerne, Black Medick and Tufted Vetch. **FIELD NOTES** Late Jun–Sep. Rests by day stretched out along a stem. Pupates in plant litter on the ground, in a cocoon. Overwinters as a pupa.

MOTHER SHIPTON
Euclidia mi

PLATE 42
72.084 (2462)

Common. Local in Scotland and Ireland. **FIELD CHARACTERS** Head brown, with lines and stripes continuous with those on the body. Body elongated, brown with numerous longitudinal wavy lines, and sometimes dark brown or blackish subdorsally. Subspiracular stripe whitish or pale brown. Prolegs on A3–A4 absent. **SIMILAR SPECIES** Burnet Companion and Four-spotted. **HABITATS** Grassy habitats, including calcareous grassland, heathland, meadows, lower slopes of moorland, and open grassland in scrub and woodland. **FOODPLANTS** Grasses, including Cock's-foot, Purple Moor-grass and Common Reed. Reports on pea family (including clovers, and Field and Ribbed melilots) are now considered doubtful as foodplants in the wild. **FIELD NOTES** Late Jun–early Sep. Pupates between spun grass leaves or on the ground, in a cocoon. Overwinters as a pupa.

NOCTUIDAE NOCTUID MOTHS

This is a very large family worldwide, with over 21,000 species described to date. There are just under 400 species recorded from the British Isles, with 303 species included in this field guide. Noctuid larvae usually have the standard full complement of prolegs on A3–A6, but they are reduced in some species such as Marbled White Spot, which has prolegs absent on A3 and reduced on A4. Larvae in most subfamilies lack conspicuous hairs, but they are more obvious in some of the Bryophilinae, such as Marbled Beauty, and may be dense in the Acronictinae, including Miller, which is exceptionally hirsute.

Dark Spectacle ×1.25

Nut-tree Tussock ×1.25

Sycamore ×1.25

Larvae in this family typically feed on plant material, although a number – such as Rosy Marbled, Grey Shoulder-knot and Dun-bar – are omnivorous, eating other larvae or insects. Silky Wainscot becomes entirely carnivorous as it grows. Feeding habits are variable; feeding openly on leaves, especially at night, is a behaviour common to many species, but feeding internally within stems is also frequent. Some species, such as the darts and allies in genera *Agrotis* and *Euxoa*, spend much of their time as larvae underground. Most species are solitary, but Blossom Underwing larvae feed gregariously when small.

Figure of Eight ×1.25

Mullein ×1.25

Sword-grass ×1.25

Bordered Sallow larva

Nutmeg larva

PLUSIINAE

SPECTACLE
Abrostola tripartita

PLATE 43
73.001 (2450)

Common. Has increased significantly in abundance in recent decades. **FIELD CHARACTERS** Head green, marked with black laterally to a variable extent and sometimes centrally. Body green or brown with abdominal segments appearing bloated, especially A1–A2, a hump on A8, and white diagonal stripes A1–A8. The green form has a white dorsal stripe formed of ovals, and a white subdorsal line T1–T3. Supraspiracular line white. The brown form is greenish brown, tinged pinkish and mottled whitish, and the darker body colour A1–A2 contrasts with the diagonal stripes. **SIMILAR SPECIES** Dark Spectacle has a yellow or white subdorsal blotch on A1, and a near-vertical white or line on A8. **HABITATS** Open habitats, including ditches, gardens, rough unmanaged ground, hedgerows, rough pasture, wetlands and woodland rides. **FOODPLANT** Common Nettle. **FIELD NOTES** Jul–Sep, and sometimes Oct–Nov. Feeds at any time of day. Pupates among plant litter on the ground or under bark. Overwinters as a pupa.

DARK SPECTACLE
Abrostola triplasia

PLATE 43
73.002 (2449)

Common; suspected immigrant. Frequent in the west; very local in Scotland. **FIELD CHARACTERS** Head black with a central white dash or white marks above, or green with black marks at the sides. Body green, blackish or purplish brown with abdominal segments appearing bloated, especially A2, and diagonal stripes A2–A7. On A8 there is a hump with a near-vertical white or pale line from the dorsum laterally and a darker patch posteriorly. The green form has a dark dorsal line with brownish-green dorsal patches on A1 and A2, and a yellow subdorsal blotch on A1 and sometimes A2. The blackish or purplish-brown forms are speckled grey and pinkish dorsally, with dark, unmarked dorsal patches on A1 and A2, and a yellow or whitish subdorsal blotch on A1. **SIMILAR SPECIES** Spectacle. **HABITATS** Open habitats, often on acidic soils, including marshy grassland, hedgerows, upland pasture and river valleys. **FOODPLANTS** Hop and Common Nettle. **FIELD NOTES** Jul–Sep, and sometimes Oct–Nov. Feeds mainly at night. Pupates in a folded leaf. Overwinters as a pupa.

SCARCE BURNISHED BRASS
Diachrysia chryson

PLATE 43
73.011 (2435)

Na. **SIMILAR SPECIES** Burnished Brass. **HABITATS** Damp habitats, including soft cliffs, fens, marshes, chalk river valleys and damp open woodland. **FOODPLANT** Hemp-agrimony. **FIELD NOTES** Late Aug–early Jun. Feeds mainly at night and rests along a stem or a leaf midrib. Prefers plants growing in shaded areas. Chews through the midrib, causing the outer leaf section to wilt. If disturbed, the larva springs away and falls to the ground. Pupates beneath a leaf in a whitish silken cocoon. Overwinters as a small larva.

BURNISHED BRASS
Diachrysia chrysitis

PLATE 43
73.012 (2434)

Common. **FIELD CHARACTERS** Head green. Body green with dark green dorsal line, edged whitish, a white subdorsal line T1–T3, and white dots and wavy diagonal lines subdorsally A1–A8. Supraspiracular stripe white. Prolegs absent A3–A4. **SIMILAR SPECIES** Indistinguishable from Scarce Burnished Brass in the field. **HABITATS** Wide variety of open habitats, including gardens, rough unmanaged ground, hedgerows and woodland rides. **FOODPLANTS** Wide variety of herbaceous plants, including Wild Angelica, Lesser Burdock, Common Comfrey, White Dead-nettle, Hemp-agrimony, Common Hemp-nettle, Hyssop, Wild Marjoram, Michaelmas-daisies, Common Nettle, Garden Parsley, Garden Pea, Spearmint, teasels, Spear Thistle and ornamental yarrows. **FIELD NOTES** Aug–Jun in the far north, Sep–May and Jun–Aug elsewhere. Feeds at night. Pupates beneath a leaf in a brown papery cocoon. Overwinters as a small larva.

GOLDEN PLUSIA
Polychrysia moneta

PLATE 43
73.014 (2437)

Common. Has declined in recent decades and is now infrequent. **FIELD CHARACTERS** Head green. Body green, with individual abdominal segments appearing bloated. Dorsal line dark green, and supraspiracular line white but indistinct T1–T3. Prolegs absent A3–A4. **HABITATS** Gardens and urban parks. **FOODPLANTS** Leaves, flower buds and unripe seeds of larkspurs and of monk's-hoods, including Wolf's-bane; also Globeflower. **FIELD NOTES** Aug–Jun. In a silk web when small and rests on the underside of a leaf when larger. Some larvae become fully grown in late summer. Pupates under a leaf in a dense yellow cocoon. Overwinters as a small larva.

SILVER Y
Autographa gamma

PLATE 43
73.015 (2441)

Immigrant. Colonises annually. **FIELD CHARACTERS** Head green, usually with longitudinal black streaks laterally. Body green, or occasionally blackish, with white hairs. Pinacula white, clearly ringed white subdorsally. Dorsal stripe dark green, edged with a white line, and with two wavy white subdorsal lines. Spiracular line white, and usually ill-defined along lower margin. Prolegs absent A3–A4. **SIMILAR SPECIES** Beautiful Golden Y, Plain Golden Y and Gold Spangle all have a more sharply defined spiracular line and usually lack such clear white rings around the subdorsal pinacula. These three species cannot be separated with certainty in the field, although there are forms of Plain Golden Y and Gold Spangle where the pale markings are yellowish, and this may not occur in Beautiful Golden Y. **HABITATS** Wide variety of open habitats. **FOODPLANTS** Wide variety of herbaceous and woody plants, including bedstraws, Broom, clovers, dandelions, docks, Flixweed, Hop, horticultural crops including Cabbage and Garden Pea, Alpine Lady-fern, limes, Common and Small nettles, Common Restharrow and Common Toadflax. **FIELD NOTES** Found most months of the year, rarely surviving winter as a larva. Pupates among foliage in a whitish silken cocoon.

BEAUTIFUL GOLDEN Y
Autographa pulchrina

PLATE 43
73.016 (2442)

Common. **FIELD CHARACTERS** Head green with a thick longitudinal black line laterally. Body green with whitish hairs. Pinacula white, sometimes ringed white. Dorsal stripe dark green, edged with a white line, and with two wavy white subdorsal lines. Spiracular line white and clearly defined. Prolegs absent A3–A4. **SIMILAR SPECIES** Silver Y, Plain Golden Y and Gold Spangle. **HABITATS** Wide variety, including gardens, grasslands, heathland, hedgerows, moorland, scrub and woodland. Prefers acidic soils. **FOODPLANTS** Wide variety of herbaceous plants, including Wood Avens, burdocks, Rough Chervil, White Dead-nettle, groundsel, Common and Small nettles, Common Ragwort and Hedge Woundwort. Also recorded on bilberry and Honeysuckle. **FIELD NOTES** Jul–May. Feeds mainly at night. Pupates among the foodplant in a brownish silken cocoon. Overwinters as a small larva.

PLAIN GOLDEN Y
Autographa jota

PLATE 43
73.017 (2443)

Common. Local in the northern half of Scotland. **SIMILAR SPECIES** Silver Y, Beautiful Golden Y and Gold Spangle. **HABITATS** Wide variety, including gardens, grasslands, hedgerows and woodland. Frequent in urban areas. **FOODPLANTS** Wide variety of herbaceous plants, including Cabbage, Rough Chervil, clovers, dandelions, Red and White dead-nettles, Groundsel, Hogweed, mints, Common Nettle, plantains and Hedge Woundwort. Also recorded on broadleaf trees, and shrubs including Honeysuckle. **FIELD NOTES** Aug–Jun. Feeds mainly at night. Pupates on the underside of a leaf in a whitish silken cocoon. Overwinters as a small larva.

GOLD SPANGLE
Autographa bractea

PLATE 43
73.018 (2444)

Common. Mainly Wales, the Midlands northwards, and Ireland. **SIMILAR SPECIES** Silver Y, Beautiful Golden Y and Plain Golden Y. **HABITATS** Wide variety, including gardens, upland grassland, hedgerows, moorland and woodland rides. **FOODPLANTS** Wide variety of herbaceous plants, including Rough Chervil, White Dead-nettle, Ground-ivy, Groundsel, Hemp-agrimony, Mouse-ear-hawkweed and Common Nettle. Also on shrubs, including Bilberry and Honeysuckle. **FIELD NOTES** Aug–early Jun. Feeds mainly at night. Pupates on the underside of a leaf in a silken cocoon. Overwinters as a small larva.

SCARCE SILVER Y
Syngrapha interrogationis

PLATE 43
73.021 (2447)

Local; immigrant. Resident in Wales and the north Midlands northwards, and in Ireland. **FIELD CHARACTERS** Head green with brown speckling. Body green with dark hairs. Pinacula white. Dorsal stripe dark green, usually edged with an irregular white stripe, and with a white subdorsal line. Spiracular stripe white or yellow. Prolegs absent A3–A4. **HABITATS** Moorland. **FOODPLANTS** Bilberry, Bog Bilberry, Cowberry and Heather. Also recorded on Common Nettle. **FIELD NOTES** Late Jul–early Jun. Feeds by day and night. Rests exposed on foliage. Pupates among the foodplant or on the ground in a white silken cocoon. Overwinters as a small larva.

GOLD SPOT
Plusia festucae

PLATE 43
73.022 (2439)

Common. **FIELD CHARACTERS** Head green. Body slender, green and with dark hairs. Pinacula darker than the body colour. Dorsal stripe green, edged with a white line, and with two white subdorsal lines. Spiracular stripe white or yellow. Prolegs absent A3–A4. **SIMILAR SPECIES** Indistinguishable from Lempke's Gold Spot. **HABITATS** Damp or wet habitats, including ditches, marshy grassland, upland grassland, fens, heathland, moorland, wetland marginal to rivers and canals, and woodland rides. **FOODPLANTS** Branched Bur-reed, Yellow Iris, rushes, Glaucous, Tufted and other sedges, Wood Small-reed and other marshland grasses, Water-plantain and Yorkshire-fog. **FIELD NOTES** Sep–May; also Jul–Aug in the south. Pupates among the foodplant in a translucent whitish silken cocoon. Overwinters as a small larva.

LEMPKE'S GOLD SPOT
Plusia putnami

PLATE 43
73.023 (2440)

Ssp. *gracilis* Local. Widespread in northern England and Scotland; local in East Anglia and Wales. **SIMILAR SPECIES** Gold Spot. **HABITATS** Damp or wet habitats, including fens, upland grassland and marshes. **FOODPLANTS** Purple and Wood small-reeds and other marshland grasses, and Yorkshire-fog. **FIELD NOTES** Aug–May. Pupates among the foodplant in a pale greyish silken cocoon. Overwinters as a small larva.

EUSTROTIINAE

MARBLED WHITE SPOT
Deltote pygarga

PLATE 43
73.024 (2410)

Common. Has increased significantly in abundance in recent decades. **FIELD CHARACTERS** Body pale green or pale brown. The green form has a dark greenish dorsal stripe, sometimes with purplish shading between segments, thickly edged whitish and with a whitish subdorsal stripe. There may be purplish lines laterally. The brown form has a dark brown or greenish-brown dorsal stripe, with a dirty whitish subdorsal stripe, and purplish-brown lines laterally. An indistinctly marked pale brownish form occurs. Prolegs absent on A3 and much reduced on A4. **HABITATS** Heathland, moorland and woodland. Prefers acidic and neutral soils.

FOODPLANTS Recorded on False Brome and Purple Moor-grass; probably also other grasses. **FIELD NOTES** Jul–Sep. Feeds mainly at night. Pupates in the ground in a cocoon. Overwinters as a pupa.

SILVER HOOK
Deltote uncula

PLATE 43
73.026 (2412)

Local. **FIELD CHARACTERS** Body slender and green. Dorsal stripe dark green, subdorsal line white and usually distinct, and subspiracular stripe white or yellowish white. Prolegs absent A3–A4. **SIMILAR SPECIES** Silver Barred has a white subdorsal stripe, and vestigial prolegs on A4; these features may be diagnostic. Confusion with Silver Barred is likely only in south-west Ireland peat bogs where both species occur. **HABITATS** Fens, wet heathland, marshes and boggy moorland. **FOODPLANTS** Grasses including Tufted Hair-grass, and sedges including Wood-sedge. **FIELD NOTES** Jul–Sep. Feeds mainly at night. Pupates in the ground in moss or soil, in a strong silken cocoon. Overwinters as a pupa.

SILVER BARRED
Deltote bankiana

PLATE 43
73.027 (2413)

RDB; immigrant. Resident in south-west Ireland, two sites in Cambridgeshire and one in Kent. **FIELD CHARACTERS** Body slender and green. Dorsal stripe dark green, subdorsal stripe white, and subspiracular stripe white or yellowish white. Prolegs absent on A3 and vestigial on A4. **SIMILAR SPECIES** Silver Hook. **HABITATS** Fens, marshes and peat bogs. In fens, may prefer regularly cut rides and other grassland areas. **FOODPLANTS** Reported on Purple Moor-grass and Smooth Meadow-grass. **FIELD NOTES** Jul–Aug. Pupates on or near the ground in a silken cocoon. Overwinters as a pupa.

AEDIINAE

FOUR-SPOTTED
Tyta luctuosa

PLATE 43
73.031 (2465)

Na; suspected immigrant. Resident in scattered small colonies. **FIELD CHARACTERS** Head brown, with lines and stripes continuous with those on the body. Body pale to mid-brown, occasionally greyish, with white subdorsal pinacula. Dorsal line brown, edged pale brown, with a pale brown subdorsal stripe and a dark brown band between them. Several dark brown lines laterally. Subspiracular line white or pale brown. Full complement of prolegs. **SIMILAR SPECIES** Burnet Companion and Mother Shipton. **HABITATS** Prefers hot, thin-soiled and sparsely vegetated habitats, including field margins, breckland and calcareous grasslands, limestone scree, old railway embankments and waste ground. **FOODPLANT** Field Bindweed; on the flowers and young leaves. **FIELD NOTES** Late Jun–Aug, and Sep–Oct. Feeds at night, and hides low down by day. Pupates in the ground in a silken cocoon. Overwinters as a pupa.

PANTHEINAE

NUT-TREE TUSSOCK
Colocasia coryli

PLATE 44
73.032 (2425)

Common. Local in the Midlands and northern England. **FIELD CHARACTERS** Body colour variable; whitish or blackish, orangey or pinkish, with pale tubercles. Tufts of hairs white or dirty whitish, with a tuft of long, forward-pointing orangey-brown or black hairs laterally on T2, and another of orangey-brown or black hairs on dorsum A1–A2 and A8. Paler examples may have a blackish dorsal band formed of blotches. **HABITATS** Broadleaf woodland. **FOODPLANTS** Most frequently Downy Birch and Hazel. Also recorded on alders, Apple, Aspen, Beech, Silver Birch, Blackthorn, Sweet Chestnut, hawthorns, Hornbeam, limes, Field Maple, Rowan, roses, Sycamore, oaks and willows. **FIELD NOTES** In the south, late May–early Jul, and Sep–early Oct; in the north, late Jun–Sep. Feeds at night, hiding by day between spun leaves. Pupates in plant litter or moss on the ground in a cocoon. Overwinters as a pupa.

DILOBINAE

FIGURE OF EIGHT
Diloba caeruleocephala

PLATE 44
73.033 (2020)

Common. Has declined severely in abundance in recent decades. **FIELD CHARACTERS** Body pale grey, with large black pinacula. Dorsal and lateral spots yellow, and a raised yellow band across the dorsum on T2. **HABITATS** Gardens, hedgerows and broadleaf woodland. **FOODPLANTS** Mainly on Blackthorn and hawthorns. Also recorded on Almond, Apple, Apricot, cherries, cotoneasters, Cherry Laurel, Peach, Pear, Japanese Quince and roses. **FIELD NOTES** Late Apr–mid-Jul. Pupates on or in the ground in a cocoon. Overwinters as an egg.

ACRONICTINAE

SCARCE MERVEILLE DU JOUR
Moma alpium

PLATE 44
73.034 (2277)

RDB. **FIELD CHARACTERS** Body black with large orange or reddish tubercles T2–A9. Hairs long and orangey brown or whitish. Large, raised white dorsal blotches on A1, A3 and A6, white marks or streaks along the dorsum, a white subdorsal line, sometimes incomplete, and other white lines laterally. **HABITATS** Prefers mature oak woodland. Also found in oak copses, scrubby oaks and hedgerow trees in well-wooded landscapes. **FOODPLANTS** Pedunculate Oak and probably Sessile Oak. A larva was found once on Sweet Chestnut, and a cocoon among Turkey Oak leaves. **FIELD NOTES** Jul–early Sep. Gregarious when young. Pupates among leaf litter on the ground in a strong silken cocoon. Overwinters as a pupa, sometimes for two winters.

REED DAGGER/POWDERED WAINSCOT
Simyra albovenosa

PLATE 44
73.035 (2290)

Nb; suspected immigrant. Resident in south-east England and East Anglia. **FIELD CHARACTERS** Body black, with large orangey verrucae. Hair tufts grey, usually mixed with white, especially laterally. Subdorsal and subspiracular stripes orange or yellowish orange. **HABITATS** Managed and neglected reedbeds, and reeds growing in grazing marsh ditches, in coastal and inland situations. **FOODPLANTS** Mainly Common Reed. Also recorded on birches, Bog-myrtle, Water Dock, Great Fen-sedge, Heather, Yellow Loosestrife, sedges including Tufted-sedge and Greater Tussock-sedge, Reed Sweet-grass, Whorl-grass, and Creeping, Grey and other willows. **FIELD NOTES** Jun–early Aug, and late Aug–Sep in a partial second generation. Feeds mainly at night. Gregarious when young. Pupates on the ground in a silken cocoon. Overwinters as a pupa.

ALDER MOTH
Acronicta alni

PLATE 44
73.036 (2281)

Local. Expanding its range in the north. **FIELD CHARACTERS** Resembles a bird's dropping in third and fourth instars. The fourth instar has a shiny body, pale brownish mixed blackish T1–T3, mainly black A1–A5, and white A6–A9, mixed with greyish and brownish on A8. The fifth instar has a black body with yellow dorsal bands T1–A10 and with long spoon-like black bristles that may break off. **HABITATS** Scrub and broadleaf woodland, often on poorly drained soils. **FOODPLANTS** Wide variety, including Alder, Crab Apple, Aspen, Beech, birches, Blackthorn, Wild Cherry, Sweet Chestnut, Dog-rose, Dogwood, elms, hawthorns, limes, oaks, Raspberry, Rowan, Sycamore, and willows including Goat Willow. Has been found on Rhododendron. **FIELD NOTES** Jun–Aug. Rests on the upperside of a leaf from third instar onwards. Pupates in rotten wood. Overwinters as a pupa.

DARK DAGGER
Acronicta tridens

PLATE 44
73.037 (2283)

Common. Less numerous than Grey Dagger. **FIELD CHARACTERS** Body grey with long, sparse black and grey hairs. Dorsal stripe irregularly margined, whitish or greyish white, sometimes orange or mixed white and orange, and often with a darker central line. Black patches laterally A1–A8, with orange blotches and white spots, and usually a red or orange transverse band on A9. Spiracular stripe whitish grey, sometimes with red or orange blotches T1–T3 and inferiorly on other segments. A short black fleshy projection on A1. **SIMILAR SPECIES** Grey Dagger has a much longer projection on A1 and sharply defined edges to the dorsal stripe. **HABITATS** Wide variety, including gardens, wetlands and woodland. **FOODPLANTS** Wide variety of broadleaf trees and shrubs, with a preference for the rose family. Recorded on Apple, birches, Blackthorn, Buckthorn, cotoneasters, hawthorns, oaks, Pear, Plum, Rowan, and Goat, Grey and other willows. **FIELD NOTES** Jul–Oct. Prefers trees growing in open situations. Pupates under loose bark or in a crevice. Overwinters as a pupa, sometimes for two winters.

GREY DAGGER
Acronicta psi

PLATE 44
73.038 (2284)

Common. Has decreased significantly in abundance in recent decades. **FIELD CHARACTERS** Body grey with long, sparse black and grey hairs. Dorsal stripe yellow or white with sharply defined edges, sometimes with a faint, darker central line. Orange patches laterally A1–A8, variably surrounded with black. Spiracular stripe greyish white. A long black fleshy projection on A1. **SIMILAR SPECIES** Dark Dagger. **HABITATS** Wide variety, including gardens, hedgerows, scrub and woodland. **FOODPLANTS** Wide variety of broadleaf trees and shrubs, including Apple, birches, Blackthorn, Highbush Blueberry, Sweet Chestnut, elms, Firethorn, hawthorns, Hazel, Juneberry, limes, oaks, Pear, Plum, roses including cultivars, Rowan and willows. Also on Bracken in the Hebrides. **FIELD NOTES** Jul–early Sep and Sep–early Nov in the south, Jul–early Oct elsewhere. Pupates among bark, in rotten wood or in the ground. Overwinters as a pupa.

SYCAMORE
Acronicta aceris

PLATE 44
73.039 (2279)

Local. **FIELD CHARACTERS** Body grey with black-edged white dorsal blotches T3–A8, and densely covered with long tufts of yellow or orange hairs. Subdorsal tufts of red or orange-brown hairs on A1 and A3–A5. **HABITATS** Mainly gardens and urban parks. Also found in scrub and open woodland. **FOODPLANTS** On young and mature trees of Horse-chestnut, Field, Norway and other maples, and Sycamore. Also recorded on birches, Laburnum, oaks, London Plane, Plum and roses. **FIELD NOTES** Jul–Sep. Rests openly on the upperside of a leaf. Pupates in a bark crevice or on the ground, in a double-layered cocoon. Overwinters as a pupa, sometimes for two winters.

MILLER
Acronicta leporina

PLATE 44
73.040 (2280)

Common. Local in Scotland and Ireland. **FIELD CHARACTERS** Body whitish green, covered with dense, long white or yellow hairs arranged asymmetrically on the abdominal segments, facing posteriorly on the left and anteriorly on the right. A variable number of short black dorsal tufts. The white-haired form appears to predominate in the south, the yellow-haired in the north. Once fully fed, the larva becomes dark greyish green or orangey brown, and, remarkably, the hairs also change colour to grey. **HABITATS** Wide variety, including heathland, moorland, scrub, wetlands and broadleaf woodland. Less often gardens and urban parks. **FOODPLANTS** Mainly Alder, and Downy and Silver birches. Also recorded on oaks, poplars including Aspen and Hybrid Black-poplar, and Bay, Grey and White willows. **FIELD NOTES** Jul–early Oct. When at rest on the underside of a leaf, the larva curls to face backwards. Pupates in rotten wood. Overwinters as a pupa, sometimes over three winters.

LIGHT KNOT GRASS
Acronicta menyanthidis

PLATE 44
73.042 (2286)

Ssp. *menyanthidis* Local. Ssp. *scotica* Local. **FIELD CHARACTERS** Body black with blackish verrucae and tufts of black or brown hairs. Spiracles white, and subspiracular spots orange T2–A8. **HABITATS** Bogs, upland grassland, wet heathland and moorland. **FOODPLANTS** Mainly woody plants, including Bearberry, Bilberry, birches, Bog-myrtle, Alder Buckthorn, Cross-leaved Heath, Heather, and Creeping, Downy, Eared and White willows. Also on Bogbean, Bramble, Yellow Iris and Soft-rush. **FIELD NOTES** Jun–Sep. Pupates on the ground. Overwinters as a pupa.

SWEET GALE MOTH
Acronicta cinerea

PLATE 44
73.044 (2288)

Na. **FIELD CHARACTERS** Body dark grey with tufts of grey or yellowish-brown hairs. Dorsal patches or band black with yellow or white subdorsal patches T3–A10, and an orange or red transverse band T2. Spiracles white, and subspiracular spots or stripe orange or red. **HABITATS** Limestone grassland and pavement in Ireland; lowland roadside grassland and moorland in Scotland. **FOODPLANTS** On moorland: Bog-myrtle and Heather. On grasslands: wide variety, including Sea Campion, dandelions, Honeysuckle, Yellow Iris, Meadowsweet, Ribwort and Sea plantains, Common Ragwort, Common Sorrel, Thrift, and Creeping and Eared willows. **FIELD NOTES** Jul–Sep. Also Sep–Oct as a second generation in Ireland. Pupates on the ground, often under a stone, and may incorporate fragments of stone into its cocoon. Overwinters as a pupa.

KNOT GRASS
Acronicta rumicis

PLATE 44
73.045 (2289)

Common. Has declined significantly in abundance in recent decades. **FIELD CHARACTERS** Body black with tufts of brown hairs. Dorsal line of red spots with transverse red stripes between. Subdorsal white patches A2–A9, and often on T3. Spiracles white, and subspiracular stripe red and orange, or red and white, or orange and white. The larva rests with A1 raised. **HABITATS** Wide variety, including coastal habitats, grassland, heathland, wetland and open woodland. **FOODPLANTS** Wide variety of woody and herbaceous plants. Frequently on Broad-leaved Dock and plantains. Also reported on Agrimony, Bilberry (fruit), birches, Bramble, Hawthorn, Heather, Hop, Stinking Iris, Knotgrass, Water Mint, Peach, Purple-loosestrife, Rhubarb, Burnet Rose, Common Sorrel, Wild Strawberry, thistles and willows. **FIELD NOTES** Jun–Sep; also Sep–Oct as a second generation in the south. Prefers sheltered places. Pupates on the ground. Overwinters as a pupa.

POPLAR GREY
Subacronicta megacephala

PLATE 45
73.046 (2278)

Common. Local in Scotland and Ireland. **FIELD CHARACTERS** Body greyish and black, heavily speckled whitish or grey, especially laterally, with long grey hairs. Dorsal and subdorsal pinacula orange or orangey brown, and lateral tubercles grey. A large white, yellowish-white or pale grey blotch on A7. **HABITATS** Gardens, river valleys, wetlands, and native and plantation woodland. **FOODPLANTS** Mainly poplars, including Aspen, Hybrid Black-poplar, Lombardy-poplar and White Poplar. Also recorded on willows, including Goat Willow. **FIELD NOTES** Jul–Sep. When at rest the larva curls to face backwards. Pupates in a bark crevice, in rotten wood or sometimes in the ground. Overwinters as a pupa, sometimes over three winters.

CORONET
Craniophora ligustri

PLATE 4
73.047 (229

Local. Widespread in the south and west. **FIELD CHARACTERS** Body green with black pinacula and long, sparse black hairs. Dorsal line yellow or white, subdorsal stripe yellow or white, and spiracles orange. **SIMILAR SPECIES** Hebrew Character and Clouded Drab both have short pale-coloured hairs, and feed much earlier in the year. **HABITATS** Fens, hedgerows, scrub on calcareous grassland and in coastal habitats, open-grown Ash trees on upland grassland and streamsides, and woodland. **FOODPLANTS** Ash and Wild Privet. Also recorded on Alder and Hazel. **FIELD NOTES** Jul–Sep. Pupates under moss in a strong greyish cocoon. Overwinters as a pupa.

METOPONIINAE

SMALL YELLOW UNDERWING
Panemeria tenebrata

PLATE 45
73.048 (2397)

Local. **FIELD CHARACTERS** Body pale yellowish brown, green or greyish, with black pinacula. Dorsal line darker, subdorsal line whitish and subspiracular stripe white. **HABITATS** Herb-rich grassland, including on soft cliffs, calcareous grassland, meadows and pastures, recently created and sparsely vegetated areas, and road verges. **FOODPLANTS** Ripening seeds of Common, Field, Little and Sticky mouse-ears, and of Greater Stitchwort. **FIELD NOTES** Jun–Jul. At first inside the seed capsule. When larger, rests along a stem below the seed capsule, and chewed holes in the capsules may indicate larvae nearby. Pupates in the ground in a cocoon. Overwinters as a pupa.

CUCULLIINAE

WORMWOOD
Cucullia absinthii

PLATE 45
73.050 (2211)

Nb. **FIELD CHARACTERS** Body green and white with brown patches and more or less distinct white dorsal and subdorsal lines. The colour and pattern make the larva remarkably cryptic among flowers of its foodplants. **HABITATS** Prefers warm, sheltered situations in coastal habitats, derelict ground, old quarries, railway and road embankments, and slag heaps. **FOODPLANTS** Flowers and developing seeds of Mugwort, Wormwood and Sea Wormwood. **FIELD NOTES** Early Aug–early Oct. Sits among the flowers and seedheads. Pupates on or in the ground in a strong cocoon. Overwinters as a pupa, sometimes over three winters.

SHARK
Cucullia umbratica

PLATE 45
73.052 (2216)

Common. **FIELD CHARACTERS** Body pale to dark brownish mixed blackish, usually with black dots and orangey-brown speckling. Dorsal and subdorsal lines and subspiracular stripe orangey brown, and often indistinct, except A9–A10, where dorsal and subspiracular stripes are pronounced. **HABITATS** Open areas, including gardens, calcareous grassland, derelict or disturbed ground, marshes and road embankments, sand dunes and vegetated shingle. **FOODPLANTS** Flowers and leaves of hawk's-beards, hawkweeds, lettuces including Garden Lettuce cultivars, and sowthistles including Marsh sowthistle. **FIELD NOTES** Jul–early Sep. Feeds at night. If disturbed, the larva convulses, springing away from the foodplant, and contracts violently from side to side. Pupates in the ground in a strong cocoon. Overwinters as a pupa.

CHAMOMILE SHARK
Cucullia chamomillae

PLATE 45
73.053 (2214)

Local. Has expanded northwards in Scotland recently. **FIELD CHARACTERS** Body white, greenish white or pale yellow, with a pattern of zigzag greenish stripes and pink shading dorsally, and pink blotches laterally. The extent of the markings varies considerably. **HABITATS** Open areas mainly on sandy or calcareous soils, including field margins, sparsely vegetated grasslands, disturbed ground, sand dunes and vegetated shingle. **FOODPLANTS** Flowers of Chamomile, Corn and Stinking chamomiles, Feverfew and mayweeds. **FIELD NOTES** Late May–mid-Jul. Feeds by day and night. Rests curled on top of a leaf or flower, or from a stem onto a flower. Pupates in the ground in a strong cocoon. Overwinters as a pupa, sometimes over two winters.

STAR-WORT
Cucullia asteris

PLATE 45
73.055 (2217)

Nb. Mainly coastal; occasionally found inland. **FIELD CHARACTERS** In two colour forms. The brown form may be pale or reddish brown, or purplish. Dorsal stripe yellow, with a yellowish subdorsal stripe and a grey band between them. Lateral lines are black and subspiracular stripe is yellow above, white below. The green form has a yellow dorsal stripe, with a whitish or yellowish-green subdorsal stripe and a dark green band between them. Lateral lines are black and subspiracular stripe is yellow above, white below. **HABITATS** Mainly saltmarsh; infrequently clearings and rides in inland woodland, and occasionally gardens. **FOODPLANTS** Sea Aster, and occasionally Sea Wormwood on the coast. Goldenrod in woodland. Has been found in gardens on China Aster and Michaelmas-daisies. **FIELD NOTES** Late Jul–mid-Oct on saltmarsh; late Jul–late Aug in woodland. Feeds by day in sunshine on flowers and sometimes leaves. On Goldenrod the larva convulses if disturbed, springing away from the plant, while on Sea Aster it holds on more tightly, presumably to avoid the risk of falling into tidal waters. Pupates in the ground in a strong cocoon. Overwinters as a pupa.

WATER BETONY
Cucullia scrophulariae

PLATE 45
73.056 (2220)

Rare immigrant; possible resident on Guernsey where larvae have been found once. **FIELD CHARACTERS** Body whitish with conspicuous yellow markings and black dots. There are black transverse lines between the segments. **SIMILAR SPECIES** Striped Lychnis and Mullein. **HABITATS** Damp open places. **FOODPLANTS** Common Figwort on Guernsey. Figworts and mulleins in Europe. **FIELD NOTES** Jul in Guernsey; Jun–Jul in Europe. Feeds on the flowers of figworts, and larger larvae hide by day among foliage at the base of the plant. Pupates in the ground. Overwinters as a pupa.

STRIPED LYCHNIS
Cucullia lychnitis

PLATE 45
73.057 (2219)

Na. **FIELD CHARACTERS** Body whitish or yellowish with variable black and yellow markings. An almost unmarked yellowish and pale green form also occurs. **SIMILAR SPECIES** Water Betony and Mullein. **HABITATS** Open, sunny, calcareous habitats, including fallow fields, chalk grassland, roadside verges, and woodland clearings and rides. **FOODPLANTS** Mainly Dark Mullein. Has also been found on Great x Dark Mullein hybrid, and White and ornamental mulleins. **FIELD NOTES** Mid-Jul–early Sep. Feeds on flowers and developing seeds, and occasionally leaves. Rests exposed on flower spikes. Pupates in the ground in a strong cocoon. Overwinters as a pupa, often for two or more winters.

MULLEIN
Cucullia verbasci

PLATE 45
73.058 (2221)

Common. **FIELD CHARACTERS** Body whitish with conspicuous yellow markings and black dots, and black vertical lines laterally. The extent of black is variable between individuals. There are black transverse lines between the segments. **SIMILAR SPECIES** Water Betony and Mullein both have black transverse lines between the segments, which Striped Lychnis does not. Water Betony lacks the vertical black lines laterally that are present in Mullein, and is less variable than the other two species. Water Betony feeds later than Mullein, and larger larvae hide by day. Striped Lychnis feeds mainly on flowers of Dark Mullein and is not fully fed until at least mid-Aug, a month later than Mullein. However, rarely they have been found fully grown together on Dark Mullein. Larvae should be reared if there is doubt. **HABITATS** Open habitats, often on disturbed calcareous soils, including ditches, gardens and urban parks (in flower borders), dry grassland, marshes, old quarries, road verges, scrub, vegetated shingle and open woodland. **FOODPLANTS** Mainly on leaves of Great Mullein. Also recorded on leaves of Butterfly-bush, Common and Water figworts, and Dark, Hoary, Moth, Olympian and White mulleins. Has been found on the flowers of Dark Mullein and of Lizard Orchid. **FIELD NOTES** Late May–Jul. Sits on or under the leaves. Pupates in the ground in a strong cocoon. Overwinters as a pupa, sometimes for up to five winters.

ONCOCNEMIDINAE

TOADFLAX BROCADE
Calophasia lunula

PLATE 45
73.059 (2223)

RDB; suspected immigrant. Expanding its range. **FIELD CHARACTERS** Body white with yellow dorsal, subdorsal and subspiracular stripes. Squarish black marks subdorsally, and black spots laterally above and below the subspiracular stripe. **HABITATS** Sparsely vegetated ground, including gardens, disturbed ground, railway embankments and vegetated shingle. **FOODPLANTS** Mainly Purple Toadflax. Also on Common, Pale and Small toadflaxes. **FIELD NOTES** Late Jun–early Aug and late Aug–Oct, in two generations. Pupates among the seedpods, roots or on posts, in a tough oval cocoon. Overwinters as a pupa.

ANOMALOUS
Stilbia anomala

PLATE 45
73.061 (2394)

Local. Has declined severely in abundance in recent decades, especially in southern England. **FIELD CHARACTERS** Larva has a prothoracic plate. In two colour forms. The green form has a green body with a greenish-white dorsal line and subdorsal stripe, both edged dark green. Subspiracular stripe whitish above, greenish white below and often edged darker above. Spiracles black, noticeably larger on T1 and A8. The brown form has a brownish body with a pinkish-white or whitish dorsal line and subdorsal stripe, both edged dark brown. Subspiracular stripe white above and pale brown below. Spiracles as for green form. **HABITATS** Upland grassland, heathland and moorland. Less often coastal grassland, including dune-slacks. **FOODPLANTS** Recorded on Tufted and Wavy hair-grasses, and Purple Moor-grass. **FIELD NOTES** Sep–May. Feeds at night. Pupates on the ground in a cocoon. Overwinters as a part-grown larva.

AMPHIPYRINAE

COPPER UNDERWING
Amphipyra pyramidea

PLATE 46
73.062 (2297)

Common. Extending its range northwards. **FIELD CHARACTERS** Body bright green or bluish green with prominent white pinacula. Dorsal stripe white, and subdorsal line white and unbroken T1 and A8–A9, comprising dots and dashes in between. Subspiracular stripe yellow above, white below, and ill-defined on T3–A2. A8 is raised to a yellow point. True legs green. **SIMILAR SPECIES** Svensson's Copper Underwing usually has a complete subspiracular line and A8 raised to a red point. Sprawler and Rannoch Sprawler have A8 slightly raised, not to a point. **HABITATS** Mainly broadleaf woodland. Also gardens and urban parks, hedgerows and scrub. **FOODPLANTS** Wide variety of broadleaf trees and shrubs, including Crab Apple, Ash, Downy Birch, Blackthorn, Bramble, hawthorns, Hazel, Hornbeam, limes, oaks, Wild and Garden privets, and willows. Also vines including Grape-vine and Honeysuckle. Prefers the shrub layer and regrowth following coppicing. **FIELD NOTES** Mid-Apr–early Jun. Rests with the anterior end lifted away from the plant, often at 90 degrees. Pupates in the ground in a cocoon. Overwinters as an egg.

SVENSSON'S COPPER UNDERWING
Amphipyra berbera

PLATE 46
73.063 (2298)

Ssp. *svenssoni* Common. Extending its range northwards. **FIELD CHARACTERS** Body bright green or bluish green with prominent white pinacula. Dorsal stripe white, and subdorsal line white and unbroken T1 and A8–A9, comprising dots and dashes in between. The subspiracular stripe is yellow above, sometimes tinged reddish, and white below. A8 raised to a red point. True legs green or black. **SIMILAR SPECIES** Copper Underwing, Sprawler and Rannoch Sprawler. **HABITATS** Mainly broadleaf woodland. Also gardens and urban parks, hedgerows and scrub. **FOODPLANTS** Frequent found on Pedunculate Oak. Also recorded on birches, Blackthorn, elms, Hornbeam, Lilac (flowers), limes, Field Maple (flowers), Rhododendron and willows. **FIELD NOTES** Mid-Apr–late May. Sometimes rests with the anterior end lifted away from the plant. Occurs in the canopy and shrub layer. Pupates in the ground in a cocoon. Overwinters as an egg.

MOUSE MOTH
Amphipyra tragopoginis

PLATE 46
73.064 (2299)

Common. Has declined significantly in abundance in recent decades in the south. **FIELD CHARACTERS** Body green, with white or greenish-white dorsal, subdorsal and spiracular stripes. Subdorsal stripe angled on A8. **SIMILAR SPECIES** Reddish Buff has pale yellow lines, an additional subspiracular line, and its subdorsal line is not angled on A8. The larva feeds only on Saw-wort. **HABITATS** Wide variety, including gardens, fens, moorland, sand dunes and woodland. **FOODPLANTS** Wide variety of wild and cultivated herbaceous and woody plants, including Barberry, Common Bird's-foot-trefoil, Salad Burnet, Greater Celandine, Fennel, hawkweeds, hawthorns, Monkeyflower, Mugwort, Garden Parsley, Californian Poppy, Saw-wort, strawberries, teasels, Common Toadflax, Goat and White willows, and Rosebay Willowherb. **FIELD NOTES** Apr–Jun. Feeds at night on flowers and leaves, hiding low down by day. Pupates on or in the ground in a tough silken cocoon. Overwinters as an egg.

PSAPHIDINAE

SPRAWLER
Asteroscopus sphinx

PLATE 46
73.065 (2227)

Common. Has declined significantly in abundance in recent decades. Local in the north and west. **FIELD CHARACTERS** In two colour forms. Body bright yellowish green, or greenish white, tinged bluish. Dorsal stripe and subdorsal line yellowish or white in the bright yellowish-green form, and white in the greenish-white form. In both forms the subdorsal line is distinctly angled on A8, and the subspiracular stripe is mainly bright yellow T1–T3, and white with yellow spots A1–A9. A8 slightly raised. True legs green. **SIMILAR SPECIES** Copper Underwing, Svensson's Copper Underwing and Rannoch Sprawler. Rannoch Sprawler lacks pale lines, has a yellow and white dash on T3 and A8–A10 and a yellow bar on A8, has brown true legs and its distribution does not overlap with Sprawler. **HABITATS** Mainly broadleaf woodland. Also well-wooded gardens and urban parks. **FOODPLANTS** Wide variety of broadleaf trees and shrubs, including Apple, Ash, Beech, birches, Blackthorn, cherries, elms, hawthorns, Hazel, limes, oaks, poplars, Wayfaring-tree and willows. **FIELD NOTES** Apr–early Jun. Active mainly at night. When alarmed, throws its head and true legs backwards over the dorsum. It is likely this action exposes a gland on the ventral surface that emits a defensive secretion, as happens in Rannoch Sprawler. Pupates deep in the ground in a cocoon. Overwinters as an egg.

RANNOCH SPRAWLER
Brachionycha nubeculosa

PLATE 46
73.066 (2228)

RDB. **FIELD CHARACTERS** Body bright green or yellowish green with yellow spots. A yellow-and-white dash T3, a yellow bar across the dorsum on A8, and a yellow-and-white dash A8–A10. A8 slightly raised. True legs brown. **SIMILAR SPECIES** Sprawler, Copper Underwing and Svensson's Copper Underwing. **HABITATS** Mature birch woodland, and small groups of old birch trees. **FOODPLANTS** Birches. **FIELD NOTES** May–early Jul. When alarmed, rears its head and true legs up, exposing the slit-like opening of a gland on the ventral surface of T1. It is likely this gland emits a defensive secretion. Pupates deep in the ground. Overwinters as a pupa, sometimes for several winters.

GREEN-BRINDLED CRESCENT
Allophyes oxyacanthae

PLATE 46
73.068 (2245)

Common. Has declined significantly in abundance in recent decades. **FIELD CHARACTERS** Body variable in colour and pattern, from uniform to resembling a lichen-covered twig. Diagnostic feature is a pair of distinctly raised points on the dorsum on A8, not present on any other noctuid larva of similar size. Body varies from pale grey to dark brown, sometimes mottled blackish, dark grey and white, with many brown, yellow or black marks. Commonly there is an orangey or whitish mark laterally on A1, and sometimes a paler or whitish patch laterally A3–A4. **HABITATS** Gardens, hedgerows, scrub and broadleaf woodland. **FOODPLANTS** Mainly found on Blackthorn and hawthorns. Also recorded on many other woody plants, including apples, birches, Wild Cherry, cotoneasters, Dog-rose, Plum, Rowan (particularly in the north) and willows. **FIELD NOTES** Apr–Jun. Pupates deep in the ground in a strong cocoon. Overwinters as an egg.

EARLY GREY
Xylocampa areola

PLATE 46
73.069 (2243)

Common. **FIELD CHARACTERS** Larva slender and tapering at both ends. Body greyish brown. Dorsal stripe pale brown, whitish from A8 posteriorly, incorporating a darker central line, and interrupted by two patches of dark grey A4–A6. Subdorsal stripe pale and indistinct. Subspiracular stripe pale brown, edged dark brown above. A8 slightly raised. **HABITATS** Gardens, hedgerows, scrub and woodland. **FOODPLANTS** Native and introduced species of honeysuckles. **FIELD NOTES** Apr–Jun. Feeds at night, and hides by day flattened along a woody stem. Pupates in the ground in a strong cocoon. Overwinters as a pupa.

HELIOTHINAE

BORDERED SALLOW
Pyrrhia umbra

PLATE 46
73.070 (2399)

Local. **FIELD CHARACTERS** Very variable; in three colour forms, all speckled whitish and with short hairs. The pale green form has a pale green body, usually with a darker dorsal stripe, edged with white lines. Subdorsal line white. Subspiracular stripe white with darker shading and black pinacula above. The dark green form has a dark green body with large black pinacula and a darker dorsal stripe edged with white lines. Subdorsal line yellow or white and subspiracular stripe yellow or greenish white. The brown form has a reddish or purplish-brown body with distinct black pinacula. Dorsal stripe dark, edged with whitish lines. Subdorsal line whitish and lateral line whitish or whitish yellow. Spiracular stripe yellow. **SIMILAR SPECIES** Marbled Clover and Shoulder-striped Clover have a pale or white supraspiracular line and are more slender at rest. Bordered Straw has longer hairs that are distinctly whitish. **HABITATS** Cliffs, breckland and calcareous grasslands, old quarries, sand dunes and vegetated shingle; also coppiced and open woodland. **FOODPLANTS** Mainly Common and Spiny restharrows. Also Henbane and Sea Sandwort. In woodland, on young regrowth of coppiced Sweet Chestnut, Hazel, oaks and willows. **FIELD NOTES** Jul–Aug. Mainly feeds at night, on flowers, seeds and shoots. Pupates just below the surface of the ground. Overwinters as a pupa.

MARBLED CLOVER
Heliothis viriplaca

PLATE 46
73.072 (2401)

RDB; suspected immigrant. Resident in East Anglia and Wiltshire. **FIELD CHARACTERS** Larva slender at rest. Body green or brownish. Dorsal stripe darker with a paler central line and edged paler, and subdorsal stripe whitish, tinged yellowish, brownish or greenish and shaded darker green or brownish below. Supraspiracular line white or pale, spiracular region pale green or brownish, and subspiracular stripe whitish. Pinacula black, and larger laterally. **SIMILAR SPECIES** Bordered Sallow. Shoulder-striped Clover is indistinguishable on field characters but has different foodplants, and the breeding areas do not overlap. **HABITATS** Field margins, breckland and chalk grasslands, disturbed ground on chalk, sand dunes, vegetated shingle, and flower-rich clearings and rides in woodland. **FOODPLANTS** Wide variety of herbaceous plants, including Bladder Campion, White Campion, Wild Carrot, Spanish Catchfly, Chicory, clovers, Flixweed, Sticky Groundsel, Smooth Hawk's-beard, hawkweeds, knapweeds, Common Restharrow, Field and Small scabiouses, and Common Toadflax. **FIELD NOTES** Late Jul–Sep, or occasionally to mid-Oct as a partial second generation. On flowers and ripening seeds. Pupates just below the ground in a flimsy cocoon. Overwinters as a pupa.

SHOULDER-STRIPED CLOVER
Heliothis maritima

PLATE 46
73.073 (2402)

Ssp. *warneckii* RDB; rare immigrant. Declining and confined to a few heaths in Dorset, Hampshire and Surrey. **SIMILAR SPECIES** Bordered Sallow and Marbled Clover. **HABITATS** Damp heathland with abundant Cross-leaved Heath. Appears to prefer areas of fairly short turf with abundant Cross-leaved Heath some five to ten years after burning. **FOODPLANTS** Mainly Cross-leaved heath. Also recorded on Bog Asphodel, Bell Heather and Heather. **FIELD NOTES** Late Jul–early Sep. Feeds mainly at night on the flowers. Pupates in ground in a silken cocoon. Overwinters as a pupa.

BORDERED STRAW
Heliothis peltigera

PLATE 46
73.074 (2403)

Immigrant. Larvae often found in summer months along the south and east coasts of England, less often inland. **FIELD CHARACTERS** Body variable shades of green, sometimes alternating with pinkish-brown transverse bands, and covered with pinpoint white speckles and sparse white hairs. Dorsal stripe dark or blackish green, with a yellow subdorsal stripe, shaded dark greenish below and with a white subspiracular line. Pinacula white, less often black. **SIMILAR SPECIES** Bordered Sallow. Scarce Bordered Straw/Old World Bollworm has many wavy longitudinal whitish streaks or lines, often with large darker patches and large black pinacula A1–A2 and A8. **HABITATS** Mainly cliffs, coastal grassland and vegetated shingle. Sometimes in gardens and urban parks near the coast. **FOODPLANTS** Frequently on flowers of Sticky Groundsel and Common Restharrow. Also on Sea Bindweed, Common Fleabane, hawk's-beards, Henbane, knapweeds, Pot Marigold, Scentless Mayweed, Ploughman's-spikenard, Corn and Sand spurreys, thistles, Thorn-apple, twinspurs and Yellow-rattle. **FIELD NOTES** Jun–Oct. Pupates on the ground in a slight cocoon. Overwintering not known in Great Britain and Ireland.

SCARCE BORDERED STRAW/
OLD WORLD BOLLWORM
Helicoverpa armigera

PLATE 47
73.076 (2400)

Immigrant. Larvae occasionally found in summer months along the south and east coasts of England. Frequently imported into florists and grocery stores. **FIELD CHARACTERS** In three colour forms. All have many wavy lines or streaks that are paler than the body colour, often large darker patches and large, raised black pinacula A1–A2 and A8, and sometimes smaller patches on other segments. The green form has a green body with a paler dorsal line. Sometimes dark shading between the wavy lines, and spiracular stripe greenish white. The brown form has a pale brownish or reddish-brown body with a paler dorsal line, edged blackish. Dark brown shading between the wavy lines laterally, and spiracular stripe creamy. The greyish form varies between grey and blackish grey with a pale grey or yellowish dorsal line. Grey or blackish-grey shading between all wavy lines, and spiracular stripe mixed pale and reddish brown, edged white. **SIMILAR SPECIES** Bordered Straw. **HABITATS** Open coastal areas. **FOODPLANTS** In the wild, reported from Scarlet Geranium, Devil's-bit Scabious, Snapdragon and Tree-mallow. As an import, on a range of flowers and fruits, especially pinks and Tomato. Has been recorded eating cooked chicken meat. **FIELD NOTES** Aug–Oct in the wild and any month as an import. Pupates in the ground. Overwintering not known in Great Britain and Ireland.

CONDICINAE

REDDISH BUFF
Acosmetia caliginosa

PLATE 47
73.078 (2393)

RDB (protected species). Confined to the Isle of Wight as a resident. **FIELD CHARACTERS** Body green with a pale yellow dorsal line, edged dark green, and pale yellow subdorsal and spiracular lines. There is a narrow, pale yellow subspiracular line. Pinacula white. **SIMILAR SPECIES** Mouse Moth. **HABITATS** Woodland. **FOODPLANT** Saw-wort. **FIELD NOTES** Jul–Aug. Feeds at night and rests under leaves by day. Pupates in the ground. Overwinters as a pupa.

BRYOPHILINAE

TREE-LICHEN BEAUTY
Cryphia algae

PLATE 47
73.082 (2292)

Immigrant; recent colonist. Established in parts of south-east England and spreading. **FIELD CHARACTERS** Body greyish green, with a whitish dorsal stripe or spots T3–A8, joining adjacent whitish spots, and with large black subdorsal marks beyond. Whitish spots laterally. Pinacula black. **HABITATS** Open habitats, including urban areas and in woodland. **FOODPLANTS** Lichens on trees and probably other substrates in Europe. **FIELD NOTES** Sep–Jun in mainland Europe; not observed in the wild in England. Pupates in a cocoon mixed with lichen and mosses, probably in a bark crevice.

MARBLED BEAUTY
Bryophila domestica

PLATE 47
73.084 (2293)

Common. Has increased significantly in abundance in recent decades. **FIELD CHARACTERS** Body black, with white speckles and a sparse covering of short white hairs. Dorsal band yellow or orange with irregular margins and incorporating a line of black spots. **HABITATS** Open habitats of man-made and natural origin, including roof tiles on buildings, cliffs, graveyards, orchards, old quarries, scrub, stone walls and woodland. **FOODPLANTS** Lichens, including *Lecidea confluens* and *Xanthoria parietina*. **FIELD NOTES** Sep–early Jun. Feeds at night, hiding by day in a tunnel formed of silk and grit. Pupates in the tunnel. Overwinters as a small larva.

MARBLED GREEN
Nyctobrya muralis

PLATE 47
73.085 (2295)

Local. Mainly coastal but inland in parts of England. **FIELD CHARACTERS** Body dark grey or blackish, speckled with white dots and dashes, and with a sparse covering of white hairs. Dorsal stripe or spots white. **HABITATS** Cliffs, man-made habitats such as drystone walls, and old quarries and rocky areas. Occasionally on trees. **FOODPLANTS** Lichens, including *Caloplaca* spp., *Diploicia canescens* and *Xanthoria parietina*. **FIELD NOTES** Sep–early Jun. Feeds at night, hiding by day in a chamber under its foodplant, sealing the entrance with frass. Pupates in the larval habitation. Overwinters as a small larva.

XYLENINAE

ROSY MARBLED
Elaphria venustula

PLATE 47
73.091 (2396)

Nb. Appears to be expanding westwards. **FIELD CHARACTERS** Body is bulbous centred on A1, tapering to the head and posteriorly. Body blackish grey or brownish, with a brown or orange dorsal line, usually edged paler, most obvious A1–A7. A subdorsal blotch of white mixed pink or orange on A1, with two small white spots posteriorly, a subdorsal black spot on A2 and another laterally on A7. A8 raised to a slight hump. **HABITATS** Open habitats on acidic soils, often associated with Bracken; also heathland, road verges, scrub and woodland. **FOODPLANTS** Probably omnivorous: Bramble, Creeping Cinquefoil, Tormentil, live and dead insects and micro-fungi. **FIELD NOTES** Jun–Sep. In captivity, has been observed to feed on fresh petals and wilted brown flowers of Bramble and cinquefoils, on live larvae, on micro-fungi, and on dead moths and flies. Pupates on or below the ground. Overwinters as a pupa.

MOTTLED RUSTIC
Caradrina morpheus

PLATE 47
73.092 (2387)

Common. Has declined significantly in abundance in recent decades. **FIELD CHARACTERS** Body greyish or brownish, paler dorsally and darker laterally. Dorsal line whitish T1–T3, and hardly visible on abdominal segments. Oblique blackish streaks laterally A2–A8, sometimes joining in a V-shape across the dorsum. **HABITATS** Wide variety of lowland habitats. **FOODPLANTS** Wide variety of herbaceous plants, including Hedge Bedstraw, dandelions, docks, goosefoots, knotgrasses, Common Nettle, Orpine, plantains, stitchworts and teasels. Also Hop and Goat Willow. **FIELD NOTES** Jul–Nov. Feeds at night, hiding in or on the ground by day. Overwinters fully fed in a cocoon in or on the ground, pupating in the spring.

CLANCY'S RUSTIC
Caradrina kadenii

PLATE 47
73.093 (2387a)

Immigrant; recent colonist in southern coastal counties. **FIELD CHARACTERS** Body brown or greenish brown, sometimes paler in the dorsal region. Yellow spots along the dorsal line, which is otherwise faint or comprises yellow dashes. Often a row of black smudges subdorsally A1–A8. Spiracles black. **HABITATS** Open habitats along the coast, including gardens. **FOODPLANTS** Wide variety of herbaceous plants in Europe; not observed in the wild in England. **FIELD NOTES** Probably Jul–Sep.

PALE MOTTLED WILLOW
Caradrina clavipalpis

PLATE 47
73.095 (2389)

Common; suspected immigrant. Has increased significantly in abundance in recent decades in much of its range. Recorded sparingly in Scotland, where it is possibly declining. **FIELD CHARACTERS** Body brown or greyish brown, paler dorsally and darker laterally. Dorsal line usually present T1–A4, but pale and hardly visible posteriorly. Subdorsal line wavy and dark brown, with or without pale edges. **HABITATS** Farmland, especially around farm buildings, gardens and grasslands. **FOODPLANTS** Grass seeds, and cereal grains in the field and in store. Also seeds of Garden Pea and plantains. **FIELD NOTES** Sep–spring, and in summer, with some larvae probably feeding up quickly to produce an often numerous partial second generation of adults end Sep. Overwinters fully fed in a cocoon in the ground, pupating in the spring.

UNCERTAIN
Hoplodrina octogenaria

PLATE 47
73.096 (2381)

Common. **FIELD CHARACTERS** Body greyish brown or brown, with obvious short hairs, some curving forwards and some backwards. Dorsal and subdorsal lines whitish, edged with dark lines. Dorsal region has abundant dark speckling. Pinacula pale or as body colour, with black centres, often surrounded by dark brown shading. **SIMILAR SPECIES** Rustic is usually paler overall, with much less dark speckling dorsally, and the hairs are slightly less conspicuous. However, in general a larva would need to be reared to be certain of its identity. Vine's Rustic has many short dark streaks in the dorsal region and orangey-brown spots laterally. **HABITATS** Wide variety of lowland habitats. **FOODPLANTS** Wide variety of herbaceous plants, including dandelions, dead-nettles, docks, plantains, Primrose, Common Sorrel and stitchworts. **FIELD NOTES** Sep–Apr. Feeds at night. Pupates in a strong cocoon in the ground.

RUSTIC
Hoplodrina blanda

PLATE 47
73.097 (2382)

Common. Has declined significantly in abundance in recent decades. **FIELD CHARACTERS** Body pale greyish brown, sometimes tinged orangey, with short hairs, some curving forwards and some backwards. Dorsal and subdorsal lines whitish, edged with dark lines. Dorsal region has some darker speckles or streaks. Pinacula pale or as body colour, with black centres. **SIMILAR SPECIES** Uncertain and Vine's Rustic. **HABITATS** Wide variety of lowland habitats **FOODPLANTS** Wide variety of herbaceous plants, including dandelions, docks, knotgrasses, plantains and stitchworts. Also reported on grasses. **FIELD NOTES** Sep–Apr. Feeds at night. Pupates in a strong cocoon in the ground.

VINE'S RUSTIC
Hoplodrina ambigua

PLATE 47
73.099 (2384)

Common; suspected immigrant. Has increased significantly in abundance in recent decades and is slowly spreading northwards. **FIELD CHARACTERS** Body pale brown across dorsal region with many oblique darker streaks, and greyish brown laterally with a row of orangey-brown spots A1–A8. Dorsal line pale, edged dark brown or blackish T1–T3, and often less well defined A1–A9. The hairs are sparse and short. **SIMILAR SPECIES** Uncertain and Rustic. **HABITATS** Wide variety of open habitats. **FOODPLANTS** Wide variety of herbaceous plants, including Groundsel, Prickly Lettuce, plantains and Primrose. **FIELD NOTES** Sep–Apr and May–Aug, in two generations. Pupates in a cocoon in the ground.

SILKY WAINSCOT
Chilodes maritima

PLATE 47
73.100 (2391)

Local. **FIELD CHARACTERS** Head brown. Antennae (segmented projections) brown with whitish bases and relatively long either side of the mouthparts. Body pale greyish or greyish brown, often tinged purplish. Dorsal line whitish on T1, comprising a row of whitish dots T2–A8, and subdorsal line a similar row of dots. Spiracles black. True legs long. **HABITATS** Reedbeds, especially the drier parts. **FOODPLANTS** Living and dead invertebrates, and feeds on dead plant tissue within broken Common Reed stems. Likely to feed on living leaves of Common Reed when young. **FIELD NOTES** Jul–Apr. Active at night. Pupates in a broken reed stem. Overwinters as a part-grown larva.

TREBLE LINES
Charanyca trigrammica

PLATE 47
73.101 (2380)

Common. Local in the north and west. **FIELD CHARACTERS** Body brownish or greyish, covered with minute warts that may be tipped white or coloured as the body. Body also with a sparse covering of short hairs. Dorsal line pale grey, usually edged with dark shading between segments. Diagonal whitish-white or pale grey subdorsal streaks A1–A7 or A8, shaded dark brown or dark grey either side. **HABITATS** Wide variety of open habitats. **FOODPLANTS** Wide variety of herbaceous plants, including dandelions, knapweeds, knotgrasses, Greater Plantain and Dwarf Thistle. **FIELD NOTES** Jun–Apr. Feeds at night at ground level, hiding in soil or under vegetation by day. Pupates in the ground. Overwinters as a small larva.

BROWN RUSTIC
Rusina ferruginea

PLATE 47
73.102 (2302)

Common. **FIELD CHARACTERS** Body various shades of brown, increasingly paler in the dorsal region from A3 posteriorly, and often noticeably yellowish or orangey brown A8–A10. There is a whitish dorsal line T1–T3, which is reduced to dots or dashes, or absent, A1–A8. Subdorsal line whitish, edged with dark brown shading. Subspiracular area brownish T1–T3, increasingly paler posteriorly and yellowish brown A7–A9. Spiracles black. **SIMILAR SPECIES** Bird's Wing has white spiracles. Saxon has white or sometimes orange spiracles, and A8 raised to a hump. **HABITATS** Most frequent in broadleaf woodland. Also recorded in open habitats, including gardens, calcareous grassland, heathland and moorland. **FOODPLANTS** Wide variety of herbaceous plants. Recorded on bistorts, dandelions, docks, Groundsel, plantains, strawberries, vetches and violets. Also recorded on Bramble. **FIELD NOTES** Aug–May. Feeds at night. Pupates in a cocoon in the ground. Overwinters as a nearly fully grown larva.

MARSH MOTH
Athetis pallustris

PLATE 47
73.103 (2392)

RDB. At two sites in Lincolnshire. **FIELD CHARACTERS** Body pale brownish grey. Dorsal region mottled dark brownish grey, especially T1–A1, and increasingly paler posteriorly with wedge-shaped marks. Dorsal line whitish, sometimes incomplete, and edged with dark shading between segments. Pale grey dashes above a pale subdorsal line. Dark brownish grey laterally. **HABITATS** Fens, marshy meadows and vegetated sand-dune slacks. Appears to prefer drier, sparsely vegetated parts and short sward heights. **FOODPLANTS** Ribwort Plantain. Probably also Meadowsweet and other herbaceous plants. **FIELD NOTES** Jun–Apr. Overwinters fully fed on or near the ground. Pupates in a cocoon.

BIRD'S WING
Dypterygia scabriuscula

PLATE 48
73.105 (2301)

Local. Recently expanded in the north-eastern part of the range. **FIELD CHARACTERS** Body various shades of brown, mottled darker. Dorsal line whitish, edged darker, and subdorsal line whitish, less well defined and edged with darker shading. Pinacula white and conspicuous. Subspiracular stripe white, whitish or pale brown, often mottled with dark brown. Spiracles white. **SIMILAR SPECIES** Brown Rustic and Saxon. **HABITATS** Heathland, parkland, scrub and broadleaf woodland. Sometimes in gardens. **FOODPLANTS** Various herbaceous plants, especially docks, Knotgrass and sorrels. **FIELD NOTES** Jul–Aug; occasionally also Sep as a partial second generation. Feeds at night. Overwinters as a pupa in a cocoon in the ground.

ORACHE MOTH
Trachea atriplicis

PLATE 48
73.106 (2304)

Immigrant; former resident; possible adventive. Resident in Channel Islands. **FIELD CHARACTERS** Body greenish, brown, greyish or blackish, speckled with small white dots. Dorsal line dark, containing small white dots. Subdorsal line comprises white dots, usually edged with dark, diagonal shading. A yellow or orange spot laterally on A8. Subspiracular stripe whitish, but yellow or orange T2–T3. **HABITATS** Fens, marshes and damp meadows. **FOODPLANTS** Various herbaceous plants, especially goosefoots, Knotgrass and oraches. **FIELD NOTES** Jul–Aug. Feeds at night. Overwinters as a pupa in a cocoon in the ground.

OLD LADY
Mormo maura

PLATE 48
73.107 (2300)

Local. **FIELD CHARACTERS** Body greyish brown with pale brown dorsal line, often broken into dots. Yellowy-orange subdorsal mark on leading edge of T1. Crossing the discontinuous, pale brown subdorsal line are pale brown subdorsal dashes A2–A8 that are distinctly angled, and shaded black on the inner angle and sometimes above. Black transverse stripe on A8, edged paler posteriorly. Spiracles bright orange. **HABITATS** Gardens, hedgerows, marshes, riverbanks, scrub and woodland. **FOODPLANTS** In autumn, on various herbaceous plants, including docks, stitchworts, Wild Strawberry and Rosebay Willowherb. In spring, mainly on woody plants, including Blackthorn, birches, elms, Hawthorn, Common Ivy, spindles and willows; also recorded on Water Dock. **FIELD NOTES** Sep–Jun. Feeds at night, hiding by day in leaf litter. Pupates in a cocoon in the ground, among Common Ivy, behind loose bark or in crevices. Overwinters as a small larva.

GUERNSEY UNDERWING
Polyphaenis sericata

PLATE 48
73.108 (2302a)

Resident in Channel Islands. **FIELD CHARACTERS** Body brown, speckled blackish brown. Dorsal line white T1–T2, then alternating thick blackish-brown and thin white dashes along the dorsum T3–A8. There is a row of lateral spots, which are orange T3–A6 and on A8, and blackish brown on A7. Spiracles white. **HABITATS** Sheltered coastal valleys. **FOODPLANTS** Honeysuckle also reported on oaks. **FIELD NOTES** Autumn–May. Feeds at night, hiding on the ground by day.

STRAW UNDERWING
Thalpophila matura

PLATE 48
73.109 (2303)

Common. Local and mainly coastal in the west and north. **FIELD CHARACTERS** Body various shades of brown. Dorsal line pale brown, edged with thick blackish streaks on anterior half of segments T3–A9. Subdorsal and subspiracular lines pale brown. Spiracles orange or white. **HABITATS** Wide variety of open grassy habitats. **FOODPLANTS** Grasses, including Silver Hair-grass, Mat-grass and Annual Meadow-grass. **FIELD NOTES** Sep–May. Feeds at night. Pupates in the ground. Overwinters as a small larva, feeding slowly throughout.

SAXON
Hyppa rectilinea

PLATE 48
73.110 (2320)

Nb. Widespread in Scotland, local in northern England and rare in Ireland. **FIELD CHARACTERS** Body orangey brown, or dark brown with a velvety-bluish hue, increasingly pale yellowish brown in the dorsal region from A2 or A3 posteriorly, and usually noticeably yellowish or orangey A7–A8. Dorsal and subdorsal lines indistinct, and pale grey or pale brown. Subspiracular stripe greyish brown T2–A7, and yellowish on T1 and A8–A11. A8 is raised into a hump. Spiracles white, or sometimes orange. **SIMILAR SPECIES** Brown Rustic and Bird's Wing. **HABITATS** Upland marshes, moorland, and open woodland including young plantations. **FOODPLANTS** Touch-me-not Balsam, Bearberry, Bilberry, Bramble, Cowberry, Raspberry and willows. **FIELD NOTES** Jul–Apr. Fully fed in Oct, overwintering as a larva in a silken chamber just below the ground, and pupating in the spring.

ANGLE SHADES
Phlogophora meticulosa

PLATE 48
73.113 (2306)

Common; immigrant. **FIELD CHARACTERS** Body bright green or brownish with faint or well-marked darker diagonal stripes A1–A9, running from the spiracular stripe to the dorsum, each crossing two segments. Dorsal line white and incomplete, and subspiracular stripe white, pale greenish or pale brown. Pinacula white. The faintly marked green form is slightly translucent. **SIMILAR SPECIES** Small Angle Shades has a pair of large white pinacula on A8, and A8 is raised to a hump. **HABITATS** Found everywhere, and often numerous in gardens. **FOODPLANTS** Wide variety of plants, but more often on herbaceous than woody species, including Touch-me-not Balsam, Blackthorn, borages, Celery, chrysanthemums, docks, Enchanter's-nightshade, Firethorn, geraniums, Groundsel, Hazel, Honeysuckle, lady's-mantles, Great Mullein, *Polyanthus*, Potato and Red Valerian. Has also been found on Bracken and Giant Fir. **FIELD NOTES** Any time of year. Feeds at night, and often seen in mild weather throughout winter. Pupates in a cocoon just under the ground.

SMALL ANGLE SHADES
Euplexia lucipara

PLATE 48
73.114 (2305)

Common. **FIELD CHARACTERS** Body dull green or purplish brown, usually with faint darker diagonal stripes A1–A9, running from the spiracular stripe to the dorsum, each crossing two segments. Dorsal and subdorsal lines paler than the body colour, usually indistinct and broken into short dashes. Subspiracular stripe well defined along its usually white lower edge, and indistinct and paler than the body colour above. Pinacula white, with a large pair on A8. A8 raised to a hump. **SIMILAR SPECIES** Angle Shades. **HABITATS** Gardens and urban parks, heathland, moorland and woodland. **FOODPLANTS** Wide variety of herbaceous and woody plants. Found on Bracken, Male-fern and other ferns. Also on Touch-me-not Balsam, birches, currants, Foxglove, Hazel, Common Ivy buds, mallows, nettles, oaks, thistles and willows. **FIELD NOTES** Jul–Sep, or later. Feeds at night. Pupates in the ground. Overwinters as a pupa.

BURREN GREEN
Calamia tridens

PLATE 48
73.116 (2366)

Ssp. *occidentalis* Ireland, where resident and widespread in the Burren, Cos Clare and Galway. Suspected immigrant elsewhere. **FIELD CHARACTERS** Head brown, and prothoracic and anal plates blackish brown. Body purplish, with green between the segments revealed as the larva stretches. Pinacula large and blackish brown. **HABITATS** Limestone pavement. **FOODPLANT** Blue Moor-grass. **FIELD NOTES** Apr–late Jun. Lives in the soil at the base of the foodplant, feeding on the rootstock and leaves. Pupates in the ground. Overwinters as an egg.

HAWORTH'S MINOR
Celaena haworthii

PLATE 49
73.118 (2367)

Local. Very local in the south, where it has declined severely in abundance in recent decades. **FIELD CHARACTERS** Prothoracic plate without central dividing line, and anal plate with slightly scalloped posterior margin. Body pale reddish brown with pale yellowish dorsal and subdorsal lines. Pinacula black and prominent, and larger laterally T2–T3. **SIMILAR SPECIES** Rosy Minor, Marbled Minor, Tawny Marbled Minor, Rufous Minor and Middle-barred Minor have a central dividing line on the prothoracic plate, an unscalloped anal plate and less prominent dorsal pinacula. Rosy Minor is distinguished from Marbled Minor, Tawny Marbled Minor, Rufous Minor and Middle-barred Minor by having a black head and larger grey pinacula laterally. Marbled Minor, Tawny Marbled Minor, Rufous Minor and the form of Middle-barred Minor with whitish markings are indistinguishable and should be reared for identification. **HABITATS** Fens, marshes and boggy moorland. **FOODPLANTS** Common Cottongrass. Probably rushes and club-rushes where Common Cottongrass is absent. **FIELD NOTES** Apr–Jul. Feeds internally in stems. A hole low down in a stem may indicate the presence of a larva within. Pupates in a cocoon near the ground. Overwinters as an egg.

CRESCENT
Helotropha leucostigma

PLATE 49
73.119 (2368)

Ssp. *leucostigma* Local; immigrant. Has decreased significantly in abundance in recent decades. Ssp. *scotica* Local. In the northern half of Scotland and the Hebrides. **FIELD CHARACTERS** Body pale purplish grey with pale grey dorsal and subdorsal lines. Pinacula black and prominent, larger dorsally T2–T3 and A8, and larger laterally T2–T3. A black transverse sclerotised strip on A9. Prothoracic plate brown, thickly edged in black, and anal plate brown with five projections. **SIMILAR SPECIES** Double Lobed has smaller dorsal pinacula and lacks projections on the anal plate. **HABITATS** Upland bogs, ditches, fens, marshes, reedbeds and carr woodland. **FOODPLANTS** Bulrushes, Great Fen-sedge, Yellow Iris, Lyme-grass, pond-sedges and Common Sedge. Ssp. *scotica* has been observed laying eggs on Purple Moor-grass. **FIELD NOTES** Mar–Jul. Feeds internally in leaves, stems and roots. Pupates in a flimsy cocoon in leaf litter. Overwinters as an egg.

DUSKY SALLOW
Eremobia ochroleuca

PLATE 49
73.120 (2352)

Common. Very local at the edge of its range. **FIELD CHARACTERS** Body pale greyish green with black pinacula. Dorsal, subdorsal and subspiracular stripes pale yellowish or whitish, the subspiracular stripe usually shaded dark grey above. **HABITATS** Grassy places, especially on calcareous soils and the coast; also embankments, road verges and woodland rides. **FOODPLANTS** Flowers and seeds of grasses, including Cock's-foot, Common Couch, oat-grasses and quaking-grasses, and sometimes cereal crops. **FIELD NOTES** Late Apr–early Jul. Pupates in the ground. Overwinters as an egg.

FROSTED ORANGE
Gortyna flavago

PLATE 49
73.121 (2364)

Common. Expanding in mainland Scotland. **FIELD CHARACTERS** Head brown, prothoracic plate with a pale central line and anal plate black. Body pale yellowish white, with large blackish pinacula. Dorsal vessel visible. More often found in an earlier instar, feeding higher in a stem. The younger larva is shiny brown with white spots or segments, and with pinacula, prothoracic and anal plates like those of the final instar. **HABITATS** Variety of open habitats, including soft cliffs, fens, coastal grassland, marshes, moorland, road verges and woodland rides. **FOODPLANTS** Wide variety of tall herbaceous plants, particularly burdocks, Foxglove, Hemp-agrimony and thistles. Also recorded on Butterfly-bush, figworts, Common Fleabane, Common Knapweed, Mugwort, Common Nettle and ragworts. **FIELD NOTES** Apr–Aug. Feeds within the lower part of a stem, causing it to droop above, or fracture at, the larval entrance hole. Pupates within the stem. Overwinters as an egg.

FISHER'S ESTUARINE MOTH
Gortyna borelii

PLATE 49
73.122 (2365)

Ssp. *lunata* RDB. Protected species. **FIELD CHARACTERS** Head orangey brown, and prothoracic plate similar, with lateral black marks. When part-grown the body is black with narrow grey bands between segments. During the final instar the larva becomes paler and when fully grown it is purplish with greyish white or yellow between segments, with black pinacula and spots. Dorsal vessel visible. **HABITATS** Dyke-banks, fields, grassland and marshy open ground. **FOODPLANT** Hog's Fennel. **FIELD NOTES** Early May–late Aug. Feeds in the stem and root. Pupates in the root in a tunnel open to the earth. Eggs are laid in batches between the stem and leaf sheath of grasses near the foodplant. Overwinters as an egg.

ROSY RUSTIC
Hydraecia micacea

PLATE 49
73.123 (2361)

Common. Has declined significantly in abundance in recent decades. **FIELD CHARACTERS** Head brown, prothoracic plate pale brown, edged black, and anal plate brown with a smooth outer edge. Body greyish or pinkish brown, and greenish between segments when feeding on green leaves, with brownish pinacula. Dorsal vessel visible. **SIMILAR SPECIES** Butterbur in last instar shows no obvious differences, but feeds on Butterbur only. **HABITATS** Wide variety, including fens, gardens, rough and weedy ground, marshes, pasture and woodland rides. **FOODPLANTS** Wide variety, including Lesser Burdock, Broad-leaved Dock, Galingale, Hop, horsetails, Yellow Iris, Meadowsweet, Ribwort Plantain, sea-lavenders, sedges and Field Woundwort. Also on crops, such as Barley, Sugar Beet, Potato, Raspberry, Garden Strawberry and wheats. **FIELD NOTES** Late Apr–early Aug. Feeds in the lower part of a stem, and in roots and rhizomes. On Yellow Iris, feeds between the opposing faces of the lower part of a leaf. Pupates in the ground, without a cocoon. Overwinters as an egg.

BUTTERBUR
Hydraecia petasitis

PLATE 49
73.124 (2362)

Local. **SIMILAR SPECIES** Rosy Rustic. **HABITATS** Fens, damp fields, marshes, mosses, peat bogs, riverbanks and roadside verges. In open places and in shade. **FOODPLANT** Butterbur. **FIELD NOTES** Apr–mid-Jul. Feeds within the petiole, stem and then the root. Pupates in the ground near the larval burrow or in an open chamber in the root. Overwinters as an egg on the withered plant.

MARSH MALLOW MOTH/GIANT EAR
Hydraecia osseola

PLATE 49
73.125 (2363)

Ssp. *hucherardi* RDB. Confined to two areas in Kent. **FIELD CHARACTERS** Head orangey brown, prothoracic plate pale orangey brown, edged black anteriorly, and anal plate grey. Body pale yellowish white with ill-defined pale pinkish subdorsal and spiracular bands. Pinacula greyish or black, and larger on A8–A9. **HABITATS** Open, damp places on saline soils, including grazing marshes, and brackish river and ditch banks. **FOODPLANT** Marsh-mallow. **FIELD NOTES** Apr–late Jul. Within a stem and later the rootstock, making affected plants look sickly. Pupates in the ground, attached to a root. Overwinters as an egg on the withered plant.

NOTE ON EAR MOTHS
Larvae of the following four species are very similar in appearance and habits, and field characters are described for Large Ear only. There are some differences in habitat and recorded foodplants. The larval skin is shiny and translucent, and what the larva eats may affect general coloration. For example, Crinan Ear and Ear Moth have a greenish tinge to the greyish body colour when feeding on Yellow Iris. Larvae of ear moths are rarely seen in the wild.

SALTERN EAR
Amphipoea fucosa

PLATE 49
73.126 (2358)

Ssp. *paludis* Local. Resident in coastal areas, and sometimes recorded inland. **SIMILAR SPECIES** Large Ear, Ear Moth and Crinan Ear. **HABITATS** Scrubby coastal grassland, wet moorland, saltmarshes and sand dunes. **FOODPLANTS** Has been found in the wild on Common Saltmarsh-grass. **FIELD NOTES** May–Jul. In stems and roots of grasses in captivity. Pupates in the ground. Overwinters as an egg.

LARGE EAR
Amphipoea lucens

PLATE 49
73.127 (2357)

Local; immigrant. Can be abundant. **FIELD CHARACTERS** Head orangey brown, prothoracic plate pale brown, edged black, and anal plate pale brown, edged black anteriorly. Body whitish grey with ill-defined purplish subdorsal band and lateral and spiracular stripes. Pinacula black, and larger at the level of the spiracles and on A8–A9 dorsally. **SIMILAR SPECIES** Saltern Ear, Ear Moth and Crinan Ear are indistinguishable in the field. **HABITATS** Marshes, wet moorland, mosses and rough pastures. **FOODPLANTS** Common Cottongrass and Purple Moor-grass. A larva of a Saltern/Large Ear was found wandering on a sandy beach in the Outer Hebrides near Marram and readily ate this plant in captivity. Despite dissection of the resultant adult, its identity is unconfirmed. **FIELD NOTES** May–Jul. Feeds within the lower stems at first, then among the roots. Pupates on the ground in leaf litter. Overwinters as an egg.

EAR MOTH
Amphipoea oculea

PLATE 49
73.128 (2360)

Common. Has decreased significantly in abundance in recent decades. Often at low density. **SIMILAR SPECIES** Saltern Ear, Large Ear and Crinan Ear. **HABITATS** Damp and dry unimproved grassland, marshes, moorland, riverbanks, saltmarshes, sand dunes and woodland rides. **FOODPLANTS** Grasses, including Tufted Hair-grass and Annual Meadow-grass. **FIELD NOTES** Apr–Jun. Feeds within the lower stems and roots. Pupates in the ground. Overwinters as an egg.

Ear Moth larva

CRINAN EAR
Amphipoea crinanensis

PLATE 49
73.129 (2359)

Local. **SIMILAR SPECIES** Saltern Ear, Large Ear and Ear Moth. **HABITATS** Dune-slacks, coastal grassland, unimproved damp grassland, moorland, mosses and vegetated sand dunes. **FOODPLANTS** Has been recorded on irises in the wild. **FIELD NOTES** May–Jul. On leaves of Yellow Iris in captivity. Pupation site not known. Overwinters as an egg.

FLOUNCED RUSTIC
Luperina testacea

PLATE 49
73.131 (2353)

Common. **FIELD CHARACTERS** Head orangey brown, prothoracic plate brownish grey, and anal plate brownish, edged black. Body shiny, and translucent whitish grey. Ill-defined dark grey transverse bands, sometimes with a purplish tinge, which are more noticeable in earlier instars. Spiracles black. **SIMILAR SPECIES** Sandhill Rustic is paler, with much paler prothoracic and anal plates; based on the limited material examined, the anal plate may lack black edging. **HABITATS** Wide variety of grasslands, but most abundant on calcareous soils, cliffs, coastal areas and sand dunes. **FOODPLANTS** Grasses, including Common Couch, fescues and Marram; also cereal crops. **FIELD NOTES** Sep–Jun. Feeds at the base of stems and among roots. Pupates in the ground.

SANDHILL RUSTIC
Luperina nickerlii

PLATE 49
73.132 (2354)

Ssp. *demuthi* Na. Kent and East Anglia. Ssp. *leechi* RDB. Cornwall. Ssp. *gueneei* RDB. North Wales and north-west England. Ssp. *knilli* Ireland. **FIELD CHARACTERS** Head orangey brown, and prothoracic and anal plates cream-coloured. Body shiny, and translucent cream-coloured, with a hint of purplish dorsally. Spiracles black. **SIMILAR SPECIES** Flounced Rustic. **HABITATS** Grassy cliffs in Ireland; saltmarshes, a vegetated sandbar and sandy beaches in England. **FOODPLANTS** Sand Couch in north Wales and Cornwall; Borrer's Saltmarsh-grass, Common Saltmarsh-grass, Bulbous Meadow-grass and other salt-tolerant grasses in Essex and Kent; unknown in Ireland. **FIELD NOTES** Sep–early Jul. In stems until Mar or Apr, later burrowing to feed on rhizomes. Tolerates saltwater inundation. In sandbar habitat, larger larvae construct chambers of silk, sand and plant material. Pupates in a flimsy cocoon in a tussock, or in sand. Overwinters as a part-grown larva.

LARGE WAINSCOT
Rhizedra lutosa

PLATE 49
73.134 (2375)

Common. Has declined significantly in abundance in recent decades, especially in northern England. Local in Scotland and Ireland. **FIELD CHARACTERS** Head reddish brown, and prothoracic and anal plates pale brown. Body elongate, shiny and pinkish brown, dappled paler. Dorsal vessel visible. **HABITATS** Reedbeds and reedy ditches, preferring drier parts away from standing water. **FOODPLANT** Common Reed. **FIELD NOTES** Apr–late Jul. Feeds among the roots. Affected plants look sickly. Pupates among the roots. Overwinters as an egg.

BLAIR'S WAINSCOT
Sedina buettneri

PLATE 49
73.135 (2376)

RDB; suspected immigrant. Resident in Dorset, and possibly elsewhere. **FIELD CHARACTERS** Body elongate, tapering at either end, and somewhat translucent white or dull whitish. Subdorsal stripe purplish brown or reddish, and a similarly coloured supraspiracular stripe, which is often incomplete. **HABITATS** Sedge-beds in marshes, pond margins and river valleys. **FOODPLANT** Lesser Pond-sedge. **FIELD NOTES** Late Apr–Aug. Feeds within the base of the growing sedge, excavating a short chamber, and frequently moves between plants. No external evidence of the larva when it is young. Later, the central growing shoot may look sickly. Pupates in the feeding site or among dead sedges. Overwinters as an egg among standing dead sedges.

BULRUSH WAINSCOT
Nonagria typhae

PLATE 49
73.136 (2369)

Common. Local in Scotland and Ireland. **FIELD CHARACTERS** Head, prothoracic and anal plates brown. Body elongate and brownish, dull purplish grey or pinkish, with greyish-white dorsal and subdorsal stripes. Spiracles black. **HABITATS** Margins of ditches, estuaries, fens, lakes, marshes and ponds. **FOODPLANTS** Mainly Bulrush, and occasionally Lesser Bulrush. **FIELD NOTES** Apr–early Aug. Feeds within the leaf at first, then in the stem, moving between plants and leaving obvious signs of feeding. Pupates head down within the stem where it has been feeding, or in a dead stem. Overwinters as an egg.

FEN WAINSCOT
Arenostola phragmitidis

PLATE 50
73.137 (2377)

Local. Most frequent on or near the coast. **FIELD CHARACTERS** Head black, prothoracic plate dark brown, and anal plate black. Body slender and cream-coloured. Transverse purplish bands T2–A8, narrowly interrupted along the dorsum on T2–A4, and with wider gaps A5–A8. Pinacula blackish, and larger on T1–T3 and A8–A9. **HABITATS** Reedbeds. **FOODPLANT** Common Reed. **FIELD NOTES** Apr–Jun. Enters a living stem above a node, excavating two or three rings within, which form dark circular scars, killing the shoot above. The larva then feeds within the stem of the dying shoot, boring up the stem and leaving a spiral tunnel filled with frass. It changes stem as it grows. Pupates on the ground. Overwinters as an egg.

LYME GRASS
Longalatedes elymi

PLATE 50
73.138 (2348)

Nb. **FIELD CHARACTERS** Head brown with bulbous dorsal lobes, and prothoracic and anal plates pale brown. Body white. **SIMILAR SPECIES** Cloaked Minor. **HABITATS** Dune-slacks and sand dunes. **FOODPLANT** Lyme-grass. **FIELD NOTES** Sep–Jun. Feeds within the lower stem, sometimes below ground level. The leading shoot of an affected plant discolours and dies. Pupates at the base of the plant. Probably overwinters as a small larva within the plant.

TWIN-SPOTTED WAINSCOT
Lenisa geminipuncta

PLATE 50
73.139 (2370)

Local. Sometimes abundant. **FIELD CHARACTERS** Head dark brown, prothoracic plate concolorous with the body, and anal plate pale grey or pale brown. Body elongate and greyish cream, with dorsal vessel visible. Pinacula black. **SIMILAR SPECIES** White-mantled Wainscot and Brown-veined Wainscot both differ from Twin-spotted Wainscot in having much smaller pinacula in the final instar. White-mantled Wainscot is distinguished from Brown-veined Wainscot by having a line of black or brown tracheal air tubes visible beneath the cuticle between the abdominal spiracles. **HABITATS** Reedbeds, and scattered patches of reeds in a variety of situations. Commonest where reeds are not cut. **FOODPLANT** Common Reed. **FIELD NOTES** May–Jul. Feeds within the stem, causing the shoot to die; a round hole indicates where a larva has entered or left. Larva changes stems as it grows. Pupates low down in a stem, head up within the larval burrow. Overwinters as an egg.

WHITE-MANTLED WAINSCOT
Archanara neurica

PLATE 50
73.140 (2372)

RDB. A coastal species. **FIELD CHARACTERS** Head dark brown, and prothoracic and anal plates brown with darker mottling. Body elongate and pinkish grey, with indistinct paler dorsal and subdorsal lines. Pinacula small and blackish. Spiracles black, with black or brown tracheal air tubes joining the spiracles; these tubes are visible beneath the cuticle. **SIMILAR SPECIES** Twin-spotted Wainscot and Brown-veined Wainscot. **HABITATS** Edges of reedbeds and reedy ditches with abundant dead stems. **FOODPLANT** Common Reed. **FIELD NOTES** Late Apr–late Jun. Feeds within the stem, about halfway up, a round hole indicating where it has entered or left. Changes stems as it grows. When fully fed it enters an old reed stem by making a small hole that it then seals from within using chewed reed. It then makes a window from within for emergence, spins a few silken threads, and pupates head down. Overwinters as an egg.

BROWN-VEINED WAINSCOT
Archanara dissoluta

PLATE 50
73.141 (2371)

Local. **FIELD CHARACTERS** Head dark brown, prothoracic plate concolorous with the body, and anal plate pale brown. Body elongate and pinkish brown, sometimes greenish between segments. Pinacula small and blackish. Spiracles black. Dorsal vessel visible. **SIMILAR SPECIES** Twin-spotted Wainscot and White-mantled Wainscot. **HABITATS** Reedbeds and reedy ditches. **FOODPLANT** Common Reed. **FIELD NOTES** Apr–early Jul. Feeds within the stem, a round hole indicating where it has entered or left. Changes stems as it grows. Pupates head down in a reed stem, close to the ground, having vacated its feeding burrow. Overwinters as an egg.

SMALL RUFOUS
Coenobia rufa

PLATE 50
73.142 (2379)

Local. **FIELD CHARACTERS** Head, prothoracic and anal plates dark brown, the prothoracic plate with a pale dorsal line. Body dull pale pinkish with sparse, moderately long hairs. Pinacula brown. **HABITATS** Bogs, fens, poorly drained fields and woodland rides, and marshes; prefers drier areas. **FOODPLANTS** Has been found in Jointed and Sharp-flowered rushes, and Soft-rush. **FIELD NOTES** Sep–Jun. Feeds within the stems, causing affected stems to wither and whiten. Larva changes stems as it grows. Pupates low down in a stem.

SMALL WAINSCOT
Denticucullus pygmina

PLATE 50
73.144 (2350)

Common. **FIELD CHARACTERS** Head, prothoracic and anal plates pale brown, the anal plate with four projections along its posterior margin. Body creamy white and translucent with some viscera visible, and a pink band dorsally with a creamy-white dorsal line and intersegmental bands. Hairs sparse and very short. Lateral stripe pink. Four brown pinacula on dorsum on A8, noticeably larger than pinacula on other segments, and a pale brown transverse sclerotised strip on A9. **SIMILAR SPECIES** Mere Wainscot and Concolorous, both of which lack the projections on the anal plate. Concolorous is similar to Mere Wainscot but more slender, does not taper towards the head and is fully fed two weeks earlier. **HABITATS** Most frequent in fens, marshes, boggy moorland and wet woodland, but also occurs in other wetland habitats. **FOODPLANTS** Cottongrasses, Great Wood-rush and sedges, including Glaucous Sedge, Lesser Pond-sedge and Tufted-sedge. Also on Reed Sweet-grass and other grasses. **FIELD NOTES** Nov or possibly earlier–Jul. Feeds within the plant, showing little external sign, or sometimes causing the shoot to look sickly. Pupates in a cocoon in a hollow stem or among the foodplant. Overwinters as an egg or larva; eggs in captivity observed to hatch Nov–late Feb.

MERE WAINSCOT
Photedes fluxa

PLATE 50
73.145 (2349)

Nb; suspected immigrant. Mainly on clay soils in central England. **FIELD CHARACTERS** Head orangey brown, and prothoracic and anal plates pale brown. Thoracic segments taper towards the head. Body cream with ill-defined markings consisting of a broad pink dorsal band, extending laterally, and a cream dorsal line. Pale brown transverse sclerotised strip on A9. **SIMILAR SPECIES** Small Wainscot and Concolorous. **HABITATS** Clearings and rides in poorly drained woodland. Also in the drier parts of broads, fens, damp unimproved grassland, marshes and reedbeds. **FOODPLANT** Wood Small-reed. **FIELD NOTES** Sep–Jun. Feeds

Larvae of Concolorous (left; p. 318) and Mere Wainscot (right)

within lower part of the stem, causing the shoot to look sickly. Pupates in a tough cocoon among the plant. Overwinters as a part-grown larva.

LEAST MINOR
Photedes captiuncula

PLATE 50

73.146 (2344)

Ssp. *expolita* RDB. Ssp. *tincta* Ireland. **FIELD CHARACTERS** Head brown, and prothoracic and anal plates pale brown. Body cream or pale yellowish and translucent, with dorsal vessel and viscera sometimes visible. Sometimes there is pinkish shading over the dorsal area posteriorly. Pale brown transverse sclerotised strip on A9. **SIMILAR SPECIES** Cloaked Minor. **HABITATS** Limestone pavement. **FOODPLANTS** Blue Moor-grass and Glaucous Sedge. **FIELD NOTES** Aug–late May. Feeds within the stem. In affected stems, the flower spike fails to develop fully. Pupates in a flimsy cocoon on the ground.

SMALL DOTTED BUFF
Photedes minima

PLATE 50

73.147 (2345)

Common. **FIELD CHARACTERS** Head brown, and prothoracic and anal plates pale brown. Body creamy white and markings ill-defined; slightly brownish dorsally with a paler dorsal line. Pale brown transverse sclerotised strip on A9. **HABITATS** Poorly drained grassland, marshes and woodland rides. **FOODPLANT** Tufted Hair-grass. **FIELD NOTES** Aug–early Jun. Feeds within the stem towards the base; in affected stems, the shoot looks sickly or dies. Pupates in a cocoon in the ground.

MORRIS'S WAINSCOT
Photedes morrisii

PLATE 50

73.148 (2346)

Ssp. *morrisii* RDB. Resident on the undercliff between Bridport and Axmouth. Bond's Wainscot ssp. *bondii* RDB. Kent; probably extinct. **FIELD CHARACTERS** Head brown, prothoracic plate pale brown, and anal plate pale brown and ending in a point. Body creamy, dorsal vessel visible, and slight pinkish markings dorsally. Transverse, pale brown sclerotised strip on A9. **SIMILAR SPECIES** Cloaked Minor. **HABITATS** Soft cliffs, preferring areas of sparsely vegetated, broken ground close to the sea. **FOODPLANT** Tall Fescue. **FIELD NOTES** Aug–late May. Feeds within the stem towards the base; in affected stems the shoot looks sickly or dies. Pupates low down among the foodplant.

CONCOLOROUS
Photedes extrema

PLATE 50

73.149 (2347)

RDB; suspected immigrant. **FIELD CHARACTERS** Head orangey brown, and prothoracic and anal plates pale brown. Body cream with ill-defined markings consisting of a broad pink dorsal band, extending laterally, and a cream dorsal line. Pale brown transverse sclerotised strip on A9. **SIMILAR SPECIES** Small Wainscot and Mere Wainscot. **HABITATS** Drier parts of fens, marshy open areas, and clearings and rides in ancient woodland. **FOODPLANTS** Purple and Wood small-reeds. **FIELD NOTES** Late Jun–May. Feeds within the lower part of the stem, and from within old stems on the growing shoots, head down, leaving much frass. Larvae are very difficult to find, leaving no external clues as to their location. Pupates in a tough cocoon spun low down among dead leaves. (See photo p. 317.)

FENN'S WAINSCOT
Protarchanara brevilinea

PLATE 50

73.150 (2351)

RDB. Norfolk Broads and Suffolk coast. **FIELD CHARACTERS** Body greenish grey with reddish-brown dorsal line and subdorsal stripe, both edged with yellowish lines. Subspiracular stripe yellowish, edged darker above. **HABITATS** Prefers drier parts of reedbeds. **FOODPLANT** Common Reed. **FIELD NOTES** Apr–Jun. At first within the upper part of the stem. In final instar it hides within a stem by day, emerging to feed on leaves at night. Pupates in a cocoon among debris on the ground. Overwinters as an egg laid on a standing reed or reed litter.

WEBB'S WAINSCOT
Globia sparganii

PLATE 50
73.151 (2373)

Nb. Spreading inland and northwards. **FIELD CHARACTERS** Head pale brown, prothoracic and anal plates pale brown or pale greenish brown. Body usually dark green, pale green below, with pale green dorsal and subdorsal stripes and an indistinct pale green spiracular stripe. Sometimes the body is pale green and unmarked apart from a dark green dorsal vessel. Spiracles with pale reddish centres. **SIMILAR SPECIES** Rush Wainscot has dark speckling on the head, but it is not certain whether this provides a consistent diagnostic feature. Where distributions overlap, a larva should be reared to confirm its identity. **HABITATS** Ditches, fens, lake margins, marshes and ponds. **FOODPLANTS** Most frequently Bulrush. Also on Lesser Bulrush, Branched Bur-reed, Common and Grey club-rushes and Yellow Iris. **FIELD NOTES** May–mid-Aug. Feeds within the stems and leaves. Pupates head up in the larval burrow. Overwinters as an egg.

RUSH WAINSCOT
Globia algae

PLATE 50
73.152 (2374)

RDB. Populations most widespread in Norfolk; very local elsewhere. **FIELD CHARACTERS** Head pale brown with darker freckling, and prothoracic and anal plates pale greenish brown, the anal plate with many short black spines. Body translucent, pale green, tinged pinkish, and sometimes with faint, paler lateral and spiracular lines. Centres of spiracles whitish. Dorsal vessel dark green. **SIMILAR SPECIES** Webb's Wainscot. **HABITATS** Edges of wetlands such as broads, gravel pits and freshwater lakes. **FOODPLANTS** Bulrush, Lesser Bulrush, Common Club-rush and Yellow Iris. The eggs are laid on Common Club-rush. **FIELD NOTES** Late May–early Aug. Feeds at first within the shoot tips of Common Club-rush, causing withering, and then moves to other foodplants. Pupates head up in a living or dead standing stem. Overwinters as an egg.

DUSKY BROCADE
Apamea remissa

PLATE 51
73.154 (2330)

Common. Has decreased significantly in abundance in recent decades. **FIELD CHARACTERS** Body greyish brown with black pinacula. Dorsal stripe whitish, and subdorsal stripe and subspiracular band pale brown. Above each spiracle is a pinaculum that is not enclosed by another mark. Prothoracic plate brown with yellowish-white dorsal and subdorsal lines, and the plate is usually paler lateral to the subdorsal lines. Anal plate brown with whitish dorsal and subdorsal lines, and this plate is also paler lateral to the subdorsal lines. **SIMILAR SPECIES** Clouded Brindle, Clouded-bordered Brindle, Large Nutmeg, Rustic Shoulder-knot and Small Clouded Brindle. Clouded Brindle and Clouded-bordered Brindle are distinguished from the other species by having a dorsal line, whereas in the other species it is broader, forming a stripe. Clouded Brindle is distinguished from Clouded-bordered Brindle by having a dorsal line on the prothoracic plate that is narrower than the subdorsal stripes and by the absence of subdorsal whitish lines on the anal plate. Rustic Shoulder-knot may differ from Dusky Brocade and Large Nutmeg by the pinaculum above each spiracle being expanded, forming an irregular, dark brown shape. Dusky Brocade and Large Nutmeg are extremely similar, but the subdorsal line on the anal plate is weaker in Large Nutmeg. The anal plate of Rustic Shoulder-knot varies between those of Dusky Brocade and Large Nutmeg. It should be noted that these differences are described on the basis of comparison of limited material, so caution is advised. Small Clouded Brindle differs from all other similar species by being fully fed in the autumn. **HABITATS** Wide variety of grassy habitats. **FOODPLANTS** Grasses, including False Brome, Reed Canary-grass, Common Couch and Annual Meadow-grass. **FIELD NOTES** Aug–Apr. Feeds at first in the flowers and on the immature seeds, and when larger feeds at night on grass blades, hiding on the ground by day. Pupates in the ground.

**Least Minor larva in stem of Blue Moor-grass
(see opposite)**

CLOUDED BRINDLE
Apamea epomidion

PLATE 51
73.155 (2327)

Common. Local in Scotland and Ireland. **FIELD CHARACTERS** Body varies from brownish to greyish, with large black pinacula. Dorsal line whitish, subdorsal stripe barely discernible and subspiracular band brownish grey. **SIMILAR SPECIES** Dusky Brocade, Clouded-bordered Brindle, Large Nutmeg, Rustic Shoulder-knot and Small Clouded Brindle. **HABITATS** Hedgerows, parkland, mature scrub and broadleaf woodland. Occasionally in gardens. **FOODPLANTS** Grasses, including Cock's-foot, Tufted Hair-grass and Annual Meadow-grass. **FIELD NOTES** Aug–Mar. Feeds at first in the flowers and on the immature seeds, and when larger feeds at night on grass blades, hiding on the ground by day. Pupates in a cocoon among grass roots or on the ground.

CLOUDED-BORDERED BRINDLE
Apamea crenata

PLATE 51
73.156 (2326)

Common. **FIELD CHARACTERS** Body varies from brownish to greyish, with large black pinacula. Dorsal line whitish, subdorsal stripe faint, and subspiracular band brownish grey. **SIMILAR SPECIES** Dusky Brocade, Clouded Brindle, Large Nutmeg, Rustic Shoulder-knot and Small Clouded Brindle. **HABITATS** Wide variety of grassy habitats. **FOODPLANTS** Grasses, including Cock's-foot and Wavy Hair-grass. **FIELD NOTES** Aug–Apr. Feeds at first in the flowers and on the immature seeds, and when larger feeds at night on grass blades, hiding on the ground by day. Pupates among grass roots.

LARGE NUTMEG
Apamea anceps

PLATE 51
73.157 (2333)

Local. Has declined severely in abundance in recent decades. Remains most frequent from the south and east Midlands to central southern England. **FIELD CHARACTERS** Body greyish brown with black pinacula. Dorsal stripe whitish, and subdorsal stripe and subspiracular band pale brown. **SIMILAR SPECIES** Dusky Brocade, Clouded Brindle, Clouded-bordered Brindle, Rustic Shoulder-knot and Small Clouded Brindle. **HABITATS** Mainly dry calcareous grassland in a variety of situations, such as arable field margins and woodland rides. **FOODPLANTS** Grasses, including Cock's-foot, Common Couch and Annual Meadow-grass, and cereal crops. **FIELD NOTES** Aug–Apr. Feeds at first in the flowers and on the immature seeds, and when larger feeds at night on grass blades, hiding on the ground by day. Pupates in the ground.

RUSTIC SHOULDER-KNOT
Apamea sordens

PLATE 51
73.158 (2334)

Common. **FIELD CHARACTERS** Body brown with black pinacula. Dorsal and subdorsal stripes and spiracular band pale brown. In the material examined the pinaculum above each spiracle is usually expanded, forming an irregular, dark brown shape. **SIMILAR SPECIES** Dusky Brocade, Clouded Brindle, Clouded-bordered Brindle, Large Nutmeg and Small Clouded Brindle. **HABITATS** Wide variety of grassy habitats. **FOODPLANTS** Grasses, including Cock's-foot and Common Couch, and cereal crops. **FIELD NOTES** Aug–Mar. Feeds at first in the flowers and on the immature seeds, and when larger feeds at night on grass blades, hiding on the ground by day. Pupates in a strong cocoon on or in the ground.

SMALL CLOUDED BRINDLE
Apamea unanimis

PLATE 51
73.159 (2331

Common. Local in northern Scotland and Ireland. **FIELD CHARACTERS** Body pale brown, with reddish shading between segments. Dorsal and subdorsal stripes whitish brown, and spiracular band pale brown. **SIMILAR SPECIES** Dusky Brocade, Clouded Brindle, Clouded-bordered Brindle, Large Nutmeg and Rustic Shoulder-knot. **HABITATS** Damp or wet grassland, including fens, margins of lakes and ponds, marshes and woodland rides. **FOODPLANTS** Grasses, including Reed Canary-grass, Wavy Hair-grass, Annual

Meadow-grass and Common Reed. Also reported on sedges. **FIELD NOTES** Jul–Oct. Ascends the plant at night to feed, hiding on the ground by day. Overwinters as a fully fed larva, dispersing in early spring to find a pupation site in the ground or in a hollow stem.

SLENDER BRINDLE
Apamea scolopacina

PLATE 51
73.160 (2335)

Common. Has increased significantly in abundance in recent decades. **FIELD CHARACTERS** Head orangey brown, often with two black frontal stripes, and a black lateral spot. Prothoracic plate concolorous with body dorsally, tinged brownish, and black laterally. Body grey or greyish green, with greyish-white dorsal and subdorsal lines. Usually a dark grey or blackish lateral band incorporating prominent black pinacula above the spiracles T2–A8. Spiracular stripe whitish or greenish white. **HABITATS** Mainly grassy clearings and rides in woodland. **FOODPLANTS** Woodland grasses, including False Brome, Wood Meadow-grass, Wood Melick and Wood Millet. Also Great Wood-rush. **FIELD NOTES** Aug–May. At first inside stems, later feeding at night on leaves and flowers and hiding by day on the ground. Pupates in a cocoon in the ground.

CRESCENT STRIPED
Apamea oblonga

PLATE 51
73.161 (2325)

Nb. **FIELD CHARACTERS** Head pale orangey brown, prothoracic plate pale brown, edged black, and anal plate pale brown, edged black anteriorly. Body creamy grey with large grey pinacula. **SIMILAR SPECIES** Northern Arches/Exile is very similar, but as the geographical distribution and habitats of these two species do not overlap, they can be identified with confidence. Dark Arches, Light Arches and Reddish Light Arches have black, not grey, pinacula, but there is no clear difference among these three species. Confused is very similar to these last three species, but the pinacula tend to be smaller and not as black. Great caution is advised and they need to be reared to be certain of their identity. **HABITATS** Ditches, estuaries, fens, coastal grazing marshes, mudflats, saltmarshes, and slacks in sand dunes. **FOODPLANTS** Grasses, including Red Fescue, Bulbous Meadow-grass, and Common and Reflexed Saltmarsh-grasses. **FIELD NOTES** Late summer–Jun. Lives in an underground chamber, feeding on roots and stem bases. Pupates in the larval chamber.

DARK ARCHES
Apamea monoglypha

PLATE 51
73.162 (2321)

Common. **FIELD CHARACTERS** Head black or brown, and prothoracic and anal plates blackish. Body mixed purplish brown and grey, with large black pinacula. **SIMILAR SPECIES** Crescent Striped, Light Arches, Reddish Light Arches, Confused and Northern Arches/Exile. **HABITATS** All types of grassland habitat. **FOODPLANTS** Grasses, including Cock's-foot and Common Couch. **FIELD NOTES** Aug–Jun. Feeds at first in the flowers and seeds, and later in a chamber among the roots, eating roots and stem bases. Pupates in the ground.

LIGHT ARCHES
Apamea lithoxylaea

PLATE 51
73.163 (2322)

Common. Has decreased significantly in abundance in recent decades. **SIMILAR SPECIES** Crescent Striped, Dark Arches, Reddish Light Arches, Confused and Northern Arches/Exile. **HABITATS** Wide variety of grassland habitats. **FOODPLANTS** Grasses, including Annual Meadow-grass. **FIELD NOTES** Aug–Jun. Feeds at first in the flowers and seeds, later eating the stem bases. Pupates in the ground.

REDDISH LIGHT ARCHES
Apamea sublustris

PLATE 51
73.164 (2323)

Local. Widespread from southern England to East Anglia, but very local elsewhere in England, Wales and Ireland. **SIMILAR SPECIES** Crescent Striped, Dark Arches, Light Arches, Confused and Northern Arches/Exile. **HABITATS** Breckland and calcareous grasslands, sand dunes and vegetated shingle. **FOODPLANTS** Grasses. **FIELD NOTES** The larva has not been found in the wild in Great Britain or Ireland. Its time of appearance is probably similar to that of Dark Arches and Light Arches.

CONFUSED
Apamea furva

PLATE 51
73.165 (2329)

Ssp. *britannica* Local. **FIELD CHARACTERS** Head, prothoracic and anal plates vary from pale orangey brown to dark brown or black. Body translucent and pale grey, usually with pale pinkish or orangey shading on abdominal segments across the dorsal area. Pinacula dark grey or blackish. **SIMILAR SPECIES** Crescent Striped, Dark Arches, Light Arches, Reddish Light Arches and Northern Arches/Exile. **HABITATS** Rocky coasts, moorland and upland pastures; occasionally sand dunes. **FOODPLANTS** Grasses, including Rough and Wood meadow-grasses. **FIELD NOTES** Sep–Jun. Feeds at night on roots and lower sections of grass stems, hiding by day among the roots. Pupates without a cocoon in the ground.

NORTHERN ARCHES/EXILE
Apamea exulis

PLATE 51
73.167 (2324)

Na. Widespread in Scotland, including Orkney and Shetland, and very local in northern England. **SIMILAR SPECIES** Crescent Striped, Dark Arches, Light Arches, Reddish Light Arches and Confused. **HABITATS** Peaty moorland and upland pastures. **FOODPLANTS** Grasses. On Purple Moor-grass in captivity. **FIELD NOTES** Sep–Jun. Feeds between the lower stem and the root, living in a pressed-out chamber at the stem bases. It has not been found in the wild in Great Britain. Pupates in the ground. Overwinters as a larva, possibly over two winters.

DOUBLE LOBED
Lateroligia ophiogramma

PLATE 5
73.168 (2330)

Common. Spreading in Scotland. **FIELD CHARACTERS** Body pinkish brown. Dorsal line, if present, ill-defined and pale grey. Pinacula brown, small on dorsum T2–A7, and large laterally and on A8. A transverse black sclerotised strip on A9. Anal plate brown, and smooth-margined posteriorly. **SIMILAR SPECIES** Crescent. **HABITATS** Fens, wet grassland, margins of lakes, marshes, riverbanks and damp woodland. **FOODPLANTS** Reed Canary-grass and Reed Sweet-grass. Also recorded on Pampas-grass. **FIELD NOTES** Aug–early Jun. Feeds within the stem. Pupates in a cocoon at the base of grass stems or on the ground.

COMMON RUSTIC
Mesapamea secalis

PLATE 5
73.169 (234)

Common. **FIELD CHARACTERS** Body pale green with a darker green dorsal vessel. Subdorsal line, if present, whitish green, above which is a reddish or purplish stripe. **SIMILAR SPECIES** Lesser Common Rustic is indistinguishable in the field. The greenest individuals of Middle-barred Minor are very similar, but smaller when fully fed, and the coloration above the subdorsal line tends to be less purple. If there is any doubt then larvae should be reared to confirm identity. **HABITATS** Wide variety of grassy habitats. **FOODPLANTS** Grasses, including Cock's-foot, Tall Fescue and Tufted Hair-grass, and cereal crops. Also recorded on Hairy Wood-rush. Has been recorded egg-laying on Sand Couch. *Mesapamea* larvae have been found, but not reared, in the stems of Yellow Iris, Sharp-flowered Rush and Soft-rush.

FIELD NOTES Aug–early Jun. Feeds within the stem; in affected stems, the shoot looks sickly or dies. May also be seen at night wandering to find a new stem. Pupates in a cocoon in the ground.

LESSER COMMON RUSTIC
Mesapamea didyma

PLATE 52
73.170 (2343a)

Common. **SIMILAR SPECIES** Common Rustic, and the greenest individuals of Middle-barred Minor. **HABITATS** Wide variety of grassy habitats. **FOODPLANTS** Grasses, including Cock's-foot and fescues. **FIELD NOTES** Sep–May. Similar to Common Rustic.

ROSY MINOR
Litoligia literosa

PLATE 52
73.171 (2342)

Common. Has declined severely in abundance in recent decades. Most frequent on coasts. **FIELD CHARACTERS** Head black and prothoracic plate brown, divided by a pale line and edged black anteriorly. Body pale yellowish brown with a purplish dorsal band, within which is a pale yellowish-brown dorsal line. Pinacula grey, and larger laterally on T2–T3. **SIMILAR SPECIES** Haworth's Minor, Marbled Minor, Tawny Marbled Minor, Rufous Minor and Middle-barred Minor. **HABITATS** Open grassy habitats, including cliffs, fens, breckland and calcareous grassland, marshes, sand dunes, scrub and waste ground. **FOODPLANTS** Grasses, including Cock's-foot, *Holcus* spp., Lyme-grass, Marram, False Oat-grass and Sheep's-fescue, and also cereal crops. Also Stinking Iris and Glaucous Sedge. **FIELD NOTES** Sep–early Jun. At first in the roots, and in spring in the stems, when they can be located by plucking faded non-flowering shoots, especially of *Holcus* spp. Pupates in a thin cocoon among leaf litter or in the ground.

CLOAKED MINOR
Mesoligia furuncula

PLATE 52
73.172 (2341)

Common. **FIELD CHARACTERS** Head brown and rather flattened, prothoracic plate pale brown, and anal plate pale brown and smoothly rounded. Body cream with a variable amount of pinkish or purplish shading. The skin is translucent, and dark viscera beneath often show through dorsally. **SIMILAR SPECIES** Lyme Grass, Least Minor and Morris's Wainscot have different foodplants from each other and non-overlapping distributions. Morris's Wainscot shares its foodplant with Cloaked Minor, but is distinguished by the anal plate ending in a point, and also the presence of a sclerotised strip on A9. Although not recorded, Cloaked Minor could share a foodplant with Lyme Grass and Least Minor, and is distinguished from Lyme Grass by its rather flat rather than bulbous head. Based on the limited material examined, Least Minor cannot be distinguished from Cloaked Minor. **HABITATS** Open, grassy habitats, often where the sward is short or the ground broken, including coastal cliffs and slopes, calcareous and sandy grasslands, and sand dunes. **FOODPLANTS** Grasses, including Tall Fescue, Tufted Hair-grass, False Oat-grass and Sheep's-fescue. **FIELD NOTES** Aug–early Jun. Feeds within the stem; in affected stems the shoot looks sickly or dies. Pupates low down among the foodplant and has been known to pupate in Jun, having finished feeding in Feb.

MARBLED MINOR
Oligia strigilis

PLATE 52
73.173 (2337)

Common. Less frequent in Scotland; uncommon in Ireland. **FIELD CHARACTERS** See Rufous Minor, from which it is indistinguishable. **SIMILAR SPECIES** Haworth's Minor, Rosy Minor, Tawny Marbled Minor, Rufous Minor and Middle-barred Minor. **HABITATS** Wide variety of grassy habitats. **FOODPLANTS** Grasses, including Reed Canary-grass, Cock's-foot and Common Couch. **FIELD NOTES** Jul–May. Feeds within the stem; in affected stems the shoot looks sickly or dies. Pupates among the roots of the foodplant.

TAWNY MARBLED MINOR
Oligia latruncula

PLATE 52
73.174 (2339)

Common. Local in the north. **FIELD CHARACTERS** See Rufous Minor, from which it is indistinguishable. **SIMILAR SPECIES** Haworth's Minor, Rosy Minor, Marbled Minor, Rufous Minor and Middle-barred Minor. **HABITATS** Wide variety of grassy habitats. **FOODPLANTS** Grasses, including Cock's-foot. **FIELD NOTES** Aug–May. Feeds within the stem; in affected stems the shoot looks sickly or dies. Pupates among the roots of the foodplant.

RUFOUS MINOR
Oligia versicolor

PLATE 52
73.175 (2338)

Local. **FIELD CHARACTERS** Head brown, prothoracic plate brown and divided centrally by a pale line, and anal plate brown, smoothly rounded posteriorly. Body pale purplish brown with whitish dorsal and subdorsal lines. Body colour laterally may be pale purplish brown, pale yellowish brown mixed purplish, or mixed whitish and purplish. **SIMILAR SPECIES** Haworth's Minor, Rosy Minor, Marbled Minor, Tawny Marbled Minor and Middle-barred Minor. **HABITATS** Wide variety of grassy habitats, including cliffs and coastal grassland, heathland, and woodland rides. **FOODPLANTS** Grasses, including Cock's-foot and Tufted and Wavy hair-grasses. **FIELD NOTES** Jul–Apr. Usually feeds within the stem, and in affected stems the shoot looks sickly or dies. Occasionally, when nearly fully fed the larva feeds externally. Pupates in a flimsy cocoon among the roots of the foodplant.

MIDDLE-BARRED MINOR
Oligia fasciuncula

PLATE 52
73.176 (2340)

Common. **FIELD CHARACTERS** Head brown, prothoracic plate brown and divided centrally by a pale line, and anal plate brown, smoothly rounded posteriorly. Body pale purplish brown with pale greenish or dirty whitish dorsal and subdorsal lines. Body colour laterally is mixed purplish brown and greenish or whitish. The intensity of the green coloration varies between individuals such that there are two forms, one with greenish markings and the other with whitish markings. **SIMILAR SPECIES** Haworth's Minor, Rosy Minor, Marbled Minor, Tawny Marbled Minor and Rufous Minor. Also, for greenest individuals, Common Rustic and Lesser Common Rustic. **HABITATS** Fens, marshy grassland, marshes, and damp woodland clearings and rides. **FOODPLANTS** Grasses, including Tufted Hair-grass and Yorkshire-fog. **FIELD NOTES** Aug–May. Hides in a leaf sheath by day, emerging to feed on leaf blades at night. Pupates in a cocoon near the ground.

BEAUTIFUL GOTHIC
Leucochlaena oditis

PLATE 5
73.178 (2226)

RDB; suspected immigrant. **FIELD CHARACTERS** Body pale brown, mottled darker. Dorsal line white, edged with a black mark or black shading anteriorly A1–A8. Subdorsal line comprises yellowish-white dots T1–A1 and a white line beyond, edged with black dashes above. Subspiracular stripe pale or orangey brown. **HABITATS** Grasslands on cliff tops and slopes. **FOODPLANTS** Grasses, including Common Couch and Annual Meadow-grass. Eggs are laid on the seedheads. **FIELD NOTES** Oct–Mar. Feeds at night and slowly throughout winter. Spins a cocoon in the ground in Feb or Mar, and pupates in Jun.

NOTE ON SALLOWS AND CHESTNUTS (GENERA *TILIACEA, XANTHIA, CIRRHIA, AGROCHOLA* AND *CONISTRA*)
Among the sallows and chestnuts, the larvae of several species are similar. Key features that help their separation are set out in the table on pp. 418–20.

ORANGE SALLOW
Tiliacea citrago

PLATE 52
73.179 (2271)

Common. Rare in Ireland. **FIELD CHARACTERS** Body dark grey with large white pinacula. Dorsal and subdorsal lines and subspiracular stripe white or greyish white, with black marks above subdorsal line and around each spiracle A1–A8. **HABITATS** Wherever limes grow, in gardens and urban parks, parkland, planted avenues of trees and woodland. **FOODPLANTS** Lime, Small-leaved Lime and other limes. Also reported on Wych Elm. **FIELD NOTES** Mar–early Jun. Feeds at night, hiding between spun leaves by day, or at the base of the tree when large. Pupates in the ground, generally remaining as a larva for at least six weeks in its cocoon before pupating, but Scottish examples have been noted to pupate soon after becoming fully fed. Overwinters as an egg on a twig.

BARRED SALLOW
Tiliacea aurago

PLATE 52
73.180 (2272)

Common. **FIELD CHARACTERS** Body purplish brown with greyish-white pinacula. Dorsal line greyish white, edged darker, and subdorsal line greyish white and usually indistinct. Subspiracular stripe mixed purplish brown and greyish white. Prothoracic plate brown, with a greyish-white dorsal line and yellowish subdorsal stripe. **SIMILAR SPECIES** See *Separating sallows and chestnuts* table (pp. 418–20). **HABITATS** Hedgerows, scrub and broadleaf woodland. Occasionally in gardens. **FOODPLANTS** Mainly Beech and Field Maple. Also recorded on Hornbeam, Pedunculate Oak and Sycamore. **FIELD NOTES** Apr–early Jun. Feeds mainly at night. At first on buds and flowers, and later on leaves. Pupates in the ground, remaining as a larva for about seven weeks before pupating. Overwinters as an egg on a twig.

PINK-BARRED SALLOW
Xanthia togata

PLATE 52
73.181 (2273)

Common. **FIELD CHARACTERS** Body pale brown, heavily speckled with darker orangey brown. Dorsal line pale brown and indistinct. Subdorsal line white or pale brown, indistinct and often only on anterior segments. No obvious patterning. Prothoracic plate dark brown, with a whitish dorsal line and subdorsal stripe. **SIMILAR SPECIES** See *Separating sallows and chestnuts* table (pp. 418–20). **HABITATS** Mainly fens, wet heathland, marshes, and carr and other wet woodlands; occasionally gardens. **FOODPLANTS** Catkins of poplars and willows, and sometimes seeds of Wych Elm. Later, herbaceous plants including docks. **FIELD NOTES** Late Mar–early Jun. Feeds in catkins and seeds until they drop. Pupates in the ground, remaining as a larva for about six weeks in its cocoon before pupating. Overwinters as an egg, in short rows on a twig.

SALLOW
Cirrhia icteritia

PLATE 52
73.182 (2274)

Common. Has declined significantly in abundance in recent decades. **FIELD CHARACTERS** Body pale brown, heavily speckled with darker orangey brown, noticeably darker along the dorsum, laterally and on A8, and paler between. Dorsal and subdorsal lines pale brown and often indistinct. Prothoracic plate brown, with a pale brown dorsal line and subdorsal stripe. **SIMILAR SPECIES** See *Separating sallows and chestnuts* table (pp. 418–20). **HABITATS** Mainly fens, wet heathland, marshes, and carr and other wet woodlands; occasionally gardens. **FOODPLANTS** Catkins of poplars and willows, and sometimes seeds Wych Elm. Later, herbaceous plants, including dandelions and docks. **FIELD NOTES** Late Mar–early Jun. Feeds in catkins and seeds until they drop. Pupates in the ground, remaining as a larva for several weeks its cocoon before pupating. Overwinters as an egg on a twig, laid in short rows and covered with hairs om the abdomen of the adult.

DUSKY-LEMON SALLOW
Cirrhia gilvago

PLATE 52

73.183 (2275)

Local. Has declined severely in abundance in recent decades, especially in southern England. **FIELD CHARACTERS** Body pale brown, heavily speckled with darker brown or orangey brown. There are forward-curving dark patches on the dorsum, most noticeable on the posterior abdominal segments, especially A8. Dorsal line pale, and subdorsal line hardly noticeable except anteriorly. Prothoracic plate dark brown or black, with a whitish dorsal line and subdorsal stripe. **SIMILAR SPECIES** See *Separating sallows and chestnuts* table (pp. 418–20). **HABITATS** Mature hedgerows, parkland and broadleaf woodland. **FOODPLANTS** Mainly Wych Elm; sometimes English Elm. **FIELD NOTES** Apr–early Jun. At first in the flower bud, then on flowers, seeds and leaves. Pupates in the ground, remaining as a larva for about 10 weeks in its cocoon before pupating. Overwinters as an egg on a twig.

PALE-LEMON SALLOW
Cirrhia ocellaris

PLATE 52

73.184 (2276)

Na; suspected immigrant. Resident in the Thames Valley and parts of the east. **FIELD CHARACTERS** Body pale greyish brown, heavily speckled darker. There is a dark M-shaped dorsal patch on A8. Dorsal line pale brown or pale grey, and subdorsal line pale and hardly noticeable. Prothoracic plate dark brown or black, with a cream dorsal line and subdorsal stripe. **SIMILAR SPECIES** See *Separating sallows and chestnuts* table (pp. 418–20). **HABITATS** Long-established groups of poplars, such as in plantations, riverbanks, roadside verges, shelterbelts and urban parks. **FOODPLANTS** Catkins of poplars, including Black-poplar, Hybrid Black-poplar and Lombardy-poplar. Later on the leaves, and on herbaceous plants, including docks. **FIELD NOTES** Apr–early Jun. Feeds on catkins in the tree and when fallen. Pupates in the ground, remaining as a larva for several weeks in its cocoon before pupating. Overwinters as an egg on a twig.

BEADED CHESTNUT
Agrochola lychnidis

PLATE 52

73.186 (2267)

Common. Has declined severely in abundance in recent decades in England and Wales. Frequent in Ireland in the south and east. **FIELD CHARACTERS** Body green or brown with white pinacula. Dorsal and subdorsal lines pale green or pale brown, edged darker. Subspiracular stripe white above and yellowish or green below, sometimes edged above with black or with black spots. The subspiracular stripe is clearly defined along both edges. **SIMILAR SPECIES** Brown-spot Pinion has a poorly defined edge below the subspiracular stripe, which is clearly defined in Beaded Chestnut. If in doubt, larvae should be reared to confirm identity. **HABITATS** Wide variety, including gardens, grasslands, heathland, hedgerows, scrub and woodland. **FOODPLANTS** Wide variety of herbaceous plants, including buttercups, clovers, dandelions, docks, Groundsel and stitchworts. Also grasses including oat-grasses, and woody species such as Bilberry, Hawthorn and willows. **FIELD NOTES** Late Mar–Jun. Mainly feeds at night. At first on herbaceous plants and grasses, but may ascend to feed on trees when larger. Pupates in the ground, remaining as a larva for several weeks in a brittle cocoon before pupating. Overwinters as an egg.

BROWN-SPOT PINION
Agrochola litura

PLATE 52

73.187 (2264)

Common. Has declined significantly in abundance in recent decades. **FIELD CHARACTERS** Body green or brown with white pinacula. Dorsal and subdorsal lines pale green, white or brown, edged darker green or brown. Subspiracular stripe white, or white above and yellow or pale yellowish brown below. The lower margin of the subspiracular stripe is ill-defined. A green final-instar caterpillar has been observed to change colour gradually as it grew, becoming pinkish brown. **SIMILAR SPECIES** Beaded Chestnut. **HABITATS** Wide variety, including gardens, heathland, hedgerows, scrub and woodland. **FOODPLANTS** Wide variety of herbaceous plants, including Bladder Campion, docks, Meadowsweet, Common Sorrel and stitchworts. Also woody species such as Ash, Bramble, Hawthorn, Honeysuckle, oak roses and willows. **FIELD NOTES** Apr–early Jun. Feeds at night. At first on herbaceous plants, but may ascend to feed on trees when larger. Pupates in the ground, remaining as a larva in its strong cocoon for several weeks before pupating. Overwinters as an egg.

FLOUNCED CHESTNUT
Agrochola helvola

PLATE 52
73.188 (2265)

Common. Has declined severely in abundance in recent decades, especially in lowland England. **FIELD CHARACTERS** Body reddish brown with white pinacula. Dorsal line whitish and subdorsal line whitish, indistinct posteriorly. Subspiracular stripe clear white. **SIMILAR SPECIES** Neglected Rustic has dark pinacula. **HABITATS** Scrubby calcareous grassland, heathland, moorland and broadleaf woodland. **FOODPLANTS** Birches, elms, Hawthorn, Heather, oaks, Burnet Rose and willows. Northern populations also on Bilberry and Heather. **FIELD NOTES** Apr–Jun. Mainly feeds at night. Pupates in the ground, remaining as a larva in its cocoon for many weeks before pupating. Overwinters as an egg.

RED-LINE QUAKER
Agrochola lota

PLATE 52
73.189 (2263)

Common. **FIELD CHARACTERS** Head orangey brown and relatively unmarked. Body pale brown or pale grey, heavily speckled darker, and with distinct white pinacula. Dorsal and subdorsal lines white. Prothoracic plate black or dark brown, with a white dorsal line and subdorsal stripe. **SIMILAR SPECIES** See *Separating sallows and chestnuts table* (pp. 418–20). **HABITATS** Fens, gardens, heathland, hedgerows, marshes, scrub, river valleys and woodland. **FOODPLANTS** Catkins and leaves of willows. **FIELD NOTES** Apr–early Jun. At first in catkins, then in spun shoots. When large, feeds at night, hiding by day between spun leaves. Pupates in the ground, remaining as a larva in its cocoon for several weeks before pupating. Overwinters as an egg on a twig.

YELLOW-LINE QUAKER
Agrochola macilenta

PLATE 52
73.190 (2264)

Common. **FIELD CHARACTERS** Body brown, speckled paler and with white pinacula. Dorsal line white and incorporating white spots A1–A7 or –A8. Subdorsal line pale. **SIMILAR SPECIES** Cousin German has blackish, not white, pinacula. **HABITATS** Wide variety, including gardens, heathland, hedgerows, moorland, scrub and woodland. **FOODPLANTS** Beech, birches, Hawthorn, Heather (in Scotland, and on lowland heaths), oaks, poplars and willows. Later, on herbaceous plants including Common Sorrel. **FIELD NOTES** Apr–Jun. At first in spun shoots of trees or Heather, then on leaves, and later feeds from the ground at night. Pupates in the ground, remaining as a larva for several weeks in its cocoon before pupating. Overwinters as an egg.

SOUTHERN CHESTNUT
Agrochola haematidea

PLATE 52
73.191 (2264a)

RDB. Appears to be spreading. **FIELD CHARACTERS** Body pinkish brown, with a whitish dorsal line and subdorsal stripe, and the subdorsal stripe edged above with black marks containing two white pinacula T3–A9, one posteriorly placed close to the stripe. Lateral line whitish, with the colour above and below the same or different tones of pinkish, brown or grey. Subspiracular stripe whitish, with black marks above. **SIMILAR SPECIES** The usual form of True Lover's Knot has the dorsal stripe either continuous or as dashes, and has black marks edging the stripe. Heath Rustic lacks a lateral line and has black marks above the subdorsal line, usually with one obvious white pinaculum on each segment, which is anteriorly placed close to the subdorsal line. Final-instar Southern Chestnut is found in midsummer, at least a month later than the other two species, and has a lateral line but no black marks edging the dorsal line. **HABITATS** Heathland. **FOODPLANTS** Cross-leaved Heath and Bell Heather. **FIELD NOTES** Late Apr–early Jul. Feeds at night, mainly on the flowers. Pupates in the ground, remaining as a larva in its cocoon for several weeks before pupating. Overwinters as an egg.

BRICK
Agrochola circellaris

PLATE 52
73.192 (2262)

Common; immigrant. **FIELD CHARACTERS** Body pale brown, heavily speckled darker, with white or pale brown pinacula. There are dark patches on the dorsum, which are confluent T1–T3 and shield-shaped A1–A8. Dorsal and subdorsal lines white. Prothoracic plate brown, with a whitish or pale grey dorsal line and subdorsal stripe, and with a pale spot between. **SIMILAR SPECIES** See *Separating sallows and chestnuts* table (pp. 418–20). Suspected has dark brown dorsal patches that are not shield-shaped, and the pale dorsal line is more distinct. **HABITATS** Gardens and urban parks, parkland, scrub and broadleaf woodland. **FOODPLANTS** Ash, Aspen, Wych Elm, poplars and willows. Larvae have also been found on Midland Hawthorn under Aspen, and on Blackthorn. On emerging from fallen catkins, they may also feed on herbaceous plants. **FIELD NOTES** Apr–Jun. At first in flowers, seeds and catkins; later on leaves. Pupates in the ground, remaining as a larva for up to six weeks before pupating. Overwinters as an egg on a twig.

LUNAR UNDERWING
Omphaloscelis lunosa

PLATE 52
73.193 (2270)

Common. Has increased significantly in abundance in recent decades. **FIELD CHARACTERS** Body dark brown dorsally and pale brown laterally, with large black pinacula. Dorsal line pale brown and subdorsal line yellowish brown. Prothoracic plate yellow. **HABITATS** A range of grassy places, including gardens and urban parks, unimproved grassland, damp meadows and pastures, parkland and woodland rides. **FOODPLANTS** Grasses, including Annual Meadow-grass and Yorkshire-fog. **FIELD NOTES** Oct–May. Feeds at night, hiding low down by day. Pupates in the ground.

CHESTNUT
Conistra vaccinii

PLATE 5
73.194 (2258)

Common. **FIELD CHARACTERS** Body pale brown, heavily speckled darker, with pale brown dorsal and subdorsal lines. Some individuals are shaded darker below the subdorsal line. Pinacula may be pale brown and inconspicuous, or white and contrasting. Prothoracic plate various shades of brown, with a pale brown dorsal line and subdorsal stripe. **SIMILAR SPECIES** See *Separating sallows and chestnuts* table (pp. 418–20). **HABITATS** Mainly woodland. Also gardens, hedgerows and scrub. **FOODPLANTS** Downy Birch, Blackthorn, Sweet Chestnut, elms, Hawthorn, European Larch, oaks, Sycamore, roses and willows. Also on herbaceous plants, including dandelions and docks. **FIELD NOTES** Late Apr–Jun. Feeds at night, at first on leaves of trees, and later may descend to feed on the ground. Pupates in the ground, remaining as a larva in the cocoon for several weeks before pupating. Overwinters as an adult, mating in spring.

DARK CHESTNUT
Conistra ligula

PLATE 5
73.195 (225

Common. Expanding in Scotland. **FIELD CHARACTERS** Indistinguishable from Chestnut. **SIMILAR SPECIES** See *Separating sallows and chestnuts* table (pp. 418–20). **HABITATS** Farmland, gardens, hedgerows, scrub and woodland. **FOODPLANTS** Birches, Blackthorn, cherries, Dogwood, elms, Gooseberry, Hawthorn, oaks and willows (especially rough-leaved species). Also on herbaceous plants, including dandelions and docks. **FIELD NOTES** Apr–Jun. Feeds at night, at first on flower buds and catkins, then tree leaves, descending to feed from the ground when larger. Pupates in the ground, remaining as a larva in the cocoon for several weeks before pupating. Overwinters as an adult at first, mating Dec–Jan and egg-laying Jan–Feb.

BLACK-SPOTTED CHESTNUT
Conistra rubiginosa

PLATE 53
73.196 (–)

Immigrant; recent colonist. **FIELD CHARACTERS** Body pale brown, heavily speckled darker, with pale dorsal and subdorsal lines. Pinacula may be pale brown and inconspicuous, or white and contrasting. Prothoracic plate black, with a whitish dorsal line and subdorsal stripe. **SIMILAR SPECIES** See *Separating sallows and chestnuts* table (pp. 418–20). **HABITATS** In Europe, woodland, and open habitats including gardens. **FOODPLANTS** In Europe, wide variety of woody trees and shrubs, completing feeding on herbaceous plants. **FIELD NOTES** Not yet found in England. Spring–early summer. Overwinters as an adult.

DOTTED CHESTNUT
Conistra rubiginea

PLATE 53
73.197 (2260)

Nb. Expanding northwards. **FIELD CHARACTERS** Body purplish grey, sparsely covered with long brown hairs. Dorsal line pale and indistinct, interrupted by or running through black spots A1–A8. Subdorsal line pale and indistinct. **HABITATS** Wooded heathland, mature hedgerows and woodland. **FOODPLANTS** Apple, including old fallen leaves. Reared in captivity on a range of woody and herbaceous plants. **FIELD NOTES** Late Apr–mid-Jun. A larva has been found on Apple, but habits poorly known in the wild. Larvae, pupae and freshly emerged adults have been found in nests of the ant *Lasius fuliginosus*, suggesting an interaction between moth and ant. Pupates in the ground, resting for several weeks in its cocoon before pupating. Overwinters as an adult.

NOTE ON PALE-STRIPED GREEN NOCTUIDS (GENERA *LITHOPHANE, IPIMORPHA, COSMIA, BRACHYLOMIA, ANTITYPE, POLYMIXIS* AND *ORTHOSIA*)

All green noctuid larvae with pale stripes could be said to look similar, but those included in the table on pp. 421–3 are considered to be the most similar in appearance and habits. The key field characters that help separate species (colour of the pinacula, colour of the true legs, and presence or absence of a lateral line) are listed. These should be read in conjunction with the full text in the species descriptions to help identify each species. Care is needed to be certain the larva to be identified is in the final instar; the listed and other species look similar before the final instar, but all change their appearance and are easier to separate in the final instar.

TAWNY PINION
Lithophane semibrunnea

PLATE 53
73.200 (2235)

Local. Extending its range northwards. **FIELD CHARACTERS** Head bluish green. Body pale green with white pinacula. Dorsal stripe white, subdorsal and lateral lines white, consisting of dashes and dots, and subspiracular stripe white. The body becomes reddish brown once feeding has stopped prior to pupation. **SIMILAR SPECIES** See *Separating readily confused pale-striped green noctuids* table (pp. 421–3). **HABITATS** Open countryside where the foodplant occurs, including woodlands. **FOODPLANT** Ash. **FIELD NOTES** May–Jul. Makes a strong cocoon in the ground in which it pupates many weeks later. Overwinters as an adult.

PALE PINION
Lithophane socia

PLATE 53
73.201 (2236)

Local. Expanding its range and becoming commoner. **FIELD CHARACTERS** Head and body bluish green with white pinacula. Dorsal stripe white, subdorsal and lateral lines white, consisting of dashes and dots, and subspiracular stripe white. **SIMILAR SPECIES** See *Separating readily confused pale-striped green noctuids* table (pp. 421–3). **HABITATS** Parkland and woodland; increasingly seen in gardens. **FOODPLANTS** Wide variety of trees and shrubs, including Ash, Apple, birches, Bramble, Horse-chestnut, Lilac, limes, Plum, Wild Privet and willows. Also reported on herbaceous plants, but not known if this is based on observations in the wild. **FIELD NOTES** May–Jul. Makes a strong cocoon in the ground in which it pupates few weeks later. Overwinters as an adult.

GREY SHOULDER-KNOT
Lithophane ornitopus

PLATE 53
73.202 (2237)

Ssp. *lactipennis* Common. Has increased very significantly in range and abundance in recent decades, although it rarely occurs in numbers. **FIELD CHARACTERS** Head bluish green. Body bluish green, speckled white, with white pinacula and noticeable whitish hairs. Dorsal and subdorsal lines white, consisting of dashes. **HABITATS** Parkland and woodland. **FOODPLANTS** Pedunculate Oak, probably Sessile Oak and possibly Turkey Oak. Feeds on other larvae. **FIELD NOTES** May–Jul. Makes a strong cocoon in the ground in which it pupates a few weeks later. Overwinters as an adult.

BLAIR'S SHOULDER-KNOT/STONE PINION
Lithophane leautieri

PLATE 53
73.206 (2240)

Ssp. *hesperica* Common. Has increased very significantly in range and abundance in recent decades. **FIELD CHARACTERS** Body green with pinacula white on green, but yellow on white markings. Dorsal stripe or dashes white, and slightly angled subdorsal dashes white, sometimes mixed yellow. Subspiracular stripe white, with red marks around the spiracles A1–A8. **HABITATS** Gardens and urban parks, and conifer plantations. **FOODPLANTS** Lawson's, Leyland and Monterey cypresses. Also Common Juniper. **FIELD NOTES** Mar–Jul. Feeds on the developing cones and leaves. Pupates in the ground. Overwinters as an egg.

GOLDEN-ROD BRINDLE
Xylena solidaginis

PLATE 53
73.207 (2233)

Local; immigrant. Resident in upland areas. **FIELD CHARACTERS** Head reddish brown with a black face. Body reddish or purplish brown with dark dorsal shading on A1–A2 and A8. A slight hump on A8. Dorsal line greyish white, and sometimes there are similar subdorsal and lateral lines. Subspiracular stripe white. Spiracles orange, shaded black above and to the sides. **HABITATS** Moorland, upland scrub and open woodland. **FOODPLANTS** Bearberry, Bilberry, birches, Cowberry, Heather and willows. **FIELD NOTES** Late Apr–Jul. Pupates in the ground or in moss. Overwinters as an egg.

SWORD-GRASS
Xylena exsoleta

PLATE 53
73.208 (2242)

Nb. Contracted as a resident to Scotland and Isle of Man. **FIELD CHARACTERS** Body pale green. Subdorsal line yellow, edged above with black marks T1–A9. Black marks contain one white pinaculum on T2–T3 and A9, and two on A1–A8. Subspiracular stripe white, edged above with orange marks T1–A9 and with white pinacula circled black. Spiracles white. **SIMILAR SPECIES** Red Sword-grass is more variable, but has orange spiracles and may have an obvious dorsal stripe. **HABITATS** Moorland, rough pasture and open woodland. **FOODPLANTS** Various herbaceous plants, including Creeping Cinquefoil, docks, Common Restharrow, stonecrops and thistles. Has also been recorded on Sugar Beet, Bog-myrtle, chrysanthemums, Black Currant, Yellow Iris and Mangel-wurzel. **FIELD NOTES** May–Jul. Feeds in sunshine and at night. Pupates in a cocoon on the ground. Overwinters as an adult.

RED SWORD-GRASS
Xylena vetusta

PLATE 53
73.209 (2241)

Local; suspected immigrant. Resident from Hampshire westwards, and in Wales, northern England and Scotland. **FIELD CHARACTERS** Body varies from shades of green to brown or black, with white pinacula across the dorsum. Dorsal stripe pale yellow but not always present, and subdorsal and subspiracular stripes white or yellow, the subspiracular stripe edged black above. Spiracles orange. **SIMILAR SPECIES** Sword-grass. **HABITATS** Boggy heathland, marshes, moorland, rough upland pastures and damp woodland. **FOODPLANTS** Various herbaceous and woody plants, including Bog-myrtle, docks, Heather, Hop, Yellow Iris, Meadowsweet, Purple Moor-grass, Devil's-bit Scabious, sedges, Marsh Thistle and low-growing willows.

Also feeds in the flower heads of Compact and Sharp-flowered rushes, and Soft-rush. **FIELD NOTES** May–Jul. Feeds fully exposed by day and night. Pupates in the ground. Overwinters as an adult.

SATELLITE
Eupsilia transversa

PLATE 54
73.210 (2256)

Common. Has increased significantly in abundance in recent decades. **FIELD CHARACTERS** Body brown to bluish black. Dorsal and subdorsal lines pale and usually indistinct, except on T1 and A10 where they are yellow or orange. Subspiracular line, if well defined, comprises variably shaped white blotches on T1–T2, A1–A2 and A8, and white dashes A3–A7. **HABITATS** Gardens and urban parks, moorland (in the north), parkland, scrub and broadleaf woodland. **FOODPLANTS** Omnivorous. Plants include Apple, Aspen, Beech, birches, Blackthorn, Sweet Chestnut, elms, Hawthorn, Hazel, limes, Field Maple, poplars, oaks and willows (including catkins). When larger also feeds on other larvae and aphids. **FIELD NOTES** Apr–Jul. Feeds at night, hiding by day between spun leaves. Makes a strong cocoon in the ground, remaining as a larva for 10–12 weeks before pupating. Overwinters as an adult.

ANGLE-STRIPED SALLOW
Enargia paleacea

PLATE 54
73.211 (2313)

Nb; suspected immigrant. Resident from central to north-east England, and in Scotland. **FIELD CHARACTERS** Head pale yellowish brown. Body whitish green to pale bluish green, with white pinacula. Dorsal, subdorsal, spiracular and subspiracular lines white. **HABITATS** Heathland and woodland; associated with large sites and long continuity of mature birch trees. **FOODPLANTS** Aspen, and Downy and Silver birches. **FIELD NOTES** Late Apr–mid-Jun. Feeds at night on young leaves, resting between spun leaves by day. Pupates in ground. Overwinters as an egg.

DOUBLE KIDNEY
Ipimorpha retusa

PLATE 54
73.212 (2311)

Local. **FIELD CHARACTERS** Head blackish or green. Body green, with a white dorsal stripe and subdorsal and subspiracular lines. **SIMILAR SPECIES** See *Separating readily confused pale-striped green noctuids* table (pp. 421–3). **HABITATS** Fens, marshes, riverbanks, scrub on heathland, and damp woodland. **FOODPLANTS** Goat, Grey, Purple and other willows. Has also been recorded on Black-poplar. **FIELD NOTES** Early Apr–late May. Lives within spun leaves. Pupates in a cocoon in the ground. Overwinters as an egg.

OLIVE
Ipimorpha subtusa

PLATE 54
73.213 (2312)

Local. Has increased significantly in abundance in recent decades. **FIELD CHARACTERS** Head black and green, with whitish markings on face. Body green, with a pale yellow, sometimes white, dorsal stripe and subdorsal and subspiracular lines. **SIMILAR SPECIES** See *Separating readily confused pale-striped green noctuids* table (pp. 421–3). **HABITATS** Gardens and urban parks, gravel pits, lakesides and broadleaf woodland. **FOODPLANTS** Poplars, including Aspen, Eastern Balsam-poplar, Lombardy-poplar and White Poplar. **FIELD NOTES** Apr–May. Lives within spun leaves, usually high in a tree. Pupates in a cocoon in the ground. Overwinters as an egg.

WHITE-SPOTTED PINION
Cosmia diffinis

PLATE 54
73.214 (2317)

pRDB. Resident in several sites in central England. **FIELD CHARACTERS** Head brown or black. Body green, with small black pinacula on white bases. Dorsal, subdorsal and subspiracular stripes white. Spiracles surrounded by thin greenish-white rings. True legs black. **SIMILAR SPECIES** See *Separating readily confused pale-striped green noctuids* table (pp. 421–3). **HABITATS** Copses, plantations, shelterbelts and woodland. **FOODPLANTS** English Elm and Small-leaved Elm, preferring sucker growth from tree trunks. Has been recorded on

Wych Elm, though not recently. **FIELD NOTES** Apr–mid-Jun. Feeds mainly at night, hiding by day in spun leaves when younger. Pupates in a cocoon in spun leaves or the bark. Overwinters as an egg.

LESSER-SPOTTED PINION
Cosmia affinis

PLATE 54
73.215 (2316)

Local. Scattered distribution following demise of elms from Dutch elm disease. **FIELD CHARACTERS** Head green. Body green, with small white or black pinacula. Dorsal, subdorsal and subspiracular stripes white. Spiracles encircled white and extended above to join a white pinaculum, and patchily edged black. True legs black. **SIMILAR SPECIES** See *Separating readily confused pale-striped green noctuids* table (pp. 421–3). **HABITATS** Hedgerows, shelterbelts and woodlands. **FOODPLANTS** Elms, including English Elm, Small-leaved Elm and Wych Elm. **FIELD NOTES** Late Apr–mid-Jun. Feeds at night. Pupates in a cocoon among leaves on the ground. Overwinters as an egg.

DUN-BAR
Cosmia trapezina

PLATE 54
73.216 (2318)

Common. **FIELD CHARACTERS** Head green. Body green, with large black pinacula on white bases. Dorsal stripe white, subdorsal line white, and subspiracular stripe greenish white or yellowish. Spiracles surrounded by obvious white rings. True legs green. **SIMILAR SPECIES** See *Separating readily confused pale-striped green noctuids* table (pp. 421–3). **HABITATS** Mainly woodland; also a wide variety of other habitats supporting scrub and trees. **FOODPLANTS** Omnivorous. Wide variety of trees and shrubs, especially Apple (blossoms and leaves), Aspen, birches, Blackthorn, Sweet Chestnut, elms, hawthorns, Hazel, larches, Field Maple, Pedunculate Oak and willows. Large larvae also feed on other larvae. **FIELD NOTES** Apr–late Jun. Pupates in a cocoon on or in the ground. Overwinters as an egg.

LUNAR-SPOTTED PINION
Cosmia pyralina

PLATE 54
73.217 (2319)

Local. **FIELD CHARACTERS** Head green. Body bright green with yellow pinacula. Dorsal, subdorsal and subspiracular lines yellow, the subspiracular line edged above with a black line T1–T2. True legs green. **SIMILAR SPECIES** See *Separating readily confused pale-striped green noctuids* table (pp. 421–3). **HABITATS** Hedgerows, parkland, scrub and woodland; less often gardens. **FOODPLANTS** Recorded on Apple, Blackthorn, Bullace, elms, hawthorns, limes, oaks and Pear. **FIELD NOTES** Apr–mid-Jun. Pupates in a cocoon in leaf litter. Overwinters as an egg.

HEART MOTH
Dicycla oo

PLATE 54
73.218 (2315)

RDB. Can occur in abundance for a short while, followed by periods of scarcity. **FIELD CHARACTERS** Head black, prothoracic plate black with a white dorsal stripe, and anal flap orangey brown. Body black or very dark brown with white pinacula. Dorsal stripe comprises large, irregular-shaped white marks. Subdorsal line white. Subspiracular stripe white or yellow. Larva becomes brownish green just before pupation. **HABITATS** Parkland, lightly wooded commons and woodland with open-grown Pedunculate Oak and understorey scrub. Also occurs in farmland with mature oaks. **FOODPLANTS** Mature and veteran Pedunculate Oak trees. **FIELD NOTES** Mid-Apr–early Jun. Lives high in the tree, feeding at night on young leaves, and hiding by day in a tight spinning of leaves. Pupates in a fragile cocoon in the ground. Overwinters as an egg.

CENTRE-BARRED SALLOW
Atethmia centrago

PLATE 54
73.219 (2269)

Common. Has decreased significantly in abundance in recent decades. **FIELD CHARACTERS** Body pale grey or brownish grey, speckled with black, and often darker between segments. Dorsal line greyish white, widening on each abdominal segment to form a spot that is edged black below. Subdorsal line greyish white, sometimes ill-defined, and subspiracular stripe pale grey, edged black above. **HABITATS** Gardens, hedgerows, riverbanks and woodland. **FOODPLANT** Ash. **FIELD NOTES** Early spring–early Jun. Eggs hatch in winter and the young larva bores into a bud, remaining concealed until bud-burst, when it feeds on the flowers. Larger larvae hide by day in bark crevices or at the base of the tree, ascending to feed at night. Pupates in a cocoon in the ground.

MINOR SHOULDER-KNOT
Brachylomia viminalis

PLATE 54
73.220 (2225)

Common. Has declined significantly in abundance in recent decades. Very local in Ireland. **FIELD CHARACTERS** Head pale greenish grey with black mouthparts. Body dull green, occasionally brown, with obvious white pinacula above the subdorsal line. Dorsal stripe, subdorsal line and subspiracular stripe white. **SIMILAR SPECIES** See *Separating readily confused pale-striped green noctuids* table (pp. 421–3). **HABITATS** Fens, scrub on heathland, lake and pond margins, marshes, river valleys and damp woodland. **FOODPLANTS** Mainly Grey Willow, but also on Eared, Goat, Purple, Tea-leaved and White willows. Also recorded on Aspen. **FIELD NOTES** Apr–Jun. At first in a spun shoot, later feeding at night on leaves, hiding by day among spun leaves. Pupates in or on the ground. Overwinters as an egg.

SUSPECTED
Parastichtis suspecta

PLATE 54
73.221 (2268)

Local; immigrant. **FIELD CHARACTERS** Body brown. Dorsal line well defined, and white or pale brown. There are block-shaped, dark brown patches between this and the subdorsal line, which is white or pale brown, and sometimes ill-defined. Subspiracular stripe white mixed with brown, edged darker above. **SIMILAR SPECIES** Brick. **HABITATS** Fens, heathland and moorland with birch scrub, and carr and other woodlands. **FOODPLANTS** Birches and willows. **FIELD NOTES** Apr–early Jun. At first in a spun shoot, later feeding at night on leaves, hiding by day within a leaf fold or spun leaves. Pupates on or in the ground. Overwinters as an egg.

DINGY SHEARS
Apterogenum ypsillon

PLATE 54
73.222 (2314)

Local. **FIELD CHARACTERS** Body brown with dark speckles, which are denser below the subdorsal line. Dorsal line white, and slightly expanded posteriorly on each segment. Subdorsal line comprises white dashes or may be continuous, with dark shaded dashes above. Subspiracular stripe wavy, orangey brown with pale and dark speckling, and edged with a white line above and below. **HABITATS** Fens, marshes, riverbanks and damp woodland. **FOODPLANTS** Poplars and willows. **FIELD NOTES** Apr–early Jun. At first within a catkin, later feeding at night on leaves, resting by day under loose bark and ascending after dark. Pupates in a cocoon under bark or on the ground. Overwinters as an egg.

OAK RUSTIC
Dryobota labecula

PLATE 54
73.223 (2246a)

Resident; recent colonist; suspected immigrant. **FIELD CHARACTERS** Body orangey brown, sometimes greyer between segments, and speckled whitish. Dorsal and subdorsal lines whitish. Spiracular band yellow mixed with whitish, sometimes greenish, the band broadly and deeply indented above and with spiracles at the bottom of indentations, except on A8 where it is within the band. Pinacula brown or black on white bases, or sometimes white on black bases. **HABITATS** Gardens, hedgerows, urban areas and woodland.

FOODPLANT Holm Oak. **FIELD NOTES** Apr–Sep in mainland Europe, growing slowly. Hides between spun leaves. Pupates in the ground. Overwinters as an egg.

MERVEILLE DU JOUR
Griposia aprilina

PLATE 54
73.224 (2247)

Common. **FIELD CHARACTERS** Body brown, sometimes tinged greenish, speckled paler, and greyish between segments. Dorsal line white, often incomplete, and edged with a fine black line. Paler, somewhat circular shading on each segment dorsally, with dark brown shading beyond containing a whitish pinaculum. Subdorsal line thin, with cream pinacula above. Body paler laterally. Subspiracular stripe indistinct, and edged with a black line above. Spiracles black. **SIMILAR SPECIES** Sombre Brocade has white spiracles, is not paler below the subdorsal line and has prominent white pinacula near the spiracular line. Twin-spotted Quaker has black spiracles, is not paler below the subdorsal line, has a white spot in the subspiracular line on A1 and sometimes A2–A4, and has A8 slightly domed. **HABITATS** Hedgerows, parkland and broadleaf woodland. **FOODPLANTS** Pedunculate Oak, probably Sessile Oak, and possibly Turkey Oak. **FIELD NOTES** Mar–Jun. At first feeds within an expanding bud; later at night on flowers and leaves, hiding by day in a bark crevice. Pupates in a strong cocoon in the ground close to the tree base. Overwinters as an egg.

BRINDLED GREEN
Dryobotodes eremita

PLATE 55
73.225 (2248)

Common. Has increased significantly in abundance in recent decades in the south. Local in northern areas and Ireland. **FIELD CHARACTERS** Body pale green, speckled yellow. Dorsal stripe and subdorsal and supraspiracular lines yellow, the subdorsal line often indistinct. **SIMILAR SPECIES** Common Quaker has a conspicuous transverse yellow stripe on the posterior margin of A8. **HABITATS** Parkland, woodland and occasionally suburban gardens. **FOODPLANTS** Holm, Pedunculate and Sessile oaks. Recorded on Hazel under oak, and on hawthorns. **FIELD NOTES** Late Feb–Jun. At first feeds in an expanding bud; later at night on leaves, hiding by day within spun terminal leaves. Pupates in a cocoon in the ground. Overwinters as an egg, hatching from late Feb.

SOMBRE BROCADE
Dryobotodes tenebrosa

PLATE 55
73.227 (2248b)

Immigrant; recent colonist. **FIELD CHARACTERS** Body pale brown or pale grey, mottled darker. Dorsal line whitish, and sometimes incomplete. There are pale diamond-shaped patches dorsally A1–A8, usually outwardly shaded blackish brown. Subdorsal line white and indistinct, sometimes replaced with blackish shading. Subspiracular stripe pale brown, edged above with a white line and black dashes. Pinacula white, and prominent near the spiracular line. Spiracles white. **SIMILAR SPECIES** Merveille du Jour and Twin-spotted Quaker. **HABITATS** Gardens and woodland. **FOODPLANT** Holm Oak. **FIELD NOTES** Spring–summer in mainland Europe. Pupates in a cocoon in the ground. Overwinters as an egg.

GREY CHI
Antitype chi

PLATE 55
73.228 (2254)

Common. Has declined significantly in abundance in recent decades in the south, where it is now confined to higher ground. **FIELD CHARACTERS** Body green with white pinacula. Dorsal line pale green, edged darker green, subdorsal line white and subspiracular stripe white, edged above with a black line. **SIMILAR SPECIES** See *Separating readily confused pale-striped green noctuids* table (pp. 421–3). **HABITATS** Mainly upland grassland and moorland; also other grassy places including gardens and parkland. **FOODPLANTS** Wide variety of plants, including dandelions, docks, Foxglove, Groundsel, Hawthorn, Yellow Iris, Laburnum, mints, Common Nettle, Ribwort Plantain, Smooth Sowthistle, thistles, Thrift and Goat Willow. **FIELD NOTES** Apr–Jun. Feeds by day and night. Pupates in a strong cocoon in the ground. Overwinters as an egg.

FLAME BROCADE
Trigonophora flammea

PLATE 55
73.229 (2251)

Immigrant; former transitory resident; recent colonist. **FIELD CHARACTERS** There are brown, greyish-brown and greenish forms. The brown form has a pinkish brown body, mottled darker, especially laterally, with white pinacula and an interrupted whitish or pale dorsal line. Darker mottling in diamond shapes across dorsal region usually discernible A2–A7, with yellowish or pale triangles above a pale, often indistinct subdorsal line. Spiracular line, if present, pale. Spiracles creamy with a whitish pinaculum behind and one above, most obvious A3–A6. The greyish-brown and green forms are mottled darker and lack the yellowish or pale triangles above the subdorsal line. **HABITATS** Open coastal areas including rough calcareous grassland, and gardens. **FOODPLANTS** Mainly Ribwort Plantain; also Broad-leaved and Curled docks, and probably a variety of other herbaceous plants. **FIELD NOTES** Nov–May. Pupates in the ground. Feeds overwinter in mild conditions.

FEATHERED BRINDLE
Aporophyla australis

PLATE 55
73.230 (2230)

Ssp. *pascuea* Nb. Mainly coastal and can be abundant. **FIELD CHARACTERS** Body pale brownish or pale yellowish dorsally, greenish mixed brownish laterally, and green below, sometimes tinged pinkish. Dorsal line white, with distinct brownish or indistinct green diamond-shaped marks across dorsal region T2–A8, these marks heavily shaded dark brown anteriorly. Subdorsal line whitish, indistinct, and edged above with dark brown dashes T2–A8. Spiracles white, part-surrounded by dark brown shading on T1 and A1–A5 or beyond. **HABITATS** Soft cliffs, rough coastal grassland, sand dunes and vegetated shingle. Also south-facing calcareous grassland. **FOODPLANTS** Various herbaceous plants, including Sea Campion, Common Chickweed, Chicory, Wood Sage, Common Sorrel, and probably grasses. Also Bramble. **FIELD NOTES** Oct–mid-May. Feeds at night, growing slowly during winter. Pupates in the ground, just below the surface.

DEEP-BROWN DART
Aporophyla lutulenta

PLATE 55
73.231 (2231)

Common. Deep-brown Dart/Northern Deep-brown Dart complex has declined significantly in abundance in recent decades. Seems to prefer lowlands. Currently these two taxa are treated as separate species, but historically northern populations were considered to be a subspecies. **FIELD CHARACTERS** See Black Rustic. **SIMILAR SPECIES** Northern Deep-brown Dart, Black Rustic and Neglected Rustic. **HABITATS** Open habitats, mainly on calcareous and sandy soils, or less often clays, including unimproved grassland, heathland, sand dunes and wide woodland rides; occasionally gardens. **FOODPLANTS** Wide variety of herbaceous and woody plants. Recorded on Blackthorn, Meadow Buttercup (flowers), Broom, cinquefoils, Broad-leaved Dock, Field Gromwell, Groundsel, Tufted Hair-grass, Heather, Annual Meadow-grass, Corn Mint, Sainfoin, sorrels and Yarrow. **FIELD NOTES** Oct–mid-May. Feeds at night, growing slowly during winter. Pupates in the ground, just below the surface.

NORTHERN DEEP-BROWN DART
Aporophyla lueneburgensis

PLATE 55
73.232 (2231a)

Common. Deep-brown Dart/Northern Deep-brown Dart complex has declined significantly in abundance in recent decades. Currently these two taxa are treated as separate species, but historically northern populations were considered to be a subspecies. Southern limit of distribution unclear owing to confusion with Deep-brown Dart. **FIELD CHARACTERS** See Black Rustic. **SIMILAR SPECIES** Deep-brown Dart, Black Rustic and Neglected Rustic. **HABITATS** Open habitats on the coast and inland at low altitude, including rough grassland and moorland. **FOODPLANTS** Herbaceous and woody plants, and grasses. Recorded on Bilberry, Common Bird's-foot-trefoil, clovers and Heather. **FIELD NOTES** Autumn–late May. Feeds at night, hiding by day. Pupates in the ground.

BLACK RUSTIC
Aporophyla nigra

PLATE 55
73.233 (2232)

Common. Has declined significantly in overall abundance in recent decades but is increasing in the east. **FIELD CHARACTERS** Body usually green, sometimes brown or pink, with patterning variable from none to striped, and with white pinacula. Dorsal line and subdorsal lines pale and often indistinct, more or less edged with brown or reddish shading in stripes, dashes or squarish marks. Subspiracular stripe white above and green or yellow below. Spiracles white, usually part-surrounded by black shading on a variable number of segments. Prolegs of all forms are pinkish above crochets. **SIMILAR SPECIES** Deep-brown Dart, Northern Deep-brown Dart and Black Rustic are variable, with no reliable characters to distinguish them in the field, except that the brown form does not seem to occur in Deep-brown Dart and Northern Deep-brown Dart. Neglected Rustic has dark pinacula, lacks a subdorsal line of dots, and has no pinkish on the prolegs. Green form of Setaceous Hebrew Character has dark pinacula, a subdorsal line of dots, and no pinkish on the prolegs. **HABITATS** Open grassy habitats on acidic, calcareous and neutral soils, including heathland and moorland. **FOODPLANTS** Wide variety of herbaceous and woody plants, including Hedge Bedstraw, Bristle Bent, clovers, dandelions, docks, Tufted Hair-grass, Heather, plantains, Common Rock-rose, stitchworts, Sweet Vernal-grass and Creeping Willow. **FIELD NOTES** Oct–May, but sometimes eggs do not hatch until Feb. Feeds at night, hiding by day. Pupates in the ground.

BRINDLED OCHRE
Dasypolia templi

PLATE 55
73.234 (2229)

Local. Has declined severely in abundance in recent decades. **FIELD CHARACTERS** Head and prothoracic plate pale orangey brown. Dorsal and lateral sclerotised plates on A9. Anal plate pale brown with four tiny projections posteriorly. Body pale pinkish brown with many black spots. **HABITATS** In the south, in rough cliff-top and coastal grasslands and sand dunes. In the north, additionally in upland grassland, marshes and moorland. **FOODPLANTS** Wild Angelica and Hogweed. **FIELD NOTES** Apr–early Aug. At first within the stems, later feeding in the roots. Pupates in the ground, just below the surface. Overwinters as an adult female, having mated in the autumn.

FEATHERED RANUNCULUS
Polymixis lichenea

PLATE 55
73.235 (2255)

Ssp. *lichenea* Local. Spreading inland in southern England. Ssp. *scillonea* Scilly. **FIELD CHARACTERS** Body brown, grey or green, heavily speckled with black, and with white pinacula. Black speckling may be diffuse, or show as forward-pointing V-shapes dorsally, and as subdorsal dashes. Dorsal line pale grey or pale green, and subdorsal line pale brown, grey or green and often indistinct. Subspiracular stripe pale brown, pale grey or pale green. **SIMILAR SPECIES** Bordered Gothic has dark brown pinacula, lacks a subspiracular stripe and feeds late Jun–early Sep. **HABITATS** Hard and soft cliffs, calcareous and coastal grasslands, sand dunes and vegetated shingle. Also in gardens. **FOODPLANTS** Wide variety of herbaceous plants, including Wild Cabbage, Hoary Cress, dandelions, docks, Foxglove, Hound's-tongue, plantains, ragworts, Biting Stonecrop, Thrift, trefoils and Red Valerian. Also on Bramble. **FIELD NOTES** Oct–May. Feeds at night, slowly through the winter. Prefers sheltered situations. Pupates in a strong cocoon in the ground.

BLACK-BANDED
Polymixis xanthomista

PLATE 55
73.236 (2253)

Ssp. *statices* Na. **FIELD CHARACTERS** Body greenish brown, speckled darker, with pinkish-brown bands between segments. Pinacula whitish, part-shaded dark brown on dorsum. Dorsal line pale, edged with darker shading, and subdorsal line pale and indistinct. Subspiracular stripe or spiracular line white. **HABITATS** Rocky coastlines, preferring areas very close to the sea; less often inland among scrub. **FOODPLANTS** Mainly Thrift. Also reported on Sea and White campions, dandelions, Harebell, Sea Plantain, Kidney Vetch and Sweet Violet. **FIELD NOTES** Mar–early Jul. Feeds at night. Pupates in a cocoon in a crevice or under the foodplant. Overwinters as an egg, and possibly also as a small larva.

LARGE RANUNCULUS
Polymixis flavicincta

PLATE 55
73.237 (2252)

Local. **FIELD CHARACTERS** Body green, speckled with tiny pale dots. Dorsal and subdorsal lines indistinct, comprising a line of pale dots. Subspiracular stripe white, edged above with a black line or black marks that may be confined to a few anterior segments. Spiracles orange or white. **SIMILAR SPECIES** See *Separating readily confused pale-striped green noctuids* table (pp. 421–3). **HABITATS** Mainly on calcareous and neutral soils. Frequently found in gardens and weedy urban areas. Also rough coastal grassland, damp meadows and river valleys. **FOODPLANTS** Wide variety of herbaceous and woody plants, including cherries, Yellow Corydalis, currants, docks, foxglove, Groundsel, Honeysuckle, Common Ivy, Londonpride, Michaelmas-daisies, mints, Mugwort, Sweet Pea, plantains, roses (flowers), spruces (seedlings), Red Valerian and Rosebay Willowherb. **FIELD NOTES** Apr–Jul. Feeds at night, hiding by day. Pupates in a strong cocoon in the ground. Overwinters as an egg.

DARK BROCADE
Mniotype adusta

PLATE 55
73.238 (2250)

Common. Has decreased significantly in abundance in recent decades. **FIELD CHARACTERS** Body green, pink or brownish, speckled whitish and with white pinacula. Dorsal and subdorsal lines are pale, and the spiracular line white. The green form sometimes has variable brownish speckling and shading to dorsal and subdorsal lines, and to the spiracular line above. The pink form is green below and pink across the dorsal region, variably extending laterally, sometimes to the spiracular line. The brown form may be speckled greenish and is brown below the spiracular line. **HABITATS** In the south, fens, chalk and cliff grasslands, heathland, and occasionally in gardens. Further north, upland grassland, moorland and sand dunes. **FOODPLANTS** Herbaceous and woody plants, including Alder, birches, Bog-myrtle, Bladder Campion, grasses, Heather, Lodgepole Pine, Sitka Spruce and Great Willowherb. **FIELD NOTES** Jun–Sep. Feeds at night. Overwinters fully fed in its cocoon underground, pupating in the spring.

HADENINAE

PINE BEAUTY
Panolis flammea

PLATE 56
73.241 (2179)

Common. Has increased significantly in abundance in recent decades. **FIELD CHARACTERS** Body dark green, rarely dark brown, and sometimes paler below subdorsal stripe. Dorsal and subdorsal stripes and lateral line white, and the subspiracular stripe white mixed with red or yellow to a variable extent, especially below. **HABITATS** Pine forests and plantations, and scrub on heathland and moorland. Also gardens and urban parks. **FOODPLANTS** Mainly on Scots Pine, and as a pest of Lodgepole Pine in Scotland. Recorded also on Corsican and Maritime pines, and larches and Dwarf Mountain-pine. **FIELD NOTES** May–Jul. Feeds on the needles, especially new shoots. Pupates on the ground or in a bark crevice. Overwinters as a pupa.

CLOUDED DRAB
Orthosia incerta

PLATE 56
73.242 (2188)

Common. **FIELD CHARACTERS** Body pale green and speckled yellow, or bluish green and speckled white. Dorsal stripe broad and yellowish white or white. Subdorsal line yellow or white. Spiracular stripe yellow below and white above, sometimes edged with a black line above. **SIMILAR SPECIES** See *Separating readily confused pale-striped green noctuids* table (pp. 421–3). **HABITATS** Commonest in woodland; occurs in most habitats. **FOODPLANTS** Wide variety of broadleaf trees, including birches, Sweet Chestnut, elms, Hawthorn, Hazel, limes, oaks, Sycamore and willows. Also reported on docks and Sitka Spruce. **FIELD NOTES** Apr–Jun. At first in expanding buds, then in spun shoots, and then openly among leaves, feeding at night. Pupates in a cocoon in the ground. Overwinters as a pupa.

BLOSSOM UNDERWING
Orthosia miniosa

PLATE 56
73.243 (2183)

Local; immigrant. **FIELD CHARACTERS** Body mixed black and blue, and occasionally tinged orangey. Dorsal stripe, subdorsal line and subspiracular stripe yellow, or occasionally orange, the subspiracular stripe containing black spots, with white marks above on A1–A8. Dorsal and subdorsal pinacula black, noticeable and large. **HABITATS** Mainly oak woodland; also hedgerows with mature oaks. Commonest in coppice regrowth, and in sunny situations in damp woodland. **FOODPLANTS** Mainly oaks. When part-grown, may feed on wasp galls on oak, and disperse to feed on birches, Blackthorn, Bramble, Hawthorn, Hazel, and herbaceous plants including Meadowsweet. **FIELD NOTES** Late Apr–mid-Jun. Gregarious in a web when small, resulting in obvious defoliation, and dispersing when larger. Pupates in a cocoon in the ground. Overwinters as a pupa.

Blossom Underwing larva

COMMON QUAKER
Orthosia cerasi

PLATE 56
73.244 (2187)

Common. **FIELD CHARACTERS** Body pale green with pale yellow or white dots and dashes. Dorsal line pale yellow or white, and subdorsal line obscure, comprising aligned dots and dashes. Supraspiracular line pale yellow or white, dipping below spiracles on T1 and A8. A conspicuous yellow transverse stripe on the posterior margin of A8. **SIMILAR SPECIES** Brindled Green. **HABITATS** Commonest in woodland; occurs in most lowland habitats. **FOODPLANTS** Wide variety of trees and shrubs, including Alder, Aspen, Beech, birches, black-poplars, Blackthorn, Sweet Chestnut, elms, Guelder-rose, Hawthorn, Hazel, oaks and willows. Has been recorded on Snow Gum. **FIELD NOTES** Apr–Jun. At first in expanding buds, then in spun shoots and leaves, and later openly among leaves, feeding at night. Pupates in a cocoon in the ground. Overwinters as a pupa.

SMALL QUAKER
Orthosia cruda

PLATE 56
73.245 (2182

Common. **FIELD CHARACTERS** Body pinkish brown or greyish green, with conspicuous black pinacula. Dorsal and subdorsal lines white or yellow, and subspiracular stripe white, mixed with green, yellow or red. A conspicuous transverse white stripe on the posterior margin of A8. **HABITATS** Most abundan in broadleaf woodland. Also wet heathland and hedgerows, and sometimes gardens. **FOODPLANTS** Mainly oaks. Also recorded on Crab Apple, Aspen, Downy Birch, Blackthorn, Sweet Chestnut, Hazel, Field Maple, roses and willows. **FIELD NOTES** Apr–early Jun. Feeds at night, hiding by day in spun leaves. Pupates in a cocoon in the ground. Overwinters as a pupa.

LEAD-COLOURED DRAB
Orthosia populeti

PLATE 5
73.246 (2185

Local. **FIELD CHARACTERS** Head pale brownish grey with black markings. Body shiny and bluish green. Dorsal line white, and thin subdorsal, supraspiracular and subspiracular lines white. **HABITATS** Mainly broadleaf woodland. Sometime isolated copses and plantations in open countryside, and gardens and urban parks. **FOODPLANTS** Mainly Aspen; occasionally other poplars including Black-poplar. **FIELD NOTES** Late Apr–early Jun. Feeds at night, hiding by day between two leaves spun together. The shape of the larva is visible as a dark object between these leaves when viewed against a bright sky. Pupates in a cocoon in the ground. Overwinters as a pupa.

POWDERED QUAKER
Orthosia gracilis

PLATE 56
73.247 (2186)

Common. Has decreased significantly in abundance in recent decades. **FIELD CHARACTERS** Body usually greyish green or brown, or sometimes pale green. Dorsal line whitish or pale, and subdorsal line comprising white dots. Subspiracular band yellowish green in greyish-green form and pale brown in brown form, with dense black shading above. This shading is absent in the pale green form. **SIMILAR SPECIES** Northern Drab shows no consistent differences, although there is no plain, pale green form. See *Separating readily confused pale-striped green noctuids* table (pp. 421–3) for species similar to pale green form. **HABITATS** Mainly bogs and marshes; also damp woodland, and sometimes gardens and other open habitats. **FOODPLANTS** Wide variety of herbaceous and woody plants, including Bilberry, Common and Greater bird's-foot-trefoils, Black-poplar, Blackthorn, Bog-myrtle, Bramble, Common Fleabane, Dyer's Greenweed, Meadowsweet, Pedunculate and Sessile oaks, Purple-loosestrife, St John's-worts, Creeping and Spear thistles, and willows. **FIELD NOTES** May–Jul. At first in spun shoots, then feeds at night, hiding low down by day. Pupates in a cocoon in the ground. Overwinters as a pupa.

NORTHERN DRAB
Orthosia opima

PLATE 56
73.248 (2184)

Local. Appears to be in decline in central and southern England. **FIELD CHARACTERS** Variable in appearance, with no obvious, consistent differences to separate from patterned forms of Powdered Quaker. **SIMILAR SPECIES** Powdered Quaker. **HABITATS** Diverse open habitats, including calcareous grassland, heathland, freshwater marshes, saltmarshes, sand dunes, river valleys and rough waste ground. **FOODPLANTS** Wide variety of herbaceous and woody plants, including birches, Dyer's Greenweed, Hound's-tongue, Marram, Mugwort, ragworts, Burnet Rose, Common Sea-lavender and willows. **FIELD NOTES** May–Jul. Feeds at night. Pupates in a cocoon in the ground. Overwinters as a pupa.

HEBREW CHARACTER
Orthosia gothica

PLATE 56
73.249 (2190)

Common. **FIELD CHARACTERS** Body pale green, speckled with yellow or white. Dorsal and subdorsal lines white or yellow. The spiracular band is broad, all white, white tinged with yellow near the spiracles, or mainly pale green with white above. The band may be edged above with a black line or shading. **SIMILAR SPECIES** See *Separating readily confused pale-striped green noctuids* table (pp. 421–3). **HABITATS** Wide variety. **FOODPLANTS** Wide variety of woody and herbaceous plants, including Alder, Bilberry, birches, Broom, Buckthorn, clovers, dandelions, docks, hawthorns, Heather, Honeysuckle, larches, Lilac, ~mes, Meadowsweet, Common Nettle, oaks, Germander Speedwell, Sitka Spruce and willows. **FIELD NOTES** Apr–Jul. Feeds mainly at night, at first on expanding buds, then on leaves. Pupates in a cocoon in the ground. Overwinters as a pupa.

TWIN-SPOTTED QUAKER
Anorthoa munda

PLATE 56
73.250 (2189)

Common. **FIELD CHARACTERS** Body pale brown or grey dorsally, and black, dark grey or dark brown laterally. Dorsal line pale and subdorsal line white, if present. In darker examples, there may be backward-pointing, V-shaped, dark brown shading dorsally on abdominal segments. Subspiracular stripe pale brown or grey, containing a white spot above on A1 and sometimes smaller white spots A2–A4. A8 is slightly domed. Spiracles are black. **SIMILAR SPECIES** Merveille du Jour and Sombre Brocade. **HABITATS** Broadleaf woodland. **FOODPLANTS** Wide variety of trees and shrubs, including Ash, birches, ~ackthorn, cherries, Sweet Chestnut, elms, Honeysuckle, Hop, Field Maple, oaks, poplars including Aspen, ~nd willows. **FIELD NOTES** Apr–Jun. Feeds at night, resting among leaves when small, and in bark crevices ~w on the trunk when larger. Pupates in a cocoon in the ground. Overwinters as a pupa.

SILVER CLOUD
Egira conspicillaris

PLATE 57
73.251 (2181)

Na. **FIELD CHARACTERS** Body brown, mottled dark brown, and often tinged greyish laterally. Prominent white pinacula across dorsal area, and a row of black pinacula or spots laterally. Dorsal and subdorsal lines pale or whitish and ill-defined. Subspiracular stripe orangey brown. Spiracles white. A black pinaculum above each abdominal spiracle. **HABITATS** Gardens, rough grassland, hedgerows, orchards, scrub and open woodland. **FOODPLANTS** Unknown in the wild in Great Britain. Egg batches have been found on dead stems of docks, and pupae under elms and oaks. In captivity, on a wide variety of herbaceous and woody plants. **FIELD NOTES** Late May–mid-Jul. Pupates in the ground. Overwinters as a pupa.

HEDGE RUSTIC
Tholera cespitis

PLATE 57
73.252 (2177)

Common. Has undergone a severe decline in abundance in recent decades. **FIELD CHARACTERS** Body dark brown, more or less speckled pale brown. Dorsal, subdorsal and subspiracular stripes white with brownish markings. Pale brown coloration laterally may be diffuse or arranged in up to three faint lateral lines. **SIMILAR SPECIES** Antler Moth has narrower dorsal and subdorsal stripes that are clearer and less mottled than those of Hedge Rustic and Feathered Gothic. These latter two species cannot be separated reliably in the field, although Hedge Rustic is rarely seen as a larva. **HABITATS** Open and rough grassy areas. **FOODPLANTS** Hard-bladed grasses, including Wavy Hair-grass and Mat-grass. **FIELD NOTES** Mar–Jul. Feeds at night, at first on blades and when larger on stems at ground level. Pupates on the ground. Overwinters as an egg.

FEATHERED GOTHIC
Tholera decimalis

PLATE 57
73.253 (2178)

Common. Has declined significantly in abundance in recent decades, especially in the north of its range. **FIELD CHARACTERS** Body dark brown, more or less speckled pale brown. Dorsal, subdorsal and subspiracular stripes white with orangey-brown or brownish markings. Pale brown laterally, often arranged in faint lateral lines. **SIMILAR SPECIES** Hedge Rustic and Antler Moth. **HABITATS** Rough grassland, including on calcareous soils, and in parkland and woodland rides. Occasionally in gardens. **FOODPLANTS** Hard-bladed grasses, including Mat-grass and Sheep's-fescue. Reported on meadow-grasses. **FIELD NOTES** Jan–Jul. Feeds at night, at first on blades and when larger on stems at ground level. Pupates on the ground. Overwinters at first as an egg, hatching from early Jan.

ANTLER MOTH
Cerapteryx graminis

PLATE 57
73.254 (2176)

Common. Population explosions occur on upland grasslands in the north. In decline in the south. **FIELD CHARACTERS** Body black, dark grey or brown, rarely speckled paler. Dorsal and subdorsal stripes white or greyish, the dorsal stripe sometimes with a broken darker line within. Subspiracular stripe whitish, speckled with brown. A pale brown lateral line. **SIMILAR SPECIES** Hedge Rustic and Feathered Gothic. **HABITATS** Commonest on acidic grassland, especially moorland and upland pastures. Less often in open countryside and on calcareous grassland. **FOODPLANTS** Grasses, including Tufted Hair-grass, Mat-grass, Purple Moor-grass and Sheep's-fescue. Also on Hare's-tail Cottongrass, Deergrass, and Heath and Jointed rushes. **FIELD NOTES** Late Jan–Jul. Feeds mainly at night. Pupates in the ground. Overwinters at first as an egg, hatching from late Jan.

Antler Moth larva

NUTMEG
Anarta trifolii

PLATE 57
73.255 (2145)

Common; immigrant. **FIELD CHARACTERS** Body various shades of green, brown or greyish brown. Dorsal line pale, indistinct or absent. Subdorsal line yellowish or whitish, sometimes with a black mark above, on T2–A8 or A9. In dark examples, the black marks may be extended across the dorsum in mottled V-shaped markings. Subspiracular stripe orange or pinkish, edged above and below with white lines. **HABITATS** Open places, especially on free-draining soils and on the coast, including allotments, fens, gardens, calcareous grassland, recently disturbed ground, river valleys, waste ground and woodland rides. **FOODPLANTS** Various herbaceous plants, especially goosefoots and oraches. Also on Beet, Field Bindweed, conifer seedlings, dandelions, docks, Flixweed and onions. **FIELD NOTES** May–Jul and Sep–Oct in two generations in the south; probably one generation further north. Feeds at night. Pupates in the soil. Overwinters as a pupa.

BROAD-BORDERED WHITE UNDERWING
Anarta melanopa

PLATE 57
73.256 (2144)

RDB. **FIELD CHARACTERS** Body varies from pale brown to purplish brown, mixed with grey. Dorsal line white, edged black. Subdorsal line whitish, thickened on each segment, and with a broad black mark above. Subspiracular stripe whitish grey, or indistinct. **SIMILAR SPECIES** Small Dark Yellow Underwing has a less distinct subdorsal line, not thickened on each segment, and a contrasting whitish subspiracular stripe. **HABITATS** High moorland, on ridges, slopes and summits; also near sea level in northern Scotland. **FOODPLANTS** Bearberry, Bilberry, Cowberry and Crowberry. **FIELD NOTES** Jul–Aug. Feeds at night. Pupates among moss. Overwinters as a pupa.

BEAUTIFUL YELLOW UNDERWING
Anarta myrtilli

PLATE 57
73.257 (2142)

Common. **FIELD CHARACTERS** Body green, with a variety of white and yellow spots and dashes. **HABITATS** Heathland and moorland. **FOODPLANTS** Heather and Bell Heather. **FIELD NOTES** Jul–Sep or later in the north. Larva any month in the south. Feeds mainly by day, resting high on the foodplant by day or night. Usually overwinters as a pupa, or sometimes as a larva. Pupates in a tough cocoon on or just below the ground.

SMALL DARK YELLOW UNDERWING
Coranarta cordigera

PLATE 57
73.258 (2143)

Na. **FIELD CHARACTERS** Body dark grey or dark brown. Dorsal stripe white or yellowish white. Subdorsal line white, and sometimes indistinct beyond T3. Black shading on each segment between dorsal and subdorsal lines. Subspiracular stripe white or yellowish white. There is also a blackish form with the markings obscured. **SIMILAR SPECIES** Broad-bordered White Underwing. **HABITATS** Moorland rich in Bearberry, mainly at altitudes of 200–650m, and associated with stony glacial moraines, dry gravels and free-draining stony road verges. **FOODPLANT** Bearberry. **FIELD NOTES** Late May–Jul. Feeds at night. Pupates on the ground in a long silken cocoon. Overwinters as a pupa.

PALE SHINING BROWN
Polia bombycina

PLATE 57
73.259 (2148)

pRDB; immigrant. Has undergone a severe decline in recent decades and is now rarely encountered. **FIELD CHARACTERS** Body pale yellowish brown, sometimes orangey brown, and speckled darker, with whitish pinacula. Dorsal line white, edged grey, and subspiracular stripe whitish, mixed brown. **SIMILAR SPECIES** Silvery Arches shows no consistent differences but is more often orangey brown. **HABITATS** Remaining populations are on calcareous soils. Recorded on arable fields, calcareous grassland, rough and scrubby grassland and open woodland. **FOODPLANTS** Recorded once in the wild, on Broad-leaved Dock. Probably on various herbaceous plants, and possibly woody species. **FIELD NOTES** Jul–Jun. Feeds at night. Pupates in the ground.

SILVERY ARCHES
Polia hepatica

PLATE 57
73.260 (2149)

Nb; suspected immigrant. In decline on the heaths of southern England. **FIELD CHARACTERS** Body pale orangey brown, speckled darker, with whitish pinacula. The darker brown speckling is often arranged in diamond-shaped marks across the dorsal area. Dorsal line white, edged grey, and subspiracular stripe poorly defined. **SIMILAR SPECIES** Pale Shining Brown. **HABITATS** Scrubby woodland on heathland, moorland and in river valleys, and open woodland on acidic or clay soils. **FOODPLANTS** In autumn, on herbaceous and woody plants, including birches, docks, grasses, plantains and willows. In spring, on expanding buds and leaves of woody species, additionally including Bilberry, Bog-myrtle, Hawthorn and Honeysuckle. **FIELD NOTES** Late Jul–May. Feeds at night. Pupates in or on the ground.

GREY ARCHES
Polia nebulosa

PLATE 57
73.261 (2150)

Common. **FIELD CHARACTERS** Body pale brown, speckled dark brown. Dorsal line whitish and ill-defined. The dark brown speckling is arranged in diamond-shaped marks across the dorsal area, each mark often darker in its posterior half A1–A8. Black diagonal dashes laterally A1–A8 reduced to two black dots on T2–T3 or A1. Spiracles orange. **HABITATS** Mainly broadleaf woodland. Also wooded countryside in the south. **FOODPLANTS** In autumn, on herbaceous plants such as dandelions, docks and Primrose, and woody species including low-growing Pedunculate Oak. In spring, recorded on birches, Blackthorn, Bramble, Hazel, Honeysuckle and willows. **FIELD NOTES** Aug–May. Feeds at night. Hides by day among foodplants when small and on the ground when larger. Pupates in the ground.

LIGHT BROCADE
Lacanobia w-latinum

PLATE 57
73.263 (2157)

Local. **FIELD CHARACTERS** Head pale brown, mottled darker, with vertical, dark brown stripes. Body pale greyish brown, speckled darker brown. Dorsal line pale, barely discernible, and subspiracular stripe pale brown and ill-defined, especially below. The dark brown speckling is often arranged in faint X-shaped marks across the dorsal area. **SIMILAR SPECIES** Pale-shouldered Brocade is similar, and most larvae, except well-marked individuals of that species, will need to be reared to confirm identity. A green form of Light Brocade is apparently unknown. **HABITATS** Open habitats mainly on calcareous soils, including open woodland; also on acidic soils such as heathland. **FOODPLANTS** Various herbaceous and woody plants, including Bramble, Broom, docks, Dyer's Greenweed, knotgrasses and Redshank. **FIELD NOTES** Late Jun–Aug. Feeds at night. Pupates in the ground. Overwinters as a pupa.

PALE-SHOULDERED BROCADE
Lacanobia thalassina

PLATE 57
73.264 (2158)

Common. **FIELD CHARACTERS** Body pale brown, less often pale green, speckled dark brown and with black pinacula. Dorsal and subdorsal lines pale and sometimes ill-defined. The dark brown speckling may be arranged in faint X-shaped or backward-facing V-shaped markings across the dorsal area. In well-marked examples there are diagonal, dark brown subdorsal dashes, especially on A7–A8. Subspiracular stripe pale brown, mixed orangey brown anteriorly. **SIMILAR SPECIES** Light Brocade. **HABITATS** Fens, moorland, scrub, wooded countryside and woodland. **FOODPLANTS** Various woody plants, including Apple, Crab Apple, Aspen, Barberry, birches, Blackthorn, Broom, Sweet Chestnut, hawthorns, Honeysuckle, oaks and willows. Recorded on herbaceous plants, including docks, Groundsel, knotgrasses, Larkspur and Potato. **FIELD NOTES** Late Jun–early Sep. Feeds at night. Pupates in a cocoon in the ground. Overwinters as a pupa.

BEAUTIFUL BROCADE
Lacanobia contigua

PLATE 58
73.265 (2156)

Local. **FIELD CHARACTERS** Body pale green or pale brown with variable markings. Well-marked examples have dark pinacula. Typically, dorsal and subdorsal lines are pale and ill-defined, there are curved, dark reddish-brown or blackish marks across the dorsal area T3–A8, and a pale subspiracular stripe that may be pale brownish, pale greenish, yellow, white or a mixture of these, and edged above with variable amounts of dark brown shading. There are plainer green or brown forms, with or without paler dorsal and subdorsal lines, with reddish-brown dorsal spots T2–A8, and with diagonal reddish-brown subdorsal dashes of varying intensity. **HABITATS** Mainly heathland and moorland; also woodland on acidic or neutral soils. **FOODPLANTS** Various woody plants, including birches, Bog-myrtle, Broom, Gorse flowers, Hazel, Heather, oaks, Rowan and willows. Also recorded on Wild Angelica (ripening seeds), Bracken, docks, Goldenrod and Dyer's Greenweed. **FIELD NOTES** Late Jul–Sep. Feeds at night and by day. Pupates in a cocoon in the ground. Overwinters as a pupa.

DOG'S TOOTH
Lacanobia suasa

PLATE 58
73.266 (2159)

Local; immigrant. Most frequent on the coast. **FIELD CHARACTERS** Body pale brown, tinged pale greyish or orangey, or pale greyish green, with black pinacula and pale dots. Dorsal and subdorsal lines comprise tiny white dots, the dorsal line edged with darker shading. The subdorsal line is edged with long diagonal dashes of darker shading. Subspiracular stripe yellowish, ill-defined below, and edged with a black line above, sometimes reduced to black marks. **SIMILAR SPECIES** Bright-line Brown-eye and Splendid Brocade have brighter white dots across the body. Splendid Brocade has a broad yellowish-cream subspiracular stripe, sharply defined above and below; in Bright-line Brown-eye the stripe tends to be narrower and yellowish, often without clear margins. Bright-line Brown-eye is commonly seen, whereas Splendid Brocade is unlikely to be encountered. **HABITATS** Coastal and estuarine grasslands, moorland, saltmarshes and river valleys; also recorded on farmland and in urban areas. **FOODPLANTS** Various herbaceous plants, including dandelions, docks, goosefoots, knotgrasses, Greater and Sea plantains and Common Sea-lavender. **FIELD NOTES** Late Jun–Jul and late Aug–Sep in two generations in the south; Aug–Sep in one generation further north. Feeds at night. Pupates in the ground. Overwinters as a pupa.

BRIGHT-LINE BROWN-EYE
Lacanobia oleracea

PLATE 58
73.267 (2160)

Common. **FIELD CHARACTERS** Body pale or dark green, or pale or pinkish brown, with black pinacula and white dots. Dorsal and subdorsal lines comprise tiny white dots, the dorsal line edged with darker shading. The subdorsal line may be edged with slightly diagonal, dark brownish or greenish dashes. Subspiracular stripe yellow or orangey, rather narrow and often with ill-defined margins, and sometimes with darker shading or, rarely, black marks above. **SIMILAR SPECIES** Dog's Tooth and Splendid Brocade. **HABITATS** Wide variety; most frequent in gardens, cultivated land and saltmarshes. **FOODPLANTS** Wide variety of herbaceous and woody plants, including bindweeds, Black-bindweed, English Elm, Fat-hen, Hazel, Hop, Common Nettle, oraches, cultivated Spinach, Reed Sweet-grass, Tamarisk, Traveller's-joy, willowherbs and willows. Also a regular pest of Tomato in glasshouses, eating leaves and fruits. **FIELD NOTES** Late Jun–Oct or later in the south as a small second generation; Aug–Sep further north. Feeds at night. Pupates in the ground. Overwinters as a pupa.

SPLENDID BROCADE
Lacanobia splendens

PLATE 58
73.268 (2160a)

Immigrant. The larva has been found once in the Channel Islands. **FIELD CHARACTERS** Body pale brown or greenish brown, with black pinacula and white dots, many of which are edged black. Dorsal and subdorsal lines comprise white dots, the dorsal line edged with darker shading. The subdorsal line is edged with long diagonal dashes of darker shading. Subspiracular stripe broad, yellowish cream, sharply defined above and below, and shaded blackish above. **SIMILAR SPECIES** Dog's Tooth and Bright-line Brown-eye. **HABITATS** In

Europe, prefers damp places, including margins of lakes and streams, meadows, moorland and woodland. **FOODPLANTS** Hedge Bindweed growing at the edge of a damp meadow in Guernsey. Various herbaceous plants in Europe, including nightshades. **FIELD NOTES** Mid–late summer. Probably pupates in the ground. Overwinters as a pupa.

DOT MOTH
Melancha persicariae

PLATE 58

73.270 (2155)

Common. Has declined severely in abundance in recent decades. **FIELD CHARACTERS** Body green, brown, or mixed greyish green and pink or purple, with A8 raised to a slight hump. Dorsal line pale. Curved dark marks across dorsal area A1–A8, most prominent A1–A2. Diagonal marks below the spiracles A3–A6. Larva rests with A1–A2 somewhat raised. **HABITATS** Wide variety of open and wooded habitats in lowlands, including gardens. **FOODPLANTS** Various wild and cultivated herbaceous and woody plants, including Barberry, Field Bindweed, Bracken, Broom, Butterfly-bush, Black Currant, Dahlia, Broad-leaved Dock, Elder, Hazel, Hollyhock, Hop, larches (seedlings), Garden Lupin, Common Nettle, Common Toadflax and willows. **FIELD NOTES** Aug–Oct. Feeds at night and by day, and rests openly on the foodplant. Pupates in the ground. Overwinters as a pupa.

BROOM MOTH
Ceramica pisi

PLATE 58

73.271 (2163)

Common. Has declined significantly in abundance in recent decades. **FIELD CHARACTERS** Body brown or green with yellow subdorsal and subspiracular stripes. **HABITATS** Mainly heathland and moorland, but occurs in a wide variety of open habitats and in woodland. **FOODPLANTS** Wide variety of herbaceous and woody plants, including Sea Aster, Bilberry, Birches, Bog-myrtle, Bracken, Bramble, Broom, docks, Dog-rose, elms, Heather, Yellow Iris, Sea-buckthorn, Creeping and Marsh thistles and Common Toadflax. Recorded in nurseries on conifers such as larches, pines and spruces, and in young plantations of Sitka Spruce. **FIELD NOTES** Jun–Sep. Rests openly on its foodplant by day. Pupates in the ground. Overwinters as a pupa.

GLAUCOUS SHEARS
Papestra biren

PLATE 58

73.272 (2162)

Local; suspected immigrant. **FIELD CHARACTERS** Body various shades of brown, speckled dark brown. Dorsal line pale and ill-defined. Dark brown shading arranged in broad diagonal dashes subdorsally, sometimes coalescing with dark shading along the dorsum to form shield-shapes. Subspiracular stripe pale brown or orangey brown, or sometimes whitish T1–T2. Spiracles white. **HABITATS** Moorland. **FOODPLANTS** Various herbaceous and woody plants, including Bearberry, Bilberry, Bog-myrtle, Colt's-foot, Heather, heaths, knotgrasses, Meadowsweet, Smooth Sowthistle, and Creeping, Eared and Grey willows. **FIELD NOTES** Jun–Aug. Feeds mainly at night. Pupates in or on the ground. Overwinters as a pupa.

SHEARS
Hada plebeja

PLATE 5

73.273 (2147)

Common. **FIELD CHARACTERS** Body brown, speckled dark brown, with prominent white pinacula. Dorsal line white, edged with dark brown shading anteriorly A1–A8. Subdorsal line white, edged above with a black dash A1–A8. Subspiracular stripe mixed whitish brown. Spiracles black. **HABITATS** Open habitats on free-draining soils, including calcareous grassland, heathland, sand dunes and open woodland. **FOODPLANTS** Various herbaceous plants, including Common Chickweed, dandelions, Smooth Hawk's-beard, Knotgrass, Lucerne and Mouse-ear-hawkweed. **FIELD NOTES** Jul–Aug, and to Sep in the south as small second generation. A difficult larva to find. Feeds at night. Pupates in the ground. Overwinters as a pupa.

CABBAGE MOTH
Mamestra brassicae

PLATE 59
73.274 (2154)

Common. **FIELD CHARACTERS** In two colour forms. Both have pale brown heads with slight pale mottling and no other markings. The brown form has a pale brown body, speckled greyish brown, with skin folds between segments often tinged reddish. Dorsal and subdorsal lines whitish and often reduced to dots and dashes, the dorsal line edged with dark shading that is densest between segments. The subdorsal line has small black marks or dashes above, and larger, diagonal, pale greyish-brown dashes. The black marks may be obscure except on A7–A8, where they are larger and triangular. A transverse line posteriorly on A8. Subspiracular stripe whitish brown or tinged orangey. Spiracles white and often surrounded by a black mark. A rare black form occurs with the brown markings replaced with black. The green form has a pale green body, speckled white, with more pronounced whitish dorsal and subdorsal lines of dots and dashes, the dorsal line edged darker green. Subspiracular stripe greenish white or barely noticeable. **SIMILAR SPECIES** Lesser Yellow Underwing, Langmaid's Yellow Underwing, Lesser Broad-bordered Yellow Underwing and Gothic all have the impression of the subdorsal lines and subspiracular stripes continuing over the head, whereas Cabbage Moth lacks such markings, having a plain, only slightly mottled head. Lesser Broad-bordered Yellow Underwing and Langmaid's Yellow Underwing are indistinguishable from each other, but usually differ from Lesser Yellow Underwing in having squarish black subdorsal marks, especially on A8, and the dorsal line usually being well defined. However, caution is advised. Gothic usually has orange spiracles, a wavier subspiracular stripe and a white spot anteriorly above the subdorsal line on T3. Of all these similar species, only Cabbage Moth has a green form. **HABITATS** Mainly in lowland cultivated areas, including gardens, but occurs in many habitats. **FOODPLANTS** Wide variety of wild and cultivated herbaceous plants, including cultivated Basil, Dahlia, docks, goosefoots, stork's-bills and tobaccos. A regular pest of leafy vegetables, especially Cabbage. Also some woody species, including birches, oaks and willows. **FIELD NOTES** Larva found throughout the year, but commonest late summer and autumn. Feeds at night. Pupates in the ground. Usually overwinters as a pupa, or occasionally as a larva.

WHITE COLON
Sideridis turbida

PLATE 59
73.275 (2152)

Nb. **FIELD CHARACTERS** Head yellowish green or orangey brown, and unmarked. Body bluish green, greyish green or bluish grey, with a dark dorsal vessel visible. Subdorsal line pale and interrupted. **HABITATS** Saltmarshes, vegetated sand dunes and vegetated shingle. Also inland on breckland grassland and heathland. **FOODPLANTS** Various herbaceous plants, including Sea Bindweed, Sea Campion (flowers), Common Chickweed, dandelions, docks, Flixweed, goosefoots, oraches, Ribwort Plantain, Sea Plantain, Common Restharrow, Sea Rocket, Sea Sandwort and Sand Spurrey. **FIELD NOTES** Late Jun–Jul, and occasionally late Aug–Sep as a small second generation. Feeds at night, hiding by day in soft ground. Pupates in the ground. Overwinters as a pupa.

CAMPION
Sideridis rivularis

PLATE 59
73.276 (2166)

Common. **FIELD CHARACTERS** Body brownish anteriorly, fading to yellowish posteriorly, and speckled dark brown or blackish. Dorsal line pale, ill-defined and edged with darker shading. V-shaped, dark brown or blackish marks across the dorsal area, and diagonal, dark brown or blackish marks laterally. Pinacula white and conspicuous. **HABITATS** Open habitats, including damp meadows, moorland, road verges, sea cliffs, waste ground and woodland rides. **FOODPLANTS** Bladder, Red, Sea and White campions, and Ragged-Robin. **FIELD NOTES** Jun–Sep, in two generations in the south and one further north. Feeds on ripening seeds within the capsule at first, later hiding by day on the ground and ascending to feed at night on petals, capsules and seeds. Pupates in the ground. Overwinters as a pupa.

BORDERED GOTHIC
Sideridis reticulata

PLATE 59
73.277 (2153)

Ssp. *marginosa* pRDB; possibly extinct; suspected immigrant. Ssp. *hibernica* Ireland. **FIELD CHARACTERS** Body pale brown or pale grey, sometimes tinged greenish, speckled dark brown and with dark brown pinacula. Dorsal and subdorsal lines pale, the subdorsal line present only anteriorly. Subspiracular stripe faint or absent. **SIMILAR SPECIES** Feathered Ranunculus. **HABITATS** Open calcareous habitats, including cliffs, breckland and chalk grasslands, and old quarries and road cuttings. Also on disturbed ground. **FOODPLANT** Has been reported in the wild pupating under Sea Campion in Ireland and feeding on it in Norfolk. **FIELD NOTES** Probably late Jun–early Sep. In Europe feeds in the seedheads. Pupates in the ground. Overwinters as a pupa.

BARRETT'S MARBLED CORONET
Conisania andalusica

PLATE 59
73.278 (2169)

Ssp. *barrettii* Nb; suspected immigrant. **FIELD CHARACTERS** Body white, with pale brown pinacula. Spiracles brown. **HABITATS** Hard and soft cliffs, and vegetated shingle. **FOODPLANTS** Sea Campion, Rock Sea-spurrey and Sand Spurrey. **FIELD NOTES** Jul–Sep. Bores down the stem and then feeds in the roots. The plant withers and dies above the affected root. Pupates in the ground. Overwinters as a pupa.

BROAD-BARRED WHITE
Hecatera bicolorata

PLATE 59
73.279 (2164)

Common. **FIELD CHARACTERS** Body usually green, with abundant dark grey squiggles and dark grey pinacula. Occasionally there is dark shading across the dorsum, forming chevrons or blotches. Dorsal line pale and ill-defined, or absent. Subspiracular stripe pale greenish or yellowish white and unmarked. Rarely there is a brown form, with darker brown squiggles. Spiracles white- or pale-centred with a darker outline. **SIMILAR SPECIES** Small Ranunculus has black spiracles. **HABITATS** Open habitats on calcareous and sandy soils, including fields reverted from arable, disturbed rough grassland, vegetated sand dunes and vegetated shingle. **FOODPLANTS** Most frequently encountered on Smooth Hawk's-beard. Also found on hawkweeds, other hawk's-beards, Prickly Lettuce, oxtongues and sowthistles. **FIELD NOTES** Late Jul–Sep. Feeds on buds, flowers and developing seeds, by day and night, resting by day on the plant. Pupates in the ground. Overwinters as a pupa.

SMALL RANUNCULUS
Hecatera dysodea

PLATE 59
73.280 (2165)

RDB; suspected immigrant; former resident. Now re-established widely in England except in the north and south-west. Established in south Wales. **FIELD CHARACTERS** Body often yellowish green, sometimes pale green or pale brown, densely speckled with dark brown or grey, and often showing strong colour contrast above and below the spiracles. Pinacula dark. Dorsal line pale, edged darker, and subdorsal line dark. Subspiracular stripe pale yellowish, pale green or pale brown, and unmarked. Spiracles black and noticeable. **SIMILAR SPECIES** Broad-barred White. **HABITATS** Recently disturbed areas, including allotments, construction sites, gardens, road verges and waste ground. **FOODPLANTS** Mainly Prickly Lettuce. Also recorded on Garden, Great and Wall lettuces, Smooth Hawk's-beard, Bristly Oxtongue and sowthistles. **FIELD NOTES** Jul–Aug. Feeds on flowers and seeds, resting high up in the flowers by day. Pupates in the ground. Overwinters as a pupa.

LYCHNIS
Hadena bicruris

PLATE 59
73.281 (2173)

Common. **FIELD CHARACTERS** Body varying shades of pale brown, speckled dark brown, with dark pinacula. The speckling is arranged in V-shaped marks across the dorsal area. Dorsal line pale and ill-defined, and subspiracular stripe pale. **SIMILAR SPECIES** Varied Coronet sometimes has V-shaped marks; if present, they are much shorter. Marbled Coronet is indistinguishable in the field. **HABITATS** Wide variety, including rough coastal areas, field margins, gardens, hedgerows, sand dunes and woodland. **FOODPLANTS** Mainly on Red and White campions, and Sweet-William. Also recorded on Bladder Campion, Night-flowering Catchfly, Ragged-Robin and soapworts. **FIELD NOTES** Late Jun–early Aug and Sep in the south in two generations; Jul–Aug further north in one generation. Feeds on developing seeds within a capsule, entirely within at first, and later externally at night with its head in the capsule, hiding by day on the ground. Hides among the seedheads of Sweet-William. Pupates in the ground. Overwinters as a pupa.

VARIED CORONET
Hadena compta

PLATE 59
73.282 (2170)

Common (possibly naturalised); suspected immigrant. Has increased significantly in range in recent decades. **FIELD CHARACTERS** Body pale brown or greyish brown, speckled dark brown or black, with dark pinacula. The speckling is concentrated along the dorsum as a band, which may form short V-shapes or diamonds. Dorsal line pale and ill-defined, and subspiracular stripe pale. **SIMILAR SPECIES** Lychnis and Marbled Coronet. **HABITATS** Gardens and urban parks, and calcareous grassland. **FOODPLANTS** Mainly Sweet-William; occasionally Bladder Campion. **FIELD NOTES** Jul–Sep. Feeds at first within a capsule; later externally at night among seedheads, hiding by day on the ground. Pupates in the ground. Overwinters as a pupa.

MARBLED CORONET
Hadena confusa

PLATE 59
73.283 (2171)

Local. **SIMILAR SPECIES** Lychnis, Varied Coronet and White Spot. **HABITATS** Open calcareous areas inland, and coastal habitats including hard cliffs and vegetated shingle. **FOODPLANTS** Mainly Bladder and Sea campions. Also recorded on Moss, Red and White campions, Nottingham Catchfly, pinks, Ragged-Robin, Rock Sea-spurrey and Sweet-William. **FIELD NOTES** Jul–Aug. Feeds at first within a capsule; later externally at night on seedheads, hiding by day on the ground. Pupates in the ground. Overwinters as a pupa, sometimes over two winters.

WHITE SPOT
Hadena albimacula

PLATE 59
73.284 (2172)

RDB. **FIELD CHARACTERS** Body pale brown, speckled dark brown, with dark pinacula. The speckling is usually concentrated along the dorsum, sometimes laterally, and as V-shaped marks across the dorsal area. Dorsal line pale, T1–T2 only, and subspiracular stripe pale. **SIMILAR SPECIES** Marbled Coronet may feed on Nottingham Catchfly and if so it would be indistinguishable in the field from well-marked examples of White Spot. **HABITATS** Cliffs and vegetated shingle. **FOODPLANT** Nottingham Catchfly. **FIELD NOTES** Jun–Aug. Feeds at first within or on a capsule; later externally at night on seedheads, hiding by day under the leaves or in shingle. Pupates in the ground. Overwinters as a pupa.

GREY
Hadena caesia

PLATE 59
73.285 (2174)

Ssp. *mananii* RDB. Protected on Isle of Man. **FIELD CHARACTERS** Body dark brown, and paler in subdorsal area. Dorsal line, if present, white, and subspiracular stripe whitish or ill-defined. Pinacula white and conspicuous. **HABITATS** Rocky coastlines and vegetated shingle, close to the strand-line. **FOODPLANTS** Sea Campion. Also recorded on Bladder Campion. **FIELD NOTES** Jun–Sep. Feeds at first within a capsule; later on leaves at night, hiding under the more isolated plants by day. Pupates in a cocoon among rocks. Overwinters as a pupa.

TAWNY SHEARS
Hadena perplexa

PLATE 59
73.286 (2167)

Ssp. *perplexa* Common. England, Wales and Scotland. Pod Lover ssp. *capsophila* Local. Ireland and Isle of Man. Protected on Isle of Man. **FIELD CHARACTERS** Body pale greyish brown with tiny dark pinacula. Dorsal, subdorsal and lateral stripes, and subspiracular band, pale yellowish brown or whitish. **HABITATS** Open areas on calcareous soils, including arable reversion to grassland, field margins and gardens. Also coastal habitats, including vegetated sand dunes, sea cliffs and vegetated shingle. Pod Lover is found on rocky coasts and saltmarshes. **FOODPLANTS** Bladder and Sea campions, Nottingham Catchfly, and sometimes White Campion and Rock Sea-spurrey. Also recorded on pinks and Sweet-William. **FIELD NOTES** May–Sep, including a small partial second generation in the south; Jul–Aug in one generation further north. Feeds at first within a capsule; later from the outside at night, usually hiding on the ground by day. Pupates in a cocoon in the ground. Overwinters as a pupa.

NOTE ON EXTERNAL-FEEDING WAINSCOTS (GENERA *MYTHIMNA, LEUCANIA* AND *SENTA*)

Typically, larvae of these genera are pale brown with paler and darker lines and stripes. They are nocturnal, and several are readily findable by torchlight at rest or feeding on grasses. Reliable distinguishing features among most of them are generally lacking, as there is little variation between species and some variation within a species. Most larvae will need to be reared to confirm identity. Species illustrated in the plate section can either be identified with certainty, or fall into one of two groups, the Smoky Wainscot group or the Clay group (see table on pp. 424–7). Note that the larva of White-point is so variable that it sits in both.

The Smoky Wainscot group comprises Common, Mathew's and Smoky wainscots, Delicate and White-point. Larvae in this group are pale brown with dark pinacula visible to the naked eye. There are alternating coloured lines on the dorsum and laterally, with a darker supraspiracular band and paler subspiracular stripe.

The Clay group comprises Brown-line Bright-eye, White-speck/American Wainscot, White-point, Clay, Cosmopolitan, and Striped, L-album, Shoulder-striped and Devonshire wainscots. Larvae in this group have a white subdorsal line with dark brown or black dashes above, often forming a near-continuous stripe A1–A8. There is also similarity between the larvae in the Clay group and Grayling, Square-spot Rustic and Six-striped Rustic.

DOUBLE LINE
Mythimna turca

PLATE 60
73.288 (2191)

Nb; suspected immigrant. Resident mainly in south-west England and Wales. **FIELD CHARACTERS** The larva is stockier than other wainscots in this group. Body orangey brown, speckled dark brown, with paler pinacula. The speckling is sometimes concentrated into indistinct X-shaped marks across the dorsal area, and in a wavy subdorsal stripe. Dorsal line and subspiracular stripe pale brown. **SIMILAR SPECIES** See *Separating external-feeding wainscots* table (pp. 424–7). **HABITATS** Upland wet grassland, ancient parkland and mature woodland. **FOODPLANTS** Grasses, including Common Bent, Cock's-foot, Wood Meadow-grass, Creeping Soft-grass and Sweet Vernal-grass. Also Carnation Sedge and Field and Hairy wood-rushes. **FIELD NOTES** Aug–May. Feeds at night. Pupates in the ground. Overwinters as a small larva.

STRIPED WAINSCOT
Mythimna pudorina

PLATE 60 (CLAY GROUP)
73.289 (2196)

Local. **SIMILAR SPECIES** See *Separating external-feeding wainscots* table (pp. 424–7). **HABITATS** Fens, acid grassland, wet heathland and marshes. **FOODPLANTS** Broad-bladed grasses, including Reed Canary-grass, Purple Moor-grass and Common Reed. **FIELD NOTES** Aug–May. Feeds at night, usually close to the ground. Pupates in a cocoon in leaf litter. Overwinters as a small larva.

BROWN-LINE BRIGHT-EYE
Mythimna conigera

PLATE 60 (CLAY GROUP)
73.290 (2192)

Common. **SIMILAR SPECIES** See *Separating external-feeding wainscots* table (pp. 424–7). **HABITATS** Various grassland habitats; commonest in woodlands and wooded countryside. **FOODPLANTS** Grasses, including Cock's-foot, Common Couch and Red Fescue. **FIELD NOTES** Aug–May. Climbs plant to feed at night. Pupates in the ground. Overwinters as a small larva.

COMMON WAINSCOT
Mythimna pallens

PLATE 60 (SMOKY WAINSCOT GROUP)
73.291 (2199)

Common. **SIMILAR SPECIES** See *Separating external-feeding wainscots* table (pp. 424–7). **HABITATS** Wide variety of dry and wet grasslands; frequent in woodlands. **FOODPLANTS** Grasses, including Cock's-foot, Common Couch, Tufted Hair-grass and Annual Meadow-grass. **FIELD NOTES** Jun–Aug and Sep–May in the south; Aug–Jun further north. At first in small groups in spun ends of grass blades, later feeding at night on blades, hiding by day at the base of the plant. Pupates in the ground. Overwinters as a small larva.

MATHEW'S WAINSCOT
Mythimna favicolor

PLATE 60 (SMOKY WAINSCOT GROUP)
73.292 (2200)

Nb. Can be numerous on saltmarshes. **SIMILAR SPECIES** See *Separating external-feeding wainscots* table (pp. 424–7). **HABITATS** Coastal and estuarine saltmarshes. **FOODPLANTS** Common Saltmarsh-grass and probably other grasses on saltmarshes. **FIELD NOTES** Aug–late May, and probably also Jul, producing a partial second generation. Climbs plant to feed at night. Pupates in the ground. Overwinters as a small larva.

SMOKY WAINSCOT
Mythimna impura

PLATE 60 (SMOKY WAINSCOT GROUP)
73.293 (2198)

Common. **FIELD CHARACTERS** Body pale brown, with dark pinacula visible to the naked eye. Dorsal line white, sometimes narrowly edged blackish. Subdorsal line white, narrowly shaded darker above, and sometimes edged with a black line. Below the subdorsal line are two orange lines, a white line and a greyish-brown supraspiracular band. The subspiracular stripe is yellowish brown. **SIMILAR SPECIES** See *Separating external-feeding wainscots* table (pp. 424–7). **HABITATS** Wide variety of grasslands, including gardens; frequent in lowland grasslands in the south, and sand dunes in the north. **FOODPLANTS** Grasses, including Cock's-foot, Tufted Hair-grass, Annual Meadow-grass and Common Reed. Also Tufted-sedge and Field and Hairy wood-rushes. **FIELD NOTES** Aug–May or Jun. Climbs plant to feed at night. Pupates in the ground. Overwinters as a small larva.

SOUTHERN WAINSCOT
Mythimna straminea

PLATE 60
73.294 (2197)

Local. Expanding northwards. **FIELD CHARACTERS** The larva is more slender than similar species, with tiny black pinacula. Body pale brown or orangey brown. Dorsal line white, edged with dark grey shading, sometimes obscuring the line. Subdorsal line white, below which is an orange line, a white lateral line and a brownish-grey supraspiracular band. The subspiracular stripe is pale brown. **SIMILAR SPECIES** See *Separating external-feeding wainscots* table (pp. 424–7). **HABITATS** Fens, marshes, fringing reedbeds to canals and rivers, and reedy ditches. **FOODPLANTS** Reed Canary-grass and Common Reed. **FIELD NOTES** Aug–May or early Jun. Climbs plant to feed at night, hiding by day in dead vegetation. Pupates between folded leaves or in the ground.

DELICATE
Mythimna vitellina

PLATE 60 (SMOKY WAINSCOT GROUP)
73.295 (2195)

Immigrant; Channel Islands resident. **SIMILAR SPECIES** See *Separating external-feeding wainscots* table (pp. 424–7). **HABITATS** Coastal grassland. **FOODPLANTS** Grasses, including Annual Meadow-grass and Cock's-foot. **FIELD NOTES** Rarely observed in the wild. Likely to be a fully fed larva in late summer. There is no evidence of overwintering.

WHITE-SPECK/AMERICAN WAINSCOT

Mythimna unipuncta

PLATE 60
(CLAY GROUP)
73.296 (2203)

Immigrant; resident in Scilly and the Channel Islands. **FIELD CHARACTERS** Body brown, usually with a dark grey dorsal band incorporating a white dorsal line. Subdorsal line white with black dashes above, a brown stripe below, and a white lateral line. Supraspiracular band grey, spiracular line white and subspiracular stripe orangey brown. **SIMILAR SPECIES** See *Separating external-feeding wainscots* table (pp. 424–7). **HABITATS** Coastal grassland. **FOODPLANTS** Not known in Great Britain or Ireland; on a wide variety of herbaceous plants elsewhere in the world. **FIELD NOTES** Rarely observed in the wild. Natural larval period not known. Pupates at the base of grass stems.

WHITE-POINT
Mythimna albipuncta

PLATE 60 (CLAY & SMOKY WAINSCOT GROUPS)
73.297 (2194)

Immigrant; recent colonist. **SIMILAR SPECIES** See *Separating external-feeding wainscots* table (pp. 424–7). **HABITATS** Open grassy areas on the coast and inland. **FOODPLANTS** Grasses, including Cock's-foot and Common Couch. **FIELD NOTES** Natural larval period not known. Many penultimate- and last-instar larvae have been found at night in Apr, and it is likely the larva feeds during the winter. In the following generation, the larva is probably fully fed in late summer. Pupates in the ground.

CLAY
Mythimna ferrago

PLATE 60 (CLAY GROUP)
73.298 (2193)

Common. **FIELD CHARACTERS** Body pale brown with a white dorsal line. Subdorsal line white with dark brown or black dashes above, often forming a near-continuous stripe A1–A8. Below the subdorsal line are two orange lines and a white line. The supraspiracular band is brownish, often speckled dark brown, and the subspiracular stripe is pale brown, edged with a white line above and below. **SIMILAR SPECIES** See *Separating external-feeding wainscots* table (pp. 424–7). **HABITATS** Wide variety of grasslands, including gardens, and frequent in woodland rides. **FOODPLANTS** Grasses, including Cock's-foot, Tall Fescue and meadow-grasses. Also recorded on Common Chickweed, dandelions and plantains. **FIELD NOTES** Aug–May. Climbs plant to feed at night. Pupates in the ground.

SHORE WAINSCOT
Mythimna litoralis

PLATE 60
73.299 (2201)

Nb. **FIELD CHARACTERS** Body pale brown with a white dorsal line. Subdorsal line white with an unbroken dark brown stripe above. Below the subdorsal line is a pale orangey-brown line and a white line. The supraspiracular band is pale greyish brown and the subspiracular stripe is white or whitish grey. **SIMILAR SPECIES** See *Separating external-feeding wainscots* table (pp. 424–7). **HABITATS** Sand dunes and sandy beaches. **FOODPLANT** Marram. **FIELD NOTES** Aug–late May. Climbs the plant to feed at night, hiding by day in the sand. Disturbing sand around the plant by day may reveal larvae or their bright green frass pellets. Pupates in sand. Overwinters as a small larva in sand.

L-ALBUM WAINSCOT
Mythimna l-album

PLATE 60 (CLAY GROUP)
73.300 (2202)

Nb; immigrant. Resident in southern and eastern coastal counties. **SIMILAR SPECIES** See *Separating external-feeding wainscots* table (pp. 424–7). **HABITATS** Rough coastal grassland, especially on cliffs. **FOODPLANTS** Has been found in the wild on Marram, but likely to feed on a range of grasses. **FIELD NOTES** Jul–Aug and Oct–May in two generations. Rarely observed in the wild. Feeds at night. Pupates in the ground. Overwinters as a small larva.

SHOULDER-STRIPED WAINSCOT
Leucania comma

PLATE 60 (CLAY GROUP)
73.301 (2205)

Common. Has decreased significantly in abundance in recent decades. **SIMILAR SPECIES** See *Separating external-feeding wainscots* table (pp. 424–7). **HABITATS** Mainly fens, marshes and damp woodland. **FOODPLANTS** Grasses, including Cock's-foot. **FIELD NOTES** Aug–Apr. Climbs the plant to feed at night. Fully fed in Sep, overwintering in a cocoon in the ground, and pupating in Apr.

OBSCURE WAINSCOT
Leucania obsoleta

PLATE 60
73.302 (2204)

Local. **FIELD CHARACTERS** Rather elongate. Body translucent pale brownish or pale greenish brown with a white dorsal line. Subdorsal and lateral lines white with a brown stripe between. Almost unmarked greyish below lateral line. Spiracles orange-centred. **SIMILAR SPECIES** See *Separating external-feeding wainscots* table (pp. 424–7). **HABITATS** Reedy ditches, fens, marshes, reedbeds, and reeds fringing estuaries, lakes, ponds and rivers. **FOODPLANT** Common Reed. **FIELD NOTES** Jul–Apr. Climbs to feed on leaves at night. Fully fed early Sep. Overwinters in a broken, dead reed stem, or in leaf litter. Pupates in the overwintering chamber in spring.

DEVONSHIRE WAINSCOT
Leucania putrescens

PLATE 60 (CLAY GROUP)
73.303 (2206)

Na. **SIMILAR SPECIES** See *Separating external-feeding wainscots* table (pp. 424–7). **HABITATS** Cliffs and coastal grassland. **FOODPLANTS** Grasses. **FIELD NOTES** Sep–May. Feeds at night throughout the winter. Fully fed late Jan–Feb, then constructs a cocoon in the ground, where the larva pupates in May.

COSMOPOLITAN
Leucania loreyi

PLATE 60 (CLAY GROUP)
73.304 (2208)

Immigrant. **SIMILAR SPECIES** See *Separating external-feeding wainscots* table (pp. 424–7). **HABITATS** Coastal grassland. **FOODPLANTS** Grasses. **FIELD NOTES** The larva has been found once in Great Britain in Sep. Natural larval period not known. Unlikely to overwinter in Great Britain or Ireland.

FLAME WAINSCOT
Senta flammea

PLATE 60
73.305 (2209)

Na; suspected immigrant. **FIELD CHARACTERS** Rather elongate. Body pale brownish with faint whitish dorsal, subdorsal and lateral lines. Obvious black pinacula below the lateral line. Subspiracular stripe yellowish brown, broadly mottled darker above. Spiracles white-centred. **SIMILAR SPECIES** See *Separating external-feeding wainscots* table (pp. 424–7). **HABITATS** Fens, wet heathland, marshes and reedbeds, preferring drier ground. **FOODPLANTS** Common Reed. **FIELD NOTES** Late Jul–Sep, or sometimes as late as Nov. Climbs to feed on leaves at night, hiding by day within a hollow stem. Pupates in a hollow stem. Overwinters as a pupa.

SILURIAN
Eriopygodes imbecilla

PLATE 60
73.306 (2175)

RDB. On hills at 450–700m in south-east Wales and adjacent parts of England. **FIELD CHARACTERS** Body pale brown, speckled dark brown, and with black pinacula, those on dorsum sometimes encircled white or grey. The speckling is concentrated in oval-shaped shading along the dorsum A2–A8. Dorsal and subdorsal lines white. Body dark brown laterally with a white lateral line. Subspiracular stripe whitish brown. **HABITATS** Gullies and hollows on moorland. **FOODPLANTS** Heath Bedstraw and Bilberry. **FIELD NOTES** Aug–May. Feeds at night, even at low temperatures. Pupates in the ground. Overwinters part-grown.

NOCTUINAE

PEARLY UNDERWING
Peridroma saucia

PLATE 60
73.307 (2119)

Immigrant. **FIELD CHARACTERS** Body pale or dark brownish grey. Dorsal line pale yellowish and ill-defined, incorporating paired pale yellowish spots T3–A3 and similar smaller spots A4–A5. Subdorsal line, if present, pale orangey brown, edged above with short black dashes. Dashes may be larger and triangular A7–A8. Additionally, A8 has a blackish triangular dorsal mark, and a pale grey or orangey transverse stripe posteriorly. Subspiracular stripe is orangey brown or whitish brown. Spiracles black. **HABITATS** Ubiquitous. **FOODPLANTS** Various herbaceous plants including clovers, dandelions, docks, Small Nettle, plantains and tobaccos. Also recorded on Cabbage, Garden Lettuce and Oil-seed Rape. **FIELD NOTES** Rarely observed in the wild. Has been found part grown mid-Sep, and probably feeds Jul–Oct. Feeds at night, hiding underground by day. Pupates in the ground. There is no evidence of overwintering.

PORTLAND MOTH
Actebia praecox

PLATE 60
73.308 (2099)

Nb; suspected immigrant. Elusive, but appears to be in decline. **FIELD CHARACTERS** Body grey or blackish grey with a white dorsal stripe that widens posteriorly on each segment. Orange shading above the subdorsal line, which is white, edged above with a black line. Subspiracular stripe white. **HABITATS** Mainly shifting sand dunes. Also on sandy heathland, and sand/shingle banks on rivers. Prefers sparsely vegetated areas on soft ground. **FOODPLANTS** Mainly Creeping Willow. Also recorded on various herbaceous plants including Sea Bindweed, Common Bird's-foot-trefoil, Common Chickweed, Rush-leaved Fescue, Tree Lupin, Marram, restharrows and Sea Wormwood. **FIELD NOTES** Sep–Jun. Feeds at night, hiding in sand by day. Small sand piles may indicate where a larva has burrowed. Pupates in the ground.

NOTE ON DARTS AND ALLIES IN GENERA *EUXOA AND AGROTIS*

Larvae of darts are all similar, being brownish or greyish in colour, and rather smooth in appearance. Some species are known to hide underground by day, coming up to feed at night (e.g. Coast Dart, White-line Dart, Heart & Dart, Archer's Dart and Sand Dart). It is probable that most, if not all, species behave in a similar way. Turnip Moth is believed to be wholly subterranean, and other species with poorly known life histories may be similar. The smooth appearance is probably an adaptation to moving through sand or soil

Heart & Dart is illustrated because it is an abundant moth in gardens and the larvae can often be encountered. Shuttle-shaped Dart is illustrated as it is a common species and the larva differs in colour from Heart & Dart. Sand Dart is also illustrated as the larva can be easily found by searching its habitat. Otherwise, larvae of individual species are not illustrated owing to lack of features that allow reliable identification. They all resemble Heart & Dart. All larvae need to be reared to the adult stage to confirm identity, with the exception of Sand Dart in locations where Coast Dart does not also occur.

COAST DART
Euxoa cursoria

NOT ILLUSTRATED
73.311 (2083)

Nb; suspected immigrant. **SIMILAR SPECIES** All *Euxoa* and *Agrotis* larvae. Sand Dart is found in more mobile dunes, especially in the foredunes closest to the sea. Coast Dart is pale brownish grey, whereas Sand Dart is pale yellowish brown. **HABITATS** Sand dunes, preferring more stable, well-vegetated areas away from the sea. **FOODPLANTS** Wide variety of herbaceous plants including Sand Couch, Early Hair-grass, Hound's-tongue, Sticky Mouse-ear, Sea Sandwort, Sea Spurge and violets. **FIELD NOTES** Mar–Jul. Rarely observed in the wild. Feeds at night, hiding by day in sand. Pupates in sand. Overwintering stage unknown; probably as an egg.

SQUARE-SPOT DART
Euxoa obelisca

NOT ILLUSTRATED
73.312 (2080)

Ssp. *grisea* Nb. Mainly coastal but with a few inland sites. **SIMILAR SPECIES** All *Euxoa* and *Agrotis* larvae. **HABITATS** Hard and soft cliffs, and inland hills. **FOODPLANTS** Poorly known, but has been reported on Lady's Bedstraw and Common Rock-rose. **FIELD NOTES** Feb–Jul. Pupates in the ground. Overwintering stage unknown; probably as an egg.

WHITE-LINE DART
Euxoa tritici

NOT ILLUSTRATED
73.313 (2081)

Common. Has declined severely in abundance in recent decades especially in the north of its range, and is less widespread in lowland England than formerly. **SIMILAR SPECIES** All *Euxoa* and *Agrotis* larvae. **HABITATS** Cliffs, calcareous grassland, heathland and wooded heathland, moorland, sand dunes and vegetated shingle. **FOODPLANTS** Various herbaceous plants including Hedge and Lady's bedstraws, Common Chickweed, mouse-ears and Corn Spurrey. **FIELD NOTES** Mar–Jul, feeding at night. Has been found hiding by day in sand. Pupates in the ground. Overwinters as an egg.

GARDEN DART
Euxoa nigricans

NOT ILLUSTRATED
73.314 (2082)

Common. Has declined severely in abundance in recent decades, especially in the south of its range. **SIMILAR SPECIES** All *Euxoa* and *Agrotis* larvae. **HABITATS** Wide variety including allotments, arable fields, calcareous and floodplain grasslands, gardens, rough open ground, marshes and open woodland. **FOODPLANTS** Various herbaceous plants including clovers, docks, plantains, and species in the carrot family such as Hogweed. **FIELD NOTES** Feb–Jun. Feeds at night. Pupates in the ground. Overwinters as an egg, hatching from early Feb.

LIGHT FEATHERED RUSTIC
Agrotis cinerea

NOT ILLUSTRATED
73.316 (2084)

Nb. Possibly in decline. **SIMILAR SPECIES** All *Euxoa* and *Agrotis* larvae. **HABITATS** Calcareous grassland, old quarries, coastal sea cliffs and vegetated shingle, where Wild Thyme grows plentifully in short turf or broken ground. **FOODPLANTS** Mainly Wild Thyme, and possibly other low-growing herbaceous plants. **FIELD NOTES** Late Jun–spring. Fully fed by late Sep, remaining as a larva and overwintering in the ground, where it pupates in the spring.

HEART & DART
Agrotis exclamationis

PLATE 60
73.317 (2089)

Common. Has declined significantly in abundance in recent decades. **FIELD CHARACTERS** Body pale brown or pale greyish brown, speckled dark brown. Dorsal line pale brown, edged with dark brown shading. The darker speckling is concentrated into a wavy, rather diffuse subdorsal stripe, and often is more extensive laterally. Spiracles black, and adjacent pinacula similar-sized and brown or black. **SIMILAR SPECIES** All *Euxoa* and *Agrotis* larvae. There are three other similar garden species that may be encountered. Heart & Club has a darker greyish-brown body colour. Shuttle-shaped Dart is yellowish brown across the dorsal area. Turnip Moth has spiracles slightly smaller than the adjacent pinacula. **HABITATS** All habitats except those at high altitude. Most frequent in arable fields, gardens and lowland pastures. **FOODPLANTS** Wide variety of herbaceous plants including Common Chickweed, docks, goosefoots and plantains. Also recorded in nurseries on conifer seedlings. **FIELD NOTES** Jul–Mar. Feeds at night. Fully fed by Oct, sometimes earlier, remaining as a larva and overwintering in the ground, where it pupates in the spring. Some larvae pupate in late summer, producing a small second generation in the autumn.

WOODS'S DART
Agrotis graslini

NOT ILLUSTRATED
73.318 (2083a)

A recent colonist on Jersey. **SIMILAR SPECIES** All *Euxoa* and *Agrotis* larvae. **HABITATS** Sand dunes. **FOODPLANTS** In Europe on docks, Tuberous Hawk's-beard, plantains and scabiouses. **FIELD NOTES** The early stages have not been found in Jersey.

TURNIP MOTH
Agrotis segetum

NOT ILLUSTRATED
73.319 (2087)

Common; immigrant. **SIMILAR SPECIES** All *Euxoa* and *Agrotis* larvae. See Heart & Dart. **HABITATS** Wide variety including farmland, gardens and urban parks, parkland, sand dunes and open woodland. **FOODPLANTS** Wide variety of wild and cultivated herbaceous plants, including arable crops. Also recorded in nurseries on conifer seedlings of Douglas Fir, other firs, larches and spruces. **FIELD NOTES** Jun–Apr with some pupating in Aug and larvae from second generation moths Oct–Apr. Believed to be almost wholly subterranean. Pupate in the ground. Overwinters as a small or well-grown larva.

HEART & CLUB
Agrotis clavis

NOT ILLUSTRATED
73.320 (208..)

Common. Much more local further north and in Ireland. **SIMILAR SPECIES** All *Euxoa* and *Agrotis* larvae. See Heart & Dart. **HABITATS** Gardens, dry grassland including calcareous grassland, and sand dunes. **FOODPLANTS** Wide variety of herbaceous plants including Wild Carrot, clovers, docks, Fat-hen, knotgrasses and mulleins. **FIELD NOTES** Aug–May. Feeds at first on leaves; later on roots underground. Fully fed in Nov, remaining as a larva and overwintering in the ground, where it pupates in the spring.

ARCHER'S DART
Agrotis vestigialis

NOT ILLUSTRATED
73.322 (208..)

Local. **SIMILAR SPECIES** All *Euxoa* and *Agrotis* larvae. **HABITATS** Mainly sand dunes. Also vegetated shingle, and locally inland on acid and breckland grasslands and heathland. Very locally on limestone grassland. **FOODPLANTS** Various herbaceous plants including bedstraws, grasses, Sea Sandwort and stitchworts. **FIELD NOTES** Sep–May. Feeds at night, and throughout the winter when mild. Has been found hiding in sand by day. Pupates in the ground.

SAND DART
Agrotis ripae

PLATE 60
73.323 (2093)

Nb. **FIELD CHARACTERS** Body very pale yellowish brown, a similar colour to the sand in which it hides. Dorsal line as body colour, edged with grey or pale brown, and there is a wavy grey or pale brown subdorsal stripe. Pinacula dark grey and spiracles black. **SIMILAR SPECIES** All *Euxoa* and *Agrotis* larvae. See Coast Dart. **HABITATS** Sand dunes, just above the foredune strand-line. **FOODPLANTS** Herbaceous plants, including Sea Bindweed, Red Goosefoot, Hound's-tongue, Common Orache, Sea Rocket, Prickly Saltwort, Annual Sea-blite, Sea-holly, Sea-milkwort and Sea-purslane. Also on sucker growth of Sea-buckthorn. **FIELD NOTES** Aug–early Jun. Feeds at night, hiding by day in sand. Can be found by day by searching the sand beneath the foodplants. Overwinters fully fed in the sand. In captivity, larvae have been noted to appear in spring on top of the sand before burrowing down again to pupate. This may be an adaptation to ensure shifting sand in winter storms has not left them too far beneath the surface for the adult to emerge safely.

CRESCENT DART
Agrotis trux

Ssp. *lunigera* Local. **SIMILAR SPECIES** All *Euxoa* and *Agrotis* larvae. **HABITATS** Mainly sea cliffs; sometimes in valleys a short distance inland from the sea. **FOODPLANTS** Rarely observed in the wild. Recorded on Thrift, and has been found fully grown among Rock Sea-spurrey. **FIELD NOTES** Aug–spring. Fully fed in Nov, remaining as a larva and overwintering at or below ground level. Pupates in the ground in spring.

SHUTTLE-SHAPED DART
Agrotis puta

PLATE 60
73.325 (2092)

Ssp. *puta* Common. Ssp. *insula* Scilly. **SIMILAR SPECIES** All *Euxoa* and *Agrotis* larvae. See Heart & Dart. **HABITATS** Wide variety of open habitats including farmland, gardens, grasslands, heathland, wetlands and open woodland. **FOODPLANTS** Rarely observed in the wild. Reported on dandelions, docks, Knotgrass and lettuces. **FIELD NOTES** May–Jul and Aug–Apr, in two or possibly three overlapping generations in the south, and Jun–Apr where there is one generation in the north. Feeds at night. Pupates in the ground.

DARK SWORD-GRASS
Agrotis ipsilon

Immigrant. **SIMILAR SPECIES** All *Euxoa* and *Agrotis* larvae. **HABITATS** Ubiquitous. **FOODPLANTS** Unknown in the wild in Great Britain and Ireland. If it does breed, then probably on herbaceous plants. **FIELD NOTES** Breeding and overwintering are unconfirmed. Feeds at night. Pupates in the ground.

FLAME
Axylia putris

PLATE 60
73.328 (2098)

Common. **FIELD CHARACTERS** Body mixed grey and brown. Dorsal line pale and ill-defined, with a yellow spot on T3 and a variable number of abdominal segments. Subdorsal line pale and ill-defined, edged above with large, dark brown or black marks A1–A2 and A7, or sometimes A1–A8. Subspiracular stripe pale, and expanded and yellowish brown A7–A8. Posterior margin of A8 has a transverse pale stripe. Larva rests with A1–A2 somewhat raised, and A8 is raised to a hump. **HABITATS** Wide variety including farmland, gardens, calcareous grassland, hedgerows and woodland rides. **FOODPLANTS** Various herbaceous plants including Hedge Bedstraw, dandelions, White Dead-nettle, docks, Fat-hen, Hop, Hound's-tongue, Knotgrass, lettuces, Common Nettle and plantains. **FIELD NOTES** Jul–Oct. Feeds at night. Pupates in the ground. Overwinters as a pupa.

FLAME SHOULDER
Ochropleura plecta

PLATE 61
73.329 (2102)

Common. **FIELD CHARACTERS** Body pale yellowish, greenish, pale brown or brown, speckled darker. Dorsal line white, edged with darker shading. Subdorsal line white, comprising dots and dashes. Subspiracular stripe pale, edged above with a white spiracular line that is shaded darker above. A8 is slightly raised. **HABITATS** Wide variety including farmland, gardens, grasslands, heathland, moorland, wetlands and woodland. **FOODPLANTS** Various herbaceous plants including Lady's Bedstraw, Common Chickweed, dandelions, docks, Groundsel, Knotgrass, Ribwort Plantain and Woodruff. Also on cultivated Beet and Garden Lettuce. **FIELD NOTES** Jun–Jul and Sep–Oct in two generations in the south; Aug–Sep in one generation in the north. Feeds at night. Pupates in the ground. Overwinters as a pupa.

BARRED CHESTNUT
Diarsia dahlii

PLATE 61
73.331 (2121)

Local. Widespread in the north. Has increased significantly in abundance in recent decades. **FIELD CHARACTERS** Body pale greyish brown or pale brown, speckled darker, especially laterally, with the dorsal area orangey brown and sometimes dark shading above the subdorsal line on the posterior segments. Pinacula black. Dorsal line pale and often interrupted, and subdorsal line pale, often ill-defined or sometimes absent. A pale transverse line posteriorly on A8. Subspiracular stripe pale and indistinct. Spiracles black. A8 is slightly swollen. **SIMILAR SPECIES** Ingrailed Clay is very similar, but the dark markings above the subdorsal line are edged posteriorly with white streaks. Larvae should be reared to confirm identity if there is any doubt. These two *Diarsia* species have dark or black spiracles, whereas similar larvae in genus *Xestia* (Dotted Clay, Square-spotted Clay, Setaceous Hebrew Character, Triple-spotted Clay and Double Square-spot) have whitish or pale spiracles. **HABITATS** Wooded heathland, moorland, and broadleaf woodland on acid soils. Also limestone pavement (the Burren, Cos Clare and Galway, Ireland). **FOODPLANTS** Various herbaceous and woody plants including Bilberry, birches, Blackthorn, Bramble, dandelions, docks, Hawthorn, plantains and willows. **FIELD NOTES** Sep–early spring. Feeds at night, hiding in leaf litter by day. Pupates in the ground.

PURPLE CLAY
Diarsia brunnea

PLATE 61
73.332 (2122)

Common. **FIELD CHARACTERS** Body orangey brown or brown, and paler dorsally, especially from A3 posteriorly. Dorsal line white and often interrupted and subdorsal line white, and conspicuous on abdominal segments to A8. White or pale subspiracular line T1–T3, and an indistinct subspiracular stripe A1–A9. There is a conspicuous yellowish-white transverse line posteriorly on A8, and A8 is slightly swollen. **HABITATS** Wooded heathland and broadleaf woodland. **FOODPLANTS** Various herbaceous plants before the winter, including docks, figworts and Foxglove. In spring, on woody species including Bilberry, birches, Blackthorn, Bramble, Heather, Hornbeam and willows; and herbaceous species including Bracken and Great Wood-rush. **FIELD NOTES** Aug–May. Feeds at night, hiding in leaf litter by day. Pupates in the ground. Overwinters as a small larva.

INGRAILED CLAY
Diarsia mendica

PLATE 61
73.333 (2123)

Ssp. *mendica* Common. Ssp. *thulei* Shetland. Ssp. *orkneyensis* Orkney. **FIELD CHARACTERS** Body brownish, sometimes mixed greyish. Dorsal line white and often interrupted. Subdorsal line white, with black or brown lozenge-shaped marks above, A1–A8. The marks are edged with white streaks posteriorly, with pale brownish in between. Subspiracular stripe paler than ground colour and spiracles dark. There is a pale transverse line posteriorly on A8. **SIMILAR SPECIES** Barred Chestnut. Also genus *Xestia* (Dotted Clay, Square-spotted Clay, Setaceous Hebrew Character, Triple-spotted Clay and Double Square-spot). **HABITATS** In the south, mainly woodland, and also open habitats including gardens. Elsewhere, most frequent on heathland and moorland. **FOODPLANTS** Various herbaceous and woody plants including

Bilberry, birches, Blackthorn, Bramble, docks, hawthorns, Hazel, Heather, Honeysuckle, Knotgrass, plantains, Primrose, violets and willows. **FIELD NOTES** Aug–May. Feeds at night, hiding by day in leaf litter. Pupates in the ground. Overwinters as a small larva.

SMALL SQUARE-SPOT
Diarsia rubi

PLATE 61
73.334 (2123)

Common. Has declined significantly in abundance in recent decades. **FIELD CHARACTERS** Head brownish, sometimes with paler or darker markings that are rarely contrasting. Body pale yellowish brown, pale brown or pale greyish brown, speckled darker, usually less so above the subdorsal line. Dorsal and subdorsal lines whitish, often incomplete, and thickly edged with dark brown shading. Subspiracular stripe pale, edged whitish above and shaded dark brown along spiracles. Spiracles dark or as body colour, hardly contrasting. **SIMILAR SPECIES** Autumnal Rustic has white spiracles, a brownish head with contrasting darker stripes and a more contrasting pale subspiracular stripe. Fen Square-spot is indistinguishable from Small Square-spot. **HABITATS** Wide variety, preferring wetter habitats such as fens, marshes, and damp pastures and woodlands; also gardens. **FOODPLANTS** Various herbaceous plants including Common Chickweed, dandelions, docks, Foxglove, grasses and plantains. Also low-growing woody species such as Heather and Creeping Willow. **FIELD NOTES** Sep–Apr and Jun–late Jul in the south, and sometimes as far north as south-west Scotland. Usually Aug–May elsewhere in Scotland. Feeds at night. Pupates in the ground.

FEN SQUARE-SPOT
Diarsia florida

PLATE 61
73.335 (2124)

Local. Believed to be a separate species from Small Square-spot, occurring in single-generation populations in East Anglia, northern England and Wales, where Small Square-spot usually has two. **SIMILAR SPECIES** Small Square-spot and Autumnal Rustic. **HABITATS** Bogs and fens. **FOODPLANTS** Unknown in the wild. **FIELD NOTES** Probably similar life history to single-generation populations of Small Square-spot.

RED CHESTNUT
Cerastis rubricosa

PLATE 61
73.336 (2139)

Common. **FIELD CHARACTERS** Body brown, speckled darker and sometimes heavily speckled, with a slight bluish hue. Dorsal line indistinct. Subdorsal line comprises yellow dashes, heavily shaded blackish above and incorporating a white dot A1–A8, and shaded dark brown or blackish below. Subspiracular stripe pale brownish or greyish. **HABITATS** Mainly hedgerows, scrub and broadleaf woodland, and moorland in northern regions. Frequently in gardens and urban parks. **FOODPLANTS** Various herbaceous and woody plants including Bog Asphodel, bedstraws, Bilberry, Common Chickweed, docks, Groundsel, Heath Spotted-orchid and willows. **FIELD NOTES** Late Apr–Jul. Rarely seen in the wild. Feeds at night, remaining on the plant by day. Overwinters as a pupa in the ground.

WHITE-MARKED
Cerastis leucographa

PLATE 61
73.337 (2140)

Local; suspected rare immigrant. **FIELD CHARACTERS** Body green, often with a brownish-yellow hue dorsally, speckled pale green and with diffuse yellow rings between segments. Dorsal line whitish green. Subdorsal line wavy, whitish green and sometimes ill-defined. Curved darker green marks, rather ill-defined, across dorsal area. Subspiracular stripe slightly paler, edged with a white line and shaded darker green above, and indistinct below. Distal ends of prolegs tinged pink. **HABITATS** Hedgerows, scrub and broadleaf woodland. **FOODPLANTS** Found once in the wild resting openly on Rosebay Willowherb by day, which it subsequently ate in captivity. Probably also on other herbaceous and woody plants. **FIELD NOTES** May–Jun. Overwinters as a pupa in the ground.

TRUE LOVER'S KNOT
Lycophotia porphyrea

PLATE 61

73.338 (2118)

Common. **FIELD CHARACTERS** Penultimate instar is variable. Body brown with a white dorsal stripe, often comprising dashes, and usually thickly shaded black or with curved black marks. Subdorsal stripe usually white, or sometimes pale brown or orangey brown, often comprising dashes. Lateral line whitish or less often brownish, comprising dashes, with black marks below. Subspiracular stripe broad, white and often mixed brown or orangey brown. There is a form with a white dorsal line, and without the subdorsal stripe, lateral line and associated black marks. Body markings on the final instar are generally less contrasting or the larva may be much paler. **SIMILAR SPECIES** Southern Chestnut and Heath Rustic. **HABITATS** Heathland and moorland. **FOODPLANTS** Heather and Bell Heather. Also Bilberry and probably Cross-leaved Heath, and has been found on Lodgepole Pine. **FIELD NOTES** Aug–May. Feeds at night. Curiously, the final instar does not feed at all, but may sometimes be found exposed on Heather at night. Pupates on or in the ground. Overwinters as a near fully grown larva.

DOTTED RUSTIC
Rhyacia simulans

PLATE 6

73.339 (2105

Local. Numbers fluctuate greatly over decades. **FIELD CHARACTERS** Body pale brown or greyish brown, sparsely covered with moderately long, dark hairs. Dorsal line white, broadly edged with dark shading. Subdorsal line white with blackish marks above A1–A8. Subspiracular stripe wavy and pale brown, with dark brown crescents above, A1–A8, each crescent edged blackish posteriorly. **SIMILAR SPECIES** Large Yellow Underwing (brown form) and Lunar Yellow Underwing have shorter pale hairs and a subdorsal stripe. Lunar Yellow Underwing differs from the other two species in having a dorsal stripe. **HABITATS** Wide variety of open habitats on calcareous and clay soils, including coastal grassland, pastures old quarries and open woodland. **FOODPLANTS** Unknown in the wild. Probably herbaceous plants. **FIELD NOTES** Sep–Apr. Pupation site unknown.

NORTHERN RUSTIC
Standfussiana lucernea

PLATE 6

73.341 (210

Local. **FIELD CHARACTERS** Body grey or dark grey, sometimes tinged greenish. Subdorsal line pale brown or whitish, sometimes indistinct, with whitish marks and dark shading above A1–A7 or A8. In paler examples the pale marks may be triangular and more extensive across the dorsum. **HABITATS** Cliffs and rocky places, old quarries, and scree and ravines in mountains. **FOODPLANTS** Various herbaceous plants including Harebell, Primrose, Purple Saxifrage, Sheep's-fescu and other grasses, and Biting Stonecrop. **FIELD NOTES** Oct–May. Feeds at nigh often sitting outstretched on rocks near foodplants. Pupates in the ground. Overwinters as a small larva.

LARGE YELLOW UNDERWING
Noctua pronuba

PLATE (

73.342 (210

Common; immigrant. Has increased significantly in abundance in recent decades. **FIELD CHARACTERS** Body varying shades of grey, brown or green, with short pale hairs. Grey and brown forms are speckled darker, with a pale or whitish dorsal line. Subdorsal stripe pale or whitish A1–A8, complete or comprising dashes, and edged with black marks above. Markings are reduced or inconspicuous on the thoracic segments. The green form is pale green or yellowish green, with lines and stripes hardly contrasting, and black marks obvious. **SIMILAR SPECIES** Dotted Rustic and Lunar Yellow Underwing. **HABITATS** Ubiquitous. **FOODPLANTS** Wide variety of wild and cultivated herbaceous plants including Cabbage, docks, Foxglove, Pot Marigold, Mind-your-own-business, cultivated Spinach, and grasses including Cock's-foot and meadow-grasses. Also on buds and foliage of various woody plants in spring, and recorded in nurseries on conifer seedlings. **FIELD NOTES** Aug–May. Feeds at night, hiding undergrou by day. Often encountered as a large larva during the winter. Pupates in a chamber in the ground.

BROAD-BORDERED YELLOW UNDERWING
Noctua fimbriata

PLATE 62
73.343 (2110)

Common. Has increased significantly in abundance in recent decades. **FIELD CHARACTERS** Body pale yellowish brown or pale greyish brown, speckled darker. Dorsal line and subspiracular stripe pale. Round black spots surrounding or adjacent to white spiracles A1–A6 or down to A8 **HABITATS** Mainly broadleaf woodland. Also wooded heathland, parkland and scrub. **FOODPLANTS** Wide variety of herbaceous and woody plants including Blackthorn, Bramble, Cleavers, dead-nettles, Broad-leaved Dock, Hawthorn, Common Nettle, Primrose, Wild Privet, Sycamore (seedlings), willows and Field Wood-rush. **FIELD NOTES** Sep–Apr. Feeds at night. At first feeds on herbaceous species, then overwinters on the ground, and n spring may climb up woody plants to feed. Pupates in the ground.

LUNAR YELLOW UNDERWING
Noctua orbona

PLATE 62
73.344 (2108)

Nb. Has declined from widespread through the twentieth century and is now very local. **FIELD CHARACTERS** Body pale brown or pale greyish brown. Dorsal stripe pale, and subdorsal stripe pale, edged above with conspicuous black marks A1–A8, these being less conspicuous or absent T1–T3. Subspiracular stripe broad, and pale or whitish. **SIMILAR SPECIES** Dotted Rustic and Large Yellow Underwing. **HABITATS** Calcareous, heathy and sandy grasslands and woodland rides, usually in dry situations, and where grazing is light or absent. **FOODPLANTS** Variety of mainly low-growing herbaceous plants including own Bent, Meadow Buttercup, Reed Canary-grass, Common Chickweed, Creeping Cinquefoil, ock's-foot, couches, Cowslip, Tufted Hair-grass, Wavy Hair-grass and Sheep's-fescue. **FIELD NOTES** Sep– te Apr, or occasionally May. Feeds at night, and throughout the winter in mild conditions. Pupates in e ground.

LESSER YELLOW UNDERWING
Noctua comes

PLATE 62
73.345 (2109)

Common. **FIELD CHARACTERS** Head various shades of brown, with the impression of the subdorsal line and subspiracular stripe continuing through it. Body pale brown or pale greyish brown, speckled darker. Dorsal line pale and often faint, except on T1–T2. Subdorsal line and adjoining lateral stripe on abdominal segments pale, ill-defined and fading anteriorly, with black triangular marks above A7–A8, and sometimes A5–A6. A pale transverse line posteriorly on A8. Subspiracular stripe broad, and pale brown or whitish. Spiracles white, sometimes edged above with dark brown marks. **SIMILAR ECIES** Cabbage Moth, Langmaid's Yellow Underwing, Lesser Broad-bordered Yellow Underwing and thic. **HABITATS** Ubiquitous. **FOODPLANTS** Wide variety of herbaceous and woody plants including ches, Blackthorn, Bog-myrtle, Bramble, Broom, Wild Cabbage, Broad-leaved Dock, Foxglove, Hawthorn, ather, Common Knapweed, Common Nettle, Red Valerian and willows. **FIELD NOTES** Aug–May, or Jun. ds at night, and throughout winter. In spring may climb up woody plants to feed on buds and leaves. oates in the ground.

LEAST YELLOW UNDERWING
Noctua interjecta

PLATE 62
73.346 (2112)

Ssp. *caliginosa* Common. Has expanded its range in the north. **FIELD CHARACTERS** Head pale greyish, sometimes slightly striped darker and lighter. Body pale yellowish or whitish, speckled grey, with strongly contrasting black pinacula. Dorsal line and subdorsal and subspiracular stripes whitish or yellowish. Spiracles black or white, clearly ringed black. **HABITATS** Open habitats including fens, hedgerows and sand dunes, and occasionally gardens, with a preference for damper conditions. **FOODPLANTS** Variety of herbaceous and woody plants including Bramble, White Dead-nettle, docks, grasses, hawthorns, nmon Mallow, Meadowsweet, Primrose, Barren Strawberry, Marsh Valerian and willows. **FIELD ES** Sep–May. Feeds at night. In spring may climb up woody plants to feed. Pupates in the ground.

LANGMAID'S YELLOW UNDERWING
Noctua janthina

PLATE 62
73.347 (2110a)

Immigrant and probable colonist. **SIMILAR SPECIES** Cabbage Moth, Lesser Yellow Underwing, Lesser Broad-bordered Yellow Underwing and Gothic. **HABITATS, FOODPLANTS and FIELD NOTES** Life history unknown in the wild in Great Britain; likely to be similar to Lesser Broad-bordered Yellow Underwing.

LESSER BROAD-BORDERED YELLOW UNDERWING
PLATE 62

Noctua janthe

73.348 (2111

Common. **FIELD CHARACTERS** Head brown, with the impression of the subdorsal line and subspiracular stripe running through it. Body pale brown or pale greyish brown, speckled darker. Dorsal line pale, usually complete or broken into long dashes. Subdorsal line and adjoining lateral stripe, if present, pale, ill-defined and fading anteriorly. Black squarish marks subdorsally A7–A8, sometimes with small black marks A5–A6. Subspiracular stripe pale, sometimes shaded blackish above. Spiracles white, or sometimes dark. There is an orangey brown form that lacks black marks. **SIMILAR SPECIES** Cabbage moth, Lesser Yellow Underwing, Langmaid' Yellow Underwing and Gothic. **HABITATS** Wide variety including gardens, grasslands, hedgerows and woodland, excluding those at high altitude. **FOODPLANTS** Wide variety of herbaceous and woody plants including birches, Blackthorn, Bramble, White Dead-nettle, Broad-leaved Dock, elms, grasses, hawthorns, Hazel, Lords-and-Ladies, Scentless Mayweed, oraches, Primrose, stitchworts and willows. **FIEL NOTES** Sep–May. Feeds at night. In spring climbs up woody plants to feed. Pupates in the ground.

STOUT DART
Spaelotis ravida

PLATE 6
73.349 (211

pRDB. In severe decline, with few reports since 2000. **FIELD CHARACTERS** Body brown, speckled darker. Dorsal line whitish, sometimes broken into dashes. Subdorsal line whitish, comprising dashes that are slightly inward-pointing posteriorly. Above the subdorsal dashes are blackish marks A2–A6, more extensive on A7–A8. There are diagonal stripes, pale greyish below and orangey brown above, running from the spiracular stripe to the subdorsal line each crossing two segments. Subspiracular stripe wavy, and whitish or pale brownish. **HABITATS** Prefers fens, marshes and damp pastures; also found in drier grasslands. **FOODPLANTS** On herbaceous plants in captivity. **FIELD NOTES** Nov or Dec–May. Unknow in the wild. Pupates in the ground.

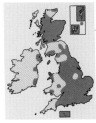

GREAT BROCADE
Eurois occulta

PLATE
73.350 (213

Nb; immigrant. Resident in the central and western Highlands of Scotland. **FIELD CHARACTERS** Body reddish or purplish brown, usually speckled blackish Dorsal line pale and indistinct. Extensive dark grey shading across the dorsal area is sometimes present. Subdorsal line usually indistinct, comprising inwa pointing pale dashes with black shading above, and black wedge-shaped marks A7–A8. Subspiracular stripe whitish, or sometimes whitish mixed yellowish or orangey, or pinkish, and edged above by a whitish-yellow line. Black smudges around the spiracles A1–A8, or more extensive black shading **HABITATS** Scrub in bogs and river valleys, and in coniferous plantations and broadleaf woodland. **FOODPLANTS** Mainly Bog-myrtle. Also a variety of herbaceous and woody plants including Bilberry, birches, Blackthorn, Bramble, docks, Heather, Primrose and willows. **FIELD NOTES** Sep–May. In Apr small larvae can be found by day high among leafless woody plants. As larvae grow, feeding becomes nocturnal. Pupates in the ground.

DOUBLE DART
Graphiphora augur

PLATE 62
73.351 (2114)

Common. Has declined severely in abundance in the south of its range. Remains widespread in Scotland and Ireland. **FIELD CHARACTERS** Body mottled brown or greyish brown, with conspicuous whitish subdorsal dots T3–A8. Transverse black bars or a stripe across the dorsum A7–A9. Subspiracular stripe slightly paler, edged with a white line and black shading above, especially around the spiracles. Spiracles whitish or orangey. **HABITATS** Fens, gardens, wet grassland, marshes, parkland, scrub and broadleaf woodland. **FOODPLANTS** Variety of woody plants including birches, Blackthorn, elms, hawthorns, oaks and willows. Also on Broad-leaved Dock. **FIELD NOTES** Aug–May. Feeds at night among scrubby vegetation. Pupates in the ground.

GREEN ARCHES
Anaplectoides prasina

PLATE 62
73.352 (2138)

Common. Has increased significantly in abundance in recent decades. **FIELD CHARACTERS** Body pinkish brown, greyish brown or grey, speckled darker. Dorsal line whitish or yellow, and subdorsal line whitish or yellow, ill-defined and sometimes hardly visible, with darker speckling often concentrated across the dorsal area into shield- or V-shaped markings or a dark band. There is a pale transverse stripe across the posterior of A8, sometimes shaded black anteriorly. Subspiracular stripe pale, usually shaded black above, and this may surround the spiracles, which are white. **HABITATS** Broadleaf and carr woodlands. **FOODPLANTS** Variety of herbaceous and woody plants including Alder, Bilberry, birches, Bramble, docks, Honeysuckle, Knotgrass, Dog's Mercury, Primrose and willows. **FIELD NOTES** Aug–May. Feeds at night and throughout the winter in mild conditions. Pupates in the ground.

DOTTED CLAY
Xestia baja

PLATE 63
73.353 (2130)

Common. Currently more frequent in the northern half of Great Britain. **FIELD CHARACTERS** Body pale brown or grey and speckled darker, sometimes densely. Dorsal line whitish, and complete or ill-defined. Subdorsal line whitish, and wavy or comprising inward-pointing dashes. Dark speckling concentrated into broad V-shaped marks, or less often shield-shaped marks, across the dorsum A1–A6, and into triangular marks A7–A8. Subspiracular stripe pale brown or pale grey. There is a pale transverse stripe across the posterior of A8. Spiracles whitish. **SIMILAR SPECIES** Barred Chestnut and Ingrailed Clay. Square-spotted Clay has a conspicuous, white spiracular line. Setaceous Hebrew Character has orange smudges below the subdorsal line and orange or yellow within the subspiracular stripe. Less well-marked individuals could be confused with Triple-spotted Clay, which has only slight orangey-brown marks below the subdorsal line and no or very little orange within the subspiracular stripe. Well-marked forms of Double Square-spot have dark shield- or X-shaped dorsal markings and black triangular subdorsal marks, and an ill-defined subspiracular stripe. Dotted Clay, Triple-spotted Clay and Double Square-spot are particularly difficult to distinguish and should be reared to confirm identity. **HABITATS** Damp grassland, heathland, scrub on calcareous grassland, wooded margins of waterbodies, and carr woodland. **FOODPLANTS** Various herbaceous plants in autumn and woody plants in spring, including Bilberry, birches, Blackthorn, Bog-myrtle, Bramble, Bird Cherry, Common Chickweed, dandelions, Red Dead-nettle, docks, Hawthorn, heathers, Hornbeam, Common Nettle, Primrose, roses and willows. **FIELD NOTES** Aug–May. Feeds at night. Pupates in the ground. Overwinters as a small larva.

SQUARE-SPOTTED CLAY
Xestia stigmatica

PLATE 63
73.354 (2131)

Nb. Increasing its range in eastern England. **FIELD CHARACTERS** Body brown or greyish brown, speckled darker. Dorsal and subdorsal lines whitish, and often broken into dots and dashes. Darker speckling is concentrated above and adjacent to the subdorsal line on abdominal segments, with increasing intensity posteriorly, forming blackish triangular marks A7–A8 and sometimes also A5–A6. Subspiracular stripe slightly paler, edged above with a white spiracular line. Spiracles whitish. **SIMILAR SPECIES** Barred Chestnut,

Ingrailed Clay, Dotted Clay, Setaceous Hebrew Character, Triple-spotted Clay and Double Square-spot. **HABITATS** Long-established broadleaf woodland on chalk, clay or gravel, especially in woodland edge habitats; also in more recent plantations. **FOODPLANTS** Has been found feeding on Bramble, Creeping Buttercup, Cleavers, Lords-and-Ladies, Dog's Mercury, Common Nettle, Oxlip, Cow Parsley and Primrose. Probably on a wide variety of herbaceous plants. **FIELD NOTES** Sep–mid-Apr. Rarely observed in the wild. Pupates in the ground, remaining as a larva within a cocoon for several weeks before pupating. Overwinters as a small larva.

NEGLECTED RUSTIC
Xestia castanea

PLATE 63

73.355 (2132)

Local. Has declined significantly in abundance in recent decades. **FIELD CHARACTERS** Body pale brown, speckled darker and with black pinacula, or green, speckled paler and with dark green pinacula. Dorsal line pale, and subspiracular stripe white, or pale edged white above. Subdorsal line absent in green form; in the brown form, pale and present only on T1 and anal flap. **SIMILAR SPECIES** Brown form: Flounced Chestnut. Green form: Black Rustic, Deep-brown Dart, Northern Deep-brown Dart and Setaceous Hebrew Character. **HABITATS** Raised bogs, heathland, wooded heathland and moorland. **FOODPLANTS** Recorded on Bog-myrtle, Cowberry, Cross-leaved Heath, Heather, Bell Heather and Grey Willow. **FIELD NOTES** Oct–Jun. Feeds at night. Pupates in the ground, remaining as a larva for several weeks before pupating. Overwinters as a small larva.

HEATH RUSTIC
Xestia agathina

PLATE 63

73.356 (2135)

Ssp. *agathina* Local. Has declined severely in abundance in recent decades, especially in lowland England. Ssp. *hebridicola* Hebrides. **FIELD CHARACTERS** Body green or brown. Dorsal stripe pale, thickened centrally on each segment and sometimes broken into dashes, or sometimes obscure. Subdorsal stripe white, edged above with black marks T3–A9, with a white pinaculum on each segment that is anteriorly placed close to or sometimes joining the stripe. Subspiracular stripe whitish or pale, mixed brown or orangey brown in the brown form, or with yellow in the green form. **SIMILAR SPECIES** Southern Chestnut and True Lover's Knot. **HABITATS** Heathland and moorland. **FOODPLANTS** Mainly on Heather, preferring tall plants. Also recorded on Bell Heather. **FIELD NOTES** Late Sep–Jun. Feeds at night. Pupates in the ground.

SQUARE-SPOT RUSTIC
Xestia xanthographa

PLATE 63

73.357 (2134)

Common. **FIELD CHARACTERS** Body pale brown, speckled darker. Dorsal line pale yellowish, sometimes whitish, edged with a dark line and shaded dark beyond. Subdorsal line white, edged above with black marks with curved margins, A1–A9. Lateral area two-tone, pale brown or orangey brown above and dark brown below. Subspiracular stripe pale brown, sometimes speckled orangey brown. **SIMILAR SPECIES** Grayling. The Clay group of wainscots (see *Separating external-feeding wainscots* table, pp. 424–7) usually have a narrower dorsal line, and black marks or a stripe with the margin parallel to the subdorsal line. Six-striped Rustic is indistinguishable in the field. **HABITATS** Grasslands of all types, including in gardens. Not found at high altitude. **FOODPLANTS** Mainly herbaceous plants, especially grasses, and also on woody plants. Recorded on Hedge Bedstraw, Bilberry, Common Chickweed, Cleavers, Crowberry, White Dead-nettle, docks, Hawthorn, Annual Meadow-grass, oaks, plantains and Creeping Willow. **FIELD NOTES** Sep–May. Feeds at night, and throughout the winter in mild weather. In spring it may feed on woody plants. Makes a cocoon in the ground, remaining as a larva for several weeks before pupating.

SIX-STRIPED RUSTIC
Xestia sexstrigata

PLATE 63
73.358 (2133)

Common. **SIMILAR SPECIES** Grayling, the Clay group of wainscots (see *Separating external-feeding wainscots* table, pp. 424–7) and Square-spot Rustic. **HABITATS** Fens, marshes, damp pastures and damp woodland; also drier habitats including gardens and urban parks, and calcareous grassland. **FOODPLANTS** Rarely recorded owing to similarity with Square-spot Rustic. Has been found on Hedge Bedstraw, Bluebell, Bramble, Water Figwort and Ribwort Plantain. **FIELD NOTES** Sep–Apr. Feeds at night, and throughout the winter in mild weather. Pupates in the ground, remaining as a larva for several weeks before pupating.

SETACEOUS HEBREW CHARACTER
Xestia c-nigrum

PLATE 63
73.359 (2126)

Common; immigrant. **FIELD CHARACTERS** Body brown, greyish brown or grey, speckled darker, or green and speckled paler. The brown or grey forms have a pale or whitish dorsal line, often interrupted and obscured. Subdorsal line pale and often ill-defined, wavy or comprising inward-pointing dashes, and edged above with black dashes A1–A8. These dashes are progressively more prominent posteriorly. Below the subdorsal line are a series of orange smudges. Subspiracular stripe pale brown or pale grey, mixed yellowish or orangey. In some examples the black marks are reduced and the speckling concentrated across the dorsal area in faint shield- or X-shaped markings. The green form has dorsal and subdorsal lines comprising pale dots, and a pale subspiracular stripe edged white above. Spiracles white. **SIMILAR SPECIES** Brown/grey forms: Barred Chestnut, Ingrailed Clay, Dotted Clay, Square-spotted Clay, Triple-spotted Clay and Double Square-spot. Green form: Black Rustic, Deep-brown Dart, Northern Deep-brown Dart and Neglected Rustic. **HABITATS** Wide variety of lowland habitats, and especially common in farmland and gardens. **FOODPLANTS** Variety of herbaceous and woody plants including Bilberry, burdocks, Common Chickweed, dandelions, White Dead-nettle, docks, Flixweed, Groundsel, Garden Lettuce, mulleins, Common Nettle, plantains, Creeping Willow and willowherbs. **FIELD NOTES** Phenology complex, with larvae likely to be found Jun–May in two generations. Feeds at night, and throughout the winter in mild weather. Pupates in the ground.

TRIPLE-SPOTTED CLAY
Xestia ditrapezium

PLATE 63
73.360 (2127)

Local. Most frequent in the west, and local and infrequent elsewhere. **FIELD CHARACTERS** Body grey or brown, speckled darker. Dorsal line whitish, consisting of dots and dashes. Subdorsal line consisting of a series of whitish dashes, edged above with black dashes, and a black triangular mark on A8. Below the subdorsal line are small orangey-brown marks. A pale transverse stripe posteriorly on A8. Spiracles white. **SIMILAR SPECIES** Barred Chestnut, Ingrailed Clay, Dotted Clay, Square-spotted Clay, Setaceous Hebrew Character and Double Square-spot. **HABITATS** Prefers open, damp areas, especially within fens, and broadleaf and carr woodlands. Sometimes in gardens and urban parks. **FOODPLANTS** Variety of herbaceous plants in autumn, and on herbaceous and woody species in spring. Recorded on birches, Blackthorn, Bramble, dandelions, docks, Dogwood, Hawthorn, Hazel, Honeysuckle, Primrose and willows. **FIELD NOTES** Aug–May. Feeds at night. Pupates in the ground.

DOUBLE SQUARE-SPOT
Xestia triangulum

PLATE 63
73.361 (2128)

Common. **FIELD CHARACTERS** Body brown or greyish brown, speckled darker. Dorsal line whitish or pale, and sometimes ill-defined. Subdorsal line whitish, comprising white dots, or ill-defined, and edged with black triangular marks above A7–A8. The subdorsal line may sometimes be absent. In some examples the black marks are reduced and the speckling concentrated across the dorsal area in shield- or X-shaped markings, while in others there are few defining marks at all. Spiracular stripe slightly paler, and ill-defined. Spiracles pale, often bright white. **SIMILAR SPECIES** Barred Chestnut, Ingrailed Clay, Dotted Clay, Square-spotted Clay, Setaceous Hebrew Character and Triple-spotted Clay. **HABITATS** Wide variety including hedgerows, meadows and pastures in river valleys, and woodland. **FOODPLANTS** Various herbaceous plants in autumn, and on herbaceous and woody plants in spring. Recorded on birches, Blackthorn, Bramble, buttercups, dandelions, docks, forget-me-nots, Hawthorn, Hazel, Cow Parsley, plantains, Primrose, Raspberry, Wood Spurge, traveller's-joys and willows. **FIELD NOTES** Aug–May. Feeds at night. Pupates in the ground.

ASHWORTH'S RUSTIC
Xestia ashworthii

PLATE 63
73.362 (2129)

Na. **FIELD CHARACTERS** Body grey or dark grey, or sometimes paler with a greenish tinge, with velvet-black subdorsal marks T2–A9. **HABITATS** Mountain and hill slopes, and old quarries, preferring patchy vegetation on rocky ground and among scree. It seems to require exposed rock of any sort, especially acidic rocks. **FOODPLANTS** Has been observed in the wild eating Heather, Bell Heather and sometimes Bilberry. In captivity, larvae readily eat Heath Bedstraw, which is present at most sites and likely to be an important foodplant in the wild. **FIELD NOTES** Aug–May or Jun. Feeds mainly at night, and may bask and feed in sunshine or sit exposed in mild conditions. Pupates in the ground, remaining as a larva within a cocoon for several weeks before pupating.

NORTHERN DART
Xestia alpicola

PLATE 63
73.363 (2125)

Ssp. *alpina* Na. **FIELD CHARACTERS** Body brown, paler dorsally, with pale dorsal and subdorsal lines that are interrupted and may be ill-defined. Paler below the level of the spiracles. **HABITATS** High slopes and tops of mountains, but has been found at much lower levels on the Outer Hebrides, Orkney and Shetland. However, there are no recent records from the Outer Hebrides or Shetland. **FOODPLANTS** Crowberry in the wild, but possibly also on other woody shrubs including Bearberry, Cowberry and Heather. **FIELD NOTES** Has a two-year life cycle. In year one larvae feed Jul–Aug, remaining small. In year two they feed spring–autumn, reaching penultimate instar. In year three they feed Mar–late May or Jun, becoming fully fed. Populations tend to be synchronised, and fully fed larvae and pupae can be found in early summer of even years under lichens and mosses growing on the ground. Pupates in moss without making a cocoon.

ROSY MARSH MOTH
Coenophila subrosea

PLATE 63
73.364 (2115)

RDB. There are five populations in Wales and one in Cumbria. **FIELD CHARACTERS** Body striped, coloured from dorsum to subspiracular region in the following order: yellow or white, grey, yellow or white, orange, grey, and white or white with pale pink. **HABITATS** Bogs and mires. **FOODPLANTS** Bilberry (leaves), Bog-myrtle (catkins, buds and leaves), Bog-rosemary, cottongrasses (flowers) and Crowberry. **FIELD NOTES** Late Aug–mid-Jun. Feeds at night, and throughout the winter in mild conditions. Pupates in a near-vertical silken cocoon among moss.

AUTUMNAL RUSTIC
Eugnorisma glareosa

PLATE 64
73.365 (2117)

Common. Has declined severely in abundance in recent decades. **FIELD CHARACTERS** Head pale brownish or brown, rarely greyish brown, usually with two contrasting darker stripes. Body pale brown or brown, with black pinacula. Dorsal and subdorsal lines pale, with a broad, pale subspiracular stripe that often contrasts with the ground colour. Spiracles white. **SIMILAR SPECIES** Small Square-spot and Fen Square-spot. **HABITATS** Lightly grazed calcareous grassland, rough grassland, heathland and moorland. Also recorded in fens, vegetated shingle and open woodland. **FOODPLANTS** Various herbaceous and woody plants including bedstraws, birches, Bluebell, Broom, docks, Heather, Bell Heather, plantains, Sheep's-fescue, Common Vetch and Creeping Willow. **FIELD NOTES** Oct–May. Feeds at night. Pupates in the ground.

PLAIN CLAY
Eugnorisma depuncta

PLATE 64
73.366 (2103)

Nb. Widespread only in the central and eastern Scottish Highlands. **FIELD CHARACTERS** Body grey or pale brown, speckled dark brown or black, the speckling less dense across the dorsum and denser laterally. Dorsal line whitish and usually ill-defined. Subspiracular stripe broad and white or cream, edged above with black or dark brown marks surrounding white spiracles. **HABITATS** Broadleaf woodland, often in river valleys. **FOODPLANTS** Various herbaceous plants including Cowslip, dead-nettles, docks, Common Nettle, Primrose, Common Sorrel, Sheep's Sorrel and stitchworts. **FIELD NOTES** Sep–Jun. Feeds at night. Hatches from the egg in Sep and immediately enters winter diapause without feeding. Pupates in a cocoon in the ground.

COUSIN GERMAN
Protolampra sobrina

PLATE 64
73.367 (2116)

Na. **FIELD CHARACTERS** Body brown, speckled darker, the speckling usually less dense subdorsally and denser laterally. Dorsal line white, incorporating a white spot on most or all segments. Subdorsal line white and ill-defined, with less obvious whitish spots. Subspiracular stripe whitish mixed with pale reddish brown. Pinacula blackish and spiracles black. **SIMILAR SPECIES** Yellow-line Quaker. **HABITATS** Woodland from c. 200m upwards, dominated by birches, with ground cover of Bilberry and Heather. Prefers open situations with young birches. **FOODPLANTS** Bilberry and Heather; also birches and Eared Willow in spring. **FIELD NOTES** Late Aug–Jun. Feeds at night. May climb woody vegetation to feed on young leaves in spring. Pupates in the ground or in moss.

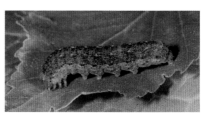

Cousin German larva

GOTHIC
Naenia typica

PLATE 64
73.368 (2136)

Local. Has declined significantly in abundance in recent decades. **FIELD CHARACTERS** Head brown, with the impression of the subdorsal line and subspiracular stripe running through it. Body pale greyish brown, speckled darker. Dorsal line pale and often ill-defined. Subdorsal line white, often reduced to a few dashes, usually with a distinct white dot above on T3 and another, less obvious, on T2, and edged above with black triangular marks A7–A8. The subdorsal line may sometimes be absent. Subspiracular stripe pale, distinctly wavy, and edged above with a black line incorporating usually orange spiracles. **SIMILAR SPECIES** Cabbage Moth, Lesser Yellow Underwing, Langmaid's Yellow Underwing and Lesser Broad-bordered Yellow Underwing. **HABITATS** Wide variety including gardens, wet grassland, hedgerows, marshes, waste ground and damp woodland. **FOODPLANTS** Various wild and cultivated herbaceous and woody plants including Apple, Auricula, Blackthorn, Butterfly-bush, Common Comfrey, Cleavers, geraniums, Groundsel, Hawthorn, Honeysuckle, Pear, sowthistles and willowherbs. **FIELD NOTES** Jul–Apr. Feeds at night, and larvae are gregarious when small. Pupates in the ground.

NOLIDAE BLACK ARCHES, SILVER-LINES AND NYCTEOLINE MOTHS

There are about 1,400 species described worldwide and eight species resident in the British Isles. All pupate in a boat-shaped or spindle-shaped cocoon. Larvae in the subfamily Nolinae lack prolegs on A3 and have tufts of hair arising from verrucae.

Short-cloaked Moth ×1.5

Scarce Silver-lines ×1.25

Kent Black Arches larva

Green Silver-lines larva

NOLINAE

SMALL BLACK ARCHES
Meganola strigula

PLATE 64
74.001 (2075)

Na. Has contracted in range in recent decades and is now confined as a breeding species to central southern England. **FIELD CHARACTERS** Body pale orange, pale pinkish or whitish, with orange verrucae and tufts of grey, yellow, pale brown and black hairs. There are longer, backward-pointing hairs on A9. Dorsal stripe pale yellow or whitish, with a black saddle on A3. Prolegs absent on A3. **HABITATS** Wooded commons with mature oaks and long-established broadleaf woodland. **FOODPLANT** Pedunculate Oak. **FIELD NOTES** Aug–early Jun. Feeds from the undersurface of a leaf, leaving the upper surface intact. Pupates in a boat-shaped cocoon that is cryptic on the bark on which it is constructed. Overwinters as a small larva.

KENT BLACK ARCHES
Meganola albula

PLATE 64
74.002 (2076)

Nb; suspected immigrant. Increasing its range inland. **FIELD CHARACTERS** Body pale grey or whitish, with yellowish verrucae and tufts of long and short grey hairs. In pale examples there is a grey or white dorsal line, and a subdorsal stripe comprising black marks on a variable number of abdominal segments. In darker examples there is a white dorsal line, and the black marks are present T1–T3 and are more extensive across the dorsum including the dorsal line A3–A7. Prolegs absent on A3. **HABITATS** Cliffs, grasslands, heathland, saltmarshes and open woodland. Also gardens and urban parks. **FOODPLANTS** Bramble, Dewberry, Raspberry and Wild Strawberry. **FIELD NOTES** Aug–late May or Jun. Overwinters when small. Pupates on a vertical plant stem, in a cryptic, spindle-shaped cocoon made of silk and plant fibres.

SHORT-CLOAKED MOTH
Nola cucullatella

PLATE 64
74.003 (2077)

Common. **FIELD CHARACTERS** Body dark grey with grey or orange verrucae and tufts of grey hairs. Dorsal line white, interrupted or narrowed by black shading on the dorsum on A1, A3, A5 and A7, and with more extensive white coloration between. Prolegs absent on A3. **HABITATS** Gardens, hedgerows, scrub and woodland. **FOODPLANTS** Mainly Blackthorn and Hawthorn. Also recorded on Apple, cherries, Midland Hawthorn and Pear. **FIELD NOTES** Aug–Jun. Overwinters when small in a crevice, covered with a few strands of silk. Pupates on a twig in a cryptic boat-shaped cocoon constructed from silk and bark.

LEAST BLACK ARCHES
Nola confusalis

PLATE 64
74.004 (2078)

Local. Has increased significantly in range and abundance in recent decades. **FIELD CHARACTERS** Body pale yellowish brown, sometimes extensively coloured dark reddish brown or blackish on dorsum on T2, A1, A3, A5 and A7–A9, and laterally on A1 and A3–A7. Orange verrucae, and tufts of hairs whitish. The hairs are long anteriorly and posteriorly. Dorsal line dark reddish brown or black. Prolegs absent on A3. **HABITATS** Gardens and urban parks, hedgerows, orchards, parkland, well-wooded countryside and woodland. **FOODPLANTS** Various broadleaf trees, including Apple, Beech, Downy Birch, Blackthorn, Buckthorn, Small-leaved Lime, and Pedunculate and Holm oaks. **FIELD NOTES** Jun–Aug. Pupates on a tree in a cryptic boat-shaped cocoon constructed from silk and bark or lichen. Overwinters as a pupa.

CHLOEPHORINAE

SCARCE SILVER-LINES
Bena bicolorana

PLATE 64
74.007 (2421)

Local. Has expanded its range recently in the north. **FIELD CHARACTERS** Body yellowish green, speckled white, with a green dorsal stripe that is edged yellow. There are diagonal yellow lines laterally, each extending across two segments. Spiracular line yellow, and thicker T1–T2. T2 is raised to a hump with two points. **HABITATS** Parkland and broadleaf woodland. Also well-wooded heathland. **FOODPLANTS** Mainly Pedunculate and Sessile oaks. Also recorded on Beech, and Downy and Silver birches. **FIELD NOTES** Aug–May. Overwinters when small, adjacent to a bud. Pupates in a boat-shaped cocoon under a leaf.

GREEN SILVER-LINES
Pseudoips prasinana

PLATE 64
74.008 (2422)

Ssp. *britannica* Common. A lowland species in the north. Has increased significantly in abundance in recent decades. **FIELD CHARACTERS** Body pale green with numerous yellow dots, dashes and pinacula. There is a transverse yellow stripe anteriorly on T1, and a yellow subdorsal stripe. Anal claspers, which rest outstretched, have noticeable red streaks. **HABITATS** Wooded heathland and broadleaf woodland. **FOODPLANTS** Mainly Beech, Downy and Silver birches, and Pedunculate and Sessile oaks. Also recorded on Alder, Aspen, Blackthorn, Sweet Chestnut, elms, Hazel and limes. **FIELD NOTES** Jul–Sep. Pupates in a strong boat-shaped cocoon under a leaf. Overwinters as a pupa.

OAK NYCTEOLINE
Nycteola revayana

PLATE 64
74.009 (2423)

Local. Usually occurs in small numbers. **FIELD CHARACTERS** Body green, with a sparse covering of long white hairs. A dark dorsal vessel is visible and there is a faint, pale green spiracular line. **HABITATS** Mainly parkland and broadleaf woodland. Also well-wooded heathland and other woodland areas. **FOODPLANTS** Holm and Pedunculate oaks, and probably Sessile Oak. Has been recorded on larches. **FIELD NOTES** May–Jul; occasionally Sep. Pupates in a tough boat-shaped cocoon under an oak leaf. Overwinters as an adult.

CREAM-BORDERED GREEN PEA
Earias clorana

PLATE 64
74.011 (2418)

Nb; suspected immigrant. **FIELD CHARACTERS** Body pale purplish brown, sometimes tinged greenish, with prominent pinacula that are often black on the dorsum on T2–T3, A2 and A8, and most prominent on A2 and A8. Dorsal line dark within a cream band with irregular margins, the band being constricted on A2 and A8. **HABITATS** Wide variety, including soft cliffs, fens, floodplains, wet heathland, marshes, reedbeds, vegetated shingle, and carr and damp woodlands. **FOODPLANTS** Willows, including Hybrid Crack-willow, Osier, and Almond, Creeping, Goat, Grey and White willows. **FIELD NOTES** Jun–Aug, and sometimes Sep–Oct. Feeds within spun terminal shoots. Pupates in a tough boat-shaped cocoon attached to a stem. Overwinters as a pupa.

CHECKLIST OF THE MACRO-MOTHS AND BUTTERFLIES OF GREAT BRITAIN AND IRELAND

This taxonomic list of macro-moths and butterflies follows Agassiz, Beavan & Heckford (2013) and subsequent corrigenda and amendments. It excludes species from the sections dealing with adventives and questionable records. Species in **bold** type are covered in the species accounts in this field guide.

Two types of brackets appear in the checklist. Conventional brackets ( ) are used around the author and date if the species is no longer in the genus in which it was first described. Square brackets [ ] are used around an author's name when the description was originally published anonymously and their identity was established by subsequent research. Square brackets are used around a date if the original publication was undated and the date was established by subsequent research. Square brackets are also used around an actual date of publication if that is different from the date stated within the publication.

HEPIALIDAE

3.001	**Orange Swift**	*Triodia sylvina* (Linnaeus, 1761)
3.002	**Common Swift**	*Korscheltellus lupulina* (Linnaeus, 1758)
3.003	**Map-winged Swift**	*Korscheltellus fusconebulosa* (De Geer, 1778)
3.004	**Gold Swift**	*Phymatopus hecta* (Linnaeus, 1758)
3.005	**Ghost Moth**	*Hepialus humuli* (Linnaeus, 1758)

COSSIDAE

50.001	**Goat Moth**	*Cossus cossus* (Linnaeus, 1758)
50.002	**Leopard Moth**	*Zeuzera pyrina* (Linnaeus, 1761)
50.003	**Reed Leopard**	*Phragmataecia castaneae* (Hübner, 1790)

SESIIDAE

52.001	**Raspberry Clearwing**	*Pennisetia hylaeiformis* (Laspeyres, 1801)
52.002	**Hornet Moth**	*Sesia apiformis* (Clerck, 1759)
52.003	**Lunar Hornet Moth**	*Sesia bembeciformis* (Hübner, [1806])
52.004	Dusky Clearwing	*Paranthrene tabaniformis* (Rottemburg, 1775)
52.005	**Welsh Clearwing**	*Synanthedon scoliaeformis* (Borkhausen, 1789)
52.006	**White-barred Clearwing**	*Synanthedon spheciformis* ([Denis & Schiffermüller], 1775)
52.007	**Large Red-belted Clearwing**	*Synanthedon culiciformis* (Linnaeus, 1758)
52.008	**Red-tipped Clearwing**	*Synanthedon formicaeformis* (Esper, 1782)
52.009	**Sallow Clearwing**	*Synanthedon flaviventris* (Staudinger, 1883)
52.010	**Orange-tailed Clearwing**	*Synanthedon andrenaeformis* (Laspeyres, 1801)
52.011	**Red-belted Clearwing**	*Synanthedon myopaeformis* (Borkhausen, 1789)
52.012	**Yellow-legged Clearwing**	*Synanthedon vespiformis* (Linnaeus, 1761)
52.013	**Currant Clearwing**	*Synanthedon tipuliformis* (Clerck, 1759)
52.014	**Six-belted Clearwing**	*Bembecia ichneumoniformis* ([Denis & Schiffermüller], 1775)
52.015	**Fiery Clearwing**	*Pyropteron chrysidiformis* (Esper, 1782)
52.016	**Thrift Clearwing**	*Pyropteron muscaeformis* (Esper, 1783)

LIMACODIDAE

53.001	**Festoon**	*Apoda limacodes* (Hufnagel, 1766)
53.002	**Triangle**	*Heterogenea asella* ([Denis & Schiffermüller], 1775)

ZYGAENIDAE

54.001	**Scarce Forester**	*Jordanita globulariae* (Hübner, 1793)
54.002	**Forester**	*Adscita statices* (Linnaeus, 1758)
54.003	**Cistus Forester**	*Adscita geryon* (Hübner, [1813])
54.004	**Transparent Burnet**	*Zygaena purpuralis* (Brünnich, 1763)
54.005	**Slender Scotch Burnet**	*Zygaena loti* ([Denis & Schiffermüller], 1775)
54.006	**Scotch Burnet/Mountain Burnet**	*Zygaena exulans* (Hohenwarth, 1792)
54.007	**New Forest Burnet**	*Zygaena viciae* ([Denis & Schiffermüller], 1775)
54.008	**Six-spot Burnet**	*Zygaena filipendulae* (Linnaeus, 1758)
54.009	**Narrow-bordered Five-spot Burnet**	*Zygaena lonicerae* (Scheven, 1777)
54.010	**Five-spot Burnet**	*Zygaena trifolii* (Esper, 1783)

PAPILIONIDAE

56.001	Apollo/Crimson-ringed	*Parnassius apollo* (Linnaeus, 1758)
56.002	Scarce Swallowtail	*Iphiclides podalirius* (Linnaeus, 1758)
56.003	**Swallowtail**	***Papilio machaon*** Linnaeus, 1758

HESPERIIDAE

57.001	**Dingy Skipper**	***Erynnis tages*** (Linnaeus, 1758)
57.002	**Grizzled Skipper**	***Pyrgus malvae*** (Linnaeus, 1758)
57.003	Large Chequered Skipper	*Heteropterus morpheus* (Pallas, 1771)
57.004	**Chequered Skipper**	***Carterocephalus palaemon*** (Pallas, 1771)
57.005	**Essex Skipper**	***Thymelicus lineola*** (Ochsenheimer, 1808)
57.006	**Small Skipper**	***Thymelicus sylvestris*** (Poda, 1761)
57.007	**Lulworth Skipper**	***Thymelicus acteon*** (Rottemburg, 1775)
57.008	**Silver-spotted Skipper**	***Hesperia comma*** (Linnaeus, 1758)
57.009	**Large Skipper**	***Ochlodes sylvanus*** (Esper, 1779)

PIERIDAE

58.001	**Wood White**	***Leptidea sinapis*** (Linnaeus, 1758)
58.002	**Cryptic Wood White**	***Leptidea juvernica*** Williams, 1946
58.003	**Orange-tip**	***Anthocharis cardamines*** (Linnaeus, 1758)
58.004	Dappled White	*Euchloe simplonia* (Freyer, 1828)
58.005	Black-veined White	*Aporia crataegi* (Linnaeus, 1758)
58.006	**Large White**	***Pieris brassicae*** (Linnaeus, 1758)
58.007	**Small White**	***Pieris rapae*** (Linnaeus, 1758)
58.008	**Green-veined White**	***Pieris napi*** (Linnaeus, 1758)
58.009	Bath White	*Pontia daplidice* (Linnaeus, 1758)
58.010	**Clouded Yellow**	***Colias croceus*** (Geoffroy, 1785)
58.011	Pale Clouded Yellow	*Colias hyale* (Linnaeus, 1758)
58.012	Berger's Clouded Yellow	*Colias alfacariensis* Ribbe, 1905
58.013	**Brimstone**	***Gonepteryx rhamni*** (Linnaeus, 1758)
58.014	Cleopatra	*Gonepteryx cleopatra* (Linnaeus, 1767)

NYMPHALIDAE

59.001	Monarch/Milkweed	*Danaus plexippus* (Linnaeus, 1758)
59.002	**Wall**	***Lasiommata megera*** (Linnaeus, 1767)
59.003	**Speckled Wood**	***Pararge aegeria*** (Linnaeus, 1758)
59.004	**Large Heath**	***Coenonympha tullia*** (Müller, 1764)
59.005	**Small Heath**	***Coenonympha pamphilus*** (Linnaeus, 1758)
59.006	Arran Brown	*Erebia ligea* (Linnaeus, 1758)
59.007	**Mountain Ringlet/ Small Mountain Ringlet**	***Erebia epiphron*** (Knoch, 1783)
59.008	**Scotch Argus**	***Erebia aethiops*** (Esper, 1777)
59.009	**Ringlet**	***Aphantopus hyperantus*** (Linnaeus, 1758)
59.010	**Meadow Brown**	***Maniola jurtina*** (Linnaeus, 1758)
59.011	**Gatekeeper/Hedge Brown**	***Pyronia tithonus*** (Linnaeus, 1771)
59.012	**Marbled White**	***Melanargia galathea*** (Linnaeus, 1758)
59.013	**Grayling**	***Hipparchia semele*** (Linnaeus, 1758)
59.014	**Pearl-bordered Fritillary**	***Boloria euphrosyne*** (Linnaeus, 1758)
59.015	**Small Pearl-bordered Fritillary**	***Boloria selene*** ([Denis & Schiffermüller], 1775)
59.016	Queen of Spain Fritillary	*Issoria lathonia* (Linnaeus, 1758)
59.017	**Silver-washed Fritillary**	***Argynnis paphia*** (Linnaeus, 1758)
59.018	Mediterranean Fritillary	*Argynnis pandora* ([Denis & Schiffermüller], 1775)
59.019	**Dark Green Fritillary**	***Argynnis aglaja*** (Linnaeus, 1758)
59.020	**High Brown Fritillary**	***Argynnis adippe*** ([Denis & Schiffermüller], 1775)
59.021	**White Admiral**	***Limenitis camilla*** (Linnaeus, 1764)
59.022	**Purple Emperor**	***Apatura iris*** (Linnaeus, 1758)
59.023	**Red Admiral**	***Vanessa atalanta*** (Linnaeus, 1758)
59.024	**Painted Lady**	***Vanessa cardui*** (Linnaeus, 1758)
59.025	American Painted Lady	*Vanessa virginiensis* (Drury, 1773)
59.026	**Peacock**	***Aglais io*** (Linnaeus, 1758)
59.027	**Small Tortoiseshell**	***Aglais urticae*** (Linnaeus, 1758)
59.028	Camberwell Beauty	*Nymphalis antiopa* (Linnaeus, 1758)
59.029	Large Tortoiseshell	*Nymphalis polychloros* (Linnaeus, 1758)
59.030	Scarce Tortoiseshell	*Nymphalis xanthomelas* ([Denis & Schiffermüller], 1775)
59.031	**Comma**	***Polygonia c-album*** (Linnaeus, 1758)
59.032	European Map	*Araschnia levana* (Linnaeus, 1758)
59.033	**Marsh Fritillary**	***Euphydryas aurinia*** (Rottemburg, 1775)
59.034	**Glanville Fritillary**	***Melitaea cinxia*** (Linnaeus, 1758)

| 59.035 | Spotted Fritillary | *Melitaea didyma* (Esper, 1779) |
| 59.036 | **Heath Fritillary** | ***Melitaea athalia*** (Rottemburg, 1775) |

RIODINIDAE
| 60.001 | **Duke of Burgundy** | ***Hamearis lucina*** (Linnaeus, 1758) |

LYCAENIDAE
61.001	**Small Copper**	***Lycaena phlaeas*** (Linnaeus, 1761)
61.002	Large Copper	*Lycaena dispar* (Haworth, 1803)
61.003	**Brown Hairstreak**	***Thecla betulae*** (Linnaeus, 1758)
61.004	**Purple Hairstreak**	***Favonius quercus*** (Linnaeus, 1758)
61.005	**Green Hairstreak**	***Callophrys rubi*** (Linnaeus, 1758)
61.006	**White-letter Hairstreak**	***Satyrium w-album*** (Knoch, 1782)
61.007	**Black Hairstreak**	***Satyrium pruni*** (Linnaeus, 1758)
61.008	**Long-tailed Blue**	***Lampides boeticus*** (Linnaeus, 1767)
61.009	Lang's Short-tailed Blue	*Leptotes pirithous* (Linnaeus, 1767)
61.010	**Small Blue**	***Cupido minimus*** (Fuessly, 1775)
61.011	Short-tailed Blue	*Cupido argiades* (Pallas, 1771)
61.012	**Holly Blue**	***Celastrina argiolus*** (Linnaeus, 1758)
61.013	**Large Blue**	***Phengaris arion*** (Linnaeus, 1758)
61.014	**Silver-studded Blue**	***Plebejus argus*** (Linnaeus, 1758)
61.015	**Brown Argus**	***Aricia agestis*** ([Denis & Schiffermüller], 1775)
61.016	**Northern Brown Argus**	***Aricia artaxerxes*** (Fabricius, 1793)
61.017	Mazarine Blue	*Cyaniris semiargus* (Rottemburg, 1775)
61.018	**Common Blue**	***Polyommatus icarus*** (Rottemburg, 1775)
61.019	**Adonis Blue**	***Polyommatus bellargus*** (Rottemburg, 1775)
61.020	**Chalk Hill Blue**	***Polyommatus coridon*** (Poda, 1761)

DREPANIDAE
65.001	**Scalloped Hook-tip**	***Falcaria lacertinaria*** (Linnaeus, 1758)
65.002	**Oak Hook-tip**	***Watsonalla binaria*** (Hufnagel, 1767)
65.003	**Barred Hook-tip**	***Watsonalla cultraria*** (Fabricius, 1775)
65.004	**Dusky Hook-tip**	***Drepana curvatula*** (Borkhausen, 1790)
65.005	**Pebble Hook-tip**	***Drepana falcataria*** (Linnaeus, 1758)
65.006	**Scarce Hook-tip**	***Sabra harpagula*** (Esper, 1786)
65.007	**Chinese Character**	***Cilix glaucata*** (Scopoli, 1763)
65.008	**Peach Blossom**	***Thyatira batis*** (Linnaeus, 1758)
65.009	**Buff Arches**	***Habrosyne pyritoides*** (Hufnagel, 1766)
65.010	**Figure of Eighty**	***Tethea ocularis*** (Linnaeus, 1767)
65.011	**Poplar Lutestring**	***Tethea or*** ([Denis & Schiffermüller], 1775)
65.012	**Satin Lutestring**	***Tetheella fluctuosa*** (Hübner, [1803])
65.013	**Common Lutestring**	***Ochropacha duplaris*** (Linnaeus, 1761)
65.014	**Oak Lutestring**	***Cymatophorina diluta*** ([Denis & Schiffermüller], 1775)
65.015	**Frosted Green**	***Polyploca ridens*** (Fabricius, 1787)
65.016	**Yellow Horned**	***Achlya flavicornis*** (Linnaeus, 1758)

LASIOCAMPIDAE
66.001	**December Moth**	***Poecilocampa populi*** (Linnaeus, 1758)
66.002	**Pale Eggar**	***Trichiura crataegi*** (Linnaeus, 1758)
66.003	**Lackey**	***Malacosoma neustria*** (Linnaeus, 1758)
66.004	**Ground Lackey**	***Malacosoma castrensis*** (Linnaeus, 1758)
66.005	**Small Eggar**	***Eriogaster lanestris*** (Linnaeus, 1758)
66.006	**Grass Eggar**	***Lasiocampa trifolii*** ([Denis & Schiffermüller], 1775)
66.007	**Oak Eggar**	***Lasiocampa quercus*** (Linnaeus, 1758)
66.008	**Fox Moth**	***Macrothylacia rubi*** (Linnaeus, 1758)
66.009	**Pine-tree Lappet**	***Dendrolimus pini*** (Linnaeus, 1758)
66.010	**Drinker**	***Euthrix potatoria*** (Linnaeus, 1758)
66.011	Small Lappet	*Phyllodesma ilicifolia* (Linnaeus, 1758)
66.012	**Lappet**	***Gastropacha quercifolia*** (Linnaeus, 1758)

ENDROMIDAE
| 67.001 | **Kentish Glory** | ***Endromis versicolora*** (Linnaeus, 1758) |

SATURNIIDAE
| 68.001 | **Emperor Moth** | ***Saturnia pavonia*** (Linnaeus, 1758) |

SPHINGIDAE
| 69.001 | **Lime Hawk-moth** | ***Mimas tiliae*** (Linnaeus, 1758) |
| 69.002 | **Eyed Hawk-moth** | ***Smerinthus ocellata*** (Linnaeus, 1758) |

69.003	Poplar Hawk-moth	*Laothoe populi* (Linnaeus, 1758)
69.004	Convolvulus Hawk-moth	*Agrius convolvuli* (Linnaeus, 1758)
69.005	Death's-head Hawk-moth	*Acherontia atropos* (Linnaeus, 1758)
69.006	Privet Hawk-moth	*Sphinx ligustri* Linnaeus, 1758
69.007	Pine Hawk-moth	*Sphinx pinastri* Linnaeus, 1758
69.008	Narrow-bordered Bee Hawk-moth	*Hemaris tityus* (Linnaeus, 1758)
69.009	Broad-bordered Bee Hawk-moth	*Hemaris fuciformis* (Linnaeus, 1758)
69.010	Humming-bird Hawk-moth	*Macroglossum stellatarum* (Linnaeus, 1758)
69.011	Oleander Hawk-moth	*Daphnis nerii* (Linnaeus, 1758)
69.012	Willowherb Hawk-moth	*Proserpinus proserpina* (Pallas, 1772)
69.013	Spurge Hawk-moth	*Hyles euphorbiae* (Linnaeus, 1758)
69.014	Bedstraw Hawk-moth	*Hyles gallii* (Rottemburg, 1775)
69.015	Striped Hawk-moth	*Hyles livornica* (Esper, [1804])
69.016	Elephant Hawk-moth	*Deilephila elpenor* (Linnaeus, 1758)
69.017	Small Elephant Hawk-moth	*Deilephila porcellus* (Linnaeus, 1758)
69.018	Silver-striped Hawk-moth	*Hippotion celerio* (Linnaeus, 1758)

GEOMETRIDAE

70.001	Ochraceous Wave	*Idaea serpentata* (Hufnagel, 1767)
70.002	Purple-bordered Gold	*Idaea muricata* (Hufnagel, 1767)
70.003	Bright Wave	*Idaea ochrata* (Scopoli, 1763)
70.004	Least Carpet	*Idaea rusticata* ([Denis & Schiffermüller], 1775)
70.005	Silky Wave	*Idaea dilutaria* (Hübner, [1799])
70.006	Dwarf Cream Wave	*Idaea fuscovenosa* (Goeze, 1781)
70.007	Isle of Wight Wave	*Idaea humiliata* (Hufnagel, 1767)
70.008	Small Dusty Wave	*Idaea seriata* (Schrank, 1802)
70.009	Satin Wave	*Idaea subsericeata* (Haworth, 1809)
70.010	Dotted Border Wave	*Idaea sylvestraria* (Hübner, [1799])
70.011	Single-dotted Wave	*Idaea dimidiata* (Hufnagel, 1767)
70.012	Treble Brown Spot	*Idaea trigeminata* (Haworth, 1809)
70.013	Small Fan-footed Wave	*Idaea biselata* (Hufnagel, 1767)
70.014	Weaver's Wave	*Idaea contiguaria* (Hübner, [1799])
70.015	Small Scallop	*Idaea emarginata* (Linnaeus, 1758)
70.016	Riband Wave	*Idaea aversata* (Linnaeus, 1758)
70.017	Portland Ribbon Wave	*Idaea degeneraria* (Hübner, [1799])
70.018	Plain Wave	*Idaea straminata* (Borkhausen, 1794)
70.019	Lewes Wave	*Scopula immorata* (Linnaeus, 1758)
70.020	Sub-angled Wave	*Scopula nigropunctata* (Hufnagel, 1767)
70.021	Lace Border	*Scopula ornata* (Scopoli, 1763)
70.022	Tawny Wave	*Scopula rubiginata* (Hufnagel, 1767)
70.023	Mullein Wave	*Scopula marginepunctata* (Goeze, 1781)
70.024	Small Blood-vein	*Scopula imitaria* (Hübner, [1799])
70.025	Lesser Cream Wave	*Scopula immutata* (Linnaeus, 1758)
70.026	Smoky Wave	*Scopula ternata* Schrank, 1802
70.027	Cream Wave	*Scopula floslactata* (Haworth, 1809)
70.028	Rosy Wave	*Scopula emutaria* (Hübner, [1809])
70.029	Blood-vein	*Timandra comae* Schmidt, 1931
70.030	Dingy Mocha	*Cyclophora pendularia* (Clerck, 1759)
70.031	Mocha	*Cyclophora annularia* (Fabricius, 1775)
70.032	Birch Mocha	*Cyclophora albipunctata* (Hufnagel, 1767)
70.033	Blair's Mocha	*Cyclophora puppillaria* (Hübner, [1799])
70.034	Jersey Mocha	*Cyclophora ruficiliaria* (Herrich-Schäffer, 1855)
70.035	False Mocha	*Cyclophora porata* (Linnaeus, 1767)
70.036	Maiden's Blush	*Cyclophora punctaria* (Linnaeus, 1758)
70.037	Clay Triple-lines	*Cyclophora linearia* (Hübner, [1799])
70.038	Vestal	*Rhodometra sacraria* (Linnaeus, 1767)
70.039	Oblique Striped	*Phibalapteryx virgata* (Hufnagel, 1767)
70.040	Lead Belle	*Scotopteryx mucronata* (Scopoli, 1763)
70.041	July Belle	*Scotopteryx luridata* (Hufnagel, 1767)
70.042	Spanish Carpet	*Scotopteryx peribolata* (Hübner, [1817])
70.043	Chalk Carpet	*Scotopteryx bipunctaria* ([Denis & Schiffermüller], 1775
70.044	Fortified Carpet	*Scotopteryx moeniata* (Scopoli, 1763)
70.045	Shaded Broad-bar	*Scotopteryx chenopodiata* (Linnaeus, 1758)
70.046	Oblique Carpet	*Orthonama vittata* (Borkhausen, 1794)
70.047	Gem	*Nycterosea obstipata* (Fabricius, 1794)
70.048	Red Carpet	*Xanthorhoe decoloraria* (Esper, [1806])
70.049	Garden Carpet	*Xanthorhoe fluctuata* (Linnaeus, 1758)

70.050	Balsam Carpet	*Xanthorhoe biriviata* (Borkhausen, 1794)
70.051	Red Twin-spot Carpet	*Xanthorhoe spadicearia* ([Denis & Schiffermüller], 1775)
70.052	Dark-barred Twin-spot Carpet	*Xanthorhoe ferrugata* (Clerck, 1759)
70.053	Flame Carpet	*Xanthorhoe designata* (Hufnagel, 1767)
70.054	Silver-ground Carpet	*Xanthorhoe montanata* ([Denis & Schiffermüller], 1775)
70.055	Large Twin-spot Carpet	*Xanthorhoe quadrifasiata* (Clerck, 1759)
70.056	Royal Mantle	*Catarhoe cuculata* (Hufnagel, 1767)
70.057	Ruddy Carpet	*Catarhoe rubidata* ([Denis & Schiffermüller], 1775)
70.058	Many-lined	*Costaconvexa polygrammata* (Borkhausen, 1794)
70.059	Yellow Shell	*Camptogramma bilineata* (Linnaeus, 1758)
70.060	Small Argent & Sable	*Epirrhoe tristata* (Linnaeus, 1758)
70.061	Common Carpet	*Epirrhoe alternata* (Müller, 1764)
70.062	Wood Carpet	*Epirrhoe rivata* (Hübner, [1813])
70.063	Galium Carpet	*Epirrhoe galiata* ([Denis & Schiffermüller], 1775)
70.064	Cloaked Carpet	*Euphyia biangulata* (Haworth, 1809)
70.065	Sharp-angled Carpet	*Euphyia unangulata* (Haworth, 1809)
70.066	Shoulder Stripe	*Earophila badiata* ([Denis & Schiffermüller], 1775)
70.067	Streamer	*Anticlea derivata* ([Denis & Schiffermüller], 1775)
70.068	Beautiful Carpet	*Mesoleuca albicillata* (Linnaeus, 1758)
70.069	Dark Spinach	*Pelurga comitata* (Linnaeus, 1758)
70.070	Mallow	*Larentia clavaria* (Haworth, 1809)
70.071	Yellow-ringed Carpet	*Entephria flavicinctata* (Hübner, [1813])
70.072	Grey Mountain Carpet	*Entephria caesiata* ([Denis & Schiffermüller], 1775)
70.073	White-banded Carpet	*Spargania luctuata* ([Denis & Schiffermüller], 1775)
70.074	July Highflyer	*Hydriomena furcata* (Thunberg, 1784)
70.075	May Highflyer	*Hydriomena impluviata* ([Denis & Schiffermüller], 1775)
70.076	Ruddy Highflyer	*Hydriomena ruberata* (Freyer, [1831])
70.077	Pine Carpet	*Pennithera firmata* (Hübner, [1822])
70.078	Chestnut-coloured Carpet	*Thera cognata* (Thunberg, 1792)
70.079	Spruce Carpet	*Thera britannica* (Turner, 1925)
70.080	Fir Carpet	*Thera vetustata* ([Denis & Schiffermüller], 1775)
70.081	Grey Pine Carpet	*Thera obeliscata* (Hübner, [1787])
70.082	Juniper Carpet	*Thera juniperata* (Linnaeus, 1758)
70.083	Cypress Carpet	*Thera cupressata* (Geyer, [1831])
70.084	Blue-bordered Carpet	*Plemyria rubiginata* ([Denis & Schiffermüller], 1775)
70.085	Barred Yellow	*Cidaria fulvata* (Forster, 1771)
70.086	Broken-barred Carpet	*Electrophaes corylata* (Thunberg, 1792)
70.087	Purple Bar	*Cosmorhoe ocellata* (Linnaeus, 1758)
70.088	Netted Carpet	*Eustroma reticulata* ([Denis & Schiffermüller], 1775)
70.089	Phoenix	*Eulithis prunata* (Linnaeus, 1758)
70.090	Chevron	*Eulithis testata* (Linnaeus, 1761)
70.091	Northern Spinach	*Eulithis populata* (Linnaeus, 1758)
70.092	Spinach	*Eulithis mellinata* (Fabricius, 1787)
70.093	Barred Straw	*Gandaritis pyraliata* ([Denis & Schiffermüller], 1775)
70.094	Small Phoenix	*Ecliptopera silaceata* ([Denis & Schiffermüller], 1775)
70.095	Red-green Carpet	*Chloroclysta siterata* (Hufnagel, 1767)
70.096	Autumn Green Carpet	*Chloroclysta miata* (Linnaeus, 1758)
70.097	Common Marbled Carpet	*Dysstroma truncata* (Hufnagel, 1767)
70.098	Dark Marbled Carpet	*Dysstroma citrata* (Linnaeus, 1761)
70.099	Beech-green Carpet	*Colostygia olivata* ([Denis & Schiffermüller], 1775)
70.100	Green Carpet	*Colostygia pectinataria* (Knoch, 1781)
70.101	Mottled Grey	*Colostygia multistrigaria* (Haworth, 1809)
70.102	Striped Twin-spot Carpet	*Coenotephria salicata* (Hübner, [1799])
70.103	Water Carpet	*Lampropteryx suffumata* ([Denis & Schiffermüller], 1775)
70.104	Devon Carpet	*Lampropteryx otregiata* (Metcalfe, 1917)
70.105	Northern Winter Moth	*Operophtera fagata* (Scharfenberg, 1805)
70.106	Winter Moth	*Operophtera brumata* (Linnaeus, 1758)
70.107	November Moth	*Epirrita dilutata* ([Denis & Schiffermüller], 1775)
70.108	Pale November Moth	*Epirrita christyi* (Allen, 1906)
70.109	Autumnal Moth	*Epirrita autumnata* (Borkhausen, 1794)
70.110	Small Autumnal Moth	*Epirrita filigrammaria* (Herrich-Schäffer, 1846)
70.111	Small White Wave	*Asthena albulata* (Hufnagel, 1767)
70.112	Dingy Shell	*Euchoeca nebulata* (Scopoli, 1763)
70.113	Waved Carpet	*Hydrelia sylvata* ([Denis & Schiffermüller], 1775)
70.114	Small Yellow Wave	*Hydrelia flammeolaria* (Hufnagel, 1767)
70.115	Welsh Wave	*Venusia cambrica* Curtis, 1839
70.116	Blomer's Rivulet	*Venusia blomeri* (Curtis, 1832)

70.117	Drab Looper	*Minoa murinata* (Scopoli, 1763)
70.118	Brown Scallop	*Philereme vetulata* ([Denis & Schiffermüller], 1775)
70.119	Dark Umber	*Philereme transversata* (Hufnagel, 1767)
70.120	Argent & Sable	*Rheumaptera hastata* (Linnaeus, 1758)
70.121	Scallop Shell	*Rheumaptera undulata* (Linnaeus, 1758)
70.122	Scarce Tissue	*Rheumaptera cervinalis* (Scopoli, 1763)
70.123	Tissue	*Triphosa dubitata* (Linnaeus, 1758)
70.124	Barberry Carpet	*Pareulype berberata* ([Denis & Schiffermüller], 1775)
70.125	Slender-striped Rufous	*Coenocalpe lapidata* (Hübner, [1809])
70.126	Small Waved Umber	*Horisme vitalbata* ([Denis & Schiffermüller], 1775)
70.127	Fern	*Horisme tersata* ([Denis & Schiffermüller], 1775)
70.128	Pretty Chalk Carpet	*Melanthia procellata* ([Denis & Schiffermüller], 1775)
70.129	Dentated Pug	*Anticollix sparsata* (Treitschke, 1828)
70.130	Chimney Sweeper	*Odezia atrata* (Linnaeus, 1758)
70.131	Twin-spot Carpet	*Mesotype didymata* (Linnaeus, 1758)
70.132	Rivulet	*Perizoma affinitata* (Stephens, 1831)
70.133	Small Rivulet	*Perizoma alchemillata* (Linnaeus, 1758)
70.134	Barred Rivulet	*Perizoma bifaciata* (Haworth, 1809)
70.135	Heath Rivulet	*Perizoma minorata* (Treitschke, 1828)
70.136	Pretty Pinion	*Perizoma blandiata* ([Denis & Schiffermüller], 1775)
70.137	Grass Rivulet	*Perizoma albulata* ([Denis & Schiffermüller], 1775)
70.138	Sandy Carpet	*Perizoma flavofasciata* (Thunberg, 1792)
70.139	Barred Carpet	*Martania taeniata* (Stephens, 1831)
70.140	Marsh Carpet	*Gagitodes sagittata* (Fabricius, 1787)
70.141	Double-striped Pug	*Gymnoscelis rufifasciata* (Haworth, 1809)
70.142	V-Pug	*Chloroclystis v-ata* (Haworth, 1809)
70.143	Sloe Pug	*Pasiphila chloerata* (Mabille, 1870)
70.144	Green Pug	*Pasiphila rectangulata* (Linnaeus, 1758)
70.145	Bilberry Pug	*Pasiphila debiliata* (Hübner, [1817])
70.146	Haworth's Pug	*Eupithecia haworthiata* Doubleday, 1856
70.147	Slender Pug	*Eupithecia tenuiata* (Hübner, [1813])
70.148	Maple Pug	*Eupithecia inturbata* (Hübner, [1817])
70.149	Cloaked Pug	*Eupithecia abietaria* (Goeze, 1781)
70.150	Toadflax Pug	*Eupithecia linariata* ([Denis & Schiffermüller], 1775)
70.151	Foxglove Pug	*Eupithecia pulchellata* Stephens, 1831
70.152	Channel Islands Pug	*Eupithecia ultimaria* Boisduval, 1840
70.153	Lead-coloured Pug	*Eupithecia plumbeolata* (Haworth, 1809)
70.154	Marsh Pug	*Eupithecia pygmaeata* (Hübner, [1799])
70.155	Netted Pug	*Eupithecia venosata* (Fabricius, 1787)
70.156	Brindled Pug	*Eupithecia abbreviata* Stephens, 1831
70.157	Oak-tree Pug	*Eupithecia dodoneata* Guenée, [1858]
70.158	Juniper Pug	*Eupithecia pusillata* ([Denis & Schiffermüller], 1775)
70.159	Cypress Pug	*Eupithecia phoeniceata* (Rambur, 1834)
70.160	White-spotted Pug	*Eupithecia tripunctaria* Herrich-Schäffer, 1852
70.161	Golden-rod Pug	*Eupithecia virgaureata* Doubleday, 1861
70.162	Dwarf Pug	*Eupithecia tantillaria* Boisduval, 1840
70.163	Larch Pug	*Eupithecia lariciata* (Freyer, 1841)
70.164	Fletcher's Pug/Pauper Pug	*Eupithecia egenaria* Herrich-Schäffer, 1848
70.165	Pimpinel Pug	*Eupithecia pimpinellata* (Hübner, [1813])
70.166	Plain Pug	*Eupithecia simpliciata* (Haworth, 1809)
70.167	Goosefoot Pug	*Eupithecia sinuosaria* (Eversmann, 1848)
70.168	Narrow-winged Pug	*Eupithecia nanata* (Hübner, [1813])
70.169	Angle-barred Pug	*Eupithecia innotata* (Hufnagel, 1767)
70.170	Marbled Pug	*Eupithecia irriguata* (Hübner, [1813])
70.171	Ochreous Pug	*Eupithecia indigata* (Hübner, [1813])
70.172	Thyme Pug	*Eupithecia distinctaria* Herrich-Schäffer, 1848
70.173	Lime-speck Pug	*Eupithecia centaureata* ([Denis & Schiffermüller], 1775)
70.174	Pinion-spotted Pug	*Eupithecia insigniata* (Hübner, 1790)
70.175	Triple-spotted Pug	*Eupithecia trisignaria* Herrich-Schäffer, 1848
70.176	Edinburgh Pug	*Eupithecia intricata* (Zetterstedt, 1839)
70.177	Satyr Pug	*Eupithecia satyrata* (Hübner, [1813])
70.178	Scarce Pug	*Eupithecia extensaria* (Freyer, 1844)
70.179	Wormwood Pug	*Eupithecia absinthiata* (Clerck, 1759)
70.180	Bleached Pug	*Eupithecia expallidata* Doubleday, 1856
70.181	Valerian Pug	*Eupithecia valerianata* (Hübner, [1813])
70.182	Currant Pug	*Eupithecia assimilata* Doubleday, 1856

70.183	**Common Pug**	*Eupithecia vulgata* (Haworth, 1809)
70.184	**Mottled Pug**	*Eupithecia exiguata* (Hübner, [1813])
70.185	**Campanula Pug**	*Eupithecia denotata* (Hübner, [1813])
70.186	**Yarrow Pug**	*Eupithecia millefoliata* Rössler, 1866
70.187	**Tawny Speckled Pug**	*Eupithecia icterata* (Villers, 1789)
70.188	**Bordered Pug**	*Eupithecia succenturiata* (Linnaeus, 1758)
70.189	**Shaded Pug**	*Eupithecia subumbrata* ([Denis & Schiffermüller], 1775)
70.190	**Grey Pug**	*Eupithecia subfuscata* (Haworth, 1809)
70.191	**Manchester Treble-bar**	*Carsia sororiata* (Hübner, [1813])
70.192	**Treble-bar**	*Aplocera plagiata* (Linnaeus, 1758)
70.193	**Lesser Treble-bar**	*Aplocera efformata* (Guenée, [1858])
70.194	Purple Treble-bar	*Aplocera praeformata* (Hübner, [1826])
70.195	**Streak**	*Chesias legatella* ([Denis & Schiffermüller], 1775)
70.196	**Broom-tip**	*Chesias rufata* (Fabricius, 1775)
70.197	**Grey Carpet**	*Lithostege griseata* ([Denis & Schiffermüller], 1775)
70.198	**Seraphim**	*Lobophora halterata* (Hufnagel, 1767)
70.199	**Small Seraphim**	*Pterapherapteryx sexalata* (Retzius, 1783)
70.200	**Yellow-barred Brindle**	*Acasis viretata* (Hübner, [1799])
70.201	**Barred Tooth-striped**	*Trichopteryx polycommata* ([Denis & Schiffermüller], 1775)
70.202	**Early Tooth-striped**	*Trichopteryx carpinata* (Borkhausen, 1794)
70.203	**Orange Underwing**	*Archiearis parthenias* (Linnaeus, 1761)
70.204	**Light Orange Underwing**	*Boudinotiana notha* (Hübner, [1803])
70.205	**Magpie**	*Abraxas grossulariata* (Linnaeus, 1758)
70.206	**Clouded Magpie**	*Abraxas sylvata* (Scopoli, 1763)
70.207	**Clouded Border**	*Lomaspilis marginata* (Linnaeus, 1758)
70.208	**Scorched Carpet**	*Ligdia adustata* ([Denis & Schiffermüller], 1775)
70.209	**Ringed Border**	*Stegania cararia* (Hübner, 1790)
70.210	Dorset Cream Wave	*Stegania trimaculata* (Villers, 1789)
70.211	**Peacock Moth**	*Macaria notata* (Linnaeus, 1758)
70.212	**Sharp-angled Peacock**	*Macaria alternata* ([Denis & Schiffermüller], 1775)
70.213	**Dusky Peacock**	*Macaria signaria* (Hübner, [1809])
70.214	**Tawny-barred Angle**	*Macaria liturata* (Clerck, 1759)
70.215	**V-Moth**	*Macaria wauaria* (Linnaeus, 1758)
70.216	**Netted Mountain Moth**	*Macaria carbonaria* (Clerck, 1759)
70.217	**Rannoch Looper**	*Macaria brunneata* (Thunberg, 1784)
70.218	**Latticed Heath**	*Chiasmia clathrata* (Linnaeus, 1758)
70.219	Tamarisk Peacock	*Chiasmia aestimaria* (Hübner, [1809])
70.220	Frosted Yellow	*Isturgia limbaria* (Fabricius, 1775)
70.221	**Little Thorn**	*Cepphis advenaria* (Hübner, 1790)
70.222	**Brown Silver-line**	*Petrophora chlorosata* (Scopoli, 1763)
70.223	**Barred Umber**	*Plagodis pulveraria* (Linnaeus, 1758)
70.224	**Scorched Wing**	*Plagodis dolabraria* (Linnaeus, 1767)
70.225	**Horse Chestnut**	*Pachycnemia hippocastanaria* (Hübner, [1799])
70.226	**Brimstone Moth**	*Opisthograptis luteolata* (Linnaeus, 1758)
70.227	**Bordered Beauty**	*Epione repandaria* (Hufnagel, 1767)
70.228	**Dark Bordered Beauty**	*Epione vespertaria* (Linnaeus, 1767)
70.229	**Speckled Yellow**	*Pseudopanthera macularia* (Linnaeus, 1758)
70.230	**Orange Moth**	*Angerona prunaria* (Linnaeus, 1758)
70.231	**Lilac Beauty**	*Apeira syringaria* (Linnaeus, 1758)
70.232	**Large Thorn**	*Ennomos autumnaria* (Werneburg, 1859)
70.233	**August Thorn**	*Ennomos quercinaria* (Hufnagel, 1767)
70.234	**Canary-shouldered Thorn**	*Ennomos alniaria* (Linnaeus, 1758)
70.235	**Dusky Thorn**	*Ennomos fuscantaria* (Haworth, 1809)
70.236	**September Thorn**	*Ennomos erosaria* ([Denis & Schiffermüller], 1775)
70.237	**Early Thorn**	*Selenia dentaria* (Fabricius, 1775)
70.238	**Lunar Thorn**	*Selenia lunularia* (Hübner, [1788])
70.239	**Purple Thorn**	*Selenia tetralunaria* (Hufnagel, 1767)
70.240	**Scalloped Hazel**	*Odontopera bidentata* (Clerck, 1759)
70.241	**Scalloped Oak**	*Crocallis elinguaria* (Linnaeus, 1758)
70.242	**Dusky Scalloped Oak**	*Crocallis dardoinaria* Donzel, 1840
70.243	**Swallow-tailed Moth**	*Ourapteryx sambucaria* (Linnaeus, 1758)
70.244	**Feathered Thorn**	*Colotois pennaria* (Linnaeus, 1761)
70.245	**March Moth**	*Alsophila aescularia* ([Denis & Schiffermüller], 1775)
70.246	**Small Brindled Beauty**	*Apocheima hispidaria* ([Denis & Schiffermüller], 1775)
70.247	**Pale Brindled Beauty**	*Phigalia pilosaria* ([Denis & Schiffermüller], 1775)

70.248	**Brindled Beauty**	*Lycia hirtaria* (Clerck, 1759)
70.249	**Rannoch Brindled Beauty**	*Lycia lapponaria* (Boisduval, 1840)
70.250	**Belted Beauty**	*Lycia zonaria* ([Denis & Schiffermüller], 1775)
70.251	**Oak Beauty**	*Biston strataria* (Hufnagel, 1767)
70.252	**Peppered Moth**	*Biston betularia* (Linnaeus, 1758)
70.253	**Spring Usher**	*Agriopis leucophaearia* ([Denis & Schiffermüller], 1775)
70.254	**Scarce Umber**	*Agriopis aurantiaria* (Hübner, [1799])
70.255	**Dotted Border**	*Agriopis marginaria* (Fabricius, [1777])
70.256	**Mottled Umber**	*Erannis defoliaria* (Clerck, 1759)
70.257	**Waved Umber**	*Menophra abruptaria* (Thunberg, 1792)
70.258	**Willow Beauty**	*Peribatodes rhomboidaria* ([Denis & Schiffermüller], 1775)
70.259	Olive-tree Beauty	*Peribatodes umbraria* (Hübner, [1809])
70.260	**Feathered Beauty**	*Peribatodes secundaria* ([Denis & Schiffermüller], 1775)
70.261	Lydd Beauty	*Peribatodes ilicaria* (Geyer, [1833])
70.262	**Bordered Grey**	*Selidosema brunnearia* (Villers, 1789)
70.263	**Ringed Carpet**	*Cleora cinctaria* ([Denis & Schiffermüller], 1775)
70.264	**Satin Beauty**	*Deileptenia ribeata* (Clerck, 1759)
70.265	**Mottled Beauty**	*Alcis repandata* (Linnaeus, 1758)
70.266	**Dotted Carpet**	*Alcis jubata* (Thunberg, 1788)
70.267	**Great Oak Beauty**	*Hypomecis roboraria* ([Denis & Schiffermüller], 1775)
70.268	**Pale Oak Beauty**	*Hypomecis punctinalis* (Scopoli, 1763)
70.269	Speckled Beauty	*Fagivorina arenaria* (Hufnagel, 1767)
70.270	**Engrailed**	*Ectropis crepuscularia* ([Denis & Schiffermüller], 1775)
70.271	**Small Engrailed**	*Ectropis* sp.
70.272	**Square Spot**	*Paradarisa consonaria* (Hübner, [1799])
70.273	**Brindled White-spot**	*Parectropis similaria* (Hufnagel, 1767)
70.274	**Grey Birch**	*Aethalura punctulata* ([Denis & Schiffermüller], 1775)
70.275	**Common Heath**	*Ematurga atomaria* (Linnaeus, 1758)
70.276	**Bordered White**	*Bupalus piniaria* (Linnaeus, 1758)
70.277	**Common White Wave**	*Cabera pusaria* (Linnaeus, 1758)
70.278	**Common Wave**	*Cabera exanthemata* (Scopoli, 1763)
70.279	**White-pinion Spotted**	*Lomographa bimaculata* (Fabricius, 1775)
70.280	**Clouded Silver**	*Lomographa temerata* ([Denis & Schiffermüller], 1775)
70.281	**Sloe Carpet**	*Aleucis distinctata* (Herrich-Schäffer, [1839])
70.282	**Early Moth**	*Theria primaria* (Haworth, 1809)
70.283	**Light Emerald**	*Campaea margaritaria* (Linnaeus, 1761)
70.284	**Barred Red**	*Hylaea fasciaria* (Linnaeus, 1758)
70.2841	**Banded Pine Carpet**	*Pungeleria capreolaria* ([Denis & Schiffermüller], 1775)
70.285	**Scotch Annulet**	*Gnophos obfuscata* ([Denis & Schiffermüller], 1775)
70.286	**Irish Annulet**	*Gnophos dumetata* Treitschke, 1827
70.287	**Annulet**	*Charissa obscurata* ([Denis & Schiffermüller], 1775)
70.288	**Brussels Lace**	*Cleorodes lichenaria* (Hufnagel, 1767)
70.289	**Black Mountain Moth**	*Glacies coracina* (Esper, 1805)
70.290	**Common Forest Looper**	*Pseudocoremia suavis* Butler, 1879
70.291	**Black-veined Moth**	*Siona lineata* (Scopoli, 1763)
70.292	**Grey Scalloped Bar**	*Dyscia fagaria* (Thunberg, 1784)
70.293	**Straw Belle**	*Aspitates gilvaria* ([Denis & Schiffermüller], 1775)
70.294	**Yellow Belle**	*Aspitates ochrearia* (Rossi, 1794)
70.295	**Grass Wave**	*Perconia strigillaria* (Hübner, [1787])
70.296	**Rest Harrow**	*Aplasta ononaria* (Fuessly, 1783)
70.297	**Grass Emerald**	*Pseudoterpna pruinata* (Hufnagel, 1767)
70.298	**Jersey Emerald**	*Pseudoterpna coronillaria* (Hübner, [1817])
70.299	**Large Emerald**	*Geometra papilionaria* (Linnaeus, 1758)
70.300	**Blotched Emerald**	*Comibaena bajularia* ([Denis & Schiffermüller], 1775)
70.301	Essex Emerald	*Thetidia smaragdaria* (Fabricius, 1787)
70.302	**Small Emerald**	*Hemistola chrysoprasaria* (Esper, 1795)
70.303	**Little Emerald**	*Jodis lactearia* (Linnaeus, 1758)
70.304	**Sussex Emerald**	*Thalera fimbrialis* (Scopoli, 1763)
70.305	**Common Emerald**	*Hemithea aestivaria* (Hübner, 1789)
70.306	**Small Grass Emerald**	*Chlorissa viridata* (Linnaeus, 1758)
70.307	**Southern Grass Emerald**	*Chlorissa cloraria* (Hübner, [1813])
70.3075	Herb Emerald	*Microloxia herbaria* (Hübner, [1813])

NOTODONTIDAE

71.001	**Oak Processionary**	*Thaumetopoea processionea* (Linnaeus, 1758)
71.002	Pine Processionary	*Thaumetopoea pityocampa* ([Denis & Schiffermüller], 1775)
71.003	**Puss Moth**	*Cerura vinula* (Linnaeus, 1758)
71.004	Feline	*Cerura erminea* (Esper, 1783)
71.005	**Sallow Kitten**	*Furcula furcula* (Clerck, 1759)
71.006	**Alder Kitten**	*Furcula bicuspis* (Borkhausen, 1790)
71.007	**Poplar Kitten**	*Furcula bifida* (Brahm, 1787)
71.008	Tawny Prominent	*Harpyia milhauseri* (Fabricius, 1775)
71.009	**Lobster Moth**	*Stauropus fagi* (Linnaeus, 1758)
71.010	**Marbled Brown**	*Drymonia dodonaea* ([Denis & Schiffermüller], 1775)
71.011	**Lunar Marbled Brown**	*Drymonia ruficornis* (Hufnagel, 1766)
71.012	**Iron Prominent**	*Notodonta dromedarius* (Linnaeus, 1767)
71.013	**Pebble Prominent**	*Notodonta ziczac* (Linnaeus, 1758)
71.014	Large Dark Prominent	*Notodonta torva* (Hübner, [1803])
71.015	Three-humped Prominent	*Notodonta tritophus* ([Denis & Schiffermüller], 1775)
71.016	**Great Prominent**	*Peridea anceps* (Goeze, 1781)
71.017	**Swallow Prominent**	*Pheosia tremula* (Clerck, 1759)
71.018	**Lesser Swallow Prominent**	*Pheosia gnoma* (Fabricius, [1777])
71.019	**White Prominent**	*Leucodonta bicoloria* ([Denis & Schiffermüller], 1775)
71.020	**Pale Prominent**	*Pterostoma palpina* (Clerck, 1759)
71.021	**Coxcomb Prominent**	*Ptilodon capucina* (Linnaeus, 1758)
71.022	**Maple Prominent**	*Ptilodon cucullina* ([Denis & Schiffermüller], 1775)
71.023	**Scarce Prominent**	*Odontosia carmelita* (Esper, [1798])
71.024	**Plumed Prominent**	*Ptilophora plumigera* ([Denis & Schiffermüller], 1775)
71.025	**Buff-tip**	*Phalera bucephala* (Linnaeus, 1758)
71.026	Dusky Marbled Brown	*Gluphisia crenata* (Esper, 1785)
71.027	**Chocolate-tip**	*Clostera curtula* (Linnaeus, 1758)
71.028	**Small Chocolate-tip**	*Clostera pigra* (Hufnagel, 1766)
71.029	**Scarce Chocolate-tip**	*Clostera anachoreta* ([Denis & Schiffermüller], 1775)

EREBIDAE

72.001	**Herald**	*Scoliopteryx libatrix* (Linnaeus, 1758)
72.002	**Straw Dot**	*Rivula sericealis* (Scopoli, 1763)
72.003	**Snout**	*Hypena proboscidalis* (Linnaeus, 1758)
72.004	**Buttoned Snout**	*Hypena rostralis* (Linnaeus, 1758)
72.005	Paignton Snout	*Hypena obesalis* Treitschke, 1829
72.006	**Bloxworth Snout**	*Hypena obsitalis* (Hübner, [1813])
72.0061	Chevron Snout	*Hypena lividalis* (Hübner, 1790)
72.007	**Beautiful Snout**	*Hypena crassalis* (Fabricius, 1787)
72.008	Black V Moth	*Arctornis l-nigrum* (Müller, 1764)
72.009	**White Satin Moth**	*Leucoma salicis* (Linnaeus, 1758)
72.010	**Black Arches**	*Lymantria monacha* (Linnaeus, 1758)
72.011	**Gypsy Moth**	*Lymantria dispar* (Linnaeus, 1758)
72.012	**Brown-tail**	*Euproctis chrysorrhoea* (Linnaeus, 1758)
72.013	**Yellow-tail**	*Euproctis similis* (Fuessly, 1775)
72.014	Reed Tussock	*Laelia coenosa* (Hübner, [1808])
72.015	**Pale Tussock**	*Calliteara pudibunda* (Linnaeus, 1758)
72.016	**Dark Tussock**	*Dicallomera fascelina* (Linnaeus, 1758)
72.017	**Vapourer**	*Orgyia antiqua* (Linnaeus, 1758)
72.018	**Scarce Vapourer**	*Orgyia recens* (Hübner, [1819])
72.019	**Buff Ermine**	*Spilosoma lutea* (Hufnagel, 1766)
72.020	**White Ermine**	*Spilosoma lubricipeda* (Linnaeus, 1758)
72.021	**Water Ermine**	*Spilosoma urticae* (Esper, 1789)
72.0211	Autumn Webworm	*Hyphantria cunea* (Drury, 1773)
72.022	**Muslin Moth**	*Diaphora mendica* (Clerck, 1759)
72.023	**Clouded Buff**	*Diacrisia sannio* (Linnaeus, 1758)
72.024	**Ruby Tiger**	*Phragmatobia fuliginosa* (Linnaeus, 1758)
72.025	**Wood Tiger**	*Parasemia plantaginis* (Linnaeus, 1758)
72.026	**Garden Tiger**	*Arctia caja* (Linnaeus, 1758)
72.027	**Cream-spot Tiger**	*Arctia villica* (Linnaeus, 1758)
72.028	Patton's Tiger	*Hyphoraia testudinaria* (Geoffroy, 1785)
72.029	**Scarlet Tiger**	*Callimorpha dominula* (Linnaeus, 1758)
72.030	**Jersey Tiger**	*Euplagia quadripunctaria* (Poda, 1761)
72.031	**Cinnabar**	*Tyria jacobaeae* (Linnaeus, 1758)
72.032	**Speckled Footman**	*Coscinia cribraria* (Linnaeus, 1758)

72.033	Feathered Footman	*Coscinia striata* (Linnaeus, 1758)
72.034	Crimson Speckled	*Utetheisa pulchella* (Linnaeus, 1758)
72.035	**Rosy Footman**	***Miltochrista miniata*** (Forster, 1771)
72.036	**Muslin Footman**	***Nudaria mundana*** (Linnaeus, 1761)
72.037	**Round-winged Muslin**	***Thumatha senex*** (Hübner, [1808])
72.038	**Four-dotted Footman**	***Cybosia mesomella*** (Linnaeus, 1758)
72.039	**Dotted Footman**	***Pelosia muscerda*** (Hufnagel, 1766)
72.040	**Small Dotted Footman**	***Pelosia obtusa*** (Herrich-Schäffer, 1851)
72.041	**Four-spotted Footman**	***Lithosia quadra*** (Linnaeus, 1758)
72.042	**Red-necked Footman**	***Atolmis rubricollis*** (Linnaeus, 1758)
72.043	**Buff Footman**	***Eilema depressa*** (Esper, 1787)
72.044	**Dingy Footman**	***Eilema griseola*** (Hübner, [1803])
72.045	**Common Footman**	***Eilema lurideola*** (Zincken, 1817)
72.046	**Scarce Footman**	***Eilema complana*** (Linnaeus, 1758)
72.047	**Hoary Footman**	***Eilema caniola*** (Hübner, 1808)
72.048	**Pigmy Footman**	***Eilema pygmaeola*** (Doubleday, 1847)
72.049	**Orange Footman**	***Eilema sororcula*** (Hufnagel, 1766)
72.050	**Dew Moth**	***Setina irrorella*** (Linnaeus, 1758)
72.051	**Clay Fan-foot**	***Paracolax tristalis*** (Fabricius, 1794)
72.052	**Dotted Fan-foot**	***Macrochilo cribrumalis*** (Hübner, 1793)
72.053	**Fan-foot**	***Herminia tarsipennalis*** Treitschke, 1835
72.054	**Shaded Fan-foot**	***Herminia tarsicrinalis*** (Knoch, 1782)
72.055	**Small Fan-foot**	***Herminia grisealis*** ([Denis & Schiffermüller], 1775)
72.056	**Common Fan-foot**	***Pechipogo strigilata*** (Linnaeus, 1758)
72.057	**Plumed Fan-foot**	***Pechipogo plumigeralis*** (Hübner, [1825])
72.058	Jubilee Fan-foot	*Zanclognatha lunalis* (Scopoli, 1763)
72.059	Dusky Fan-foot	*Zanclognatha zelleralis* (Wocke, 1850)
72.060	**Marsh Oblique-barred**	***Hypenodes humidalis*** Doubleday, 1850
72.061	**Pinion-streaked Snout**	***Schrankia costaestrigalis*** (Stephens, 1834)
72.062	**White-line Snout**	***Schrankia taenialis*** (Hübner, [1809])
72.063	**Blackneck**	***Lygephila pastinum*** (Treitschke, 1826)
72.064	**Scarce Blackneck**	***Lygephila craccae*** ([Denis & Schiffermüller], 1775)
72.065	Levant Blackneck	*Tathorhynchus exsiccata* (Lederer, 1855)
72.066	**Waved Black**	***Parascotia fuliginaria*** (Linnaeus, 1761)
72.067	**Small Purple-barred**	***Phytometra viridaria*** (Clerck, 1759)
72.068	Lesser Belle	*Colobochyla salicalis* ([Denis & Schiffermüller], 1775)
72.069	**Beautiful Hook-tip**	***Laspeyria flexula*** ([Denis & Schiffermüller], 1775)
72.070	**Olive Crescent**	***Trisateles emortualis*** ([Denis & Schiffermüller], 1775)
72.071	Scarce Marbled	*Eublemma minutata* (Fabricius, 1794)
72.072	**Purple Marbled**	***Eublemma ostrina*** (Hübner, [1808])
72.073	**Small Marbled**	***Eublemma parva*** (Hübner, [1808])
72.074	Beautiful Marbled	*Eublemma purpurina* ([Denis & Schiffermüller], 1775)
72.075	Oak Yellow Underwing	*Catocala nymphagoga* (Esper, 1787)
72.076	**Clifden Nonpareil/Blue Underwing**	**Catocala fraxini** (Linnaeus, 1758)
72.077	Minsmere Crimson Underwing	*Catocala conjuncta* (Esper, 1787)
72.078	**Red Underwing**	***Catocala nupta*** (Linnaeus, 1767)
72.079	Rosy Underwing	*Catocala electa* (Vieweg, 1790)
72.080	French Red Underwing	*Catocala elocata* (Esper, 1787)
72.081	**Dark Crimson Underwing**	***Catocala sponsa*** (Linnaeus, 1767)
72.082	**Light Crimson Underwing**	***Catocala promissa*** ([Denis & Schiffermüller], 1775)
72.083	**Burnet Companion**	***Euclidia glyphica*** (Linnaeus, 1758)
72.084	**Mother Shipton**	***Euclidia mi*** (Clerck, 1759)
72.085	Alchymist	*Catephia alchymista* ([Denis & Schiffermüller], 1775)
72.0855	Green Drab	*Ophiusa tirhaca* (Cramer, 1773)
72.086	Lunar Double-stripe	*Minucia lunaris* ([Denis & Schiffermüller], 1775)
72.087	Passenger	*Dysgonia algira* (Linnaeus, 1767)
72.088	Geometrician	*Grammodes stolida* (Fabricius, 1775)

NOCTUIDAE

73.001	**Spectacle**	***Abrostola tripartita*** (Hufnagel, 1766)
73.002	**Dark Spectacle**	***Abrostola triplasia*** (Linnaeus, 1758)
73.003	Ni Moth	*Trichoplusia ni* (Hübner, [1803])
73.004	Slender Burnished Brass	*Thysanoplusia orichalcea* (Fabricius, 1775)
73.0041	Boathouse Gem	*Thysanoplusia daubei* (Boisduval, 1840)
73.005	Scar Bank Gem	*Ctenoplusia limbirena* (Guenée, 1852)
73.006	Accent Gem	*Ctenoplusia accentifera* (Lefebvre, 1827)
73.007	Streaked Plusia	*Vittaplusia vittata* (Wallengren, 1856)

73.008	Golden Twin-spot	*Chrysodeixis chalcites* (Esper, [1803])
73.009	Tunbridge Wells Gem	*Chrysodeixis acuta* (Walker, 1857)
73.010	Dewick's Plusia	*Macdunnoughia confusa* (Stephens, 1850)
73.011	**Scarce Burnished Brass**	***Diachrysia chryson*** (Esper, 1798)
73.012	**Burnished Brass**	***Diachrysia chrysitis*** (Linnaeus, 1758)
73.013	Purple-shaded Gem	*Euchalcia variabilis* (Piller & Mitterpacher, 1783)
73.014	**Golden Plusia**	***Polychrysia moneta*** (Fabricius, 1787)
73.015	**Silver Y**	***Autographa gamma*** (Linnaeus, 1758)
73.016	**Beautiful Golden Y**	***Autographa pulchrina*** (Haworth, 1809)
73.017	**Plain Golden Y**	***Autographa jota*** (Linnaeus, 1758)
73.018	**Gold Spangle**	***Autographa bractea*** ([Denis & Schiffermüller], 1775)
73.019	Stephens' Gem	*Megalographa biloba* (Stephens, 1830)
73.020	Essex Y	*Cornutiplusia circumflexa* (Linnaeus, 1767)
73.021	**Scarce Silver Y**	***Syngrapha interrogationis*** (Linnaeus, 1758)
73.022	**Gold Spot**	***Plusia festucae*** (Linnaeus, 1758)
73.023	**Lempke's Gold Spot**	***Plusia putnami*** Grote, 1873
73.024	**Marbled White Spot**	***Deltote pygarga*** (Hufnagel, 1766)
73.025	Pretty Marbled	*Deltote deceptoria* (Scopoli, 1763)
73.026	**Silver Hook**	***Deltote uncula*** (Clerck, 1759)
73.027	**Silver Barred**	***Deltote bankiana*** (Fabricius, 1775)
73.028	Pale Shoulder	*Acontia lucida* (Hufnagel, 1766)
73.029	Spotted Sulphur	*Acontia trabealis* (Scopoli, 1763)
73.030	Sorcerer	*Aedia leucomelas* (Linnaeus, 1758)
73.0301	Druid	*Aedia funesta* (Esper, 1786)
73.031	**Four-spotted**	***Tyta luctuosa*** ([Denis & Schiffermüller], 1775)
73.032	**Nut-tree Tussock**	***Colocasia coryli*** (Linnaeus, 1758)
73.033	**Figure of Eight**	***Diloba caeruleocephala*** (Linnaeus, 1758)
73.034	**Scarce Merveille du Jour**	***Moma alpium*** (Osbeck, 1778)
73.035	**Reed Dagger/Powdered Wainscot**	***Simyra albovenosa*** (Goeze, 1781)
73.036	**Alder Moth**	***Acronicta alni*** (Linnaeus, 1767)
73.037	**Dark Dagger**	***Acronicta tridens*** ([Denis & Schiffermüller], 1775)
73.038	**Grey Dagger**	***Acronicta psi*** (Linnaeus, 1758)
73.039	**Sycamore**	***Acronicta aceris*** (Linnaeus, 1758)
73.040	**Miller**	***Acronicta leporina*** (Linnaeus, 1758)
73.041	Marsh Dagger	*Acronicta strigosa* ([Denis & Schiffermüller], 1775)
73.042	**Light Knot Grass**	***Acronicta menyanthidis*** (Esper, 1798)
73.043	Scarce Dagger	*Acronicta auricoma* ([Denis & Schiffermüller], 1775)
73.044	**Sweet Gale Moth**	***Acronicta cinerea*** (Hufnagel, 1766)
73.045	**Knot Grass**	***Acronicta rumlcis*** (Linnacus, 1758)
73.046	**Poplar Grey**	***Subacronicta megacephala*** ([Denis & Schiffermüller], 1775)
73.047	**Coronet**	***Craniophora ligustri*** ([Denis & Schiffermüller], 1775)
73.048	**Small Yellow Underwing**	***Panemeria tenebrata*** (Scopoli, 1763)
73.049	Goldwing	*Synthymia fixa* (Fabricius, 1787)
73.050	**Wormwood**	***Cucullia absinthii*** (Linnaeus, 1761)
73.051	Scarce Wormwood	*Cucullia artemisiae* (Hufnagel, 1766)
73.052	**Shark**	***Cucullia umbratica*** (Linnaeus, 1758)
73.0527	Marigold Shark	*Cucullia calendulae* Treitschke, 1835
73.053	**Chamomile Shark**	***Cucullia chamomillae*** ([Denis & Schiffermüller], 1775)
73.054	Cudweed	*Cucullia gnaphalii* (Hübner, [1813])
73.055	**Star-wort**	***Cucullia asteris*** ([Denis & Schiffermüller], 1775)
73.056	**Water Betony**	***Cucullia scrophulariae*** ([Denis & Schiffermüller], 1775)
73.057	**Striped Lychnis**	***Cucullia lychnitis*** Rambur, 1833
73.058	**Mullein**	***Cucullia verbasci*** (Linnaeus, 1758)
73.059	**Toadflax Brocade**	***Calophasia lunula*** (Hufnagel, 1766)
73.060	Antirrhinum Brocade	*Calophasia platyptera* (Esper, 1788)
73.061	**Anomalous**	***Stilbia anomala*** (Haworth, 1812)
73.062	**Copper Underwing**	***Amphipyra pyramidea*** (Linnaeus, 1758)
73.063	**Svensson's Copper Underwing**	***Amphipyra berbera*** Rungs, 1949
73.064	**Mouse Moth**	***Amphipyra tragopoginis*** (Clerck, 1759)
73.0645	Languard Ochre	*Amphipyra effusa* Boisduval, [1828]
73.065	**Sprawler**	***Asteroscopus sphinx*** (Hufnagel, 1766)
73.066	**Rannoch Sprawler**	***Brachionycha nubeculosa*** (Esper, 1785)
73.067	Double-spot Brocade	*Meganephria bimaculosa* (Linnaeus, 1767)
73.068	**Green-brindled Crescent**	***Allophyes oxyacanthae*** (Linnaeus, 1758)
73.069	**Early Grey**	***Xylocampa areola*** (Esper, 1789)
73.070	**Bordered Sallow**	***Pyrrhia umbra*** (Hufnagel, 1766)

73.071	Spotted Clover	*Protoschinia scutosa* ([Denis & Schiffermüller], 1775)
73.072	**Marbled Clover**	***Heliothis viriplaca*** (Hufnagel, 1766)
73.073	**Shoulder-striped Clover**	***Heliothis maritima*** Graslin, 1855
73.074	**Bordered Straw**	***Heliothis peltigera*** ([Denis & Schiffermüller], 1775)
73.075	Eastern Bordered Straw	*Heliothis nubigera* Herrich-Schäffer, 1851
73.076	**Scarce Bordered Straw/ Old World Bollworm**	***Helicoverpa armigera*** (Hübner, [1808])
73.077	Pease Blossom	*Periphanes delphinii* (Linnaeus, 1758)
73.078	**Reddish Buff**	***Acosmetia caliginosa*** (Hübner, [1813])
73.079	Silvery Gem	*Eucarta virgo* (Treitschke, 1835)
73.080	Latin	*Callopistria juventina* (Stoll, 1782)
73.081	Latreille's Latin	*Callopistria latreillei* (Duponchel, 1827)
73.0811	Florida Fern Moth	*Callopistria floridensis* (Guenée, 1852)
73.082	**Tree-lichen Beauty**	***Cryphia algae*** (Fabricius, 1775)
73.083	Marbled Grey	*Bryophila raptricula* ([Denis & Schiffermüller], 1775)
73.084	**Marbled Beauty**	***Bryophila domestica*** (Hufnagel, 1766)
73.085	**Marbled Green**	***Nyctobrya muralis*** (Forster, 1771)
73.086	Shining Marbled	*Pseudeustrotia candidula* ([Denis & Schiffermüller], 1775)
73.087	Small Mottled Willow	*Spodoptera exigua* (Hübner, [1808])
73.088	Dark Mottled Willow	*Spodoptera cilium* Guenée, 1852
73.089	Mediterranean Brocade/ African Cotton Leafworm	*Spodoptera littoralis* (Boisduval, 1833)
73.090	Wedgeling	*Galgula partita* Guenée, 1852
73.091	**Rosy Marbled**	***Elaphria venustula*** (Hübner, 1790)
73.092	**Mottled Rustic**	***Caradrina morpheus*** (Hufnagel, 1766)
73.093	**Clancy's Rustic**	***Caradrina kadenii*** (Freyer, [1836])
73.094	Lorimer's Rustic	*Caradrina flavirena* Guenée, 1852
73.095	**Pale Mottled Willow**	***Caradrina clavipalpis*** (Scopoli, 1763)
73.096	**Uncertain**	***Hoplodrina octogenaria*** (Goeze, 1781)
73.097	**Rustic**	***Hoplodrina blanda*** ([Denis & Schiffermüller], 1775)
73.098	Powdered Rustic	*Hoplodrina superstes* (Ochsenheimer, 1816)
73.099	**Vine's Rustic**	***Hoplodrina ambigua*** ([Denis & Schiffermüller], 1775)
73.100	**Silky Wainscot**	***Chilodes maritima*** (Tauscher, 1806)
73.101	**Treble Lines**	***Charanyca trigrammica*** (Hufnagel, 1766)
73.102	**Brown Rustic**	***Rusina ferruginea*** (Esper, 1785)
73.103	**Marsh Moth**	***Athetis pallustris*** (Hübner, [1808])
73.104	Porter's Rustic	*Athetis hospes* (Freyer, [1831])
73.105	**Bird's Wing**	***Dypterygia scabriuscula*** (Linnaeus, 1758)
73.106	**Orache Moth**	***Trachea atriplicis*** (Linnaeus, 1758)
73.107	**Old Lady**	***Mormo maura*** (Linnaeus, 1758)
73.108	**Guernsey Underwing**	***Polyphaenis sericata*** (Esper, 1787)
73.109	**Straw Underwing**	***Thalpophila matura*** (Hufnagel, 1766)
73.110	**Saxon**	***Hyppa rectilinea*** (Esper, 1796)
73.111	Purple Cloud	*Actinotia polyodon* (Clerck, 1759)
73.112	Pale-shouldered Cloud	*Chloantha hyperici* ([Denis & Schiffermüller], 1775)
73.113	**Angle Shades**	***Phlogophora meticulosa*** (Linnaeus, 1758)
73.114	**Small Angle Shades**	***Euplexia lucipara*** (Linnaeus, 1758)
73.115	Berber	*Pseudenargia ulicis* (Staudinger, 1859)
73.116	**Burren Green**	***Calamia tridens*** (Hufnagel, 1766)
73.117	Cameo	*Crypsedra gemmea* (Treitschke, 1825)
73.118	**Haworth's Minor**	***Celaena haworthii*** (Curtis, 1829)
73.119	**Crescent**	***Helotropha leucostigma*** (Hübner, [1808])
73.120	**Dusky Sallow**	***Eremobia ochroleuca*** ([Denis & Schiffermüller], 1775)
73.121	**Frosted Orange**	***Gortyna flavago*** ([Denis & Schiffermüller], 1775)
73.122	**Fisher's Estuarine Moth**	***Gortyna borelii*** Pierret, 1837
73.123	**Rosy Rustic**	***Hydraecia micacea*** (Esper, 1789)
73.124	**Butterbur**	***Hydraecia petasitis*** Doubleday, 1847
73.125	**Marsh Mallow Moth/Giant Ear**	***Hydraecia osseola*** Staudinger, 1882
73.126	**Saltern Ear**	***Amphipoea fucosa*** (Freyer, 1830)
73.127	**Large Ear**	***Amphipoea lucens*** (Freyer, 1845)
73.128	**Ear Moth**	***Amphipoea oculea*** (Linnaeus, 1761)
73.129	**Crinan Ear**	***Amphipoea crinanensis*** (Burrows, 1908)
73.130	Dumeril's Rustic	*Luperina dumerilii* (Duponchel, 1826)
73.131	**Flounced Rustic**	***Luperina testacea*** ([Denis & Schiffermüller], 1775)
73.132	**Sandhill Rustic**	***Luperina nickerlii*** (Freyer, 1845)
73.133	Scarce Arches	*Fabula zollikoferi* (Freyer, [1836])

73.134	**Large Wainscot**	*Rhizedra lutosa* (Hübner, [1803])
73.135	**Blair's Wainscot**	*Sedina buettneri* (Hering, 1858)
73.136	**Bulrush Wainscot**	*Nonagria typhae* (Thunberg, 1784)
73.137	**Fen Wainscot**	*Arenostola phragmitidis* (Hübner, [1803])
73.138	**Lyme Grass**	*Longalatedes elymi* (Treitschke, 1825)
73.139	**Twin-spotted Wainscot**	*Lenisa geminipuncta* (Haworth, 1809)
73.140	**White-mantled Wainscot**	*Archanara neurica* (Hübner, [1808])
73.141	**Brown-veined Wainscot**	*Archanara dissoluta* (Treitschke, 1825)
73.142	**Small Rufous**	*Coenobia rufa* (Haworth, 1809)
73.143	Brighton Wainscot	*Oria musculosa* (Hübner, [1808])
73.144	**Small Wainscot**	*Denticucullus pygmina* (Haworth, 1809)
73.145	**Mere Wainscot**	*Photedes fluxa* (Hübner, [1809])
73.146	**Least Minor**	*Photedes captiuncula* (Treitschke, 1825)
73.147	**Small Dotted Buff**	*Photedes minima* (Haworth, 1809)
73.148	**Morris's Wainscot**	*Photedes morrisii* (Dale, 1837)
73.149	**Concolorous**	*Photedes extrema* (Hübner, [1809])
73.150	**Fenn's Wainscot**	*Protarchanara brevilinea* (Fenn, 1864)
73.151	**Webb's Wainscot**	*Globia sparganii* (Esper, 1789)
73.152	**Rush Wainscot**	*Globia algae* (Esper, 1788)
73.153	Union Rustic	*Pabulatrix pabulatricula* (Brahm, 1791)
73.154	**Dusky Brocade**	*Apamea remissa* (Hübner, [1809])
73.155	**Clouded Brindle**	*Apamea epomidion* (Haworth, 1809)
73.156	**Clouded-bordered Brindle**	*Apamea crenata* (Hufnagel, 1766)
73.157	**Large Nutmeg**	*Apamea anceps* ([Denis & Schiffermüller], 1775)
73.158	**Rustic Shoulder-knot**	*Apamea sordens* (Hufnagel, 1766)
73.159	**Small Clouded Brindle**	*Apamea unanimis* (Hübner, [1813])
73.160	**Slender Brindle**	*Apamea scolopacina* (Esper, 1788)
73.161	**Crescent Striped**	*Apamea oblonga* (Haworth, 1809)
73.162	**Dark Arches**	*Apamea monoglypha* (Hufnagel, 1766)
73.163	**Light Arches**	*Apamea lithoxylaea* ([Denis & Schiffermüller], 1775)
73.164	**Reddish Light Arches**	*Apamea sublustris* (Esper, 1788)
73.165	**Confused**	*Apamea furva* ([Denis & Schiffermüller], 1775)
73.166	Scarce Brindle	*Apamea lateritia* (Hufnagel, 1766)
73.167	**Northern Arches/Exile**	*Apamea exulis* (Lefebvre, 1836)
73.168	**Double Lobed**	*Lateroligia ophiogramma* (Esper, 1794)
73.169	**Common Rustic**	*Mesapamea secalis* (Linnaeus, 1758)
73.170	**Lesser Common Rustic**	*Mesapamea didyma* (Esper, 1788)
73.171	**Rosy Minor**	*Litoligia literosa* (Haworth, 1809)
73.172	**Cloaked Minor**	*Mesoligla furuncula* ([Denis & Schiffermüller], 1775)
73.173	**Marbled Minor**	*Oligia strigilis* (Linnaeus, 1758)
73.174	**Tawny Marbled Minor**	*Oligia latruncula* ([Denis & Schiffermüller], 1775)
73.175	**Rufous Minor**	*Oligia versicolor* (Borkhausen, 1792)
73.176	**Middle-barred Minor**	*Oligia fasciuncula* (Haworth, 1809)
73.177	Maize Wainscot	*Sesamia nonagrioides* (Lefebvre, 1827)
73.178	**Beautiful Gothic**	*Leucochlaena oditis* (Hübner, [1822])
73.179	**Orange Sallow**	*Tiliacea citrago* (Linnaeus, 1758)
73.180	**Barred Sallow**	*Tiliacea aurago* ([Denis & Schiffermüller], 1775)
73.181	**Pink-barred Sallow**	*Xanthia togata* (Esper, 1788)
73.182	**Sallow**	*Cirrhia icteritia* (Hufnagel, 1766)
73.183	**Dusky-lemon Sallow**	*Cirrhia gilvago* ([Denis & Schiffermüller], 1775)
73.184	**Pale-lemon Sallow**	*Cirrhia ocellaris* (Borkhausen, 1792)
73.185	Pale Stigma	*Mesogona acetosellae* ([Denis & Schiffermüller], 1775)
73.186	**Beaded Chestnut**	*Agrochola lychnidis* ([Denis & Schiffermüller], 1775)
73.187	**Brown-spot Pinion**	*Agrochola litura* (Linnaeus, 1761)
73.188	**Flounced Chestnut**	*Agrochola helvola* (Linnaeus, 1758)
73.189	**Red-line Quaker**	*Agrochola lota* (Clerck, 1759)
73.190	**Yellow-line Quaker**	*Agrochola macilenta* (Hübner, [1809])
73.191	**Southern Chestnut**	*Agrochola haematidea* (Duponchel, 1827)
73.192	**Brick**	*Agrochola circellaris* (Hufnagel, 1766)
73.193	**Lunar Underwing**	*Omphaloscelis lunosa* (Haworth, 1809)
73.194	**Chestnut**	*Conistra vaccinii* (Linnaeus, 1761)
73.195	**Dark Chestnut**	*Conistra ligula* (Esper, 1791)
73.196	**Black-spotted Chestnut**	*Conistra rubiginosa* (Scopoli, 1763)
73.197	**Dotted Chestnut**	*Conistra rubiginea* ([Denis & Schiffermüller], 1775)
73.198	Red-headed Chestnut	*Conistra erythrocephala* ([Denis & Schiffermüller], 1775)
73.199	Orange Upperwing	*Jodia croceago* ([Denis & Schiffermüller], 1775)
73.200	**Tawny Pinion**	*Lithophane semibrunnea* (Haworth, 1809)

73.201	**Pale Pinion**	*Lithophane socia* (Hufnagel, 1766)
73.202	**Grey Shoulder-knot**	*Lithophane ornitopus* (Hufnagel, 1766)
73.203	Conformist	*Lithophane furcifera* (Hufnagel, 1766)
73.204	Softly's Shoulder-knot	*Lithophane consocia* (Borkhausen, 1792)
73.205	Nonconformist	*Lithophane lamda* (Fabricius, 1787)
73.206	**Blair's Shoulder-knot/Stone Pinion**	*Lithophane leautieri* (Boisduval, 1829)
73.207	**Golden-rod Brindle**	*Xylena solidaginis* (Hübner, [1803])
73.208	**Sword-grass**	*Xylena exsoleta* (Linnaeus, 1758)
73.209	**Red Sword-grass**	*Xylena vetusta* (Hübner, [1813])
73.210	**Satellite**	*Eupsilia transversa* (Hufnagel, 1766)
73.211	**Angle-striped Sallow**	*Enargia paleacea* (Esper, 1791)
73.212	**Double Kidney**	*Ipimorpha retusa* (Linnaeus, 1761)
73.213	**Olive**	*Ipimorpha subtusa* ([Denis & Schiffermüller], 1775)
73.214	**White-spotted Pinion**	*Cosmia diffinis* (Linnaeus, 1767)
73.215	**Lesser-spotted Pinion**	*Cosmia affinis* (Linnaeus, 1767)
73.216	**Dun-bar**	*Cosmia trapezina* (Linnaeus, 1758)
73.217	**Lunar-spotted Pinion**	*Cosmia pyralina* ([Denis & Schiffermüller], 1775)
73.218	**Heart Moth**	*Dicycla oo* (Linnaeus, 1758)
73.219	**Centre-barred Sallow**	*Atethmia centrago* (Haworth, 1809)
73.220	**Minor Shoulder-knot**	*Brachylomia viminalis* (Fabricius, [1777])
73.221	**Suspected**	*Parastichtis suspecta* (Hübner, [1817])
73.222	**Dingy Shears**	*Apterogenum ypsillon* ([Denis & Schiffermüller], 1775)
73.223	**Oak Rustic**	*Dryobota labecula* (Esper, 1788)
73.224	**Merveille du Jour**	*Griposia aprilina* (Linnaeus, 1758)
73.225	**Brindled Green**	*Dryobotodes eremita* (Fabricius, 1775)
73.226	Southern Brindled Green	*Dryobotodes roboris* (Boisduval, [1828])
73.227	**Sombre Brocade**	*Dryobotodes tenebrosa* (Esper, 1789)
73.228	**Grey Chi**	*Antitype chi* (Linnaeus, 1758)
73.229	**Flame Brocade**	*Trigonophora flammea* (Esper, 1785)
73.230	**Feathered Brindle**	*Aporophyla australis* (Boisduval, 1829)
73.231	**Deep-brown Dart**	*Aporophyla lutulenta* ([Denis & Schiffermüller], 1775)
73.232	**Northern Deep-brown Dart**	*Aporophyla lueneburgensis* (Freyer, 1848)
73.233	**Black Rustic**	*Aporophyla nigra* (Haworth, 1809)
73.234	**Brindled Ochre**	*Dasypolia templi* (Thunberg, 1792)
73.235	**Feathered Ranunculus**	*Polymixis lichenea* (Hübner, [1813])
73.236	**Black-banded**	*Polymixis xanthomista* (Hübner, [1819])
73.237	**Large Ranunculus**	*Polymixis flavicincta* ([Denis & Schiffermüller], 1775)
73.238	**Dark Brocade**	*Mniotype adusta* (Esper, 1790)
73.239	Bedrule Brocade	*Mniotype solieri* (Boisduval, 1840)
73.240	**Beautiful Arches**	*Mniotype satura* ([Denis & Schiffermüller], 1775)
73.241	**Pine Beauty**	*Panolis flammea* ([Denis & Schiffermüller], 1775)
73.242	**Clouded Drab**	*Orthosia incerta* (Hufnagel, 1766)
73.243	**Blossom Underwing**	*Orthosia miniosa* ([Denis & Schiffermüller], 1775)
73.244	**Common Quaker**	*Orthosia cerasi* (Fabricius, 1775)
73.245	**Small Quaker**	*Orthosia cruda* ([Denis & Schiffermüller], 1775)
73.246	**Lead-coloured Drab**	*Orthosia populeti* (Fabricius, 1781)
73.247	**Powdered Quaker**	*Orthosia gracilis* ([Denis & Schiffermüller], 1775)
73.248	**Northern Drab**	*Orthosia opima* (Hübner, [1809])
73.249	**Hebrew Character**	*Orthosia gothica* (Linnaeus, 1758)
73.250	**Twin-spotted Quaker**	*Anorthoa munda* ([Denis & Schiffermüller], 1775)
73.251	**Silver Cloud**	*Egira conspicillaris* (Linnaeus, 1758)
73.252	**Hedge Rustic**	*Tholera cespitis* ([Denis & Schiffermüller], 1775)
73.253	**Feathered Gothic**	*Tholera decimalis* (Poda, 1761)
73.254	**Antler Moth**	*Cerapteryx graminis* (Linnaeus, 1758)
73.255	**Nutmeg**	*Anarta trifolii* (Hufnagel, 1766)
73.256	**Broad-bordered White Underwing**	*Anarta melanopa* (Thunberg, 1791)
73.257	**Beautiful Yellow Underwing**	*Anarta myrtilli* (Linnaeus, 1761)
73.258	**Small Dark Yellow Underwing**	*Coranarta cordigera* (Thunberg, 1788)
73.259	**Pale Shining Brown**	*Polia bombycina* (Hufnagel, 1766)
73.260	**Silvery Arches**	*Polia hepatica* (Clerck, 1759)
73.261	**Grey Arches**	*Polia nebulosa* (Hufnagel, 1766)
73.262	Feathered Ear	*Pachetra sagittigera* (Hufnagel, 1766)
73.263	**Light Brocade**	*Lacanobia w-latinum* (Hufnagel, 1766)
73.264	**Pale-shouldered Brocade**	*Lacanobia thalassina* (Hufnagel, 1766)
73.265	**Beautiful Brocade**	*Lacanobia contigua* ([Denis & Schiffermüller], 1775)
73.266	**Dog's Tooth**	*Lacanobia suasa* ([Denis & Schiffermüller], 1775)

73.267	**Bright-line Brown-eye**	*Lacanobia oleracea* (Linnaeus, 1758)
73.268	**Splendid Brocade**	*Lacanobia splendens* (Hübner, [1808])
73.269	Stranger	*Lacanobia blenna* (Hübner, [1824])
73.270	**Dot Moth**	*Melanchra persicariae* (Linnaeus, 1761)
73.271	**Broom Moth**	*Ceramica pisi* (Linnaeus, 1758)
73.272	**Glaucous Shears**	*Papestra biren* (Goeze, 1781)
73.273	**Shears**	*Hada plebeja* (Linnaeus, 1761)
73.274	**Cabbage Moth**	*Mamestra brassicae* (Linnaeus, 1758)
73.275	**White Colon**	*Sideridis turbida* (Esper, 1790)
73.276	**Campion**	*Sideridis rivularis* (Fabricius, 1775)
73.277	**Bordered Gothic**	*Sideridis reticulata* (Goeze, 1781)
73.278	**Barrett's Marbled Coronet**	*Conisania andalusica* (Staudinger, 1859)
73.279	**Broad-barred White**	*Hecatera bicolorata* (Hufnagel, 1766)
73.280	**Small Ranunculus**	*Hecatera dysodea* ([Denis & Schiffermüller], 1775)
73.281	**Lychnis**	*Hadena bicruris* (Hufnagel, 1766)
73.282	**Varied Coronet**	*Hadena compta* ([Denis & Schiffermüller], 1775)
73.283	**Marbled Coronet**	*Hadena confusa* (Hufnagel, 1766)
73.284	**White Spot**	*Hadena albimacula* (Borkhausen, 1792)
73.285	**Grey**	*Hadena caesia* ([Denis & Schiffermüller], 1775)
73.286	**Tawny Shears**	*Hadena perplexa* ([Denis & Schiffermüller], 1775)
73.287	Viper's Bugloss	*Hadena irregularis* (Hufnagel, 1766)
73.288	**Double Line**	*Mythimna turca* (Linnaeus, 1761)
73.289	**Striped Wainscot**	*Mythimna pudorina* ([Denis & Schiffermüller], 1775)
73.290	**Brown-line Bright-eye**	*Mythimna conigera* ([Denis & Schiffermüller], 1775)
73.291	**Common Wainscot**	*Mythimna pallens* (Linnaeus, 1758)
73.292	**Mathew's Wainscot**	*Mythimna favicolor* (Barrett, 1896)
73.293	**Smoky Wainscot**	*Mythimna impura* (Hübner, [1808])
73.294	**Southern Wainscot**	*Mythimna straminea* (Treitschke, 1825)
73.295	**Delicate**	*Mythimna vitellina* (Hübner, [1808])
73.296	**White-speck/American Wainscot**	*Mythimna unipuncta* (Haworth, 1809)
73.297	**White-point**	*Mythimna albipuncta* ([Denis & Schiffermüller], 1775)
73.298	**Clay**	*Mythimna ferrago* (Fabricius, 1787)
73.299	**Shore Wainscot**	*Mythimna litoralis* (Curtis, 1827)
73.300	**L-album Wainscot**	*Mythimna l-album* (Linnaeus, 1767)
73.301	**Shoulder-striped Wainscot**	*Leucania comma* (Linnaeus, 1761)
73.302	**Obscure Wainscot**	*Leucania obsoleta* (Hübner, [1803])
73.303	**Devonshire Wainscot**	*Leucania putrescens* (Hübner, [1824])
73.304	**Cosmopolitan**	*Leucania loreyi* (Duponchel, 1827)
73.305	**Flame Wainscot**	*Senta flammea* (Curtis, 1828)
73.306	**Silurian**	*Eriopygodes imbecilla* (Fabricius, 1794)
73.307	**Pearly Underwing**	*Peridroma saucia* (Hübner, [1808])
73.308	**Portland Moth**	*Actebia praecox* (Linnaeus, 1758)
73.309	Eversmann's Rustic	*Actebia fennica* (Tauscher, 1806)
73.310	Black Collar	*Dichagyris flammatra* ([Denis & Schiffermüller], 1775)
73.311	**Coast Dart**	*Euxoa cursoria* (Hufnagel, 1766)
73.312	**Square-spot Dart**	*Euxoa obelisca* ([Denis & Schiffermüller], 1775)
73.313	**White-line Dart**	*Euxoa tritici* (Linnaeus, 1761)
73.314	**Garden Dart**	*Euxoa nigricans* (Linnaeus, 1761)
73.315	Great Dart	*Agrotis bigramma* (Esper, 1790)
73.316	**Light Feathered Rustic**	*Agrotis cinerea* ([Denis & Schiffermüller], 1775)
73.317	**Heart & Dart**	*Agrotis exclamationis* (Linnaeus, 1758)
73.318	**Woods's Dart**	*Agrotis graslini* Rambur, 1848
73.319	**Turnip Moth**	*Agrotis segetum* ([Denis & Schiffermüller], 1775)
73.320	**Heart & Club**	*Agrotis clavis* (Hufnagel, 1766)
73.321	Spalding's Dart	*Agrotis herzogi* Rebel, 1911
73.322	**Archer's Dart**	*Agrotis vestigialis* (Hufnagel, 1766)
73.323	**Sand Dart**	*Agrotis ripae* (Hübner, [1823])
73.324	**Crescent Dart**	*Agrotis trux* (Hübner, [1824])
73.325	**Shuttle-shaped Dart**	*Agrotis puta* (Hübner, [1803])
73.326	Grouville Dart	*Agrotis catalaunensis* (Millière, 1873)
73.327	**Dark Sword-grass**	*Agrotis ipsilon* (Hufnagel, 1766)
73.328	**Flame**	*Axylia putris* (Linnaeus, 1761)
73.329	**Flame Shoulder**	*Ochropleura plecta* (Linnaeus, 1761)
73.330	Radford's Flame Shoulder	*Ochropleura leucogaster* (Freyer, [1831])
73.331	**Barred Chestnut**	*Diarsia dahlii* (Hübner, [1813])
73.332	**Purple Clay**	*Diarsia brunnea* ([Denis & Schiffermüller], 1775)
73.333	**Ingrailed Clay**	*Diarsia mendica* (Fabricius, 1775)

73.334	**Small Square-spot**	*Diarsia rubi* (Vieweg, 1790)
73.335	**Fen Square-spot**	*Diarsia florida* (Schmidt, 1859)
73.336	**Red Chestnut**	*Cerastis rubricosa* ([Denis & Schiffermüller], 1775)
73.337	**White-marked**	*Cerastis leucographa* ([Denis & Schiffermüller], 1775)
73.338	**True Lover's Knot**	*Lycophotia porphyrea* ([Denis & Schiffermüller], 1775)
73.339	**Dotted Rustic**	*Rhyacia simulans* (Hufnagel, 1766)
73.340	Southern Rustic	*Rhyacia lucipeta* ([Denis & Schiffermüller], 1775)
73.341	**Northern Rustic**	*Standfussiana lucernea* (Linnaeus, 1758)
73.342	**Large Yellow Underwing**	*Noctua pronuba* (Linnaeus, 1758)
73.343	**Broad-bordered Yellow Underwing**	*Noctua fimbriata* (Schreber, 1759)
73.344	**Lunar Yellow Underwing**	*Noctua orbona* (Hufnagel, 1766)
73.345	**Lesser Yellow Underwing**	*Noctua comes* Hübner, [1813]
73.346	**Least Yellow Underwing**	*Noctua interjecta* Hübner, [1803]
73.347	**Langmaid's Yellow Underwing**	*Noctua janthina* [Denis & Schiffermüller], 1775
73.348	**Lesser Broad-bordered Yellow Underwing**	*Noctua janthe* (Borkhausen, 1792)
73.349	**Stout Dart**	*Spaelotis ravida* ([Denis & Schiffermüller], 1775)
73.350	**Great Brocade**	*Eurois occulta* (Linnaeus, 1758)
73.351	**Double Dart**	*Graphiphora augur* (Fabricius, 1775)
73.352	**Green Arches**	*Anaplectoides prasina* ([Denis & Schiffermüller], 1775)
73.353	**Dotted Clay**	*Xestia baja* ([Denis & Schiffermüller], 1775)
73.354	**Square-spotted Clay**	*Xestia stigmatica* (Hübner, [1813])
73.355	**Neglected Rustic**	*Xestia castanea* (Esper, 1798)
73.356	**Heath Rustic**	*Xestia agathina* (Duponchel, 1827)
73.357	**Square-spot Rustic**	*Xestia xanthographa* ([Denis & Schiffermüller], 1775)
73.358	**Six-striped Rustic**	*Xestia sexstrigata* (Haworth, 1809)
73.359	**Setaceous Hebrew Character**	*Xestia c-nigrum* (Linnaeus, 1758)
73.360	**Triple-spotted Clay**	*Xestia ditrapezium* ([Denis & Schiffermüller], 1775)
73.361	**Double Square-spot**	*Xestia triangulum* (Hufnagel, 1766)
73.362	**Ashworth's Rustic**	*Xestia ashworthii* (Doubleday, 1855)
73.363	**Northern Dart**	*Xestia alpicola* (Zetterstedt, 1839)
73.364	**Rosy Marsh Moth**	*Coenophila subrosea* (Stephens, 1829)
73.365	**Autumnal Rustic**	*Eugnorisma glareosa* (Esper, 1788)
73.366	**Plain Clay**	*Eugnorisma depuncta* (Linnaeus, 1761)
73.367	**Cousin German**	*Protolampra sobrina* (Duponchel, [1843])
73.368	**Gothic**	*Naenia typica* (Linnaeus, 1758)

NOLIDAE

74.001	**Small Black Arches**	*Meganola strigula* ([Denis & Schiffermüller], 1775)
74.002	**Kent Black Arches**	*Meganola albula* ([Denis & Schiffermüller], 1775)
74.003	**Short-cloaked Moth**	*Nola cucullatella* (Linnaeus, 1758)
74.004	**Least Black Arches**	*Nola confusalis* (Herrich-Schäffer, 1847)
74.005	Scarce Black Arches	*Nola aerugula* (Hübner, 1793)
74.006	Jersey Black Arches	*Nola chlamitulalis* (Hübner, [1813])
74.007	**Scarce Silver-lines**	*Bena bicolorana* (Fuessly, 1775)
74.008	**Green Silver-lines**	*Pseudoips prasinana* (Linnaeus, 1758)
74.009	**Oak Nycteoline**	*Nycteola revayana* (Scopoli, 1772)
74.010	Eastern Nycteoline	*Nycteola asiatica* (Krulikovsky, 1904)
74.011	**Cream-bordered Green Pea**	*Earias clorana* (Linnaeus, 1761)
74.012	Egyptian Bollworm	*Earias insulana* (Boisduval, 1833)

Checklist of the micro-moths mentioned in this field guide

The following species are either mentioned in the *Introduction* or are described in the species accounts where they are similar to macro-moth species.

PSYCHIDAE

| 11.016 | | *Acanthopsyche atra* (Linnaeus, 1767) |

TINEIDAE

| 12.001 | | *Myrmecozela ochraceella* (Tengström, 1848) |

GELECHIIDAE

| 35.060 | | *Apodia bifractella* (Duponchel, [1843]) |
| 35.061 | | *Ptocheuusa paupella* (Zeller, 1847) |

COLEOPHORIDAE
37.004   *Coleophora albella* (Thunberg, 1788)
37.044   *Coleophora discordella* Zeller, 1849
37.060   *Coleophora ochrea* (Haworth, 1828)

PTEROPHORIDAE
45.030   White Plume   *Pterophorus pentadactyla* (Linnaeus, 1758)
45.008   Yarrow Plume   *Gillmeria pallidactyla* (Haworth, 1811)
45.023   Crescent Plume   *Marasmarcha lunaedactyla* (Haworth, 1811)

TORTRICIDAE
49.185   *Lobesia littoralis* (Westwood & Humphreys, 1845)
49.200   Cherry Bark Tortrix   *Enarmonia formosana* (Scopoli, 1763)
49.279   *Gypsonoma dealbana* (Frölich, 1828)
49.339   *Cydia servillana* (Duponchel, 1836)

PYRALIDAE
62.028   *Dioryctria abietella* ([Denis & Schiffermüller], 1775)
62.059   *Phycitodes saxicola* (Vaughan, 1870)

SCIENTIFIC NAMES OF PLANTS AND THEIR ASSOCIATED BUTTERFLY AND MOTH SPECIES

The butterfly and moth species listed under each plant taxon in the table below are those whose larvae we believe have been confirmed as feeding on that foodplant in the wild in Great Britain and Ireland, or that can reasonably be inferred as doing so. We have not listed plant associations where larvae have been reared in captivity. Also, we have not listed foodplants where it is clear to us that these apply in mainland Europe or further afield, where foodplant range can be much greater. It is likely that there are many more associations to be discovered in the wild than are currently listed, so those in the table should be used as a guide only. Further explanation is given in the section 'What do larvae eat?' of the *Introduction* (see p. 40). The plant names follow Stace (2019) wherever possible. There are a few occasions in the literature where the common name of a plant is represented by multiple genera, so we cannot know from the source which genus was intended. In such cases no scientific name has been applied (e.g. goosefoots).

It should be noted that for polyphagous moth and butterfly species, the number of foodplants in the species accounts, and therefore also in the table below, has been limited to approximately 20. The taxa are separated into algae, conifers, ferns and horsetails, flowering plants, fungi and slime moulds, lichens and mosses. For conifers and flowering plants, they are arranged within alphabetical groups of related species where it is thought helpful to do so. Where it is considered that the reader may not immediately know which group to look at, the plant name is interspersed alphabetically between groups and has a signpost to the group for details (for example, Aspen is listed alphabetically but the entry redirects to poplars). Stand-alone plants are likewise interspersed.

FOODPLANT	BUTTERFLY AND MOTH CHECKLIST NUMBERS
ALGAE	
algae	72.035, 72.037, 72.038, 72.041, 72.042, 72.043, 72.044, 72.045, 72.046, 72.049
Pleurococcus naegelii	72.041, 72.042, 72.043
CONIFERS	
Cedars	
Cedar, Atlas *Cedrus atlantica*	69.007
Cedar-of-Lebanon *Cedrus libani*	69.007
cedars *Cedrus* spp.	70.284
Red-cedar, Japanese *Cryptomeria japonica*	70.214
Red-cedar, Western *Thuja plicata*	70.079, 70.081, 70.162, 70.176, 70.240
red-cedars *Thuja* spp.	70.158
Conifers	
conifer seedlings	73.255
conifers	73.271, 73.317, 73.342
Cypresses	
Cypress, Lawson's *Cupressus lawsoniana*	70.079, 70.081, 70.162, 70.240, 73.206
Cypress, Leyland *Cupressus × leylandii*	70.258, 73.206
Cypress, Monterey *Cupressus macrocarpa*	70.081, 70.083, 70.159, 70.258, 73.206
cypresses *Cupressus* spp.	70.158, 70.176, 70.265
Firs and Spruces	
Fir, Douglas *Pseudotsuga menziesii*	70.079, 70.081, 70.162, 70.176, 70.214, 70.240, 70.264, 70.276, 70.284, 73.319
Fir, Giant *Abies grandis*	70.079, 70.162, 73.113
Fir, Noble *Abies procera*	70.079, 70.149
firs *Abies* spp.	69.007, 73.319
Hemlock-spruce, Western *Tsuga heterophylla*	70.079, 70.081, 70.162, 70.214, 70.264, 70.284
Silver-fir, European *Abies alba*	70.079, 70.081, 70.149, 70.264, 70.276

FOODPLANT	BUTTERFLY AND MOTH CHECKLIST NUMBERS
Spruce, Norway *Picea abies*	69.007, 70.079, 70.081, 70.149, 70.162, 70.163, 70.213, 70.214, 70.258, 70.260, 70.276, 70.284, 72.010, 72.026
Spruce, Sitka *Picea sitchensis*	70.074, 70.079, 70.106, 70.141, 70.149, 70.162, 70.214, 70.244, 70.256, 70.270, 72.017, 73.238, 73.242, 73.249
spruces *Picea* spp.	70.171, 70.240, 70.252, 70.264, 70.265, 73.237, 73.271, 73.319
Junipers	
Juniper, Common *Juniperus communis*	70.078, 70.158, 70.162, 70.171, 70.176, 70.240, 70.265, 73.206
junipers *Juniperus* spp.	70.082, 70.158, 70.176
Larches	
Larch, European *Larix decidua*	70.109, 70.163, 70.171, 70.284, 72.012, 73.194
larches *Larix* spp.	70.106, 70.110, 70.149, 70.162, 70.212, 70.214, 70.240, 70.244, 70.247, 70.252, 70.254, 70.264, 70.268, 70.270, 70.276, 73.216, 73.241, 73.249, 73.270, 73.271, 73.319, 74.009
Pines	
Mountain-pine, Dwarf *Pinus mugo*	73.241
Pine, Corsican *Pinus nigra*	70.077, 70.214, 70.276, 70.284, 73.241
Pine, Lodgepole *Pinus contorta*	70.072, 70.074, 70.077, 70.106, 70.131, 70.141, 70.168, 70.284, 73.238, 73.241, 73.338
Pine, Maritime *Pinus pinaster*	69.007, 73.241
Pine, Monterey *Pinus radiata*	69.007
Pine, Scots *Pinus sylvestris*	66.009, 69.007, 70.077, 70.079, 70.081, 70.109, 70.162, 70.171, 70.213, 70.214, 70.217, 70.264, 70.270, 70.276, 70.284, 72.010, 72.026, 73.241
pines *Pinus* spp.	70.171, 70.240, 70.258, 70.265, 70.276, 73.271
Spruce, Norway *see* Firs and Spruces	
Spruce, Sitka *see* Firs and Spruces	
spruces *see* Firs and Spruces	
Thuja, Chinese *Platycladus orientalis*	70.176
Yew *Taxus baccata*	70.258, 70.264, 70.270
FERNS AND HORSETAILS	
Bracken *Pteridium aquilinum*	3.001, 3.003, 3.004, 3.004, 70.222, 72.017, 72.026, 73.038, 73.113, 73.114, 73.265, 73.270, 73.271, 73.332
ferns	72.019, 73.114
Horsetail, Water *Equisetum fluviatile*	72.026
horsetails *Equisetum* spp.	72.029, 73.123
Lady-fern, Alpine *Athyrium distentifolium*	73.015
Male-fern *Dryopteris filix-mas*	73.114
FLOWERING PLANTS	
Agrimony *Agrimonia eupatoria*	57.002, 72.012
Alders	
Alder *Alnus glutinosa*	50.001, 52.006, 52.007, 65.005, 65.012, 65.013, 66.001, 66.007, 67.001, 70.030, 70.075, 70.084, 70.096, 70.097, 70.105, 70.106, 70.108, 70.109, 70.112, 70.113, 70.114, 70.115, 70.184, 70.202, 70.212, 70.227, 70.244, 70.247, 70.247, 70.248, 70.251, 70.254, 70.255, 70.270, 70.273, 70.274, 70.277, 70.278, 70.299, 71.006, 71.009, 71.012, 71.021, 71.025, 72.012, 72.018, 72.055, 73.036, 73.040, 73.047, 73.238, 73.244, 73.249, 73.352, 74.008
Alder, Grey *Alnus incana*	71.012
alders *Alnus* spp.	73.032
Alison, Sweet *Lobularia maritima*	70.004, 70.049
Alkanet, Green *Pentaglottis sempervirens*	72.029, 72.030
Almond *see* Cherries	

FOODPLANT	BUTTERFLY AND MOTH CHECKLIST NUMBERS
Anenome, Wood *Anemone nemorosa*	70.127, 70.131
Angelica, Wild *Angelica sylvestris*	56.003, 70.142, 70.160, 70.161, 70.173, 70.175, 70.190, 70.265, 73.012, 73.234, 73.265
Apples	
Apple *Malus domestica*	50.001, 50.002, 52.011, 66.003, 66.005, 69.002, 70.084, 70.095, 70.105, 70.106, 70.107, 70.144, 70.174, 70.184, 70.240, 70.247, 70.256, 70.280, 71.009, 72.010, 72.011, 72.012, 72.013, 72.019, 72.022, 72.026, 73.032, 73.033, 73.037, 73.038, 73.065, 73.197, 73.201, 73.210, 73.216, 73.217, 73.264, 73.368, 74.003, 74.004
Apple, Crab *Malus sylvestris*	52.011, 65.007, 66.002, 69.002, 70.107, 70.144, 70.174, 70.205, 70.241, 70.244, 70.255, 70.268, 70.280, 71.009, 72.015, 73.036, 73.062, 73.245, 73.264
apples *Malus* spp.	66.012, 70.226, 70.245, 72.045, 73.068
Apricot *see* Cherries	
Arabis, Garden *Arabis caucasica*	70.059
Archangel, Yellow *Lamiastrum galeobdolon*	70.229
Arrowgrass, Sea *Triglochin maritima*	66.004
Artichoke, Globe *Cynara cardunculus*	59.024
Ash *Fraxinus excelsior*	50.001, 50.002, 66.001, 69.005, 69.006, 70.095, 70.107, 70.141, 70.169, 70.184, 70.201, 70.221, 70.223, 70.231, 70.235, 70.247, 70.254, 70.265, 70.270, 73.047, 73.062, 73.065, 73.187, 73.192, 73.200, 73.201, 73.219, 73.250
Aspen *see* Poplars	
Asphodel, Bog *Narthecium ossifragum*	73.073, 73.336
Asters	
Aster, China *Callistephus chinensis*	73.055
Aster, Sea *Tripolium pannonicum*	70.141, 73.055, 73.271
Michaelmas-daisies *Symphyotrichum* spp.	70.252, 73.012, 73.055, 73.237
Aubrieta *Aubrieta deltoidea*	70.059
Auricula *see* Primroses	
Avens, Mountain *Dryas octopetala*	68.001
Avens, Wood *Geum urbanum*	57.002, 70.016, 73.016
Balm *Melissa officinalis*	72.019
Balsam-poplar, Eastern *see* Poplars	
balsam-poplars *see* Poplars	
Balsams	
Balsam, Himalayan *Impatiens glandulifera*	69.016, 70.094
Balsam, Orange *Impatiens capensis*	69.016, 70.050
Balsam, Small *Impatiens parviflora*	70.050
Balsam, Touch-me-not *Impatiens noli-tangere*	70.088, 70.094, 73.110, 73.113, 73.114
Baneberry *Actaea spicata*	70.127
Barberries	
Barberry *Berberis vulgaris*	70.122, 70.124, 70.184, 70.190, 70.240, 70.265, 72.015, 72.019, 73.064, 73.264, 73.270
Barberry, Hedge *Berberis* × *stenophylla*	70.122
Barberry, Mrs Wilson's *Berberis wilsoniae*	70.122
Barberry, Thunberg's *Berberis thunbergii*	70.122
barberries *Berberis* spp.	70.122, 70.305
Berberis turcomanica	70.124
Barley *see* Grasses	
Bartsia, Red *Odontites vernus*	70.134
Basil *Ocimum basilicum*	73.274
Bearberry *Arctostaphylos uva-ursi*	70.216, 73.042, 73.110, 73.207, 73.256, 73.258, 73.272

FOODPLANT	BUTTERFLY AND MOTH CHECKLIST NUMBERS
Bedstraws	
Bedstraw, Heath *Galium saxatile*	69.017, 70.046, 70.051, 70.060, 70.063, 70.087, 70.099, 70.100, 70.101, 70.102, 70.103, 73.306
Bedstraw, Hedge *Galium album*	69.010, 69.015, 69.017, 70.011, 70.054, 70.056, 70.057, 70.061, 70.062, 70.063, 70.064, 70.087, 70.093, 70.099, 70.100, 70.102, 70.103, 73.092, 73.233, 73.313, 73.328, 73.357, 73.358
Bedstraw, Lady's *Galium verum*	69.010, 69.017, 70.039, 70.051, 70.056, 70.057, 70.061, 70.062, 70.063, 70.087, 70.093, 70.099, 70.100, 70.101, 70.102, 70.103, 73.312, 73.313, 73.329
bedstraws *Galium* spp.	69.009, 69.014, 69.015, 69.016, 70.015, 70.016, 70.027, 70.052, 70.055, 70.059, 72.021, 73.015, 73.322, 73.336, 73.365
Cleavers *Galium aparine*	69.010, 69.017, 70.051, 70.054, 70.061, 70.093, 70.101, 70.103, 73.343, 73.354, 73.357, 73.368
Marsh-bedstraw, Common *Galium palustre*	70.046, 70.104
marsh-bedstraws *Galium* spp.	69.017, 70.087
Woodruff *Galium odoratum*	70.027, 70.051, 70.093, 70.100, 73.329
Beech *Fagus sylvatica*	50.002, 52.012, 53.001, 53.002, 65.003, 70.037, 70.105, 70.106, 70.170, 70.203, 70.206, 70.224, 70.230, 70.236, 70.241, 70.243, 70.248, 70.252, 70.254, 70.255, 70.256, 70.264, 70.271, 70.299, 71.005, 71.009, 71.021, 71.025, 72.010, 72.013, 72.015, 72.018, 72.053, 72.070, 72.070, 73.032, 73.036, 73.065, 73.180, 73.190, 73.210, 73.244, 74.004, 74.007, 74.008
Beets	
Beet *Beta vulgaris*	73.255, 73.329
Beet, Sea *Beta vulgaris*	59.034
Beet, Sugar *Beta vulgaris*	73.123, 73.208
Mangel-wurzel *Beta vulgaris*	73.208
Bellflowers	
Bellflower, Clustered *Campanula glomerata*	70.173
Bellflower, Giant *Campanula latifolia*	70.185
Bellflower, Nettle-leaved *Campanula trachelium*	70.185, 70.190
bellflowers *Campanula* spp.	70.185
Harebell *Campanula rotundifolia*	73.236, 73.341
Bent, Bristle *see* Grasses	
Bent, Brown *see* Grasses	
Bent, Common *see* Grasses	
Bent, Creeping *see* Grasses	
bents *see* Grasses	
Betony *Betonica officinalis*	70.190
Bilberries	
Bilberry *Vaccinium myrtillus*	54.006, 61.005, 66.002, 66.007, 66.008, 68.001, 70.026, 70.072, 70.074, 70.090, 70.091, 70.097, 70.098, 70.106, 70.110, 70.121, 70.131, 70.145, 70.179, 70.183, 70.191, 70.217, 70.221, 70.240, 70.241, 70.244, 70.245, 70.249, 70.255, 70.256, 70.263, 70.265, 70.282, 70.303, 72.007, 72.017, 72.032, 73.016, 73.018, 73.021, 73.042, 73.110, 73.186, 73.188, 73.207, 73.232, 73.247, 73.249, 73.256, 73.260, 73.271, 73.272, 73.306, 73.331, 73.332, 73.333, 73.336, 73.350, 73.352, 73.353, 73.357, 73.359, 73.362, 73.364, 73.367
Bilberry, Bog *Vaccinium uliginosum*	73.021

FOODPLANT	BUTTERFLY AND MOTH CHECKLIST NUMBERS
Blueberry, Highbush *Vaccinium corymbosum*	73.038
Cowberry *Vaccinium vitis-idaea*	54.006, 70.091, 70.191, 73.021, 73.110, 73.207, 73.256, 73.355
Cranberry *Vaccinium oxycoccos*	70.191
Bindweeds	
Bindweed, Field *Convolvulus arvensis*	69.004, 70.015, 70.141, 73.031, 73.255, 73.270
Bindweed, Hedge *Calystegia sepium*	69.004, 69.016, 73.268
Bindweed, Sea *Calystegia soldanella*	69.004, 73.074, 73.275, 73.308, 73.323
bindweeds	73.267
Birches	
Birch, Downy *Betula pubescens*	52.005, 52.007, 65.001, 65.005, 65.016, 67.001, 70.032, 70.074, 70.086, 70.105, 70.109, 70.120, 70.203, 70.223, 70.224, 70.241, 70.247, 70.248, 70.268, 70.270, 70.271, 70.273, 70.274, 70.277, 70.299, 70.303, 71.012, 71.018, 71.023, 72.055, 73.032, 73.040, 73.062, 73.194, 73.211, 73.245, 74.004, 74.007, 74.008
Birch, Silver *Betula pendula*	52.005, 52.007, 53.001, 53.002, 65.001, 65.002, 65.005, 65.016, 66.003, 67.001, 70.032, 70.105, 70.109, 70.120, 70.203, 70.223, 70.224, 70.241, 70.247, 70.248, 70.268, 70.270, 70.271, 70.273, 70.274, 70.277, 70.299, 70.303, 71.012, 71.018, 71.023, 73.032, 73.040, 73.211, 74.007, 74.008
birches *Betula* spp.	50.001, 50.002, 52.006, 52.012, 65.007, 65.012, 65.013, 66.001, 66.002, 66.005, 66.007, 66.008, 68.001, 70.084, 70.090, 70.095, 70.096, 70.097, 70.098, 70.106, 70.107, 70.108, 70.111, 70.113, 70.115, 70.120, 70.184, 70.202, 70.211, 70.226, 70.230, 70.236, 70.240, 70.244, 70.245, 70.246, 70.251, 70.252, 70.254, 70.255, 70.256, 70.258, 70.263, 70.264, 70.265, 70.267, 70.278, 70.280, 70.305, 70.306, 71.006, 71.009, 71.019, 71.021, 71.025, 72.010, 72.011, 72.013, 72.016, 72.017, 72.018, 72.019, 72.022, 72.029, 72.055, 73.035, 73.036, 73.037, 73.038, 73.039, 73.042, 73.063, 73.065, 73.066, 73.068, 73.107, 73.114, 73.188, 73.190, 73.195, 73.201, 73.207, 73.210, 73.216, 73.221, 73.238, 73.242, 73.243, 73.244, 73.248, 73.249, 73.250, 73.260, 73.261, 73.264, 73.265, 73.271, 73.274, 73.331, 73.332, 73.333, 73.345, 73.348, 73.350, 73.351, 73.352, 73.353, 73.360, 73.361, 73.365, 73.367
Bird's-foot *see* Clovers and Trefoils	
bistorts *Bistorta* spp.	73.102
Bittersweet *Solanum dulcamara*	69.005
Black-bindweed *Fallopia convolvulus*	73.267
Blackthorn *see* Cherries	
Bladder-senna *Colutea arborescens*	61.008
Bluebell *Hyacinthoides non-scripta*	73.358, 73.365
Blueberry, Highbush *see* Bilberries	
Bogbean *Menyanthes trifoliata*	69.016, 73.042
Bog-myrtle *Myrica gale*	66.008, 68.001, 70.106, 70.120, 70.131, 70.212, 70.241 70.244, 70.249, 70.254, 70.255, 70.263, 70.275, 72.013 72.017, 72.023, 73.035, 73.042, 73.044, 73.208, 73.209 73.238, 73.247, 73.260, 73.265, 73.271, 73.272, 73.345 73.350, 73.353, 73.355, 73.364
Bog-rosemary *Andromeda polifolia*	73.364
Borages	
Borage *Borago officinalis*	72.029, 72.030
borages *Borago* spp.	73.113

FOODPLANT	BUTTERFLY AND MOTH CHECKLIST NUMBERS
Brambles	
Bramble *Rubus fruticosus*	57.002, 61.005, 61.012, 65.007, 65.008, 65.009, 66.002, 66.003, 66.006, 66.007, 66.008, 68.001, 70.068, 70.097, 70.142, 70.183, 70.205, 70.221, 70.226, 70.243, 70.252, 70.258, 70.265, 70.303, 70.306, 72.012, 72.013, 72.016, 72.018, 72.022, 72.024, 72.029, 72.030, 72.038, 72.045, 72.053, 72.055, 73.042, 73.062, 73.091, 73.102, 73.110, 73.187, 73.201, 73.230, 73.235, 73.243, 73.247, 73.261, 73.263, 73.271, 73.331, 73.332, 73.333, 73.343, 73.345, 73.346, 73.348, 73.350, 73.352, 73.353, 73.354, 73.358, 73.360, 73.361, 74.002
Dewberry *Rubus caesius*	65.009, 70.068, 74.002
Raspberry *Rubus idaeus*	52.001, 57.002, 61.012, 65.008, 65.009, 66.003, 68.001, 70.068, 70.097, 70.183, 70.254, 70.268, 72.053, 72.055, 73.036, 73.110, 73.123, 73.361, 74.002
brideworts *Spiraea* spp.	69.006, 70.241
Brome, False *see* Grasses	
Brome, Upright *see* Grasses	
Broom *Cytisus scoparius*	61.005, 61.008, 61.014, 66.006, 66.007, 70.040, 70.042, 70.141, 70.195, 70.196, 70.230, 70.240, 70.250, 70.252, 70.258, 70.262, 70.265, 70.270, 70.275, 70.295, 70.297, 70.298, 70.303, 72.016, 72.024, 73.015, 73.231, 73.249, 73.263, 73.264, 73.265, 73.270, 73.271, 73.345, 73.365
Buckthorns	
Buckthorn *Rhamnus cathartica*	58.013, 61.005, 66.012, 70.118, 70.119, 70.123, 70.200, 70.247, 70.270, 70.286, 73.037, 73.249, 74.004
Buckthorn, Alder *Frangula alnus*	58.013, 61.005, 61.012, 66.012, 68.001, 70.119, 70.123, 70.200, 70.212, 70.248, 70.251, 70.258, 72.013, 72.018, 73.042
Buckwheat *Fagopyrum esculentum*	69.015
Bullace *see* Cherries	
Bulrushes	
Bulrush *Typha latifolia*	73.136, 73.151, 73.152
Bulrush, Lesser *Typha angustifolia*	73.136, 73.151, 73.152
bulrushes *Typha* spp.	73.119
Burdocks	
Burdock, Greater *Arctium lappa*	59.024
Burdock, Lesser *Arctium minus*	59.024, 73.012, 73.123
burdocks *Arctium* spp.	3.005, 72.025, 72.026, 73.016, 73.121, 73.359
Burnet, Salad *Poterium sanguisorba*	57.002, 66.008, 68.001, 70.287, 72.025, 73.064
Burnet-saxifrages	
Burnet-saxifrage *Pimpinella saxifraga*	56.003, 61.018, 70.011, 70.165, 70.175, 70.190
Burnet-saxifrage, Greater *Pimpinella major*	70.165
burnet-saxifrages *Pimpinella* spp.	70.173
Bur-reed, Branched *Sparganium erectum*	73.022, 73.151
Butterbur *Petasites hybridus*	73.124
Buttercups	
Buttercup, Creeping *Ranunculus repens*	73.354
Buttercup, Meadow *Ranunculus acris*	70.127, 73.231, 73.344
buttercups *Ranunculus* spp.	73.186, 73.361
pearwort, Lesser *Ranunculus flammula*	70.125
butterfly-bush *Buddleja davidii*	69.006, 70.141, 73.058, 73.121, 73.270, 73.368
Cabbages/other *Brassica* spp.	
roccoli *Brassica oleracea*	58.006
russels-sprout *Brassica oleracea*	58.006
abbage *Brassica oleracea*	58.006, 58.007, 58.008, 69.016, 70.049, 73.015, 73.017, 73.274, 73.307, 73.342

FOODPLANT	BUTTERFLY AND MOTH CHECKLIST NUMBERS
Cabbage, Wild *Brassica oleracea*	58.007, 58.008, 70.059, 73.235, 73.345
Rape, Oil-seed *Brassica napus*	58.007, 73.307
Turnip *Brassica rapa*	58.003
Cactus	70.183
Campions	
Campion, Bladder *Silene vulgaris*	70.138, 70.155, 70.183, 73.072, 73.187, 73.238, 73.276, 73.281, 73.282, 73.283, 73.285, 73.286
Campion, Moss *Silene acaulis*	70.155, 73.283
Campion, Red *Silene dioica*	69.009, 69.017, 70.131, 70.132, 70.138, 70.155, 70.161, 73.276, 73.281, 73.283
Campion, Sea *Silene uniflora*	66.004, 70.131, 70.155, 70.287, 73.044, 73.230, 73.236, 73.275, 73.276, 73.277, 73.278, 73.283, 73.285, 73.286
Campion, White *Silene latifolia*	69.009, 70.132, 70.138, 70.155, 73.072, 73.236, 73.276, 73.281, 73.283, 73.286
Catchfly, Night-flowering *Silene noctiflora*	73.281
Catchfly, Nottingham *Silene nutans*	70.155, 70.294, 73.283, 73.284, 73.286
Catchfly, Small-flowered *Silene gallica*	70.155
Catchfly, Spanish *Silene otites*	70.189, 70.294, 73.072
Ragged-Robin *Silene flos-cuculi*	69.009, 70.132, 73.276, 73.281, 73.283
Caraway *Carum carvi*	56.003
Carrots	
Carrot *Daucus carota*	56.003
Carrot, Wild *Daucus carota*	56.003, 66.004, 70.051, 70.160, 70.173, 70.294, 70.304, 73.072, 73.320
Catchfly, Night-flowering *see* Campions	
Catchfly , Nottingham *see* Campions	
Catchfly, Small-flowered *see* Campions	
Catchfly, Spanish *see* Campions	
cat's-ears *Hypochaeris* spp.	70.250
Celandine, Greater *Chelidonium majus*	73.064
Celandine, Lesser *Ficaria verna*	59.036, 70.059, 70.131
Celery *Apium graveolens*	73.113
Cereals *see* Grasses	
Chamomiles	
Chamomile *Chamaemelum nobile*	73.053
Chamomile, Corn *Anthemis arvensis*	73.053
Chamomile, Stinking *Anthemis cotula*	73.053
Mayweed, Scentless *Tripleurospermum inodorum*	73.074, 73.348
mayweeds *Tripleurospermum* spp.	70.179, 73.053
Charlock *Sinapis arvensis*	58.003, 58.007, 58.008
Cherries	
Almond *Prunus dulcis*	52.008, 52.011, 66.005, 73.033
Apricot *Prunus armeniaca*	73.033
Blackthorn *Prunus spinosa* (continued opposite)	50.002, 61.003, 61.007, 65.007, 66.001, 66.002, 66.003 66.005, 66.006, 66.007, 66.008, 66.012, 68.001, 69.002 70.067, 70.084, 70.086, 70.095, 70.106, 70.107, 70.108 70.113, 70.143, 70.144, 70.169, 70.184, 70.190, 70.205 70.212, 70.226, 70.230, 70.240, 70.241, 70.243, 70.244 70.245, 70.247, 70.252, 70.254, 70.255, 70.256, 70.265 70.279, 70.280, 70.281, 70.282, 70.295, 70.303, 70.305 71.009, 71.025, 72.012, 72.013, 72.015, 72.017, 72.018 72.019, 72.026, 72.029, 73.032, 73.033, 73.036, 73.037 73.038, 73.062, 73.063, 73.065, 73.068, 73.107, 73.113 73.192, 73.194, 73.195, 73.210, 73.216, 73.217, 73.231 73.243, 73.244, 73.245, 73.247, 73.250, 73.261, 73.264

FOODPLANT	BUTTERFLY AND MOTH CHECKLIST NUMBERS
Blackthorn *Prunus spinosa* (continued)	73.331, 73.332, 73.333, 73.343, 73.345, 73.348, 73.350, 73.351, 73.353, 73.360, 73.361, 73.368, 74.003, 74.004, 74.008
Bullace *Prunus domestica*	61.003, 73.217
cherries *Prunus* spp.	50.002, 52.011, 52.012, 66.003, 66.003, 66.007, 66.012, 70.024, 70.084, 70.084, 70.095, 70.105, 70.105, 70.107, 70.144, 70.226, 70.226, 70.241, 70.245, 70.245, 71.025, 72.012, 72.012, 72.027, 72.029, 73.033, 73.033, 73.065, 73.195, 73.237, 73.250, 74.003
Cherry, Bird *Prunus padus*	70.256, 70.280, 72.011, 72.055, 73.353
Cherry, Dwarf *Prunus cerasus*	70.279
Cherry, Wild *Prunus avium*	70.223, 70.280, 73.036, 73.068
Laurel, Cherry *Prunus laurocerasus*	73.033
laurels *Prunus* spp.	70.258
Peach *Prunus persica*	52.011, 73.033
Plum *Prunus domestica*	50.001, 66.005, 70.205, 70.247, 70.248, 70.258, 70.280, 73.037, 73.038, 73.039, 73.068, 73.201
Plum, Wild *Prunus domestica*	61.007, 66.006, 70.230, 70.240, 70.279, 70.282, 71.025, 72.016, 72.019, 72.078
Chervils	
Chervil, Bur *Anthriscus caucalis*	70.130
Chervil, Rough *Chaerophyllum temulum*	70.130, 70.131, 73.016, 73.017, 73.018
Parsley, Cow *Anthriscus sylvestris*	56.003, 70.011, 70.130, 70.131, 70.161, 70.161, 73.354, 73.361
Chestnut, Sweet *Castanea sativa*	50.001, 52.012, 53.002, 70.037, 70.086, 70.106, 70.113, 70.142, 70.224, 70.226, 70.246, 70.252, 70.255, 70.256, 70.268, 70.273, 70.277, 70.303, 71.021, 71.025, 72.013, 72.070, 73.032, 73.034, 73.036, 73.038, 73.070, 73.194, 73.210, 73.216, 73.242, 73.244, 73.245, 73.250, 73.264, 74.008
Chickweed, Common *see* Stitchworts	
Chicory *Cichorium intybus*	73.072, 73.230
chrysanthemums *Chrysanthemum* spp.	73.113, 73.208
Cinquefoils	
Cinquefoil, Creeping *Potentilla reptans*	57.002, 66.008, 70.287, 70.293, 73.091, 73.208, 73.344
Cinquefoil, Marsh *Comarum palustre*	68.001, 70.002
Cinquefoil, Shrubby *Dasiphora fruticosa*	66.003
cinquefoils *Potentilla* spp.	70.305, 73.231
Silverweed *Potentilla anserina*	57.002
Strawberry, Barren *Potentilla sterilis*	57.002, 73.346
Tormentil *Potentilla erecta*	57.002, 68.001, 70.306, 73.091
Cleavers *see* Bedstraws	
Clovers and Trefoils	
Bird's-foot *Ornithopus perpusillus*	61.018, 61.020
Bird's-foot-trefoil, Common *Lotus corniculatus*	52.014, 54.005, 54.007, 54.008, 54.009, 54.010, 58.001, 58.002, 58.010, 61.005, 61.014, 61.018, 61.020, 66.006, 66.007, 70.043, 70.250, 70.262, 70.263, 70.287, 70.291, 70.293, 70.294, 72.083, 73.064, 73.232, 73.247, 73.308
Bird's-foot-trefoil, Greater *Lotus pedunculatus*	54.008, 54.009, 54.010, 58.001, 58.002, 61.018, 66.008, 73.247
Bird's-foot-trefoil, Hairy *Lotus subbiflorus*	58.010
Clover, Hare's-foot *Trifolium arvense*	70.294
Clover, Red *Trifolium pratense*	54.009, 61.018, 61.020
Clover, White *Trifolium repens*	54.009, 61.018, 61.020, 70.218

FOODPLANT	BUTTERFLY AND MOTH CHECKLIST NUMBERS
clovers *Trifolium* spp.	54.008, 58.010, 66.006, 70.043, 70.045, 70.218, 70.250, 70.275, 70.305, 72.083, 73.015, 73.017, 73.072, 73.186, 73.232, 73.233, 73.249, 73.307, 73.314, 73.320
Medick, Black *Medicago lupulina*	58.010, 61.018, 70.043, 70.293, 72.083
Medick, Sickle *Medicago sativa*	66.006
Medick, Spotted *Medicago arabica*	58.010
Trefoil, Lesser *Trifolium dubium*	61.018
trefoils	70.043, 70.218, 70.275, 73.235
Club-rushes	
Club-rush, Common *Schoenoplectus lacustris*	73.151, 73.152
Club-rush, Grey *Schoenoplectus tabernaemontani*	73.151
Cock's-foot *see* Grasses	
Colt's-foot *Tussilago farfara*	70.250, 72.031, 73.272
Comfreys	
Comfrey, Common *Symphytum officinale*	73.012, 73.368
comfreys *Symphytum* spp.	70.011, 72.029
Corydalis, Yellow *Pseudofumaria lutea*	73.237
Cotoneasters	
Cotoneaster, Wall *Cotoneaster horizontalis*	61.012, 66.003
cotoneasters *Cotoneaster* spp.	70.226, 70.241, 72.011, 72.017, 73.033, 73.037, 73.068
Cottongrasses	
Cottongrass, Common *Eriophorum angustifolium*	59.004, 73.118, 73.127
Cottongrass, Hare's-tail *Eriophorum vaginatum*	59.004, 73.254
cottongrasses *Eriophorum* spp.	73.144, 73.364
Couch, Common *see* Grasses	
Couch, Sand *see* Grasses	
couches *see* Grasses	
Cowberry *see* Bilberries	
Cowslip *see* Primroses	
Cow-wheats	
Cow-wheat, Common *Melampyrum pratense*	59.036, 70.153
Cow-wheat, Field *Melampyrum arvense*	70.153
Cranberry *see* Bilberries	
Crane's-bills and Stork's-bill	
Crane's-bill, Bloody *Geranium sanguineum*	66.008
Crane's-bill, Dove's-foot *Geranium molle*	61.015
Crane's-bill, Shining *Geranium lucidum*	70.287
Stork's-bill, Common *Erodium cicutarium*	61.015
Cresses	
Bitter-cress, Hairy *Cardamine hirsuta*	58.008, 70.049
Bitter-cress, Large *Cardamine amara*	58.003, 58.008
Cress, Hoary *Lepidium draba*	58.007, 73.235
Rock-cress, Hairy *Arabis hirsuta*	58.003
Water-cress *Rorippa officinale*	58.003, 58.007, 58.008
Winter-cress *Barbarea vulgaris*	58.003, 58.008
Crosswort *Cruciata laevipes*	70.093
Crowberry *Empetrum nigrum*	54.006, 70.014, 70.072, 70.289, 73.256, 73.357, 73.363, 73.364
Cuckooflower *Cardamine pratensis*	58.003, 58.008
Cudweed, Common *Filago germanica*	59.024

FOODPLANT	BUTTERFLY AND MOTH CHECKLIST NUMBERS
Currants	
Currant, Black *Ribes nigrum*	50.002, 52.013, 59.031, 70.089, 70.092, 70.097, 70.182, 70.205, 70.215, 70.243, 72.017, 73.208, 73.270
Currant, Red *Ribes rubrum*	52.013, 59.031, 70.089, 70.092, 70.097, 70.182, 70.205, 70.215
currants *Ribes* spp.	70.184, 70.245, 70.252, 70.305, 73.114, 73.237
Gooseberry *Ribes uva-crispa*	52.013, 59.031, 66.003, 70.089, 70.092, 70.182, 70.205, 70.215, 72.013, 73.195
Dahlia *Dahlia x hortensis*	70.161, 73.270, 73.274
Daisy, Oxeye *Leucanthemum vulgare*	72.031
Dame's-violet *Hesperis matronalis*	58.003, 58.006
dandelions *Taraxacum* spp.	3.001, 3.005, 70.016, 70.052, 70.059, 70.250, 72.022, 72.023, 72.024, 72.025, 72.026, 72.027, 72.030, 73.015, 73.017, 73.044, 73.092, 73.096, 73.097, 73.101, 73.102, 73.182, 73.186, 73.194, 73.195, 73.228, 73.233, 73.235, 73.236, 73.249, 73.255, 73.261, 73.266, 73.273, 73.275, 73.298, 73.307, 73.325, 73.328, 73.329, 73.331, 73.334, 73.353, 73.359, 73.360, 73.361
Dead-nettles	
Dead-nettle, Red *Lamium purpureum*	3.002, 72.022, 73.017, 73.353
Dead-nettle, White *Lamium album*	3.002, 70.100, 70.229, 72.022, 72.027, 72.030, 73.012, 73.016, 73.017, 73.018, 73.328, 73.346, 73.348, 73.357, 73.359
dead-nettles *Lamium* spp.	3.005, 72.026, 73.096, 73.343, 73.366
Dewberry *see* Brambles	
Dill *Anethum graveolens*	56.003
Docks and Sorrels	
Dock, Broad-leaved *Rumex obtusifolius*	3.001, 73.123, 73.229, 73.231, 73.259, 73.270, 73.343, 73.345, 73.348, 73.351
Dock, Curled *Rumex crispus*	52.015, 66.004, 73.229
Dock, Water *Rumex hydrolapathum*	52.015, 72.018, 72.021, 73.035, 73.107
docks *Rumex* spp.	3.002, 3.005, 69.015, 70.016, 70.029, 70.052, 70.059, 70.097, 70.131, 70.250, 70.265, 72.012, 72.020, 72.022, 72.023, 72.024, 72.025, 72.026, 72.027, 72.029, 73.015, 73.092, 73.096, 73.097, 73.102, 73.105, 73.107, 73.113, 73.181, 73.182, 73.184, 73.186, 73.187, 73.194, 73.195, 73.208, 73.209, 73.228, 73.233, 73.235, 73.237, 73.242, 73.249, 73.255, 73.260, 73.261, 73.263, 73.264, 73.265, 73.266, 73.271, 73.274, 73.275, 73.307, 73.314, 73.317, 73.320, 73.325, 73.328, 73.329, 73.331, 73.332, 73.333, 73.334, 73.336, 73.342, 73.346, 73.350, 73.352, 73.353, 73.357, 73.359, 73.360, 73.361, 73.365, 73.366
Sorrel, Common *Rumex acetosa*	52.015, 54.002, 70.029, 72.018, 73.044, 73.096, 73.187, 73.190, 73.230, 73.366
Sorrel, Sheep's *Rumex acetosella*	52.015, 54.002, 66.006, 72.023, 73.366
sorrels *Rumex* spp.	69.015, 70.059, 70.262, 73.105, 73.231
Dog's-tail, Crested *see* Grasses	
Dogwoods	
Dogwood *Cornus sanguinea*	61.005, 61.012, 66.007, 69.006, 70.184, 70.200, 70.221, 70.247, 70.303, 72.027, 72.045, 73.036, 73.195, 73.360
dogwoods *Cornus* spp.	69.005
Elder *Sambucus nigra*	70.142, 70.160, 70.169, 70.184, 70.231, 70.243, 72.019, 73.270
elephant-ears *Bergenia* spp.	72.017

FOODPLANT	BUTTERFLY AND MOTH CHECKLIST NUMBERS
Elms	
Elm, English *Ulmus procera*	50.001, 70.206, 70.246, 70.254, 70.255, 73.183, 73.214, 73.215, 73.217, 73.267
Elm, Japanese *Ulmus davidiana*	70.206
Elm, Small-leaved *Ulmus minor*	73.214, 73.215, 73.217
Elm, Wych *Ulmus glabra*	52.012, 61.006, 70.116, 70.206, 70.243, 70.246, 70.247, 70.255, 70.270, 70.280, 72.029, 73.179, 73.181, 73.182, 73.183, 73.192, 73.214, 73.215, 73.217
elms *Ulmus* spp.	50.002, 59.031, 61.006, 66.001, 66.003, 66.005, 68.001, 70.107, 70.108, 70.116, 70.205, 70.226, 70.244, 70.245, 70.248, 70.251, 70.252, 70.256, 71.025, 72.010, 72.013, 72.015, 72.017, 72.018, 72.030, 72.055, 73.036, 73.038, 73.063, 73.065, 73.107, 73.188, 73.194, 73.195, 73.210, 73.215, 73.216, 73.217, 73.242, 73.244, 73.250, 73.271, 73.348, 73.351, 74.008
Enchanter's-nightshade *Circaea lutetiana*	69.016, 70.094, 73.113
Escallonia *Escallonia rubra*	61.012, 72.024
Evening-primrose, Common *Oenothera biennis*	69.016, 72.029
Everlasting-pea, Broad-leaved *see* Vetches, Tares and Peas	
Everlasting-pea, Narrow-leaved *see* Vetches, Tares and Peas	
eyebrights *Euphrasia* spp.	70.134, 70.135, 70.136
False-acacia *Robinia pseudoacacia*	71.025
Fat-hen *see* Goosefoots and Oraches	
Fennel *Foeniculum vulgare*	56.003, 73.064
Fennel, Hog's *Peucedanum officinale*	56.003, 73.122
Fescue, Red *see* Grasses	
Fescue, Rush-leaved *see* Grasses	
Fescue, Tall *see* Grasses	
fescues *see* Grasses	
Feverfew *Tanacetum parthenium*	73.053
Figworts	
Figwort, Common *Scrophularia nodosa*	73.056, 73.058
Figwort, Water *Scrophularia auriculata*	3.005, 73.058, 73.358
figworts *Scrophularia* spp.	73.121, 73.332
Firethorn *Pyracantha coccinea*	70.243, 72.017, 73.038, 73.113
Flax, Fairy *Linum catharticum*	70.293
Fleabane, Common *Pulicaria dysenterica*	70.173, 70.179, 70.190, 72.012, 72.024, 72.073, 73.074, 73.121, 73.247
Flixweed *Descurainia sophia*	58.007, 70.049, 70.061, 70.189, 70.197, 72.031, 73.015, 73.072, 73.255, 73.275, 73.359
Forget-me-nots	
Forget-me-not, Water *Myosotis scorpioides*	72.029
forget-me-nots *Myosotis* spp.	70.243, 72.030, 73.361
Forsythia *Forsythia* x *intermedia*	69.005, 69.006
Foxglove *Digitalis purpurea*	59.036, 70.151, 72.029, 73.114, 73.121, 73.228, 73.235, 73.237, 73.332, 73.334, 73.342, 73.345
Foxtail, Meadow *see* Grasses	
fuchsias *Fuchsia* spp.	69.014, 69.015, 69.016
Galingale *Cyperus longus*	73.123
Geraniums	
Geranium, Scarlet *Pelargonium* x *hybridum*	73.076
geraniums *Pelargonium* spp.	3.002, 58.006, 70.097, 72.029, 73.113, 73.274, 73.368
glassworts *Salicornia* spp.	70.166
Globeflower *Trollius europaeus*	73.014

FOODPLANT	BUTTERFLY AND MOTH CHECKLIST NUMBERS
Godetia *Clarkia amoena*	69.014, 69.016
Goldenrods	
Goldenrod *Solidago virgaurea*	70.142, 70.160, 70.161, 70.161, 70.173, 70.180, 70.183, 70.190, 70.252, 72.024, 73.055, 73.265
Goldenrod, Canadian *Solidago canadensis*	70.173, 70.243
goldenrods *Solidago* spp.	70.179
Golden-samphire *Limbarda crithmoides*	66.004
Gooseberry *see* Currants	
Goosefoots and Oraches	
Fat-hen *Chenopodium album*	73.267, 73.320, 73.328
Goosefoot, Red *Oxybasis rubra*	73.323
goosefoots	70.069, 70.166, 70.179, 70.190, 73.092, 73.106, 73.255, 73.266, 73.274, 73.275, 73.317
Orache, Common *Atriplex patula*	70.029, 73.323
Orache, Grass-leaved *Atriplex littoralis*	66.004
oraches *Atriplex* spp.	70.069, 70.141, 70.166, 73.106, 73.255, 73.267, 73.275, 73.348
Sea-purslane *Atriplex portulacoides*	66.004, 73.323
Gorses	
Gorse *Ulex europaeus*	61.005, 66.006, 66.007, 70.040, 70.041, 70.042, 70.141, 70.258, 70.295, 70.297, 70.306, 72.016, 72.027, 72.045, 72.046, 73.265
Gorse, Dwarf *Ulex minor*	61.005
gorses *Ulex* spp.	61.012, 61.014
Grape-vine *Vitis vinifera*	69.015, 69.016, 73.062
Grasses	
Barley *Hordeum* sp.	73.123
Bent, Bristle *Agrostis curtisii*	59.013, 72.032, 73.233
Bent, Brown *Agrostis vinealis*	73.344
Bent, Common *Agrostis capillaris*	59.008, 73.288
Bent, Creeping *Agrostis stolonifera*	59.003, 59.009
bents *Agrostis* spp.	59.002, 59.005, 59.010, 59.011
Brome, False *Brachypodium sylvaticum*	57.004, 57.005, 57.006, 57.009, 59.002, 59.003, 59.009, 59.010, 59.013, 66.010, 72.002, 73.024, 73.154, 73.160
Brome, Upright *Bromopsis erecta*	57.004
Canary-grass, Reed *Phalaris arundinacea*	66.010, 73.154, 73.159, 73.168, 73.173, 73.289, 73.294, 73.344
Cereals	73.095, 73.120, 73.131, 73.157, 73.158, 73.169, 73.171
Cock's-foot *Dactylis glomerata*	57.005, 57.006, 57.009, 59.002, 59.003, 59.009, 59.010, 59.011, 59.012, 66.010, 72.027, 72.084, 73.120, 73.155, 73.156, 73.157, 73.158, 73.162, 73.169, 73.170, 73.171, 73.173, 73.174, 73.175, 73.288, 73.290, 73.291, 73.293, 73.295, 73.297, 73.298, 73.301, 73.344
Couch, Common *Elymus repens*	57.005, 57.009, 59.002, 59.003, 59.009, 59.010, 59.011, 59.013, 73.120, 73.131, 73.154, 73.157, 73.158, 73.162, 73.173, 73.178, 73.290, 73.291, 73.297
Couch, Sand *Elymus junceiformis*	73.132, 73.311
couches *Elymus* spp.	66.010, 73.344
Deergrass *Trichophorum germanicum*	73.254
Dog's-tail, Crested *Cynosurus cristatus*	59.005
Fescue, Red *Festuca rubra*	3.003, 57.009, 59.012, 59.013, 73.161, 73.290
Fescue, Rush-leaved *Festuca arenaria*	73.308
Fescue, Tall *Schedonorus arundinaceus*	73.148, 73.169, 73.172, 73.298
fescues *Festuca* spp.	59.005, 59.010, 59.011, 73.131, 73.170
Foxtail, Meadow *Alopecurus pratensis*	57.005, 57.006

FOODPLANT	BUTTERFLY AND MOTH CHECKLIST NUMBERS
grasses	3.001, 3.002, 3.005, 66.004, 70.131, 72.012, 72.013, 73.022, 73.023, 73.026, 73.095, 73.097, 73.109, 73.120, 73.128, 73.131, 73.144, 73.154, 73.155, 73.156, 73.157, 73.158, 73.159, 73.160, 73.161, 73.162, 73.163, 73.164, 73.165, 73.167, 73.169, 73.170, 73.171, 73.172, 73.173, 73.174, 73.175, 73.176, 73.178, 73.186, 73.193, 73.232, 73.238, 73.252, 73.253, 73.254, 73.260, 73.288, 73.289, 73.290, 73.291, 73.293, 73.295, 73.297, 73.298, 73.301, 73.303, 73.304, 73.322, 73.334, 73.341, 73.342, 73.346, 73.348, 73.357
Hair-grass, Early *Aira praecox*	59.013, 73.311
Hair-grass, Silver *Aira caryophyllea*	73.109
Hair-grass, Tufted *Deschampsia cespitosa*	59.003, 59.008, 59.009, 59.013, 66.010, 73.026, 73.061, 73.128, 73.147, 73.155, 73.169, 73.172, 73.175, 73.176, 73.231, 73.233, 73.254, 73.291, 73.293, 73.344
Hair-grass, Wavy *Avenella flexuosa*	59.002, 59.008, 73.061, 73.156, 73.159, 73.175, 73.252, 73.344
Hairy-brome *Bromopsis ramosa*	57.004
Holcus sp.	73.171
Lyme-grass *Leymus arenarius*	73.119, 73.138, 73.171
Maize *Zea mays*	70.141
Marram *Ammophila arenaria*	59.013, 66.006, 66.010, 73.131, 73.171, 73.248, 73.299, 73.300, 73.308
Mat-grass *Nardus stricta*	59.005, 59.007, 73.109, 73.252, 73.253, 73.254
Meadow-grass, Annual *Poa annua*	59.002, 59.013, 70.059, 73.109, 73.128, 73.154, 73.155, 73.157, 73.159, 73.163, 73.178, 73.193, 73.231, 73.291, 73.293, 73.295, 73.357
Meadow-grass, Bulbous *Poa bulbosa*	73.132, 73.161
Meadow-grass, Rough *Poa trivialis*	73.165
Meadow-grass, Smooth *Poa pratensis*	59.010, 73.027
Meadow-grass, Wood *Poa nemoralis*	73.160, 73.165, 73.288
meadow-grasses *Poa* spp.	59.003, 59.005, 59.009, 59.011, 66.010, 73.253, 73.298, 73.342
Melick, Wood *Melica uniflora*	73.160
Millet, Wood *Milium effusum*	59.009, 73.160
Moor-grass, Blue *Sesleria caerulea*	59.008, 73.116, 73.146
Moor-grass, Purple *Molinia caerulea*	57.004, 57.009, 59.004, 59.008, 66.010, 72.002, 72.024, 72.084, 73.024, 73.027, 73.061, 73.127, 73.209, 73.254, 73.289
Oat-grass, Downy *Avenula pubescens*	59.010
Oat-grass, False *Arrhenatherum elatius*	66.006, 73.171, 73.172
oat-grasses	73.120, 73.186
Pampas-grass *Cortaderia selloana*	73.168
quaking-grasses *Briza* spp.	73.120
Reed, Common *Phragmites australis*	50.003, 66.010, 72.084, 73.035, 73.1, 73.134, 73.137, 73.139, 73.140, 73.141, 73.150, 73.159, 73.289, 73.293, 73.294, 73.302, 73.305
Ribbon-grass *Phalaris arundinacea*	66.010
rye-grasses *Lolium* spp.	59.010
Saltmarsh-grass, Borrer's *Puccinellia fasciculata*	73.132
Saltmarsh-grass, Common *Puccinellia maritima*	73.126, 73.132, 73.161, 73.292
Saltmarsh-grass, Reflexed *Puccinellia distans*	73.161
Sheep's-fescue *Festuca ovina*	57.008, 59.008, 59.012, 59.013, 73.171, 73.172, 73.253, 73.254, 73.341, 73.344, 73.365

FOODPLANT	BUTTERFLY AND MOTH CHECKLIST NUMBERS
Small-reed, Purple *Calamagrostis canescens*	73.023, 73.149
Small-reed, Wood *Calamagrostis epigejos*	57.009, 66.010, 73.022, 73.023, 73.145, 73.149
Soft-grass, Creeping *Holcus mollis*	57.005, 57.006, 57.009, 73.288
Sweet-grass, Reed *Glyceria maxima*	73.035, 73.144, 73.168, 73.267
Timothy *Phleum pratense*	57.005, 57.006, 57.009, 59.012
Tor-grass *Brachypodium rupestre*	57.004, 57.005, 57.007, 57.009, 59.002, 59.005, 59.012, 72.002
Vernal-grass, Sweet *Anthoxanthum odoratum*	59.008, 73.233, 73.288
wheats *Triticum* spp.	73.123
Whorl-grass *Catabrosa aquatica*	73.035
Yorkshire-fog *Holcus lanatus*	57.006, 57.009, 59.002, 59.003, 59.012, 73.022, 73.023, 73.176, 73.193
Greenweeds	
Greenweed, Dyer's *Genista tinctoria*	61.005, 70.040, 70.041, 73.247, 73.248, 73.263, 73.265
Whin, Petty *Genista anglica*	61.005, 70.040, 70.041, 70.285, 70.295, 70.297, 70.306
Gromwell, Field *Buglossoides arvensis*	73.231
Ground-ivy *Glechoma hederacea*	70.051, 70.052, 72.030, 73.018
Groundsel *see* Ragworts and Groundsels	
Groundsel, Heath *see* Ragworts and Groundsels	
Groundsel, Sticky *see* Ragworts and Groundsels	
Guelder-rose *Viburnum opulus*	52.010, 69.006, 70.184, 70.200, 73.244
Gum, Snow *Eucalyptus niphophila*	73.244
Gypsywort *Lycopus europaeus*	70.179
Hairy-brome *see* Grasses	
Harebell *see* Bellflowers	
Hawkbits	
Hawkbit, Autumn *Scorzoneroides autumnalis*	70.250
hawkbits	70.173, 70.189
Hawk's-beards	
Hawk's-beard, Beaked *Crepis vesicaria*	70.294
Hawk's-beard, Smooth *Crepis capillaris*	73.072, 73.273, 73.279, 73.280
hawk's-beards *Crepis* spp.	70.189, 70.190, 73.052, 73.074, 73.279
Hawkweeds	
hawkweeds *Hieracium* spp.	59.034, 70.173, 72.027, 73.052, 73.064, 73.072, 73.279
Mouse-ear-hawkweed *Pilosella officinarum*	72.023, 73.018, 73.273
Hawthorns	
Hawthorn *Crataegus monogyna*	50.002, 52.011, 65.007, 65.009, 66.001, 66.002, 66.003, 66.005, 66.007, 66.012, 68.001, 70.024, 70.067, 70.086, 70.097, 70.106, 70.107, 70.109, 70.141, 70.142, 70.144, 70.157, 70.161, 70.161, 70.174, 70.183, 70.190, 70.200, 70.205, 70.223, 70.226, 70.230, 70.241, 70.243, 70.245, 70.246, 70.247, 70.248, 70.252, 70.255, 70.258, 70.268, 70.271, 70.273, 70.279, 70.280, 70.282, 70.303, 70.306, 71.009, 71.021, 71.025, 72.012, 72.019, 73.107, 73.186, 73.187, 73.188, 73.190, 73.194, 73.195, 73.210, 73.228, 73.242, 73.243, 73.244, 73.260, 73.331, 73.343, 73.345, 73.353, 73.357, 73.360, 73.361, 73.368, 74.003
Hawthorn, Midland *Crataegus laevigata*	70.086, 70.205, 70.226, 70.247, 70.248, 70.255, 70.268, 70.273, 70.279, 70.280, 70.282, 73.192, 74.003

FOODPLANT	BUTTERFLY AND MOTH CHECKLIST NUMBERS
hawthorns *Crataegus* spp.	70.084, 70.108, 70.156, 70.169, 70.184, 70.240, 70.244, 70.254, 70.256, 70.265, 70.270, 70.305, 72.010, 72.013, 72.015, 72.016, 72.017, 72.018, 72.020, 72.045, 72.055, 73.032, 73.033, 73.036, 73.037, 73.038, 73.062, 73.064, 73.065, 73.068, 73.216, 73.217, 73.225, 73.249, 73.264, 73.333, 73.346, 73.348, 73.351
Hazel *Corylus avellana*	59.031, 65.009, 65.013, 66.002, 66.003, 66.007, 68.001, 70.068, 70.074, 70.090, 70.106, 70.107, 70.108, 70.111, 70.113, 70.156, 70.205, 70.207, 70.223, 70.226, 70.227, 70.240, 70.244, 70.245, 70.246, 70.247, 70.248, 70.251, 70.254, 70.255, 70.256, 70.265, 70.268, 70.270, 70.273, 70.274, 70.277, 70.299, 70.303, 70.305, 71.009, 71.012, 71.021, 71.025, 72.012, 72.013, 72.015, 72.016, 72.017, 72.018, 72.055, 73.032, 73.038, 73.047, 73.062, 73.065, 73.070, 73.113, 73.114, 73.210, 73.216, 73.225, 73.242, 73.243, 73.244, 73.245, 73.261, 73.265, 73.267, 73.270, 73.333, 73.348, 73.360, 73.361, 74.008
Heather/Heaths	
Heath, Cross-leaved *Erica tetralix*	61.005, 61.014, 66.008, 68.001, 70.026, 70.072, 70.225, 70.249, 70.262, 70.263, 70.275, 70.285, 70.292, 70.306, 72.016, 73.042, 73.073, 73.191, 73.355
Heather *Calluna vulgaris*	61.012, 61.014, 66.002, 66.006, 66.007, 66.008, 68.001, 70.014, 70.026, 70.072, 70.074, 70.076, 70.090, 70.097, 70.098, 70.106, 70.109, 70.110, 70.131, 70.141, 70.161, 70.168, 70.179, 70.205, 70.225, 70.230, 70.241, 70.249, 70.262, 70.263, 70.265, 70.275, 70.285, 70.287, 70.292, 70.295, 70.306, 72.007, 72.013, 72.016, 72.017, 72.023, 73.021, 73.035, 73.042, 73.044, 73.073, 73.188, 73.188, 73.190, 73.207, 73.209, 73.231, 73.232, 73.233, 73.238, 73.249, 73.257, 73.265, 73.271, 73.272, 73.332, 73.333, 73.334, 73.338, 73.345, 73.350, 73.355, 73.356, 73.362, 73.365, 73.367
Heather, Bell *Erica cinerea*	61.014, 66.002, 66.008, 68.001, 70.072, 70.110, 70.249, 70.262, 70.263, 70.275, 70.285, 70.292, 70.295, 72.023, 72.025, 73.073, 73.191, 73.257, 73.338, 73.355, 73.356, 73.362, 73.365
heathers	54.006, 70.097, 72.018, 72.024, 72.032, 73.353
heaths *Erica* spp.	73.272
Hemp-agrimony *Eupatorium cannabinum*	68.001, 70.142, 70.173, 70.179, 70.190, 72.029, 72.030, 73.011, 73.012, 73.018, 73.121
Hemp-nettle, Common *Galeopsis tetrahit*	70.133, 73.012
Henbane *Hyoscyamus niger*	73.070, 73.074
Hogweed *Heracleum sphondylium*	70.160, 70.175, 70.183, 73.017, 73.234, 73.314
Holcus sp. see grasses	
Holly *Ilex aquifolium*	61.012, 69.006, 70.141, 70.200, 70.243
Hollyhock *Alcea rosea*	70.070, 73.270
Honesty *Lunaria annua*	58.003, 70.049
Honeysuckles	
Honeysuckle *Lonicera periclymenum*	50.002, 59.021, 59.033, 66.007, 69.006, 69.009, 70.024, 70.067, 70.202, 70.230, 70.231, 70.241, 70.243, 70.256, 70.258, 70.265, 70.268, 70.270, 70.305, 72.019, 72.029, 72.030, 73.016, 73.018, 73.044, 73.062, 73.108, 73.113, 73.187, 73.237, 73.249, 73.250, 73.260, 73.261, 73.264, 73.333, 73.352, 73.360, 73.368
honeysuckles *Lonicera* spp.	73.069
Hop *Humulus lupulus*	3.005, 59.023, 59.026, 59.031, 69.006, 70.182, 70.252, 72.004, 72.015, 72.019, 72.031, 73.002, 73.015, 73.092, 73.123, 73.208, 73.209, 73.250, 73.267, 73.270, 73.328

FOODPLANT	BUTTERFLY AND MOTH CHECKLIST NUMBERS
Horehound, Black *Ballota nigra*	3.002, 3.005, 70.179, 72.027
Hornbeam *Carpinus betulus*	70.095, 70.106, 70.107, 70.108, 70.111, 70.245, 70.246, 70.254, 70.255, 70.256, 70.270, 70.303, 71.021, 71.025, 72.010, 72.055, 73.032, 73.062, 73.063, 73.180, 73.332, 73.353
Horse-chestnut *Aesculus hippocastanum*	50.002, 70.243, 73.039, 73.201
Horse-radish *Armoracia rusticana*	58.006, 58.007, 58.008, 70.049
Hound's-tongue *Cynoglossum officinale*	72.025, 72.026, 72.029, 73.235, 73.248, 73.311, 73.323, 73.328
Hyssop *Hyssopus officinalis*	73.012
Irises	
Iris, Stinking *Iris foetidissima*	73.171
Iris, Yellow *Iris pseudacorus*	70.250, 72.021, 73.022, 73.042, 73.044, 73.119, 73.123, 73.151, 73.152, 73.208, 73.209, 73.228, 73.271
irises *Iris* spp.	73.129
Ironwood, Persian *Parrotia persica*	71.025
Ivy, Common *Hedera helix*	61.012, 66.007, 70.004, 70.012, 70.016, 70.141, 70.200, 70.205, 70.243, 70.258, 72.019, 72.053, 73.107, 73.114, 73.237
Jasmines	
Jasmine, Summer *Jasminum officinale*	69.005
Jasmine, Winter *Jasminum nudiflorum*	70.257
jasmines *Jasminum* spp.	69.006, 70.305, 72.019
Juneberry *Amelanchier lamarckii*	66.005, 73.038
Knapweeds	
Knapweed, Common *Centaurea nigra*	54.001, 59.024, 70.291, 73.121, 73.345
Knapweed, Greater *Centaurea scabiosa*	54.001, 59.024, 59.033
knapweeds *Centaurea* spp.	70.173, 70.190, 70.250, 73.072, 73.074, 73.101
Knotgrasses	
Knotgrass *Polygonum aviculare*	66.008, 69.015, 70.016, 70.051, 70.052, 70.250, 70.305, 73.105, 73.106, 73.273, 73.325, 73.328, 73.329, 73.333, 73.352
knotgrasses *Polygonum* spp.	73.092, 73.097, 73.101, 73.263, 73.264, 73.266, 73.272, 73.320
Knotweeds	
Knotweed, Himalayan *Koenigia polystachya*	70.120
Knotweed, Japanese *Reynoutria japonica*	72.013
Laburnum *Laburnum anagyroides*	71.025, 73.039, 73.228
Lady's-mantles	
Lady's-mantle, Alpine *Alchemilla alpina*	70.098
Lady's-mantles *Alchemilla* spp.	70.048, 73.113
Larkspurs	
Larkspur *Consolida ajacis*	73.264
Larkspurs *Consolida* spp.	73.014
Laurel, Cherry *see* Cherries	
Laurels *see* Cherries	
Laurustinus *Viburnum tinus*	69.006
Lavenders *Lavandula* spp.	70.241
Lettuces	
Lettuce, Garden *Lactuca sativa*	73.280, 73.359
Lettuce, Great *Lactuca virosa*	73.280
Lettuce, Prickly *Lactuca serriola*	73.099, 73.279, 73.280
Lettuces *Lactuca* spp.	72.030, 73.307, 73.325, 73.328, 73.329
Lettuce, Wall *Mycelis muralis*	70.190, 73.280
Lilac *Syringa vulgaris*	50.002, 69.005, 69.006, 70.230, 70.231, 70.243, 70.245, 70.257, 70.258, 73.063, 73.201, 73.249

FOODPLANT	BUTTERFLY AND MOTH CHECKLIST NUMBERS
lilies	72.017
Limes	
Lime *Tilia* x *europaea*	70.164, 70.251, 73.179
Lime, Large-leaved *Tilia platyphyllos*	70.164
Lime, Small-leaved *Tilia cordata*	53.002, 65.006, 70.164, 70.248, 72.055, 73.179, 74.004
limes *Tilia* spp.	66.001, 70.086, 70.095, 70.096, 70.226, 70.236, 70.240, 70.245, 70.247, 70.254, 70.255, 70.273, 70.305, 71.009, 71.021, 71.025, 72.010, 72.015, 72.017, 73.015, 73.032, 73.036, 73.038, 73.062, 73.063, 73.065, 73.201, 73.210, 73.217, 73.242, 73.249, 74.008
Liquorice, Wild *Astragalus glycyphyllos*	61.020, 72.063
Loosestrife, Yellow *Lysimachia vulgaris*	70.129, 70.142, 70.161, 72.021, 73.035
Lords-and-ladies *Arum maculatum*	73.348, 73.354
Louseworts	
Lousewort *Pedicularis sylvatica*	72.067
louseworts *Pedicularis* spp.	72.021
Lucerne *Medicago sativa*	58.010, 61.012, 66.006, 70.218, 72.083, 73.273
Lupins	
Lupin, Garden *Lupinus polyphyllus*	73.270
Lupin, Tree *Lupinus arboreus*	66.006, 70.195, 73.308
Madder, Wild *Rubia peregrina*	69.010, 69.014
Maize *see* Grasses	
Mallows	
Mallow, Common *Malva sylvestris*	70.070, 73.346
mallows *Malva* spp.	59.024, 73.114
Marsh-mallow *Althaea officinalis*	70.070, 73.125
Tree-mallow *Malva arborea*	70.070, 73.076
Mangel-wurzel *see* Beets	
Maples	
Maple, Field *Acer campestre*	70.031, 70.106, 70.108, 70.114, 70.148, 70.184, 70.244, 70.245, 70.255, 70.256, 71.021, 71.022, 71.024, 73.032, 73.039, 73.063, 73.180, 73.210, 73.216, 73.245, 73.250
Maple, Norway *Acer platanoides*	73.039
maples *Acer* spp.	71.022, 73.039
Sycamore *Acer pseudoplatanus*	50.002, 70.095, 70.106, 70.113, 70.114, 70.184, 70.200, 70.243, 70.244, 70.245, 70.253, 70.254, 70.256, 70.268, 70.303, 71.021, 71.022, 71.024, 71.025, 72.015, 72.017, 72.055, 73.032, 73.036, 73.039, 73.180, 73.194, 73.242, 73.343
Marigold, Pot *Calendula officinalis*	73.074, 73.342
Marjorams	
Marjoram, Pot *Origanum majorana*	70.059
Marjoram, Wild *Origanum vulgare*	61.013, 70.021, 70.023, 70.100, 70.141, 70.179, 70.189, 70.291, 73.012
Marram *see* Grasses	
Mayweed, Scentless *see* Chamomiles	
mayweeds *see* Chamomiles	
Meadow-rues	
Meadow-rue, Common *Thalictrum flavum*	70.140
Meadow-rue, Lesser *Thalictrum minus*	70.140
Meadowsweet *Filipendula ulmaria*	65.008, 66.008, 68.001, 70.025, 70.097, 72.012, 72.018, 72.029, 73.044, 73.123, 73.187, 73.209, 73.243, 73.247, 73.249, 73.272, 73.346
Medick, Black *see* Clovers and Trefoils	
Medick, Sickle *see* Clovers and Trefoils	
Medick, Spotted *see* Clovers and Trefoils	
Melick, Wood *see* Grasses	

FOODPLANT	BUTTERFLY AND MOTH CHECKLIST NUMBERS
Melilot, Ribbed *Melilotus officinalis*	57.005, 58.010, 66.006
Mercury, Dog's *Mercurialis perennis*	72.025, 73.352, 73.354
Michaelmas-daisies *see* Asters	
Mignonettes	
Mignonette, Wild *Reseda lutea*	58.007, 58.008
Weld *Reseda luteola*	58.003
Milk-parsley *Thysselinum palustre*	56.003
Milkworts	
Milkwort, Common *Polygala vulgaris*	72.067
Milkwort, Heath *Polygala serpyllifolia*	72.067
Millet, Wood *see* Grasses	
Mind-your-own-business *Soleirolia soleirolii*	73.342
Mints	
Mint, Corn *Mentha arvensis*	73.231
Mint, Round-leaved *Mentha suaveolens*	70.097
Mint, Water *Mentha aquatica*	72.021
mints *Mentha* spp.	70.230, 73.017, 73.228, 73.237
Spearmint *Mentha spicata*	73.012
mock-privets *Phillyrea* spp.	69.006
Monkeyflower *Erythranthe guttata*	73.064
Monk's-hoods	
monk's-hoods *Aconitum* spp.	73.014
Wolf's-bane *Aconitum lycoctonum*	73.014
montbretias *Crocosmia* spp.	66.007
morning-glories *Ipomoea* spp.	69.004
Mouse-ears	
Mouse-ear, Common *Cerastium fontanum*	73.048
Mouse-ear, Field *Cerastium arvense*	70.154, 73.048
Mouse-ear, Sticky *Cerastium glomeratum*	73.048, 73.311
mouse-ears *Cerastium* spp.	73.313
Mugwort *see* Wormwoods	
Mulleins	
Mullein, Dark *Verbascum nigrum*	70.189, 73.057, 73.058
Mullein, Great *Verbascum thapsus*	72.022, 72.031, 73.058, 73.113
Mullein, Great x Dark hybrid *Verbascum x emialbum*	73.057
Mullein, Hoary *Verbascum pulverulentum*	73.058
Mullein, Moth *Verbascum blattaria*	73.058
Mullein, Olympian *Verbascum olympicum*	73.058
Mullein, White *Verbascum lychnitis*	73.057, 73.058
mulleins *Verbascum* spp.	73.057, 73.320, 73.359
Mustards	
Mustard, Garlic *Alliaria petiolata*	58.003, 58.007, 58.008, 70.049
Mustard, Hedge *Sisymbrium officinale*	58.003, 58.007, 58.008
Mustard, Tower *Turritis glabra*	58.003
Myrtle, Chilean *Luma apiculata*	70.033
nasturtium *Tropaeolum majus*	58.006, 58.007, 58.008, 70.049
navelwort *Umbilicus rupestris*	70.014, 70.205
Nettles	
Nettle, Common *Urtica dioica*	59.023, 59.024, 59.026, 59.027, 59.031, 70.131, 72.003, 72.012, 72.019, 72.020, 72.022, 72.025, 72.026, 72.027, 72.029, 72.030, 73.001, 73.002, 73.012, 73.015, 73.016, 73.017, 73.018, 73.021, 73.092, 73.121, 73.228, 73.249, 73.267, 73.270, 73.328, 73.343, 73.345, 73.353, 73.354, 73.359, 73.366

FOODPLANT	BUTTERFLY AND MOTH CHECKLIST NUMBERS
Nettle, Small *Urtica urens*	59.023, 59.026, 59.027, 73.015, 73.016, 73.307
nettles *Urtica* spp.	3.005, 72.013, 73.114
Nightshade, Deadly *Atropa belladonna*	69.005
Nipplewort *Lapsana communis*	72.019
Oaks	
Oak, Holm *Quercus ilex*	52.012, 61.004, 66.003, 69.006, 70.033, 70.156, 70.248, 70.270, 71.001, 71.009, 73.223, 73.225, 73.227, 74.004, 74.009
Oak, Pedunculate *Quercus robur*	50.001, 52.012, 53.001, 53.002, 61.004, 65.002, 65.014, 65.015, 66.008, 70.035, 70.036, 70.086, 70.156, 70.157, 70.170, 70.184, 70.246, 70.248, 70.253, 70.255, 70.267, 70.268, 70.273, 70.300, 71.001, 71.010, 71.011, 71.016, 72.019, 72.022, 72.055, 72.056, 72.081, 72.082, 73.034, 73.063, 73.180, 73.202, 73.216, 73.218, 73.224, 73.225, 73.247, 73.261, 74.001, 74.004, 74.007, 74.008, 74.009
Oak, Sessile *Quercus petraea*	52.012, 61.004, 65.002, 65.014, 65.015, 70.156, 70.170, 70.246, 70.253, 70.300, 71.010, 71.011, 71.016, 73.225, 73.247, 74.007, 74.008
Oak, Turkey *Quercus cerris*	61.004, 71.001
oaks *Quercus* spp.	50.002, 53.001, 65.005, 65.013, 66.001, 66.002, 66.003, 66.007, 70.037, 70.095, 70.096, 70.097, 70.106, 70.107, 70.108, 70.161, 70.203, 70.223, 70.224, 70.226, 70.236, 70.240, 70.241, 70.243, 70.244, 70.245, 70.247, 70.251, 70.252, 70.254, 70.256, 70.264, 70.265, 70.270, 70.277, 70.282, 70.303, 70.305, 71.009, 71.012, 71.021, 71.025, 72.010, 72.011, 72.013, 72.015, 72.017, 72.018, 72.041, 72.045, 72.051, 72.053, 72.055, 72.070, 73.032, 73.036, 73.037, 73.038, 73.039, 73.040, 73.062, 73.065, 73.070, 73.108, 73.114, 73.187, 73.188, 73.190, 73.194, 73.195, 73.210, 73.217, 73.242, 73.243, 73.244, 73.245, 73.249, 73.250, 73.264, 73.265, 73.274, 73.351, 73.357
Olive *Olea europaea*	70.200
onions *Allium* spp.	73.255
Orache, Common *see* Goosefoots and Oraches	
Orache, Grass-leaved *see* Goosefoots and Oraches	
oraches *see* Goosefoots and Oraches	
Orchids	
Orchid, Lizard *Himantoglossum hircinum*	73.058
Spotted-orchid, Heath *Dactylorhiza maculata*	73.336
twayblades *Neottia* spp.	72.024
Oregon-grape *Mahonia aquifolium*	70.122
Orpine *Hylotelephium telephium*	70.183, 70.205, 73.092
Oxlip *see* Primroses	
Oxtongues	
Oxtongue, Bristly *Helminthotheca echioides*	73.280
oxtongues	73.279
Pansy, Wild *see* Violets	
Parsley, Cow *see* Chervils	
Parsley, Garden *Petroselinum crispum*	56.003, 73.012, 73.064
Parsnips	
Parsnip *Pastinaca sativa*	56.003
Parsnip, Wild *Pastinaca sativa*	70.160, 70.175, 70.190, 70.293
Pea, Garden *see* Vetches, Tares and Peas	

FOODPLANT	BUTTERFLY AND MOTH CHECKLIST NUMBERS
Pea, Marsh *see* Vetches, Tares and Peas	
Pea, Sweet *see* Vetches, Tares and Peas	
Peach *see* Cherries	
Pears	
Pear *Pyrus communis*	50.001, 50.002, 52.011, 65.007, 66.012, 70.144, 70.184, 70.243, 70.248, 71.009, 72.012, 72.013, 73.033, 73.037, 73.038, 73.217, 73.368, 74.003
pears *Pyrus* spp.	70.174
Pellitory-of-the-wall *Parietaria judaica*	59.023, 72.006
Pepper, Chilli *Capsicum annuum*	69.005
Pignut *Conopodium majus*	70.130, 70.161, 70.161
Pinks	
pinks *Dianthus* spp.	73.076, 73.283, 73.286
Sweet-William *Dianthus barbatus*	73.281, 73.282, 73.283, 73.286
Plane, London *Platanus* x *hispanica*	73.039
Plantains	
Plantain, Buck's-horn *Plantago coronopus*	59.034, 70.294
Plantain, Greater *Plantago major*	70.173, 73.101, 73.266
Plantain, Ribwort *Plantago lanceolata*	59.034, 59.036, 70.016, 73.044, 73.103, 73.123, 73.228, 73.229, 73.275, 73.329, 73.358
Plantain, Sea *Plantago maritima*	59.034, 66.004, 70.250, 73.044, 73.236, 73.266, 73.275
plantains *Plantago* spp.	59.033, 70.100, 70.305, 72.022, 72.023, 72.024, 72.025, 72.026, 72.030, 73.017, 73.092, 73.095, 73.096, 73.097, 73.099, 73.102, 73.233, 73.235, 73.237, 73.260, 73.298, 73.307, 73.314, 73.317, 73.328, 73.331, 73.333, 73.334, 73.357, 73.359, 73.361, 73.365
Ploughman's-spikenard *Inula conyzae*	72.046, 72.073, 73.074, 73.208
Plum *see* Cherries	
Plum, Wild *see* Cherries	
Polyanthus *see* Primroses	
Poplars	
Aspen *Populus tremula*	52.002, 59.022, 65.005, 65.010, 65.011, 66.001, 69.002, 69.003, 70.090, 70.107, 70.121, 70.190, 70.198, 70.204, 70.207, 70.228, 70.248, 70.251, 70.254, 70.255, 70.256, 70.270, 70.278, 70.280, 70.305, 71.003, 71.005, 71.007, 71.013, 71.017, 71.020, 71.021, 71.027, 71.028, 71.029, 72.001, 72.010, 72.022, 72.076, 72.078, 73.032, 73.036, 73.040, 73.046, 73.192, 73.210, 73.211, 73.213, 73.216, 73.220, 73.244, 73.245, 73.246, 73.250, 73.264, 74.008
Balsam-poplar, Eastern *Populus balsamifera*	73.213
balsam-poplars *Populus* spp.	52.002
Black-poplar *Populus nigra*	52.002, 52.003, 70.198, 70.227, 72.009, 72.078, 73.184, 73.212, 73.246, 73.247
Black-poplar, Hybrid *Populus* x *canadensis*	52.002, 72.009, 73.040, 73.046, 73.184
black-poplars *Populus nigra*	65.010, 73.244
Lombardy-poplar *Populus nigra*	52.002, 52.003, 73.046, 73.184, 73.213
poplar, Grey *Populus* x *canescens*	52.002, 66.003, 72.009
poplar, White *Populus alba*	52.002, 59.022, 65.010, 72.009, 72.078, 73.046, 73.213
poplars *Populus* spp.	50.001, 53.002, 65.011, 66.001, 66.002, 69.002, 69.003, 70.074, 70.198, 70.207, 70.244, 70.247, 70.252, 70.254, 70.278, 71.003, 71.005, 71.007, 71.013, 71.017, 71.020, 71.021, 71.027, 71.028, 71.029, 72.001, 72.009, 72.076, 72.078, 73.040, 73.046, 73.065, 73.181, 73.182, 73.190, 73.192, 73.210, 73.213, 73.222, 73.246, 73.250
poppy, Californian *Eschscholzia californica*	73.064
potato *Solanum tuberosum*	69.005, 73.113, 73.123, 73.264

FOODPLANT	BUTTERFLY AND MOTH CHECKLIST NUMBERS
Primroses	
Auricula *Primula auricula*	73.368
Cowslip *Primula veris*	60.001, 70.054, 70.059, 73.344, 73.366
Oxlip *Primula elatior*	73.354
Polyanthus *Primula x polyantha*	73.113
Primrose *Primula vulgaris*	60.001, 70.016, 70.054, 70.055, 70.131, 73.096, 73.099, 73.261, 73.333, 73.341, 73.343, 73.346, 73.348, 73.350, 73.352, 73.353, 73.354, 73.360, 73.361, 73.366
Privets	
Privet, Garden *Ligustrum ovalifolium*	69.006, 70.024, 70.205, 70.230, 70.231, 70.243, 70.257, 70.258, 73.062
Privet, Wild *Ligustrum vulgare*	69.002, 69.006, 70.200, 70.201, 70.231, 70.244, 70.245, 70.257, 70.270, 73.047, 73.062, 73.201, 73.343
privets *Ligustrum* spp.	50.002, 70.097
Purple-loosestrife *Lythrum salicaria*	68.001, 69.016, 69.017, 70.142, 70.275, 73.247
Quince, Japanese *Chaenomeles japonica*	73.033
Radish, Wild *Raphanus raphanistrum*	58.008
Ragged-Robin *see* Campions	
Ragworts and Groundsels	
Groundsel *Senecio vulgaris*	70.004, 70.173, 72.025, 72.027, 72.029, 72.030, 72.031, 73.016, 73.017, 73.018, 73.099, 73.102, 73.113, 73.186, 73.208, 73.228, 73.231, 73.237, 73.264, 73.329, 73.336, 73.359, 73.368
Groundsel, Heath *Senecio sylvaticus*	72.031
Groundsel, Sticky *Senecio viscosus*	73.072, 73.074
Ragwort, Common *Jacobaea vulgaris*	70.160, 70.161, 70.161, 70.173, 70.179, 70.187, 70.188, 70.190, 70.304, 72.012, 72.019, 72.020, 72.021, 72.026, 72.031, 73.016, 73.044
Ragwort, Hoary *Jacobaea erucifolia*	70.304, 72.031
Ragwort, Marsh *Jacobaea aquatica*	72.021, 72.026, 72.031
Ragwort, Oxford *Senecio squalidus*	72.031
ragworts	70.141, 70.183, 70.189, 72.024, 72.025, 72.027, 73.121, 73.235, 73.248
Rape, Oil-seed *see* Cabbages/other *Brassica* spp.	
Raspberry *see* Brambles	
Redshank *Persicaria maculosa*	70.029, 73.263
Reed, Common *see* Grasses	
Restharrows	
Restharrow, Common *Ononis repens*	61.018, 70.262, 70.294, 70.296, 73.015, 73.070, 73.072, 73.074, 73.208, 73.275
Restharrow, Spiny *Ononis spinosa*	66.006, 73.070
restharrows *Ononis* spp.	61.014, 70.059, 73.308
Rhododendron *Rhododendron ponticum*	70.107, 72.055, 73.036, 73.063
Roble *Nothofagus obliqua*	71.025
Rocket, Sea *Cakile maritima*	58.008, 73.275, 73.323
Rock-rose, Common *Helianthemum nummularium*	54.003, 61.005, 61.014, 61.015, 61.016, 70.005, 70.287, 72.025, 73.233, 73.312
Roses	
Dog-rose *Rosa canina*	57.002, 66.003, 66.005, 70.066, 70.067, 70.085, 70.095, 70.107, 70.142, 70.221, 70.244, 70.254, 70.255, 70.256, 70.305, 71.009, 72.012, 73.036, 73.068, 73.271
Downy-rose, Sherard's *Rosa sherardii*	70.067
Rose, Burnet *Rosa spinosissima*	66.008, 70.066, 70.085, 70.250, 73.188, 73.248

FOODPLANT	BUTTERFLY AND MOTH CHECKLIST NUMBERS
roses *Rosa* spp.	66.007, 69.016, 70.090, 70.096, 70.097, 70.111, 70.141, 70.241, 70.245, 70.247, 70.252, 70.258, 71.021, 72.013, 72.017, 72.018, 72.022, 72.027, 72.030, 73.032, 73.033, 73.038, 73.039, 73.187, 73.194, 73.237, 73.245, 73.353
Sweet-briar *Rosa rubiginosa*	70.066
Rowan *see* Whitebeams	
Rushes	
Rush, Compact *Juncus conglomeratus*	73.209
Rush, Heath *Juncus squarrosus*	73.254
Rush, Jointed *Juncus articulatus*	59.004, 73.142, 73.254
Rush, Sharp-flowered *Juncus acutiflorus*	73.142, 73.209
rushes *Juncus* spp.	73.022
Soft-rush *Juncus effusus*	73.042, 73.142, 73.209
Sage, Wood *Teucrium scorodonia*	59.036, 66.008, 70.023, 70.131, 70.229, 72.031, 73.230
Sainfoin *Onobrychis viciifolia*	54.009, 70.218, 73.231
Saltwort, Prickly *Salsola kali*	73.323
Sandwort, Sea *Honckenya peploides*	73.070, 73.275, 73.311, 73.322
Saw-wort *Serratula tinctoria*	73.064, 73.078
Saxifrages	
Londonpride *Saxifraga* x *urbium*	73.237
Saxifrage, Alpine *Micranthes nivalis*	70.131
Saxifrage, Mossy *Saxifraga hypnoides*	70.071
Saxifrage, Purple *Saxifraga oppositifolia*	70.071, 73.341
Saxifrage, Yellow *Saxifraga aizoides*	70.071, 70.285
saxifrages *Saxifraga* spp.	70.285
Scabiouses	
Scabious, Devil's-bit *Succisa pratensis*	59.033, 69.008, 69.015, 70.179, 72.023, 73.076, 73.209
Scabious, Field *Knautia arvensis*	59.033, 69.008, 69.009, 70.173, 70.189, 73.072
Scabious, Small *Scabiosa columbaria*	59.033, 69.008, 73.072
Sea-blite, Annual *Suaeda maritima*	73.323
Sea-buckthorn *Hippophae rhamnoides*	66.007, 70.169, 70.212, 70.305, 72.012, 73.271, 73.323
Sea-holly *Eryngium maritimum*	73.323
Sea-lavenders	
Sea-lavender, Common *Limonium vulgare*	66.004, 73.248, 73.266
Sea-lavender, Rock *Limonium binervosum*	70.173
Sea-lavenders *Limonium* spp.	73.123
Sea-milkwort *Lysimachia maritima*	73.323
Sea-purslane *see* Goosefoots and Oraches	
Sedges	
Beak-sedge, White *Rhynchospora alba*	59.004
Fen-sedge, Great *Cladium mariscus*	73.035, 73.119
Pond-sedge, Greater *Carex riparia*	66.010
Pond-sedge, Lesser *Carex acutiformis*	66.010, 73.135, 73.144
Pond-sedges *Carex* spp.	73.119
Sedge, Carnation *Carex panicea*	73.288
Sedge, Common *Carex nigra*	73.119
Sedge, Glaucous *Carex flacca*	73.022, 73.144, 73.146, 73.171
Sedge, Pendulous *Carex pendula*	66.010
sedges *Carex* spp.	73.026, 73.035, 73.123, 73.144, 73.159, 73.209
Tufted-sedge *Carex elata*	59.003, 59.012, 73.022, 73.035, 73.144, 73.293
Tussock-sedge, Greater *Carex paniculata*	66.010, 73.035
Wood-sedge *Carex sylvatica*	59.009, 72.052, 73.026
Service-tree, Wild *see* Whitebeams	
Sheep's-bit *Jasione montana*	70.185
Sheep's-fescue *see* Grasses	
Shepherd's-purse *Capsella bursa-pastoris*	70.049

FOODPLANT	BUTTERFLY AND MOTH CHECKLIST NUMBERS
Silverweed *see* Cinquefoils	
Small-reed, Purple *see* Grasses	
Small-reed, Wood *see* Grasses	
Snapdragon *Antirrhinum majus*	69.015, 70.150, 73.076
Sneezewort *see* Yarrows	
Snowberry *Symphoricarpos albus*	69.005, 69.006, 69.009, 70.184, 70.231
Soapworts *Saponaria officinalis*	73.281
Sorrel, Common *see* Docks and Sorrels	
Sorrel, Sheep's *see* Docks and Sorrels	
sorrels *see* Docks and Sorrels	
Southernwood *see* Wormwoods	
Sowthistles	
Sowthistle, Marsh *Sonchus palustris*	73.052
Sowthistle, Perennial *Sonchus arvensis*	69.015
Sowthistle, Smooth *Sonchus oleraceus*	72.026, 73.228, 73.272
sowthistles *Sonchus* spp.	73.052, 73.279, 73.280, 73.368
Spearwort, Lesser *see* Buttercups	
Speedwells	
Speedwell, Germander *Veronica chamaedrys*	59.036, 73.249
Speedwell, Ivy-leaved *Veronica hederifolia*	59.036
Spiderflower *Tarenaya hassleriana*	58.007
Spinach *Spinacia oleracea*	73.267, 73.342
Spindles	
Spindle *Euonymus europaeus*	66.005, 69.005, 70.205, 70.208, 70.270, 72.024
Spindle, Evergreen *Euonymus japonicus*	70.205
spindles *Euonymus* spp.	73.107
Spurges	
Spurge, Sea *Euphorbia paralias*	73.311
Spurge, Wood *Euphorbia amygdaloides*	70.117, 73.361
spurges *Euphorbia* spp.	69.013
Spurreys	
Sea-spurrey, Rock *Spergularia rupicola*	73.278, 73.283, 73.286
Spurrey, Corn *Spergula arvensis*	73.074, 73.313
Spurrey, Sand *Spergularia rubra*	73.074, 73.275, 73.278
Stitchworts	
Chickweed, Common *Stellaria media*	70.016, 70.029, 70.064, 73.230, 73.273, 73.275, 73.298 73.308, 73.313, 73.317, 73.329, 73.334, 73.336, 73.344 73.353, 73.357, 73.359
Stitchwort, Greater *Stellaria holostea*	70.131, 70.154, 73.048
stitchworts *Stellaria* spp.	70.064, 72.022, 72.023, 72.024, 72.027, 73.092, 73.096 73.097, 73.107, 73.186, 73.187, 73.233, 73.322, 73.348 73.366
St John's-worts	
St John's-wort, Perforate *Hypericum perforatum*	70.142
St John's-worts *Hypericum* spp.	70.189, 70.192, 70.193, 73.247
Stonecrops	
Stonecrop, Biting *Sedum acre*	73.235, 73.341
Stonecrop, English *Sedum anglicum*	70.071
stonecrops *Sedum* spp.	70.023, 70.205, 70.285, 73.208
Stranvaesia *Photinia davidiana*	70.184
Strawberries	
Strawberry, Garden *Fragaria ananassa*	73.123
Strawberry, Wild *Fragaria vesca*	3.005, 57.002, 66.008, 70.059, 70.068, 70.097, 70.098, 70.287, 73.107, 74.002

FOODPLANT	BUTTERFLY AND MOTH CHECKLIST NUMBERS
strawberries *Fragaria* spp.	69.015, 73.064, 73.102
Strawberry, Barren *see* Cinquefoils	
Sweet-briar *see* Roses	
Sweet-William *see* Pinks	
Sycamore *see* Maples	
Tamarisk *Tamarix gallica*	70.152, 70.169, 70.252, 73.267
Tansy *Tanacetum vulgare*	70.054, 70.141, 70.179, 70.188
Tare, Smooth *see* Vetches, Tares and Peas	
Teaplant, Duke of Argyll's *Lycium barbarum*	69.005
Teasels	
Teasel, Wild *Dipsacus fullonum*	59.033
teasels *Dipsacus* spp.	69.006, 73.012, 73.064, 73.092
Thistles	
Thistle, Carline *Carlina vulgaris*	59.024, 72.072
Thistle, Creeping *Cirsium arvense*	59.024, 66.008, 72.024, 73.247, 73.271
Thistle, Dwarf *Cirsium acaule*	73.101
Thistle, Marsh *Cirsium palustre*	59.024, 73.209, 73.271
Thistle, Musk *Carduus nutans*	59.024
Thistle, Spear *Cirsium vulgare*	59.024, 73.012, 73.247
thistles	70.250, 72.026, 73.074, 73.114, 73.121, 73.208, 73.228
Thorn-apple *Datura stramonium*	73.074
Thrift *Armeria maritima*	52.016, 66.004, 66.006, 70.287, 73.044, 73.228, 73.235, 73.236, 73.324
Thyme, Wild *Thymus drucei*	54.004, 61.013, 70.021, 70.142, 70.172, 70.250, 70.287, 70.293, 73.316
Timothy *see* Grasses	
Toadflaxes	
Toadflax, Common *Linaria vulgaris*	69.015, 70.150, 73.015, 73.059, 73.064, 73.072, 73.270, 73.271
Toadflax, Ivy-leaved *Cymbalaria muralis*	70.023
Toadflax, Pale *Linaria repens*	70.150, 73.059
Toadflax, Purple *Linaria purpurea*	73.059
Toadflax, Small *Chaenorhinum minus*	73.059
toadflaxes *Linaria* spp.	70.161, 70.294
tobaccos *Nicotiana* spp.	69.016, 73.274, 73.307
Tomato *Solanum lycopersicum*	73.076, 73.267
Tormentil *see* Cinquefoils	
Traveller's-joy *Clematis vitalba*	70.004, 70.126, 70.127, 70.128, 70.141, 70.142, 70.146, 70.173, 70.230, 70.258, 70.265, 70.302, 72.055, 73.267, 73.361
Turnip *see* Cabbages/other *Brassica* spp.	
twayblades *see* Orchids	
twinspurs *Diascia* spp.	73.074
Valerians	
Valerian, Common *Valeriana officinalis*	70.025, 70.142, 70.181
Valerian, Marsh *Valeriana dioica*	59.033, 70.181, 73.346
Valerian, Red *Centranthus ruber*	73.113, 73.235, 73.237, 73.345
Vetches, Tares and Peas	
Bitter-vetch *Lathyrus linifolius*	54.009, 58.001, 58.002
Everlasting-pea, Broad-leaved *Lathyrus latifolius*	61.008
Everlasting-pea, Narrow-leaved *Lathyrus sylvestris*	61.008
milk-vetches *Astragalus* spp.	72.063
Pea, Garden *Lathyrus oleraceus*	73.012, 73.015, 73.095

FOODPLANT	BUTTERFLY AND MOTH CHECKLIST NUMBERS
Pea, Marsh *Lathyrus palustris*	72.063
Pea, Sweet *Lathyrus odoratus*	73.237
Tare, Smooth *Ervum tetrasperma*	70.003, 70.294
Vetch, Bush *Vicia sepium*	70.027
Vetch, Common *Vicia sativa*	73.365
Vetch, Crown *Securigera varia*	61.020
Vetch, Horseshoe *Hippocrepis comosa*	52.014, 54.008, 61.014, 61.019, 61.020, 70.023, 70.043
Vetch, Kidney *Anthyllis vulneraria*	52.014, 54.008, 61.010, 61.020, 66.006, 70.250, 70.287, 73.236
Vetch, Tufted *Vicia cracca*	58.001, 70.218, 72.063, 72.064, 72.083
Vetch, Wood *Ervilia sylvatica*	72.063, 72.064
vetches	59.036, 70.043, 70.045, 70.218, 70.275, 70.285, 73.102
Vetchling, Meadow *Lathyrus pratensis*	54.007, 54.009, 58.001, 58.002, 70.218, 70.250
Violets	
Dog-violet, Common *Viola riviniana*	59.014, 59.015, 59.017, 59.019, 59.020, 72.023
Dog-violet, Heath *Viola canina*	59.014, 59.020
Dog-violet, Pale *Viola lactea*	59.020
Pansy, Wild *Viola tricolor*	59.014
Violet, Hairy *Viola hirta*	59.019, 59.020
Violet, Marsh *Viola palustris*	59.014, 59.015, 59.019
Violet, Sweet *Viola odorata*	59.014, 59.017, 59.020, 73.236
violets *Viola* spp.	70.055, 72.025, 73.102, 73.311, 73.333
Viper's-buglosses	
Viper's-bugloss *Echium vulgare*	59.024
viper's-buglosses *Echium* spp.	3.001
Virginia-creepers *Parthenocissus* spp.	69.016, 72.019
Walnut *Juglans regia*	52.012, 71.009
water-lilies	69.016
Water-plantain *Alisma plantago-aquatica*	73.022
Wayfaring-tree *Viburnum lantana*	50.002, 52.010, 69.006, 70.226, 73.065
Weigelia *Weigela florida*	70.184
Weld *see* Mignonettes	
wheats *see* Grasses	
Whin, Petty *see* Greenweeds	
Whitebeams	
Rowan *Sorbus aucuparia*	50.002, 52.011, 65.007, 66.007, 68.001, 69.006, 70.090, 70.095, 70.096, 70.105, 70.106, 70.114, 70.115, 70.141, 70.184, 70.200, 70.203, 70.224, 70.226, 70.241, 70.245, 70.254, 70.256, 70.258, 71.021, 71.025, 72.001, 72.019, 72.026, 73.032, 73.036, 73.037, 73.038, 73.068, 73.265
Service-tree, Wild *Sorbus torminalis*	70.226, 70.244
whitebeams *Sorbus* spp.	72.019
Willows	
Crack-willow, Hybrid *Salix x fragilis*	52.003, 59.022, 70.017, 72.078, 74.011
Osier *Salix viminalis*	52.008, 70.147, 74.011
Violet-willow, Siberian *Salix acutifolia*	52.002
Willow, Almond *Salix triandra*	74.011
Willow, Bay *Salix pentandra*	72.009, 73.040
Willow, Creeping *Salix repens*	52.008, 66.006, 70.030, 70.090, 70.228, 70.250, 70.295, 70.306, 71.028, 72.009, 72.016, 73.035, 73.042, 73.044, 73.233, 73.272, 73.308, 73.334, 73.357, 73.359, 73.365, 74.011
Willow, Downy *Salix lapponum*	73.042
Willow, Eared *Salix aurita*	70.030, 70.076, 70.090, 70.147, 70.249, 70.275, 71.012, 71.028, 72.024, 72.026, 73.042, 73.044, 73.220, 73.272, 73.367

FOODPLANT	BUTTERFLY AND MOTH CHECKLIST NUMBERS
Willow, Goat *Salix caprea*	52.003, 52.008, 52.009, 59.022, 69.003, 70.030, 70.090, 70.091, 70.097, 70.121, 70.147, 70.199, 70.211, 70.243, 70.247, 70.263, 70.278, 71.005, 72.009, 72.016, 72.053, 73.036, 73.037, 73.046, 73.064, 73.092, 73.212, 73.220, 73.228, 74.011
Willow, Grey *Salix cinerea*	52.003, 52.008, 52.009, 59.022, 61.012, 66.005, 69.003, 70.030, 70.076, 70.091, 70.097, 70.120, 70.121, 70.147, 70.161, 70.161, 70.211, 70.278, 71.005, 71.012, 71.029, 72.009, 72.016, 72.019, 72.026, 72.027, 73.035, 73.037, 73.040, 73.212, 73.220, 73.272, 73.355, 74.011
Willow, Purple *Salix purpurea*	73.212, 73.220
Willow, Tea-leaved *Salix phylicifolia*	52.008, 70.076, 73.220
Willow, White *Salix alba*	65.005, 70.199, 70.292, 71.005, 72.009, 72.010, 72.078, 73.040, 73.042, 73.064, 73.220, 74.011
willows *Salix* spp.	50.001, 50.002, 52.002, 52.003, 52.012, 59.031, 66.001, 66.002, 66.003, 66.004, 66.006, 66.008, 66.012, 69.002, 69.003, 70.074, 70.086, 70.096, 70.098, 70.106, 70.107, 70.108, 70.110, 70.113, 70.131, 70.183, 70.184, 70.190, 70.198, 70.199, 70.202, 70.204, 70.205, 70.207, 70.212, 70.221, 70.223, 70.224, 70.227, 70.240, 70.241, 70.244, 70.245, 70.248, 70.251, 70.252, 70.254, 70.255, 70.256, 70.264, 70.267, 70.268, 70.271, 70.273, 70.277, 70.278, 70.303, 70.305, 71.003, 71.005, 71.007, 71.009, 71.013, 71.017, 71.020, 71.021, 71.025, 71.027, 71.028, 71.029, 72.001, 72.009, 72.011, 72.012, 72.013, 72.015, 72.017, 72.018, 72.078, 73.032, 73.035, 73.036, 73.037, 73.038, 73.046, 73.062, 73.063, 73.065, 73.068, 73.070, 73.107, 73.110, 73.114, 73.181, 73.182, 73.186, 73.187, 73.188, 73.189, 73.190, 73.192, 73.194, 73.195, 73.201, 73.207, 73.209, 73.210, 73.216, 73.221, 73.222, 73.242, 73.244, 73.245, 73.247, 73.248, 73.249, 73.250, 73.260, 73.261, 73.264, 73.265, 73.267, 73.270, 73.274, 73.331, 73.332, 73.333, 73.336, 73.343, 73.345, 73.346, 73.348, 73.350, 73.351, 73.352, 73.353, 73.360, 73.361
Willowherbs	
Willowherb, Broad-leaved *Epilobium montanum*	70.094
Willowherb, Great *Epilobium hirsutum*	69.016, 70.094, 73.238
Willowherb, Rosebay *Chamaenerion angustifolium*	69.014, 69.015, 69.016, 70.073, 70.094, 72.018, 73.064, 73.107, 73.237, 73.337
willowherbs *Epilobium* spp.	69.014, 69.015, 69.016, 69.017, 73.267, 73.359, 73.368
Wolf's-bane *see* Monk's-hoods	
Woodruff *see* Bedstraws	
Wood-rushes	
Wood-rush, Field *Luzula campestris*	73.288, 73.293, 73.343
Wood-rush, Great *Luzula sylvatica*	73.144, 73.160, 73.332
Wood-rush, Hairy *Luzula pilosa*	57.009, 73.169, 73.288, 73.293
wood-rushes *Luzula* spp.	70.131, 72.052
Wood-sorrel *Oxalis acetosella*	70.131
Wormwoods	
Mugwort *Artemisia vulgaris*	70.023, 70.053, 70.142, 70.173, 70.179, 70.187, 70.188, 70.190, 70.252, 70.305, 73.050, 73.064, 73.121, 73.237, 73.248
Southernwood *Artemisia abrotanum*	70.187, 70.188
Wormwood *Artemisia absinthium*	70.187, 73.050
Wormwood, Sea *Artemisia maritima*	66.004, 70.173, 70.178, 70.294, 73.050, 73.055, 73.308
wormwoods *Artemisia* spp.	70.059, 70.179, 70.188

FOODPLANT	BUTTERFLY AND MOTH CHECKLIST NUMBERS
Woundworts	
Woundwort, Field *Stachys arvensis*	70.133, 73.123
Woundwort, Hedge *Stachys sylvatica*	73.016, 73.017
woundworts *Stachys* spp.	70.229
Yarrows	
Sneezewort *Achillea ptarmica*	70.187, 70.188
Yarrow *Achillea millefolium*	59.036, 61.018, 70.023, 70.054, 70.059, 70.161, 70.179, 70.183, 70.186, 70.187, 70.188, 70.190, 70.250, 70.265, 70.293, 72.024, 72.031, 73.231
yarrows *Achillea* spp.	73.012
Yellow-rattle *Rhinanthus minor*	70.137, 70.153, 73.074
Yorkshire-fog *see* Grasses	
FUNGI AND SLIME MOULDS	
Botryobasidium spp.	72.066
Cladonia fimbriata	72.066
Cylindrobasidium laeve	72.066
Daldinia concentrica	72.066
Diploicia canescens	73.085
fungi, bracket	72.066
moulds, slime	72.066
Phaeolus schweinitzii	72.066
Piptoporus betulinus	72.066
Stereum hirsutum	72.066
Tapinella panuoides	72.066
Trametes versicolor	72.066
Trichaptum abietinum	72.066
LICHENS	
Caloplaca spp.	73.085
Flavoparmelia caperata	72.041
Flavoparmelia spp.	72.043
Lecidea confluens	73.084
lichens	70.240, 70.288, 72.035, 72.036, 72.037, 72.038, 72.041, 72.042, 72.043, 72.044, 72.045, 72.046, 72.049, 72.050, 72.069, 73.082, 73.084, 73.085
lichens, beard *Usnea* spp.	70.266
Peltigera membranacea	72.035, 72.041, 72.044
Peltigera spp.	72.037
Physcia stellaris	72.069
Ramalina sp.	70.288
Xanthoria parietina	72.069, 73.084, 73.085
MOSSES	
Barbula sp.	72.044
Feather-moss, Silky Wall *Homalothecium sericeum*	72.037
mosses	3.004, 70.139, 72.035, 72.037
Pincushion, Common *Dicranoweisia cirrata*	72.037
Thyme-moss, Swan's-neck *Mnium hornum*	3.004

PHOTOGRAPHIC CREDITS

Bloomsbury Publishing would like to thank the following for providing images and for permission to reproduce copyright material. While every effort has been made to trace and acknowledge all copyright holders, we would like to apologise for any errors or omissions and invite readers to inform us so that corrections can be made in any future editions of the book.

All images © Barry Henwood except the following: 17 left © John Walters; 28 bottom © Mandy Henwood; 29 © Mandy Henwood; 31 C © Phil Sterling; 51 C © Professor Daniel Janzen; 62 bottom left © John Walters; 73 © Bob Heckford; 76 bottom © Phil Sterling; 79 both © Phil Sterling; 80 top right, bottom left and right © Phil Sterling; 81 top left and right © Phil Sterling; 82 bottom left and right © Phil Sterling; 83 top right © Bob Heckford, bottom ©Tony Davis/Butterfly Conservation; 90 ©Peter Eeles; 108 © Peter Eeles.

APPENDIX 1

SEPARATING *XANTHORHOE* CARPETS					
Species (bold = illustrated)	Key field characters	Habitats	Foodplants	Larval period	Comments on identification and similar species
Red Carpet *Xanthorhoe decoloraria*	• Body green or brown • Pinacula whitish • Green form has a green proleg	Usually at higher altitudes on grasslands in rocky situations and moorland. In the Northern Isles also on road verges and sand dunes	Lady's-mantles	• Aug–late May • Fully fed in spring	• Red Carpet is likely to be the only *Xanthorhoe* on lady's-mantles with whitish panicula • Silver-ground Carpet has brown pinacula with white centres and a pale subdorsal stripe • Oblique Carpet has reddish or brown proleg
Garden Carpet *Xanthorhoe fluctuata*	• Body green, or greyish brown • Pale subdorsal stripe variable and may be faint or clearly visible • Pinacula whitish	Wide variety, especially allotments, gardens and rough ground, and including woodland	Cabbage family	• Apr–early Nov • One to three generations • Fully fed in autumn	• Red Carpet is fully fed in spring. Its green form with reddish bands is sufficiently dissimilar to be identifiable in the field • Possible Garden Carpet larvae must be reared to confirm identity
Balsam Carpet *Xanthorhoe biriviata*	• Body green, brown or grey • Pinacula whitish	Damp pastures, scrub and woodland, and along banks of rivers and canals	Orange Balsam; less often Small Balsam	• Jun, and Aug–Oct in a partial second generation • Fully fed in autumn	Larvae found on listed foodplants can be identified in the field
Red Twin-spot Carpet *Xanthorhoe spadicearia*	• Body brown • Pale subdorsal stripe variable, usually visible • Pinacula whitish	Wide variety, including calcareous grassland, fens, hedgerows, moorland, sand dunes	Variety of herbaceous plants	• Jun–Jul and Sep in two generations as far north as south-west Scotland, and Jun–late Aug elsewhere • Fully fed in autumn	Must be reared to confirm identity

Species	Description	Habitat	Period	Notes
Dark-barred Twin-spot Carpet *Xanthorhoe ferrugata*	• Body brown • Pale subdorsal stripe variable, usually visible • Pinacula whitish	Wide variety, including calcareous grassland, fens, hedgerows, moorland, sand dunes and woodland	• Jun–Jul and Sep–Oct • Fully fed in autumn	Must be reared to confirm identity
Flame Carpet *Xanthorhoe designata*	• Body brown • Pale subdorsal stripe variable and may be faint or clearly visible • Pinacula whitish	Wide variety, including calcareous grassland, upland grassland, hedgerows, moorland and lowland woodlands	• Jun–Jul and Sep, in two generations • Fully fed in autumn	Must be reared to confirm identity
Silver-ground Carpet *Xanthorhoe montanata*	• Body greyish brown • Subdorsal stripe whitish or pale, wide, and contrasting with darker body colour • Pinacula brown with white centres • Spiracles with pale centres	Prefers sheltered areas among tall herbaceous vegetation within fens, gardens, grasslands, heathland, hedgerows, scrub and woodland rides	Herbaceous plants, including Cleavers, Hedge Bedstraw and Primrose	• Jul–May • Fully fed in spring	• Red Twin-spot Carpet and Dark-barred Twin-spot Carpet have a narrower and less obvious subdorsal stripe, and have black spiracles • Large Twin-spot Carpet has the subdorsal stripe less constant in width along its length. Its larva is fully fed a little later in spring, but there is potential for confusion where ranges overlap • See Red Carpet
Large Twin-spot Carpet *Xanthorhoe quadrifasiata*	• Body brown or grey, occasionally greyish green • Subdorsal stripe slightly paler than body colour, and of irregular width • Pinacula whitish	Scrub on heathland, ancient woodland, and carr and other wet woodlands	Herbaceous plants, including bedstraws, Primrose and violets	• Aug–May • Fully fed in spring	• See Silver-ground Carpet • Red Carpet unlikely to occur in same habitats as Large Twin-spot Carpet

Note: The "Herbaceous plants" column applies as larval foodplant. For Dark-barred Twin-spot Carpet the foodplant is "Variety of herbaceous plants"; for Flame Carpet "Has been found feeding on Mugwort".

APPENDIX 2

SEPARATING PUG MOTHS (GENERA *GYMNOSCELIS* AND *EUPITHECIA*)					
Species (bold = illustrated)	Body colour	Description of variation	Foodplants	Number of generations	Comments on identification and similar species
Double-striped Pug *Gymnoscelis rufifasciata*	Pink, yellow, white or green	• Plain green and plain white forms occur • Patterned forms have dorsal arrows • If ground colour pale then may have dark dorsal and lateral lines • If ground colour dark then may have white dorsal and lateral lines	Wide variety	One to three	• More stumpy and smaller when fully fed than others listed in table • With experience, likely to be identifiable as this species; otherwise must be reared to confirm identity
White-spotted Pug *Eupithecia tripunctaria*	Whitish green, greyish green, brown or whitish	• All forms have dorsal triangles • May have brown lateral patches	Mainly Elder in first generation and wide variety in second, most often Wild Angelica	Two	Must be reared to confirm identity
Golden-rod Pug *Eupithecia virgaureata*	Brown or grey	• All forms have dorsal triangles • Obvious diagonal white or whitish lateral and subspiracular stripes	Wide variety of woody and herbaceous plants in first generation, and especially Goldenrod and Common Ragwort in second	Two	• Lateral stripes are a helpful clue to identity, but other species have them to some extent, especially Satyr Pug, Wormwood Pug and Bleached Pug • Must be reared to confirm identity
Lime-speck Pug *Eupithecia centaureata*	Plain green, or patterned yellowish or whitish	• Very variable • Plain green form has dark dorsal line • Patterned forms have red, purple or brown markings, often in geometric shapes	Wide variety of herbaceous plants	Two	Geometric-patterned forms likely to be this species, but all must be reared to confirm identity

Species	Colour	Description	Foodplant	Generations	Notes
Satyr Pug *Eupithecia satyrata*	Whitish green to yellowish green, or whitish pink to dark pink	• Very variable • Plain green form has dark dorsal line • Patterned forms have a dark pink or brown diagonal stripe and dorsal triangles, with diagonal whitish or yellowish lateral and subspiracular stripes. These stripes may be indistinct	Wide variety of herbaceous plants	One or two	So variable that all must be reared to confirm identity
Wormwood Pug *Eupithecia absinthiata*	Greenish, yellowish green or brownish	• Very variable • Plain yellowish-green form occurs • Patterned forms have brown dorsal ovals with lateral extensions, or triangles • Pale subspiracular line more or less continuous	Wide variety of herbaceous plants, including Goldenrod	One	Must be reared to confirm identity
Bleached Pug *Eupithecia expallidata*	Green, yellowish green or whitish	• Very variable • Plain green or yellowish-green forms have darker dorsal and subdorsal lines • Patterned forms are whitish with a pale brown dorsal line, dark brown ovals or diamond shapes on the dorsum, a dark brown subdorsal line, and a whitish subspiracular line	Goldenrod in woodland situations	One	Must be reared to confirm identity (but adult very similar to Wormwood Pug, so may require further investigation)
Shaded Pug *Eupithecia subumbrata*	Green or brown	• Invariable • Larva long and thin with a dark dorsal stripe	Wide variety	One	Although invariable, Shaded Pug is so similar to plain forms of Lime-speck Pug and Satyr Pug that all must be reared to confirm identity

APPENDIX 3

SEPARATING SALLOWS AND CHESTNUTS

Species (bold = illustrated)	Key field characters	Habitats	Foodplants	Comments on identification and similar species
Barred Sallow *Tiliacea aurago*	• Body purplish brown with greyish-white pinacula • Subdorsal line greyish white, usually indistinct • Prothoracic plate brown, with greyish-white dorsal line and yellowish subdorsal stripe	Mainly hedgerows, scrub and broadleaf woodland	Mainly Beech and Field Maple	Barred Sallow, Pink-barred Sallow, Sallow, Dusky-lemon Sallow, Pale-lemon Sallow, Chestnut, Dark Chestnut, Black-spotted Chestnut, Red-line Quaker and Brick are all similar. Differences described in literature between Pink-barred Sallow and Sallow based on prothoracic and anal plates are no longer considered reliable. If in doubt, larvae should be reared to confirm identity of all species in this group
Pink-barred Sallow *Xanthia togata*	• Body pale brown, heavily speckled with darker orangey brown • No obvious patterning • Prothoracic plate dark brown, with whitish dorsal line and subdorsal stripe	Mainly fens, wet heathland, marshes, carr and other wet woodlands	Catkins of poplars and willows, and seeds of Wych Elm. Later, herbaceous plants	See Barred Sallow
Sallow *Cirrhia icteritia*	• Body pale brown, heavily speckled with darker orangey brown, noticeably darker along the dorsum, laterally and on A8, and paler between • Prothoracic plate brown, with pale brown dorsal line and subdorsal stripe	Mainly fens, wet heathland, marshes, carr and other wet woodlands	Catkins of poplars and willows, and seeds of Wych Elm. Later, herbaceous plants	See Barred Sallow. Well-marked examples likely to be identifiable to species

Species	Description	Habitat	Foodplant	Notes
Dusky-lemon Sallow *Cirrhia gilvago*	• Forward-curving dark patches on the dorsum, most noticeable on posterior abdominal segments, especially A8 • Prothoracic plate dark brown or black, with whitish dorsal line and subdorsal stripe and no pale spot between	Mature hedgerows, parkland and broadleaf woodland	Mainly Wych Elm; sometimes English Elm	See Barred Sallow. Most likely to be confused with Brick, but well-marked examples on elms likely to be identifiable to species
Pale-lemon Sallow *Cirrhia ocellaris*	• Dark M-shaped dorsal patch on A8 • Prothoracic plate dark brown or black, with cream dorsal line and subdorsal stripe and no pale spot between	Long-established groups of poplars in open countryside	Catkins of Black-poplar and hybrids. Later, on the leaves, and on herbaceous plants	See Barred Sallow. Most likely to be confused with Brick, but well-marked examples on poplars likely to be identifiable to species
Red-line Quaker *Agrochola lota*	• Body with distinct white pinacula • Dorsal and subdorsal lines white • Prothoracic plate black or dark brown, with white dorsal line and subdorsal stripe	Wide variety	Catkins and leaves of willows	See Barred Sallow. Most likely to be confused with Chestnut, Dark Chestnut and Black-spotted Chestnut, but well-marked examples likely to be identifiable to species
Brick *Agrochola circellaris*	• White or pale brown pinacula • Dark patches on the dorsum, confluent T1–T3, and shield-shaped A1–A8 • Dorsal and subdorsal lines white • Prothoracic plate brown, with whitish or pale grey dorsal line and subdorsal stripe, and with a pale spot between	Wide variety of situations with trees	Mainly Ash, Aspen, Wych Elm, poplars and willows. Later, may also feed on herbaceous plants	See Barred Sallow. Most likely to be confused with Dusky-lemon Sallow and Pale-lemon Sallow, but well-marked examples likely to be identifiable to species

continued overleaf

SEPARATING SALLOWS AND CHESTNUTS *continued*				
Species (bold = illustrated)	Key field characters	Habitats	Foodplants	Comments on identification and similar species
Chestnut *Conistra vaccinii*	• Pinacula may be pale brown and inconspicuous, or white and contrasting • Body with pale brown dorsal and subdorsal lines • Prothoracic plate various shades of brown, with pale brown dorsal line and subdorsal stripe	Mainly broadleaf woodland	Wide variety of woody and herbaceous plants	See Barred Sallow. Chestnut and Dark Chestnut are indistinguishable in the field; Black-spotted Chestnut has a blacker prothoracic plate. Also likely to be confused with Red-line Quaker
Dark Chestnut *Conistra ligula*	• As for Chestnut	Farmland, gardens, hedgerows, scrub and woodland	Wide variety of woody and herbaceous plants	See Barred Sallow. Chestnut and Dark Chestnut are indistinguishable in the field; Black-spotted Chestnut has a blacker prothoracic plate. Also likely to be confused with Red-line Quaker
Black-spotted Chestnut *Conistra rubiginosa*	• Pinacula may be pale brown and inconspicuous, or white and contrasting • Body with pale dorsal and subdorsal lines • Prothoracic plate black, with whitish dorsal line and subdorsal stripe	In Europe, woodland and open habitats, including gardens	In Europe, wide variety of woody and herbaceous plants	See Barred Sallow. Chestnut and Dark Chestnut are indistinguishable in the field; Black-spotted Chestnut has a blacker prothoracic plate than these two species. Red-line Quaker may also have a black prothoracic plate and could be confused

APPENDIX 4

SEPARATING READILY CONFUSED PALE-STRIPED GREEN NOCTUIDS

Species (bold = illustrated)	Key field characters			Habitats	Foodplants	Comments on identification and similar species
	Pinacula	True leg	Lateral line			
Tawny Pinion *Lithophane semibrunnea*	White	Green	Yes	Open countryside	Ash	Only Tawny Pinion and Pale Pinion have a lateral line. Pale Pinion has a bluish-green body; Tawny Pinion has a pale green body
Pale Pinion *Lithophane socia*	White	Green	Yes	Gardens, parkland and woodland	Wide variety of trees and shrubs	See Tawny Pinion
Double Kidney *Ipimorpha retusa*	As body colour	Green usually	No	Variety of mainly wetland habitats	Black-poplar and willows	Olive has a blackish-and-green head with white markings, yellow or sometimes white body lines, and doesn't feed on willows. Double Kidney has a green or black head but without white markings, and has white body lines. Minor Shoulder-knot has obvious white pinacula
Olive *Ipimorpha subtusa*	As body colour	Black	No	Wide variety	Poplars, including Aspen	See Double Kidney
White-spotted Pinion *Cosmia diffinis*	Black	Black	No	Woodlands, including plantations	Elms	Combination of brown or black head and black true legs is diagnostic
Lesser-spotted Pinion *Cosmia affinis*	Black or white	Black	No	Hedgerows, shelterbelts and woodlands	Elms	Dun-bar has green true legs and the black pinacula are encircled white

continued overleaf

SEPARATING READILY CONFUSED PALE-STRIPED GREEN NOCTUIDS *continued*

Species (bold = illustrated)	Key field characters			Habitats	Foodplants	Comments on identification and similar species
	Pinacula	True leg	Lateral line			
Dun-bar *Cosmia trapezina*	Black centre, white surround	Green	No	Mainly woodland	Wide variety of trees and shrubs	See Lesser-spotted Pinion
Lunar-spotted Pinion *Cosmia pyralina*	Yellow	Green	No	Hedgerows, parkland, scrub and woodland	Wide variety of trees	Combination of yellow pinacula and subspiracular line edged above with black on T1–T2 is diagnostic
Minor Shoulder-knot *Brachylomia viminalis*	White	Green (black in earlier instars)	No	Wide variety of mainly wetland habitats	Mainly Grey Willow	See Double Kidney
Grey Chi *Antitype chi*	White	Green	No	Mainly upland grassland and moorland	Wide variety of deciduous and woody plants	Large Ranunculus, pale green form of Powdered Quaker and Hebrew Character all have distinct speckling, which Grey Chi lacks. Grey Chi has white pinacula. Large Ranunculus and Grey Chi differ from pale green form of Powdered Quaker and Hebrew Character by having a narrower dorsal line and spiracles positioned immediately above the subspiracular stripe, whereas the other two species have the spiracles within the spiracular stripe. Could also be confused with Clouded Drab

Species						Notes
Large Ranunculus *Polymixis flavicincta*	As body colour	Green	No	Wide variety, and frequently in urban areas	Wide variety of herbaceous and woody plants	See Grey Chi and Clouded Drab
Clouded Drab *Orthosia incerta*	As body colour	Green	No	Wide variety	Wide variety of broadleaf trees	Most similar to Hebrew Character and pale green form of Powdered Quaker, which themselves are indistinguishable. Hebrew Character has a dorsal line, not a stripe, and a spiracular band, and if there is black above the band it may be a line or shading. Clouded Drab has a broader dorsal stripe and a spiracular stripe, and if there is black above the stripe, this is a black line. Also see Grey Chi and Large Ranunculus
Powdered Quaker *Orthosia gracilis* (pale green form)	As body colour	Green	No	Mainly bogs and marshes	Wide variety	See Clouded Drab. This form of Powdered Quaker is indistinguishable from Hebrew Character
Hebrew Character *Orthosia gothica*	As body colour	Green	No	Wide variety	Wide variety	See Clouded Drab. Indistinguishable from pale green form of Powdered Quaker

APPENDIX 5

Species (bold = illustrated)	Wainscot larval group and key field characters	Habitats	Foodplants	Larval period	Comments on identification and similar species
SEPARATING EXTERNAL-FEEDING WAINSCOTS					
Double Line *Mythimna turca*	Larva is stockier than other species. Body orangey brown, speckled dark brown, with paler pinacula	Upland wet grassland, ancient parkland and mature woodland	Grasses, Carnation Sedge and Field and Hairy wood-rushes	Fully fed in May; overwinters as a small larva	Unlikely to be confused with another species listed in this table
Striped Wainscot *Mythimna pudorina*	Clay group	Fens, acid grassland, wet heathland and marshes	Broad-bladed grasses	Fully fed in May; overwinters as a small larva	Cannot be identified with certainty in the field
Brown-line Bright-eye *Mythimna conigera*	Clay group	Various grassland habitats	Grasses	Fully fed in May; overwinters as a small larva	Cannot be identified with certainty in the field
Common Wainscot *Mythimna pallens*	Smoky Wainscot group	Various grassland habitats	Grasses	Fully fed in Aug and May in the south, Jun in the north; overwinters as a small larva	Cannot be identified with certainty in the field
Mathew's Wainscot *Mythimna favicolor*	Smoky Wainscot group	Coastal and estuarine saltmarshes	Common Saltmarsh-grass	Fully fed in May, and probably Jul; overwinters as a small larva	Likely to be identifiable to this species if found on Common Saltmarsh-grass

Smoky Wainscot *Mythimna impura*	Smoky Wainscot group	Various grassland habitats	Grasses, Tufted-sedge and Field and Hairy wood-rushes	Fully fed in May or Jun; overwinters as a small larva	Cannot be identified with certainty in the field
Southern Wainscot *Mythimna straminea*	Similar to Smoky Wainscot group, but more slender and rather more greyish or greyish green than species in that group, and has a continuous greyish-brown stripe above the subdorsal line	Wetland habitats with reeds	Reed Canary-grass and Common Reed	Fully fed in May or Jun; overwinters as a part-grown larva	Can be separated in the field based on slender shape, markings and habitat
Delicate *Mythimna vitellina*	Smoky Wainscot group	Coastal grassland	Grasses	Likely to be a fully fed larva in late summer	Cannot be identified with certainty in the field
White-speck/ American Wainscot *Mythimna unipuncta*	Clay group. Body brown, usually with a dark grey dorsal band incorporating a white dorsal line	Coastal grassland	Not known in the British Isles	Larval period in the wild not known	Larva generally darker than others in Clay group but cannot be identified with certainty in the field
White-point *Mythimna albipuncta*	Clay group and Smoky Wainscot group. Larva is variable	Various grassland habitats	Grasses	Large larvae have been found at night in Apr, but larval period in the wild not known	Cannot be identified with certainty in the field

continued overleaf

SEPARATING EXTERNAL-FEEDING WAINSCOTS *continued*

Species (bold = illustrated)	Wainscot larval group and key field characters	Habitats	Foodplants	Larval period	Comments on identification and similar species
Clay *Mythimna ferrago*	Clay group	Various grassland habitats	Grasses	Fully fed in May; overwinters when small	• Cannot be identified with certainty in the field • Also similar to Grayling (see Grayling), and Square-spot Rustic and Six-striped Rustic (see Square-spot Rustic)
Shore Wainscot *Mythimna litoralis*	Larva has a pale body, and a white subdorsal line with an unbroken dark brown stripe above	Sand dunes and sandy beaches	Marram	Fully fed in late May; overwinters as a small larva in sand	Can be separated in the field based on markings and habitat
L-album Wainscot *Mythimna l-album*	Clay group	Rough coastal grassland, especially on cliffs	Has been found in the wild on Marram	Fully fed in late May and Aug; overwinters as a small larva	Cannot be identified with certainty in the field
Shoulder-striped Wainscot *Leucania comma*	Clay group	Mainly fens, marshes and damp woodland	Grasses	Fully fed in Sep; overwinters in a cocoon in the ground	Larva is fully fed in Sep when other similar species are likely to be adults or small larvae

Species	Larva	Habitat	Foodplant	Life cycle	Notes
Obscure Wainscot *Leucania obsoleta*	Larva elongate, translucent, pale brownish or pale greenish brown, with white dorsal, subdorsal and lateral lines, and grey below. Spiracles orange-centred	Wetland habitats with reeds	Common Reed	Fully fed in early Sep; overwinters in a hollow stem or leaf litter	Similar to Flame Wainscot. Obscure Wainscot can be separated in the field based on markings
Devonshire Wainscot *Leucania putrescens*	Clay group	Cliffs and coastal grassland	Grasses	Fully fed late Jan–Feb, then constructs a cocoon in the ground	Devonshire Wainscot can be separated in the field based on a larva found fully fed in winter in the right coastal location
Cosmopolitan *Leucania loreyi*	Clay group. Larva has dark dorsal dots that are edged white laterally	Coastal grassland	Grasses	Larval period in the wild not known; likely to be a larva only in summer or autumn	Cannot be identified with certainty in the field
Flame Wainscot *Senta flammea*	Larva elongate and pale brownish, with whitish lines, black pinacula laterally, and a yellowish-brown subspiracular stripe. Spiracles white-centred	Wetland habitats with reeds	Common Reed	Fully fed Sep–Nov; overwinters as a pupa in a hollow stem	See Obscure Wainscot. Flame Wainscot can be separated in the field based on markings

INDEX OF ENGLISH NAMES

Bold numbers prefixed with 'Pl' refer to colour artworks (those in the plate section).

Adonis Blue **Pl 8**, 60, 115
Alcon Blue 60
Alder Kitten **Pl 34**, 206
Alder Moth **Pl 44**, 32, 53, 298
American Wainscot 350, 425
Angle Shades **Pl 48**, 311
Angle-barred Pug **Pl 24**, 171
Angle-striped Sallow **Pl 54**, 331
Annulet **Pl 33**, 199
Anomalous **Pl 45**, 303
Antler Moth **Pl 57**, 340
Archer's Dart 30, 354
Argent & Sable **Pl 21**, 159
Ashworth's Rustic **Pl 63**, 364
August Thorn **Pl 28**, 186
Autumnal Moth **Pl 20**, 157
Autumnal Rustic **Pl 64**, 364
Autumn Green Carpet **Pl 20**, 154

Balsam Carpet **Pl 18**, 143, 414
Banded Pine Carpet **Pl 33**, 198
Barberry Carpet **Pl 21**, 20, 160
Barred Carpet **Pl 22**, 164
Barred Chestnut **Pl 61**, 356
Barred Hook-tip **Pl 9**, 117
Barred Red **Pl 33**, 198
Barred Rivulet **Pl 22**, 163
Barred Sallow **Pl 52**, 325, 418
Barred Straw **Pl 20**, 153
Barred Tooth-striped **Pl 26**, 179
Barred Umber **Pl 27**, 183
Barred Yellow **Pl 19**, 151
Barrett's Marbled Coronet **Pl 59**, 346
Beaded Chestnut **Pl 52**, 326
Beautiful Brocade **Pl 58**, 343
Beautiful Carpet **Pl 18**, 147
Beautiful Golden Y **Pl 43**, 295
Beautiful Gothic **Pl 52**, 324
Beautiful Hook-tip **Pl 42**, 290
Beautiful Snout **Pl 37**, 278
Beautiful Yellow Underwing **Pl 57**, 341
Bedstraw Hawk-moth **Pl 14**, 130
Beech-green Carpet **Pl 20**, 154
Belted Beauty **Pl 30**, 61, 190
Bilberry Pug **Pl 23**, 42, 43, 62, 166
Birch Mocha **Pl 17**, 139
Bird's Wing **Pl 48**, 310
Black Arches **Pl 37**, 278
black arches, silver-lines and nycteoline moths **Pl 64**, 366–8
Black Hairstreak **Pl 8**, 111
Black Mountain Moth **Pl 33**, 200
Black Rustic **Pl 55**, 336
Black-banded **Pl 55**, 336
Black-spotted Chestnut **Pl 53**, 329, 420
Black-veined Moth **Pl 33**, 20, 200

Blackneck **Pl 41**, 289
Blair's Mocha **Pl 17**, 139
Blair's Shoulder-knot **Pl 53**, 330
Blair's Wainscot **Pl 49**, 315
Bleached Pug **Pl 25**, 174, 417
Blomer's Rivulet **Pl 21**, 159
Blood-vein **Pl 17**, 52, 138
Blossom Underwing **Pl 56**, 338
Blotched Emerald **Pl 34**, 48, 202
Bloxworth Snout **Pl 37**, 277
Blue Underwing **Pl 42**, 291
Blue-bordered Carpet **Pl 19**, 151
Bond's Wainscot 318
Bordered Beauty **Pl 28**, 184
Bordered Gothic **Pl 59**, 346
Bordered Grey **Pl 31**, 193
Bordered Pug **Pl 25**, 176
Bordered Sallow **Pl 46**, 293, 305
Bordered Straw **Pl 46**, 306
Bordered White **Pl 32**, 196
Brick **Pl 52**, 328, 419
Bright Wave **Pl 16**, 133
Bright-line Brown-eye **Pl 58**, 343
Brimstone **Pl 4**, 41, 97
Brimstone Moth **Pl 27**, 9, 48, 184
Brindled Beauty **Pl 30**, 132, 190
Brindled Green **Pl 55**, 334
Brindled Ochre **Pl 55**, 336
Brindled Pug **Pl 23**, 40, 168
Brindled White-spot **Pl 32**, 195
Broad-barred White **Pl 59**, 346
Broad-bordered Bee Hawk-moth **Pl 14**, 58, 59, 130
Broad-bordered White Underwing **Pl 57**, 341
Broad-bordered Yellow Underwing **Pl 62**, 359
Broken-barred Carpet **Pl 19**, 151
Broom Moth **Pl 58**, 344
Broom-tip **Pl 26**, 178
Brown, fritillary, admiral and tortoiseshell butterflies **Pl 5–7**, 98–107
Brown Argus **Pl 8**, 113
Brown Hairstreak **Pl 8**, 109, 110
Brown Rustic **Pl 47**, 309
Brown Scallop **Pl 21**, 159
Brown Silver-line **Pl 27**, 183
Brown-line Bright-eye 349, 424
Brown-spot Pinion **Pl 52**, 326
Brown-tail **Pl 37**, 31, 32, 38, 40, 55, 56, 61, 62, 279
Brown-veined Wainscot **Pl 50**, 16, 317
Brussels Lace **Pl 33**, 46, 199
Buff Arches **Pl 9**, 118
Buff Ermine **Pl 38**, 280
Buff Footman **Pl 41**, 286
Buff-tip **Pl 36**, 210
Bulrush Wainscot **Pl 49**, 316

Burnet Companion **Pl 42**, 292
Burnished Brass **Pl 43**, 294
Burren Green **Pl 48**, 312
Butterbur **Pl 49**, 313
Buttoned Snout **Pl 37**, 277

Cabbage Moth **Pl 59**, 345
Campanula Pug **Pl 25**, 175
Campion **Pl 59**, 345
Canary-shouldered Thorn **Pl 28**, 186
Centre-barred Sallow **Pl 54**, 39, 333
chafer beetle 18
Chalk Carpet **Pl 17**, 142
Chalk Hill Blue **Pl 8**, 60, 115
Chamomile Shark **Pl 45**, 17, 301
Channel Islands Pug **Pl 23**, 167
Chequered Skipper **Pl 3**, 92
Cherry Bark Tortrix 81
Chestnut **Pl 53**, 328, 420
Chestnut-coloured Carpet **Pl 19**, 149
Chevron **Pl 20**, 152
Chimney Sweeper **Pl 22**, 30, 162
Chinese Character **Pl 9**, 118
Chocolate-tip **Pl 36**, 211
Cinnabar **Pl 40**, 50, 56, 283
Cistus Forester **Pl 2**, 87
Clancy's Rustic **Pl 47**, 308
Clay 350, 426
Clay Fan-foot **Pl 41**, 288
Clay group **Pl 60**, 424–7
Clay Triple-lines **Pl 17**, 140
clearwing moths **Pl 1**, 76–84
Clifden Nonpareil **Pl 42**, 291
Cloaked Carpet **Pl 18**, 146
Cloaked Minor **Pl 52**, 323
Cloaked Pug **Pl 23**, 39, 167
Clouded Border **Pl 26**, 181
Clouded Brindle **Pl 51**, 320
Clouded Buff **Pl 39**, 281
Clouded Drab **Pl 56**, 337, 423
Clouded Magpie **Pl 26**, 180
Clouded Silver **Pl 32**, 39, 197
Clouded Yellow **Pl 4**, 24, 97
Clouded-bordered Brindle **Pl 51**, 320
Coast Dart 353
Comma **Pl 7**, 106
Common Blue **Pl 8**, 114
Common Carpet **Pl 18**, 145
Common Emerald **Pl 34**, 40, 48, 203
Common Fan-foot **Pl 41**, 289
Common Footman **Pl 41**, 286
Common Forest Looper **Pl 33**, 200
Common Heath **Pl 32**, 196
Common Lutestring **Pl 9**, 116, 119
Common Marbled Carpet **Pl 20**, 154
Common Pug **Pl 25**, 175
Common Quaker **Pl 56**, 338
Common Rustic **Pl 52**, 322
Common Swift **Pl 1**, 72

Common Wainscot 349, 424
Common Wave **Pl 32**, 197
Common White Wave **Pl 32**, 196
Concolorous **Pl 50**, 317, 318
Confused **Pl 51**, 322
Convolvulus Hawk-moth **Pl 12**, 127, 128
copper, hairstreak and blue butterflies **Pl 8**, 109–115
Copper Underwing **Pl 46**, 303
Coronet **Pl 45**, 300
Cosmopolitan 351, 427
Cousin German **Pl 64**, 365
Coxcomb Prominent **Pl 36**, 6, 209
Cream Wave **Pl 16**, 137
Cream-bordered Green Pea **Pl 64**, 368
Cream-spot Tiger **Pl 39**, 282
Crescent **Pl 49**, 312
Crescent Dart 355
Crescent Plume 277
Crescent Striped **Pl 51**, 321
Crinan Ear **Pl 49**, 315
Cryptic Wood White **Pl 4**, 95
Currant Clearwing 82
Currant Pug **Pl 25**, 175
Cypress Carpet **Pl 19**, 150
Cypress Pug **Pl 23**, 169

Dark Arches **Pl 51**, 321
Dark Bordered Beauty **Pl 28**, 185
Dark Brocade **Pl 55**, 337
Dark Chestnut **Pl 53**, 328, 420
Dark Crimson Underwing **Pl 42**, 292
Dark Dagger **Pl 44**, 299
Dark Green Fritillary **Pl 6**, 26, 103
Dark Marbled Carpet **Pl 20**, 39, 154
Dark Spectacle **Pl 43**, 50, 51, 294
Dark Spinach **Pl 18**, 147
Dark Sword-grass 355
Dark Tussock **Pl 38**, 279
Dark Umber **Pl 21**, 159
Dark-barred Twin-spot Carpet 144, 415
Death's-head Hawk-moth **Pl 13**, 129
December Moth **Pl 10**, 39, 121
Deep-brown Dart **Pl 55**, 335
Delicate 350, 425
Dentated Pug **Pl 22**, 43, 162
Devon Carpet **Pl 20**, 24, 156
Devonshire Wainscot 351, 427
Dew Moth **Pl 41**, 287
Dingy Footman **Pl 41**, 33, 286
Dingy Mocha **Pl 17**, 138
Dingy Shears **Pl 54**, 333
Dingy Shell **Pl 21**, 158
Dingy Skipper **Pl 3**, 91
Dog's Tooth **Pl 58**, 343
Dot Moth **Pl 58**, 344
Dotted Border **Pl 30**, 192
Dotted Border Wave **Pl 16**, 134
Dotted Carpet **Pl 31**, 194
Dotted Chestnut **Pl 53**, 59, 329

Dotted Clay **Pl 63**, 361
Dotted Fan-foot **Pl 41**, 288
Dotted Footman **Pl 40**, 285
Dotted Rustic **Pl 61**, 358
Double Dart **Pl 62**, 361
Double Kidney **Pl 54**, 331, 421
Double Line **Pl 60**, 348, 424
Double Lobed **Pl 51**, 322
Double Square-spot **Pl 63**, 363
Double-striped Pug **Pl 22**, 165, 416
Drab Looper **Pl 21**, 159
Drinker **Pl 11**, 56, 124
Duke of Burgundy **Pl 7**, 108
Dun-bar **Pl 54**, 42, 332, 422
Dusky Brocade **Pl 51**, 319
Dusky Hook-tip **Pl 9**, 117
Dusky Peacock **Pl 27**, 182
Dusky Sallow **Pl 49**, 312
Dusky Scalloped Oak **Pl 29**, 188
Dusky Thorn **Pl 28**, 186
Dusky-lemon Sallow **Pl 52**, 326, 419
Dwarf Cream Wave **Pl 16**, 133
Dwarf Pug **Pl 24**, 170

Ear Moth **Pl 49**, 314
Early Grey **Pl 46**, 305
Early Moth **Pl 32**, 198
Early Thorn **Pl 29**, 44, 45, 187
Early Tooth-striped **Pl 26**, 179
Edinburgh Pug **Pl 25**, 173
eggar and lappet moths **Pl 10–11**, 121–4
Elephant Hawk-moth **Pl 15**, 32, 50, 51, 131
Emperor Moth **Pl 11**, 36, 39, 49, 126
emperor moths **Pl 11**, 126
Engrailed **Pl 32**, 31, 195
Essex Skipper **Pl 3**, 92
Exile **Pl 51**, 322
Eyed Hawk-moth **Pl 12**, 44, 45, 49, 128

False Mocha **Pl 17**, 140
Fan-foot **Pl 41**, 288
Feathered Beauty **Pl 31**, 193
Feathered Brindle **Pl 55**, 335
Feathered Gothic **Pl 57**, 340
Feathered Ranunculus **Pl 55**, 336
Feathered Thorn **Pl 29**, 189
Fen Square-spot **Pl 61**, 357
Fen Wainscot **Pl 50**, 316
Fenn's Wainscot **Pl 50**, 318
Fern **Pl 21**, 161
Festoon **Pl 2**, 85
Fiery Clearwing 20, 83
Figure of Eight **Pl 44**, 298
Figure of Eighty **Pl 9**, 118
Fisher's Estuarine Moth **Pl 49**, 20, 41, 313
Five-spot Burnet **Pl 2**, 89
Flame **Pl 60**, 355
Flame Brocade **Pl 55**, 335

Flame Carpet 144, 415
Flame Shoulder **Pl 61**, 356
Flame Wainscot **Pl 60**, 352, 427
Fletcher's Pug **Pl 24**, 170
Flounced Chestnut **Pl 52**, 327
Flounced Rustic **Pl 49**, 26, 315
Forester **Pl 2**, 87
forester and burnet moths **Pl 2**, 86–9
Four-dotted Footman **Pl 40**, 33, 34, 284
Four-spotted **Pl 43**, 297
Four-spotted Footman **Pl 40**, 276, 285
Fox Moth **Pl 11**, 38, 121, 123
Foxglove Pug **Pl 23**, 167
Frosted Green **Pl 9**, 119
Frosted Orange **Pl 49**, 26, 27, 313

Galium Carpet **Pl 18**, 146
Garden Carpet **Pl 18**, 143, 414
Garden Dart 353
Garden Tiger **Pl 39**, 55, 282
Gatekeeper **Pl 5**, 101
Ghost Moth **Pl 1**, 73
Giant Ear **Pl 49**, 314
Glanville Fritillary **Pl 7**, 106
Glaucous Shears **Pl 58**, 344
goat and leopard moths **Pl 1**, 74
Goat Moth **Pl 1**, 26, 38, 74, 75
Gold Spangle **Pl 43**, 296
Gold Spot **Pl 43**, 296
Gold Swift 73
Golden Plusia **Pl 43**, 295
Golden-rod Brindle **Pl 53**, 330
Golden-rod Pug **Pl 23**, 170, 416
Gothic **Pl 64**, 365
Grass Eggar **Pl 10**, 39, 55, 123
Grass Emerald **Pl 33**, 202
Grass Rivulet **Pl 22**, 164
Grass Wave **Pl 33**, 201
Grayling **Pl 5**, 102
Great Brocade **Pl 62**, 360
Great Oak Beauty **Pl 31**, 194
Great Prominent **Pl 35**, 208
Green Arches **Pl 62**, 361
Green Carpet **Pl 20**, 155
Green Hairstreak **Pl 8**, 60, 110
Green Pug **Pl 22**, 166
Green Silver-lines **Pl 64**, 366, 368
Green-brindled Crescent **Pl 46**, 304
Green-veined White **Pl 4**, 97
Grey **Pl 59**, 347
Grey Arches **Pl 57**, 342
Grey Birch **Pl 32**, 196
Grey Carpet **Pl 26**, 178
Grey Chi **Pl 55**, 334, 422
Grey Dagger **Pl 44**, 23, 299
Grey Mountain Carpet **Pl 19**, 148
Grey Pine Carpet **Pl 19**, 150
Grey Pug **Pl 26**, 177
Grey Scalloped Bar **Pl 33**, 200

Grey Shoulder-knot **Pl 53**, 330
Grizzled Skipper **Pl 3**, 92
Ground Lackey **Pl 10**, 122
Guernsey Underwing **Pl 48**, 310
Gypsy Moth **Pl 37**, 34, 62, 278

hawk-moths **Pl 12–15**, 127–31
Haworth's Minor **Pl 49**, 312
Haworth's Pug **Pl 23**, 166
Heart & Club 354
Heart & Dart **Pl 60**, 26, 354
Heart Moth **Pl 54**, 332
Heath Fritillary **Pl 7**, 6, 20, 107
Heath Rivulet **Pl 22**, 163
Heath Rustic **Pl 63**, 362
Hebrew Character **Pl 56**, 339, 423
Hedge Brown **Pl 5**, 101
Hedge Rustic **Pl 57**, 340
Herald **Pl 37**, 276
High Brown Fritillary **Pl 6**, 20, 39, 103
Hoary Footman **Pl 41**, 287
Holly Blue **Pl 8**, 40, 59, 112
Honeysuckle Sawfly 17
hook-tip and lutestring moths **Pl 9**, 116–20
Hornet Moth 77
Horse Chestnut **Pl 27**, 184
Humming-bird Hawk-moth **Pl 14**, 35, 130

Ingrailed Clay **Pl 61**, 356
Irish Annulet **Pl 33**, 199
Iron Prominent **Pl 35**, 208

Jersey Emerald **Pl 33**, 202
Jersey Mocha **Pl 17**, 37, 139
Jersey Tiger **Pl 40**, 283
July Belle **Pl 17**, 141
July Highflyer **Pl 19**, 148
Juniper Carpet **Pl 19**, 150
Juniper Pug **Pl 23**, 169

Kent Black Arches **Pl 64**, 366, 367
Kentish Glory **Pl 11**, 125
Knot Grass **Pl 44**, 300

L-album Wainscot 351, 426
Lace Border **Pl 16**, 136
Lackey **Pl 10**, 122
Langmaid's Yellow Underwing **Pl 62**, 360
Lappet **Pl 11**, 31, 44, 45, 124
Larch Pug **Pl 24**, 170
Large Blue 20, 42, 60, 113
Large Ear **Pl 49**, 16, 314
Large Emerald **Pl 33**, 48, 202
Large Heath **Pl 5**, 98, 99
Large Nutmeg **Pl 51**, 320
Large Ranunculus **Pl 55**, 337, 423
Large Red-belted Clearwing 28, 79
Large Skipper **Pl 3**, 35, 91, 94
Large Thorn **Pl 28**, 186

Large Twin-spot Carpet 144, 415
Large Wainscot **Pl 49**, 315
Large White **Pl 4**, 6, 96
Large Yellow Underwing **Pl 62**, 26, 31, 358
Latticed Heath **Pl 27**, 183
Lead Belle **Pl 17**, 141
Lead-coloured Drab **Pl 56**, 338
Lead-coloured Pug **Pl 23**, 168
Least Black Arches **Pl 64**, 367
Least Carpet **Pl 16**, 133
Least Minor **Pl 50**, 318, 319
Least Yellow Underwing **Pl 62**, 359
Lempke's Gold Spot **Pl 43**, 296
Leopard Moth **Pl 1**, 75
Lesser Broad-bordered Yellow Underwing **Pl 62**, 360
Lesser Common Rustic **Pl 52**, 323
Lesser Cream Wave **Pl 16**, 137
Lesser Swallow Prominent **Pl 35**, 209
Lesser Treble-bar **Pl 26**, 177
Lesser Yellow Underwing **Pl 62**, 24, 359
Lesser-spotted Pinion **Pl 54**, 332, 421
Light Arches **Pl 51**, 321
Light Brocade **Pl 57**, 342
Light Crimson Underwing **Pl 42**, 292
Light Emerald **Pl 32**, 39, 198
Light Feathered Rustic 353
Light Knot Grass **Pl 44**, 300
Light Orange Underwing **Pl 26**, 180
Lilac Beauty **Pl 28**, 36, 132, 185
Lime Hawk-moth **Pl 12**, 35, 128
Lime-speck Pug **Pl 24**, 172, 416
Little Emerald **Pl 34**, 203
Little Thorn **Pl 27**, 183
Lobster Moth **Pl 35**, 33, 52, 205, 207
Long-tailed Blue **Pl 8**, 49, 109, 111
looper moths **Pl 16–34**, 132–204
Lulworth Skipper **Pl 3**, 35, 93
Lunar Hornet Moth **Pl 1**, 77
Lunar Marbled Brown **Pl 35**, 207
Lunar Thorn **Pl 29**, 187
Lunar Underwing **Pl 53**, 328
Lunar Yellow Underwing **Pl 62**, 359
Lunar-spotted Pinion **Pl 54**, 332, 422
Lychnis **Pl 59**, 347
Lyme Grass **Pl 50**, 316

Magpie **Pl 26**, 43, 50, 180
Maiden's Blush **Pl 17**, 140
Mallow **Pl 19**, 147
Manchester Treble-bar **Pl 26**, 177
Map-winged Swift **Pl 1**, 72
Maple Prominent **Pl 36**, 209
Maple Pug **Pl 23**, 166
Marbled Beauty **Pl 47**, 307
Marbled Brown **Pl 35**, 207
Marbled Clover **Pl 46**, 305
Marbled Coronet **Pl 59**, 347
Marbled Green **Pl 47**, 307
Marbled Minor **Pl 52**, 27, 323

Marbled Pug **Pl 24**, 172
Marbled White **Pl 5**, 30, 35, 101
Marbled White Spot **Pl 43**, 296
March Moth **Pl 29**, 189
Marsh Carpet **Pl 22**, 164
Marsh Fritillary **Pl 7**, 20, 31, 106
Marsh Mallow Moth **Pl 49**, 314
Marsh Moth **Pl 47**, 310
Marsh Oblique-barred 289
Marsh Pug **Pl 23**, 168
Mathew's Wainscot 349, 424
May Highflyer **Pl 19**, 149
Meadow Brown **Pl 5**, 37, 101
Mere's Pug 173
Mere Wainscot **Pl 50**, 317
Merveille du Jour **Pl 54**, 334
metalmark butterflies **Pl 7**, 108
Middle-barred Minor **Pl 52**, 324
Miller **Pl 44**, 299
Minor Shoulder-knot **Pl 54**, 333, 422
Mocha **Pl 17**, 139
Morris's Wainscot **Pl 50**, 318
Mother Shipton **Pl 42**, 292
Mottled Beauty **Pl 31**, 38, 194
Mottled Grey **Pl 20**, 155
Mottled Pug **Pl 25**, 174, 175
Mottled Rustic **Pl 47**, 308
Mottled Umber **Pl 31**, 192
Mountain Burnet **Pl 2**, 86, 88
Mountain Ringlet **Pl 5**, 100
Mouse Moth **Pl 46**, 304
Mullein **Pl 45**, 302
Mullein Wave **Pl 16**, 136
Muslin Footman **Pl 40**, 284
Muslin Moth **Pl 39**, 41, 281

Narrow-bordered Bee Hawk-moth **Pl 14**, 28, 129
Narrow-bordered Five-spot Burnet **Pl 2**, 89
Narrow-winged Pug **Pl 24**, 171
Neglected Rustic **Pl 63**, 362
Netted Carpet **Pl 19**, 152
Netted Mountain Moth **Pl 27**, 182
Netted Pug **Pl 23**, 168
New Forest Burnet **Pl 2**, 20, 88
noctuid moths **Pl 43–64**, 293–365
Northern Arches **Pl 51**, 322
Northern Brown Argus **Pl 8**, 114
Northern Dart **Pl 63**, 364
Northern Deep-brown Dart **Pl 55**, 335
Northern Drab **Pl 56**, 339
Northern Ruby Tiger 282
Northern Rustic **Pl 61**, 358
Northern Spinach **Pl 19**, 152
Northern Winter Moth **Pl 20**, 156
November Moth **Pl 20**, 157
Nut-tree Tussock **Pl 44**, 49, 50, 297
Nutmeg **Pl 57**, 293, 341
nycteoline moths **Pl 64**, 366

Oak Beauty **Pl 30**, 191
Oak Eggar **Pl 10**, 123
Oak Hook-tip **Pl 9**, 116
Oak Lutestring **Pl 9**, 119
Oak Nycteoline **Pl 64**, 368
Oak Processionary **Pl 34**, 205
Oak Rustic **Pl 54**, 333
Oak-tree Pug **Pl 23**, 169
Oblique Carpet **Pl 17**, 142
Oblique Striped **Pl 17**, 141
Obscure Wainscot **Pl 60**, 351, 427
Ochreous Pug **Pl 24**, 172
Old Lady **Pl 48**, 310
Old World Bollworm **Pl 47**, 306
Olive **Pl 54**, 331, 421
Olive Crescent **Pl 42**, 291
Orache Moth **Pl 48**, 310
Orange Footman **Pl 41**, 287
Orange Moth **Pl 28**, 185
Orange Sallow **Pl 52**, 325
Orange Swift **Pl 1**, 72
Orange Underwing **Pl 26**, 35, 36, 180
Orange-tailed Clearwing 81
Orange-tip **Pl 4**, 36, 96

Painted Lady **Pl 7**, 6, 105
Pale Brindled Beauty **Pl 30**, 190
Pale Eggar **Pl 10**, 121
Pale Mottled Willow **Pl 47**, 308
Pale November Moth **Pl 20**, 157
Pale Oak Beauty **Pl 31**, 194
Pale Pinion **Pl 53**, 329, 421
Pale Prominent **Pl 36**, 209
Pale Shining Brown **Pl 57**, 341
Pale Tussock **Pl 38**, 56, 279
Pale-lemon Sallow **Pl 52**, 326, 419
Pale-shouldered Brocade **Pl 57**, 342
Pauper Pug **Pl 24**, 170
Peach Blossom **Pl 9**, 54, 118
Peacock **Pl 7**, 39, 49, 105
Peacock Moth **Pl 27**, 181
Pearl-bordered Fritillary **Pl 6**, 102
Pearly Underwing **Pl 60**, 352
Pebble Hook-tip **Pl 9**, 117
Pebble Prominent **Pl 35**, 6, 208
Peppered Moth **Pl 30**, 6, 191
Phoenix **Pl 19**, 152
Pigmy Footman **Pl 41**, 287
Pimpinel Pug **Pl 24**, 171
Pine Beauty **Pl 56**, 337
Pine Carpet **Pl 19**, 149
Pine Hawk-moth **Pl 14**, 129
Pine-tree Lappet **Pl 11**, 124
Pinion-spotted Pug **Pl 24**, 173
Pinion-streaked Snout 289
Pink-barred Sallow **Pl 52**, 29, 325, 418
Plain Clay **Pl 64**, 38, 365
Plain Golden Y **Pl 43**, 295
Plain Pug **Pl 24**, 44, 45, 171

Plain Wave **Pl 16**, 136
Plumed Fan-foot **Pl 41**, 289
Plumed Prominent **Pl 36**, 210
Pod Lover 348
Poplar Grey **Pl 45**, 300
Poplar Hawk-moth **Pl 12**, 37, 128
Poplar Kitten **Pl 34**, 6, 207
Poplar Lutestring **Pl 9**, 119
Portland Moth **Pl 60**, 352
Portland Ribbon Wave **Pl 16**, 135
Powdered Quaker **Pl 56**, 339, 423
Powdered Wainscot **Pl 44**, 298
Pretty Chalk Carpet **Pl 22**, 161
Pretty Pinion **Pl 22**, 163
Privet Hawk-moth **Pl 13**, 129
prominent, kitten and processionary moths **Pl 34–6**,
    205–11
Purple Bar **Pl 19**, 151
Purple Clay **Pl 61**, 356
Purple Emperor **Pl 6**, 104
Purple Hairstreak **Pl 8**, 30, 33, 60, 110
Purple Marbled **Pl 42**, 291
Purple Thorn **Pl 29**, 187
Purple-bordered Gold **Pl 16**, 133
Puss Moth **Pl 34**, 34, 37, 54, 55, 206

Rannoch Brindled Beauty **Pl 30**, 190
Rannoch Looper **Pl 27**, 182
Rannoch Sprawler **Pl 46**, 55, 304
Raspberry Clearwing 76
Red Admiral **Pl 7**, 104
Red Carpet **Pl 18**, 143, 414
Red Chestnut **Pl 61**, 357
Red Sword-grass **Pl 53**, 330
Red Twin-spot Carpet 143, 414
Red Underwing **Pl 42**, 44, 45, 291
Red-belted Clearwing 76, 81
Red-green Carpet **Pl 20**, 39, 153
Red-line Quaker **Pl 52**, 29, 327, 419
Red-necked Footman **Pl 41**, 285
Red-tipped Clearwing 79, 80
Reddish Buff **Pl 47**, 20, 306
Reddish Light Arches **Pl 51**, 322
Reed Dagger **Pl 44**, 298
Reed Leopard **Pl 1**, 75
Rest Harrow **Pl 33**, 201
Riband Wave **Pl 16**, 52, 135
Ringed Border 181
Ringed Carpet **Pl 31**, 193
Ringlet **Pl 5**, 100
Rivulet **Pl 22**, 162
Rosy Footman **Pl 40**, 33, 34, 36, 37, 284
Rosy Marbled **Pl 47**, 42, 50, 51, 307
Rosy Marsh Moth **Pl 63**, 6, 364
Rosy Minor **Pl 52**, 323
Rosy Rustic **Pl 49**, 313
Rosy Wave **Pl 16**, 138
Round-winged Muslin **Pl 40**, 33, 34, 284
Royal Mantle **Pl 18**, 144

Ruby Tiger **Pl 39**, 282
Ruddy Carpet **Pl 18**, 145
Ruddy Highflyer **Pl 19**, 149
Rufous Minor **Pl 52**, 324
Rush Wainscot **Pl 50**, 319
Rustic **Pl 47**, 308
Rustic Shoulder-knot **Pl 51**, 320

Sallow **Pl 52**, 29, 31, 325, 418
Sallow Clearwing 80
Sallow Kitten **Pl 34**, 206
Saltern Ear **Pl 49**, 314
Sand Dart **Pl 60**, 30, 38, 355
Sandhill Rustic **Pl 49**, 315
Sandy Carpet **Pl 22**, 164
Satellite **Pl 54**, 331
Satin Beauty **Pl 31**, 41, 193
Satin Lutestring **Pl 9**, 119
Satin Wave **Pl 16**, 16, 50, 51, 134
Satyr Pug **Pl 25**, 173, 417
Saxon **Pl 48**, 311
Scalloped Hazel **Pl 29**, 46, 188
Scalloped Hook-tip **Pl 9**, 34, 37, 54, 116
Scalloped Oak **Pl 29**, 188
Scallop Shell **Pl 21**, 160
Scarce Blackneck **Pl 41**, 290
Scarce Bordered Straw **Pl 47**, 306
Scarce Burnished Brass **Pl 43**, 294
Scarce Chocolate-tip **Pl 36**, 211
Scarce Footman **Pl 41**, 6, 286
Scarce Forester **Pl 2**, 87
Scarce Hook-tip **Pl 9**, 117
Scarce Merveille du Jour **Pl 44**, 298
Scarce Prominent **Pl 36**, 210
Scarce Pug **Pl 25**, 174
Scarce Silver Y **Pl 43**, 296
Scarce Silver-lines **Pl 64**, 47, 367
Scarce Tissue **Pl 21**, 160
Scarce Umber **Pl 30**, 191
Scarce Vapourer **Pl 38**, 280
Scarlet Tiger **Pl 40**, 6, 283
Scorched Carpet **Pl 26**, 181
Scorched Wing **Pl 27**, 184
Scotch Annulet **Pl 33**, 199
Scotch Argus **Pl 5**, 100
Scotch Burnet **Pl 2**, 86, 88
September Thorn **Pl 28**, 44, 45, 187
Seraphim **Pl 26**, 178
Setaceous Hebrew Character **Pl 63**,
    363
Shaded Broad-bar **Pl 17**, 142
Shaded Fan-foot **Pl 41**, 288
Shaded Pug **Pl 26**, 176, 417
Shark **Pl 45**, 37, 301
Sharp-angled Carpet **Pl 18**, 146
Sharp-angled Peacock **Pl 27**, 181
Shears **Pl 58**, 344
Shore Wainscot **Pl 60**, 30, 350, 426
Short-cloaked Moth **Pl 64**, 367

Shoulder Stripe **Pl 18**, 147
Shoulder-striped Clover **Pl 46**, 306
Shoulder-striped Wainscot 351, 426
Shuttle-shaped Dart **Pl 60**, 355
Silky Wainscot **Pl 47**, 42, 309
Silky Wave **Pl 16**, 133
Silurian **Pl 60**, 352
Silver Barred **Pl 43**, 297
Silver Cloud **Pl 57**, 340
Silver Hook **Pl 43**, 297
Silver Y **Pl 43**, 295
Silver-ground Carpet 144, 415
Silver-spotted Skipper **Pl 3**, 35, 93
Silver-studded Blue **Pl 8**, 41, 60, 113
Silver-washed Fritillary **Pl 6**, 41, 103
Silvery Arches **Pl 57**, 342
Single-dotted Wave **Pl 16**, 134
Six-belted Clearwing 83
Six-spot Burnet **Pl 2**, 33, 89
Six-striped Rustic **Pl 63**, 363
skippers **Pl 3**, 91–4
Slender Brindle **Pl 51**, 321
Slender Pug **Pl 23**, 29, 166
Slender Scotch Burnet **Pl 2**, 88
Slender-striped Rufous **Pl 21**, 161
Sloe Carpet **Pl 32**, 197
Sloe Pug **Pl 22**, 165
slug moths **Pl 2**, 85
Small Angle Shades **Pl 48**, 311
Small Argent & Sable **Pl 18**, 145
Small Autumnal Moth **Pl 20**, 157
Small Black Arches **Pl 64**, 366
Small Blood-vein **Pl 16**, 137
Small Blue **Pl 8**, 112
Small Brindled Beauty **Pl 30**, 189
Small Chocolate-tip **Pl 36**, 27, 211
Small Clouded Brindle **Pl 51**, 320
Small Copper **Pl 8**, 109
Small Dark Yellow Underwing **Pl 57**, 341
Small Dotted Buff **Pl 50**, 318
Small Dotted Footman **Pl 40**, 33, 285
Small Dusty Wave **Pl 16**, 134
Small Eggar **Pl 10**, 122
Small Elephant Hawk-moth **Pl 15**, 32, 43, 131
Small Emerald **Pl 34**, 31, 203
Small Engrailed **Pl 32**, 195
Small Fan-foot **Pl 41**, 276, 288
Small Fan-footed Wave **Pl 16**, 135
Small Grass Emerald **Pl 34**, 204
Small Heath **Pl 5**, 99
Small Marbled **Pl 42**, 291
Small Mountain Ringlet **Pl 5**, 100
Small Pearl-bordered Fritillary **Pl 6**, 39, 102
Small Phoenix **Pl 20**, 153
Small Purple-barred **Pl 42**, 290
Small Quaker **Pl 56**, 338
Small Ranunculus **Pl 59**, 346
Small Rivulet **Pl 22**, 163
Small Rufous **Pl 50**, 317

Small Scallop **Pl 16**, 135
Small Seraphim **Pl 26**, 179
Small Skipper **Pl 3**, 93
Small Square-spot **Pl 61**, 357
Small Tortoiseshell **Pl 7**, 105
Small Wainscot **Pl 50**, 317
Small Waved Umber **Pl 21**, 161
Small White **Pl 4**, 95, 96
Small White Wave **Pl 21**, 157
Small Yellow Underwing **Pl 45**, 301
Small Yellow Wave **Pl 21**, 158
Smoky Wainscot 349, 425
Smoky Wainscot group **Pl 60**, 424–5
Smoky Wave **Pl 16**, 137
Snout **Pl 37**, 277
Sombre Brocade **Pl 55**, 334
Southern Chestnut **Pl 52**, 327
Southern Grass Emerald **Pl 34**, 204
Southern Wainscot **Pl 60**, 349, 425
Spanish Carpet **Pl 17**, 141
Speckled Footman **Pl 40**, 283
Speckled Wood **Pl 5**, 99
Speckled Yellow **Pl 28**, 185
Spectacle **Pl 43**, 294
Spinach **Pl 20**, 153
Splendid Brocade **Pl 58**, 343
Sprawler **Pl 46**, 304
Spring Usher **Pl 30**, 191
Spruce Carpet **Pl 19**, 150
Spurge Hawk-moth **Pl 14**, 130
Square Spot **Pl 32**, 41, 195
Square-spot Dart 353
Square-spot Rustic **Pl 63**, 38, 362
Square-spotted Clay **Pl 63**, 361
Star-wort **Pl 45**, 43, 302
Stone Pinion **Pl 53**, 330
Stout Dart **Pl 62**, 360
Straw Belle **Pl 33**, 201
Straw Dot **Pl 37**, 277
Straw Underwing **Pl 48**, 311
Streak **Pl 26**, 178
Streamer **Pl 18**, 147
Striped Hawk-moth **Pl 15**, 131
Striped Lychnis **Pl 45**, 302
Striped Twin-spot Carpet **Pl 20**, 155
Striped Wainscot 348, 424
Sub-angled Wave **Pl 16**, 136
Suspected **Pl 54**, 333
Sussex Emerald **Pl 34**, 20, 203
Svensson's Copper Underwing **Pl 46**, 303
Swallow Prominent **Pl 35**, 208
Swallowtail **Pl 3**, 20, 53, 90
swallowtail butterflies **Pl 3**, 90
Swallow-tailed Moth **Pl 29**, 189
Sweet Gale Moth **Pl 44**, 300
swift moths **Pl 1**, 72–3
Sword-grass **Pl 53**, 330
Sycamore **Pl 44**, 299

Talisker Burnet 89
Tawny Marbled Minor **Pl 52**, 324
Tawny Pinion **Pl 53**, 329, 421
Tawny Shears **Pl 59**, 348
Tawny Speckled Pug **Pl 25**, 176
Tawny Wave **Pl 16**, 136
Tawny-barred Angle **Pl 27**, 182
Thrift Clearwing 84
Thyme Pug **Pl 24**, 172
Tissue **Pl 21**, 160
Toadflax Brocade **Pl 45**, 303
Toadflax Pug **Pl 23**, 167
Transparent Burnet **Pl 2**, 88
Treble Brown Spot **Pl 16**, 134
Treble Lines **Pl 47**, 309
Treble-bar **Pl 26**, 177
Tree-lichen Beauty **Pl 47**, 307
Triangle **Pl 2**, 85
Triple-spotted Clay **Pl 63**, 363
Triple-spotted Pug **Pl 24**, 173
True Lover's Knot **Pl 61**, 32, 358
Turnip Moth 354
tussock, ermine, tiger, footman, snout, fan-foot,
      marbled, blackneck and underwing
      moths **Pl 37–42**, 276–92
Twin-spot Carpet **Pl 22**, 162
Twin-spotted Quaker **Pl 56**, 339
Twin-spotted Wainscot **Pl 50**, 316

Uncertain **Pl 47**, 308

V-Moth **Pl 27**, 182
V-Pug **Pl 22**, 39, 165
Valerian Pug **Pl 25**, 174
Vapourer **Pl 38**, 34, 49, 280
Varied Coronet **Pl 59**, 347
Vestal **Pl 17**, 140
Vine's Rustic **Pl 47**, 309

Wall **Pl 5**, 98
Water Betony **Pl 45**, 302
Water Carpet **Pl 20**, 155
Water Ermine **Pl 38**, 281
Waved Black **Pl 42**, 290
Waved Carpet **Pl 21**, 158

Waved Umber **Pl 31**, 192
Weaver's Wave **Pl 16**, 135
Webb's Wainscot **Pl 50**, 319
Welsh Clearwing 78
Welsh Wave **Pl 21**, 158
White Admiral **Pl 6**, 35, 36, 38, 57, 58, 98, 104
white butterflies **Pl 4**, 95–7
White Colon **Pl 59**, 345
White Ermine **Pl 38**, 281
White Plume **Pl 40**, 284
White Prominent **Pl 35**, 209
White Satin Moth **Pl 37**, 31, 276, 278
White Spot **Pl 59**, 41, 347
White-banded Carpet **Pl 19**, 148
White-barred Clearwing 78
White-letter Hairstreak **Pl 8**, 111
White-line Dart 353
White-line Snout 289
White-mantled Wainscot **Pl 50**, 16, 316
White-marked **Pl 61**, 357
White-pinion Spotted **Pl 32**, 197
White-point 350, 425
White-speck 350, 425
White-spotted Pinion **Pl 54**, 331, 421
White-spotted Pug **Pl 23**, 39, 169, 416
Willow Beauty **Pl 31**, 192
Winter Moth **Pl 20**, 39, 156
Wood Carpet **Pl 18**, 146
Wood Tiger **Pl 39**, 67, 282
Wood White **Pl 4**, 95
Woods's Dart 354
Wormwood **Pl 45**, 44, 301
Wormwood Pug **Pl 25**, 174, 417

Yarrow Plume 277
Yarrow Pug **Pl 25**, 176
Yellow Belle **Pl 33**, 201
Yellow Horned **Pl 9**, 120
Yellow Shell **Pl 18**, 144, 145
Yellow-barred Brindle **Pl 26**, 179
Yellow-legged Clearwing 82
Yellow-line Quaker **Pl 52**, 40, 327
Yellow-ringed Carpet **Pl 19**, 148
Yellow-tail **Pl 37**, 31, 38, 279

INDEX OF SCIENTIFIC NAMES

Bold numbers prefixed with 'Pl' refer to colour artworks (those in the plate section).

abbreviata, Eupithecia **Pl 23**, 168
abietaria, Eupithecia **Pl 23**, 167
abietella, Dioryctria 167
Abraxas **Pl 26**, 180
Abrostola **Pl 43**, 294
abruptaria, Menophra **Pl 31**, 192
absinthiata, Eupithecia **Pl 25**, 174, 417
absinthii, Cucullia **Pl 45**, 301
Acanthopsyche 56
Acasis **Pl 26**, 179
aceris, Acronicta **Pl 44**, 299
Acherontia **Pl 13**, 129
Achlya **Pl 9**, 120
Acosmetia **Pl 47**, 306
Acronicta **Pl 44**, 298, 299, 300
Acronictinae 298–301
Actebia **Pl 60**, 352
acteon, Thymelicus **Pl 3**, 93
adippe, Argynnis **Pl 6**, 103
Adscita **Pl 2**, 87
adusta, Mniotype **Pl 55**, 337
adustata, Ligdia **Pl 26**, 181
advenaria, Cepphis **Pl 27**, 183
Aediinae 297
aegeria, Pararge **Pl 5**, 99
aescularia, Alsophila **Pl 29**, 189
aestivaria, Hemithea **Pl 34**, 203
Aethalura **Pl 32**, 196
aethiops, Erebia **Pl 5**, 100
affinis, Cosmia **Pl 54**, 332, 421
affinitata, Perizoma **Pl 22**, 162
agathina, Xestia **Pl 63**, 362
agestis, Aricia **Pl 8**, 113
Aglais **Pl 7**, 105
aglaja, Argynnis **Pl 6**, 103
Agriopis **Pl 30**, 191, 192
Agrius **Pl 12**, 128
Agrochola **Pl 52**, 324, 326, 327, 328, 419
Agrotis **Pl 60**, 352, 353, 354, 355
albella, Coleophora 31
albicillata, Mesoleuca **Pl 18**, 147
albimacula, Hadena **Pl 59**, 347
albipuncta, Mythimna 350, 425
albipunctata, Cyclophora **Pl 17**, 139
albovenosa, Simyra **Pl 44**, 298
albula, Meganola **Pl 64**, 367
albulata, Asthena **Pl 21**, 157
albulata, Perizoma **Pl 22**, 164
alchemillata, Perizoma **Pl 22**, 163
Alcis **Pl 31**, 194
alcon, Phengaris 60
Aleucis **Pl 32**, 197
algae, Cryphia **Pl 47**, 307
algae, Globia **Pl 50**, 319
Allophyes **Pl 46**, 304
alni, Acronicta **Pl 44**, 298

alniaria, Ennomos **Pl 28**, 186
alpicola, Xestia **Pl 63**, 364
alpium, Moma **Pl 44**, 298
Alsophila **Pl 29**, 189
alternata, Epirrhoe **Pl 18**, 145
alternata, Macaria **Pl 27**, 181
ambigua, Hoplodrina **Pl 47**, 309
Amphipoea **Pl 49**, 314, 315
Amphipyra **Pl 46**, 303, 304
Amphipyrinae 303–4
anachoreta, Clostera **Pl 36**, 211
Anaplectoides **Pl 62**, 361
Anarta **Pl 57**, 341
anceps, Apamea **Pl 51**, 320
anceps, Peridea **Pl 35**, 208
andalusica, Conisania **Pl 59**, 346
andrenaeformis, Synanthedon 81
Angerona **Pl 28**, 185
annularia, Cyclophora **Pl 17**, 139
anomala, Stilbia **Pl 45**, 303
Anorthoa **Pl 56**, 339
Anthocharis **Pl 4**, 96
Anticlea **Pl 18**, 147
Anticollix **Pl 22**, 162
antiqua, Orgyia **Pl 38**, 280
Antitype **Pl 55**, 329, 334, 422
Apamea **Pl 51**, 319, 320, 321, 322
Apatura **Pl 6**, 104
Apaturinae 104
Apeira **Pl 28**, 185
Aphantopus **Pl 5**, 100
apiformis, Sesia 77
Aplasta **Pl 33**, 201
Aplocera **Pl 26**, 177
Apocheima **Pl 30**, 189
Apoda **Pl 2**, 85
Apodia 291
Aporophyla **Pl 55**, 335, 336
aprilina, Griposia **Pl 54**, 334
Apterogenum **Pl 54**, 333
Archanara **Pl 50**, 316, 317
Archiearinae 180
Archiearis **Pl 26**, 180
Arctia **Pl 39**, 282
Arctiinae 280–7
Arenostola **Pl 50**, 316
areola, Xylocampa **Pl 46**, 305
argiolus, Celastrina **Pl 8**, 112
argus, Plebejus **Pl 8**, 113
Argynnis **Pl 6**, 103
Aricia **Pl 8**, 113, 114
arion, Phengaris 113
armigera, Helicoverpa **Pl 47**, 306
artaxerxes, Aricia **Pl 8**, 114
asella, Heterogenea **Pl 2**, 85
ashworthii, Xestia **Pl 63**, 364

Aspitates **Pl 33**, 201
assimilata, Eupithecia **Pl 25**, 175
asteris, Cucullia **Pl 45**, 302
Asteroscopus **Pl 46**, 304
Asthena **Pl 21**, 157
atalanta, Vanessa **Pl 7**, 104
Atethmia **Pl 54**, 333
athalia, Melitaea **Pl 7**, 107
Athetis **Pl 47**, 310
Atolmis **Pl 41**, 285
atomaria, Ematurga **Pl 32**, 196
atra, Acanthopsyche 56
atrata, Odezia **Pl 22**, 162
atriplicis, Trachea **Pl 48**, 310
atropos, Acherontia **Pl 13**, 129
augur, Graphiphora **Pl 62**, 361
aurago, Tiliacea **Pl 52**, 325, 418
aurantiaria, Agriopis **Pl 30**, 191
aurinia, Euphydryas **Pl 7**, 106
australis, Aporophyla **Pl 55**, 335
Autographa **Pl 43**, 295, 296
autumnaria, Ennomos **Pl 28**, 186
autumnata, Epirrita **Pl 20**, 157
aversata, Idaea **Pl 16**, 135
Axylia **Pl 60**, 355

badiata, Earophila **Pl 18**, 147
baja, Xestia **Pl 63**, 361
bajularia, Comibaena **Pl 34**, 202
bankiana, Deltote **Pl 43**, 297
batis, Thyatira **Pl 9**, 118
bellargus, Polyommatus **Pl 8**, 115
Bembecia 83
bembeciformis, Sesia **Pl 1**, 77
Bena **Pl 64**, 367
berbera, Amphipyra **Pl 46**, 303
berberata, Pareulype **Pl 21**, 160
betulae, Thecla **Pl 8**, 110
betularia, Biston **Pl 30**, 191
biangulata, Euphyia **Pl 18**, 146
bicolorana, Bena **Pl 64**, 367
bicolorata, Hecatera **Pl 59**, 346
bicoloria, Leucodonta **Pl 35**, 209
bicruris, Hadena **Pl 59**, 347
bicuspis, Furcula **Pl 34**, 206
bidentata, Odontopera **Pl 29**, 188
bifaciata, Perizoma **Pl 22**, 163
bifida, Furcula **Pl 34**, 207
bifractella, Apodia 291
bilineata, Camptogramma **Pl 18**, 145
bimaculata, Lomographa **Pl 32**, 197
binaria, Watsonalla **Pl 9**, 116
bipunctaria, Scotopteryx **Pl 17**, 142
biren, Papestra **Pl 58**, 344
biriviata, Xanthorhoe **Pl 18**, 143, 414
biselata, Idaea **Pl 16**, 135
Biston **Pl 30**, 191
blanda, Hoplodrina **Pl 47**, 308
blandiata, Perizoma **Pl 22**, 163

blomeri, Venusia **Pl 21**, 159
boeticus, Lampides **Pl 8**, 111
Boletobiinae 290–1
Boloria **Pl 6**, 102
bombycina, Polia **Pl 57**, 341
Bombycoidea 125–31
borelii, Gortyna **Pl 49**, 313
Boudinotiana **Pl 26**, 180
Brachionycha **Pl 46**, 304
Brachylomia **Pl 54**, 329, 333, 422
bractea, Autographa **Pl 43**, 296
brassicae, Mamestra **Pl 59**, 345
brassicae, Pieris **Pl 4**, 96
brevilinea, Protarchanara **Pl 50**, 318
britannica, Thera **Pl 19**, 150
brumata, Operophtera **Pl 20**, 156
brunnea, Diarsia **Pl 61**, 356
brunnearia, Selidosema **Pl 31**, 193
brunneata, Macaria **Pl 27**, 182
Bryophila **Pl 47**, 307
Bryophilinae 307
bucephala, Phalera **Pl 36**, 210
buettneri, Sedina **Pl 49**, 315
Bupalus **Pl 32**, 196

c-album, Polygonia **Pl 7**, 106
c-nigrum, Xestia **Pl 63**, 363
Cabera **Pl 32**, 196, 197
caeruleocephala, Diloba **Pl 44**, 298
caesia, Hadena **Pl 59**, 347
caesiata, Entephria **Pl 19**, 148
caja, Arctia **Pl 39**, 282
Calamia **Pl 48**, 312
caliginosa, Acosmetia **Pl 47**, 306
Callimorpha **Pl 40**, 283
Calliteara **Pl 38**, 279
Callophrys **Pl 8**, 110
Calophasia **Pl 45**, 303
cambrica, Venusia **Pl 21**, 158
camilla, Limenitis **Pl 6**, 104
Campaea **Pl 32**, 198
Camptogramma **Pl 18**, 145
caniola, Eilema **Pl 41**, 287
capreolaria, Pungeleria **Pl 33**, 198
captiuncula, Photedes **Pl 50**, 318
capucina, Ptilodon **Pl 36**, 209
Caradrina **Pl 47**, 308
cararia, Stegania 181
carbonaria, Macaria **Pl 27**, 182
cardamines, Anthocharis **Pl 4**, 96
cardui, Vanessa **Pl 7**, 105
carmelita, Odontosia **Pl 36**, 210
carpinata, Trichopteryx **Pl 26**, 179
Carsia **Pl 26**, 177
Carterocephalus **Pl 3**, 92
castaneae, Phragmataecia **Pl 1**, 75
castanea, Xestia **Pl 63**, 362
castrensis, Malacosoma **Pl 10**, 122
Catarhoe **Pl 18**, 144, 145

Catocala **Pl 42**, 291, 292
Celaena **Pl 49**, 312
Celastrina **Pl 8**, 112
centaureata, Eupithecia **Pl 24**, 172, 416
centrago, Atethmia **Pl 54**, 333
Cepphis **Pl 27**, 183
Ceramica **Pl 58**, 344
Cerapteryx **Pl 57**, 340
cerasi, Orthosia **Pl 56**, 338
Cerastis **Pl 61**, 357
Cerura **Pl 34**, 206
Cerurinae 206–7
cervinalis, Rheumaptera **Pl 21**, 160
cespitis, Tholera **Pl 57**, 340
chamomillae, Cucullia **Pl 45**, 301
Charanyca **Pl 47**, 309
Charissa **Pl 33**, 199
chenopodiata, Scotopteryx **Pl 17**, 142
Chesias **Pl 26**, 178
chi, Antitype **Pl 55**, 334, 422
Chiasmia **Pl 27**, 183
Chilodes **Pl 47**, 309
Chloephorinae 367–8
chloerata, Pasiphila **Pl 22**, 165
Chlorissa **Pl 34**, 204
Chloroclysta **Pl 20**, 153, 154
Chloroclystis **Pl 22**, 164, 165
chlorosata, Petrophora **Pl 27**, 183
christyi, Epirrita **Pl 20**, 157
chrysidiformis, Pyropteron 83
chrysitis, Diachrysia **Pl 43**, 294
Chrysomelidae 18
chryson, Diachrysia **Pl 43**, 294
chrysoprasaria, Hemistola **Pl 34**, 203
chrysorrhoea, Euproctis **Pl 37**, 279
Cidaria **Pl 19**, 151
Cilix **Pl 9**, 118
cinctaria, Cleora **Pl 31**, 193
cinerea, Acronicta **Pl 44**, 300
cinerea, Agrotis 353
cinxia, Melitaea **Pl 7**, 106
circellaris, Agrochola **Pl 52**, 328, 419
Cirrhia **Pl 52**, 324, 325, 326, 418, 419
citrago, Tiliacea **Pl 52**, 325
citrata, Dysstroma **Pl 20**, 154
clathrata, Chiasmia **Pl 27**, 183
clavaria, Larentia **Pl 19**, 147
clavipalpis, Caradrina **Pl 47**, 308
clavis, Agrotis 354
Cleora **Pl 31**, 193
Cleorodes **Pl 33**, 199
clorana, Earias **Pl 64**, 368
cloraria, Chlorissa **Pl 34**, 204
Clostera **Pl 36**, 211
Coenobia **Pl 50**, 317
Coenocalpe **Pl 21**, 161
Coenonympha **Pl 5**, 99
Coenophila **Pl 63**, 364
Coenotephria **Pl 20**, 155

cognata, Thera **Pl 19**, 149
Coleophora 31, 171
Coleophoridae 17
Coliadinae 97
Colias **Pl 4**, 97
Colocasia **Pl 44**, 297
Colostygia **Pl 20**, 154, 155
Colotois **Pl 29**, 189
comae, Timandra **Pl 17**, 138
comes, Noctua **Pl 62**, 359
Comibaena **Pl 34**, 202
comitata, Pelurga **Pl 18**, 147
comma, Hesperia **Pl 3**, 93
comma, Leucania 351, 426
complana, Eilema **Pl 41**, 286
compta, Hadena **Pl 59**, 347
Condicinae 306
confusa, Hadena **Pl 59**, 347
confusalis, Nola **Pl 64**, 367
conigera, Mythimna 349, 424
Conisania **Pl 59**, 346
Conistra **Pl 53**, 324, 328, 329, 420
consonaria, Paradarisa **Pl 32**, 195
conspicillaris, Egira **Pl 57**, 340
contigua, Lacanobia **Pl 58**, 343
contiguaria, Idaea **Pl 16**, 135
convolvuli, Agrius **Pl 12**, 128
coracina, Glacies **Pl 33**, 200
Coranarta **Pl 57**, 341
cordigera, Coranarta **Pl 57**, 341
coridon, Polyommatus **Pl 8**, 115
coronillaria, Pseudoterpna **Pl 33**, 202
corylata, Electrophaes **Pl 19**, 151
coryli, Colocasia **Pl 44**, 297
Coscinia **Pl 40**, 283
Cosmia **Pl 54**, 329, 331, 332, 421, 422
Cosmorhoe **Pl 19**, 151
Cossidae **Pl 1**, 74–5
Cossinae 74
Cossoidea 74–84
Cossus **Pl 1**, 74
cossus, Cossus **Pl 1**, 74
costaestrigalis, Schrankia 289
craccae, Lygephila **Pl 41**, 290
Craniophora **Pl 45**, 300
crassalis, Hypena **Pl 37**, 278
crataegi, Trichiura **Pl 10**, 121
crenata, Apamea **Pl 51**, 320
crepuscularia, Ectropis **Pl 32**, 195
cribraria, Coscinia **Pl 40**, 283
cribrumalis, Macrochilo **Pl 41**, 288
crinanensis, Amphipoea **Pl 49**, 315
Crocallis **Pl 29**, 188
croceus, Colias **Pl 4**, 97
cruda, Orthosia **Pl 56**, 338
Cryphia **Pl 47**, 307
cuculata, Catarhoe **Pl 18**, 144
cucullatella, Nola **Pl 64**, 367
Cucullia **Pl 45**, 301, 302

Cuculliinae 301–2
cucullina, Ptilodon **Pl 36**, 209
culiciformis, Synanthedon 79
cultraria, Watsonalla **Pl 9**, 117
Cupido **Pl 8**, 112
cupressata, Thera **Pl 19**, 150
cursoria, Euxoa 353
curtula, Clostera **Pl 36**, 211
curvatula, Drepana **Pl 9**, 117
Cybosia **Pl 40**, 284
Cyclophora **Pl 17**, 35, 138, 139, 140
Cymatophorina **Pl 9**, 119

dahlii, Diarsia **Pl 61**, 356
dardoinaria, Crocallis **Pl 29**, 188
Dasypolia **Pl 55**, 336
dealbana, Gypsonoma 34, 35
debiliata, Pasiphila **Pl 23**, 166
decimalis, Tholera **Pl 57**, 340
decoloraria, Xanthorhoe **Pl 18**, 143, 414
defoliaria, Erannis **Pl 31**, 192
degeneraria, Idaea **Pl 16**, 135
Deilephila **Pl 15**, 131
Deileptenia **Pl 31**, 193
Deltote **Pl 43**, 296, 297
Dendrolimus **Pl 11**, 124
denotata, Eupithecia **Pl 25**, 175
dentaria, Selenia **Pl 29**, 187
Denticucullus **Pl 50**, 317
depressa, Eilema **Pl 41**, 286
depuncta, Eugnorisma **Pl 64**, 365
derivata, Anticlea **Pl 18**, 147
designata, Xanthorhoe 144, 415
Diachrysia **Pl 43**, 294
Diacrisia **Pl 39**, 281
Diaphora **Pl 39**, 281
Diarsia **Pl 61**, 356, 357
Dicallomera **Pl 38**, 279
Dicranurinae 207
Dicycla **Pl 54**, 332
didyma, Mesapamea **Pl 52**, 323
didymata, Mesotype **Pl 22**, 162
diffinis, Cosmia **Pl 54**, 331, 421
Diloba **Pl 44**, 298
Dilobinae 298
diluta, Cymatophorina **Pl 9**, 119
dilutaria, Idaea **Pl 16**, 133
dilutata, Epirrita **Pl 20**, 157
dimidiata, Idaea **Pl 16**, 134
Dioryctria 167
discordella, Coleophora 114
Dismorphiinae 95
dispar, Lymantria **Pl 37**, 278
dissoluta, Archanara **Pl 50**, 317
distinctaria, Eupithecia **Pl 24**, 172
distinctata, Aleucis **Pl 32**, 197
ditrapezium, Xestia **Pl 63**, 363
dodonaea, Drymonia **Pl 35**, 207
dodoneata, Eupithecia **Pl 23**, 169

dolabraria, Plagodis **Pl 27**, 184
domestica, Bryophila **Pl 47**, 307
dominula, Callimorpha **Pl 40**, 283
Drepana **Pl 9**, 117
Drepanidae **Pl 9**, 116–20
Drepaninae 116–18
Drepanoidea 116–20
dromedarius, Notodonta **Pl 35**, 208
Drymonia **Pl 35**, 207
Dryobota **Pl 54**, 333
Dryobotodes **Pl 55**, 334
dubitata, Triphosa **Pl 21**, 160
dumetata, Gnophos **Pl 33**, 199
duplaris, Ochropacha **Pl 9**, 119
Dypterygia **Pl 48**, 310
Dyscia **Pl 33**, 200
dysodea, Hecatera **Pl 59**, 346
Dysstroma **Pl 20**, 154

Earias **Pl 64**, 368
Earophila **Pl 18**, 147
Ecliptopera **Pl 20**, 153
Ectropis **Pl 32**, 194, 195
Ectropis sp. **Pl 32**, 195
efformata, Aplocera **Pl 26**, 177
egenaria, Eupithecia **Pl 24**, 170
Egira **Pl 57**, 340
Eilema **Pl 41**, 286, 287
Elaphria **Pl 47**, 307
Electrophaes **Pl 19**, 151
elinguaria, Crocallis **Pl 29**, 188
elpenor, Deilephila **Pl 15**, 131
elymi, Longalatedes **Pl 50**, 316
emarginata, Idaea **Pl 16**, 135
Ematurga **Pl 32**, 196
emortualis, Trisateles **Pl 42**, 291
emutaria, Scopula **Pl 16**, 138
Enargia **Pl 54**, 331
Endromidae **Pl 11**, 125
Endromis **Pl 11**, 125
Ennominae 180–201
Ennomos **Pl 28**, 16, 186, 187
Entephria **Pl 19**, 148
Epione **Pl 28**, 184, 185
epiphron, Erebia **Pl 5**, 100
Epirrhoe **Pl 18**, 145, 146
Epirrita **Pl 20**, 156, 157
epomidion, Apamea **Pl 51**, 320
Erannis **Pl 31**, 192
Erebia **Pl 5**, 100
Erebidae **Pl 37–42**, 276–92
Erebinae 291–2
eremita, Dryobotodes **Pl 55**, 334
Eremobia **Pl 49**, 312
Eriogaster **Pl 10**, 122
Eriopygodes **Pl 60**, 352
erosaria, Ennomos **Pl 28**, 187
Erynnis **Pl 3**, 91
Eublemma **Pl 42**, 291

Euchoeca **Pl 21**, 158
Euclidia **Pl 42**, 292
Eugnorisma **Pl 64**, 364, 365
Eulithis **Pl 19–20**, 152, 153
euphorbiae, Hyles **Pl 14**, 130
euphrosyne, Boloria **Pl 6**, 102
Euphydryas **Pl 7**, 106
Euphyia **Pl 18**, 146
Eupithecia **Pl 23–6**, 164, 166–77, 416, 417
Euplagia **Pl 40**, 283
Euplexia **Pl 48**, 311
Euproctis **Pl 37**, 279
Eupsilia **Pl 54**, 331
Eurois **Pl 62**, 360
Eustroma **Pl 19**, 152
Eustrotiinae 296–7
Euthrix **Pl 11**, 124
Euxoa 352, 353
exanthemata, Cabera **Pl 32**, 197
exclamationis, Agrotis **Pl 60**, 354
exiguata, Eupithecia **Pl 25**, 175
expallidata, Eupithecia **Pl 25**, 174, 417
exsoleta, Xylena **Pl 53**, 330
extensaria, Eupithecia **Pl 25**, 174
extrema, Photedes **Pl 50**, 318
exulans, Zygaena **Pl 2**, 88
exulis, Apamea **Pl 51**, 322

fagaria, Dyscia **Pl 33**, 200
fagata, Operophtera **Pl 20**, 156
fagi, Stauropus **Pl 35**, 207
Falcaria **Pl 9**, 116
falcataria, Drepana **Pl 9**, 117
fascelina, Dicallomera **Pl 38**, 279
fasciaria, Hylaea **Pl 33**, 198
fasciata, Zaraea 17
fasciuncula, Oligia **Pl 52**, 324
favicolor, Mythimna 349, 424
Favonius **Pl 8**, 110
ferrago, Mythimna 350, 426
ferrugata, Xanthorhoe 144, 415
ferruginea, Rusina **Pl 47**, 309
festucae, Plusia **Pl 43**, 296
filigrammaria, Epirrita **Pl 20**, 157
filipendulae, Zygaena **Pl 2**, 89
fimbrialis, Thalera **Pl 34**, 203
fimbriata, Noctua **Pl 62**, 359
firmata, Pennithera **Pl 19**, 149
flammea, Panolis **Pl 56**, 337
flammea, Senta **Pl 60**, 352, 427
flammea, Trigonophora **Pl 55**, 335
flammeolaria, Hydrelia **Pl 21**, 158
flavago, Gortyna **Pl 49**, 313
flavicincta, Polymixis **Pl 55**, 337, 423
flavicinctata, Entephria **Pl 19**, 148
flavicornis, Achlya **Pl 9**, 120
flaviventris, Synanthedon 80
flavofasciata, Perizoma **Pl 22**, 164

flexula, Laspeyria **Pl 42**, 290
florida, Diarsia **Pl 61**, 357
floslactata, Scopula **Pl 16**, 137
fluctuata, Xanthorhoe **Pl 18**, 143, 414
fluctuosa, Tetheella **Pl 9**, 119
fluxa, Photedes **Pl 50**, 317
formicaeformis, Synanthedon 79
formosana, Enarmonia 81
fraxini, Catocala **Pl 42**, 291
fuciformis, Hemaris **Pl 14**, 130
fucosa, Amphipoea **Pl 49**, 314
fuliginaria, Parascotia **Pl 42**, 290
fuliginosa, Phragmatobia **Pl 39**, 282
fulvata, Cidaria **Pl 19**, 151
furcata, Hydriomena **Pl 19**, 148
Furcula **Pl 34**, 206, 207
furcula, Furcula **Pl 34**, 206
furuncula, Mesoligia **Pl 52**, 323
furva, Apamea **Pl 51**, 322
fuscantaria, Ennomos **Pl 28**, 186
fusconebulosa, Korscheltellus **Pl 1**, 72
fuscovenosa, Idaea **Pl 16**, 133

Gagitodes **Pl 22**, 164
galathea, Melanargia **Pl 5**, 101
galiata, Epirrhoe **Pl 18**, 146
gallii, Hyles **Pl 14**, 130
gamma, Autographa **Pl 43**, 295
Gandaritis **Pl 20**, 153
Gastropacha **Pl 11**, 124
geminipuncta, Lenisa **Pl 50**, 316
Geometra **Pl 33**, 202
Geometridae **Pl 16–34**, 132–204
Geometrinae 201–4
Geometroidea 132–204
geryon, Adscita **Pl 2**, 87
Gillmeria 277
gilvago, Cirrhia **Pl 52**, 326, 419
gilvaria, Aspitates **Pl 33**, 201
Glacies **Pl 33**, 200
glareosa, Eugnorisma **Pl 64**, 364
glaucata, Cilix **Pl 9**, 118
Globia **Pl 50**, 319
globulariae, Jordanita **Pl 2**, 87
glyphica, Euclidia **Pl 42**, 292
gnoma, Pheosia **Pl 35**, 209
Gnophos **Pl 33**, 199
Gonepteryx **Pl 4**, 97
Gortyna **Pl 49**, 313
gothica, Orthosia **Pl 56**, 339, 423
gracilis, Orthosia **Pl 56**, 339, 423
graminis, Cerapteryx **Pl 57**, 340
Graphiphora **Pl 62**, 361
graslini, Agrotis 354
Griposia **Pl 54**, 334
grisealis, Herminia **Pl 41**, 288
griseata, Lithostege **Pl 26**, 178
griseola, Eilema **Pl 41**, 286
grossulariata, Abraxas **Pl 26**, 180

Gymnoscelis **Pl 22**, 164, 165, 416
Gypsonoma 34, 35

Habrosyne **Pl 9**, 118
Hada **Pl 58**, 344
Hadena **Pl 59**, 347, 348
Hadeninae 337–52
haematidea, Agrochola **Pl 52**, 327
halterata, Lobophora **Pl 26**, 178
Hamearis **Pl 7**, 108
harpagula, Sabra **Pl 9**, 117
hastata, Rheumaptera **Pl 21**, 159
haworthiata, Eupithecia **Pl 23**, 166
haworthii, Celaena **Pl 49**, 312
Hecatera **Pl 59**, 346
hecta, Phymatopus 73
Heliconiinae 102–3
Helicoverpa **Pl 47**, 306
Heliothinae 305–6
Heliothis **Pl 46**, 305, 306
Helotropha **Pl 49**, 312
helvola, Agrochola **Pl 52**, 327
Hemaris **Pl 14**, 129, 130
Hemeroplanes 50, 51
Hemistola **Pl 34**, 203
Hemithea **Pl 34**, 203
hepatica, Polia **Pl 57**, 342
Hepialidae **Pl 1**, 72–3
Hepialoidea 72–3
Hepialus **Pl 1**, 73
Herminia **Pl 41**, 288
Herminiinae 288–9
Hesperia **Pl 3**, 93
Hesperiidae **Pl 3**, 91–4
Hesperiinae 92–4
Heterogenea **Pl 2**, 85
Heteropterinae 92
Hipparchia **Pl 5**, 102
hippocastanaria, Pachycnemia **Pl 27**, 184
hirtaria, Lycia **Pl 30**, 190
hispidaria, Apocheima **Pl 30**, 189
Hoplodrina **Pl 47**, 308, 309
Horisme **Pl 21**, 161
humidalis, Hypenodes 289
humuli, Hepialus **Pl 1**, 73
Hydraecia **Pl 49**, 313, 314
Hydrelia **Pl 21**, 158
Hydriomena **Pl 19**, 148, 149
Hylaea **Pl 33**, 198
hylaeiformis, Pennisetia 76
Hyles **Pl 14–15**, 130, 131
Hypena **Pl 37**, 277, 278
Hypeninae 277–8
Hypenodes 289
Hypenodinae 289
hyperantus, Aphantopus **Pl 5**, 100
Hypomecis **Pl 31**, 194
Hyppa **Pl 48**, 311

icarus, Polyommatus **Pl 8**, 114
ichneumoniformis, Bembecia 83
icterata, Eupithecia **Pl 25**, 176
icteritia, Cirrhia **Pl 52**, 325, 418
Idaea **Pl 16**, 132, 133, 134, 135, 136
imbecilla, Eriopygodes **Pl 60**, 352
imitaria, Scopula **Pl 16**, 137
immutata, Scopula **Pl 16**, 137
impluviata, Hydriomena **Pl 19**, 149
impura, Mythimna 349, 425
incerta, Orthosia **Pl 56**, 337, 423
indigata, Eupithecia **Pl 24**, 172
innotata, Eupithecia **Pl 24**, 171
insigniata, Eupithecia **Pl 24**, 173
interjecta, Noctua **Pl 62**, 359
interrogationis, Syngrapha **Pl 43**, 296
intricata, Eupithecia **Pl 25**, 173
inturbata, Eupithecia **Pl 23**, 166
io, Aglais **Pl 7**, 105
Ipimorpha **Pl 54**, 329, 331, 421
ipsilon, Agrotis 355
iris, Apatura **Pl 6**, 104
irriguata, Eupithecia **Pl 24**, 172
irrorella, Setina **Pl 41**, 287

jacobaeae, Tyria **Pl 40**, 283
janthe, Noctua **Pl 62**, 360
janthina, Noctua **Pl 62**, 360
Jodis **Pl 34**, 203
Jordanita **Pl 2**, 87
jota, Autographa **Pl 43**, 295
jubata, Alcis **Pl 31**, 194
juniperata, Thera **Pl 19**, 150
jurtina, Maniola **Pl 5**, 101
juvernica, Leptidea **Pl 4**, 95

kadenii, Caradrina **Pl 47**, 308
Korscheltellus **Pl 1**, 72

l-album, Mythimna 351, 426
labecula, Dryobota **Pl 54**, 333
Lacanobia **Pl 57–8**, 342, 343
lacertinaria, Falcaria **Pl 9**, 116
lactearia, Jodis **Pl 34**, 203
Lampides **Pl 8**, 111
Lampropteryx **Pl 20**, 155, 156
lanestris, Eriogaster **Pl 10**, 122
Laothoe **Pl 12**, 128
lapidata, Coenocalpe **Pl 21**, 161
lapponaria, Lycia **Pl 30**, 190
Larentia **Pl 19**, 147
Larentiinae 141–79
lariciata, Eupithecia **Pl 24**, 170
Lasiocampa **Pl 10**, 123
Lasiocampidae **Pl 10–11**, 121–4
Lasiocampinae 122–3
Lasiocampoidea 121–4
Lasiommata **Pl 5**, 98
Laspeyria **Pl 42**, 290

Lateroligia **Pl 51**, 322
latruncula, Oligia **Pl 52**, 324
leautieri, Lithophane **Pl 53**, 330
legatella, Chesias **Pl 26**, 178
Lenisa **Pl 50**, 316
leporina, Acronicta **Pl 44**, 299
Leptidea **Pl 4**, 95
Leucania **Pl 60**, 348, 351, 426, 427
Leucochlaena **Pl 52**, 324
Leucodonta **Pl 35**, 209
leucographa, Cerastis **Pl 61**, 357
Leucoma **Pl 37**, 278
leucophaearia, Agriopis **Pl 30**, 191
leucostigma, Helotropha **Pl 49**, 312
libatrix, Scoliopteryx **Pl 37**, 276
lichenaria, Cleorodes **Pl 33**, 199
lichenea, Polymixis **Pl 55**, 336
Ligdia **Pl 26**, 181
ligula, Conistra **Pl 53**, 328, 420
ligustri, Craniophora **Pl 45**, 300
ligustri, Sphinx **Pl 13**, 129
limacodes, Apoda **Pl 2**, 85
Limacodidae **Pl 2**, 85
Limenitidinae 104
Limenitis **Pl 6**, 104
linariata, Eupithecia **Pl 23**, 167
linearia, Cyclophora **Pl 17**, 140
lineata, Siona **Pl 33**, 200
lineola, Thymelicus **Pl 3**, 92
literosa, Litoligia **Pl 52**, 323
Lithophane **Pl 53**, 329, 330, 421
Lithosia **Pl 40**, 285
Lithostege **Pl 26**, 178
lithoxylaea, Apamea **Pl 51**, 321
Litoligia **Pl 52**, 323
litoralis, Mythimna **Pl 60**, 350, 426
littoralis, Lobesia 84
litura, Agrochola **Pl 52**, 326
liturata, Macaria **Pl 27**, 182
livornica, Hyles **Pl 15**, 131
Lobophora **Pl 26**, 178
Lomaspilis **Pl 26**, 181
Lomographa **Pl 32**, 197
Longalatedes **Pl 50**, 316
lonicerae, Zygaena **Pl 2**, 89
loreyi, Leucania 351, 427
lota, Agrochola **Pl 52**, 327, 419
loti, Zygaena **Pl 2**, 88
lubricipeda, Spilosoma **Pl 38**, 281
lucens, Amphipoea **Pl 49**, 314
lucernea, Standfussiana **Pl 61**, 358
lucina, Hamearis **Pl 7**, 108
lucipara, Euplexia **Pl 48**, 311
luctuata, Spargania **Pl 19**, 148
luctuosa, Tyta **Pl 43**, 297
lueneburgensis, Aporophyla **Pl 55**, 335
lunaedactyla, Marasmarcha 277
lunosa, Omphaloscelis **Pl 53**, 328
lunula, Calophasia **Pl 45**, 303

lunularia, Selenia **Pl 29**, 187
Luperina **Pl 49**, 315
lupulina, Korscheltellus **Pl 1**, 72
luridata, Scotopteryx **Pl 17**, 141
lurideola, Eilema **Pl 41**, 286
lutea, Spilosoma **Pl 38**, 280
luteolata, Opisthograptis **Pl 27**, 184
lutosa, Rhizedra **Pl 49**, 315
lutulenta, Aporophyla **Pl 55**, 335
Lycaena **Pl 8**, 109
Lycaenidae **Pl 8**, 109–15
Lycaeninae 109
lychnidis, Agrochola **Pl 52**, 326
lychnitis, Cucullia **Pl 45**, 302
Lycia **Pl 30**, 190
Lycophotia **Pl 61**, 358
Lygephila **Pl 41**, 289, 290
Lymantria **Pl 37**, 278
Lymantriinae 278–80

Macaria **Pl 27**, 181, 182
machaon, Papilio **Pl 3**, 90
macilenta, Agrochola **Pl 52**, 327
Macrochilo **Pl 41**, 288
Macroglossinae 129–31
Macroglossum **Pl 14**, 130
Macrothylacia **Pl 11**, 123
macularia, Pseudopanthera **Pl 28**, 185
Malacosoma **Pl 10**, 122
Malacosomatinae 122
malvae, Pyrgus **Pl 3**, 92
Mamestra **Pl 59**, 345
Maniola **Pl 5**, 101
Marasmarcha 277
margaritaria, Campaea **Pl 32**, 198
marginaria, Agriopis **Pl 30**, 192
marginata, Lomaspilis **Pl 26**, 181
marginepunctata, Scopula **Pl 16**, 136
maritima, Chilodes **Pl 47**, 309
maritima, Heliothis **Pl 46**, 306
Martania **Pl 22**, 164
matura, Thalpophila **Pl 48**, 311
maura, Mormo **Pl 48**, 310
megacephala, Subacronicta **Pl 45**, 300
Meganola **Pl 64**, 366, 367
megera, Lasiommata **Pl 5**, 98
Melanargia **Pl 5**, 101
Melanchra **Pl 58**, 344
melanopa, Anarta **Pl 57**, 341
Melanthia **Pl 22**, 161
Melitaea **Pl 7**, 106, 107
mellinata, Eulithis **Pl 20**, 153
mendica, Diaphora **Pl 39**, 281
mendica, Diarsia **Pl 61**, 356
Menophra **Pl 31**, 192
menyanthidis, Acronicta **Pl 44**, 300
Mesapamea **Pl 52**, 322, 323
Mesoleuca **Pl 18**, 147
Mesoligia **Pl 52**, 323

mesomella, *Cybosia* **Pl 40**, 284
Mesotype **Pl 22**, 162
meticulosa, *Phlogophora* **Pl 48**, 311
Metoponiinae 301
miata, *Chloroclysta* **Pl 20**, 154
micacea, *Hydraecia* **Pl 49**, 313
mi, *Euclidia* **Pl 42**, 292
millefoliata, *Eupithecia* **Pl 25**, 176
Miltochrista **Pl 40**, 284
Mimas **Pl 12**, 128
miniata, *Miltochrista* **Pl 40**, 284
minima, *Photedes* **Pl 50**, 318
minimus, *Cupido* **Pl 8**, 112
miniosa, *Orthosia* **Pl 56**, 338
Minoa **Pl 21**, 159
minorata, *Perizoma* **Pl 22**, 163
Mniotype **Pl 55**, 337
Moma **Pl 44**, 298
monacha, *Lymantria* **Pl 37**, 278
moneta, *Polychrysia* **Pl 43**, 295
monoglypha, *Apamea* **Pl 51**, 321
montanata, *Xanthorhoe* 144, 415
Mormo **Pl 48**, 310
morpheus, *Caradrina* **Pl 47**, 308
morrisii, *Photedes* **Pl 50**, 318
mucronata, *Scotopteryx* **Pl 17**, 141
multistrigaria, *Colostygia* **Pl 20**, 155
munda, *Anorthoa* **Pl 56**, 339
mundana, *Nudaria* **Pl 40**, 284
muralis, *Nyctobrya* **Pl 47**, 307
muricata, *Idaea* **Pl 16**, 133
murinata, *Minoa* **Pl 21**, 159
muscaeformis, *Pyropteron* 84
muscerda, *Pelosia* **Pl 40**, 285
myopaeformis, *Synanthedon* 81
Myrmecozela 59
myrtilli, *Anarta* **Pl 57**, 341
Mythimna **Pl 60**, 348, 349, 350, 351, 424, 425, 426

Naenia **Pl 64**, 365
nanata, *Eupithecia* **Pl 24**, 171
napi, *Pieris* **Pl 4**, 97
nebulata, *Euchoeca* **Pl 21**, 158
nebulosa, *Polia* **Pl 57**, 342
neurica, *Archanara* **Pl 50**, 316
neustria, *Malacosoma* **Pl 10**, 122
nickerlii, *Luperina* **Pl 49**, 315
nigra, *Aporophyla* **Pl 55**, 336
nigricans, *Euxoa* 353
nigropunctata, *Scopula* **Pl 16**, 136
Noctua **Pl 62**, 358, 359, 360
Noctuidae **Pl 43–64**, 293–365
Noctuinae 352–65
Noctuoidea 205–368
Nola **Pl 64**, 367
Nolidae **Pl 64**, 366
Nolinae 366–7
Nonagria **Pl 49**, 316
notata, *Macaria* **Pl 27**, 181

notha, *Boudinotiana* **Pl 26**, 180
Notodonta **Pl 35**, 208
Notodontidae **Pl 34–6**, 205–11
Notodontinae 207–10
nubeculosa, *Brachionycha* **Pl 46**, 304
Nudaria **Pl 40**, 284
nupta, *Catocala* **Pl 42**, 291
Nycteola **Pl 64**, 368
Nyctobrya **Pl 47**, 307
Nymphalidae **Pl 5–7**, 98–107
Nymphalinae 104–7

obelisca, *Euxoa* 353
obeliscata, *Thera* **Pl 19**, 150
obfuscata, *Gnophos* **Pl 33**, 199
oblonga, *Apamea* **Pl 51**, 321
obscurata, *Charissa* **Pl 33**, 199
obsitalis, *Hypena* **Pl 37**, 277
obsoleta, *Leucania* **Pl 60**, 351, 427
obtusa, *Pelosia* **Pl 40**, 285
occulta, *Eurois* **Pl 62**, 360
ocellaris, *Cirrhia* **Pl 52**, 326, 419
ocellata, *Cosmorhoe* **Pl 19**, 151
ocellata, *Smerinthus* **Pl 12**, 128
Ochlodes **Pl 3**, 94
ochraceella, *Myrmecozela* 59
ochrata, *Idaea* **Pl 16**, 133
ochrea, *Coleophora* 87, 114
ochrearia, *Aspitates* **Pl 33**, 201
ochroleuca, *Eremobia* **Pl 49**, 312
Ochropacha **Pl 9**, 119
Ochropleura **Pl 61**, 356
octogenaria, *Hoplodrina* **Pl 47**, 308
ocularis, *Tethea* **Pl 9**, 118
oculea, *Amphipoea* **Pl 49**, 314
Odezia **Pl 22**, 162
oditis, *Leucochlaena* **Pl 52**, 324
Odontopera **Pl 29**, 188
Odontosia **Pl 36**, 210
oleracea, *Lacanobia* **Pl 58**, 343
Oligia **Pl 52**, 26, 323, 324
olivata, *Colostygia* **Pl 20**, 154
Omphaloscelis **Pl 53**, 328
Oncocnemidinae 303
ononaria, *Aplasta* **Pl 33**, 201
oo, *Dicycla* **Pl 54**, 332
Operophtera **Pl 20**, 156
ophiogramma, *Lateroligia* **Pl 51**, 322
opima, *Orthosia* **Pl 56**, 339
Opisthograptis **Pl 27**, 184
orbona, *Noctua* **Pl 62**, 359
Orgyia **Pl 38**, 280
ornata, *Scopula* **Pl 16**, 136
ornitopus, *Lithophane* **Pl 53**, 330
or, *Tethea* **Pl 9**, 119
Orthonama **Pl 17**, 142
Orthosia **Pl 56**, 329, 337, 338, 339, 423
osseola, *Hydraecia* **Pl 49**, 314
ostrina, *Eublemma* **Pl 42**, 291

otregiata, *Lampropteryx* **Pl 20**, 156
Ourapteryx **Pl 29**, 189
oxyacanthae, *Allophyes* **Pl 46**, 304

Pachycnemia **Pl 27**, 184
palaemon, *Carterocephalus* **Pl 3**, 92
paleacea, *Enargia* **Pl 54**, 331
pallens, *Mythimna* 349, 424
pallidactyla, *Gillmeria* 277
pallustris, *Athetis* **Pl 47**, 310
palpina, *Pterostoma* **Pl 36**, 209
pamphilus, *Coenonympha* **Pl 5**, 99
Panemeria **Pl 45**, 301
Panolis **Pl 56**, 337
Pantheinae 297
Papestra **Pl 58**, 344
paphia, *Argynnis* **Pl 6**, 103
Papilio **Pl 3**, 90
papilionaria, *Geometra* **Pl 33**, 202
Papilionidae **Pl 3**, 90
Papilioninae 90
Papilionoidea 90–115
Paracolax **Pl 41**, 288
Paradarisa **Pl 32**, 195
Pararge **Pl 5**, 99
Parascotia **Pl 42**, 290
Parasemia **Pl 39**, 282
Parastichtis **Pl 54**, 333
Parectropis **Pl 32**, 195
Pareulype **Pl 21**, 160
parthenias, *Archiearis* **Pl 26**, 180
parva, *Eublemma* **Pl 42**, 291
Pasiphila **Pl 22–3**, 164, 165, 166
pastinum, *Lygephila* **Pl 41**, 289
paupella, *Ptocheuusa* 291
pavonia, *Saturnia* **Pl 11**, 126
Pechipogo **Pl 41**, 289
pectinataria, *Colostygia* **Pl 20**, 155
Pelosia **Pl 40**, 285
peltigera, *Heliothis* **Pl 46**, 306
Pelurga **Pl 18**, 147
pendularia, *Cyclophora* **Pl 17**, 138
pennaria, *Colotois* **Pl 29**, 189
Pennisetia 76
Pennithera **Pl 19**, 149
pentadactyla, *Pterophorus* **Pl 40**, 284
Perconia **Pl 33**, 201
Peribatodes **Pl 31**, 192, 193
peribolata, *Scotopteryx* **Pl 17**, 141
Peridea **Pl 35**, 208
Peridroma **Pl 60**, 352
Perizoma **Pl 22**, 162, 163, 164
perplexa, *Hadena* **Pl 59**, 348
persicariae, *Melanchra* **Pl 58**, 344
petasitis, *Hydraecia* **Pl 49**, 313
Petrophora **Pl 27**, 183
Phalera **Pl 36**, 210
Phalerinae 210
Phengaris 60, 113

Pheosia **Pl 35**, 208, 209
Phibalapteryx **Pl 17**, 141
Phigalia **Pl 30**, 190
Philereme **Pl 21**, 159
phlaeas, *Lycaena* **Pl 8**, 109
Phlogophora **Pl 48**, 311
phoeniceata, *Eupithecia* **Pl 23**, 169
Photedes **Pl 50**, 317, 318
Phragmataecia **Pl 1**, 75
Phragmatobia **Pl 39**, 282
phragmitidis, *Arenostola* **Pl 50**, 316
Phycitodes **Pl 42**, 291
Phymatopus 73
Phytometra **Pl 42**, 290
Pieridae **Pl 4**, 95–7
Pierinae 96–7
Pieris **Pl 4**, 96, 97
pigra, *Clostera* **Pl 36**, 211
pilosaria, *Phigalia* **Pl 30**, 190
pimpinellata, *Eupithecia* **Pl 24**, 171
Pinarinae 124
pinastri, *Sphinx* **Pl 14**, 129
pini, *Dendrolimus* **Pl 11**, 124
piniaria, *Bupalus* **Pl 32**, 196
pisi, *Ceramica* **Pl 58**, 344
plagiata, *Aplocera* **Pl 26**, 177
Plagodis **Pl 27**, 183, 184
plantaginis, *Parasemia* **Pl 39**, 282
plebeja, *Hada* **Pl 58**, 344
Plebejus **Pl 8**, 113
plecta, *Ochropleura* **Pl 61**, 356
Plemyria **Pl 19**, 151
plumbeolata, *Eupithecia* **Pl 23**, 168
plumigeralis, *Pechipogo* **Pl 41**, 289
plumigera, *Ptilophora* **Pl 36**, 210
Plusia **Pl 43**, 296
Plusiinae 294–6
Poecilocampa **Pl 10**, 121
Poecilocampinae 121
Polia **Pl 57**, 341, 342
Polychrysia **Pl 43**, 295
polycommata, *Trichopteryx* **Pl 26**, 179
Polygonia **Pl 7**, 106
Polymixis **Pl 55**, 329, 336, 337, 423
Polyommatinae 111–15
Polyommatus **Pl 8**, 114, 115
Polyphaenis **Pl 48**, 310
Polyploca **Pl 9**, 119
populata, *Eulithis* **Pl 19**, 152
populeti, *Orthosia* **Pl 56**, 338
populi, *Laothoe* **Pl 12**, 128
populi, *Poecilocampa* **Pl 10**, 121
porata, *Cyclophora* **Pl 17**, 140
porcellus, *Deilephila* **Pl 15**, 131
porphyrea, *Lycophotia* **Pl 61**, 358
potatoria, *Euthrix* **Pl 11**, 124
praecox, *Actebia* **Pl 60**, 352
prasina, *Anaplectoides* **Pl 62**, 361
prasinana, *Pseudoips* **Pl 64**, 368

primaria, Theria **Pl 32**, 198
proboscidalis, Hypena **Pl 37**, 277
procellata, Melanthia **Pl 22**, 161
processionea, Thaumetopoea **Pl 34**, 205
Procridinae 87
promissa, Catocala **Pl 42**, 292
pronuba, Noctua **Pl 62**, 358
Protarchanara **Pl 50**, 318
Protolampra **Pl 64**, 365
pruinata, Pseudoterpna **Pl 33**, 202
prunaria, Angerona **Pl 28**, 185
prunata, Eulithis **Pl 19**, 152
pruni, Satyrium **Pl 8**, 111
Psaphidinae 304–5
Pseudocoremia **Pl 33**, 200
Pseudoips **Pl 64**, 368
Pseudopanthera **Pl 28**, 185
Pseudoterpna **Pl 33**, 202
psi, Acronicta **Pl 44**, 299
Pterapherapteryx **Pl 26**, 179
Pterophoridae 17
Pterophorus **Pl 40**, 284
Pterostoma **Pl 36**, 209
Ptilodon **Pl 36**, 209
Ptilophora **Pl 36**, 210
Ptocheuusa 291
pudibunda, Calliteara **Pl 38**, 279
pudorina, Mythimna 348, 424
pulchellata, Eupithecia **Pl 23**, 167
pulchrina, Autographa **Pl 43**, 295
pulveraria, Plagodis **Pl 27**, 183
punctaria, Cyclophora **Pl 17**, 140
punctinalis, Hypomecis **Pl 31**, 194
punctulata, Aethalura **Pl 32**, 196
Pungeleria **Pl 33**, 198
puppillaria, Cyclophora **Pl 17**, 139
purpuralis, Zygaena **Pl 2**, 88
pusaria, Cabera **Pl 32**, 196
pusillata, Eupithecia **Pl 23**, 169
puta, Agrotis **Pl 60**, 355
putnami, Plusia **Pl 43**, 296
putrescens, Leucania 351, 427
putris, Axylia **Pl 60**, 355
Pygaerinae 211
pygarga, Deltote **Pl 43**, 296
pygmaeata, Eupithecia **Pl 23**, 168
pygmaeola, Eilema **Pl 41**, 287
pygmina, Denticucullus **Pl 50**, 317
pyraliata, Gandaritis **Pl 20**, 153
pyralina, Cosmia **Pl 54**, 332, 422
pyramidea, Amphipyra **Pl 46**, 303
Pyrginae 91–2
Pyrgus **Pl 3**, 92
pyrina, Zeuzera **Pl 1**, 75
pyritoides, Habrosyne **Pl 9**, 118
Pyronia **Pl 5**, 101
Pyropteron 83, 84
Pyrrhia **Pl 46**, 305

quadra, Lithosia **Pl 40**, 285
quadrifasiata, Xanthorhoe 144, 415
quadripunctaria, Euplagia **Pl 40**, 283
quercifolia, Gastropacha **Pl 11**, 124
quercinaria, Ennomos **Pl 28**, 186
quercus, Favonius **Pl 8**, 110
quercus, Lasiocampa **Pl 10**, 123

rapae, Pieris **Pl 4**, 96
ravida, Spaelotis **Pl 62**, 360
recens, Orgyia **Pl 38**, 280
rectangulata, Pasiphila **Pl 22**, 166
rectilinea, Hyppa **Pl 48**, 311
remissa, Apamea **Pl 51**, 319
repandaria, Epione **Pl 28**, 184
repandata, Alcis **Pl 31**, 194
reticulata, Eustroma **Pl 19**, 152
reticulata, Sideridis **Pl 59**, 346
retusa, Ipimorpha **Pl 54**, 331, 421
revayana, Nycteola **Pl 64**, 368
rhamni, Gonepteryx **Pl 4**, 97
Rheumaptera **Pl 21**, 159, 160
Rhizedra **Pl 49**, 315
Rhodometra **Pl 17**, 140
rhomboidaria, Peribatodes **Pl 31**, 192
Rhyacia **Pl 61**, 358
ribeata, Deileptenia **Pl 31**, 193
ridens, Polyploca **Pl 9**, 119
Riodinidae **Pl 7**, 108
Riodininae 108
ripae, Agrotis **Pl 60**, 355
rivata, Epirrhoe **Pl 18**, 146
Rivula **Pl 37**, 277
rivularis, Sideridis **Pl 59**, 345
Rivulinae 277
roboraria, Hypomecis **Pl 31**, 194
rostralis, Hypena **Pl 37**, 277
ruberata, Hydriomena **Pl 19**, 149
rubi, Callophrys **Pl 8**, 110
rubidata, Catarhoe **Pl 18**, 145
rubi, Diarsia **Pl 61**, 357
rubiginata, Plemyria **Pl 19**, 151
rubiginata, Scopula **Pl 16**, 136
rubiginea, Conistra **Pl 53**, 329
rubiginosa, Conistra **Pl 53**, 329, 420
rubi, Macrothylacia **Pl 11**, 123
rubricollis, Atolmis **Pl 41**, 285
rubricosa, Cerastis **Pl 61**, 357
rufa, Coenobia **Pl 50**, 317
rufata, Chesias **Pl 26**, 178
ruficiliaria, Cyclophora **Pl 17**, 139
ruficornis, Drymonia **Pl 35**, 207
rufifasciata, Gymnoscelis **Pl 22**, 165, 416
rumicis, Acronicta **Pl 44**, 300
Rusina **Pl 47**, 309
rusticata, Idaea **Pl 16**, 133

Sabra **Pl 9**, 117
sacraria, Rhodometra **Pl 17**, 140

sagittata, Gagitodes **Pl 22**, 164
salicata, Coenotephria **Pl 20**, 155
salicis, Leucoma **Pl 37**, 278
sambucaria, Ourapteryx **Pl 29**, 189
sannio, Diacrisia **Pl 39**, 281
Saturnia **Pl 11**, 126
Saturniidae **Pl 11**, 126
Saturniinae 126
satyrata, Eupithecia **Pl 25**, 173, 417
Satyrinae 98–102
Satyrium **Pl 8**, 111
saucia, Peridroma **Pl 60**, 352
saxicola, Phycitodes **Pl 42**, 291
scabriuscula, Dypterygia **Pl 48**, 310
Schrankia 289
scoliaeformis, Synanthedon 78
Scoliopteryginae 276
Scoliopteryx **Pl 37**, 276
scolopacina, Apamea **Pl 51**, 321
Scopula **Pl 16**, 132, 136, 137, 138
Scotopteryx **Pl 17**, 141, 142
scrophulariae, Cucullia **Pl 45**, 302
secalis, Mesapamea **Pl 52**, 322
secundaria, Peribatodes **Pl 31**, 193
Sedina **Pl 49**, 315
segetum, Agrotis 354
selene, Boloria **Pl 6**, 102
Selenia **Pl 29**, 16, 187
Selidosema **Pl 31**, 193
semele, Hipparchia **Pl 5**, 102
semibrunnea, Lithophane **Pl 53**, 329, 421
senex, Thumatha **Pl 40**, 284
Senta **Pl 60**, 348, 352, 427
seriata, Idaea **Pl 16**, 134
sericata, Polyphaenis **Pl 48**, 310
sericealis, Rivula **Pl 37**, 277
servillana, Cydia 79, 80
Sesia **Pl 1**, 77
Sesiidae **Pl 1**, 9, 76–84
Sesiinae 77–84
Setina **Pl 41**, 287
sexalata, Pterapherapteryx **Pl 26**, 179
sexstrigata, Xestia **Pl 63**, 363
Sideridis **Pl 59**, 345, 346
signaria, Macaria **Pl 27**, 182
silaceata, Ecliptopera **Pl 20**, 153
similaria, Parectropis **Pl 32**, 195
similis, Euproctis **Pl 37**, 279
simpliciata, Eupithecia **Pl 24**, 171
simulans, Rhyacia **Pl 61**, 358
Simyra **Pl 44**, 298
sinapis, Leptidea **Pl 4**, 95
Siona **Pl 33**, 200
siterata, Chloroclysta **Pl 20**, 153
Smerinthinae 128
Smerinthus **Pl 12**, 128
sobrina, Protolampra **Pl 64**, 365
socia, Lithophane **Pl 53**, 329, 421
solidaginis, Xylena **Pl 53**, 330

sordens, Apamea **Pl 51**, 320
sororcula, Eilema **Pl 41**, 287
sororiata, Carsia **Pl 26**, 177
spadicearia, Xanthorhoe 143, 414
Spaelotis **Pl 62**, 360
Spargania **Pl 19**, 148
sparganii, Globia **Pl 50**, 319
sparsata, Anticollix **Pl 22**, 162
spheciformis, Synanthedon 78
Sphingidae **Pl 12–15**, 127–31
Sphinginae 128–9
Sphinx **Pl 13**, 129
sphinx, Asteroscopus **Pl 46**, 304
Spilosoma **Pl 38**, 280, 281
splendens, Lacanobia **Pl 58**, 343
sponsa, Catocala **Pl 42**, 292
Standfussiana **Pl 61**, 358
statices, Adscita **Pl 2**, 87
Stauropus **Pl 35**, 207
Stegania 181
stellatarum, Macroglossum **Pl 14**, 130
Sterrhinae 132–40
stigmatica, Xestia **Pl 63**, 361
Stilbia **Pl 45**, 303
straminata, Idaea **Pl 16**, 136
straminea, Mythimna **Pl 60**, 349, 425
strataria, Biston **Pl 30**, 191
strigilata, Pechipogo **Pl 41**, 289
strigilis, Oligia **Pl 52**, 323
strigillaria, Perconia **Pl 33**, 201
strigula, Meganola **Pl 64**, 366
suasa, Lacanobia **Pl 58**, 343
suavis, Pseudocoremia **Pl 33**, 200
Subacronicta **Pl 45**, 300
subfuscata, Eupithecia **Pl 26**, 177
sublustris, Apamea **Pl 51**, 322
subrosea, Coenophila **Pl 63**, 364
subsericeata, Idaea **Pl 16**, 134
subtusa, Ipimorpha **Pl 54**, 331, 421
subumbrata, Eupithecia **Pl 26**, 176, 417
succenturiata, Eupithecia **Pl 25**, 176
suffumata, Lampropteryx **Pl 20**, 155
suspecta, Parastichtis **Pl 54**, 333
sylvanus, Ochlodes **Pl 3**, 94
sylvata, Abraxas **Pl 26**, 180
sylvata, Hydrelia **Pl 21**, 158
sylvestraria, Idaea **Pl 16**, 134
sylvestris, Thymelicus **Pl 3**, 93
sylvina, Triodia **Pl 1**, 72
Synanthedon 78, 79, 80, 81, 82
Syngrapha **Pl 43**, 296
syringaria, Apeira **Pl 28**, 185

taenialis, Schrankia 289
taeniata, Martania **Pl 22**, 164
tages, Erynnis **Pl 3**, 91
tantillaria, Eupithecia **Pl 24**, 170
tarsicrinalis, Herminia **Pl 41**, 288
tarsipennalis, Herminia **Pl 41**, 288

temerata, *Lomographa* **Pl 32**, 197
templi, *Dasypolia* **Pl 55**, 336
tenebrata, *Panemeria* **Pl 45**, 301
tenebrosa, *Dryobotodes* **Pl 55**, 334
tenuiata, *Eupithecia* **Pl 23**, 166
ternata, *Scopula* **Pl 16**, 137
tersata, *Horisme* **Pl 21**, 161
testacea, *Luperina* **Pl 49**, 315
testata, *Eulithis* **Pl 20**, 152
Tethea **Pl 9**, 118, 119
Tetheella **Pl 9**, 119
tetralunaria, *Selenia* **Pl 29**, 187
thalassina, *Lacanobia* **Pl 57**, 342
Thalera **Pl 34**, 203
Thalpophila **Pl 48**, 311
Thaumetopoea **Pl 34**, 205
Thaumetopoeinae 205–6
Thecla **Pl 8**, 110
Theclinae 110–11
Thera **Pl 19**, 149, 150
Theria **Pl 32**, 198
Tholera **Pl 57**, 340
Thumatha **Pl 40**, 284
Thyatira **Pl 9**, 118
Thyatirinae 118–20
Thymelicus **Pl 3**, 92, 93
Tiliacea **Pl 52**, 324, 325, 418
tiliae, *Mimas* **Pl 12**, 128
Timandra **Pl 17**, 138
Tinthiinae 76–7
tipuliformis, *Synanthedon* 82
tithonus, *Pyronia* **Pl 5**, 101
tityus, *Hemaris* **Pl 14**, 129
togata, *Xanthia* **Pl 52**, 325, 418
Toxocampinae 289–90
Trachea **Pl 48**, 310
tragopoginis, *Amphipyra* **Pl 46**, 304
transversa, *Eupsilia* **Pl 54**, 331
transversata, *Philereme* **Pl 21**, 159
trapezina, *Cosmia* **Pl 54**, 332, 422
tremula, *Pheosia* **Pl 35**, 208
triangulum, *Xestia* **Pl 63**, 363
Trichiura **Pl 10**, 121
Trichopteryx **Pl 26**, 179
tridens, *Acronicta* **Pl 44**, 299
tridens, *Calamia* **Pl 48**, 312
trifolii, *Anarta* **Pl 57**, 341
trifolii, *Lasiocampa* **Pl 10**, 123
trifolii, *Zygaena* **Pl 2**, 89
trigeminata, *Idaea* **Pl 16**, 134
Trigonophora **Pl 55**, 335
trigrammica, *Charanyca* **Pl 47**, 309
Triodia **Pl 1**, 72
tripartita, *Abrostola* **Pl 43**, 294
Triphosa **Pl 21**, 160
triplasia, *Abrostola* **Pl 43**, 294
triptolemus, *Hemeroplanes* 50, 51
tripunctaria, *Eupithecia* **Pl 23**, 169, 416
Trisateles **Pl 42**, 291

trisignaria, *Eupithecia* **Pl 24**, 173
tristalis, *Paracolax* **Pl 41**, 288
tristata, *Epirrhoe* **Pl 18**, 145
tritici, *Euxoa* 353
truncata, *Dysstroma* **Pl 20**, 154
trux, *Agrotis* 355
tullia, *Coenonympha* **Pl 5**, 99
turbida, *Sideridis* **Pl 59**, 345
turca, *Mythimna* **Pl 60**, 348, 424
typhae, *Nonagria* **Pl 49**, 316
typica, *Naenia* **Pl 64**, 365
Tyria **Pl 40**, 283
Tyta **Pl 43**, 297

ultimaria, *Eupithecia* **Pl 23**, 167
umbra, *Pyrrhia* **Pl 46**, 305
umbratica, *Cucullia* **Pl 45**, 301
unangulata, *Euphyia* **Pl 18**, 146
unanimis, *Apamea* **Pl 51**, 320
uncula, *Deltote* **Pl 43**, 297
undulata, *Rheumaptera* **Pl 21**, 160
unipuncta, *Mythimna* 350, 425
urticae, *Aglais* **Pl 7**, 105
urticae, *Spilosoma* **Pl 38**, 281

v-ata, *Chloroclystis* **Pl 22**, 165
vaccinii, *Conistra* **Pl 53**, 328, 420
valerianata, *Eupithecia* **Pl 25**, 174
Vanessa **Pl 7**, 104, 105
venosata, *Eupithecia* **Pl 23**, 168
Venusia **Pl 21**, 158, 159
venustula, *Elaphria* **Pl 47**, 307
verbasci, *Cucullia* **Pl 45**, 302
versicolora, *Endromis* **Pl 11**, 125
versicolor, *Oligia* **Pl 52**, 374
vespertaria, *Epione* **Pl 28**, 185
vespiformis, *Synanthedon* 82
vestigialis, *Agrotis* 354
vetulata, *Philereme* **Pl 21**, 159
vetusta, *Xylena* **Pl 53**, 330
viciae, *Zygaena* **Pl 2**, 88
villica, *Arctia* **Pl 39**, 282
viminalis, *Brachylomia* **Pl 54**, 333, 422
vinula, *Cerura* **Pl 34**, 206
viretata, *Acasis* **Pl 26**, 179
virgata, *Phibalapteryx* **Pl 17**, 141
virgaureata, *Eupithecia* **Pl 23**, 170, 416
viridaria, *Phytometra* **Pl 42**, 290
viridata, *Chlorissa* **Pl 34**, 204
viriplaca, *Heliothis* **Pl 46**, 305
vitalbata, *Horisme* **Pl 21**, 161
vitellina, *Mythimna* 350, 425
vittata, *Orthonama* **Pl 17**, 142
vulgata, *Eupithecia* **Pl 25**, 175

w-album, *Satyrium* **Pl 8**, 111
w-latinum, *Lacanobia* **Pl 57**, 342
Watsonalla **Pl 9**, 116, 117
wauaria, *Macaria* **Pl 27**, 182

Xanthia **Pl 52**, 324, 325, 418
xanthographa, Xestia **Pl 63**, 362
xanthomista, Polymixis **Pl 55**, 336
Xanthorhoe **Pl 18**, 142, 143, 144, 414, 415
Xestia **Pl 63**, 361, 362, 363, 364
Xylena **Pl 53**, 330
Xyleninae 307–37
Xylocampa **Pl 46**, 305

ypsillon, Apterogenum **Pl 54**, 333

Zaraea 17
Zeuzera **Pl 1**, 75
Zeuzerinae 75
ziczac, Notodonta **Pl 35**, 208
zonaria, Lycia **Pl 30**, 190
Zygaena **Pl 2**, 88, 89
Zygaenidae **Pl 2**, 86–9
Zygaeninae 87–9
Zygaenoidea 85–9